Governed by Affect

New Histories of Psychology
Michael Pettit, Series Editor

Associate Editors

Saulo Araujo   Alexandra Hui
Sunal Bhatia   Sarah Igo
Cathy Faye   Edward Jones-Imhotep
Peter Hegarty   Dana Simmons

Governed by Affect:
Hot Cognition and the End of Cold War Psychology
Michael Pettit

Governed by Affect

Hot Cognition and the End of Cold War Psychology

MICHAEL PETTIT

OXFORD
UNIVERSITY PRESS

Oxford University Press is a department of the University of Oxford. It furthers
the University's objective of excellence in research, scholarship, and education
by publishing worldwide. Oxford is a registered trade mark of Oxford University
Press in the UK and certain other countries.

Published in the United States of America by Oxford University Press
198 Madison Avenue, New York, NY 10016, United States of America.

© Oxford University Press 2024

All rights reserved. No part of this publication may be reproduced, stored in
a retrieval system, or transmitted, in any form or by any means, without the
prior permission in writing of Oxford University Press, or as expressly permitted
by law, by license, or under terms agreed with the appropriate reproduction
rights organization. Inquiries concerning reproduction outside the scope of the
above should be sent to the Rights Department, Oxford University Press, at the
address above.

You must not circulate this work in any other form
and you must impose this same condition on any acquirer.

Library of Congress Cataloging-in-Publication Data
Names: Pettit, Michael (Michael John), author.
Title: Governed by affect : hot cognition and the end of cold war psychology / Michael Pettit.
Description: 1 edition. | New York, NY : Oxford University Press, [2024] |
Series: New histories of psychology |
Includes bibliographical references and index. |
Identifiers: LCCN 2024001015 (print) | LCCN 2024001016 (ebook) |
ISBN 9780197621851 (hardback) | ISBN 9780197621875 (epub) |
ISBN 9780197621882
Subjects: LCSH: Psychology—History.
Classification: LCC BF105 .P428 2024 (print) | LCC BF105 (ebook) |
DDC 150.9—dc23/eng/20240315
LC record available at https://lccn.loc.gov/2024001015
LC ebook record available at https://lccn.loc.gov/2024001016

DOI: 10.1093/oso/9780197621851.001.0001

Printed by Sheridan Books, Inc., United States of America

CONTENTS

Preface: A Float on a Sea of Affect   vii
Acknowledgments   xi

Introduction   1

1. A New Look for Psychology: The Antifascist Roots of a New Discipline   27

2. Rational Living and Straight Thinking: Therapeutic Cultures and Their Promise of Liberty   60

3. The Tragedy of American Psychology: Racial Justice and Professionalism on the Expanding Frontier of Mental Health   95

4. Vigilant Minds, Thoughtless Brains: Warfare, Welfare, and the Remaking of Cognition   128

5. Why Linda Was Not a Feminist: Expertise, Activism, and the Crisis of Confidence   161

6. Rethinking the Politics of Self-Esteem   192

7. How Faces Became Special: Perceiving Others in a Digital Age   230

8. The Coming Crisis of Affective Science   263

Conclusion   297

Bibliography   301
Index   347

PREFACE: A FLOAT ON A SEA OF AFFECT

We live in a world awash in affect. Snap decisions, gut reactions, instant determinations of like/dislike govern our actions. These primitive dispositions operating beyond awareness seemingly overrule even the most careful and reasoned thinking. How could it be any other way? Such are the demands of both our evolved natures honed in the deep past and our sped-up technological society. Since each individual decision taxes our limited cognitive capacities, our organic machine must largely run on automatic, constantly optimized toward the pleasurable with little time or opportunity for conscious deliberation.

Affect's pull is seemingly inescapable. Personal success hinges on the individual's ability to delay gratification in a world of tempting distractions. Intergroup relations require that we not succumb to those "implicit biases" activated by first impressions. Even economics, once the realm of the invisible hand guaranteeing rational choices in the aggregate, has been remade in affective terms since the 2008 financial crisis, with unthinking plebeians needing benevolent "nudges" to push their behavior onto the optimal path. These powerful feelings extended beyond the skin. Affect saturates and even organizes the infrastructure of our networked, globalized public sphere. Computational analytics in both commerce and politics circumvent the self-knowing subject, predicting their future choices from data gathered on their past wants. The internet itself has been recast from a library of universal knowledge to a social web that constantly solicits, distributes, and manipulates emotions. The internet assemblage of minds and devices saps attention, isolates people into tribal echo chambers, then mobilizes them as digital mobs. Even the humanities, ever suspicious of the sciences' reductionism and claims to universality, have undergone their own affective turn as feminist and queer theorists have embraced the role of feelings and other embodied experiences as immediate, primary, constitutive forms of being human, which defy the Enlightenment's obsession with reason, language, and representation.[1]

---

1. Constantina Papoulias and Felicity Callard, "Biology's Gift: Interrogating the Turn to Affect," *Body & Society* 16, no. 1 (2010): 29–56.

Given this current state, who has not succumbed to spells of catastrophizing about the future? But we must set aside such automatic associations.

In this context, psychology has come to supply policymakers, experts in adjacent fields, and ordinary people with a seemingly inexhaustible array of tools, concepts, and practices for making individuals healthier, wealthier, and happier. The identification of mental health as a "hidden burden" on late modern economies is one obvious indicator, but central to affect's current reign is extension far beyond the realm of pathology by demonstrating how even healthy reasoning is defective and deficient.[2] The opening years of the twenty-first century saw the consolidation of a new form of psychology that promoted an understanding of the person where deliberative reason functioned as an energy in short supply and a process constantly besieged by barbaric emotions gathered at the gates. This genre of colloquial science extends beyond "mere" popularizers, journalists, and clinical practitioners with a striking amount of supposedly "basic" research activity organized around designing applications for the new affective science of self-help.[3] Their gospel of self-improvement through emotional regulation travels far, diffracted through those same modularized networks of the social web whose activity they also seek to explain. Affective science features prominently in viral lectures and the self-talk found on social media platforms, along with more traditional venues of cultural influence like the *New York Times* editorial page and its bestseller list. Regardless of the medium, affective science's presentation follows a familiar script that hinges on the surprising counterintuitive finding or "effect," which defies expectations while offering the consumer a simple fix for self-improvement. This hypermodularized knowledge offers an often-contradictory understanding of affective life that at once underscores the ubiquity, and even reasonableness, of affective dispositions, while also decrying the failures of those persons who too easily succumb to their quick, gut feelings.

This supposedly novel science of affect may strike some as oddly familiar and maybe even old fashioned. Often couched as promissory neuroscience, this hypermediated psychology harkens back to the kind of psychology popularized during the last fin-de-siècle. The emphasis on the automaticity of our action is reminiscent of long-standing challenges to the separation of humanity from the rest of the animals. Cutting-edge dual process theories of cognition recall the Victorian duality between our reasonable and emotional nature, a conflict made famous by Sigmund Freud's psychoanalysis, if not Robert Louis Stevenson's Jekyll and Hyde. In our second Gilded Age, leading psychologists are once again

---

2. J. L. Christopher Murray, Alan D. Lopez, and World Health Organization. *The Global Burden of Disease: A Comprehensive Assessment of Mortality and Disability from Diseases, Injuries, and Risk Factors in 1990 and Projected to 2020*. World Health Organization, 1996.

3. This genre is sometimes discussed in terms of the "Gladwell effect" on social science, dubbed after the Canadian-born science journalist whose bestsellers helped craft this style of exposition. On colloquial science in the age of print media, see Erika Lorraine Milam, *Creatures of Cain: The Hunt for Human Nature in Cold War America*. Princeton, NJ: Princeton University Press, 2020.

entering the public sphere to champion a gospel of self-help through the mastery of willpower over our baser natures.[4]

How should we make sense of this recurrence? Does psychology have nothing new to offer? Is the discipline itself bent on mindlessly repeating its own errors of the past? This book advances a historical perspective on contemporary psychology and the varieties of personhood this science works to enact. The echoes of psychology's long past certainly continue to structure the present, but the familiarity of certain tropes risks obscuring the rather dramatic ways in which the profession has been remade in recent decades as psychology and psychologists have acquired an unprecedented—if always unstable and contested—role in public life.

---

4. On the first iteration of this public psychology, see Michael Pettit, *The Science of Deception: Psychology and Commerce in America*. Chicago: University of Chicago Press, 2013.

ACKNOWLEDGMENTS

Acknowledgments furnish a wonderful opportunity to reflect upon the debts one accrues over time, to realize the profoundly distributed nature of the knowledge which goes into making a book. This one developed out of many conversations held over many years in several countries. I am grateful to have this opportunity to give an accounting of the people and places which sustained me and allowed me to complete it.

Portions of this book has previously appeared in different versions. Sections of chapters 1 and chapter 7 have previously appeared in an earlier form as a chapter in Laurens Schlicht, Carla Seemann, and Christian Kassung (eds.), *Mind Reading as Cultural Practice* (Palgrave, 2020). A section of Chapter 3 appeared "'Angela's psych squad': Black psychology against the American carceral state in the 1970s." *Journal of the History of the Behavioral Sciences* 58, no. 4 (2022): 365-382. An earlier version of Chapter 6 appeared as an entry for *The Oxford Research Encyclopedia of Psychology* (New York: Oxford University Press, 2020) edited by Wade Pickren. I thank the publishers for their permission to reprint this material.

Research began in earnest as part of a Social Science and Humanities Research Council (SSHRC) Insight Grant I held with Chris Green on the digital history of psychology and a SSHRC Connection Grant held with Mark Solovey and Alex Rutherford to support a workshop on the history of American social sciences and social policy since the 1960s. Another SSHRC Insight Grant supported much of the archival research for this book. I benefited from the assistance of the staff at the Cummings Center for the History of Psychology (especially Lizette Royer Barton), the Manuscript Room at the Library of Congress, Rare Book and Manuscript Library, Columbia University, and the National Archives at Kew who provided me with both virtual and physical access to the archival materials at the heart of this book. Paul Slovic and John Monahan kindly answered questions I had about their research. Writing was supported by an extended stay at the Max Planck Institute for the History of Science in Berlin and an abbreviated one at the National Humanities Center in Durham, NC. I am grateful to both institutions and their staff. The bulk of the writing happened during a near year of lockdown in Broadbottom, a small village outside of Manchester.

Despite the isolation of lockdown, I remained embedded in a community of scholars who sharpened by thinking and provided feedback of various drafts. Numerous friends have read various proposals and chapter drafts leading the final manuscript. Many thanks go out to Glenn Adams, Jeremy Burman, Ian Burney, Jennifer Derr, Dave Devonis, Cathy Faye, Joel Isaac, Kira Lussier, Raymond Mar, Mikey McGovern, Erika Milam, Amy Milne-Smith, Lamia Moghnieh, Jill Morawski, Kieran O'Doherty, Wade Pickren, Rachael Rosner, Dana Simmons, Mark Solovey, Thomas Teo, C. J. Valasek, Andrew Winston, and Jacy Young. I have also learned much from the students in my history of psychology and research methods courses. I especially benefited from a number of students who worked as research assistants or completed theses closely related to this book: Nataly Beribisky, David Berman, Ian Davidson, Shayna Fox Lee, Loren Gaudet, Crystal Heidari, Tyler Hnatuk, Eric Oosenbrug, Shivrang Setlur, Hanna Smolyanitsky, and Jana Vigor. At Oxford University Press, I am grateful to Sarah Harrington for shepherding the manuscript through the review process and the editorial staff who oversaw the book through production. Along with the helpful anonymous reviewers for the press, I am especially grateful to Peter Hegarty, Sarah Igo, Edward Jones-Imhotep, and Alex Rutherford who each read the entire manuscript and offered countless helpful suggestions for improving it during a stimulating online workshop. Finally, I am always grateful for the ongoing support from my family, my mother Kathie and the extended Yates family.

My greatest debt is to partner Alexia Yates for her constant intellectual camaraderie, insightful conversation, and emotional support.

Introduction

When it comes to understanding affect's contemporary pull, psychology and history make for an uneasy (if ultimately a necessary) pairing. Psychologists strive to go beyond the contingencies and particularities of any given historical context to derive universal laws of mental life. Historians remain largely wary of psychologists' propensity for individualistic explanations rooted in the variation of traits and motivations found within the person. This mutual incomprehension makes this book's dual ambition something of a challenge. My aim is to make historical sense of recent developments in psychology and show how these shifts within psychology can cast new light on the changing historical experience of personhood. That so many of us today around the globe not only feel awash in affect seemingly beyond our control in our everyday lives is both a cause and an effect of this entanglement of psychology and history. This sense derives not only from our experience of certain bodily states, but also from our relating to them as they increasingly serve as the site of governance. In other words, this book concerns itself with the historical matrix from which affective science emerged alongside examining a range of its cultural effects.

Existing histories told both within and outside of psychology have touched on this story, but the main lines of these narratives obscure several strands that need foregrounding to properly illuminate the intertwined history of psychology as a profession and the emergence of an affective self. One persistent way psychologists understand their own history is in terms of competing "schools" or "systems." This approach documents the rise and fall of faculty, structuralist, and functionalist psychologies and focuses especially on the midcentury battles between behaviorism and psychoanalysis as meta-theories.[1] This latter conflict, which took

---

1. Thomas Leahey, "The Mythical Revolutions of American Psychology," *American Psychologist* 47, no. 2 (1992): 308–318; Richard W. Robins, Samuel D. Gosling, and Kenneth H. Craik, "An Empirical Analysis of Trends in Psychology," *American Psychologist* 54, no. 2 (1999): 117–128; Joseph H. Spear, "Prominent Schools or Other Active Specialties? A Fresh Look at Some Trends in Psychology," *Review of General Psychology* 11, no. 4 (2007): 363–380; Christopher D. Green, "Why Psychology Isn't Unified, and Probably Never Will Be," *Review of General Psychology* 19, no. 3 (2015): 207–214.

Governed by Affect. Michael Pettit, Oxford University Press. © Oxford University Press 2024.
DOI: 10.1093/oso/9780197621851.003.0001

shape in the interwar years and reached a crescendo in the 1950s, often served as a proxy war over whether psychology was first and foremost an academic science or a therapeutic practice. Behaviorists gave primacy to the laboratory where they accounted for psychological phenomena by operationalizing them in terms of directly observed, finely measurable activity. In contrast, psychoanalysis defined itself as the clinical art of interpreting human mental life in terms of unconscious motivations buried below the surface. Both behaviorism and psychoanalysis proved seductive, expansive empires. The behaviorists used their experiments to derive practical interventions targeting specific symptoms, while psychoanalysis captured the imagination of countless experimenters who wished to materialize its dynamics in controlled settings.

The schools and systems approach has tended to culminate in a triumphant cognitive revolution at midcentury. According to this oft-told tale, the hedonic psychologies of behaviorism and psychoanalysis are moribund things best left in the past. In their place, psychology embraced a more elevated picture of how the mind works, with the computer serving as the dominant model for our mental machinery. This metaphor allowed psychologists to see what the flexible, adaptive human thinker could achieve as it received, processed, stored, and retrieved information from the surrounding world. According to this narrative, information processing was first established in experimental psychology and was then extended into the applied domains of child development, social relations, and finally the therapies offered by clinicians. Even the best historical analyses largely bolster this narrative about psychology's recent past, telling how Cold War cybernetics inspired the adoption of an austere and deliberative rationality as their norm for human thinking.[2] Alongside this story of cognition's ascendancy runs a parallel one psychologists tell about their own growing smartness. This narrative holds

---

2. See especially Paul Erickson, Judy L. Klein, Lorraine Daston, Rebecca Lemov, Thomas Sturm, and Michael D. Gordin. *How Reason Almost Lost Its Mind: The Strange Career of Cold War Rationality*. Chicago: University of Chicago Press, 2013. On cybernetics, see Donna Haraway, *Simians, Cyborgs, and Women: The Reinvention of Nature*. New York: Routledge, 1991; Steven J. Heims, *Constructing a Social Science for America: The Cybernetics Group 1946–1953*. Cambridge, MA: MIT Press, 1991; Peter Galison, "The Ontology of the Enemy: Norbert Wiener and the Cybernetic Vision," *Critical Inquiry* 21, no. 1 (1994): 228–266; Paul N. Edwards, *Closed World: Computers and the Politics of Discourse in Cold War America*. Cambridge, MA: MIT Press, 1996; N. Katherine Hayles, *How We Became Posthuman: Virtual Bodies in Cybernetics, Literature, and Informatics*. Chicago: University of Chicago Press, 1999; Rhodri Hayward, "The Tortoise and the Love-Machine: Grey Walter and the Politics of Electroencephalography," *Science in Context* 14, no. 4 (2001): 615–641; Andrew Pickering, *The Cybernetic Brain: Sketches of Another Future*. Chicago: University of Chicago Press, 2010; Ronald R. Kline, *The Cybernetics Moment: Or Why We Call Our Age the Information Age*. Baltimore: Johns Hopkins University Press, 2015; Tara Abraham, *Rebel Genius: Warren S. McCulloch's Transdisciplinary Life in Science*. Cambridge: MIT Press, 2016. On the cognitive revolution, see Howard Gardner, *The Mind's New Science: A History of the Cognitive Revolution*. New York: Basic Books, 1985; George Mandler, "Origins of the Cognitive (R)evolution," *Journal of the History of the Behavioral Sciences* 38, no. 4 (2002): 339–353; John D. Greenwood, "Understanding the 'Cognitive Revolution' in Psychology." *Journal of the History of the Behavioral Sciences* 35, no. 1 (1999): 1–22; Jamie Cohen-Cole, *The*

that psychology is unique among the human sciences in terms of its methodological sophistication. The field may have flirted at one time with Freud's armchair speculations, but it demarcated itself from other human sciences by its in-depth training in both experimental design and statistical analysis. This dual toolbox allowed the psychologist to explain the causes of human conduct in objective terms. The "inference revolution" of advanced statistics secured the psychologist's advantage over the layperson in properly interpreting their conduct.[3] In sum, the received view holds that the start of the Cold War spelled the end of the history of psychology as the field escaped its past and entered a timeless, scientific present.

As someone who exists simultaneously as both an insider and an outsider to contemporary psychology, I find much that is recognizable in this flattering self-portrait, but it fails to capture certain features of the field which intrigue and puzzle me. I come to this history as someone formally trained as a historian of science (with a strong philosophical and anthropological bent) but who is now employed in a Canadian department of psychology. In Canada, the reach of American psychology is felt strongly if experienced as somewhat culturally peculiar. (This tension partly explains the existence of my research area, one dedicated to critically reflecting on the field from within.) As I learned to perform as a passable professor of psychology, I undertook something of an informal ethnography of my adopted field. I read textbooks, I attended conferences, I followed science bloggers, I began teaching research methods to better understand how psychologists thought. This book started as part of my own attempt to make sense of this world I was entering and getting acculturated into. From my partial vantage point, I found that the received view missed much of what I observed about the organization of own department, what I overheard in corridor talk, what I saw when pursuing the proceedings of the annual convention, and what topics I understood as prioritized by the leading journals.

The ground was shifting. The greater prevalence given to "health mental" in public life partly accounts for this, as does a new interest in observing and manipulating people using the behavioral measures derived from Big Data. However, these stories and others are too easily siloed from one another. My central contention is that these oft-told stories misconstrue important aspects of this

---

Open Mind: Cold War Politics and the Sciences of Human Nature. Chicago: University of Chicago Press, 2014; Hunter Heyck, *Age of System: Understanding the Development of Modern Social Science*. Baltimore: Johns Hopkins University Press, 2015.

3. On the inference revolution, see Gerd Gigerenzer and Julian N. Marewski, "Surrogate Science: The Idol of a Universal Method for Scientific Inference." *Journal of Management* 41, no. 2 (2015): 421–440. This interpretation builds on a large literature on the rise of statistical thinking, see Theodore M. Porter, *The Rise of Statistical Thinking, 1820–1900*. Princeton, NJ: Princeton University Press, 1986; Gerd Gigerenzer, Zeno Swijtink, Theodore Porter, Lorraine Daston, and Lorenz Kruger. *The Empire of Chance: How Probability Changed Science and Everyday Life*. Cambridge: Cambridge University Press, 1989; Ian Hacking, *The Taming of Chance*. Cambridge: Cambridge University Press, 1990; Theodore M. Porter, *Trust in Numbers: The Pursuit of Objectivity in Science and Public Life*. Princeton, NJ: Princeton University Press, 1995.

recent history. They impede our ability to properly understand psychology's current cultural role and the intertwined sense in which we are all governed by affect, at both an individual and societal level.

I want to underscore three major limitations to the received view of the history of psychology that hinder our understanding of the field's current reach. The first has to do with the question of periodization discussed above. Did cognitive science neatly supplant behaviorism and psychoanalysis (never mind other understandings of personhood)? Has little changed since the first rumblings of the cognitive revolution? Given broader experience of historical change during this period, this seemed unlikely. Put simply, psychology's history did not end in the 1970s (as the "history of psychology" as a specialty took off). Yet we lack a framework for understanding how the field has changed since then.

This leads us to the second major problem with the still dominant "schools" approach: it offers a very poor understanding of how various subspecialties or areas have historically interacted with one another. The most obvious example of this limitation is the too neat cleavage between experimental and clinical psychology. Historical accounts tend to privilege experimental psychology, and the growth and extension of the psychological laboratory structure the narrative. Typically, chapters dedicated to clinical psychology (as well as social, developmental, and industrial psychology among others) are awkwardly inserted as distinct chapters into this narrative, but their presence does little to change the overall story told. Yet, a general experimental psychology is a rare beast today, so we need a better understanding of the dynamics of specializations.

Third, the privileging of the laboratory as a cherished space suggests that insider histories largely continue to do a poor job of integrating the more contextualist interpretations offered by professional historians. How psychology relates to a larger world and how these relations might shape, if not drive, historical change remains largely occluded. This finds expression in the often-hidden geography of the field (as the center of influence shifts from central Europe to the United States) but also in how psychology's growth was invariably altered by the field's engagement with a wide range of publics, whether subjects, patients, or policymakers. The spread of psychology is not simply a story of transmission or diffusion. Its greater public presence has significantly transformed basic theory as well as applied practice.

As an alternative to these internal histories, this book offers a tripartite interpretation for the turn-of-the-millennium preponderance of the affective, the automatic, the beyond conscious awareness; a framework grounded in the interplay between the scientific discipline and the clinical profession in postwar psychology and how they related to various publics. Three overlapping transformations cutting across the field's varied specialties (e.g., clinical, experimental, social, developmental) fundamentally recast their relationship with each other while also reorienting psychology's relationship with society. These changes did not result in a new "paradigm" or meta-theory so much as a distributed network of concrete interventions (such as cognitive behavior therapy, the identification of cognitive biases in decision making, connectionist models of thought, and Big

Data analytics for harvesting behavioral responses) which shared a family resemblance with one another and allowed psychology to relate the self to public life in novel ways.

These three transformations were (1) a switch in psychology's disciplinary identity from that of a social or natural science to a health one; (2) an increasing orientation of university-based psychological scientists and their organizations toward the realms of self-help and public policy; and (3) the overshadowing of cognitive science by theories of affect. These three transformations—in psychology's political economy, in its public engagement, and in its theories of self—constitute distinct but interconnected areas of analysis for constructing a new history of the psychological society. These transformations unfolded gradually, sequentially, and interdependently. This book foregrounds the rise and circulation of affective science but sees the other two transformations as crucial prerequisites for this reorientation of psychological thought and practice.

The first transformation started in earnest during the Great Depression, accelerated in the years following World War II, and crystallized in the 1970s as psychology shifted from a small, narrowly defined academic discipline to a mass health profession. First, the combination of a scarcity of academic jobs and the popular appeal of mental tests as sorting tools pushed many young psychologists into applied roles in schools, industry, and other settings. The United States' entry into World War II further oriented psychologists toward practical applications, forever changing the field's political economy. Many did not wish to return to the prewar status quo. Both the American Psychological Association (APA) and individual departments underwent major reorganizations, giving an unprecedented representation to professionals working in applied settings.[4] The military patronage tied to psychologists' role in rehabilitating returning veterans provided the crucial funding for expanding the discipline's domain. However, the first generation of clinical psychologists resisted easy incorporation into a medical establishment dominated by psychiatrists.[5] They understood their profession as offering viable alternatives to the "medical model" of mental health. Shaped by the radical ethos of the Popular Front and its struggle against global fascism, they argued that their version of counseling was a democratic encounter among equals and a generalizable tool of human understanding that was not limited to the treatment of psychopathology.

If psychology began as an outgrowth of philosophy (albeit deploying physiological equipment to answer old questions), by the 1960s the field had decidedly

---

4. The best overview of this transformation remains James H. Capshew. *Psychologists on the March: Science, Practice, and Professional Identity in America, 1929–1969.* Cambridge: Cambridge University Press, 1999. On its Depression-era roots, see Lorenz J. Finison, "The Psychological Insurgency: 1936–1945," *Journal of Social Issues* 42, no. 1 (1986): 21–33.

5. Roderick D. Buchanan, "Legislative Warriors: American Psychiatrists, Psychologists, and Competing Claims over Psychotherapy in the 1950s." *Journal of the History of the Behavioral Sciences* 39, no. 3 (2003): 225–249.

entered the system of health professions.[6] However, the APA remained largely fixed on the concerns of the academics who founded it. The influx of younger psychologists schooled in the "new" social movements inspired by the civil rights struggle and demanding greater relevance for their science brought the tension between these two groups to the forefront. The 1970s saw a self-described "crisis" in many areas of psychology, alongside a flourishing of radical experiments with democracy as Black, humanistic, antiwar, community, feminist, gay and lesbian psychologists strove to remake their chosen field. They wanted to create not only a more inclusive psychology, but also a more accountable and democratic one. They redesigned their own research to make it more deliberative and consultative in order to "give voice" to the silenced and marginalized.[7] Such agitation and experimentation was short-lived. By decade's end, changes in the American political landscape meant the conflict over psychology's public role had resolved in a much more conservative manner, with the now numerically predominant clinicians mobilizing psychology's organizational bodies as lobbies for their narrow professional interests.

These competing efforts led to the second transformation whereby organized psychology embraced its role as a policy science demonstrating its relevance to legislators and other publics as part of a concerted effort to increase its market share. The timing of this turn to policy mattered. Heightened demands for inclusivity at the table and greater transparency in the process bolstered skepticism about the legitimacy of governmental decision making and even a wariness toward state-based solutions.[8] By the 1980s, psychology's radical experiments with democracy had largely collapsed (or at least been relegated to the disciplinary margins).[9] Instead, the conception of laypeople who were institutionalized in

---

6. Andrew Abbott, *The System of Professions: An Essay on the Division of Expert Labor*. Chicago: University of Chicago Press, 1988.

7. Ellen Herman, *The Romance of American Psychology: Political Culture in the Age of Experts*. Oakland: University of California Press, 1995, 238–303; Wade Pickren, "Tension and Opportunity in Post-World War II American Psychology." *History of Psychology* 10, no. 3 (2007): 279–299; Jessica Grogan, *Encountering America: Humanistic Psychology, Sixties Culture and the Shaping of the Modern Self*. New York: Harper Perennial, 2013; Peter Hegarty, *A Recent History of Lesbian and Gay Psychology: From Homophobia to LGBT*. London: Routledge, 2017; Alexandra Rutherford, *Psychology at the Intersections of Gender, Feminism, History, and Culture*. New York: Cambridge University Press, 2021.

8. Hugh Heclo, "The Sixties' False Dawn: Awakenings, Movements, and Postmodern Policy-Making," *Journal of Policy History* 8, no. 1 (1996): 34–63.

9. After 1980, the qualitative methods movement (found largely outside the United States) captured much of this sensibility. These practitioners fashioned themselves as more ethical than their quantitative counterparts. A major argument of this book is that the experiments with democracy, although framed as a rejection of certain received psychometric approaches, were not limited to qualitative methods. For a critical account of the ethical exceptionalism qualitative methods, see Svend Brinkmann and Steinar Kvale. "Confronting the Ethics of Qualitative Research," *Journal of Constructivist Psychology* 18, no. 2 (2005): 157–181.

Introduction

these policy interventions reflected a broader late-modern pessimism about the possibilities of self-rule, a suspicion of the state, and general incredulity toward modernity's metanarratives about progress.[10]

The reorganization of psychology around the imperatives of health and its pursuit of policy relevance drove the third transformation: a major theoretical reorientation across the supposedly "basic" areas of psychological science. In contrast to a triumphant cognitive science taking its cues from cybernetic information theory and documenting the mind's successes, the new affective science took inspiration from clinical and social settings and foregrounded the ubiquity of cognitive biases that compromised human judgment and even functioning. Contact with this new set of "applied" problems fundamentally, if quietly, altered the basic tenets of cognitive theory. Cognitive scientists in the 1950s, led by Herbert Simon, argued that human rationality was limited or "bounded" by the demands of the task environment and the mind's processing power. Ruled by a series of shortcuts known as heuristics, thinking was inevitably constrained, if largely dependable. In the 1970s, across an array of applied realms, the perceived balance between the mind's successes and failures shifted dramatically. Clinical psychologists working with anxious and depressed clients experienced their own cognitive revolution and recast these mood disorders as distorted patterns of thinking. They gave unprecedented attention to the mind's many "cognitive biases" which compromised the person's perception of the world and themselves. In turn, forensic psychologists documented the inability of clinicians and other mental health professionals to successfully predict future violence in patients encountered through the criminal justice system. In parallel to these developments, feminist and radical community psychologists challenged the ways in which biased, prejudicial attitudes had become built into legal and educational institutions, perpetuating inequity along lines of gender and race. Finally, as mathematical psychologists interested in judgment and decision making applied cognitive theory to the practical problems of mitigating the risks generated by large-scale technological and economic systems, the problem of bias and the human propensity to avoid dreaded, averse consequences came to the fore.[11] The cumulative effect of these local revolts in the 1970s was a quiet revolution when it came to psychology's meta-theory in the 1990s.

10. Jean-François Lyotard, *The Postmodern Condition: A Report on Knowledge*. Minneapolis: University of Minnesota Press, 1984; Daniel T. Rodgers, *Age of Fracture*. Cambridge, MA: Harvard University Press, 2011; Melinda Cooper, *Family Values: Between Neoliberalism and the New Social Conservatism*. Cambridge, MA: MIT Press, 2017.

11. This shift to managing failures owes much to the logics of the risk society. See Ulrich Beck, *Risk Society: Towards a New Modernity*. Thousand Oaks, CA: SAGE, 1992.

THE AFFECTIVE REVOLUTION

This final transformation, which forms the centerpiece of this book, dovetails with what the intellectual historian Ruth Leys calls "the ascent of affect."[12] Around the year 2000, affect was suddenly and seemingly everywhere. A few definitions are necessary to understand the nature of this transformation. Part of affect's appeal is its conceptual plasticity, so that it connotes different things to different audiences. For example, many individuals in the humanities looked to affect for its promise to go beyond reason and words to capture intense emotional states typically denigrated by the tastemakers of modernity. The term means something very different in academic psychology; there, affect and emotion are conceptually related, but they are not synonymous terms. Affect refers to a set of basic dispositions or moods that are more primitive than complex emotional states. An affect possesses a valence (either positive or negative), which arouses the organism on a physiological level, thereby establishing motivation as an impulse to act. Operating on a preconscious level, affect skirts deliberate intentionality. Psychologists' embrace of affect embodies (literally) a counterrevolution against cognitive science's commitment to medium-agnostic models of the thinking mind.[13] Leys traced much contemporary affect theory back to the early 1960s' work of the personality psychologist Silvan Tomkins. He pursued these interests in comparative intellectual isolation for two decades, eventually finding support in fellow emotions researchers Paul Ekman and Carroll Izard. By 1980, a wide range of psychologists turned to affect, seeing in it a key resource to resist cognitivism's overly rationalistic approach to mental life. Surveying this heightened interest, in 1981 Tomkins boldly declared that "the next decade or so belongs to affect."[14] His prediction proved largely accurate. Many psychologists came to embrace his emotional primitives as the true source of motivation rather than as an outcome of action. In the influential formulation of social psychologist Robert Zajonc, "preference need no inferences."[15] Affect, often linked to the growing cultural salience of evolutionary biology and neuroscience, offered a radically different account of how people came to their decisions, one that was distinct from earlier meta-theories such as behaviorism, psychoanalysis, and cognitivism.

In the 1970s, psychology faced major competition from sociobiology when it came to explaining the conduct of humans and other species. Sharing with cognitivism a grounding mathematical game theory, sociobiology broke with its view

---

12. Ruth Leys, *The Ascent of Affect: Genealogy and Critique*. Chicago: University of Chicago Press, 2017.

13. Constantina Papoulias and Felicity Callard, "Biology's Gift: Interrogating the Turn to Affect," *Body and Society* 16, no. 1 (2010): 29–56.

14. Silvan Tomkins, "The Quest for Primary Motives: Biography and Autobiography of an Idea," *Journal of Personality and Social Psychology* 41, no. 2 (1981): 306–329, 314.

15. Robert Zajonc, "Feeling and Thinking: Preferences Need no Inferences," *American Psychologist* 35, no. 2 (1980): 151–175.

of the mind as a computer deliberately executing operations. Instead, people were seen as fleshy machines, the unwitting carriers of their own genetic material, motivated by deep Darwinian logics unavailable to conscious reflection. Altruism, seemingly unselfish kindness, provided sociobiologists with the greatest puzzle. If maximizing the propagation of one's own genes governed all behavior, why be nice? The gene's eye view (rather than the organismic one) revealed parental investment in their offspring and sacrifices for other conspecifics (even at the risk of their own life) represented a "rational" evolutionary strategy. In one swoop, sociobiology placed powerful, inchoate, universal, affective dispositions (the "love" for a child or a mate) at the center of the struggle for existence.[16] Neither sociobiology nor its successor ever became the dominant meta-theory in psychology. However, much subsequent psychology adopted a thin evolutionary veneer; evoking Darwin signaled a broad commitment to scientific naturalism and materialism amid mounting culture wars of the late twentieth century.

The biologization of psychology (in terms of a vague evolutionary background and a more proximate set of neuroimaging methods) certainly contributed to the ascent of affect, but this explanation still misses much of the story. It neglects the realignment of the experimental and the clinical in psychology as a major factor pushing the affective to the foreground. Historian Paul Forman has pointed to a broad reversal that was experienced across the industrial West around 1980 when it came to the primacy of science over technology. Where the moderns venerated "basic research," knowledge for its own sake, and maintained a clear demarcation between supposedly pure science and practical technology, their postmodern counterparts rejected these dichotomies, seeing the most valuable knowledge (at both a theoretical and commercial level) deriving from the solution to practical problems.[17] This change almost exactly parallels psychology's experience around 1980 when the applied areas of clinical and professional psychology eclipsed the parent discipline. The numerical prominence of clinicians changed the priorities of psychology's organizational bodies, created new funding opportunities, and pushed the affective (in the form of pathological mood disorders) to the forefront of the discipline's research agenda.[18] Simply put, psychology became a health science after 1980 when it had not been one before.[19] Many psychologists bemoaned this growing indebtedness to the "medical model." However, even the proposed

---

16. Donna Haraway, *Primate Visions: Gender, Race, and Nature in the World of Modern Science*. London: Routledge, 1989; Amanda Rees, *The Infanticide Controversy: Primatology and the Art of Field Science*. Chicago: University of Chicago Press, 2009; Erika Lorraine Milam, *Creatures of Cain: The Hunt for Human Nature in Cold War America*. Princeton, NJ: Princeton University Press, 2020.

17. Paul Forman, "The Primacy of Science in Modernity, of Technology in Postmodernity, and of Ideology in the History of Technology," *History and Technology* 23, no. 1–2 (2007): 1–152.

18. Wade Pickren, *Psychology and Health: Culture, Place, History*. London: Routledge, 2019.

19. Jonathan Metzl and Anna Kirkland (eds.), *Against Health: How Health Became the New Morality*. New York: New York University Press, 2010.

alternatives to it, such as the positive psychology with its enthusiasm on character, resilience, and strength, maintained a commitment to the imperatives of health.[20]

With its increased proximity to health, psychology also forged new relationships with neuroscience. This development came in the form of the biologization of mood disorders (a process started by a new National Institute of Mental Health (NIMH) funding initiative in 1969 and culminating with the release of a new generation of antidepressant medication in the late 1980s) and the management of patients suffering from neurological damages. Psychological theory increasingly attended to the distinction between controlled and automatic processes, the former belonging to conscious mind and the latter governed by the nervous system.[21] What changed, then, was a shift from midcentury admonishments of "speculative neurology" as being beyond the bounds of positivist science given the current state of knowledge to a cultivation of "anticipatory neuroscience" in the 1990s. With ambiguous and often contested evidence, invoking the brain gave wholly psychological theories not only greater realism but also heightened credibility.[22] The eclipse of cognitive science by neuroscience provides one of the more common and plausible narratives in the recent history of psychology.[23]

Leys tells us much about affect theory's limits, but her largely intellectual history offers an overly narrow perspective on its ascendency. However, there are at least two problems with this line of argument. First, "neuroscience" as both a concept and a field actually predated "cognitive science." When, in the late 1970s, the Sloan Foundation granted money to organize cognitive science into an interdisciplinary field, it modeled this project on the earlier success of its neuroscience initiative. Furthermore, brainhood, the notion that our individuality and identity are localized in our nervous system, served the historical antecedent for scientific psychology.[24] No psychologist denied *that* the brain was somehow involved in psychological processes; where they differed was in the attention they paid to *how* psychological function got substantiated on biological matter. Part of the innovativeness of midcentury cognitive science lay in its agnosticism when it came to the

---

20. Jeffery Yen, "Authorizing Happiness: Rhetorical Demarcation of Science and Society in Historical Narratives of Positive Psychology." *Journal of Theoretical and Philosophical Psychology* 30, no. 2 (2010): 67; Daniel Horowitz, *Happier?: The History of a Cultural Movement That Aspired to Transform America*. Oxford: Oxford University Press, 2017.

21. Richard M. Shiffrin and Walter Schneider, "Controlled and Automatic Human Information Processing: II. Perceptual Learning, Automatic Attending and a General Theory," *Psychological Review* 84, no. 2 (1977): 127–190.

22. David P. McCabe and Alan D. Castel. "Seeing Is Believing: The Effect of Brain Images on Judgments of Scientific Reasoning," *Cognition* 107, no. 1 (2008): 343–352.

23. The most thorough version of this narrative is Nikolas Rose and Joelle M. Abi-Rached. *Neuro: The New Brain Sciences and the Management of the Mind*. Princeton, NJ: Princeton University Press, 2013.

24. Fernando Vidal, "Brainhood, Anthropological Figure of Modernity." *History of the Human Sciences* 22, no. 1 (2009): 5–36.

medium for the mind. The alliance with artificial intelligence meant that cognitive theorists did not care whether the mind's program ran on a living brain or on its electronic counterpart. Cognitive science and neuroscience existed in parallel as contemporary alternatives rather than in a line of historical succession. Second, sociological studies suggest that laypeople tend to accommodate novel neuroscience claims to their existing understandings of the self, others, and society rather than having them overturned.[25] Given that theories of cool, serial, deliberative thinking are just as easily substantiated on neurological models as hot, automatic, affective ones, the rise of neuroscience alone does not provide a sufficient explanation for psychology's affective revolution.

A number of factors beyond affect theory's (questionable) intellectual merits contributed to contemporary interest. Something else changed when psychologists abandoned medium-agnostic computationalism in favor of live, fleshy, hot models of the brain's neurocircuitry. This shift very much involved the recycling and repacking of older ideas in new neurological clothing. Self-control represented an extreme example. It resurrected a concept from Victorian self-help. In the 1950s and 1960s, these same authors freely cited Freud, but removed these references in the 1990s, while the theories themselves remained largely untouched. No singular discovery or piece of evidence drove this sudden embrace of anticipatory neuroscience. The impetus came largely from new forms of patronage (e.g., funding the National Institutes of Health's "decade of the brain" initiatives), the availability of new imagining technologies in hospitals, and the push from pharmaceutical companies to classify mental illness as diseases of the brain amenable to chemical intervention. In other words, the turn to neuroscience and affect is better understood as the effects of the realignment of clinical over experimental priorities in postwar psychology.

By 2000, affect came to dominate scientific conceptualizations of (good) decision making, even when it came to something as refined and seemingly intentional as morality. Reviewing this "affective revolution," psychologist Jonathan Haidt argued for "the 'affective primacy' principle" for understanding moral decision making. Drawing support from sociobiology, Haidt contended that the human mind had two components: "an ancient, automatic, and very fast affective system and a phylogenetically newer, slower, and motivationally weaker cognitive system." People make moral decisions intuitively, drawing on their fast, automatic affective dispositions, and subsequently "rationalize" their choices using the slow cognitive system. Morality, for Haidt, was action oriented and functioned to bind individuals into tribal groups to augment the survival of their genetic material.[26] In many ways, Haidt's dual process theory was old, even synonymous with

---

25. Cliodhna O'Connor and Helene Joffe, "How Has Neuroscience Affected Lay Understandings of Personhood? A Review of the Evidence," *Public Understanding of Science* 22, no. 3 (2013): 254–268.

26. Jonathan Haidt, "The New Synthesis in Moral Psychology," *Science* 316, no. 5827 (2007): 998–1002, 998.

psychology itself. The prominence of such an idea bookended the "psychological century." Both William James and Sigmund Freud had endorsed such views, but they became marginalized and forgotten among scientific psychologists, only to come back with a vengeance beginning in the 1990s, often cloaked in the language of promissory neuroscience.[27]

Organized around dichotomies like hot–cold, fast–slow, primitive–rational, and affective–cognitive, dual process theories received an unprecedented public airing after Daniel Kahneman received the Nobel Prize in Economics in 2003. He made the theory the centerpiece of his acceptance speech (reprinted in both *American Psychologist* and *American Economic Review*) and a subsequent bestseller. He posited the existence of two reasoning systems: one fast, associative, automatic, unconscious; the other slow, rule-based, deliberative, conscious.[28] Affect did not replace true cognition but encircled it. Rather than a computer-like machine, the human mind became an evolutionary-honed brain, error-prone and misled by its barely articulated wants. When it came to decision making, psychologists ultimately saw intentional reasoning (or "executive function") not only as a scarce resource, but as one besieged by affect-laden dispositions and automatic processes. This dual process theory could explain poor impulse control, group prejudice, the dangers of inflated self-worth, the seductions of digital technologies, and even the irrationality of financial markets. Affective science, then, is a historically particular model of emotional expression and predominance over conscious, "rational" decision making. It is also a theory of embodied emotions that carries distinct political consequences.

FROM AMERICAN COOL TO AMERICAN RED AND BLUE

This still rather inward-looking intellectual history of affect produces a narrative that coincides with an important sociological critique of psychic life under neoliberalism. First, social and political problems get psychologized, so that they become a trouble localized to the interior of the lone person's mind. Psychologization also renders conflicts into problems of misperceived communication, poor attitudes, or failures to motivate rather than resulting from unequal and unjust socioeconomic structures requiring change through collective action. Psychological interventions sustain the kind of hyperindividualism characteristic of neo-liberal ideology: a person unencumbered by reciprocal obligations, disembedded from

---

27. Steven A. Sloman, "The Empirical Case for Two Systems of Reasoning," *Psychological Bulletin* 119, no. 1 (1996): 3–22; Janet Metcalfe and Walter Mischel. "A Hot/Cool-System Analysis of Delay of Gratification: Dynamics of Willpower," *Psychological Review* 106, no. 1 (1999): 3–19.

28. Daniel Kahneman, "A Perspective on Judgment and Choice: Mapping Bounded Rationality." *American Psychologist* 58, no. 9 (2003): 697; Kahneman, "Maps of Bounded Rationality: Psychology for Behavioral Economics." *American Economic Review* 93, no. 5 (2003): 1449–1475; Daniel Kahneman, *Thinking, Fast and Slow*. New York: Macmillan, 2011.

their historical community, and empowered as a self-responsible agent over their own actions.[29] Along with the "punctual" individual comes the proliferation of evaluative metrics and tools designed to monitor, regulate, and control the self. These began with the inexact and burdensome information-gathering technologies of midcentury universities, governments, and corporations, but they increasingly derive from how the Big Data analytics of surveillance capitalism discretely captures the self-revelations secreted through computer-mediated social lives.[30] Finally, these instruments not only quantify the self but orient it toward optimization. A significant component of living under late capitalism is a coercive "promise of happiness." Postindustrial, service sector jobs do not produce tangible goods, but rather sell pleasing experiences to the consumer. Austerity often denied working-class persons the traditional markers of adulthood such as steady employment and home ownership. Instead, these inhabitants of "the mood economy" mark the transition to adulthood in terms of overcoming a childhood trauma or youthful addiction.[31]

By taking a historical approach, this book departs from this sociological critique by rejecting the assumption that contemporary psychology resulted simply or directly from the inevitable working out of the cunning of neoliberal reason or an unchanging suspicion of mass democracy among elite intellectuals. Charting the historical transformation of postwar American psychology as it became a truly global force foregrounds actors and contexts that trouble this appealing narrative. Namely, the push for health, broader public relevance, and even theories of affect did not come primarily from the established academic centers of the discipline, but rather from a series of significant challenges to their power in the decades following 1945. This book takes seriously the inspiration and insights American psychologists derived from the Popular Front of the 1930s and the New Left of the 1960s. Without denying the importance of the patronage of the military-industrial complex and the profound influence of capitalist norms on psychology, these political movements and their radical experiments with democracy disrupted

---

29. Nikolas Rose, *Inventing Our Selves: Psychology, Power, and Personhood*. Cambridge: Cambridge University Press, 1998; Barbara Cruikshank, *The Will to Empower: Democratic Citizens and Other Subjects*. Ithaca, NY: Cornell University Press, 1999; Eva Illouz, *Saving the Modern Soul: Therapy, Emotions, and the Culture of Self-help*. Oakland: University of California Press, 2008. This version of person can be traced back to the "possessive individualism" of the liberal social contract theories that created the precondition for the psychological; see Charles Taylor, *Sources of the Self: The Making of the Modern Identity*. Cambridge, MA: Harvard University Press, 1989.

30. Sarah E. Igo, *The Averaged American: Surveys, Citizens, and the Making of a Mass Public*. Cambridge, MA: Harvard University Press, 2007.

31. Sara Ahmed, *The Promise of Happiness*. Durham, NC: Duke University Press, 2010; Jennifer M. Silva, *Coming Up Short: Working-class Adulthood in an Age of Uncertainty*. Oxford: Oxford University Press, 2013; William Davies, *The Happiness Industry: How the Government and Big Business Sold Us Well-Being*. London: Verso Books, 2015; Thomas Teo, "Homo Neoliberalus: From Personality to Forms of Subjectivity," *Theory and Psychology* 28, no. 5 (2018): 581–599.

business as usual at key historical junctures as members entered the field of psychology and altered its assumptions and practices. This history casts psychology as a contested political space rather than a site of corporate liberal hegemony.

This history also suggests reasons for the contemporary embrace of mental health among those on the left as the predominant language for articulating political complaint.[32] In austere times of retrenchment, health serves as the last refuge for the utopian aspirations of the welfare state and its radical critics. This took the form of an implicit promise of delivering psychological justice. This promise took seriously postwar psychology's demand to improve human welfare as a crucial aspect of universal rights. It centered on the recognition of how unequal systems caused psychic harm, not merely material deprivation. Moreover, it advanced a theory of social change whereby uplifting a person or group's mental outlook formed a necessary precedent for social action. The pursuit of psychological justice served as a persistent and stable self-understanding of the liberal psychologist's social role. Certain periods, such as the early 1940s and especially the 1970s, saw more radical approaches for justifying psychology. This entailed considering psychology's constructive contributions in these systems of inequality and the adoption of alternative methods and epistemologies to make the discipline more accountable to those on the margins whom it sought to represent. At best, these moments were rare and fleeting. They marked alternatives that were available but largely not pursued in the discipline. The discipline's comparative political quietude, if not compliance with state authority after September 11 and the 2008 financial crisis represents something of a dog that did not bark. In contrast, affect as a meta-theory has largely delivered justice psychologized. Instead of achieving psychological welfare as a universal, equitably distributed good, it rendered it as individualized models of human capital, personal responsibility, and mental health. In late modernity, demands made against the system increasingly take the form of "complaints" in a psychological register. A corollary of this form of resistance has been the expansion of what two critics call "the empire of trauma" wherein documenting wrongs made against persons requires evidence of psychic harm.[33] In sum, psychology provided an appealing language for registering the damage done by a hierarchical, unequal, and discriminatory society. At the same time, this history also acknowledges how rendering this utopian project through the language of the psychological ultimately compromised and even undermined it.

This matter opens a new understanding of emotional life in late modernity. Broadly speaking, the past fifty years have witnessed a shift from "American cool" to what we might call "American red and blue." The cultural historian Peter Stearns coined the former term to capture the dominant "emotional style" of the mid-twentieth century, one revolving around the masculine forms restraint,

---

32. Sara Ahmed, *Complaint!*. Durham, NC: Duke University Press, 2021.

33. Didier Fassin and Richard Rechtman, *The Empire of Trauma: An Inquiry into the Condition of Victimhood*. Princeton, NJ: Princeton University Press, 2009.

detachment, and management and an unmarked yet universalizing whiteness.[34] Born out of the Enlightenment's "republic of letters," the bourgeois public sphere was predicated on the fiction of deliberative, communication action through the self-expression of rational actors. This narrative certainly risks veering into a false nostalgia where midcentury "consensus liberalism" masked an unspoken white supremacy, patriarchal control, and heteronormativity. Indeed, it was feminist and queer scholars who first noticed this new public prominence of the emotions and developed sophisticated accounts which they refused to dichotomize between mood and sound reason. Although "cool" had its forms in African American art forms like jazz, the norms of this emotional style delegitimized oppositional forms of political affective expressiveness, namely, the angry Black woman and the feminist killjoy for whom enlightenment through consciousness-raising only attenuated them to the persistence of inequality.[35] In contrast, "American red and blue" underscores a new openness and demand for candor across the social spectrum. The political convulsions of the 1960s and the resulting "culture wars" led to a new public emotionality driven by frank expressiveness in the form of "uncivil," "hot," tribal emotions. In other words, "American red and blue" is a structure of feeling that speaks to the incomplete, uneven, and often halted inroads made by radical political interventions seeking greater equality in a supposedly "post-scarcity," "post-materialist" society.

At the risk of reifying the kinds of problematic dichotomies favored by psychologists, Table 0.1 outlines some of the ground traveled between cognitive and affect theory in terms of intellectual content, interdisciplinary alliances, and political contexts. Cognitivism was always more than a theory about how the mind works. It extended into a political philosophy built around not only the homology between human and machine minds, but also between organic and administrative bodies. The keywords *system, structure, function*, and *process* defined this high modernist social science at both the organismal and organizational scale.[36] This worldview was born out of reactions to the geopolitical catastrophes of midcentury and the constant threat of nuclear annihilation if cooler heads did not prevail.[37] It was embodied and promulgated by a generation of largely male

---

34. Peter N. Stearns, *American Cool: Constructing a Twentieth-century Emotional Style*. New York: New York University Press, 1994.

35. Eve Kosofsky Sedgwick, *Touching Feeling: Affect, Pedagogy, Performativity*. Durham, NC: Duke University Press, 2003; Ann Cvetkovich, *Archive of Feelings*. Durham, NC: Duke University Press, 2003; Sara Ahmed, *Cultural Politics of Emotion*. Edinburgh: Edinburgh University Press, 2004; Berlant, Lauren. *Cruel Optimism*. Durham, NC: Duke University Press, 2011.

36. Hunter Heyck, *Age of System: Understanding the Development of Modern Social Science*. Baltimore: Johns Hopkins University Press, 2015.

37. Paul Erickson, Judy L. Klein, Lorraine Daston, Rebecca Lemov, Thomas Sturm, and Michael D. Gordin. *How Reason Almost Lost Its Mind: The Strange Career of Cold War Rationality*. Chicago: University of Chicago Press, 2013.

Table 0.1: Cognitive and Affective Science Contrasted.

	Cognitive Science	Affective Science
Key process	Thinking	Feeling
Circa	1956–2000	1980–present
Core subarea	Perception and memory	Clinical and Social psychology
How the mind works	Computation	Automaticity
Speed	Slow	Fast
Decision-making	Manipulation of symbols (mental representations)	Intuitive or implicit reaction
Nature of errors	Noise, channel capacity	Affective dispositions
Role of Culture	Universalism	Tribalism, parochialism
Interdisciplinary conversations	Artificial intelligence, linguistics, philosophy	Neuroimaging, economics, psychiatry, sociobiology
Geopolitics	Cold War	War on Terror
Domestic politics	Consensus liberalism	Red/Blue state culture wars
Central metaphor	The computer	The network
Human analog	Scientist	Polarized group, digital crowd

and (at least passably) white academics whose careers flourished in the comparative largesse of the rapidly expanding postwar university system. They adopted the consensus liberalism of their governmental and private foundation patrons. They universalized their own experience as scientists, crafting and testing hypotheses about the world. Putting a premium on consensus achieved through method and scholarly deliberation, they often dismissed and silenced radical difference as irrational conflict.[38] Culture, especially language and highbrow pursuits like chess, mattered greatly to them, but they understood the term rather flatly. Culture, like education, primarily served as a medium for transmitting information. These academics equated cultural differences with miscommunication, something they theorized would be eradicated by unrelenting modernization.[39] To become a computer for these men was not to become a robot, a mechanical serf beholden to another's will. Instead, such a form embodied the pinnacle of progress, the closest thing to transcending the bounds of biological limits and imbibing the language of thought itself—mathematics, logic, and reason. It offered the hope of becoming the best (albeit still bounded and limited) player of the game.

Affective science is more recent, so both its political influences and consequences necessarily remain more opaque to historians. However, imagining the human as a

---

38. Jamie Cohen-Cole, *The Open Mind: Cold War Politics and the Sciences of Human Nature*. Chicago: University of Chicago Press, 2014.

39. Michael E. Latham, *Modernization as Ideology: American Social Science and" Nation Building" in the Kennedy Era*. Chapel Hill: University of North Carolina Press, 2000.

machine running on automatic is much older than affective science.[40] Whether we were "merely" automata (a soulless thing to be played rather than a skilled player) has troubled a certain class of so-called moderns from (at least) René Descartes onward. His introduction of the problematic mind–body dualism was meant to preserve humanity's God-given dignity in the face of this mechanical onslaught. Three hundred years later, T. H. Huxley, in championing Darwin's displacement of humanity's unique place in the order of things, famously declared humanity was nothing more than a fancy machine with conscious thought, an epiphenomenon of our automated organic machinery. William James's rejection of Huxley's automata theory by embracing "the utility of consciousness" for humanity's survival value, in important ways marked the birth of "the psychological." Identifying the properties of this consciousness as effective decision-maker bestowed meaning and purpose on the fledging discipline. It also established for it a unique object of study, making it more impervious to reduction to mere physiology. Yet, as a historian of technology, Edward Jones-Imhotep argues that the dream (or nightmare) of autonomous machinery was predicated on "*not* seeing certain kinds of labor and the people performing." The philosophe's handwringing over automata (concerns strikingly absent from the artisans who crafted, demonstrated, and worked with these machines) functioned as a disappearing act. It secreted away an elite's fears and imaginings about the psychic lives of those they deemed lowly, persons often marked by race.[41]

Such tensions between autonomy and automaticity find expression in psychologists' methodological choices. In this area, their continued epistemological commitments have done much to obscure the significant transformation traced in this book. The discipline has largely remained dedicated to a marriage of behaviouristic (if not strictly behaviorist) experimental designs prioritizing control and eugenics-born quantitative methods for measuring variations in individual difference. Behaviorism, as David Bakan persuasively argued, represented white, Protestant, rural folk's horrified response to the cosmopolitanism of urban modernity using tools familiar to them from animal husbandry.[42] Humans, like rats, pigeons, and livestock, were simply automata, trainable by following a few basic schedules of punishment or reward. They intended an even distribution of their technologies of control throughout society. Many, especially midcentury European intellectuals, saw behaviorism as a parody of American crassness, practicality, and brute utilitarianism. Yet, the movement's unrelenting materialism and

---

40. On automatism marking the boundary of the human, see Paul Christopher Johnson, *Automatic Religion: Nearhuman Agents of Brazil and France*. Chicago: University of Chicago Press, 2021; Heather Murray, *Asylum Ways of Seeing: Psychiatric Patients, American Thought and Culture*. Philadelphia: University of Pennsylvania Press, 2022.

41. Edward Jones-Imhotep, "The Ghost Factories: Histories of Automata And Artificial Life." *History and Technology* 36, no. 1 (2020): 3–29, 11.

42. David Bakan, "Behaviorism and American Urbanization," *Journal of the History of the Behavioral Sciences* 2, no. 1 (1966): 5–28.

reductionism met with unease from liberal, conservative, and radical humanists. The affective revolution recalls the behaviorist fascination with technologies of control, but now with an even less democratic distribution. Instead, the new psychology is organized around the bifurcation between a cognition as reserved for the few and an affective rule for the many.

Despite this methodological continuity, the affective revolution led to profound changes in the kind of psychology ordinary persons encountered in their daily lives. If intelligence tests defined psychology's public face between 1920 and 1970, a host of new measures began outstripping its reach. This included the Beck Depression Inventory (1961), the Rosenberg Self-Esteem Scale (1965), the Positive Affect and Negative Affect Schedule (1988), online quizzes for the "Big 5" personality traits, and the Implicit Association Test (1998). Again, this list illustrates a splintering of psychology. None of these measures has the I.Q.'s singular reach. Nevertheless, these novel measures came from a shared cultural place where implicit, unconscious, primitive, and affective dispositions took precedence over acquired cognitive abilities. These newer measures traveled along the psychometric infrastructure built for and by I.Q., allowing them to enter a wide range of educational, medical, and vocational settings. Through their circulation, psychology concretized its reach into everyday life.

However, wanting behavioristic methods to deliver findings from a deeper and deeper place in the psyche has put psychologists in a difficult spot. The fundamental mismatch between the questions they wish to ask about people's hidden, affective motivations and having the answers framed in terms of the demands of laboratory rigor has been an ongoing source of trouble. It helps explain why some of psychologists' most cherished concepts and interventions have failed to be replicated, and yet remain central to the discipline's imaginary. Affective science offers so much to so many different publics. History, then, can explain that it has failed to deliver.

TOWARD A MULTISITED HISTORY

To what extent is the rise of the new affective science a uniquely American story? One of the thornier interpretive issues in writing the recent history of psychology concerns the field's implicit yet problematic geography. Psychologists have long sought universality in order to establish general truths about human thought and conduct, laws of mental function and behavior akin to the Newtonian laws governing all matter in the cosmos. Despite these ambitions, over the course of the twentieth century, psychological science became co-equivalent with American culture. The field went from having a polycentric structure rooted in different national traditions in Europe to American hegemony after World War II (with some contestation in a Communist world, whose leadership remained largely disdainful of the field's explanatory power).[43]

---

43. On the polycentric history of psychology, see Kurt Danziger, "Universalism and Indigenization in the History of Modern Psychology" in Adrian Brock (ed.), *Internationalizing the History of Psychology*. New York: New York University Press, 2006, 208–225.

What first appeared as exclusively "American" was a more complex cultural bricolage. This transnational quilting began in the 1870s with the importation of European psychologies by affluent intellectuals who traveled to leading universities on the continent to receive doctoral training.[44] In the interwar years, newly established patrons like the Rockefeller Foundation brought European scientists to America. The forced migration resulting from the rise of fascism made these exchanges more urgent and permanent. American institutions and various publics selectively adopted and reinterpreted those aspects of this émigré science that were most amenable to the local culture.[45] An Americanized version of psychoanalysis, liberated from Freud's considerable pessimism, exemplifies this moment.[46] After World War II, reconstructing the sciences became a concerted project of American "soft" diplomacy, with English becoming the new universal language of scientific exchange. Internationalism also required methodological accommodations to the new American norms. This largesse created centers of power in Europe amenable to American understanding of the psyche.[47]

"Psychological science," then, was not only plural in origin but formed an archipelago of English-speaking locales centered in the United States but extending to the United Kingdom, Canada, Israel, and beyond. National differences continued to matter. When Brazil embraced American psychology in the 1960s, it chose behavior analysis rather than the ascendant cognitive science.[48] Psychology in Canada and Great Britain remained more open to neurology.[49] Indeed, many Canadian and British psychologists saw neurology as an alternative to American psychology, which became globally influential due in part to the ease of transmission in a common English tongue, albeit with distinct national concepts and vocabularies. Nor was this affective science wholly "Western" in origin. Starting

---

44. Daniel T. Rodgers, *Atlantic Crossings: Social Politics in a Progressive Age*. Cambridge, MA: Harvard University Press, 1998.

45. On interwar patronage bringing European psychologists to the United States, see Christian Fleck, *A Transatlantic History of the Social Sciences: Robber Barons, the Third Reich and the Invention of Empirical Social Research*. London: Bloomsbury, 2011. On the selective uptake of émigré psychology, see Michael M. Sokal, "The Gestalt Psychologists in Behaviorist America." *The American Historical Review* 89, no. 5 (1984): 1240–1263.

46. Dagmar Herzog, *Cold War Freud*. Cambridge: Cambridge University Press, 2017.

47. Sandra G. L. Schruijer, "Whatever Happened to the 'European' in European Social Psychology? A Study of the Ambitions in Founding the European Association of Experimental Social Psychology." *History of the Human Sciences* 25, no. 3 (2012): 88–107; Thomas Teo, "Backlash against American Psychology: An Indigenous Reconstruction of the History of German Critical Psychology." *History of Psychology* 16, no. 1 (2013): 1–18.

48. Sérgio Cirino, Rodrigo Miranda, and Robson Cruz, "The Beginnings of Behavior Analysis Laboratories in Brazil: A Pedagogical View," *History of Psychology* 15, no. 3 (2012): 263–272.

49. Yvan Prkachin, "'The Sleeping Beauty of the Brain': Memory, MIT, Montreal, and the Origins of Neuroscience." *Isis* 112, no. 1 (2021): 22–44.

in the 1970s, psychologists eagerly adopted (or perhaps culturally appropriated) Eastern meditative practices into their therapeutic toolbox as routinized "mindfulness."[50]

After 1991, this assembled psychology was globally ascendant, seemingly making good on the discipline's universalizing pretensions. Psychological interventions traveled along the same circuits, promoting Hollywood films, Coca-Cola, and other products of American cultural imperialism.[51] To somewhat recast historian Kate Brown's question about the modernist landscapes, why did people in Kazakhstan and Montana come to be seen as possessing nearly the same mind?[52] The affective science of personality assessment, impression management, and happiness industries took hold in places as different as London, England, and Pune, India.[53] Beyond this "corporate cross-cultural psychology," the discipline transformed the lives of illegal detainees scooped up in the War on Terror and global poor were subjected to behavioral experiments to maximize the effectiveness of developmental aid. At this moment of peak influence, some did warn of the field's remarkable provinciality. Economic competition from East Asia starting in the late 1980s inspired the revival of a cultural psychology of the self. In 2009, developmental psychologist Jeffrey Arnett surveyed the flagship journals of numerous subfields, showing ridiculous overrepresentation of American researchers and samples.[54] A team of cultural psychologists coined the term "WEIRD" (Western, Educated, Industrialized, Rich, and Democratic) to capture a persistence bias in the kinds of people psychologists preferred studying when constructing their theories. They also collected field experiment data suggesting that people who were not from these cultures differed not only in terms of high-level culture but also in basic perception and decision making.[55] Yet, these widely cited criticisms hid a much longer history of marginalized psychologists, underscoring the discipline's first

---

50. Jeff Wilson, *Mindful America: Meditation and the Mutual Transformation of Buddhism and American Culture*. Oxford: Oxford University Press, 2014; Anne Harrington and John Dunne, "When Mindfulness Is Therapy: Ethical Qualms, Historical Perspectives." *American Psychologist* 70, no. 7 (2015): 621–631; Shayna Fox Lee, "Psychology's Own Mindfulness: Ellen Langer and the Social Politics of Scientific Interest in 'Active Noticing,'" *Journal of the History of the Behavioral Sciences* 55, no. 3 (2019): 216–229; Evan Thompson, *Why I Am not a Buddhist*. New Haven, CT: Yale University Press, 2020.

51. Victoria De Grazia, *Irresistible empire: America's advance through twentieth-century Europe*. Harvard University Press, 2005.

52. Kate Brown, "Gridded lives: Why Kazakhstan and Montana Are Nearly the Same Place. *American Historical Review* 106, no. 1 (2001): 17–48.

53. Sunil Bhatia, *Decolonizing Psychology: Globalization, Social Justice, and Indian Youth Identities*. New York: Oxford University Press, 2017.

54. Jeffrey Jensen Arnett, "The Neglected 95%, a Challenge to Psychology's Philosophy of Science." *American Psychologist* 64, no. 6 (2009): 571–574.

55. Joseph Henrich, Steven J. Heine, and Ara Norenzayan, "The Weirdest People in the World?" *Behavioral and Brain Sciences* 33, no. 2–3 (2010): 61–83.

world bias. This newfound commitment to diversifying psychology also masked how this methodological critique facilitated the exportation and extension of an American psychology under the rubric of global mental health.[56]

The psychology traced in this book, then, is neither a global, universal science nor a uniquely American peculiarity. Both are myths that obscure psychology's geographic reach. My approach has been to take up different strands of this globally dominant form of psychology which denies their cultural particularity and trace them back to their localities. Provincializing this knowledge allows me to attend to counter-stories that were present when the dominant theories were still in flux. Despite psychologists' disavowal of their discipline's embedded in history, the stories they tell about themselves matter. These stories are often contradictory and depend on the teller's perspective on events. This book does not necessarily try to resolve these contradictions, but it does dwell on them and elucidates what they mean about psychology's place in the world.[57] By juxtaposing familiar, oft-told stories about psychology with narratives about foreclosed possible futures brings the discipline's political history into focus. This book also seeks to repopulate the history of psychology by dwelling on the possible experience of participants and publics, not just the authoritative words of scientists. Such a historical approach reveals how local conditions and demands grow into universalizing theories and practices, as some places come to matter more than others while also becoming invisible in the process.

This approach builds upon yet challenges in important ways another influential line of sociological critique of "the psychological." One can trace this standpoint back to Theodor Adorno's condemnation of empirical social science as complacent "administrative research" in the service of the capitalist state as opposed to his own "critical" approach. It became common sense among critical scholars that mainstream social scientists functioned as "the servants of power."[58] But this sociological critique of psychology risks given too much voice to the dominant, re-silencing the marginalized. The history presented in this book tries to deal with the psychologized: participants in studies and clients in therapy, eager consumers of psychological knowledge, and those unwillingly subjected to psychological interventions. What possibilities does psychology open and which does it foreclose? The answer to this question requires going beyond what psychologists say to consider what psychology does to different populations, whether or not these consequences are intended. It also means not assuming a transparent and uniform uptake of knowledge. As psychology has become an omnipresent feature of the

---

56. Elise Klein and China Mills, "Psy-Expertise, Therapeutic Culture and the Politics of the Personal in Development," *Third World Quarterly* 38, no. 9 (2017): 1990–2008.

57. The book has a decidedly and purposefully *Roshoman*-like quality that it does not seek to resolve. See Karl G. Heider, "The Rashomon Effect: When Ethnographers Disagree," *American Anthropologist* 90, no. 1 (1988): 73–81.

58. Loren Baritz, *The Servants of Power: A History of the Use of Social Science in American Industry*. Middletown, CT: Wesleyan University Press, 1960.

public sphere, presenting concepts for self-understanding as well as technologies of measurement and control, various and varied publics have adapted it to their own local needs in the process of adopting its insights. Grappling with psychology's tremendous cultural impact requires attending to this circuitry and mediation among experts and publics—what the communication theorist Stuart Hall called the encoding of messages by mass media and their variegated decodings by different subcultural groups.[59] This Hallian perspective resonates with what some critical scholars call "the social lives of methods" or attending not only to how an experiment gets put together to generate a fact but also to how these experiments move as tools beyond the immediate context of discovery, are adopted by different communities, and are given new interpretive meanings.

Concretizing the question of agency (on the part of both human and nonhuman actors) creates a less conspiratorial narrative than those narratives where the inevitable logic of capitalism rules. Instead, knowledge remains located in particular groups, with their interests and contingent upon certain sociotechnical arrangements that are not necessarily so. The field's content is as much about how a set of intellectuals grappled and made sense of these cultural changes than about seeing it as unwitting instruments of it. Moreover, naming these psychologists and tracing their local histories reveal a more inclusive history, shaped by progressive social movements. Antifascism, sexual liberation, Black power, and feminism (and not just corporate interests and the demands of the security state) have shaped psychology not only in terms of ideology but at the level of mundane design. Psychology rather than consensus was the product of the contestation among these forces.

The chapters that follow offer a multisited framework for understanding the history of psychology since World War II. No single actor, institution, or theory appears consistently across the chapters. Each chapter delves into a close reading of how different components of affective science got made and assembled together in distinct locales. The major transformations psychology has experienced are present throughout. However, the book does advance an overall historical argument. Chapters 1 through 3 examine psychology's gradual alignment with medicine and the resistance this move encountered. Chapters 4 and 5 grapple with psychology's new publicness by comparing two applied cognitive psychology groups dedicated to solving the practical problems of late modern, technological societies. Finally, Chapters 6 through 8 delve into the affective science in its ascendancy, excavating its vision of personhood, society, and health along with the crises this approach faced.

Chapter 1 starts with a new origin story for postwar psychology by rereading the history of the late 1940s "New Look" approach to perception. Rather than simply a precursor to cognitive science, the New Look movement represented an antifascist alliance among radical and liberal clinicians, social psychologists,

---

59. Stuart Hall, 'Encoding/Decoding' in Stuart Hall, Dorothy Hobson, Andrew Lowe, and Paul Willis (eds.), *Culture, Media, Language*. London: Hutchinson, 1980, pp. 128–138.

and experimental researchers to advance a psychological theory of ideology and prejudice. They understood all cognition as "hot": governed by an individual's personality and motivation. They redeployed a host of existing perceptual instruments to capture this dangerous facet of human subjectivity. The Red Scare led to the "cooling" of cognition, a narrowing of focus to the decontextualized processing of information, and a forgetting of these radical roots. By 1956, cognitive psychologists adopted the computerized chess player as the favored model of thinking rather than the prejudiced and affective individual.

Chapter 2 examines the contested meaning of reason and rationality in postwar psychology by focusing on the career of America's leading psychotherapist, Albert Ellis. His rational therapy understood emotions as a category of distorted thinking, one that got people into trouble, especially around their sexual inhibitions. Through his New York City practice and his voluminous writings in the mainstream, pornographic, and underground presses, Ellis called upon ordinary Americans to abandon their hang-ups and think straight about themselves. The people responded through individual and shared self-exploration, experimentation, and expression. Ellis's reputation rose in connection to his advocacy of freedom of expression in the 1960s, but feminists, gay liberationists, and Objectivist libertarians all challenged his authority over sexual and psychological matters. These intense political critiques of therapy's authoritarian potential facilitated a reconciliation among different modalities of treatment and led to the "psychological détente" known as cognitive-behavioral therapy as a means of eliding this contentious history.

Chapter 3 continues the story of clinical psychology as a profession, examining how its rank and file came to eclipse the academic, scientific side of the discipline. The 1970s saw two competing strategies for expanding clinical psychology by politicizing mental health. The first strategy was "the battle for professionalism" represented by the "Dirty Dozen," a coterie of white, male clinicians in private practice seeking to seize control of the American Psychological Association (APA) to transform it into a lobby for securing compensation from insurance providers. In contrast, the second strategy was initiated by the Black psychologists affiliated with the Westside Community Mental Health Center in San Francisco who offered a radical alternative to professionalism grounded in community participation and control. These two groups articulated very different visions of training, credentialing, and compensation as well as psychology's relationship to the law. Both worked to advance psychology as a health field and to secure its domain over psychotherapy as an intervention. Professionalism proved triumphant, but theirs was something of a pyrrhic victory given the growth of psychopharmacology and the fissure of the APA in the 1980s.

The next two chapters focus on the breakdown of the cool, computational understanding of cognition as the sequential processing of information. This story is traced through the parallel history of two different research organizations on either side of the Atlantic. Adjacent to but independent from the nearby universities, both organizations were dedicated at once to applying psychology to everyday problems while developing basic theories seen as fundamental to the cognitive science. Chapter 4 looks at the Applied Psychology Unit (APU) in the United Kingdom in order to trace the rise of theories of automatic, parallel, unconscious processes localized in the brain. From the 1940s onward, the APU advanced influential, functionalist models of memory and attention. Despite this superficial continuity, cognitive theory at the APU changed significantly as its researchers grounded the theories in a historically shifting set of different experimental participants: (1) the competent naval recruit of the 1950s; (2) the "unskilled," female technology worker of the 1960s; and (3) the amnesic neuropsychological patient of the 1970s. Starting in the late 1980s, psychologists in the English-speaking world began adopting this model of "implicit memory" which was activated by subtle "priming" cues beyond immediate attention, seeing everyone as running on automatic and acting without much conscious thought.

Chapter 5 tackles the cultural origins of "cognitive bias," a concept most closely tied to the Nobel Prize-winning research of Daniel Kahneman and Amos Tversky on judgment and decision making under uncertainty. Existing accounts tend to focus on their contributions in isolation, neglecting their close collaboration in studying risk perception at Decision Research in Eugene, Oregon. This group's engagement with the controversy over domestic nuclear power opens an alternative history of heuristics and biases where statistical norms of risk met post-1960s social movements dedicated to participatory democracy. The Oregon group's attempts to balance the prevalence of cognitive biases with demands of public deliberation illuminate how cognition reheated in the 1970s amid a wider crisis of faith in democracy fed by the culture wars and the political realignment resulting from the Watergate scandal, the Vietnam War, the Arab-Israeli conflict, and the energy crisis.

The final three chapters delve into some of the cultural and political consequences of the new affective science of automaticity and self-regulation. Self-esteem ranks among the most studied of all of psychology's many constructs. Emerging out of reactions to the Great Depression and the rise of fascism by psychoanalysts and social action researchers, the English-speaking world hit peak self-esteem in the early 1990s. The state-funded California Task Force on Self-Esteem promoted the concept as a social vaccine; the popular daytime talk show host Oprah Winfrey made the term nearly ubiquitous. Feelings of low self-worth (often the result of societal prejudice) purportedly lay at the root of a host of problems, ranging from poor school performance to teenage pregnancy to addiction. Self-esteem crystallized as a means allowing marginalized and minoritized groups (African Americans, women, gays) to articulate the harms caused by unacknowledged white, male privilege in a language amenable to liberal policymakers. But psychologists largely reacted negatively to their newfound cultural influence. In response, the new field of positive psychology preached a secular gospel of self-control grounded in moral character as the real solution to society's woes.

The act of looking at human faces illuminates the extent to which the most rudimentary forms of cognition became affect-laden social judgments. Around the year 2000, facial recognition suddenly became a prominent, widely heralded mental ability leading midcentury psychologists to declare face perception an uninteresting problem. Facial recognition emerged out of the crisis of Cold War artificial intelligence, presenting a task that humans (even infants) could accomplish easily, quickly, and without conscious thought but that bested advanced computers. At the heart of this reversal are two computerized technologies of visual display and rapid recording of responses: functional Magnetic Resonance Imaging (fMRI) in neuroscience and the Implicit Association Test (IAT) in social psychology. The new psychology of discriminating different faces anticipated and helped constitute the infrastructure for a new digital landscape where interpersonal relations consisted of snap decisions about people made on social media platforms.

The book concludes by examining how psychology acquired an unprecedented status in mass culture and public policy following the 2008 financial crisis by offering tools for explaining and governing irrational behavior. Psychology in the form of unconscious behavioral nudges entered the halls of government and corporations as never before. This newfound influence proved something of a false victory, as the new affective science found itself mired in a pair of crises that threatened its legitimacy as a reliable and ethical field. In the summer of 2015, a widely publicized attempt to replicate a hundred high-profile experiments questioned the evidentiary basis of psychological knowledge. However, psychologists' preoccupation with method obscured even more troubling findings about the public role of affective science in the twenty-first century. The near simultaneous release of the Hoffman Report revealed uncomfortable truths about the collusion between psychology's largest organizational body and the Department of Defense to allow the torture of detainees during the American government's "War on Terror" campaign.

What follows then is neither a history of affective science narrowly conceived nor a comprehensive, global history of psychology since 1945. Instead, this genealogy (necessarily partial and incomplete) offers a critical and historically informed framework for understanding how and why psychology has come to matter for a range of publics and the form of personhood this has enabled. While each substantive chapter takes up a distinct theme or problem, they converge in the 1970s as a shared inflection point, one unappreciated by most psychologists and their critics as well. As radicals schooled in 1960s grassroots social movements entered the profession in unprecedented numbers, psychologists engaged in a wide range of experiments with democracy. As members of the civil rights, antiwar, feminist, gay liberation, and other post-1960s movements entered graduate school to join the ranks of the profession, they carried with them sensibilities honed by these transformative political experiences. Throughout the 1970s, they tried to incorporate these lessons into research designs (both qualitative and quantitative) which both gave voice to those who were frequently silenced and worked to mobilize (rather than control) various publics. The community psychology approach to mental health represented the best-known example, but this approach proved influential in areas of social, developmental, and cognitive psychology. The moment was short-lived. The tensions between psychologists' progressive ambitions and their actions bolstering the status quo drives much of this history. By the early

1980s, the growing malaise of the cultural war diminished psychologists' faith in activating these publics and the discipline returned to a more passive understanding of the individual. The "psychologist's advantage" as a detached knower (and manipulator) of others' psyches proved triumphant by decade's end.[60] The widespread adoption of this imperious stance had damaging consequences for the discipline, the profession, and democracy itself.

60. Karl Scheibe, "The Psychologist's Advantage and its Nullification: Limits of Human Predictability," *American Psychologist* 33, no. 10 (1978): 869–881.

1

A New Look for Psychology

The Antifascist Roots of a New Discipline

In 1950, *American Psychologist* published a letter from a newly minted PhD from Arkansas, praising what he called "psychology's New Look." For Gabriel Elias, the New Look entailed a generational revolt against an older, university-oriented, experimental science by "the more practically minded people in the fields of clinical, applied, industrial, and social psychology." He rejected suggestions made by the old guard that clinical psychology belonged in medical schools. No, his chosen speciality belonged in existing departments as "ours are psychological methods." Instead, the old guard needed to expand their definition of psychology and embrace those clinicians, opinion experts, and other practical men who had been put into action by wartime mobilization. Psychology's future lay as one field where "all strive equally to further human knowledge and welfare; and each borrows from, and aids, the other in pursuit of this common selfless end." This radical recasting of what counted as psychology represented "the progressivism of the New Look."[1]

In subsequent decades, the New Look has acquired a narrower meaning, becoming synonymous with a series of experiments conducted by Harvard psychologist Jerome Bruner in the late 1940s. According to Bruner, these experiments "helped turn the tide of American psychology toward a more cognitive emphasis." After several decades in exile during the behaviorist heyday, psychologists were again permitted to speak of private mental representations as genuine objects amenable to scientific investigation.[2] In this interpretation, the new respectability granted to the mind owed a tremendous debt to the cybernetic concept of information as a universal medium of communication and the electronic computer as a live metaphor for the human mind.[3] However, this framing of postwar

---

1. Gabriel Elias, "A Clinician Answers Guthrie," *American Psychologist* 5, no. 9 (1950): 495.

2. Jerome S. Bruner, "Jerome S. Bruner," in Gardner Lindzey (ed.), *A History of Psychology in Autobiography*, vol. 4. San Francisco: W. H. Freeman, 1980, 75–151, quote 107.

3. Alan Collins, "From H=log s (n) to Conceptual Framework: A Short History of Information," *History of Psychology* 10, no. 1 (2007): 44–72.

psychology as culminating in the cognitive revolution is incomplete, if not misleading. Textbooks tend to narrate the discipline's history as a succession of "isms," with the consensus position arguing that cognitivism represented a revolt against the behaviorism of Clark Hull, E. C. Tolman, and B. F. Skinner. According to this version of events, the revolution centered on a rejection of the behaviorists' denial of ephemeral mental states.[4] Here the revolution begins in 1956 with a pair of interdisciplinary conferences bringing together psychologists, linguists, and computer scientists. Cognitivism originated in the laboratories of experimentalists, then got extended to social and clinical applications in the 1980s. These accounts remain steadfast in their focus on psychology as an academic, experimental science, albeit one transformed by its encounters with the military.[5]

Such a narrative erases what a working psychologist like Elias identified as the "New Look." He did not see it as a revolt against behaviorism, but rather as the rejection of an asocial psychology. Radicalized by the Great Depression, and then in the next decade mobilized with the United States' entry into the Second World War, psychologists sought a new start for their discipline. Not wishing to return to the older hierarchies that placed experimental research over clinical and social application, a younger generation demanded a new perceptual psychology to help make sense of their catastrophic age.[6] Indeed, the New Look's uneven impact on psychology was one of the most lasting legacies of "the cultural front": the organizing of American cultural production around antifascist aesthetics between 1936 and 1948.[7] The New Look as a historically specific mode of "experimenting from the Left" is largely invisible to a partisan historiography pitting empirical social science as "administrative research" in the service of the capitalist state against the radical alternative of critical theory.[8] The career of Else Frenkel-Brunswik illustrates how the new direction taken by psychology took its cues

---

4. For a critical account of this narrative sequence, see Thomas H. Leahey, "The Mythical Revolutions of American Psychology," *American Psychologist* 47, no. 2 (1992): 308–318.

5. The writing of social psychology out of this history began with Howard Gardner, *The Mind's New Science: A History of the Cognitive Revolution*. New York: Basic Books, 1985. When not neglected entirely, contributions from social and clinical psychology get resigned to the contextual background for the true cognitive revolution. For example, *The Authoritarian Personality* is read as part of the cultural context for the cognitive revolution but separates from it in Jamie Cohen-Cole, *The Open Mind: Cold War Politics and the Sciences of Human Nature*. Chicago: University of Chicago Press, 2014.

6. Katherine Pandora, *Rebels within the Ranks: Psychologists' Critique of Scientific Authority and Democratic Realities in New Deal America*. Cambridge: Cambridge University Press, 2002.

7. Michael Denning, *The Cultural Front: The Laboring of American Culture in the Twentieth Century*. London: Verso, 1997.

8. This distinction came out of this historical milieu of émigré intellectuals responding to capitalism and fascism. The most complete history of critical theory remains Martin Jay, *The Dialectical Imagination: A History of the Frankfurt School and the Institute of Social Research, 1923–1950*. Berkeley: University of California Press, 1996. The most sympathetic history of administrative research is Christian Fleck, *A Transatlantic History of the Social Sciences: Robber*

from the radicalism of the cultural front. Often overshadowed by the powerful men surrounding her, Frenkel-Brunswik embodied this alternative origin story for postwar psychology: one that was centered on émigré intellectuals, antifascist commitments, and mobilization of the tools of perceptual psychology to achieve applied, clinical, and political ends.

Attending to the unrealized ambitions of these reformers helps clarify what aspects of the mind did and did not return to psychology in the second half of the twentieth century. A long line of criticisms have lamented how cognitivism's information-processing model unmoored thinking from its cultural context and neglected "hot," affective, unconscious, motivational processes.[9] Revisiting the New Look reveals that this silence was not an accident, but a disciplinary choice with a political history. The cooling of cognition into the processing of information was itself an accommodation to the Red Scare rather than a direct outcome of wartime mobilization.

THE PSYCHOLOGICAL FRONT

World War II is often seen as the main pivot in the history of psychology as the field grew from a narrow scientific discipline to a mass profession focused on the provision of (mental) health care. The most notable aspects of this transformation were both the introduction of psychologists who provided mental assessments to Veterans Administration hospitals and the resulting training programs for clinical psychologists. However, psychologists from numerous branches mobilized their talents as part of the war effort. Perceptual psychologists helped accustom human operators to new signal detection technologies like radar. Social psychologists studied morale, the diffusion of rumors, and the effects of propaganda.[10] Although the demands of the warfare state dramatically increased their number, for many the consciousness of the applied psychologist had been forged by the Great Depression. The economic collapse of the 1930s had greatly diminished the number of academic positions, driving many recent PhDs into practical fields whose social contributions they ultimately found rewarding.[11] It was this generation that voiced concerns about returning to the older hierarchy of pure, experimental psychology, which was now held above the fields of clinical,

Barons, the Third Reich and the Invention of Empirical Social Research. London: Bloomsbury Publishing, 2011.

9. Their subsequent inclusion would in some ways undo the cognitive revolution. See Christopher D. Green, "Where Did the Word "Cognitive" Come from Anyway?" *Canadian Psychology* 37, no. 1 (1996): 31–39.

10. James H. Capshew, *Psychologists on the March: Science, Practice, and Professional Identity in America, 1929–1969*. New York: Cambridge University Press, 1999.

11. Lorenz J. Finison, "Unemployment, Politics, and the History of Organized Psychology," *American Psychologist* 31, no. 11 (1976): 747–755.

industrial, and social psychology. Their concerns took institutional form. In 1946, the American Psychological Association (APA) incorporated once competing organizations dedicated to applied psychology and redefined its mission as the advancement of psychology as a science, a profession, and "a means of promoting human welfare."[12]

David Krech was one of the most eloquent advocates of not returning to prewar ways. Born Isidore Krechevsky, he first made his reputation using the standard tools of interwar learning theory: running rats in mazes. He diverged from behaviorist orthodoxy by suggesting that these rats paid attention to their circumstances, weighing and discarding "wrong" solutions to the maze until they hit upon the correct one. Such an interpretation coincided with Tolman's "purposeful behaviorism" who was Krech's dissertation supervisor at Berkeley. Krech received accolades for his doctoral research, but because of the scarcity of academic positions combined with mounting antisemitism was unable to secure a professorship upon graduating in 1933. Precariously employed, Krechevsky became "disaffected" and then radicalized while holding a series of temporary contracts in a neuropsychology laboratory at the University of Chicago. He came to see his stalled career not as a personal failing, but as a symptom of a sick society. In 1935, he joined New America, "an avowed Marxist revolutionary organization" but a "self-consciously indigenous" one whose "members took an exceedingly dim view of the Communist Party and of the USSR."[13] Krech soon began organizing his fellow psychologists like the workers he valorized.[14] In 1936, he cofounded the Society for the Psychological Study of Social Issues (SPSSI) to create a platform for psychologists wishing to mobilize their knowledge for progressive causes. It was around this time that Krech, fearful of mounting antisemitism, changed his name from Krechevsky to Krech. His own work shifted from the neurology of rats to social psychology, or what he tellingly described as "the socialization of perceptual theory."[15]

Krech carried these radical commitments into peacetime, leading the demand for a new psychology fit for the new global order. He warned that demobilization would lead to the fission of the "experimental" and "professional" branches, to the impoverishment of both. In particular, he challenged the old hierarchy where perceptual psychology constituted fundamental research, which then got applied to the domains of clinical, social, and personality psychology. His polemics

---

12. James H. Capshew and Ernest R. Hilgard, "The Power of Service: World War II and Professional Reform in the American Psychological Association." In *The American Psychological Association: A Historical Perspective*. Washington, DC: American Psychological Association, 1992, pp. 149–175, quote 162.

13. David Krech, "David Krech" in Gardner Lindzey (ed.), *A History of Psychology in Autobiography*, vol. 3 (Englewood Cliffs, NJ: Prentice-Hall, 1974): 221–250, 235.

14. Lorenz J. Finison, "The Psychological Insurgency: 1936–1945," *Journal of Social Issues* 42, no. 1 (1986): 21–33.

15. Krech, "David Krech," 244.

criticized both rat psychologists, who were more adept at handling rodents than their co-specifics, and perceptual psychologists, who were in love with the recall of a nonsense syllabus. Krech proposed that "'pure' experimental work can be done with *material* that is 'practically' important."[16] He encouraged scientists to study basic psychological processes using socially relevant situations. Where the prewar leadership seemed content in keeping the domains of perception, motivation, and behavior separate, the world in which psychology found itself after the war demanded their fusion.

It was Krech who dubbed this unifying perspective the "New Look," a term he appropriated from popular culture. In 1947, a *Life Magazine* pictorial spread had used the phrase to describe French fashion designer Christian Dior's bold Corolle Line. Dior's use of excess fabric, womanly contours, and nonfunctional hats signified the end to wartime austerity, conveying a sense of possibility and renewal in the wake of global devastation. Krech first used the term in a psychological context in the introductory manifesto for a special issue of *The Journal of Personality* he edited in 1949. The whole issue functioned as a clarion call for reorganizing psychology. It offered readers what Krech understood as a "complete" psychological theory as opposed to a series of proliferating domain-specific "theorettes." In his "Notes toward a Psychological Theory," Krech listed those psychologists whom he saw as exemplifying the New Look: Jerome Bruner, Gardner Murphy, George Klein, Heinz Werner, David McClelland, Leo Postman, Herman Witkin, Muzafer Sherif, Henry Gleitman, Julian Hochberg, and Else Frenkel-Brunswik. He did not name Kurt Lewin (likely because of his passing in 1947), but Lewin's conceptualization of the social field as a kind of Gestalt and his championing of action research certainly influenced the entire group. Yet, these were not his direct students. Krech's chorus of reformers does not fit easily into existing narratives about the discipline. It freely intermingled scientists from disparate intellectual traditions, including the second generation of Gestalt psychologists trained in America (e.g., Werner, Witkin, Gleitman, and Hochberg), pioneering social psychologists (e.g., Murphy, Sherif, and Frenkel-Brunswik), and those later associated with the cognitive revolution (e.g., Bruner, Postman).

This eclecticism mirrored the most distinct feature of Krech's proposed "complete" psychological theory: its rejection of the dichotomy between cognition and emotion. Surveying his field, he found learning psychologists, perceptual psychologists, and motivational psychologists, "each working only one side of nature's street in splendid isolation and each refraining from getting involved in jurisdictional disputes with one another."[17] Isolationism as a political ideology had led to the global catastrophe; now, it threatened the scientist's ability to truly comprehend the human. Krech argued that "there can be no behaviour which is not

16. David Krech, "A Note on Fission," *American Psychologist* 1, no. 9 (1946): 402–404, 404.

17. Krech, "Notes toward a Psychological Theory," *Journal of Personality* 18, no. 1 (1949): 66–87, 69.

at one and the same time 'cognitive' and 'emotional.' "[18] Throughout Krech riddled his exposition with political metaphors. He rejected both the "parliamentary" solution of mutual coexistence and the "imperialistic" one with one area claiming explanatory sovereignty over another. Instead, he proposed a "revolutionary" response, a fundamental recasting of psychological concepts beyond existing, common-sense definitions.[19] The New Look approach would follow the path of international cooperation through a new kind of global government holding together the perceptual, the behavioral, and the affective by examining the human in action through socially and clinically relevant situations.

Put simply, Krech championed a vision of psychology that might be termed "experimenting from the left." In a wide-ranging analysis of the literature, film, and art of the 1930s, historian Michael Denning reevaluated the impact of the Popular Front on American culture, arguing that it had a greater impact than is traditionally thought. It was a historical bloc with a political aesthetics extending beyond agitprop. Its members included émigré intellectuals and artists fleeing the Nazi seizure of power alongside the proletarian children of European immigrants. These individuals organized themselves into insurgent unions and represented the radical wing of Franklin Delano Roosevelt's New Deal coalition, pushing its politics leftward. The turning point came in 1936, the year of SPSSI's founding. The victory of the insurgent Congress of Industrial Organizations (CIO) in Flint, Michigan, and Akron, Ohio, led to massive "sit down" labor action across the country. Both Spain and France elected Popular Front governments; Franco's actions against the Spanish Republicans served as a rallying point in the United States. By 1936, fellow travelers rather than hard-line members of the Communist Party made up its rank and file.[20] The cultural front united liberals, democratic socialists, and communists and generated a mass culture (radio, film, magazines), with forms and themes that Denning calls "writing from the Left." This decidedly antifascist aesthetic denounced the corrupting influence of monopolistic corporations, venerated the working class, and pushed liberal Democrats toward antiracist policies. It represented an attack on long-standing American ideology of individualism, instead depicting the person as embedded in structures and circumstances beyond their control.

Alongside this role in the arts, the cultural front had a parallel (and perhaps more profound) impact on the social sciences. In its early years, SPSSI was a radical activist organization; with a membership often facing precarious employment, members publicly allied themselves with striking workers at home. They also pursued an internationalist vision, with the comparative psychologist T. C. Schneirla coordinating the Psychologists' Committee of the Medical Bureau to Aid Spanish Democracy, which sought to assist the Republican forces in 1937.[21]

18. Krech, "Notes toward a Psychological Theory," 82.

19. Krech, "Notes toward a Psychological Theory," 69–73.

20. Denning, *The Cultural Front*, 23.

21. Lorenz J. Finison, "Psychologists and Spain," *American Psychologist* 32, no. 12 (1977): 1080–1084.

The new psychology described by Krech was not simply one that aimed to pour an already existing practice into new organizational forms. Instead, the encounter with the Popular Front changed the very questions psychologists asked and how they arranged their existing laboratory equipment to ask a new set of questions. This new way of doing psychology flourished between 1936 and 1950 and then seemingly vanished following the Red Scare.

EXPERIMENTING FROM THE LEFT

Prior to 1935, social and perceptual psychology shared little common ground. Perceptual psychology involved experiments on the psychophysics of the sensory organs and their mental representation. It assumed a universal human subject, although in practice data were derived from highly trained, educated, white men.[22] In contrast, social psychology consisted of speculations about the character of different social groups, with the problem of social control looming large. Social psychology usually organized these racialized groups hierarchically, with the then newly discovered measure of general intelligence used as a sorting mechanism. Coming out of World War I, racialized differences in intelligence appeared to white psychologists to be a self-evident metric for organizing society along meritocratic lines. In one of the most radical reversals in the history of science, postwar psychologists not only rejected the eugenic notion of innate intelligence as overly simplistic but argued that a belief in such racial differences was a symptom of an "irrational" prejudice.[23]

This shift started during the Great Depression when the composition of psychology as a discipline changed, with many non-WASPs entering its ranks for the first time. This new generation brought new sensibilities and new approaches to the subject matter. At Columbia University, Muzafer Sherif, an émigré from Turkey, showed how a classic perceptual phenomenon manifested itself differently under social influences. The autokinetic effect, by which a stationary light in a darkened room would appear to move, was well known to psychologists. By having participants perform the experiment both individually and in small groups, Sherif showed how the presence of other observers altered one's judgments about the direction and nature of the movement.[24] His success in demonstrating

---

22. Kurt Danziger, *Constructing the Subject: Historical Origins of Psychological Research*. New York: Cambridge University Press, 1990.

23. Franz Samelson, "From "Race Psychology" to "Studies in Prejudice": Some Observations on the Thematic Reversal in Social Psychology." *Journal of the History of the Behavioral Sciences* 14, no. 3 (1978): 265–278.

24. Muzafer Sherif, "A Study of Some Social Factors in Perception," *Archives of Psychology* 187 (1935).

how social circumstances altered basic perceptual processes soon spread to other psychologists.[25]

The New Look approach took up these Depression-era studies and their common commitment to integrating the disparate areas of perception, learning, and motivation. However, contributors to the movement differed on what aspect of the synthesis deserved the most attention. Frenkel-Brunswik distinguished between "perception-centered" and "personality-centered" approaches.[26] The perception-centered New Look, exemplified by Bruner, represented a critique of classic perception research from the standpoint of social psychology. It argued against a long-held assumption of human universality when it came to basic cognitive processes. Instead, Bruner and his associates demonstrated how a person's social background shaped their learning experience and motivation, altering what was perceivable to them. Frenkel-Brunswik saw herself as exemplifying the personality-centered approach as she redeployed the existing perceptual apparatus to serve as a diagnostic tool for individual personality traits and psychopathologies.

Bruner established the "perception-centered" approach in a study the press dubbed the "big money" experiment.[27] He and his co-author, Cecile Goodman, identified two determinants of perception: the *autochthonous* (the physiological properties of the sensory and nervous sensory systems) and the *behavioral* (adaptive functions that included both the laws of learning and psychodynamic personality traits). Perceptual psychology tended to focus exclusively on the autochthonous at the expense of the behavioral. Bruner and Goodman opened by rejecting the universalist, acultural assumptions of prior perceptual theory where the human observer served as "a passive recording instrument of rather complex design."[28] Treating the human machinery as indifferent and interchangeable excluded how a person's motivations shaped their perceptual processes. For Bruner and Goodman, these motivational differences derived from lived experience rather than from the body's inborn physiological capacity. They sought to demonstrate the organism's selective, adaptive, and functionally relevant perception "in a world of more or less ambiguously organized sensory stimuli."[29] Despite its embeddedness in these technical, seemingly esoteric, disciplinary disputes, the

---

25. On hunger and perception, see R. Nevitt Sanford, "The Effects of Abstinence from Food upon Imaginal Processes: A Preliminary Experiment." *The Journal of Psychology* 2, no. 1 (1936): 129–136; Sanford, "The Effects of Abstinence from Food upon Imaginal Processes: A Further Experiment." *The Journal of Psychology* 3, no. 1 (1937): 145–159.

26. Else Frenkel-Brunswik, "Intolerance of Ambiguity as an Emotional and Perceptual Personality Variable," *Journal of Personality* 18, no. 1 (1949): 108–143.

27. "Big Money," *New York Times*, September 29, 1946, 103.

28. Jerome S. Bruner and Cecile C. Goodman, "Value and Need as Organizing Factors in Perception," *Journal of Abnormal and Social Psychology* 42, no. 1 (1947): 33–44.

29. Bruner and Goodman, "Value and Need," 35.

experiment attracted considerable interest. Indeed, it made national headlines even before it was published. Here the content of the stimuli mattered. Their study focused on how two groups of children (one rich, the other poor) perceived the size of coins differently due to their class background.

Bruner's perception-centered approach served as a double political intervention. On one level, he offered an empirical account of ideology written in the vernacular of American functionalism. "Big Money" was antifascist experimental proof of how class became embodied through developmental experience and then channeled what was perceivable. Bruner made legible the perceptual system's purpose not only in preserving the organism as a biological entity, but also in portraying the person as a psychological and political being. Later experiments focused on how perception functioned to channel threats to personal identity. Individuals held consistent (even rigid) worldviews tied to their identity, and perception literally filtered sensory experience to sustain them.

On second level, Bruner's perception-centered approach had more to do with the small-p politics of academic institutions than with global geopolitics.

He received his PhD from Harvard in 1941, mentored by the personality psychologist Gordon W. Allport. By the late 1930s, Harvard's psychology department had split into two camps: the biotropic group led by E. G. Boring and organized around the Psychological Laboratory and the sociotropic group led by Henry A. Murray and organized around the Psychological Clinic. In 1946, the sociotropic group (Murray, Allport, and Bruner) joined the anthropology and sociology faculty to help form the Department of Social Relations, a new interdisciplinary program. A core member of the Social Relations cluster, Bruner argued that human perception was too important a topic to leave to the perceptual psychologists. His 1940s publications repeatedly make the case that perception as an object of study and the laboratory as an investigatory space belonged as much to the new area of Social Relations as it did to the old guard in the Department of Psychology.[30]

The local turf wars echoed throughout Bruner's coin article. Its conclusion railed against the then current allocation of laboratory resources at Harvard: "For too long now, perception has been virtually the exclusive domain of the Experimental psychologists with a capital *E*. If we are to reach an understanding of the way in which perception works in everyday life, we social psychologists and students of personality will have to join with the experimental psychologists and reexplore much of this ancient field of perception whose laws for too long have been taken for granted."[31]

An eclectic range of psychoanalytic references pervaded Bruner's early articles. He made little distinction among Freudian, Jungian, or neo-Freudian schools, focusing on their common ground, their common gift, to American experimental psychology. He described a 1947 experiment demonstrating how people's

---

30. Joel Isaac, *Working Knowledge: Making the Human Sciences from Parsons to Kuhn*. Cambridge, MA: Harvard University Press, 2012, 92–124.

31. Bruner and Goodman, "Value and Need," 43.

emotional reactions to a word affected its future perceptibility as inspired by "the dramatic experiments of Jung."[32] A year later, Bruner described his ambition to develop "a model or paradigm of the nature of perception which is both adequate generally and apposite specifically to an explanation of 'why the Rorschach works.'" The ambiguous inkblots had captured the imagination of those affiliated with Harvard's Psychological Clinic as a means of circumventing a person's defenses against candid self-revelation. Yet, Bruner warned that there "cannot be an independent theory of the perception of ink blots any more than there can be independent theories of the perception of Picasso collages, the phi phenomenon, or autokinetic movement."[33] As these examples suggest, Bruner's ambition was to develop a general theory of perception to unify the socially and clinically relevant work of the new Department of Social Relations.

Bruner remains the best remembered spokesman for the New Look, but the University of California at Berkeley served as the nexus for a distinct but complementary approach. The west coast "personality-centered" approach led by Frenkel-Brunswik drew inspiration from the same antifascist politics of the cultural front but developed in a distinct institutional niche with its own demands. Frenkel-Brunswik, along with her Harvard colleagues, was interested in repurposing the ready-at-hand equipment of the perception laboratory into projective devices for probing hidden, psychic depths. However, her interests were diagnostic. Her contribution to Krech's 1949 special issue focused on her recent work adapting the kinds of ambiguous figures made famous by Gestalt psychologists to detect the presence of authoritarianism and prejudice.

"Intolerance to ambiguity" lay at the heart of Frenkel-Brunswik's personality-centered science. She argued that the prejudiced perceived the world differently. Intolerant of uncertainty, they recoiled at qualified statements. When it came to problem-solving, they could not abandon the established mental set, even after it lost its appropriateness to the situation at hand. In contrast, healthy psychological and political development resulted in the capacity to perceive authority figures like parents in both a negative and positive light rather than in terms of moral absolutes. Connecting moral ambivalence in emotional relationships to the perceptual ambiguity that fascinated the Gestalt psychologists, Frenkel-Brunswik proposed a simple test using familiar ambiguous images to diagnose this authoritarian syndrome. Figures like Rubin's figure–ground reversal demonstrated the role of the perceiver in organizing sensory information, while ambiguous figures like the Rorschach ink blots served as stimuli onto which the patient projected associations in psychoanalysis. Frenkel-Brunswik suggested the former could be used for similar diagnostic purposes as the latter. In her "experiments on perceptual ambiguity," Frenkel-Brunswik turned to a class of

---

32. Jerome S. Bruner and Leo Postman, "Emotional Selectivity in Perception and Reaction," *Journal of Personality* 16, no. 1 (1947): 69–77, 69.

33. Jerome S. Bruner, "IV. Perceptual Theory and the Rorschach Test," *Journal of Personality* 17, no. 2 (1948): 157–168, 158.

stimuli that were supposedly devoid of social or emotional content to see if such materials could function as a diagnostic tool for the rigid mentality that interested her. Using lower-middle-class children who scored on the extreme ends of an ethnic prejudice scale, she presented them with a sequence of images in which a drawing of a dog gradually transitioned into that of a cat. The card sequence captured the Gestalt switch in material form. The highly prejudiced group held onto the original perceptual object (the dog) long after its features had transmogrified into those of a cat. Frenkel-Brunswik argued that this tenacity exhibited a reluctance to surrender one's preconceived judgments in the light of new empirical evidence. The rigid-minded person stuck to the definite and safe.[34]

In contrast, embracing uncertainty provided the leitmotif for Frenkel-Brunswik's own biography. Born in present-day Poland, her family moved to Austria to avoid the pogroms. She received her academic training at the University of Vienna, studying under Karl Bühler, and she later served as chief assistant to his wife Charlotte.[35] She also underwent psychoanalysis twice and participated in the Vienna Circle of logical positivists. In 1938, she fled to the United States following the Anschluss, where she soon married fellow Viennese psychologist Egon Brunswik. Fortuitously, Tolman had spent a previous sabbatical year in Vienna and found he had much in common with Brunswik's probabilistic functionalism. Tolman helped secure a position for his collaborator at Berkeley. However, the school's anti-nepotism rule prevented Frenkel-Brunswik from receiving a faculty appointment. She instead continued her career through a series of grant-funded research contracts mainly at the university's Institute of Child Welfare (ICW). In 1943, Berkeley's Institute for Social Research received funding from the American Jewish Committee to study the pressing problem of antisemitism as an ideology. Frenkel-Brunswik quickly joined this project, which was officially co-directed by the social psychologist N. Sanford Nevitt and the sociologist-in-exile Theodor Adorno. The group's efforts culminated in 1950 with the publication of *The Authoritarian Personality* (*TAP*), a unique encounter between German critical theory and American empirical social research. The authorship order and each collaborator's contribution to *TAP* became a matter of considerable dispute. Historians tend to credit Adorno with the theoretical framework and the social psychologists with the methods.[36]

---

34. Frenkel-Brunswik, "Intolerance of Ambiguity," 128.

35. Mitchell G. Ash, "Psychology and Politics in Interwar Vienna: The Vienna Psychological Institute, 1922–1942," in Mitchell G. Ash and William R. Woodward (eds.), *Psychology in Twentieth-Century Thought and Society*. New York: Cambridge University Press, 1987, 143–164.

36. Jay, *The Dialectical Imagination*, 219–252; John P. Jackson Jr., *Social Scientists for Social Justice: Making the Case against Segregation*. New York: New York University Press, 2001, 52–54, Fleck, *A Transatlantic History of the Social Sciences*, 221–272.

But such a neat division of labor does a disservice to Frenkel-Brunswik's sophistication as a theorist.[37] Take *TAP*'s contrarian stance on the psycho-political dangers of upholding dichotomous sex roles and submitting to patriarchal authority. Rather than benign mechanisms of social control, *TAP* suggested that the valorizing tradition, authority, and power played a central role in the authoritarian personality structure. Antisemitism, and even ethnocentrism, were not isolated phenomena, but rather were the product of an individual's weak ego structure. Such individuals found refuge in conventionalism, projecting their insecurities by stereotyping the most vulnerable. This interpretation derived, in part, from the Frankfurt School's Freudo-Marxist critique of bourgeois mores.

But it was hardly a lesson Frenkel-Brunswik needed to learn from Adorno. In pursuing an academic career on two continents, she was precisely the kind of woman who flaunted gender norms, and like other women psychologists of her era, she dwelled both publicly and privately on the implications of such choices.[38] Her own psychoanalysis revealed how "she was displaying in her life the role [of] Cordelia," from Shakespeare's *King Lear*. She came to identify with this character, "the best and most generous daughter of King Lear, who nevertheless preferred his other two daughters because of their flattering attitude."[39] Unlike her more conventionally beautiful sisters who found fulfillment in traditional familial roles, Frenkel-Brunswik immersed herself in the transformative possibilities of Viennese intellectual life. Her older sister recalled that their parents "wanted their children being settled in a 'normal' way . . . this scientific career did not impress them."[40] According to a fellow graduate student, Frenkel-Brunswik differentiated herself from her siblings who "lived exclusively for her husband and her baby." The tension between family and intellect was an acute and recurring point of reflection for Frenkel-Brunswik, but "her career came first."[41]

A rejection of motherliness extended into Frenkel-Brunswik's professional persona. How she embodied the female intellect captivated her fellow psychologists.

---

37. M. Brewster Smith, "Else Frenkel-Brunswik," in Barbara Sicherman and Carol Hurd Green (eds.), *Notable American Women: The Modern Period*. Cambridge, MA: Harvard University Press, 1980, 250–252. In writing this encyclopedia entry, Smith solicited and archived numerous recollections of Frenkel-Brunswik.

38. Elizabeth Johnston and Ann Johnson, "Balancing Life and Work by Unbending Gender: Early American Women Psychologists' Struggles and Contributions," *Journal of the History of the Behavioral Sciences* 53, no. 3 (2017): 246–264; Alexandra Rutherford, "'Making Better Use of US Women': Psychology, Sex Roles, and Womanpower in post-WWII America," *Journal of the History of the Behavioral Sciences* 53, no. 3 (2017): 228–245.

39. Else Frenkel-Brunswik, "Psychoanalysis and Personality Research," *Journal of Abnormal and Social Psychology* 35, no. 2 (1940): 176–197, 192.

40. Johanna Urabin to M. Brewster Smith, August 24, 1978, Box M849, Folder 2, M. Brewster Smith Papers, The Drs. Nicholas and Dorothy Cummings Center for the History of Psychology, the University of Akron. Hereafter cited as MBSP.

41. Edith Weisskopf-Joelson to Smith, May 11, 1978. Box M849, Folder 2, MBSP.

While she was an accomplished and confident dancer (an invaluable attribute in a "courtier" navigating the informalities of Buhler's Psychological Institute), her intellectual assertiveness as a Jewish woman pushed the limits of acceptability as Red Vienna succumbed to Austrofascism.[42] Gendered expectations profoundly shaped life in exile. Berkeley's anti-nepotism rule not only denied Frenkel-Brunswik the status and security she once held in Vienna but also pushed her into an applied research area deemed especially suitable to the female temperament, child study. However, her contemporaries stressed that "Else's interest was not in children," either personally or professionally. Concerned with life course development since her time in Vienna, the childless (or perhaps childfree) Frenkel-Brunswik "would say that her interests were theoretical."[43] Child development served as a means of continuing her intellectual career, but in a feminized guise that Frenkel-Brunswik seemingly rejected.

TAP, then, provided respite for Frenkel-Brunswik and gave her the opportunity to assert herself as a theorist capable of synthesizing her various Viennese influences. Her New Look approach took concrete form in redeploying Gestalt images for psychoanalytic ends. However, the aim was not the diagnosis of individual psychopathology. Echoing the politics of the Popular Front, she turned projective techniques into a psychological tool for identifying Fascist (or authoritarian) tendencies hidden in the population. She understood that the prejudiced were not just biased in their attitudes and behaviors toward particular groups. Instead, prejudice was a *symptom* of deeper cognitive deficiencies (and vice versa). In developing her intolerance of the ambiguity typology, Frenkel-Brunswik cited the German psychologist Erich Jaensch as a precedent. In 1938, the year of Frenkel-Brunswik's forced migration, Jaensch had proposed the existence of two personality types: a rigid, rule-bent J-type and a loose, malleable S-type. Frenkel-Brunswik's citation was not an innocent one, for Jaensch ranked among those "at the forefront when it came to assigning psychology a role as a buttress to Nazi policies."[44] His highly politicized personality theory venerated the clear-minded J-type and condemned the waffling liberalism of the S-type. Later commentators noted the irony of American psychologists retaining Jaensch's schema while merely inverting its valuation.[45] However, this was not a serendipitous discovery by a later generation. Frenkel-Brunswik, aware of Jaensch's political commitments, readily addressed them in her original article.

---

42. Hedda Bolgar to Smith, August 26, 1978, Box M849, Folder 2, MBSP.

43. Marjorie Honzik to Smith, May 11, 1978. Box M849, folder 2, MBSP.

44. Ulfried Geuter, *The Professionalization of Psychology in Nazi Germany*. Translated by Richard J. Holmes (1984; New York Cambridge University Press, 1992), 169.

45. Kenneth J. Gergen, "Social Psychology as History," *Journal of Personality and Social Psychology* 26, no. 2 (1973): 309–320, 312.

Rather than an earnest attempt at empirical science, her article is better read as a playful inversion, if not an outright parody, of Nazi typologies. Her "intolerance of ambiguity" article largely adhered to the norms of the postwar social scientific report, but at important junctures it flouts them. Frenkel-Brunswik was forthright about the speculative nature of the document. For example, at a time when reporting inferential statistics was something of a novelty, she made clear that she never secured statistically significant results for her chief construct. Certainly, she could not seriously suggest that American social scientists should emulate Jaensch's racial psychology in a straightforward manner. Instead, Frenkel-Brunswik self-consciously appropriated the theory of a leading Nazi ideologue, repurposing it much like she did with the Gestalt images. Hers was a call to recast the politics that had disrupted her life and forced her into exile. This very act of subversion, quietly embedded in a canonical work of social science, represented the culmination of the cultural front's impact on psychology and was the clearest manifestation of what experimenting from the left might entail. Despite her own continued precarity, Frenkel-Brunswik offered a unique synthesis of clinical, developmental, social, and perceptual psychology, generating one of the most productive research programs of the postwar era.

Whether the East Coast or West Coast variant, certain features held the New Look together. Rather than a palace revolt against behaviorism, the movement sought a synthesis of learning theory and psychoanalysis to ground the study of perception not only in lived experience but also in the possibilities of antifascist action. Combining research on children and adults, their work traced the ontogenetic development of a self-motivated perception that selectively misconstrued the world. Overwhelmed by the ambiguous texture of the environment, the mind simplified in a patterned matter. This emphasis on how the human organism managed (later processed) complexity became the defining feature of cognitive science, but the latter shed the New Look's commitment to radical politics.

THE RED SCARE AND THE COOLING OF COGNITION

The erasure of the New Look owed much to Americans' lost appetite for cultural front sensibilities. Enthusiasm peaked with Henry Wallace's failed 1948 presidential bid on the Progressive Party ticket and his attempt to keep alive the radicalism of the New Deal. Support for this alternative vision of American society collapsed owing to both international and domestic events.[46] In 1947, the House Un-American Activities Committee (HUAC) convened hearings to investigate the supposed communist infiltration of Hollywood and the entertainment industry. International tensions mounted in February 1948 when the Soviet-backed Communist Party staged a coup in Czechoslovakia, ending the last remaining

---

46. Denning, *Cultural Front*, 24.

democracy in Eastern Europe. In response, the United States launched the Marshall Plan in April in the hopes of reconstructing Europe along democratic and capitalist lines.[47] The social sciences, which many American politicians equated with socialism, came under considerable scrutiny.[48] In 1951, Congressman E. E. Cox, a southern anti-New Deal Democrat, established a committee to investigate tax-exempt philanthropic foundations dedicated to "social reform and international relations." Republican Congressman B. Carroll Reece initiated an even more thoroughgoing investigation the following year. The 1954 final report of the Reece Committee charged the social sciences' purported value-neutrality as a cover for promoting such morally corrupting doctrines as "scientism, moral relativism, social engineering, socialism, collectivism, internationalism, and world government."[49]

The mounting Cold War dispersed the adherents of the New Look. The Red Scare hit the Berkeley Psychology Department particularly hard. As the *Journal of Personality* special issue went to press, University of California president Robert Gordon Sproul proposed a loyalty oath requiring faculty members to swear that they were not members of the Communist Party or explain why they refused to sign the pledge. Purportedly designed to fend off scrutiny from conservative members of the state legislature, the loyalty oath had a dramatic effect on the Berkeley campus as it posed a major challenge to freedom of expression. Tolman led the nonsigners, organizing resistance in the university senate and recruiting assistance from professional organizations.[50] A somewhat reluctant political actor, the lifelong pacifist had participated in numerous antifascist activities in the late 1930s. He numbered among SPSSI's charter members, and his 1940 chairman's address had been replete with the cultural front's anti-elite rhetoric and calls for a new social order.[51] Despite Tolman's support, the university dismissed Nevitt for his continued refusal to sign. As the pressure mounted, a unique opportunity presented itself to Krech. A student visiting Berkeley from Norway approached him with an invitation to consult with an emerging group of social scientists there. Krech secured one of the first Fulbright Awards to spend the academic year in Oslo. Relocating allowed him to temporarily

---

47. Michael J. Hogan, *The Marshall Plan: America, Britain and the Reconstruction of Western Europe, 1947–1952*. Cambridge: Cambridge University Press, 1987.

48. Andrew S. Winston, "Value Neutrality and SPSSI: The Quest for Policy, Purity, and Legitimacy," *Journal of Social Issues* 67, no. 1 (2011): 59–72.

49. Mark Solovey, *Shaky Foundations: The Politics-Patronage-Social Science Nexus in Cold War America*. New Brunswick, NJ: Rutgers University Press, 2013, 120–127, quote 126.

50. Nancy K. Innis, "Lessons from the Controversy over the Loyalty Oath at the University of California," *Minerva* 30, no. 3 (1992): 337–365; David W. Carroll, *Purpose and Cognition: Edward Tolman and the Transformation of American Psychology*. New York: Cambridge University Press, 2017, 190–210.

51. Edward Chace Tolman, "Psychological Man," *Journal of Social Psychology* 13, no. 1 (1941): 203–218.

avoid the question of whether to sign the oath. Abroad, Krech inexplicably found that his "zest for social psychology was waning" and his research returned to neuropsychology.[52] He eventually signed before spending the following year at Harvard, while his Berkeley colleagues filed a successful challenge with the California Supreme Court.

Soon after, Frenkel-Brunswik's personal life unraveled. Her husband's suicide in 1955 left her a widow. She struggled with practical matters, having a "hard time dealing with the 'political' aspects of everyday life."[53] She also sought refuge in Oslo, spending a year there on a Fulbright fellowship to escape Berkeley. In 1958, she died by overdose.[54]

As the repeated invitations to Norway indicated, the West Coast take on the New Look certainly attracted enthusiasts. A 1952 survey counted Frenkel-Brunswik the most frequently cited scientist in the *Journal of Abnormal and Social Psychology*, ahead of Bruner and even Freud.[55] Berkeley alumnae like Milton Rokeach kept research on open-mindedness alive, so that it eventually became a defining characteristic of mental health and a personality trait on which people naturally varied.[56] However, the Berkeley group's influence was a contested one, with later researchers struggling to replicate the correlation among intolerance to ambiguity, ethnocentrism, and authoritarianism. As the Soviet Union replaced Nazi Germany as the immediate international threat, American sociologist Edward Shils and the British psychologist Hans Eysenck criticized *TAP* for ignoring the authoritarianism of the left.[57] After 1950, the Berkeley approach became a diffuse presence spread thinly throughout the social sciences. Lacking a stable institutional base, they did not bring about the (cognitive) revolution.

Very different dynamics on the Harvard campus led to the distillation of select aspects of the New Look into cognitive science. As the Cold War heated, Bruner distanced himself from social psychology. In November 1948, he declined a job offer from the University of Chicago. In explaining his decision, Bruner noted: "I discover that my primary interest is in the field of psychology in general. . . . Chicago needs a social psychologist, and, to be perfectly frank about it, I have no idea whether five years from now, Chicago would have one such in the person of me."[58] Despite his unwillingness to relocate, Bruner found himself unhappy as a

---

52. Krech, "David Krech," 244.

53. Norma Haan to Smith, April 29, 1978. Box M849, folder 2, MBSP.

54. "Maid Finds U.C. Psychologist Dead," *Oakland Tribune*, April 1, 1958, 6.

55. Kenneth E. Clark, "The APA Study of Psychologists," *American Psychologist* 9, no. 3 (1954): 117–120.

56. See Cohen-Cole, *The Open Mind*, 40–44.

57. On the reception of *TAP*, see Martin Roiser and Carla Willig, "The Strange Death of the Authoritarian Personality: 50 Years of Psychological and Political Debate," *History of the Human Sciences* 15, no. 4 (2002): 71–96.

58. Bruner, cited in Lawrence T. Nichols, "Social Relations Undone: Disciplinary Divergence and Departmental Politics at Harvard, 1946–1970," *American Sociologist* 29, no. 2 (1998): 83–107, 87.

member of Social Relations, chafing under the leadership of Talcott Parsons and his "'sociologization' of psychology."[59] Alienated from his departmental colleagues, Bruner found an intellectual kinship with George A. Miller, a psychologist trained in the perceptual laboratory of S. S. Stevens.[60] In the language of the Harvard community, Bruner wanted to transform biotropic psychology rather than remain in the social psychology tribe. In 1951, following a year at the Institute for Advanced Study, Bruner initiated "the Cognition Project" at Harvard.[61]

The Cold War's cooling of cognition altered the very design of Bruner's experiments and the psychic phenomena they sought to capture. Through the early 1950s, Bruner reperceptualized his research. Three experiments using a tachistoscope illustrate this transition. The tachistoscope, consisting of a slide deck and a shutter system for viewing one stimulus at a time, was a venerable psychological apparatus dating back to the mid-nineteenth century. The device became a staple of any respectable perception laboratory because it allowed for the exposure to varying stimuli for a fraction of a second. Despite its reliability and durability, the tachistoscope was not a stable piece of machinery. It was a "fluid technology," highly adaptable to local circumstances.[62] As Raymond Dodge, the psychologist who designed the type used by Bruner, remarked in 1907, "No psychological instrument is subject to greater modification in response to special experimental conditions than exposure apparatus"[63] Depending on what item flashed before the viewing hood, the very nature of the device changed.

When Bruner began working with the tachistoscope, he used it in a manner very similar to Frenkel-Brunswik's redeployment of the Gestalt figures. In 1947, Bruner and his collaborator Leo Postman took a piece of ready-at-hand perceptual equipment and remade it into a projective test. They did so in two phases. First, they gave their subjects a word association test, measuring reaction times for ninety-nine short words. Using this technique, they identified a set of emotionally charged words for that subject. Invariably, these words dealt with sexuality and violence. Two weeks later, they brought the participants back and exposed them to the same list via the tachistoscope. They found "sensitization in the presence of "dangerous" stimulus objects. The words compromising the slow reaction–fast recognition group were almost uniformly linked with prevailing taboos. One may cite as examples the following: *penis, crime, bitch, dream, anger,*

---

59. Bruner, "Jerome S. Bruner," 122.

60. Isaac, *Working Knowledge*, 182–183.

61. Jerome Bruner, Jacquelin J. Goodnow, and George A. Austin, *A Study of Thinking*. New York: Wiley, 1956.

62. Marianne De Laet and Annemarie Mol, "The Zimbabwe Bush Pump: Mechanics of a Fluid Technology," *Social Studies of Science* 30, no. 2 (2000): 225–263.

63. Raymond Dodge, "An Improved Exposure Apparatus," *Psychological Bulletin* 4, no. 1 (1907): 10–13, 10.

fairy (male subject), *death,* and *fight*."[64] The unconscious provided "a perceptual defense" from these external threats by making them more difficult to perceive.

Two years later, in 1949, their experimental design had changed dramatically. Bruner and Postman still used the tachistoscope for a word association test but gone were the emotionally charged items. Now, they were interested in comparing a participant's accuracy when identifying items drawn from a single set (color–word associations) versus multiple sets (alternating color or food associations).[65] They remained interested in how a word's meaning shaped its perception, but they chose to deal with decidedly cooler topics than those of just a few years previously.

By 1954, Bruner and Postman began formally collaborating with George Miller. The result represented a full return to the kind of designs championed by early memory researcher Herrmann Ebbinghaus, with participants presented with nonsense syllables devoid of meaning. Their vocabulary also shifted. Rather than affective words invoking unconscious dynamics, they were concerned with "the amount of information obtained from a tachistoscopic exposure." The amount depended on "conditions of illumination and exposure duration, and are independent of the order of approximation to English letter sequences."[66] This last experiment design treated the participants as another piece of mechanistic equipment, the stance Bruner had explicitly rejected in 1947. In the early days of the Red Scare, Bruner followed a sharp trajectory from experimentalizing psychoanalysis as a way of understanding ideology to the cold cognitions of information theory. He did so with little public fanfare and while preserving a superficially similar experimental design. However, his theory and practice of the observing participant changed dramatically in less than a decade.

Bruner's widely cited article "On Perceptual Readiness" (1957) offered a thorough rewriting of his early career. He described his coin experiment, whose findings had appeared in numerous daily newspapers across the country, as "an innocent enough paper" dealing "with what at that time was the rather obscure problem of how extra-stimulus factors influenced perception, a subject then of interest to only a small band of us."[67] The 1957 paper also excised earlier citations to Jung, Rorschach, and psychoanalysis as the theoretical bedrock for his experiments, replacing them with references to psychophysics. Bruner retained the notion that the person mattered to perception; the processing of sensations (now understood as "information") was lawful but idiosyncratic based on a person's learning and

---

64. Jerome S. Bruner and Leo Postman, "Emotional Selectivity in Perception and Reaction," *Journal of Personality* 16, no. 1 (1947): 69–77, 75.

65. Leo Postman and Jerome S. Bruner, "Multiplicity of Set as a Determinant of Perceptual Behavior," *Journal of Experimental Psychology* 39, no. 3 (1949): 369–377.

66. George A. Miller, Jerome S. Bruner, and Leo Postman, "Familiarity of Letter Sequences and Tachistoscopic Identification," *Journal of General Psychology* 50, no. 1 (1954): 129–139, 138.

67. Jerome Bruner, "On Perceptual Readiness," *Psychological Review* 64, no. 2 (1957): 123–152, 123.

experience. What Bruner carried forward from his earliest experiments was how an input's "symbolic value" mattered in how a participant selected and attended to them, but information theory drained all emotional color and political immediacy from the laboratory.

The perceptual defense controversy of the late 1950s put an end to the New Look. The criticisms raised were not new. Back in Krech's 1949 symposium, the Gestalt psychologists Hochberg and Gleitman had criticized the concept of perceptual defense for positing a vitalist, metaphysical homunculus, an infinite regress of miniature persons inside the head who actively selected or ignored inputs based on their desirability.[68] Such criticisms gained traction almost a decade later but not because of some general distaste for psychoanalysis. Instead, as critics noted, Bruner's methodology of mere exposure collided with mounting political concerns about the "commercial exploitation of subliminal perception."[69] In September 1957, a New Jersey advertising firm announced it had been covertly inserting messages into a film reel suggesting viewers should "Eat Popcorn" and "Drink Coca-Cola." These "subliminal" messages lasted less than a second, but the firm reported great success in increasing sales for these products after a trial run at a local cinema. Subliminal advertising met with immediate condemnation. Republican lawmakers demanded the Federal Communications Commission investigate.[70] As the controversy swirled, journalist Vance Packard's bestselling exposé *The Hidden Persuaders* (1957) situated the subliminal advertising in an even more troubling political context: totalitarian techniques like the brainwashing of American soldiers captured during the Korean War. If advertisers could implant desires against the consumer's will, governments could do the same.[71] As one critical review of perceptual defense warned, "the further application of subliminal perception is certain to embroil psychology in a dispute not of its own choosing."[72] The cultural baggage of unvoluntary mind control through brief manipulations beyond a person's awareness made perceptual defense research untenable for a respectable Harvard professor of the liberal persuasion. By 1958, conflation with subliminal advertising meant the antifascist political psychology of the New Look had become its opposite.

68. Julian E. Hochberg and Henry Gleitman, "Towards a Reformulation of the Perception-Motivation Dichotomy," *Journal of Personality*, 18 (1949): 180–191, 184.

69. Israel Goldiamond, "Indicators of Perception: I. Subliminal Perception, Subception, Unconscious Perception: An Analysis in Terms of Psychophysical Indicator Methodology," *Psychological Bulletin* 55, no. 6 (1958): 373–411, 373.

70. "Psychic Hucksterism Stirs Call for Inquiry," *New York Times*, October 6, 1957, 38.

71. Catherine Lutz, "Epistemology of the Bunker: The Brainwashed and Other New Subjects of Permanent War," in Joel Pfister and Nancy Schnog, eds. *Inventing the Psychological: Toward a Cultural History of Emotional Life in America*. New Haven, CT: Yale University Press, 1997, 245–267.

72. James McConnell, Richard Cutler, and Elton McNeil, "Subliminal Stimulation: An Overview," *American Psychologist* 13, no. 5 (1958): 229–242, 239.

COLD WAR CHESS

As the heating of the Cold War sundered certain alliances, it forged others. The launch of the Sputnik satellite in 1957 stoked worries among policymakers that the United States was falling behind the Soviets. This perceived technology gap meant "Congress opened the purse strings for science, engineering, and education," Miller later observed. "Enough of this funding spilled over into computers, psychology, and even linguistics that we were able to pursue our ideas as fast as we think could of them." For Miller, this unprecedented windfall, not the Depression or the war, enabled the generational shift within psychology. Before Sputnik, "positions of academic power were still in the hands of behavioristic psychologists who would have been reluctant to invest limited resources in mentalistic speculations."[73] In Sputnik's aftermath, the social sciences needed to appear value neutral but broadly useful. Three interdisciplinary areas received considerable interest from the government funders and private foundations: communication studies, decision sciences, and the science of strategy.[74] Miller and his allies were poised to take advantage of this opportunity and made each of these areas their own.

In 1956, Miller's landmark paper "Magical Number Seven, Plus or Minus Two" appeared in the *Psychological Review*. With deft humor, he documented how this innocuous integer haunted him as he moved from the psychophysics of judging magnitudes to a person's capacity for remembering a string of digits. The solution to this puzzle lay in recasting human psychology in light of information theory. Communication engineers provided a universal, quantitative language for expressing a medium's limited capacity to receive, process, and recall the inputs from the world. Whether organic or mechanical, overloading the system created errors. However, humans, like machines, could overcome "this informational bottleneck" by actively processing the inputs they received, "chunking" them into meaningful sequences. This "recoding," according to Miller, was "the very lifeblood of the thought processes."[75] As his *Psychological Review* went to press, Miller participated in a two-day symposium at MIT organized by the Special Interest Group in Information Theory. Other presenters included Simon Newell and Herbert Simon, then employed by the RAND corporation, on their early computer program which operated as a "logic machine" for solving problems, and the MIT linguist Noam Chomsky who explained his theory of transformational generative grammar. Miller "left the symposium with a conviction, more intuitive than rational, that experimental psychology, theoretical linguistics, and the

---

73. George A. Miller, "A Very Personal History," Talk to Cognitive Science Workshop, MIT, June 1, 1979, 9.

74. Solovey, *Shaky Foundations*, 54–102.

75. George Miller, "The Magical Number Seven, Plus or Minus Two: Some Limits on Our Capacity for Processing Information," *Psychological Review* 63, no. 2 (1956): 81–97, 95.

computer simulation of cognitive processes were all pieces from a larger whole."[76] As the New Look became politically distasteful with its links to both Marxism and corporate mind control, the Cambridge-area cognitive scientists promised a new science of humans grounded in the individual's rationality, flexibility, independence.

The MIT symposium was not an isolated happening. Newell and Simon had arrived fresh from a ten-week summer workshop at nearby Dartmouth College dedicated to artificial intelligence. The collaborative research project started from "the conjecture that every aspect of learning or any other feature of intelligence can in principle be so precisely described that a machine can be made to simulate it. An attempt will be made to find how to make machines use language, form abstractions and concepts, solve kinds of problems now reserved for humans, and improve themselves."[77] The starting point for this multidisciplinary effort was the coupling of "natural and artificial intelligence," although, as the Dartmouth proposal made clear, the distinction between the two was uninteresting for many. These two realms constituted a common problem.

Bruner, who remained closest to educational psychology, demonstrated how the new cognitive science rejected the eugenic assumptions about intelligence found in interwar psychometrics, emphasizing instead its growth and flexibility. Intelligence was a series of (learnable) processes rather than a trait fixed over the life course or knowledge of a specific content domain. If the distinction between natural and artificial intelligence seemed uninteresting, then the one between experts and novices seemed pivotal. Driven by post-Sputnik funding to improve American science education, cognitive psychologists dedicated their efforts to understanding the acquisition of expertise in different domains. Rather than the unfolding of an innate, inborn ability, intelligence came through the cultural transmission of skills via the medium of language.[78] The magical year 1956 heralded the arrival of *homo adaptivus*, a bounded yet flexible decision maker.[79]

Cognitive science departed from the New Look in important ways. In contrast to the Berkeley campus, behaviorism (embodied by the bete noir B. F. Skinner) posed an immediate threat around Cambridge, Massachusetts. In the 1950s, Skinner's behavior analysis dominated experimental psychology at Harvard, a position Miller wished to usurp. Linguistics provided a key resource in this struggle. In 1959, Chomsky penned a devastating critique of Skinner's *Verbal Behavior*.

---

76. George A. Miller, "The Cognitive Revolution: A Historical Perspective," *Trends in Cognitive Sciences* 7, no. 3 (2003): 141–144, 143.

77. John McCarthy, "A Proposal for the Dartmouth Summer Research Project on Artificial Intelligence," August 31, 1955. http://www-formal.stanford.edu/jmc/history/dartmouth/dartmouth.html

78. Jerome Bruner, "The Course of Cognitive Growth," *American Psychologist* 19, no. 1 (1964): 1–15.

79. Heyck, *Age of System: Understanding the Development of Modern Social Science*. Baltimore: Johns Hopkins University Press, 2015, 81–125.

The senior scientist's unwillingness to even read the criticisms when sent to him in advance of publication, never mind engage with them, exemplified his close-minded rigidity. Skinner's disciplinary chauvinism contrasted with the openness and interdisciplinarity of the cognitive scientists. In their eyes, such actions made Skinner very much the authoritarian, a perverse engineer of human conduct rather than a curious scientist. Dissatisfaction with arrangements in both the departments of psychology and social relations led Bruner and Miller to create the Center for Cognitive Studies in 1960 as a distinct physical and intellectual space to promote a fundamentally optimistic vision of the human being.[80]

Chess held a unique place in the new cognitivist imaginary.[81] Between 1948 and 1953, leading cyberneticians Norbert Wiener, Claude Shannon, and Alan Turing each published accounts of a chess-playing machine, reviving the Enlightenment dream of realizing Maelzel's Chess Playing Automaton. From their shared cybernetic perspective, the best way to understand the mind was to build one, whether as an electronic or a paper machine. Chess's easily formalized rules analyzed in an extensive body of theory facilitated its enrollment into early computing.[82] As historian Paul Edwards observed, programs "manipulate symbols according to well-defined, sequentially executed rules to achieve some desired transformation of input symbols into output symbols. Rule-oriented, abstract games such as checkers and chess also have this structure. As a result, all computer programming, in any language, is gamelike."[83] In 1955, Simon, Newell, and J. C. Shaw started writing one of the first chess-playing programs. Simon went even further, later suggesting that chess served as cognition's *drosophila*. Like the fruit fly in the geneticist's laboratory, he argued the game provided a "standard task environment" for formulating the common questions for cognitive science and artificial intelligence.[84]

Unlike fruit fly genetics, chess simulations never became a mundane pedagogical activity on which every student trained, but they did provide a ready-at-hand platform for disaggregating rapid perception from the slower processing of

---

80. Cohen-Cole, *The Open Mind*, 155–158.

81. Neil Charness, "The Impact of Chess Research on Cognitive Science," *Psychological research* 54, no. 1 (1992): 4–9; Hunter Crowther-Heyck, *Herbert A. Simon: The Bounds of Reason in Modern America*. Baltimore: Johns Hopkins University Press, 2005, 293–295; Nathan Ensmenger, "Is Chess the Drosophila of Artificial Intelligence? A Social History of an Algorithm," *Social Studies of Science* 42, no. 1 (2012): 5–30.

82. These proposals appeared in the wake of mathematician John von Neumann and economist Oskar Morgenstern recasting all decision making in terms of games with calculable "optimal action." See Paul Erickson, *The World the Game Theorists Made*. Chicago: University of Chicago Press, 2015.

83. Edwards, *The Closed World: Computers and the Politics of Discourse in Cold War America*. Cambridge, MA: MIT Press, 1996, 170.

84. Herbert A. Simon and William G. Chase, "Skill in Chess," *American Scientist* 61, no. 4 (1973): 394–403.

information. Methodological inspiration came from the Dutch psychologist and chess master Adriaan de Groot. For his 1946 dissertation, de Groot had recruited players of various ranks and had them relate their thought process as they solved different mid-game problems. This think-aloud method revealed that experts did not venture further down the decision tree of options compared to amateurs, but they more readily recognized patterns and interpreted them in light of considerable experience. Simon saw these recorded protocols as the very act of processing information. After meeting the Dutch psychologist in 1960, Simon secured a grant to oversee the translation of de Groot's book into English and began emulating his method for conveying the contents of the seemingly intangible mind, returning expert introspection to the psychological mainstream after its supposed banishment by the behaviorists.[85]

Chess appealed due its timely timelessness. The ancient and abstract strategy game seemed to evade the constraints of any one culture. For aficionados, deep play represented the purest form of human intellect in action; the game's austere beauty served as a refuge from the messiness of the world, a place where the mind directly interacted with mathematized rules.[86] The game also possessed heightened cultural visibility during the Cold War, with the Americans and Soviets using international tournaments to stage their nation's respective intelligence in dramatic but consequence-free proxy wars. Indeed, many analogized the conflict itself to a grand match. Chess functioned as a model of cognition since play involved rational choices; correct and incorrect decisions led to better or worse outcomes as measured by the criterion of wins or losses. In contrast to logic puzzles, chess was a social activity. Winning required anticipating an opponent's actions as one planned, prospected, and delayed immediate gains for future advantage. These players varied considerably in skill, with an established ranking system placing individuals on a scale from novice to grandmaster. Involving neither chance nor hidden elements, the game operated as decision scientists imagined the marketplace with free agents competing with "perfect information."[87]

Chess also made evident the limits of any cognitive system. The earliest computers performed terribly. An organizer of an early human–machine tournament rated the computer as a "fish," a title given by players "when one of their peers exhibits a singular skill in losing chess games."[88] Simon found this weakness revelatory. Early programs relied on brute computational power to forecast future

---

85. Herbert A. Simon to Adriaan de Groot, August 15, 1960. Herbert A. Simon Papers, Carnegie Mellon University Libraries Digital Collections. Hereafter cited as HASP.

86. In contrast, de Groot abandoned chess research by 1970, having become more "concerned about the 'relevance' of what we are doing in and with science." De Groot to Simon, July 23, 1970, HASP.

87. Robert Leonard, *Von Neumann, Morgenstern, and the Creation of Game Theory: From Chess to Social Science, 1900–1960*. Cambridge: Cambridge University Press, 2010, 9–29.

88. George R. R. Martin, "The Computer Was a Fish," *Analog Science Fiction/Science Fact*, July 1972, 61–74, 61.

scenarios, but it was impossible for any mind (whether organic or mechanical) to compute every possible move. Still decisions must be made. Smartness resided not in perfectly executed algorithms, but in well-honed shortcuts or heuristics that allowed the mind to select certain pathways and discard others.[89]

The slow deliberateness of expert chess captured what most fascinated Simon about thinking. In the mid-1960s, Soviet psychologists challenged this view by using rudimentary eye-tracking equipment to measure thought in terms of a player's fixation on particular squares on the board. This experimental setup suggested that decision making was a rapid affair. A player's immediate perception of the board determined subsequent play as the brain processed the possibilities in parallel rather than deliberating on possible decisions in a sequence.[90] Simon's laboratory used eye-tracking equipment only sporadically, largely to refute the Soviets on their own ground.[91] Despite his own cybernetic inclinations, Simon showed little interest in technologies for circumventing the participant's conscious self-reflection. He championed instead the superiority of verbal protocol analysis as a method for conveying thought as a sequential and purposeful process accessible to the player and the scientist.[92]

Chess, then, helped establish cognition as bounded yet disembodied. The anthropologist Robert Desjarlais has described deep play's immersion as a "ludic fabulation" where "a person is looking at a specific position on the board, but in his mind's eye he is giving thought to—constructing, enacting—a series of imaginary riffs on that concrete reality."[93] This constructive intellect was the dimension of the human experience that most captivated early cognitive scientists. Theirs was an optimistic psychology of the forward-looking planner, open to future possibilities; an agent no longer defined by their past. This cybernetician's dream of transcending one's organic body to become an unlocatable mind capable of universal surveillance was itself a seductive male fantasy grounded in the Cold War militarization of everyday life.[94] A later generation of psychologists would take the overwhelming maleness of chess mastery as an entry point to arbitrate the controversy over sex differences in

---

89. Allen Newell, J. C. Shaw, and H. A. Simon, "Chess-Playing Programs and the Problem of Complexity," *IBM Journal of Research and Development* 2, no. 4 (1958): 320–335.

90. O. K. Tikhomirov and E. D. Poznyanskaya, "An Investigation of Visual Search as a Means of Analyzing Heuristics," *Soviet Psychology* 5, no. 2 (1966): 3–15.

91. Simon to Charles N. Cofer, October 23, 1968, HASP.

92. Herbert A. Simon and Michael Barenfeld, "Information-Processing Analysis of Perceptual Processes in Problem Solving," *Psychological Review* 76, no. 5 (1969): 473–483.

93. Robert R. Desjarlais, *Counterplay: An Anthropologist at the Chessboard*. Berkeley: University of California Press, 2011, 107.

94. Donna Haraway, *Simians, Cyborgs, and Women: The Reinvention of Nature*. London: Routledge, 1991.

cognitive ability, attributing superior male achievement to a statistical effect of the highly skewed sex ratios in participation.[95] In contrast, the cyberneticians found the maleness of chess self-evident and uninteresting. Its unquestioned manliness (and unspoken whiteness) was what made it an unassailable site of intellectual achievement. Their chess forever remained the refined world of contemplative tournaments, the cool calculations of the Soviet-American rivalry, and not the rapid, intuitive game of the predominantly Black blitz players hustling marks in city parks.[96] At least that was how Simon spoke publicly about chess simulations.

But passion drew men like Simon to the game. Those who put in the hours needed to acquire expertise did not experience chess as a cool, intellectual undertaking but rather as an obsession. Simon, who at his peak ranked as a skilled amateur cusping on expert proficiency, often experienced chess as an unhealthy compulsion.[97] In 1955, Newell wrote his collaborator to report "a mild flirtation with chess itself." Instead of coding the promised program, he found himself "spending a good deal of time just playing and learning the game."[98] Simon responded emphatically: "the idea is for the *machine* to play chess, not AI. Beware of temptations and the rationalizations thereof. (And beware of tempting me with chess when you return). It is a loathsome disease."[99] A joke, no doubt, but Simon slipped at other times. The calm, gray-suited organization man described playing against a computer in highly emotive terms to his favorite chess confidant de Groot. Competing against a program running on a JOHNNIAC machine, "the computer had perhaps the upper hand for ten mores or so." Then "in the middle game it ran out of ideas, began fidgeting, and I clobbered it."[100] Simon did not simply anthropomorphize the computer as an intentional agent as he frequently did elsewhere. He imagined his mechanical opponent as overwhelmed by its embodied emotions. Simon's own experience of computing was highly emotive,

---

95. Neil Charness and Yigal Gerchak, "Participation Rates and Maximal Performance: A Log-Linear Explanation for Group Differences, such as Russian and Male Dominance in Chess," *Psychological Science* 7, no. 1 (1996): 46–51; Christopher F. Chabris and Mark E. Glickman. "Sex Differences in Intellectual Performance: Analysis of a Large Cohort of Competitive Chess Players," *Psychological Science* 17, no. 12 (2006): 1040–1046; Merim Bilalić, Kieran Smallbone, Peter McLeod, and Fernand Gobet. "Why Are (the Best) Women So Good at Chess? Participation Rates and Gender Differences in Intellectual Domains," *Proceedings of the Royal Society B: Biological Sciences* 276, no. 1659 (2009): 1161–1165.

96. Desjarlais, *Counterplay*, 19–25.

97. On Simon's chess proficiency, see Simon to Herbert Barry, January 31, 1984, HASP.

98. Newell to Simon, July 12, 1955, HASP.

99. Simon to Newell, July 29, 1955, HASP.

100. Simon to de Groot, February 4, 1961, HASP.

yet he refused this move in print, even when responding to those who criticized the appropriateness of his central metaphor.[101]

Like all analogies, chess constrained cognitive science by directing it toward certain problems while limiting what questions seemed posable. In 1963, Ulric Neisser, a junior associate at Harvard's Center for Cognitive Studies, enumerated "three fundamental and interrelated characteristics of human thought that are conspicuously absent from existing or contemplated computer programs." He complained that his own field neglected human development, emotion, and conflicting motivations when it simulated the thinking process with computer programs.[102] In short, cognitive studies presented a passionless mind. Neisser's list was remarkable because each of these elements once lay at the heart of the New Look. Both Bruner and Frenkel-Brunswik had worked with children to ascertain how social values led to conflicting motivations affecting perception. Those elements excluded by the computer metaphor were available to cognitive scientists in the not-so-distant past and yet had seemingly disappeared. Even more tellingly, Neisser repeated these very lacunae in his 1967 field-defining textbook *Cognitive Psychology*. A summa of cutting-edge research, none of these neglected domains, so worrisome in 1963, featured in the book's organization.[103] Despite Bruner's continued work with children, Neisser excluded cognitive development from his survey while limiting coverage of emotion to a brief mention of the "perceptual defense" controversy and concluding the book by noting that carefully controlled laboratory experiments on cognitions tended to elide the problem of conflicting motives. Neisser dedicated the vast majority of his book to recent advances in visual and auditory perception (where the computational, information-processing stance had achieved its greatest victories) and confined the unanswered question of "higher mental processes" to a speculative final chapter.

As cognitive science gained footholds beyond the Rand Corporation and Harvard Yard, the field largely adhered to the constraints imposed by Neisser's textbook. If 1956 represented the year of the revolutionary insurrection, the late 1970s marked the height of cognitivism's imperial reach. New interdisciplinary journals like *Cognitive Science* (started in 1977) and *Brain and Behavioral Science* (1978) joined psychology-specific ones like *Cognitive Psychology* (1970) and *Cognition* (1972) to provide interdisciplinary platforms for discussion. In 1978, Simon received one of the first Nobel Prizes in Economics for his research on "the decision-making process." In 1979, the University of California at San Diego hosted the first meeting of the Cognitive Science Society. Perhaps no document better captured the new consensus than "Cognitive Science, 1978," a report Miller prepared for the Alfred P. Sloan Foundation. Reflecting his own interests, Miller foregrounded

---

101. Herbert Simon, "Motivational and Emotional Controls of Cognition," *Psychological Review* 74, no. 1 (1967): 29–39.

102. Ulric Neisser, "The Imitation of Man by Machine," *Science* 139, no. 3551 (1963): 193–197, 195.

103. Neisser, *Cognitive Psychology*. New York: Appleton-Century-Crofts, 1967.

advances in psychology and linguistics inspired by computer science with an anticipatory gaze directed on their neurological substantiation. A common impulse "to discover the representational and computational capacities of the mind and their structural and functional representation in the brain" held the field together.[104] By this time, cognitive science's original entanglements with social psychology, studies of prejudice, and psychoanalysis were but a dim memory. This political quietude was not unique. Neighboring fields followed a similar ascent "to the icy slopes of logic," with technical formalism replacing social engagement under the harsh gaze of McCarthyism.[105]

THE COCA-COLONIZATION OF THE MIND

In 1955, the Eisenhower administration independently adopted the name New Look to describe its new diplomatic policy of nuclear deterrence or "mass retaliation" against foreign enemies. Likewise, the cooled version of psychology's New Look came to feature prominently in American Cold War diplomacy as a leading cultural export. A significant part of the chess-playing computer's appeal lay in its universality, its promise to deliver the mind from the messiness of history. Reacting against the hypernationalism that led to war, psychologists saw their own brand of scientific inquiry as a potential model for international cooperation in pursuit of common goals. They embraced the United Nations as a political body whose structures might enable a "view from everywhere" in which all could contribute to the scientific enterprise.[106] This universalism was not only methodological but extended to their understanding of human nature as a concerted rejection of eugenics with its genocidal conviction in innate and hierarchical human differences. However, a debate persisted around the extent to which cognitive processes (and cognitive psychologists themselves) remained culture bound. The question touched every area of psychology from clinical to comparative but was particularly vexed in social psychology.

Once at the center of the New Look approach, social psychology found itself relegated to the outskirts of the cognitive empire, where it, too, took on chesslike qualities. Leon Festinger, an American-born student of Kurt Lewin, became the undisputed leader of American social psychologists upon his mentor's death. Festinger schooled a generation in the aesthetics of experimental realism: the staging of dramatic situations to reveal people's hidden motivations. Festinger

---

104. Miller, "A Very Personal History," 6.

105. George A. Reisch, *How the Cold War Transformed Philosophy of Science: To the Icy Slopes of Logic*. New York: Cambridge University Press, 2005.

106. Perrin Selcer, "The View from Everywhere: Disciplining Diversity in Post–World War II International Social Science," *Journal of the History of the Behavioral Sciences* 45, no. 4 (2009): 309–329.

also epitomized the methodological individualism of American psychology. Experiments revolved around how the lone person perceived others and judged the social world, eschewing the psyche's embeddedness in community or tradition. For Festinger, the social was but a situation, a laboratory construct populated with role-playing stooges and other fictional props. Beneath all the exciting dramaturgy lay the coolness characteristic of midcentury cognitivism. His theory of cognitive dissonance (first outlined in 1957) explained the reason behind humanity's apparent irrationality. Much like the international system, a functioning mind required balance. The pursuit of consistency motivated people, and their aberrant acts resulted from attempts to resolve the discomfort from holding competing, discrepant beliefs. Most telling, inconsistent beliefs need not have strong ties to a person's sense of self. Any discrepant cognitions could produce the dissonance that motivated action.[107]

The 1950 UNESCO statement on race captured the contradictions of this universal psychology, seemingly underwritten by international cooperation. Crafting the statement brought together over a hundred scientists from around the world, experts in anthropology, population biology, sociology, and psychology. In the North Atlantic, the Holocaust provided the immediate point of reference, and the statement represented a refutation of eugenics. Rather than eliminating race from the scientific vocabulary, the statement relocated the site of human difference from genetics to cultural variation.[108] Along with culture, the statement defined race as a problem of *relations*, of how people from different nations or groups might peaceably relate to one another. Resolving intergroup "tensions" represented a different political project for those scientists from the Global South on whose expertise on race relations the document drew heavily. Their primary reference point was not sovereign nations relating to one another as equals in an international system. Attuned to the problems of administrating settler colonial societies with heterogeneous populations of indigenous peoples, former slaves, and colonizers, they did not view cultural differences through a relativist prism but through a Lamarckian lens of "backwardness" and uneven development. Schooled in the problematics of late colonial administration, they sought to bring "the people without history" into industrial society through modernization.[109]

---

107. Frances Cherry, *Stubborn Particulars of Social Psychology: Essays on the Research Process*. London: Routledge, 1995; John D. Greenwood, *The Disappearance of the Social in American Social Psychology*. New York: Cambridge University Press, 2003; Javier Lezaun, Fabian Muniesa, and Signe Vikkelsø. "Provocative Containment and the Drift of Social-Scientific Realism," *Journal of Cultural Economy* 6, no. 3 (2013): 278–293.

108. Michelle Brattain, "Race, Racism, and Antiracism: UNESCO and the Politics of Presenting Science to the Postwar Public," *American Historical Review* 112, no. 5 (2007): 1386–1413.

109. Sebastián Gil-Riaño, "Relocating Anti-Racist Science: The 1950 UNESCO Statement on Race and Economic Development in the Global South," *British Journal for the History of Science* 51, no. 2 (2018): 281–303.

In general, American psychologists' cross-cultural imagination barely lingered on the decolonizing world. One exception was a combative collaboration conducted by the anthropologist Melville Herskovits and the psychologist Donald T. Campbell (a former Frenkel-Brunswik protégé at Berkeley). At the Northwestern faculty club, the pair debated how to test whether culture shaped even the most basic perceptual processes. Herskovits thought so; Campbell remained skeptical. To settle their gentlemen's disagreement, Campbell proposed the now-familiar move of redeploying a set of geometric optical illusions to measure higher functions. Starting in 1956, they set out to compare the reactions of inhabitants of various small-scale societies to those of Evanston locals. The non-American respondents proved less prone to the supposedly universal angular illusions. A note made near the end of their study hinted at why liberal social scientists may have rarely undertaken such projects. The team cautioned against interpreting the variation observed in their samples as constituting an essential "racial" difference. Any measurable differences resulted wholly from culture, or, in the psychologist's terminology, the learning experience of developing in a less carpentered world.[110] Tellingly, ethnographers (not psychologists) administered these tests. With Herskovits securing the funding and managing the team, the workforce consisted largely of graduate students conducting more extensive fieldwork in Africa. The tests represented a brief diversion from their in-depth observation of cultural patterns rather than a sustained effort. This project mirrored the extractive practices of colonial administrators, leaving behind no lasting psychological infrastructure in terms of local personnel or data collection facilities.[111]

The situation in Europe, especially the Nordic countries, was quite different. That both Krech and Frenkel-Brunswik found temporary refuge in Oslo was no accident. Vilhelm Aubert, the student who recruited Krech, was part of a small group of social scientists trying to reorient Norwegian academic life away from its Germanic foundations toward what they saw as the more promising and democratic "American" alternative. By the time Frenkel-Brunswik arrived, this group had established its own Institute for Social Relations, inspired as much by empirical survey methods of Lazarsfeld (the first visitor invited after the war) as the namesake institute at Frankfurt. With a steady flow of prominent Fulbright awardees, Oslo provided a beachhead for introducing American-style social psychology to Western Europe. On one such fellowship, Stanley Schacter (a student of Festinger) oversaw a Ford Foundation grant to coordinate the replication of an experiment on group conformity in seven different European countries. Beyond attempting

---

110. Marshall H. Segall, Donald T. Campbell, and Melville J. Herskovits, *The Influence of Culture on Visual Perception*. Indianapolis: Bobbs-Merrill, 1966.

111. On the underdevelopment of African psychology, see Yusuf Omer Abdi, "The Problems and Prospects of Psychology in Africa," *International Journal of Psychology* 10, no. 3 (1975): 227–234.

to establish the cross-cultural validity of the phenomenon, the experiment's stated goals included promoting scientific cooperation across national borders and familiarizing the Europeans with American methods.[112] The study failed to achieve its first objective, and the second was given more lip service than sustained support, but the final one proved most successful. Virtually unknown before the war, the ranks of applied (and later clinical) psychologists increased dramatically in the Nordic countries, tied to the administration of their distinct vision of the welfare state, until they had more psychologists per capita than any country in the world.[113]

Festinger oversaw a more sustained effort at inter-European cooperation as chair of the Committee on Transnational Social Psychology. Both the American government (through the Office of Naval Research) and major philanthropic organizations (especially the Ford Foundation) invested considerable sums into integrating European experimental social psychologists, seeing their approach to intergroup relations as a bulwark against the considerable communist sympathies of European intellectuals.[114] Festinger's Committee led to the founding of the European Society for Experimental Social Psychology (ESESP) in 1966, which empowered a new generation of psychologists largely sympathetic to American methodologies. The Society's first president, Serge Moscovici, secured a further $240,000 from the Ford Foundation to support three centers for experimental social psychology in Europe: his own in Paris, Henri Tajfel at Bristol, and Jozef Nuttin in Leuven.

Moscovici and Tajfel, in particular, envisioned a distinctly European social psychology. Both men contended that the Americans offered an impoverished understanding of "the social," one overly individualistic on both a methodological and conceptual level. Their laboratories focused on the analysis of beliefs distributed in social collectives rather than the attitudes held by individuals.[115] They embraced the anti-Americanization rhetoric of the European Left wherein residents of the former imperial centers somehow became colonialism's true victims. Writing in the aftermath of the dissolution of Europe's overseas empires, Moscovici now decried the acceptance of American money as a "colonial pact"

---

112. Stanley Schachter, Josef Nuttin, Cecily De Monchaux, Paul H. Maucorps, Diedrich Osmer, Hubertus Duijker, Ragnar Rommetveit, and Joachim Israel, "Cross-Cultural Experiments on Threat and Rejection: A Study of the Organization for Comparative Social Research," *Human Relations* 7, no. 4 (1954): 403–439.

113. Ole Jacob Madsen, *The Psychologization of Society: On the Unfolding of the Therapeutic in Norway*. London: Routledge, 2018.

114. On American funding remaking European science, see John Krige, *American Hegemony and the Postwar Reconstruction of Science in Europe*. Cambridge, MA: MIT Press, 2008.

115. Serge Moscovici and Ivana Marková, *The Making of Modern Social Psychology: The Hidden Story of How an International Social Science Was Created*. Cambridge: Polity Press, 2006.

that placed indigenous knowledge in existential jeopardy.[116] These developments led David Berlyne to make a telling analogy: "American psychologists have earned the abundant gratitude of the rest of the world. But like all parents of ambitious children, or like those who program computers that might beat them at chess, they had better not expect much in the way of thanks. Most of the important advances in psychology of the next few decades will, it is safe to predict, grow out of American psychology. But many of these will take place outside the United States."[117] Born in Britain, Berlyne had completed his doctorate at Yale before accepting a permanent position at the University of Toronto; a transnational trajectory that sensitized him to psychology's unspoken Americanness. Psychology's deterritorialization as a global science meant the discipline became "imprisoned in English" when it came to how psychologists conceived of the nature of the person.[118]

Geopolitics led to a highly uneven distribution of psychology. Writing amid the final reheating of the Cold War, the Iranian-born Fathali Moghaddam could rightly speak of "psychology in three worlds." With its overwhelming numeric and financial presence, the United States alone occupied the first. In the second world (consisting of much of Europe, Canada, Israel, and certain Latin American countries like Argentina and Brazil), the tensions between American dominance presented as an unmarked universalism and local ways of knowing the person created a series of backlashes and the veneration of so-called "indigenous psychologies."[119] The rest of the globe lacked any sustained psychological infrastructure. On those rare occasions when these places and their people featured in psychology, they did so as sites of data extraction, as locations for conducting impossible experiments, and as targets of benevolent development to adhere to American norms.[120]

The backlash Moghaddam described was genuine if short-lived. After a brief flourishing in the 1970s, the hope of maintaining a distinctly European social psychology largely ended in failure. ESESP and its journal became numerically dominated by contributors from America working exclusively in its national

---

116. Serge Moscovici, "Quelles histoires?" *Canadian Psychology* 33, no. 3 (1992): 540–547, 542.

117. David E. Berlyne, "American and European Psychology," *American Psychologist,* 23, no. 6 (1968): 447–452.

118. Anna Wierzbicka, *Imprisoned in English: The Hazards of English as a Default Language.* New York: Oxford University Press, 2013.

119. This was most pronounced in West Germany with a flourishing Marxist critical psychology. Thomas Teo, "Backlash against American Psychology: An Indigenous Reconstruction of the History of German Critical Psychology," *History of Psychology* 16, no. 1 (2013): 1–18.

120. Fathali Moghaddam, "Psychology in the Three Worlds: As Reflected by the Crisis in Social Psychology and the Move toward Indigenous Third-World Psychology," *American Psychologist* 42, no. 10 (1987): 912–920.

idiom.[121] Such a result was perhaps unsurprising given that there were more psychologists in the United States than in the rest of the world combined.[122] When cross-cultural concerns again resurfaced toward the end of the 1980s, pressure to secure American funding and to appear in the most influential English-language journals had largely muted critiques from the second world. Due to competition from the "tiger economies," interest shifted to comparisons with East Asia (usually organized around an immutable and eternal dichotomy between individualist-collectivist civilizations rather than in the lived history of democratic and totalitarian polities), but the methodologies used were exclusively American.

The once "Unamerican" science of the cultural front (with its bricolage of émigré influences) came to exemplify the "coca-colonization" of Western Europe and beyond.[123] Social psychology traveled along the same cultural circuits bringing Hollywood films and jazz to the world. Its extension represented the exercise of American soft power as part of the Cold War project of winning hearts and minds.[124] Psychology shared much in common with those cultural products. It, too, foregrounded individual expression and choice. Like Hollywood cinema, psychology seduced audiences with its posthistorical fantasy of a classless society where atomistic players of the game competed on a level playing field.[125] If universality once appealed as a buttress against the eugenics of individual and national differences, it came to carry very different political connotations as utopian internationalism ceded ground to the American economic hegemony flowing from the Marshall Plan. To psychologize meant to think in peculiarly American terms.

---

121. Sandra Schruijer, "Whatever Happened to the 'European' in European Social Psychology? A Study of the Ambitions in Founding the European Association of Experimental Social Psychology." *History of the Human Sciences* 25, no. 3 (2012): 88–107; Valentina Rizzoli, Paula Castro, Arjuna Tuzzi, and Alberta Contarello, "Probing the History of Social Psychology, Exploring Diversity and Views of the Social: Publication Trend in the *European Journal of Social Psychology* from 1971 to 2016." *European Journal of Social Psychology* 49, no. 4 (2019): 671–687.

122. Mark R. Rosenzweig, "Trends in Development and Status of Psychology: An International Perspective," *International Journal of Psychology* 17, no. 1–4 (1982): 117–140.

123. Pieter J. van Strien, "The American 'Colonization' of Northwest European Social Psychology after World War II." *Journal of the History of the Behavioral Sciences* 33, no. 4 (1997): 349–363.

124. Reinhold Wagnleitner, *Coca-Colonization and the Cold War: The Cultural Mission of the United States in Austria after the Second World War*. Chapel Hill: University of North Carolina Press, 1994; Kristin Ross, *Fast Cars, Clean Bodies: Decolonization and the Reordering of French culture*. MIT Press, 1996; Uta G. Poiger, *Jazz, Rock, and Rebels: Cold War Politics and American Culture in a Divided Germany*. Oakland: University of California Press, 2000.

125. Victoria De Grazia, *Irresistible Empire: America's Advance through Twentieth-Century Europe*. Cambridge, MA: Harvard University Press, 2005.

CONCLUSION

No one doubted that psychology emerged from World War II with a New Look. However, many disagreed about what counted as the revolt's figure and its ground. In the late 1940s, the political aesthetics of the Popular Front provided the most immediate point of departure for this new thinking about thinking rather than the human–machine couplings of cybernetics. The New Look started with an antifascist repudiation of the eugenics of innate racial differences and recast intergroup relations in terms of errors in social judgment. This was as dramatic an epistemic shift as any in the history of psychology. This was the first postwar "revolution" in psychology, followed by the more widely heralded revolt against behaviorism a decade later. The Red Scare largely pushed the historical memory of this initial, radical break to the background, foregrounding instead the later ascendancy of cognitive science.

While the New Look remained resolutely focused on humanity's failings both emotional and political, the cognitivism that displaced it gravitated toward the pinnacles of human achievement and capacity for reasoning. These attributes were invariably found wanting in their implementation, subject to processing errors that led judgment astray, but cognitive scientists embraced a hopeful, optimistic view of the possibility of human perfectibility. Doing so required them to detach perception from the social and clinical settings, the so-called daily life, which was at the heart of Krech's vision for a unified psychology. Throughout its history, the darker yet more complex vision of humanity found in the New Look approach served as a temptation to scientific psychologists. Psychologists as different as Krech and Neisser concurred that a satisfactory theory of perception must account for affect, development, and motivation. Yet, integrating these domains elided the exactitude demanded by the laboratory. In place of a "complete theory," cognitive science championed the flexible problem solver (on fairly limited range of tasks). Thinking remained "bounded," but cognitive science represented a flight from the kinds of relations in which the New Look sought to embed the perceiving subject. The electronic computer replaced the ambiguous figure as the ready-at-hand instrument for theorizing the human mind.

2

Rational Living and Straight Thinking

Therapeutic Cultures and Their Promise of Liberty

In January 1966, an enigmatic notice appeared among the classifieds of the *Berkeley Barb*, the mouthpiece for the Bay Area counterculture. It read: "YOUNG mature couples—students of theories of Dr. Albert Ellis—seek other couples interested in coterie living or get togethers" and included a local phone number.[1] Intrigued by the advertisement, the editors published an explanation by the ad's author in the following issue. Richard Thorne, the nominal leader of the East Bay Sexual Freedom League, described what he saw as an imminent revolution in social mores in a city "fast becoming the great experimental "freedom lab" for the whole country and the world!" Beyond unmarried couples "shacking" and the "orgy-ism" promoted by his group, Thorne envisioned a better future when everyone might experience sex without guilt.[2] Undergirding this new freedom was a more profound commitment, both most desirable and most difficult, "to tell the truth particularly about (and to) oneself." Despite the elusiveness of this self-reckoning, Thorne insisted some success had been achieved. Namely, "in psychotherapy it has been employed with far too great success for it to be reasonably considered absurd."[3] Bringing together telling the truth about and to himself, the evidence of psychotherapy, and the very person of Albert Ellis, Thorne declared his allegiance to a new mode of rational living.

The chess-playing computer provided an influential model of rationality in Cold War America, but it far from exhausted the possibilities. In 1956, the magical year

---

1. *Berkeley Barb*, 2, no. 4, January 28, 1966, 7.

2. Andrew Lester, "'This Was My Utopia': Sexual Experimentation and Masculinity in the 1960s Bay Area Radical Left," *Journal of the History of Sexuality* 29, no. 3 (2020): 364–387.

3. Richard Thorne, "A Step Toward Sexual Freedom in Berkeley," *Berkeley Barb*, 2, no. 5, February 4, 1966, 5.

of the cognitive revolution on Ivy League campuses, Ellis independently unveiled his "rational psychotherapy" at the annual meeting of the American Psychological Association (APA). Steeped in the teachings of the New York neo-Freudians, Ellis had formally broken with psychoanalysis in 1953, soon after becoming a full-time psychotherapist in private practice. His rational therapy built upon and elevated the popular genre of "practical psychology," which aimed at personal improvement through techniques such as autosuggestion.[4] He replaced the psychoanalytic search for childhood traumas hidden in the psyche's depths with "teaching these clients to organize and discipline their thinking."[5] His was a "highly active, intensive, unorthodox rational-persuasive-directive psychotherapy focussed on the current feelings and behavior of the client."[6] Like the New Look academics, Ellis challenged the long-standing Western dichotomy between thought and emotion, arguing against the premise they represented distinct mental processes. Instead, he subsumed the affective into the cognitive; emotions represented "a certain kind—a biased, prejudiced, or strongly evaluative kind—of thinking." As a result, "disordered emotions can often (though not always) be ameliorated by changing one's thinking."[7] Rebranding the therapy as rational-emotive therapy (RET) a few years later, Ellis challenged his clients to disrupt these patterns.

If Ellis elevated practical psychology to new levels of scientific legitimacy, he continued to embroil psychotherapy in controversy.[8] A flexible technology of improvement through verbal communication and other nonphysical methods, psychotherapy at that time existed on the boundary between established medicine and popular quackery.[9] Its best-known form, psychoanalysis, fascinated the moderns by combining an evocative set of concepts about the repressed secrets governing the self and a technique for excavating this self's hidden depths. Yet, Sigmund Freud's theories of childhood psychosexual development challenged the limits of bourgeois politesse. Psychoanalysis achieved considerable cultural respectability in the aftermath of World War II as American ego psychologists downplayed its sexual moorings in the hopes of making the technique amenable to the medical establishment of a largely Christian nation. As the advertisement in the *Berkeley Barb* indicated, Ellis's rational living troubled this trend, braiding mental health to new forms of sexual freedom and expression. Seeing American

---

4. Mathew Thomson, *Psychological Subjects: Identity, Culture, and Health in Twentieth-Century Britain*. Oxford: Oxford University Press, 2006, chapter 1.

5. Albert Ellis, "Rational Psychotherapy," *Journal of General Psychology* 59 (1958): 35–49, 35.

6. Albert Ellis, "The Private Practice of Psychotherapy: A Clinical Psychologist's Report," *Journal of General Psychology* 58 (1958): 207–216, 207.

7. Ellis, "Rational Psychotherapy," 36.

8. On psychotherapy's historical liminality, see Rachael I. Rosner, "History and the Topsy-Turvy World of Psychotherapy," *History of Psychology* 21, no. 3 (2018): 177–186.

9. Sonu Shamdasani, "'Psychotherapy': The Invention of a Word," *History of the Human Sciences* 18, no. 1 (2005): 1–22.

sexual mores as the source of much irrational, guilt-ridden thinking, Ellis pushed the boundaries of professional respectability. Purposefully blurring the lines that separated professional care from self-help, he designed RET as a mode of psychological intervention communicable through the mass market. He frequently appeared in magazines (mainstream, underground, and pornographic), on radio and television, and in evening lectures on college campuses. He performed Friday evening group psychotherapy sessions before Manhattan audiences, released instructional tape recordings, and hosted "marathon" weekend retreats. Ellis summoned a range of publics to join him in living rationally, cultivating a network of individuals who both adopted and adapted his concepts to give meaning to their lives.

A number of critics argue that the postwar United States became a "psychological society" where the therapeutic pursuit of the self eclipsed traditional sources of social cohesion such as organized religion. Everyday problems became psychologized, understood by using the apparatus of disciplinary psychology which also furnished ready-at-hand solutions.[10] This omnipresence of the psychological in American self-talk contrasts with the insular, divisive, doctrinaire, and often outright cult-like character of the early psychoanalytic movement.[11] However, these two stories intersect in illuminating ways. The infrastructure for the psychological society was built through the spread of overlapping networks of competing therapeutic communities. Led by charismatic leaders, their remit extended well beyond formal treatment. The therapeutic ethos in postwar America involved inviting ordinary people to recast their own lived experience using a novel conceptual vocabulary. Ellis exemplified this trend like no other before him had done. For five decades, he preached a secular gospel of rational living, of "thinking straight" and getting over "hang-ups" as the cure for America's psychic woes. In the process, he became one of the most visible—if ever controversial—spokespersons for clinical psychology at midcentury. Then, rather abruptly, Ellis joined forces with those seeking psychotherapy's return to the medical fold. In the

10. Philip Rieff, *The Triumph of the Therapeutic: Uses of Faith after Freud*. Chicago: University of Chicago Press, 1987; Philip Cushman, *Constructing the Self, Constructing America: A Cultural History of Psychotherapy*. Reading, MA: Addison-Wesley, 1995; Nikolas Rose, *Inventing Our Selves: Psychology, Power, and Personhood*. Cambridge: Cambridge University Press, 1998; Eva Illouz, *Saving the Modern Soul: Therapy, Emotions, and the Culture of Self-Help*. Oakland: University of California Press, 2008.

11. Richard Noll, *The Jung Cult: The Origins of a Charismatic Movement*. New York: Simon and Schuster, 1997; Sonu Shamdasani, *Cult Fictions: C. G. Jung and the Founding of Analytical Psychology*. London: Routledge, 2003; Lydia Marinelli and Andreas Mayer. *Dreaming by the Book: Freud's "The Interpretation of Dreams" and the History of the Psychoanalytic Movement*. New York: Other Press, 2003; George Makari, *Revolution in Mind: The Creation of Psychoanalysis*. New York: HarperCollins, 2008.

1970s, hostile external scrutiny discouraged sectarian struggles in favor of measurable outcomes in a moment described as "psychological détente."[12]

This reconciliation resolved certain political problems facing psychotherapy. It made good on the libertarian desire to disentangle psychological care from an ever expanding "therapeutic state" organized around the involuntary confinement of the mentally ill. The therapeutic archive generated by Ellis's considerable correspondence with clients, clinicians, and critics reveals a countermove: the cultivation of a psychological society where a wide range of persons "freely" adapted expert advice to their own mundane, everyday self-talk. Finally, the scientific rhetoric surrounding psychological détente obscured how an unmarked manly, white heterosexism continued to undergird therapy's promised freedom to think rationally.

THE POSTWAR RECONSTRUCTION OF SEX

Breaking with psychoanalysis did not mean Ellis rejected the centrality of sexuality to psychic life. Indeed, the contradictory sexual mores of postwar society animated much of his career. As part of the wartime mobilization, American women had entered the paid workforce in unprecedented numbers. Peace brought a supposed return to prewar norms: a veneration of heterosexual marriage, an idealization of the nuclear family, a renewed religiosity. In turn, the "traditional" family was seen as providing a bulwark on the Cold War's domestic front against godless communism. Following the scarcity of the depression and the spousal separation of the war, the size of families grew as the age at marriage decreased. A baby boom housed in a suburban and consumerist domesticity represented a kind of "containment at home," in historian Elaine May Tyler's apt phrase.[13] Not everyone concurred with the postwar sexual consensus.[14] Most famously, Betty Friedan's *The Feminine Mystique* (1963) catalogued the psychic toll postwar domesticity had taken on middle-class women.[15] More immediately, new gender norms intensified the policing of those deemed sexually deviant. The Lavender Scare of

---

12. Michael J. Mahoney, Aaron T. Beck, Marvin R. Goldfried, and Donald Meichenbaum, "Editorial," *Cognitive Therapy and Research* 1, no. 1 (1977): 1–3, 2.

13. Elaine Tyler May, *Homeward Bound: American Families in the Cold War Era*. New York: Basic Books, 1988.

14. Joanne Meyerowitz (ed.), *Not June Cleaver: Women and Gender in Postwar America, 1945–1960*. Philadelphia: Temple University Press, 1994.

15. On the radical roots of Friedan's liberal feminism, see Daniel Horowitz, *Betty Friedan and the Making of* The Feminine Mystique: *The American Left, the Cold War, and Modern Feminism*. Amherst: University of Massachusetts Press, 1998. Her analysis of housewives' psyches drew upon humanistic psychology. See Ellen Herman, *The Romance of American Psychology: Political Culture in the Age of Experts*. Oakland: University of California Press, 1995, 290–292.

the early 1950s purged the civil service of homosexuals on the pretext that these individuals were vulnerable to blackmail from foreign agents.[16]

In 1947, the year Ellis received his PhD from Teachers College, a renewed panic over sex crimes swept across the United States. Fed by sensational media coverage of particularly violent incidents, fears crystallized around male deviants whose "utter lack of power to control his sexual impulses" led them to commit unconscionable acts of violence, especially against children. The panic had begun in 1937, subsided during World War II, then reached a fevered pitch between 1947 and 1955. State legislatures passed "sexual psychopath" statutes as police cracked down on a range of illegal sexual acts, including exposure and consensual sodomy.[17] In 1949, New Jersey followed the national trend. Its Sex Offender Act stipulated that all persons convicted of even minor sexual offenses must submit to psychological assessment to determine whether they should be sent for indefinite treatment in a psychiatric hospital rather than receive a prison sentence. A 1950 revision mandated that all such evaluations had to take place at a recently created Diagnostic Center at Menlo Park, where Ellis found employment as chief psychologist.[18]

Sexual psychopaths made headlines, but these statutes exemplified a wider "divestment" from criminal law which ceded its jurisdiction over certain troublesome persons to psychiatry.[19] Spared imprisonment due to a mental illness beyond their control, a diagnosis of sexual psychopathology entailed potentially indefinite confinement to a state hospital with little treatment or recourse for challenging this assessment before the law. The number of persons institutionalized due to mental illness ballooned at midcentury, peaking in 1955 with nearly 500 per 100,000 adults over the age of 15 confined to psychiatric hospitals.[20] Civil libertarians, most famously Thomas Szasz, denounced this rapidly encroaching "therapeutic state" that intentionally confused social norms with disease.[21] Indeed, examining these "deviants" made Ellis and his colleagues skeptical of the sexual psychopath diagnosis and the threat posed by sex crimes. Instead of the violent fiends of

---

16. David K. Johnson, *The Lavender Scare: The Cold War Persecution of Gays and Lesbians in the Federal Government*. Chicago: University of Chicago Press, 2009.

17. Estelle B. Freedman, "'Uncontrolled Desires': The Response to the Sexual Psychopath, 1920–1960," *Journal of American History* 74, no. 1 (1987): 83–106.

18. Simon A. Cole, "From the Sexual Psychopath Statute to "Megan's Law": Psychiatric Knowledge in the Diagnosis, Treatment, and Adjudication of Sex Criminals in New Jersey, 1949–1999," *Journal of the History of Medicine and Allied Sciences* 55, no. 3 (2000): 292–314.

19. Nicholas N. Kittrie, *The Right to Be Different: Deviance and Enforced Therapy*. Baltimore: Johns Hopkins Press, 1971.

20. Bernard E. Harcourt, "From the Asylum to the Prison: Rethinking the Incarceration Revolution," *Texas Law Review* 84 (2005): 1751–1786.

21. Thomas S. Szasz, *Law, Liberty, and Psychiatry: An Inquiry into the Social Uses of Mental Health Practices*. New York: Macmillan, 1963.

popular lore, the majority of individuals assessed at Menlo Park were "innocuous, inadequate, passive, and minor offenders."[22]

During these formative years, Ellis made common cause with Abraham Maslow, then a young professor at Brooklyn College. Both men wanted their fellow Americans to rethink sex. During the war, each had published innovative questionnaire-based research linking sexuality to personality among young, college-educated women. The émigré neo-Freudians living in New York City inspired both of their sexological endeavors. Led by the charismatic feminist analyst Karen Horney, the neo-Freudians challenged the orthodox view that the sexual libido and its repression lay at the root of psychic drives. In bestsellers like *Neurotic Personality of Our Time* (1937), Horney argued that generalized feelings of anxiety in a status-obsessed society drove psychosocial development and its pathologies. Ellis and Maslow concurred. Their surveys showed sexuality to be a "subpattern" of a more general "dominance-feeling," or assured self-confidence in the lives of college women. Maslow canonized this neo-Freudian, sociological approach with his famous hierarchy of needs which placed the pursuit of "esteem" near the pinnacle of individual drives.[23] However, as antisemitism continued to shape academic hiring practices and other opportunities for professional advancement, Maslow and Ellis found themselves neither at home in academic psychology nor fitting into America's growing psychoanalytic community.[24]

Nor could they secure support from the leading sexology network in the country, the Rockefeller-funded Committee for Research on Problems of Sex (CPRS) chaired by the Yale primatologist and eugenicist Robert M. Yerkes. Created in 1922, the CPRS sought to avoid scandal by focusing on a natural science approach, initially funding endocrinology research almost exclusively. In the late 1930s, the CRPS renewed its commitment to behavioral studies, yet Yerkes rebuffed Maslow's interest during the primatology phase of his career. When the CRPS did venture into the arena of human sexuality in 1942, it sponsored the Midwestern zoologist Alfred Kinsey's interview-based surveys. This decision clearly upset Maslow and Ellis, who criticized Kinsey on methodological grounds while supporting his findings about the diversity of ordinary Americans' sexual pursuits.

---

22. Ralph Brancale, Albert Ellis, and Ruth R. Doorbar, "Psychiatric and Psychological Investigations of Convicted Sex Offenders: A Summary Report," *American Journal of Psychiatry* 109, no. 1 (1952): 17–21.

23. Abraham H. Maslow, "Self-esteem (Dominance-feeling) and Sexuality in Women," *Journal of Social Psychology* 16, no. 2 (1942): 259–294; Albert Ellis, "Questionnaire versus Interview Methods in the Study of Human Love Relationships," *American Sociological Review* 12, no. 5 (1947): 541–553.

24. Andrew Winston, "'The Defects of His Race': E. G. Boring and Antisemitism in American Psychology, 1923–1953," *History of Psychology* 1, no. 1 (1998): 27–51; Ben Harris, "Jewish Quotas in Clinical Psychology?: *The Journal of Clinical Psychology* and the Scandal of 1945," *Review of General Psychology* 13, no. 3 (2009): 252–261.

Psychoanalysis likewise failed to provide a refuge for the pair. In the 1930s, both Nazis and Christian conservatives criticized psychoanalysis as a decadent Jewish science promoting sexual promiscuity. After the war, the project of making psychodynamic psychiatry medically acceptable involved downplaying sex. The Kinsey report became a flashpoint as it documented the American male pursuing a plenum of sexual outlets. Analysts declared his direct interview techniques inadequate for revealing candid responses on such a sensitive topic. Against Kinsey's empirical findings, they advanced their "love doctrine": healthy sexuality was not about the frequency of outlet but about the love from sustained heterosexual couplings. They took the historically recent phenomenon of "companionate marriage" and naturalized it, downplaying Freud's more sympathetic views on homosexuality to make psychoanalysis palatable.[25]

Lost between these two camps, Ellis and Maslow tried organizing a Society for the Scientific Study of Sex as an alternative to the CRPS's more open approach to clinical perspectives.[26] Their eclecticism had roots in the Institute for Sexology established by Magnus Hirschfeld in 1919. Unlike most interwar sexologists bent on the eugenic elimination of deviancy, Hirschfeld dedicated his Berlin institute and the journal he edited to the curation of sexual diversity in support of minority rights. Hirschfeld became the first target of the Nazis following their consolidation of power in 1933. Casting the institute as an icon of Weimar degeneracy, the Nazis destroyed its building, burned its library, and led Hirschfeld to flee into exile.[27] At this time, the Indian physician A. J. Pillay took up the sexologist mantle.[28] He continued to edit Hirschfeld's journal into the 1950s, with Ellis's assistance as the American corresponding editor after the war.[29]

As part of his general sexual permissiveness, Ellis defended the civil liberties of gay and lesbians at a time when few did so publicly. In a position more aligned with Freud than with the American analysts who spoke in his name, Ellis rejected both the religious condemnation and criminalization of same-sex relations.[30] As Kinsey's survey showed, a complete absence of homoerotic desires (if

---

25. Dagmar Herzog, *Cold War Freud*. Cambridge University Press, 2017, 21–55.

26. Ellis to Yerkes, December 15, 1949, Robert Yerkes Papers, Box 17, folder 299. This organization did not come into existence until 1957.

27. Heike Bauer, *The Hirschfeld Archives: Violence, Death, and Modern Queer Culture*. Philadelphia: Temple University Press, 2017.

28. Veronika Fuechtner, "Indians, Jews, and Sex: Magnus Hirschfeld and Indian Sexology," *Imagining Germany, Imagining Asia: Essays in Asian-German Studies*. Rochester, NY: Camden House, 2013, 111–130.

29. Ellis to Pillay, November 3, 1952, Albert Ellis Papers, Box 118, folder 8.

30. Henry Abelove, "Freud, Male Homosexuality, and the Americans" in Henry Abelove, Michèle Aina Barale, and David M. Halperin (eds.), *The Lesbian and Gay Studies Reader*. New York: Routledge, 1993, 381–393; Matthew Tontonoz, "Sandor Rado, American Psychoanalysis, and the Question of Bisexuality," *History of Psychology* 20, no. 3 (2017): 263–289; Herzog, *Cold War Freud*, 56–86.

not experience) was rare. Humans were born "plurisexual." Nevertheless, Ellis perpetuated the homophobia of much American psychoanalysis. He deemed the "exclusive homosexual" a troubled individual needing psychotherapeutic care. Because contemporary culture discriminated against homosexual activity, these individuals, Ellis maintained, should conform to societal norms to avoid the psychic stress of prejudice. Here Ellis applied a double standard as he encouraged freeing various forms of heterosexual expression from moral constrictions. He justified this contradiction with the belief that homosexuality, even though not innate itself, became fixed due to an inborn neurotic disposition. A fearful avoidance of rejection from a heterosexual partner, he stated, led to adoption of the homosexual lifestyle. Ellis felt that exclusive homosexuals (even those once married and with children) had failed to give heterosexual relations a chance. Rational therapy focused on practical techniques for encouraging such encounters.[31]

Given his libertine beliefs, Ellis did not last long as a functionary of the therapeutic state. He complained about how the Chief Psychologist of the State of New Jersey lacked "complete freedom from censorship in my researches and writings on sexual topics."[32] In 1953, he resigned from his position at Menlo Park.

Upon his resignation and now back in Manhattan, Ellis pioneered a new professional identity: the psychologist in private practice. He championed the establishment of clinical psychology as a profession distinct from psychiatry and psychoanalysis and independent from physicians, the hospital system, and the state. This field took its cues more from neo-Freudian dissidents than from mainline psychoanalysis. In *Self-Analysis* (1942), published soon after her expulsion from the New York Psychoanalytic Society for heterodoxy, Horney promoted an expansive view of the therapeutic. People turned to analysis not simply because they suffered from specific disorders, but to resolve general feelings of dissatisfaction that were holding them back. Analysis offered an opportunity for "self-realization" freeing one of unhealthy compulsions.[33] Carl Rogers, APA's president in 1947, did much to incorporate such views into the new profession of clinical psychology and its New Look for psychotherapy. Rejecting the psychiatrist's "fascist" modes of control, Rogers conceived of a more agentful role for the patient (or, as he preferred to call this individual, the client) in their treatment. He championed a nondirective psychotherapy where the counselor served as a catalyst for the client's own self-discovery. The new clinical psychology would be democratic in both form and purpose as Rogers recast psychotherapy as a nonmedical intervention applicable to numerous everyday troubles. The very design of the

---

31. Albert Ellis, "On the Cure of Homosexuality," *International Journal of Sexology*, 55 (1952): 135–138; Ellis, "Are Homosexuals Necessarily Neurotic?" *One: The Homosexual Magazine*, 3, no. 4 (1955): 8–12; Ellis, "The Effectiveness of Psychotherapy with Individuals Who Have Severe Homosexual Problems," *Journal of Consulting Psychology*, 20 (1956): 191–195.

32. Ellis to Robert M. Yerkes, November 21, 1953. Robert M. Yerkes Papers, Yale University. Box 17, folder 299.

33. Karen Horney, *Self-Analysis*. New York: Norton, 1942.

therapist's office reflected this more egalitarian ethos. Rather than a passive patient reclining on a sofa, the active client sat across a desk, face-to-face with their equal, the therapist.[34] Where psychoanalysis remained somewhat shrouded in mystery, American clinical psychologists strove to make therapy open, transparent, and efficient.

Reflecting his own commitment to rational thinking, Ellis carefully documented the early years of his practice. In 1955, he saw 306 individuals for a total of 2,748 therapy sessions with an average of fifty-five sessions per work week. Marital, courtship, and sexual problems counted as the most common issue bringing clients to his door. His clientele was overwhelmingly young (in their twenties and thirties), intelligent, and college educated. In terms of religion, Jewish clients outnumbered Protestant and Catholic ones combined. Perhaps the most telling piece of data Ellis collected related to referrals. Only 3 percent of new clients came at the direction of their physician. In contrast, 9 percent found Ellis through public talks and writings, and 16 percent were referred by other psychologists or counselors. However, the vast majority, 54 percent, came for treatment at the personal recommendation of other clients.[35] This data suggested that clinical psychology could achieve autonomy from the medical establishment and the therapeutic state. A successful private practice need not depend on referrals from doctors. A clientele enthusiastically sharing its positive experiences of therapy with peers sufficed for creating a market of adults voluntarily submitting to psychotherapy. Already by 1955, rational living consisted of building and activating a network of likeminded individuals.

ALBERT ELLIS'S COGNITIVE REVOLUTION

In 1959, Ellis incorporated his practice as the Institute for Rational Living, a nonprofit center for research, therapy, and training. Along with conducting individual and group psychotherapy, he channeled the growing revenue from royalties and speaker's fees into supporting the center. Independent of any university, the Institute more closely resembled the training centers established by competing psychoanalytic sects, but one wholly under Ellis's control. Building his Institute, Ellis grew distant from his academic colleagues. During the late 1950s and throughout much of the 1960s, his extensive correspondence (consisting of dozens of letters received and responses dictated per week) included none of the academics associated with the cognitive revolution. When Ellis returned to campuses in the late

---

34. Carl R. Rogers, "'Client-Centered' Psychotherapy," *Scientific American* 187, no. 5 (1952): 66–75. On the couch as key technology of the psychoanalytic setting, see Andreas Mayer, *Sites of the Unconscious: Hypnosis and the Emergence of the Psychoanalytic Setting*. Chicago: University of Chicago Press, 2013, 198–221.

35. Albert Ellis, "The Private Practice of Psychotherapy: A Clinical Psychologist's Report," *Journal of General Psychology*, 58 (1958): 207–216, 210.

1960s, he was as likely to give an evening lecture on sexual freedom at the invitation of a student club as he was to appear in a departmental research seminar.[36] Given this isolation, Ellis did not initially use the word "cognitive" to describe his 1956 revolution in therapy. Yet, he noted the kinship as early as 1962, stressing how "it is difficult to think of any major social science where an absorbing interest in the cognitive-rational processes has not become pronounced in the last two decades."[37] The transformation he introduced shared many common features with the cognitive sciences gaining sway within universities. First and foremost, Ellis believed in the constitutive power of language as the great mediator of feeling and behavior.[38] Humanity's capacity to verbalize their thoughts granted them the unique ability to solve problems through reason. As a clinician, however, Ellis specialized in how this rationality went astray. His therapy consisted in getting clients to articulate their (negative) thoughts on pressing matters of concern and then directly challenging the accuracy of their statements through an aggressive form of debate modeled on philosophical disputation.

A philosophy of life, a way of (re)conceiving oneself, lay at the heart of Ellis's therapy. Like the cognitivists, he understood ordinary humans as creators of meaning and rational predictors of the future. All effective psychotherapeutic interventions operated on the level of thought and efforts to "teach or induce their patients to reperceive or rethink their life events and philosophies and thereby to change their unrealistic and illogical thought, emotion, and behavior."[39] However, existing psychoanalytic techniques such as dream analysis, free association, catharsis, and transference only did so indirectly. As a result, psychoanalysis remained largely "ineffectual and wasteful," if occasionally successful by happenstance. In contrast, RET unabashedly embraced "more direct, persuasive, suggestive, active, and logical techniques."[40] This confrontational approach contrasted with Rogers's nondirective client-centered therapy, then the preferred modality among clinical psychologists. The two began sparring as early as 1952, with Rogers sometimes adopting a remarkably personal tone: "your dislike for me and everything I stand for is so strong that you are much more interested in tearing down what we do than in attempting to understand it."[41] Indeed, the correspondence captured the split between America's two leading psychotherapists, with Rogers requesting an empathetic hearing and Ellis committed to pointing out and demolishing his opponent's errors. Ellis recognized that their differences carried political overtones, noting his "more 'authoritarian' reactions to your

36. Ellis to Virginia Miller, March 13, 1969, Box 133, folder 2.

37. Albert Ellis, *Reason and Emotion in Psychotherapy* (New York: Lyle Stuart, 1962), 108.

38. Luke Stark, "Albert Ellis, Rational Therapy, and the Media of 'Modern' Emotional Management," *History of the Human Sciences* 30, no. 4 (2017): 54–74.

39. Ellis, *Reason and Emotion in Psychotherapy*, 36–37.

40. Ellis, *Reason and Emotion in Psychotherapy*, 37.

41. Carl R. Rogers to Ellis, July 9, 1952, Box 118, folder 12.

'democratic' theories of therapy."[42] Exhortation on the rational therapists' part tore down the client's damaging self-image, disrupted the negative narratives they constructed about themselves, and tried to replace these with a truer, yet more forgiving, self-understanding.

Ellis retained from his exposure to the neo-Freudians the view that "societally-induced superstitions and prejudices have caused widespread human disturbances."[43] Anxiety derived from one's relations with others lay at the heart of most neuroses. Rather than the universal, biological libido of classic psychoanalysis, Ellis understood these dynamics in culturally specific terms. In language echoing Horney's, he argued: "Ours, in other words, is a generally neuroticizing civilization, in which most people are more or less emotionally disturbed because they are brought up to believe, and then to internalize and to keep reinfecting themselves with, arrant nonsense which must inevitably lead them to become ineffective, self-defeating, and unhappy."[44] As a remedy, Ellis sought to disabuse his clients of those false beliefs that made them neurotic. Along with face-to-face argumentation, he used practical instruction, what he called homework, to challenge and break down these cognitive tendencies. Assignments often involved the client writing out lists as a distancing technique to obtain an "objective" perspective on their own life.

As was always his approach, Ellis built RET from his own experience and modeled its solutions in the self-help books he published. In *Reason and Emotion in Psychotherapy* (1962), the most comprehensive statement of RET, Ellis broke down "irrational ideas" into a nested set of lists. The major incorrect beliefs causing psychic harm included (1) the necessity of universal approval from every member of the community; (2) universal competence and achievement across all of life's domains; (3) the notion that certain people are innately bad or evil, deserving of punishment; (4) the conviction that when things do not go as one wanted this represents a catastrophe; (5) the idea that human unhappiness has an external cause over which the individual has no control; and (6) the recognition that if something is fearsome, one should dwell upon it. To combat these damaging ideas, Ellis preached a secular gospel of radical self-acceptance. It embraced "human beings as fallible, limited, biologically rooted animals. But it also accepts them as unique, symbol-producing and thought-creating persons who have unusual potentials, in most instances to build or rebuild their own emotions and behaviors."[45] To live rationally was to fundamentally live on one's own, to become self-reliant for one's own emotional well-being. In the densely interconnected world of postwar New York City, Ellis reasserted rugged individualism: he proclaimed that "the rational individual should do his best to stand on his own

---

42. Ellis to Rogers, August 5, 1952, Box 118, folder 12.

43. Ellis, *Reason and Emotion in Psychotherapy*, 60.

44. Ellis, *Reason and Emotion in Psychotherapy*, 94.

45. Ellis, *Reason and Emotion in Psychotherapy*, 130.

two feet and to do his own thinking and acting."[46] Men were free. They should not depend on others or abstract principles (whether God or the state) to find their own fulfillment. If Ellis's exhortation method of analysis bordered on the authoritarian, it resulted in personal emancipation from others.

Ellis was not alone in promoting this line of self-help. Businessman and future Libertarian Party presidential candidate Harry Browne published a widely syndicated letter entitled "A Gift to My Daughter" around Christmas 1966. Unable to decide how to fulfill her many material wants and selfishly desiring to bestow upon her an enduring gift, Browne gave her (and the public) a simple truth: "No one owes you anything." Browne intended this simple message of diminished expectations to be read as emancipatory. Because no one was obligated to give her their "moral conduct, respect, friendship, love, courtesy, or intelligence," his daughter was free to make her own choices. No one else could grant her happiness; it was entirely in her own hands.[47] For both Ellis and Browne, reasonable people did not look to others for fulfillment. It could only be found inside oneself. Responsibility to others bred an unhealthy dependency, antithetical to freedom and happiness.

RET had much in common with this strand of popular libertarianism, exemplified by the novelist Ayn Rand.[48] As both movements gained a foothold in the affluent society, Ellis entered into a proxy war with the "goddess of the market." During the writing of *Atlas Shrugged* (1957), Rand began convening weekly meetings of her admirers, a group known as the Collective. Chief among these disciples was Nathaniel Branden, who led the effort to systematize her writings into the Objectivist philosophy.[49] In 1958, he founded the Nathaniel Branden Institute (NBI) to promote Objectivism by organizing lectures on college campuses, distributing a newsletter, and creating a book service. Branden was also a student of clinical psychology and translated Rand's thought into a therapeutic practice. Branden's efforts meant Rand's influence spread through the same networks as RET.[50] By 1966, a number of early RET advocates formally converted to Objectivism. Ellis acknowledged he and Rand had much in common, starting with their shared atheism. He noted that both held "enlightened self interest—or what they [the Objectivists] call selfishness—should be the basis for sane human behavior." However, the two movements parted ways over what constituted "rationality." Ellis argued that the Objectivists "believe in the absoluteness of reason

---

46. Ellis, *Reason and Emotion in Psychotherapy*, 82.

47. https://www.harrybrowne.org/articles/GiftDaughter.htm

48. Angus Burgin, *The Great Persuasion: Reinventing Free Markets since the Depression*. Cambridge, MA: Harvard University Press, 2012.

49. Jennifer Burns, *Goddess of the Market: Ayn Rand and the American Right*. Oxford University Press, 2009.

50. Nathaniel Branden, "The Benefits and Hazards of the Philosophy of Ayn Rand: A Personal Statement," *Journal of Humanistic Psychology* 24, no. 4 (1984): 39–64.

and they, as far as I can see, are arrant blamers of human beings when they go wrong." He also disagreed with their economic philosophy, as "they believe in the free market of Adam Smith which never has existed and never will and are somewhat on the fascistic republic side."[51]

Ellis pledged to "iron out my differences with the Objectivists" in a public debate with Branden.[52] In this debate, he dismissed Objectivism as a secular religion demanding rigid devotion from its adherents rather than free thinking and self-determination.[53] This encounter pushed Ellis to articulate what exactly he meant by rationality. His answer was unsurprisingly psychological. He rejected any "absolute criterion of "rationality," asserting that what is deemed "rational" by one person, group, or community can easily be seen as being "irrational" by another person or group. In RET, "rational" has always meant cognition that is effective or self-helping, not merely cognition that is empirically and logically valid."[54] Living rationally did not mean adopting the god's eye view from nowhere, but, rather, learning to live free of social judgment and obligations to others. The "rationality" of RET also meant the freedom to treat others instrumentally in service of one's own needs.

This alignment of psychology with libertarianism had consequences for the cultural relocation of the therapeutic at the end of the 1960s.[55] Psychotherapists expanded their remit amid intense political opposition to psychiatric authority: its incursion into civil liberties despite its documented inability either to predict dangerous conduct or to improve mental health. Psychological libertarians, espousing a patient's "right to treatment," were among the more vocal opponents of involuntary commitment in psychiatric hospitals.[56] Unlike more radical critics like Thomas Szasz, therapists like Ellis and Branden did not seek to categorically abolish the notion of mental illness, although they acknowledged the arbitrariness of existing psychiatric labels.[57] Instead, these clinicians fragmented and proliferated those sites deemed psychological. Working in private practice for fee rather than as salaried public employees meant they could promote

---

51. Ellis to Albert V. Freeman, January 10, 1966. Box 129, folder 2.

52. Ellis to James F. Smith, October 26, 1966. Box 124, folder 19.

53. Albert Ellis, *Is Objectivism a Religion?* New York: Lyle Stuart, 1968.

54. Ellis, "Changing Rational-Emotive Therapy (RET) to Rational Emotive Behavior Therapy (REBT)," *Journal of Rational-Emotive and Cognitive-Behavior Therapy* 13, no. 2 (1995): 85–89, 85.

55. Greg Eghigian, "Deinstitutionalizing the History of Contemporary Psychiatry," *History of Psychiatry* 22, no. 2 (2011): 201–214.

56. Joseph M. Livermore, Carl P. Malmquist, and Paul E. Meehl, "On the Justifications for Civil Commitment," *University of Pennsylvania Law Review* 117, no. 1 (1968): 75–96.

57. Ellis and Szasz publicly debated each other in 1977. See the videorecording *A Debate between Albert Ellis and Thomas Szasz: Mental Illness, Fact or Myth?* Baldwin, NY: William E. Simon, 1977.

the psychologization of everyday problems in print and through lectures while seeking to limit the power of the therapeutic state. This move reinforced the individualism of psychotherapy. It remade psychological care as the preserve of the lone individual freely seeking help for their personal problems, a person largely unburdened by history and disembedded from any community. Indeed, rather than signifying the alienation of modernity, atomism came to characterize mental health. The self promoted by psychotherapy, then, was not so much "empty" as had been marked by historically specific forms of postwar white, male, heterosexual privilege, but was rendered as a natural and universal good.

ALBERT ELLIS'S SEXUAL REVOLUTION

This expansion of the psychological led Ellis to flirt with the boundaries of professional respectability. He built his Manhattan practice by representing himself as an expert in sexual and marital difficulties, but such a reputation pushed the limits of acceptable public discourse. Ellis carved a cultural niche for rational therapy by making common cause with sexologists, pornographers, sex reformers, free speech advocates, and sexual minorities persecuted under the law. He saw his disputational methods as emancipatory for all, but, at its core, his therapy privileged male heterosexual liberation. Ellis became a full-time clinician in private practice in 1953, the same year *Playboy* hit the newsstands. Although he would not appear in its pages for almost another decade, his pop psychology fit *Playboy*'s brand of consumerist, urban bachelorhood.[58] The rationality in RET centered on the imperative to "think straight" about oneself. For Ellis, "thinking straight" invariably focused on sex, the source of many guilt-ridden hang-ups. This thinking was "straight" in a second sense. Ellis's sexology facilitated how the implicit heterosexual norms undergirding the public sphere became explicit during these years. Talk about sex became more overt rather than coded. However, the new sexual freedoms granted under the law were not distributed evenly throughout society.[59] Certainly in the age of Emmett Till, the greater male assertiveness Ellis encouraged was not experienced equally across the color line.[60] As a therapist and public intellectual, Ellis championed a racialized, male-centric view of the modern individual that venerated its fulsome self-expression unencumbered by the needs or desires of others. RET operated as part of the system that perpetuated this sexual double standard all the while that Ellis was personally preaching against it.

58. Elizabeth Fraterrigo, *Playboy and the Making of the Good Life in Modern America*. Oxford: Oxford University Press, 2009.

59. Margot Canaday, *The Straight State: Sexuality and Citizenship in Twentieth-Century America*. Princeton, NJ: Princeton University Press, 2009.

60. Danielle L. McGuire, *At the Dark End of the Street: Black Women, Rape, and Resistance*. New York: Vintage, 2010.

Lyle Stuart served as the publisher for both Ellis's sex advice and his early rational psychotherapy manuals. Stuart started as a journalist but switched to publishing in 1951, launching a tabloid known as *The Independent*, which sought stories that would offend his rivals' advertisers. This paper included a regular column from Ellis starting in 1956 where he propounded his libertine views on nonmonogamy, adultery, premarital sex, masturbation, and censorship. This was Ellis's first sustained mass market platform, a direct and often crude mode of communication he came to prefer over decorous professional publications. When Stuart turned to books, his catalogue ran the gamut from radical political commentary to mafia exposés to straight-up pornography. Yet, Ellis's titles dominated the list; he was "Stuart's most lucrative and long-term author."[61] The first title was the frequently reprinted *Sex without Guilt* (1958), whose ads faced censorship from both the *New York Times* and *Esquire* magazine. Despite this resistance, Ellis confided in a friend that the book's success meant "I really may make some gelt out of sex."[62]

Ellis came to publish about a book a year with Stuart, including titles such as *The Art and Science of Love* (1960), *Creative Marriage* (1961), *If This Be Sexual Heresy* (1963), *The Origins and Development of the Incest Taboo* (1963), and *Sex and Single Man* (1963). In 1962, Stuart published *Reason and Emotion in Psychotherapy*, Ellis's most important and widely cited theoretical text. Together, Ellis and Stuart pursued a publication strategy that conflated professional expertise and titillation. By the 1960s, Ellis's sexual advice and opinions on censorship would feature regularly in the columns of men's magazines ranging from the sophisticated *Playboy* and its competitor *Rogue* to the hardcore *Penthouse* by 1970. His position took him to the Supreme Court. As the author of the introduction to the seized edition of the eighteenth-century erotic novel *Fanny Hill*, Ellis became involved in the resulting obscenity case. Decisions such as *Memoirs v. Massachusetts* (1966) expanded the space for erotic material in the public sphere, if often narrowly cast in the right to privacy for heterosexual adults.[63] Ellis's involvement made him a free speech celebrity, a fixture of the college lecture circuit.[64]

Ellis's boundary-pushing approach antagonized clinical psychologists worried about their shared profession's public image. Both the APA's Committee on Science and Professional Ethics and Conduct and the New York Society of Clinical Psychologists filed complaints against Ellis in January 1966, following an

---

61. Marcia Seligson, "The Bad Boy of Publishing: Lyle Stuart," *New York Times Book Review*, November 30, 1969, 34.

62. Ellis to Michael Amrine, June 3, 1958. Box 119, folder 21.

63. Marc Stein, *Sexual Injustice: Supreme Court Decisions from Griswold to Roe*. Chapel Hill: University of North Carolina Press, 2010; Whitney Strub, *Obscenity Rules: Roth v. United States and the Long Struggle over Sexual Expression*. Lawrence: University Press of Kansas, 2013; Sarah E. Igo, *The Known Citizen: A History of Privacy in Modern America*. Cambridge, MA: Harvard University Press, 2018.

64. Natalie Gittelson, "No Business Like Lecture Business," *New York Times Magazine*, June 9, 1968.

ad in the *Village Voice* that invited people to attend a special holiday celebration at his Institute. The evening started with a live demonstration of group psychotherapy followed by a party. His fellow professionals felt the "advertisement could be interpreting clinical services as entertainment and has a commercial rather than professional ring to it."[65] The APA committee complained that this latest instance represented "a consistent pattern of advertising practices which have been the subject of ethical complaint by your colleagues" and threatened Ellis's expulsion from the Association.[66] Faced with professional censure, Ellis demurred and promised to reform. But his justification revealed the social world of clinical psychology in 1960s New York. The local press, he pointed out, frequently featured advertisements for lectures and symposia by prominent clinicians. The live demonstrations of RET were a fixture of his Institute's educational outreach and were no different than the "Theatre of Psychodrama" advertised by the competing Moreno Institute. With regard to the planned party, he reasoned that other educational and religious groups promoted similar gatherings. Rational living was a community not so different in kind.[67] In the midcentury metropolis, clinical psychology advanced as much as an accoutrement of the fashionable social scene as carefully designated medical treatment.

Ellis's approach became even more pronounced in counterculture enclaves like the Esalen Institute in Big Sur, California. Founded by two Stanford graduates, Esalen provided a retreat for those interested in realizing their "human potential" through a combination of humanistic psychology, Eastern meditative practices, and the consumption of psychedelic drugs.[68] Ellis's former associate Maslow served as the major inspiration for Esalen, and the émigré psychotherapist Fritz Perl lived in residence there for five years starting in 1964. Ellis visited for a weekend sojourn in 1968 as part of a trip promoting RET on the west coast.[69] Ultimately, he took a dim view of Esalen's approach as it taught "people that they do need to be loved in order to accept themselves."[70] Esalen and other countercultural therapeutics became a topic of national conversation that same summer. *Life Magazine* published an extensive pictorial essay featuring the children of the American bourgeoisie abandoning their inhibitions at Esalen and similar locales. The psychic excess released in such pursuits contrasted with the cover story depicting the deprivations of the "starving children of Biafra War," a stark

65. Kenneth Helfant to Ellis, January 24, 1966, Box 123, folder 17.

66. Richard F. Docter to Ellis, January 17, 1966, Box 123, folder 17.

67. Ellis to Docter, February 12, 1966, Box 123, folder 17.

68. Jeffrey J. Kripal, *Esalen: America and the Religion of No Religion*. Chicago: University of Chicago Press, 2011.

69. Ellis to Henry L. Drake, March 22, 1968, Box 130, folder 11.

70. Ellis to Bryan Sharkey, December 1, 1969, Box 132, folder 6.

illustration of the racial and geographic limits of the counterculture's empathetic consciousness.[71]

The marathon weekend soon emerged as the most intensive, if controversial, technology for human encountering. George Bach, a Los Angeles-based psychotherapist in private practice, pioneered in the technique. Bach long advocated the "influence-pressure" of group therapy to get clients "to stop playing games and start interacting truthfully, authentically, and transparently." However, he found the typical group session inadequate. A marathon, then, consisted of a dozen or so individuals retreating to a secluded setting for twenty-four hours or longer. The weekend involved "no interruptions, continuous meetings for 2 days, no subgrouping, no socializing, minimal breaks, clear-cut ground rules, and admission of people seriously interested in changing themselves rather than the universe."[72] Carl Rogers, then the dean of American clinical psychologists, embraced the encounter movement, understanding it in epochal terms. Echoing Maslow, he noted how the "affluent society" satisfied the individual's "survival needs." Gifted an excess of leisure time, such an individual came to realize their alienation as they simply wore a series of societally demanded "masks" hiding their true selves. Yet, Rogers remained optimistic, as "for the first time he is aware that this is not a *necessary* tragedy of life, that he does not have to live out his days in this fashion. So he is seeking, with great determination and inventiveness, ways of modifying this existential loneliness. The intensive group experience, perhaps the most significant social invention of this century, is an important one of the ways."[73] Ellis, too, embraced the marathon, formally collaborating with Bach to adopt the technique for RET.[74] He pitched his "weekend of rational encounter" as an anecdote to the excesses of the human potential movement.[75]

Ellis revealed his expectations for these weekends through his reaction to one of the famous variants on the encounter group: nude psychotherapy. In 1967, the California psychotherapist Paul Bindrim proposed this variation whereby participants literally shed their clothing to facilitate the revelation of their repressed, authentic selves to others.[76] Soon after, Bindrim, on the pretext of joining an APA symposium, wrote Ellis about the value of nudity in group therapy. The letter extended an invitation to participate in one of Bindrim's sessions.[77] However,

---

71. Jane Howard, "Inhibitions Thrown to the Gentle Winds," *Life* 65, July 12, 1968, 48–65.

72. George R. Bach, "The Marathon Group: Intensive Practice of Intimate Interaction," *Psychological Reports* 18, no. 3 (1966): 995–1002.

73. Carl R. Rogers, "Interpersonal Relationships: U.S.A. 2000," *Journal of Applied Behavior Science* 4, no. 3 (1968): 265–280, 268.

74. Ellis to Albert Freeman, September 19, 1967, Box 128, folder 6.

75. Albert Ellis, "A Weekend of Rational Encounter," *Rational Living*, 4, no. 2 (1969): 1–8.

76. Ian Nicholson, "Baring the Soul: Paul Bindrim, Abraham Maslow and 'Nude Psychotherapy,'" *Journal of the History of the Behavioral Sciences* 43, no. 4 (2007): 337–359.

77. Paul Bindrim to Ellis, February 8, 1968. Box 130, folder 11.

the pair quickly diverged. Ellis concluded that "Paul Bindrim is not to be trusted very far in regard to sexual freedom.... he insists very clearly, that a nudist marathon means that the individuals are only allowed to look and touch lightly and not at all to have sex relations of any kind. Secondly, he over-emphasizes the love bit as against the sex bit in a very typical meely-mouthed ministerial manner. His old background as a preacher comes out very clearly in what he says and the net result is quite puritanical and even hypocritically so, since on the surface he seems to be liberal."[78]

As his reaction to Bindrim made evident, sex permeated rational living. Ellis's books, articles, and lectures became touchstones of the sexual revolution. Some readers experienced his writing as transformative. After attending a campus lecture, a college senior wrote seeking advice about "any psychiatrists of your school of thought and/or liberal point of view." Having left the Catholic Church at nineteen, she had experienced "premarital relations" with various partners without ever finding much satisfaction, a fact that bothered her. Upon the advice of the school psychologist, she had entered therapy with two different psychiatrists, but these men only added to her "guilt feeling about sex."[79] Ellis responded that he knew no one in her area with such an outlook. Despite the disappointing response, her letter revealed a canny consumer of psychological wares. Unhappy with her situation, she refused to accept the care (and judgment) offered her and sought a therapist who suited her needs. Another "enthusiastic supporter of your rational-emotive psychotherapy" expressed her ongoing reservations about sex. A self-identified atheist, she still worried about the moral judgments of her peers (as well as the risk of pregnancy).[80] In this case, Ellis explained that he could not fully answer her questions as it was unethical to offer therapeutic advice without first interviewing a client in person. However, reiterating the advice in his popular books, he urged her to "start thinking for yourself and find the kind of males for you, who also think for themselves and do not go along with conventional morality." To do otherwise, she risked becoming "emotionally disturbed."[81] Others looked to Ellis to connect with a community espousing his views. A twenty-year-old woman wrote, asking "could you put me in contact with any individuals and/or organizations in the Miami or Miami Beach, FLD area who share in this enlightened and liberated, yet spiritually clean thinking?"[82] Others spoke of their excitement to recast their lives in Ellis's terms. A heterosexual male student wrote to express his desire "in meeting you and working with you and preparing myself for the task of presenting a sexual gospel. I have a keen interest in how sex influences and is influential to man. In light of this, I want to be an evangelist for

---

78. Ellis to Ed Lange, October 10, 1968, Box 130, folder 2.

79. Juliet L. Cafaro to Ellis, April 4, 1968, Box 129, folder 3.

80. Christine Grahm to Ellis, March 26, 1968, Box 129, folder 6.

81. Ellis to Grahm, April 1, 1968, Box 129, folder 6.

82. VH to Ellis, May 19, 1968, Box 129, folder 8.

a more knowledgeable country."[83] These university students testified to how Ellis provided a secular alternative to religion, which furnished them with new modes of self-exploration.

Ellis's promise of sexual freedom remained unevenly distributed. In 1967, a couple from Allentown, Pennsylvania, shared their experiences in pursuing "exogamous sex," a decision they had made after consulting with Ellis. They not only sought to practice this alternative to monogamous marriage, but they wanted to document, analyze, and report their self-experiment. As their letter revealed, things had gone awry. They presented their experience as a dialogue, a dialectic of their relationship's deterioration. As the wife's portion of the letter made evident, their exogamy was not always consensual. She got "emotionally upset" when the husband "goes out independently, or even worse, when we go out together and he starts looking around for prey." The husband countered in language couched in Ellis's gospel of rational living. "Because you can acknowledge intellectually that it is a sound moral system; and because you love me, I think you can do it. Reason is on your side; only emotion stands in the way." Yet, the wife remained resistant. She concluded: "I want domestic tranquility, but I'm not positive that I sincerely want to have my thinking modified."[84] Rational living granted the husband freedom from an outdated morality and the opportunity to delve into new sexual pleasures while maintaining the comforts of his companionate marriage. This same rationality manifested itself for the wife as having her thoughts "modified" against her will to conform to what she experienced as heterosexist norms. Using language that would gain political salience over the coming decade, she viewed rational therapy not as an emancipation from unwanted tradition but as the coercive imposition of the patriarchy's latest guise.

By the end of the 1960s, members of both the gay and women's liberation movements publicly challenged Ellis's authority to make unquestioned pronouncements about their psyches. Based on his experience at the Diagnostic Center, Ellis positioned himself as an ally of homophile organizations such as the Mattachine Society. Following a 1953 schism between the radical leadership, which was openly critical of heterosexism, and the rank-and-file membership, which was not, the Mattachine Society publicly adopted an accommodationist strategy of adjusting homosexual lives to homophobic social norms. Part of this "retreat to respectability" involved cultivating relationships with sexologists and sex radicals like Ellis to slowly ameliorate American attitudes toward homosexuality.[85] Ellis's "defense" of homosexuality remained entangled with his immersion in psychoanalysis. Always distancing himself from those analysts who saw homosexuality as a sickness, Ellis nevertheless maintained that something was amiss.

---

83. MVH to Ellis, December 5, 1969, Box 133, folder 1.

84. BEM to Ellis, December 29, 1967, Box 128, folder 10.

85. Martin Meeker, "Behind the Mask of Respectability: Reconsidering the Mattachine Society and Male Homophile Practice, 1950s and 1960s," *Journal of the History of Sexuality* 10, no. 1 (2001): 78–116.

Fortunately, he was well positioned to fix the problem. In 1955, the *Mattachine Review* reprinted an essay by Ellis explaining his cure for exclusive homosexuality using psychoanalytic methods. The complete elimination of homoerotic attraction was impossible (and undesirable), but directed psychotherapy could encourage such individuals to also pursue more socially accepted heterosexual outlets. Tellingly, this persistent homophobia was one of the stances Ellis retained from his analytic training.[86] Despite his self-professed rationality, he did not follow the evidence provided by psychologist Evelyn Hooker, who in 1957 demonstrated the inability of trained analysts to make good on their claim to distinguish between exclusive homosexuals and heterosexuals using Rorschach responses as an index of their personalities. Collaborating with Mattachine Society volunteers, Hooker circulated the results of his experiment widely among gay rights activists as crucial counterevidence to psychoanalysts' claims about the obvious maladjustment of homosexual men.[87] Instead, Ellis trusted his own clinical judgment.

If anything, his position on homosexuality hardened as others questioned his authority. When outlining his position to the Philadelphia-based leader of the Homosexual Law Reform Society, Ellis affirmed that he did not consider "homosexual behavior in itself is in the least pathological," but that, in his view, exclusive homosexuality "maybe and often is pathological." It could not be otherwise, as "in our culture most individuals who are fixed homosexuals are neurotically or psychotically obsessed with homosexual behavior."[88] Ellis was even more forthright with friendly colleagues. He believed that "a predisposition to emotional disturbance of a severe nature is inherited and that most though not all homosexuals have this predisposition." This meant "homosexuals are usually exceptionally disturbed individuals more frequently than not in the borderline psychotic or psychotic class." Homosexual men "inherit a tendency to think crookedly and be supersensitive." This tendency resulted in their becoming "inordinately afraid of failing and in dire need of love." RET with such individuals involved helping with this general neurotic tendency and during this process encouraging their seductive behaviors with women to mitigate their innate fear of failing.[89] He objected when the popular advice columnist Ann Landers wrote of the slim chances of "curing" homosexuality. In disagreement with Landers, Ellis insisted that "if you are only keeping psychoanalytic psychotherapy in mind, there are other approaches to the treatment of homosexuality such as the rational-emotive psychotherapy which I and my associates use which are much more effective in curing homosexuality."[90]

---

86. On conversion therapy, see Tom Waidzunas, *The Straight Line: How the Fringe Science of Ex-Gay Therapy Reoriented Sexuality*. Minneapolis: University of Minnesota Press, 2015.

87. Peter Hegarty, "Homosexual Signs and Heterosexual Silences: Rorschach Research on Male Homosexuality from 1921 to 1969," *Journal of the History of Sexuality* 12, no. 3 (2003): 400–423.

88. Ellis to Clark P. Polak, December 9, 1966, Box 124, folder 6.

89. Ellis to Charles L. Odom, June 23, 1967, Box 128, folder 11.

90. Ellis to Ann Landers, March 20, 1967, Box 128, folder 19.

He declared that the exclusive homosexual had "the right to be wrong," but Ellis remained adamant that his rational therapy could cure those who wished.[91]

Ellis's widely promoted claims resulted in his receiving numerous letters from young men in distress. Often writing from small towns in the rural heartland, these men shared their desperation, sense of isolation, and self-hatred due to their same-sex desires. They spoke of conflicts with their religious convictions and frequently expressed thoughts of suicide. They looked to Ellis as a sympathetic expert who recognized their "condition" when no one else did. One teenager even pleaded with Ellis to "just come and get me" at an appointed time at a post office outside Kansas City.[92]

Ellis's tenacity put him increasingly at odds with the more militant gay liberationists who rejected accommodationism and, taking their cue from the Black freedom struggle, began asserting their rights and publicly proclaiming their identity.[93] In 1963, the audience at the conference of the East Coast Homophile Organization heckled Ellis's presentation.[94] In 1968, Elver Barker wrote an extensive letter on behalf of the Mattachine Society, outlining their differences with Ellis. Barker condemned "the racket in which you and many other counsellors are engaged." When it came to RET, he argued that its narrow pursuit of self-interest left no room for romantic love. Barker had "no doubt that when the basic human need to love and be loved is not adequately met that this deprivation is the core of practically all serious emotional disturbances. That you deny this most important fact of the love need places you in a category of inadequate counsellors and writers on the subject of love, including sexual love. Human life holds deep meanings to people who are emotionally and socially free to love and be loved and who think deeply beneath the surface of things. Our modern age is characterized by superficiality in every area of living, and your minimizing the importance of the need for love is but a reflection of that superficiality."[95] Barker refused the psychotherapist's certain dismissal of queer love, but he did not reject psychology wholesale. His letter advanced a highly psychologized understanding of homosexual rights, one grounded in the universalizing humanism of Maslow's hierarchy of needs. Barker invoked Ellis's former ally to condemn RET as crass and shallow, characteristic of a superficial modernity opposed to authentic connections. By the early 1970s, Ellis numbered among "one of a New York five-man rogues' gallery of shrinks

---

91. Albert Ellis, "Homosexuality: The Right to Be Wrong," *Journal of Sex Research* 4, no. 2 (1968): 96–107.

92. FL to Ellis, January 10, 1967, Box 128, folder 4; JTJ to Ellis, January 5, 1967, Box 128, folder 13; DVJ, February 22, 1968, Box 129, folder 2; JS to Ellis, August 8, 1968, Box 130, folder 10.

93. Abram J. Lewis, "'We Are Certain of Our Own Insanity': Antipsychiatry and the Gay Liberation Movement, 1968–1980," *Journal of the History of Sexuality*, 25, no. 1 (2016): 83–113.

94. Kristin Gay Esterberg, "From Illness to Action: Conceptions of Homosexuality in *The Ladder*, 1956–1965," *Journal of Sex Research* 27, no. 1 (1990): 65–80, 74.

95. Elver Barker to Ellis, February 15, 1968, Box 129, folder 7.

who are most responsible for the 'scientific' façade which covers the oppression of homosexuals."[96]

Ellis did not attract the same ire from the feminist movement, but a number of his women readers echoed similar criticisms. In 1967, six self-identified "girls" at a large co-ed university wrote to challenge the tenets of his sexology. They questioned whether "*The Art of Erotic Seduction* was addressed with sincerity to American males. We were unable to believe that a supposedly well-educated *doctor* could have the idea that a male should get as much sex as he possibly can without the growth of emotional love. Our only conclusion is that you wrote the book for financial gain."[97] The lead correspondent followed up a year later, psychologizing the psychologist: "I wonder what kind of person you are to devote your whole being to the act of sex—I mean, in essence, do you really believe sex is all *that* important? Maybe if people like you put sex in its proper (natural, healthy) perspective and didn't spend their whole lives blowing it up into a major catastrophe, it wouldn't *be* such a trauma."[98] Ellis defensively retorted that, contrary to his public persona, he did not "devote my whole being to the art of sex." He spent most of his days working on clients' nonsexual problems. He conceded that "sex is not all-important, but it does seem to me that you have quite a problem in this area and I would sincerely advise you to get some psychological help with it."[99] Another female fan wrote to Ellis to report she had purchased a number of his books as Christmas gifts. She thanked him for "writing all those sensible rational living-type books," but complained that this beneficial material came after "the commercial for free love, free sex, and just generally making whoopee."[100] These women refused to believe Ellis was sincere in his promotion of sex freed of affection. They dismissed his casualization of sex as mere showmanship, a technique for selling books to the credulous and titillated masses.

The leaders of the women's liberation movement frequently cited the masculine, heterosexist psychotherapist as a major source of oppressive ideology.[101] After lumping Ellis's advice together with that of *Cosmopolitan* and *Playboy* as essential sources for the sexually liberated, one feminist journalist observed in 1971 how the new freedom "seems oddly like a jail."[102] Psychologist Arlynn Miller's encounter with Ellis illustrates the complexity of these dynamics. They met in 1971, shortly after her divorce, when Miller attended a conference where Ellis

---

96. Craig A. Hanson to Ellis, September 14, 1972, Box 140, folder 6.

97. M. Finn to Ellis, November 11, 1967, Box 128, folder 3.

98. M. Finn to Ellis, April 24, 1968, Box 129, folder 5.

99. Ellis to M. Finn, May 2, 1968, Box 129, folder 5.

100. Martha Beck to Ellis, December 16, 1967, Box 128, folder 5.

101. Mari Jo Buhle. *Feminism and Its Discontents: A Century of Struggle with Psychoanalysis.* Cambridge, MA: Harvard University Press, 2009, 206–239.

102. Michele Clark, "Women's Liberation and the Sexual Revolution," *Everywoman* 1, no. 13 (January 22, 1971), 13.

was presenting. During the question-and-answer session, he delivered "an impassioned statement" describing her frustrations with a life heretofore defined by her status as a wife, mother, and housekeeper, roles she lost in her divorce. Ellis invited her to lunch, after which they had sex. Miller later recalled, "In those days Ellis believed that sometimes sex with a patient could be Therapeutic." Miller found the sexual encounter "perfunctory. But that whole experience was very significant. It helped me mature sexually. Prior to this, I only had had sex with my husband. Now that I was single, I didn't know how or when I would be sexual again. So I can thank Albert Ellis for that. He helped open me to new experiences."[103] Decades later, Miller still understood Ellis's approach to sexuality as beneficial, and she incorporated their brief encounter into a personal narrative of liberation. Others were less sanguine. Such open secrets led the APA to convene the Task Force on Sex Roles and Sex Bias Stereotyping on Psychotherapeutic Practice in 1974. One of its major outcomes was the prohibition of sex with clients in APA ethics code, curtailing the kind of excess found at marathon weekends.[104] The 1970s also saw the development of a self-consciously feminist therapy in the Boston area, which focused on improving women's health by acknowledging their embeddedness in relationships rather than promoting detachment like RET.[105]

Whereas he was once at the sexual vanguard, Ellis now occupied the tired riptide of comfortable, male heterosexual privilege. His "right to be sick" argument may (or may not) have read as progressive in the 1950s, but gay liberationists now demanded he cease and desist from speaking on their behalf. Similarly, many of his women readers called out the masculine assumptions Ellis built into sexology. Rather than emancipation from conservative mores, his public science made them beholden to a new set of demands as compulsory heterosexuality became an even more explicit feature of everyday life. Based on his own youthful shyness, Ellis preached a gospel of persistence that pushed against the decorum of Victorian courtship. He encouraged young men to expect sexual gratification without consequence or even consideration of others. His freedom of thought and expression expanded the number of public spaces and situations deemed sexual. However, many experienced this "rational" yet unrelenting pursuit of sex

---

103. Arlynn Miller, "Interview by Alexandra Rutherford [Video Recording]," *Psychology's Feminist Voices Oral History and Online Archive Project*. Philadelphia, October 25, 2007. http://www.feministvoices.com/assets/Feminist-Presence/Miller/Arlyn-Millerfinal.pdf

104. Susanna Kim and Alexandra Rutherford. "From Seduction to Sexism: Feminists Challenge the Ethics of Therapist–Client Sexual Relations in 1970s America," *History of Psychology* 18, no. 3 (2015): 283–296. Sexual harassment structured inclusion within psychology. See Jacy L. Young and Peter Hegarty, "Reasonable Men: Sexual Harassment and Norms of Conduct in Social Psychology," *Feminism and Psychology* 29, no. 4 (2019): 453–474.

105. Christina Robb, *This Changes Everything: The Relational Revolution in Psychology*. New York: Farrar, Straus, Giroux, 2006.

divorced from affection not as freedom but as unwanted scrutiny, surveillance, and oppression.[106]

PSYCHOLOGICAL DÉTENTE

As Ellis shed allies as the sexual revolution expanded beyond its original remit of liberating male, heterosexual libidos, support came from a surprising corner. The establishment reached out and embraced rational-emotive therapy as the evidence-backed key to a compromise among psychodynamic, behavioral, and cognitive practitioners. RET had flourished as a self-contained, if not insular, superpower detached from the rest of the discipline. Ellis remained a fixture of the annual APA conventions, where he ran workshops to recruit followers, but he largely ceased publishing in psychology journals, preferring high-circulation magazines, mass market self-help books, and eventually his own inhouse organ, *Rational Living*. As his eventual ally Michael Mahoney noted, it was Ellis's prolific literary production that "succeeded in forcing recognition of cognitive therapy as a serious ideological competitor." He won not by persuading other professionals. Rather, "Ellis was deemed more acceptable by the lay public than by academic and clinical psychologists. In many ways, professional recognition of rational-emotive therapy (RET) was given only grudgingly in response to public demand."[107] Much to his colleagues' surprise, once adopted and evaluated, RET seemingly worked, or at least it proved effective in terms of the new demands placed on psychotherapy. As Ellis entered the 1970s, he muted (though never entirely abandoned) his countercultural cache and used his considerable showmanship to secure RET's place in the competitive psychotherapy market. After two decades on the fringe, Ellis suddenly became respectable.

Ellis's foremost ally in this transformation was his polar opposite in terms of persona. The bowtie-wearing, soft-spoken, federal grant-wielding, academic psychiatrist Aaron T. Beck oozed respectability. Where Ellis focused on sex, depression served as Beck's bread and butter. Both began their careers as psychoanalysts but chafed under the movement's strictures. As a professor at the University of Pennsylvania, Beck remained ensconced within one of psychodynamic psychiatry's most prestigious institutions. Yet, in the early 1960s, he found himself frustrated and isolated from his colleagues. After a period of departmental infighting and professional disappointment, Beck withdrew and undertook an intense period of self-analysis. He found refuge in cognitive psychologists who shared his commitment to rendering the contents of the mind communicable through experimentation and measurement. These scientists looked at how the

---

106. Carolyn Bronstein, *Battling Pornography: The American Feminist Anti-Pornography Movement, 1976–1986*. Cambridge University Press, 2011.

107. Michael Mahoney, "Reflections on the Cognitive-Learning Trend in Psychotherapy," *American Psychologist* 32, no. 1 (1977): 5–13, 7.

mind successfully *functioned* as an information-processing computer, but the breakdown of these processes captivated Beck the clinician. Publicly, he focused on how cognitive errors led rational thinking astray and how therapists might set it again on the logical path. Privately, he filled notebooks with his own intrusive, unwanted, affective "automatic thoughts" which he sought to document and measure.[108] In 1963, Beck first suggested depression consisted of a series of "cognitive distortions" that altered the patient's very perception. The depressed experienced a "distortion of reality" and repeatedly demonstrated "a bias against themselves" when interpreting the information they received from the world.[109] As Beck emerged from his personal depression, he committed himself to remaking psychotherapy in light of his own experience.

If Beck's cognitive therapy broke with mainline American psychoanalysis, it offered a number of gifts to psychologists. He first made his reputation among psychologists with an assessment tool rather than with his skill as a therapist. In 1961, Beck published an inventory that provided a standardized criteria for assessing depression, even if the self-report questionnaire did not rise to the behaviorist ideal of a truly objective measure.[110] Consisting of twenty-one questions, this easy-to-use instrument was readily embraced by clinical psychologists. Like Ellis, Beck found graded tasks, list-making, and homework assignments powerful tools for getting clients to recognize and then manage their own cognitions. After reading a summary of Beck's first article on the cognitive features of depression, Ellis contacted the Philadelphia psychiatrist in late 1963 asking for a reprint of the article (as well as an earlier one from Beck's abandoned research on homosexuality). Finding that Beck's cognitive approach resonated with his own rational therapy, Ellis started recommending his work to colleagues. Yet, only in the late 1960s did the pair begin regular correspondence accompanied by frequent, reciprocal trips to each other's workplaces. After Ellis's initial visit to the Philadelphia clinic in 1969, Beck wrote hurriedly about how he "found our discussions stimulating and look forward to sharing my ideas with you again before too long."[111] Two years later, Beck insisted the two of them were "getting close to breaking through the iron curtain of the irrational therapies."[112] Beck had the legitimacy of an academic appointment in a leading psychiatry department which came with access to NIMH funds for research and a large pool of trainees. As America's leading psychotherapeutic showman, Ellis still maintained a wide audience through mass

---

108. Rachael I. Rosner, "The 'Splendid Isolation' of Aaron T. Beck," *Isis* 105, no. 4 (2014): 734–758.

109. Aaron T. Beck, "Thinking and Depression: I. Idiosyncratic Content and Cognitive Distortions," *Archives of General Psychiatry* 9, no. 4 (1963): 324–333, 328.

110. Aaron T. Beck, Calvin H. Ward, Mock Mendelson, Jeremiah Mock, and John Erbaugh, "An Inventory for Measuring Depression," *Archives of General Psychiatry* 4, no. 6 (1961): 561–571.

111. Beck to Ellis, n.d. [1969], Box 132, folder 4.

112. Beck to Ellis, April 9, 1971, Box 137, folder 10.

media outlets and a growing legion of practitioners who were adopting his cognitive techniques.

In the 1970s, Beck drew Ellis back into the fold, seeing in him a key ally in making psychotherapy accountable. The talking cure was undoubtedly popular. Amid the nation's political convulsions of the Vietnam War and the Watergate scandal, the affluent retreated into introspective self-exploration as they had never done before. The number and variety of practitioners proliferated, with Americans seeking guidance from a growing array of professional and popular sources.

However, the enthusiasm for talk therapy said nothing about its efficacy, a pressing concern for Ellis and Beck who staked so much of their self-image on their own rationality, as well as for insurance companies which were increasingly being asked to cover psychotherapy services. As early as 1952, the iconoclastic British clinical psychologist Hans Eysenck had launched a polemical attack on the benefits of psychotherapy. Eysenck demanded clear baselines and benchmarks for saying psychoanalysis worked. Collecting data from various studies, he compared the subsequent improvement of neurotics receiving psychoanalysis with clients abandoned to custodial care in state hospitals. Within two years of their illness, about two-thirds of neurotic patients improved whether with or without the benefit of psychoanalysis.[113] In light of Eysenck's damning result, clinical psychologists earnestly sought to demonstrate factors that might contribute to a patient's recovery. Ellis made an early contribution to this effort with a paper comparing the outcomes from three techniques as he transitioned from orthodox psychoanalysis to his own rational therapy.[114] Judicial rulings such as *Wyatt v. Stickney* (1971), the first legal victory for securing institutionalized persons' "right to treatment," made the accountability of psychotherapy a more immediate concern. The courts increasingly deemed custodial care inadequate. Psychiatry (on behalf of the state) could not simply confine the mentally ill but must effect change. The efficacy question weighed particularly on Beck. When he asked his colleague if he knew of any such research on RET, Ellis confessed: "there are damn few of these studies that I ever come across, which deal with therapy, itself."[115] His passive response, a rarity for Ellis, suggested that his interest in conducting such research himself had long ago waned. Yet, after decades of psychotherapeutic practice and its analysis in graduate training programs for clinical psychologists, these outcome studies were coming to fruition.[116]

---

113. Hans Eysenck, "The Effects of Psychotherapy: An Evaluation," *Journal of Consulting Psychology* 16, no. 5 (1952): 319–324.

114. Albert Ellis, "Outcome of Employing Three Techniques of Psychotherapy," *Journal of Clinical Psychology* 13 (1957): 344–350.

115. Ellis to Aaron T. Beck, May 27, 1969, Box 131, folder 12.

116. Lester Luborsky, Barton Singer, and Lise Luborsky, "Comparative Studies of Psychotherapies: Is it True that Everyone Has Won and All Must Have Prizes?" *Archives of General Psychiatry* 32, no. 8 (1975): 995–1008.

Ellis and Beck found an unexpectedly friendly reception among hardnosed behavior therapists. Maladaptive, learned habits lay at the root of neuroses, according to these clinicians, and simple conditioning procedures could eliminate unwanted behavioral patterns ranging from stuttering to alcoholism. Behavior therapies were highly directed, focused on the concrete problem troubling the patient. Outcomes came with clear criteria in terms of improved daily function. Among the most popular techniques was the systematic desensitization developed by the South African psychiatrist Joseph Wolpe. This intervention involved a low-level but gradually increasing exposure to an anxiety-inducing stimulus until the stimulus no longer produced anxiety in the client.[117] Following Wolpe's lead, behavior therapy developed in the hierarchically organized, even autocratic, atmosphere of psychiatric medicine of the British commonwealth before arriving on American shores in the mid-1960s. There, the neo-behaviorism of B. F. Skinner shaped the movement's reception. In the immediate postwar years, Skinner exemplified the American notion of better living through technology. Just as novel gadgets and appliances seemingly improved home life, Skinner offered the public a technology of behavior to improve child-rearing and education. He extended his famous operant conditioning experiments on pigeons into a tripartite science of behavior. In 1947, he hosted the first Conference for the Experimental Analysis of Behavior, building a network of young scientists interested in his laboratory methods. As a professor at Harvard in the early 1960s, he articulated his philosophy of radical behaviorism. Finally, in 1968, the first volume of the *Journal of Applied Behavior Analysis* appeared, publicizing practical efforts to deploy Skinner's technology.

As cognitive science came to dominate Ivy League psychology departments, behavior analysis flourished at public universities where the applied field resonated with these schools' practical missions.[118] Where talk therapies spoke to comparatively affluent neurotics looking for self-understanding, behavior analysis served as technology for managing unruly populations deemed beneath the psychoanalyst's remit. The use of these programs with involuntarily confined individuals in prisons and psychiatric hospitals led to significant litigation as these technologies risked violating the civil liberties of the most vulnerable.[119] This was especially true of children with intellectual disabilities, both inside and outside residential institutions.[120]

117. John Grossberg, "Behavior Therapy: A Review," *Psychological Bulletin* 62, no. 2 (1964): 73–88.

118. Alexandra Rutherford, *Beyond the Box: BF Skinner's Technology of Behaviour from Laboratory to Life, 1950s–1970s*. Toronto: University of Toronto Press, 2009.

119. On the new attentiveness to human rights in the 1970s, see Jeremi Suri, *Power and Protest: Global Revolution and the Rise of Détente*. Cambridge, MA: Harvard University Press, 2009; Samuel Moyn, *The Last Utopia: Human Rights in History*. Cambridge, MA: Harvard University Press, 2012; Michael Pettit, "The Great Cat Mutilation: Sex, Social Movements, and the Utilitarian Calculus in 1970s New York City," *BJHS Themes* 2 (2017): 57–78.

120. Gil Eyal, *The Autism Matrix*. Cambridge, UK: Polity, 2010; Chloe Silverman, *Understanding Autism: Parents, Doctors, and the History of a Disorder*. Princeton, NJ: Princeton University Press,

Increasingly prominent players in the mental health marketplace, behavior therapists struggled with a major public relations problem. Their interventions may have been efficacious, but they carried troubling political baggage. Having rejected the mushiness of psychoanalysis and humanism, they developed a technology of behavior that came to be seen as cold, rigid, even authoritarian. The publication of Skinner's *Beyond Freedom and Dignity* (1971) did much to solidify this view. There the Harvard professor called for the abolition of "autonomous man." Such an individual, "the inner man, the homunculus, the possessing demon, the man defended by the literatures of freedom and dignity," was a mere fiction, a "device used to explain what we cannot explain in any other way."[121] Relinquishing this egoistical illusion of self-possession promised to save humanity from self-destruction through war, overpopulation, and other planetary threats. His bestseller gave Skinner a wider audience than he had ever received, but one that largely rejected his message as being out of step with the countercultural, antitechnocratic mood ever suspicious of authority. Readers questioned whose interests the radical control of behavior served. Rather than announcing the liberation of humans from themselves, they denounced Skinnerian behaviorism as a totalitarianism trampling over dissidents and the elimination of all human values by reducing society to a mindless anthill.[122]

The problem was that, rather ironically, "behavior modification" lacked a precise definition. The term encompassed interventions ranging from the mundane to the inhumane, with psychosurgery undoubtedly the most controversial. First proposed in the mid-1930s, lobotomies became a popular therapeutic option to treat the symptoms of severe mental illnesses in the 1950s; the technique aroused much opposition, and its use faded by decade's end.[123] Following the urban unrest of the late 1960s and the increased political organization of Black prisoners, a team of psychiatrists suggested reviving psychosurgery as a technique for curbing antisocial violence. Their proposed Center for the Study and Reduction of Violence would disproportionality target Blacks, a fact not lost on organizations such as the Black Panther Party.[124] Political opposition to behavior modification was polyvalent. Its most vocal critic within the federal government was Senator Sam Ervin Jr., a southern conservative and fierce critic of both civil rights legislation and the Equal Rights Amendment. He opposed the therapeutic state

2011; Rémy Amouroux, "Beyond Indifference and Aversion: The Critical Reception and Belated Acceptance of Behavior Therapy in France," *History of Psychology* 20, no. 3 (2017): 313–329.

121. B. F. Skinner, *Beyond Freedom and Dignity*, Indianapolis, IN: Hackett Publishing, 1971/2002, 200.

122. Alexandra Rutherford, *Beyond the Box: BF Skinner's Technology of Behaviour from Laboratory to Life, 1950s–1970s*. Toronto: University of Toronto Press, 2009.

123. Mical Raz, *The Lobotomy Letters: The Making of American Psychosurgery*. Rochester, NY: University of Rochester Press, 2013.

124. A. Nelson, *Body and Soul: The Black Panther Party and the Fight against Medical Discrimination*. Minneapolis: University of Minnesota Press, 153–180.

as part of an antimodernist crusade against the behavioral sciences' intrusive gaze into the lives of ordinary citizens.[125] In 1971, Ervin convened a three-year, fact-finding subcommittee to examine federal sponsorship of behavior modification programs. The 1974 report that resulted decried the proliferation of federally supported behavior control technologies as a mounting threat to civil liberties and recommended more legislative oversight to protect citizens' privacy.[126] The report left unclear which technologies fell under its remit. Interventions such as physical punishment, electroshock treatments, drugs, and psychosurgery drew the most attention, but the report acknowledged behavior modification might include something as general as "any learned response to any stimulus."[127] As federal regulation of biomedical research expanded, the "behavioral sciences" decidedly fell within its purview.[128]

Given this unwanted outside scrutiny, behavior therapists needed to rebrand or risk losing their tentative hold on the medical market. The 1974 meeting of the Association for the Advancement of Behavior Therapy (AABT) saw a "surge of interest in the integration of cognitive psychology and behavioral approaches to clinical problems" with an audience of over six hundred members attending a symposium on "cognitive behavior modification."[129] Cognitivism, with its emphasis on the active processing of information, promised a more humane if still scientific face. Around Cambridge, Massachusetts, Skinner and the cognitivists held each other in mutual contempt; away from Harvard Yard, more creative arrangements seemed possible. Problem solving provided the platform for the détente between behavior and cognitive therapies. Where their fellow behaviorists saw trial-and-error conditioning and rote learning as keys to the organism's overcoming of obstacles, a younger generation of reformers within the ranks of behavior therapists foregrounded the "transfer-of-training phenomenon" or the person's ability to conceptualize and then apply solutions across the various situations they faced. Rather than having the client dependent on the therapist for treating discrete symptoms, an open and consensual cognitive behavior modification would

---

125. Sam Ervin, "Why Senate Hearings on Psychological Tests in Government," *American Psychologist* 20, no. 11 (1965): 879–880. See also Roderick Buchanan, "On Not "Giving Psychology Away": The Minnesota Multiphasic Personality Inventory and Public Controversy over Testing in the 1960s." *History of Psychology* 5, no. 3 (2002): 284–309.

126. *Individual Rights and the Federal Role in Behavior Modification: A Study*. Prepared by the Staff of the Subcommittee on Constitutional Rights of the Committee on the Judiciary, United States Senate, Ninety-Third Congress, Second Session. Washington, DC: U.S. Government Printing Office, 1974, 45.

127. *Individual Rights and the Federal Role in Behavior Modification*, 1.

128. Alexandra Rutherford, "The Social Control of Behavior Control: Behavior Modification, Individual Rights, and Research Ethics in America, 1971–1979," *Journal of the History of the Behavioral Sciences* 42, no. 3 (2006): 203–220.

129. Michael Mahoney to Ellis, November 10, 1975, Box 144, folder 10.

empower the client as a general problem solver in their lives.[130] Addressing the client as an active agent in their own treatment, one responsible for choosing their improvement, circumvented much of the Senate Subcommittee's concerns about behavioral control as secretive and involuntary, even if the actual interventions differed little. This move returned behavior modification to "the reasoned exchange of information" between equals rather than the "authoritarian" imposition of another's will through direct manipulation.[131]

Treatment had to meet the exacting standards of the behavior therapists. In post-World War II America, randomized controlled trials (RCTs) held the key to medical legitimacy. RCTs tested the efficacy of new therapies by randomly assigning subjects to one of two groups. Under a veil of ignorance, one group would receive the treatment, and the other a placebo.[132] Reformers pushed the experiments as a means of taming the pharmaceutical market by eliminating unethical entrepreneurs offering ineffective and dangerous wares. Federal regulators and funding bodies wanted to subject psychotherapy to RCTs. However, many psychoanalysts resisted attempts to disenchant their process into a series of discrete procedures. Methodologically, assigning patients to the placebo control group without their knowledge seemed challenging. Beck and the behavior therapists provided the pathway. A true placebo group trial was impossible (although often comparisons were made with patients being left on a waitlist for the duration of the treatment), but competing modalities could be compared to one another using a similar experimental design. By the late 1960s, Beck had sufficiently standardized his treatment procedures and codified them in teaching manuals so that they could be implemented in comparison experiments with pharmacotherapies. With NIMH funding and an array of graduate students, Beck's depression clinic at Pennsylvania housed this research.[133] Likewise, different behavior and cognitive therapies could compete with one another in similarly designed experiments. In 1977, Beck joined Mahoney, Marvin Goldfried, and Donald Meichenbaum in co-founding the Institute of Cognitive Therapy and Research as an ecumenical home for these competitive trials and other outcomes research. Early experiments showed that his cognitive therapy outperformed both behavioral techniques and even pharmacology.[134]

---

130. Thomas D'Zurilla and Marvin Goldfried, "Problem Solving and Behavior Modification," *Journal of Abnormal Psychology* 78, no. 1 (1971): 107–126.

131. *Individual Rights and the Federal Role in Behavior Modification*, 1.

132. Harry M. Marks, *The Progress of Experiment: Science and Therapeutic Reform in the United States, 1900–1990*. Cambridge University Press, 2000.

133. Rachael I. Rosner, "Manualizing Psychotherapy: Aaron T. Beck and the Origins of Cognitive Therapy of Depression." *European Journal of Psychotherapy and Counselling* 20, no. 1 (2018): 25–47.

134. Brian Shaw, "Comparison of Cognitive Therapy and Behavior Therapy in the Treatment of Depression," *Journal of Consulting and Clinical Psychology* 45, no. 4 (1977): 543–551; Augustus

This combative solution appealed to Ellis. Ever confident in his methods, he gladly allowed RET to compete. Long outside the academic establishment, he knew a good marketing tool when he saw one, and he and the other men recommending therapeutic détente clearly relished their jocular sparring, issuing a continual stream of commentaries in clinical and counseling journals. Ellis conducted little to no outcomes research himself. Instead, he welcomed doctoral students and other RET novices to visit his institute, familiarize themselves with his techniques, and write dissertations assessing its effectiveness. Intimate matters, on which Ellis staked so much of his career, rarely (if ever) featured in these outcome studies. For comparative purposes, these studies inevitably operationalized RET as a treatment for anxiety, often among students and usually tied to worry about some kind of public performance.[135] When compared to other modes of therapy using new statistical procedures such as meta-analysis, RET fared remarkably well, garnering the largest effect size of any modality.[136] At a time when legislators and insurance providers were looking askance at psychotherapy, statistics offered a powerful tool of persuasion. In the shifting mental health marketplace of the 1970s, outcome studies offered the gift of giving therapy precision.

This promissory precision appealed to others who were trying to reform their own mental health professions. Many psychiatrists blamed their specialty's low status among physicians on its fuzzy diagnostic standards. The antipsychiatry movement had charged the field with confusing mental illness with social impropriety. Homosexuality exemplified this classificatory problem like no other condition had. Eager to supplant psychoanalysis, behavior therapists boasted of the superior efficacy of treating sexual "problems": deploying electric shocks as an "aversion therapy" in a failed attempt to extinguish homosexual tendencies, fetishism, and "transvestism."[137] However, as Ellis experienced, an increasingly vocal gay liberation movement was unwilling to acquiesce to professional condemnation. In 1970, gay rights advocates disrupted a screening depicting aversion therapy at the AABT meeting, condemning this "treatment" as simply torture. That same year, activists started picketing the American Psychiatric Association's annual meetings, seeking to have homosexuality no longer identified as a mental

---

J. Rush, Aaron T. Beck, Maria Kovacs, and Steven Hollon, "Comparative Efficacy of Cognitive Therapy and Pharmacotherapy in the Treatment of Depressed Outpatients," *Cognitive Therapy and Research* 1, no. 1 (1977): 17–37.

135. Raymond A. DiGiuseppe, Norman J. Miller, and Larry D. Trexler, "A Review of Rational-Emotive Psychotherapy Outcome Studies," *The Counseling Psychologist* 7, no. 1 (1977): 64–72.

136. Mary Smith and Gene Glass, "Meta-Analysis of Psychotherapy Outcome Studies," *American Psychologist* 32, no. 9 (1977): 752–760.

137. This approach started in Czechoslovakia and became especially prominent in Britain and its commonwealth; see Waidzunas, *The Straight Line*, chapter 1; Nathan Ha, "Detecting and Teaching Desire: Phallometry, Freund, and Behaviorist Sexology," *Osiris* 30, no. 1 (2015): 205–227; Kate Davison, "Cold War Pavlov: Homosexual Aversion Therapy in the 1960s." *History of the Human Sciences* 34, no. 1 (2021): 89–119.

disorder in the association's *Diagnostic and Statistical Manual* (DSM). Witnessing a demonstration at the 1972 AABT meeting convinced psychiatrist Robert Spitzer to convene a task force to resolve the dispute.[138] In 1973, the American Psychiatric Association declassified homosexuality as a "mental disorder," suggesting "sexual orientation disturbance" as a milder replacement.[139] Spitzer mobilized this political success to remake the entire DSM. As Evelyn Hooker had demonstrated in the case of homosexuality, the field's diagnostic capacity was unreliable. Every diagnostician elicited information from their patients in an idiosyncratic manner, and the nomenclature itself was highly ambiguous. Rigor demanded expunging the omnipresent psychoanalytic concept of "neuroses" and replacing it with specified disorders defined by the unique symptoms. Published in 1980, DSM-III pushed against psychiatry's exceptionalism among medical specialties. It focused on identifying discrete disorders and then treating them in a specified manner amenable to insurance claims.[140]

The need to neutralize the political controversies engulfing psychotherapy dulled the differences among behavior, cognitive, and rational-emotive therapies. A common retreat from what came to be seen as coercive, involuntary "modifications" laid the groundwork for "psychological détente."[141] Therapy was the handmaiden of civil liberties and must, above all, guarantee a client's freedom of mind, self-efficacy, and self-determination. In this context, the more authoritarian therapeutic styles of both Ellis and the behavior therapists represented a serious liability. A new consensus modality, or peace treaty, called cognitive-behavior therapy (later known as cognitive-behavioral therapy or CBT) facilitated an escape from a contentious recent past. The term originated with Beck's group, but a host of clinicians soon adopted it as their own.[142] Ellis began adopting it as early as 1972, but, true to form, he demurred about certain facets of the new synthesis.[143] He appreciated and shared his colleagues' eclecticism when it came to permissible forms of treatment, but unlike their unrelenting pragmatism, he insisted RET constituted a unique and specific "philosophical system." The therapist's direct exhortation upon the client still played a larger role in RET

---

138. Ronald Bayer, *Homosexuality and American Psychiatry: The Politics of Diagnosis*. Princeton, NJ: Princeton University Press, 1987, 99, 115.

139. On Spitzer's continued commitment to conversion therapy, see Waidzunas, *The Straight Line*, chapter 2.

140. Rick Mayes and Allan V. Horwitz, "DSM-III and the Revolution in the Classification of Mental Illness," *Journal of the History of the Behavioral Sciences* 41, no. 3 (2005): 249–267.

141. The 1974 AABT presidential address urged behavior therapists to get out of the sexuality game on civil liberties grounds. Gerald Davison, "Homosexuality: The Ethical Challenge," *Journal of Consulting and Clinical Psychology* 44, no. 2 (1976): 157–162.

142. Larry Trexler to Ellis, December 13, 1971, Box 137, folder 7. On CBT's later expansion, see Sarah Marks, "CBT in Britain: Historical Development and Contemporary Situation" in Windy Dryden (ed.), *Cognitive Behaviour Therapies*. London: Sage, 2012, 1–24.

143. Ellis to Stephen Neiger, March 6, 1972, Box 138, folder 9.

than did its competitors.[144] Yet, no one disputed that Ellis had largely entered the CBT fold.

These parallel transformations felt across America's mental health professions had several consequences. With the elimination of neuroses as psychiatry's primary etiology, the clinically depressed replaced the habitually neurotic as the default therapeutic subject. Depression was at once indelible going back to antiquity and utterly modern. In 1972, revelations about past hospitalizations for depressive episodes led the Democratic vice-presidential candidate Thomas Eagleton to withdraw from the national ticket. A history with the affective disorder was thought to undercut his ability to make sound judgments, disqualifying him for higher office. In light of the Eagleton revelations, depression went mainstream, described by journalists just the next year as the "common cold of mental ills."[145] Psychiatric epidemiologists insisted that incidents rose dramatically between 1960 and 1975, especially among women and the young.[146] A generously funded NIMH program (started in 1969) dedicated to the disorder's psychobiology made it an attractive topic for researchers.[147] Instead of electroconvulsive therapy in hospitals, a new generation of pharmaceuticals and talk therapies managed the illness among outpatients. As numerous critics have convincingly argued, this rapid expansion of depression's reach medicalized otherwise normal (and even healthy) negative affective states. Ordinary feelings of sadness and loss became symptoms of a recognizable and treatable disorder, leading to a so-called depression epidemic. Increasingly seen as biological, the root of such negative affects lay inside the damaged individual rather than in the larger structures governing their lives. Favored treatments like CBT likewise particularized and individualized instead of targeting social transformation.[148]

An oft-neglected feature of CBT was its success in desexualizing psychotherapy. After World War II, ego psychologists, especially the Menninger brothers at their family clinic in Topeka, Kansas, strove to disentangle the talking cure from psychosexual theories of personhood.[149] Psychotherapy's embeddedness within the

---

144. Albert Ellis, "Rational-Emotive Therapy and Cognitive Behavior Therapy: Similarities and Differences," *Cognitive Therapy and Research* 4, no. 4 (1980): 325–340.

145. Rona Cherry and Laurence B. Cherry, "Depression: Common Cold of Mental Ills," *New York Times*, November 25, 1973, 38; Donald C. Drake, "Can Severe Depression Be Prevented?" *Philadelphia Inquirer*, November 7, 1973, 3C. See Jane White, "Depression Epidemic in United States," *Tyler Courier-Times*, February 8, 1981, 49.

146. Gerald L. Klerman and Myrna M. Weissman, "Increasing Rates of Depression," *Journal of the American Medical Association* 261, no. 15 (1989): 2229–2235.

147. Martin M. Katz, Steven K. Secunda, Robert M. A. Hirschfeld, and Stephen H. Koslow, "NIMH Clinical Research Branch Collaborative Program on the Psychobiology of Depression," *Archives of General Psychiatry* 36, no. 7 (1979): 765–771.

148. Allan V. Horwitz and Jerome C. Wakefield, *The Loss of Sadness: How Psychiatry Transformed Normal Sorrow into Depressive Disorder*. Oxford: Oxford University Press, 2007.

149. Rebecca Jo Plant, "William Menninger and American Psychoanalysis, 1946–48," *History of Psychiatry* 16, no. 2 (2005): 181–202.

counterculture did much to resexualize it and bring it into disrepute. The CBT brand allowed for the denial (if not disavowal) of this troubled past. The psychological management of sex did not disappear, but remarkably sex (as identity, orientation, or source of satisfaction) fell outside CBT's ever-expanding empire.[150] As psychotherapy's geographic center in America shifted from hippie California and neurotic New York to the mid-Atlantic and the Washington beltway, sexuality disappeared from a literature now narrowly focused on evaluating outcomes. A psychotherapy finally freed of sex was a prerequisite for its acceptance as a medical treatment, analogous to a dosage of medication, rather than an indulgent and wasteful self-obsession. The psychological détente of the late 1970s granted psychotherapy a respectability denied it since the term's coinage. Rather than a directionless plumbing of the depths, talking cures were now tied to specified diagnoses demarcated by clear criteria. The course of treatment was also limited with carefully specified outcomes. This dual specificity made CBT particularly amenable to the demands of third-party insurance providers, an increasingly important part of any practitioner's business model.

CONCLUSION

Despite his often-outré statements and cultivation of the countercultural, Ellis and the communities he fostered in fact exemplified certain trends in postwar psychology. Like that of his academic counterparts, Ellis's approach to psychotherapy underwent a "cognitive revolution" in the mid-1950s that gradually became the consensus position by the 1970s. Like them, Ellis valorized rationality as the key to well-being by subsuming emotions as a subset of thinking. Bad feelings represented distorted thought patterns, but as mere thoughts they could be deliberately combatted and altered through the medium of cognition.

A striking feature of this cognitivism was its unrelenting individualism. At a fundamental level, Ellis told a wide variety of audiences that other people were of no consequence to one's own mental health. All that mattered was how the individual perceived the world. Even more so than the psychoanalysts with whom he broke, Ellis made the individual the locus of their own destiny. For behaviorists, the organism responded to the environment. For experimental cognitivists, the organism responded to its *perceptions* of the environment. Ellis further narrowed the focus and *internalized* responsibility for one's own emotional state. Nobody—not parents, friends, neighbors, or society as different variations of

---

150. Deborah Weinstein, "Sexuality, Therapeutic Culture, and Family Ties in the United States after 1973," *History of Psychology* 21, no. 3 (2018): 273–289. On the new psychological management of sex around "misaligned" bodies, see Eve Kosofsky Sedgwick, "How to Bring Your Kids up Gay," *Social Text* 29 (1991): 18–27; David Valentine, *Imagining Transgender: An Ethnography of a Category*. Durham, NC: Duke University Press, 2007; Lisa Downing, Iain Morland, and Nikki Sullivan, *Fuckology: Critical Essays on John Money's Diagnostic Concepts*. Chicago: University of Chicago Press, 2015.

psychoanalysis taught—could grant happiness. Cognition became how one related to one's self, even when something as necessarily relational as sex was involved. Ellis's approach was libertarian in a second sense in that he helped carve a space of psychological care that was outside the surveillance of the therapeutic state and the apparatus of state hospitals. Like many postwar psychologists, Ellis held ambivalent attitudes toward the medical establishment. These professionals understood psychotherapy as a more general tool of social facilitation, distinct from biomedicine's cures. Only after 1970 did Ellis join forces with those who were seeking to integrate psychotherapy into the biomedical norms of National Institutes of Health (NIH) funding, RCTs, and discrete variables with measurable outcomes. In the intervening years, Ellis pioneered new modes of giving away psychology. His efforts led both to publics becoming eager to consume his wares and to counter-publics becoming schooled in psychology and yet skeptical of the claims he advanced.

By drawing thinking, reason, and cognition into this medically adjacent, public arena, Ellis lay the foundation for their remaking. In such applied and contested realms, the academic dispute with behaviorism became muted as the pragmatic eclecticism of the therapeutic underground held sway. This led to the reevaluation of cognition itself as it became connected to affect in new ways. Experimental cognitive scientists tended to document the mind's many successes. In their hands, the limited or bounded information processor remained a talented problem solver. Beck, Ellis, and their fellow behavior therapists shifted the balance. The clinical realm brought to the fore the many ways in which the mind habitually failed, even among largely healthy, if troubled, individuals seen in his private practice. Omnipresent cognitive distortions caused human unhappiness. Problem solving was a therapeutic skill, but Ellis popularized a version of cognitive science that stressed humanity's distance from computers rather than its proximity. This gap would become increasingly important to psychologists by the 1970s. Here their marriage of convenience with behavior therapy was telling. From certain academic perspectives, the break with behaviorism loomed large (often due to personal acrimonies among the victors writing the first draft of history). In the more practical world of therapy, behaviorism did not dissolve amid cognitive revolution. The synthesis of the two would loop back to shape academic research agendas. By the 1970s, the tide shifted from documenting the mind's many successes to attending to biases and errors that led it astray.

3

The Tragedy of American Psychology

Racial Justice and Professionalism on the Expanding Frontier of Mental Health

On February 1, 1979, Ron Dellums, Oakland's Black, Democratic Socialist representative, read a tribute to Thomas O. Hilliard, one of his constituents on the floor of Congress. Hilliard embodied professional psychology's radical potential to transform society by informing public policy and empowering the marginalized. Trained and licensed as a clinical psychologist, Hilliard looked beyond the individual therapeutic relationship to effect change. He was a founding member of the Association of Black Psychologists, a health care worker serving underrepresented communities, and a consummate organizer within his chosen profession, but his most distinct contribution was an innovative line of forensic psychology dedicated to mitigating the racial prejudice endemic to the criminal justice system. He consulted on jury selection; he testified to the damage caused by solitary confinement; and he explained how imminent threats like the visible presence of the Ku Klux Klan diminished the capacity of young Black men to make sound judgments. Hilliard advanced a collaborative, preventative, and thoroughly politicized community psychology dedicated to rectifying the psychic harms caused by the discrimination that was built into the very structure of American society.[1]

Hilliard was far from a lone figure. The politics of mental health was a live issue in the 1970s. Upon assuming office in 1977, Jimmy Carter convened a massive presidential commission on the topic, the latest in a series of postwar efforts to rationalize and augment the nation's mental health resources. The 1978 report challenged the ethos of professional autonomy, foregrounded the rights of patients, detailed the psychic costs of racism and poverty, and demanded equal access and preventative care. The Mental Health Systems Act, passed in 1980, promised free

---

1. Ronald V. Dellums, "Tribute to Thomas O. Hilliard," *Congressional Record: Proceedings and Debates of the 96th Congress First Session*, vol. 125, part 2, February 1, 1979, 1739.

Governed by Affect. Michael Pettit, Oxford University Press. © Oxford University Press 2024.
DOI: 10.1093/oso/9780197621851.003.0004

mental health care of their choosing for the poorest and most disenfranchised. Yet, by the time of Hilliard's death in 1985 at the age of forty-three, such hopes were largely dashed.[2] Carter's successor, Ronald Reagan, quickly repealed most of the 1980 Act before it took effect.[3] Reagan administration policies recast "freedom of choice" in narrower, free market, consumerist terms, sundered from human rights and preventative care.

After a period of expansive, youthful optimism, the profession dedicated to probing the darkest facets of the human psyche experienced something of its own midlife crisis. American psychology sold itself by furnishing the uncomfortably affluent with a seductive vocabulary for performing (if not exactly plumbing) their depths.[4] As finding oneself became the subject of journalistic ridicule during the so-called me decade, American clinical psychology seemed outwardly triumphant. It secured legal recognition as a profession distinct from the medical establishment. Its practitioners were aligning around an evidence-based mode of treatment. These same clinicians seized control of the American Psychological Association (APA), the field's major organization, from their academic rivals. By the end of the 1980s, each of professional psychology's apparent victories would be seriously undercut.

Some have characterized these postwar struggles in terms of "tensions and opportunities," but what happened to American psychology is better understood as a tragedy when a fundamental flaw in the protagonist leads to their downfall.[5] Such tragedies can be larger than persons. Historian William Appleman Williams famously described "the tragedy of American diplomacy." Arguing against the nation's self-image as an exporter of freedom, Appleman showed how American politicians sought to evade problems of class and race by pursuing policies of economic imperialism which opened "new frontiers" by expanding the markets for the nation's wares.[6] American psychology followed an almost identical path of tragic growth. The discipline entered the decade confronting problems of racialized inequality. The psychological leadership largely evaded these concerns by focusing on expanding the discipline's reach into new markets by creating new

---

2. "Thomas Hilliard Rites Saturday," *Tyler Courier-Times*, December 5, 1985, 8.

3. Gerald N. Grob, "Public Policy and Mental Illnesses: Jimmy Carter's Presidential Commission on Mental Health," *The Milbank Quarterly* 83, no. 3 (2005): 425–456.

4. Jessica Grogan, *Encountering America: Humanistic Psychology, Sixties Culture & the Shaping of the Modern Self*. New York: Harper Perennial, 2013; Elizabeth Lunbeck, *The Americanization of Narcissism*. Cambridge, MA: Harvard University Press, 2014; Susanne Schmidt, *Midlife Crisis: The Feminist Origins of a Chauvinist Cliché*. Chicago: University of Chicago Press, 2020. Along with talking cures for the comparatively affluent, clinical psychologists offered behavior modification for those (once) institutionalized. See Gil Eyal, *The Autism Matrix*. Cambridge: Polity, 2010.

5. Wade Pickren, "Tension and Opportunity in Post-World War II American Psychology," *History of Psychology* 10, no. 3 (2007): 279–299.

6. William Appleman Williams, *The Tragedy of American Diplomacy*. New York: Norton, 1959.

services where its professional expertise could hold sway.[7] This victory excluded voices within organized psychology like Hilliard's, concerned with social justice and community control. As the controversies over use of behavior modification for prisoners and other institutionalized populations revealed, psychology's ever-expanding remit was not without consequences. As was the case with the American state, psychology's imperialism undercut the profession's progressive, democratic pretensions. Reckoning with psychology's postwar transformation requires tracing both of these bold experiments with democracy and showing how a narrow professionalism came to triumph.

REVOLT OF THE PROFESSIONALS

The decades following World War II represented a period of unprecedented growth for psychology as the field progressed from a small discipline ensconced in universities to a mass, helping profession. In 1942, the United States Public Health Service (USPHS) and the Veterans Administration (VA) banded together to expand the pool of mental health professionals. World War I had taught them that the existing psychiatric profession was too small to handle the large number of returning soldiers experiencing various forms of trauma and distress from their deployment. In the interwar period, psychologists (with academic doctorates) had made tentative (if largely unsuccessful) moves to establish their field as a recognized health profession.[8] The USPHS provided the funds, and the VA hospitals created opportunities for paid practicum and internship experiences with clinical populations in need. American psychology departments reluctantly accepted the call. In 1946, two hundred clinical trainees were admitted to programs at twenty-two universities. By 1949, the program had expanded to fifteen hundred trainees in fifty different degree-granting programs.[9]

Psychologist scientists uneasy with the potential impurity of these new recruits needed a way of controlling them. In 1949, the APA convened a conference in Boulder, Colorado, to discuss the future of clinical training. Psychologist David Shakow oversaw the compromise that was reached. Psychology would promote a scientist-practitioner model of training, which would proceed in four steps. (1) The first involved an immersion in the latest experimental training existing in the department. Psychologists were first and foremost scientists. (2) Next, students would undertake a practicum in a clinical setting. The burgeoning counseling centers at universities designed to help veterans accommodate themselves

---

7. On psychology's turn to health, see Wade Pickren, *Psychology and Health: Culture, Place, History*. New York: Routledge, 2019.

8. Ludy T. Benjamin Jr., "A History of Clinical Psychology as a Profession in America (and a Glimpse at its Future)," *Annual Review of Clinical Psychology* 1 (2005): 1–30, 10–14.

9. James H. Capshew. *Psychologists on the March: Science, Practice, and Professional Identity in America, 1929–1969*. New York: Cambridge University Press, 1999.

to civilian life provided a most desirable setting.[10] (3) After that came an internship in a more formal medical setting (almost always a VA hospital dealing with returning soldiers in the early years) where the trainee would study under experienced psychiatrists. (4) Finally, these doctoral students would complete a PhD dissertation on an academically respectable topic, reasserting their identity as scientists.[11]

Psychology's entry into the health professions, a result of its interwar successes with mental testing, started with standardized intelligence tests for sorting underperforming and exceptional school children and soon expanded to offering employers various inventories and questionnaires to screen workers for undesirable personality traits. Clinical psychologists defined their expertise in terms of measurement, evaluation, and assessment. Treatment, namely, psychotherapy, lay beyond their purview. This arrangement was not satisfactory to the expanding ranks of postwar clinical psychologists. With an increasing number working in standalone private practices, they sought the right to offer their clients the full-suite services from diagnosis to therapy. Psychiatrists opposed this incursion, or at the very least they expected psychologists to maintain a subvariant position. A pitched battle started in the 1950s as psychologists succeeded in lobbying state legislatures for recognition as a full and licensed profession while medical associations countered these moves.[12]

Clinical psychologists were not simply health care providers but scientific evaluators of tests, therapies, and even clinical judgment itself. Carl Rogers, the APA president who convened the Boulder conference, embodied this duality. He became an icon of the therapist as a humanist who encountered clients on an equal and empathetic footing. He also contributed to the demystification of psychotherapy when he started tape-recording sessions in 1942. Recording allowed for the dissection of these conversations into discrete variables to evaluate what specific elements of treatment led to improved outcomes.[13] Such evaluation projects provided much fodder for students in the scientist-practitioner stream.

Unlike other social and natural sciences, psychology's bubble did not burst in the 1970s. Its rate of growth slowed somewhat from the early 1950s, but the ranks

---

10. Tom McCarthy, "Great Aspirations: The Postwar American College Counseling Center," *History of Psychology* 17, no. 1 (2014): 1–18.

11. David B. Baker and Ludy T. Benjamin Jr., "The Affirmation of the Scientist-Practitioner: A Look Back at Boulder," *American Psychologist* 55, no. 2 (2000): 241–247.

12. Roderick D. Buchanan, "Legislative Warriors: American Psychiatrists, Psychologists, and Competing Claims over Psychotherapy in the 1950s," *Journal of the History of the Behavioral Sciences* 39, no. 3 (2003): 225–249. American licensing legislation provided a model for efforts in other countries. See Manfred Fichter and Hans-Ulrich Wittchen, "Clinical Psychology and Psychotherapy: A Survey of the Present State of Professionalization in 23 Countries," *American Psychologist* 35, no. 1 (1980): 16–25.

13. Carl R. Rogers, "The Use of Electrically Recorded Interviews in Improving Psychotherapeutic Techniques," *American Journal of Orthopsychiatry* 12, no. 3 (1942): 429–434.

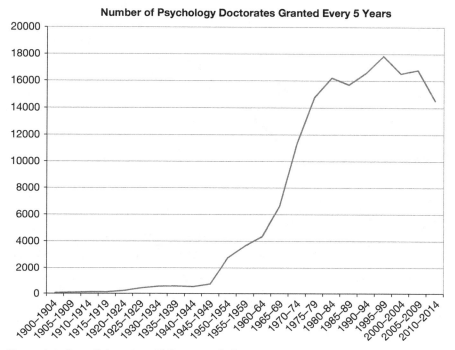

Figure 3.1 Overall American PhDs in psychology.
Data from Capshew (1999) and NSF Survey of Doctorates Earned (https://www.nsf.gov/statistics/srvydoctorates/).

of psychology continued to increase every year, except for a brief setback in the late 1980s (Figure 3.1). Psychology's sustained growth was uneven across specialties. The field did not experience the common "Cold War bubble" because psychology expanded as a health profession rather than an academic specialty dependent on university enrolments from the GI bill and the post-Sputnik investments in education.[14] Already by 1960, the number of new clinical psychologists outnumbered those specializing in academic areas such as social, developmental, and experimental psychology, but these other areas were truly eclipsed in the 1970s (Figure 3.2).

This meant that whoever counted as a professional psychologist also changed dramatically. In 1966, women accounted for a little more than a fifth of new PhDs. Many of them chose to specialize in traditional areas of research, but longstanding sexism in academic hiring frequently pushed these women to pursue careers in applied settings such as schools where they found distinct networks established by an earlier generation.[15] The number of women obtaining PhDs in

---

14. David Kaiser, "Booms, Busts, and the World of Ideas: Enrollment Pressures and the Challenge of Specialization," *Osiris* 27, no. 1 (2012): 276–302.

15. Elizabeth Johnston and Ann Johnson, "Searching for the Second Generation of American Women Psychologists," *History of Psychology* 11, no. 1 (2008): 40–72; Alexandra Rutherford,

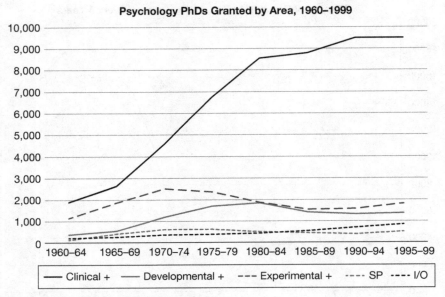

Figure 3.2 Psychology PhDs by specialty.
Data from NSF Survey of Doctorates Earned (https://www.nsf.gov/statistics/srvydoctorates/).

psychology accelerated in the early 1970s, marking an early victory for second-wave feminism unique among the sciences. By 1986, the number of women receiving PhDs in psychology surpassed the number of men for the first time. By the mid-1990s, women accounted for two-thirds of new doctorates (Figure 3.3).[16] Psychology's diversification had limits. Starting in the late 1960s, Black activists documented the unspoken, yet overwhelming, whiteness of the profession and offered solutions for amelioration. Despite their efforts, the so-called minority pipeline problem persisted into the twenty-first century with the recruitment of Black and Latino doctoral students stalling in the late 1990s.[17]

The mounting tensions between academics and practitioners resulting from psychology's uneven growth were evident when George Albee delivered his 1970 presidential address to the APA. As a member of the 1946 cohort of VA trainees whose last name began with "A," he joked that he counted as the first true

---

"'Making better use of US Women': Psychology, Sex Roles, and Womanpower in Post-WWII America," *Journal of the History of the Behavioral Sciences* 53, no. 3 (2017): 228–245.

16. Ann Howard, Georgine Pion, Gary Gottfredson, Pamela Flattau, Stuart Oskamp, Sheila Pfaffin, Douglas Bray, and Alvin Burstein, "The Changing Face of American Psychology: A Report from the Committee on Employment and Human Resources," *American Psychologist* 41, no. 12 (1986): 1311–1327.

17. Kenneth Maton, Jessica Kohout, Marlene Wicherski, George Leary, and Andrey Vinokurov, "Minority Students of Color and the Psychology Graduate Pipeline: Disquieting and Encouraging Trends, 1989–2003," *American Psychologist* 61, no. 2 (2006): 117–131.

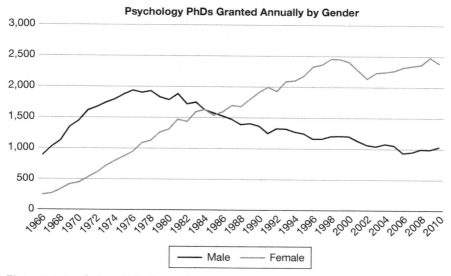

Figure 3.3 Psychology PhDs by gender.
Data from NSF Survey of Doctorates Earned (https://www.nsf.gov/statistics/srvydoctorates/).

clinical psychologist.[18] Few had a clearer vision of postwar psychology's political economy; an insight that made Albee the profession's leading critic. Ever an organization man, he offered a pessimistic evaluation of his chosen vocation. He described the postwar clinical psychologist as a cuckoo bird; "it has had to place its eggs in the other birds' nests."[19] Clinical psychology started as "a small offshoot of academic, scientific psychology" and for its first twenty-five years had to accommodate itself to graduate programs that were often hostile to professional training. Nor did clinicians control the facilities where their trainees conducted their internships. These facilities remained the domain of psychiatry. This dual indebtedness to universities and hospitals distorted clinicians' understanding of mental health. They focused either on "the white middle-class neurotic who seeks prolonged psychotherapeutic relationships" or "the seriously disturbed poor who are incarcerated in tax-supported state and Veterans Administration hospitals" to the exclusion of the rest of humanity.[20] For the sake of actually improving human welfare, Albee urged his fellow psychologists to "forget 'psychiatric patients' for a century and turn our attention to the psychological causes of racism, sexism, and of the profit motive as sources of danger to the human-centered life."[21] At the time

18. Jim Kelly, "Interview with George Albee," 1996. https://vimeo.com/68178065, quote at 2:30.

19. George Albee, "The Uncertain Future of Clinical Psychology," *American Psychologist* 25, no. 12 (1970): 1071–1080, 1072.

20. Albee, "The Uncertain Future of Clinical Psychology," 1073.

21. Albee, "The Uncertain Future of Clinical Psychology," 1074.

Albee delivered his address, APA faced two internal revolts as the pressure from this rapid and uneven growth intersected with the wider political upheavals felt throughout the United States.

The first came from marginalized Black members.[22] At the 1968 APA meeting in San Francisco, Joseph White gathered a number of fellow Black psychologists to share their concerns about organized psychology's failure to address their needs. Rather than a beacon of progress, professional psychology remained a largely segregated field.[23] The group quickly decided to create its own organization, the Association of Black Psychologists (ABPsi), a few months after the assassination of Martin Luther King Jr. in 1968. As Blacks in a variety of professions established their own caucuses to forward their personal and their community's interest, these Black intellectuals rejected the integration versus segregation framework characteristic of white political thought on race relations. Instead, they embraced a strand of Black nationalism extending back to Marcus Garvey (1887–1940), which argued that Black freedom required separation and control over their own organizations.[24] At thirty-five, White was among the oldest of ABPsi's founders, whose members specialized largely in social and clinical psychology. Like many Black nationalist movements, ABPsi was male dominated at the outset and advanced through performances of virile, militant masculinity.[25] White's "Towards a Black Psychology," published in the mass market periodical *Ebony*, served as their manifesto. Eurocentric models of psychic development threatened their community by giving scientific credence to popular assumptions of Black inferiority and pathology.[26] Combatting these models required bringing Blacks to the center of the psychological complex to rebuild the field from nonprejudicial sources. At the following convention, the newly organized Black Graduate Students Association challenged APA president George A. Miller at the podium and presented the organization with a series of demands for improving Black representation within psychology.[27]

22. Wade Pickren, "Liberating History: The Context of the Challenge of Psychologists of Color to American Psychology," *Cultural Diversity and Ethnic Minority Psychology* 15, no. 4 (2009): 425–433.

23. Eligio Padilla, Russell Boxley, and Nathaniel Wagner, "The Desegregation of Clinical Psychology Training," *Professional Psychology* 4, no. 3 (1973): 259–264.

24. Robert Williams, "A History of the Association of Black Psychologists: Early Formation and Development," *Journal of Black Psychology* 1, no. 1 (1974): 9–24.

25. A trend reversed in 1975 with the election of Ruth King as president. On gender and Black Power, see Robyn C. Spencer, *The Revolution Has Come: Black Power, Gender, and the Black Panther Party in Oakland*. Durham, NC: Duke University Press, 2016; Ashley D. Farmer, *Remaking Black Power: How Black Women Transformed an Era*. Chapel Hill: University of North Carolina Press Books, 2017.

26. Joseph White, "Toward a Black Psychology," *Ebony*, September 1970, 45–52.

27. Gary Simpkins and Phillip Raphael, "Black Students, APA, and the Challenge of Change," *American Psychologist* 25, no. 5 (1970): xxi.

The second, initially quieter rebellion came from the ranks of clinical psychologists, led by a group calling itself "the Dirty Dozen" (although it actually included fourteen members).[28] Born in the interwar years, these men received their PhDs in the mid-1950s at the height of psychology's initial boom. Despite the norms of the Boulder model, they conducted no formal research upon graduation, having dedicated themselves wholly to the practice of psychology.[29] Unlike Albee, who held an academic appointment throughout his career, they made a living in free-standing private practices, independent of universities and hospitals, by collecting fees from individual clients for services rendered. In this setting, reimbursement from third-party insurance providers was the key to their sustained livelihood. Without state-level credentials, many insurers refused to honor claims for psychological services; a plight toward which salaried academics seemed indifferent. In 1962, the California State Psychological Association assembled a "Political Action Booklet" to instruct professionals on how to approach their elected representatives and make them aware that psychologists formed an organized group with interests.[30]

Angered by their exclusion from reimbursement from third-party insurance providers, the Community Mental Health Act (1963), led to their first mobilization. A centerpiece of John F. Kennedy's "New Frontier" reforms, the Act promised federal funding for mental health services outside of state hospitals. At issue was who would staff these new federally supported organizations.[31] On the one hand, the Act promised to empower persons to live more autonomous lives in their own community. However, many psychologists worried that the medical profession would assert control over populations traditionally under psychologists' remit, namely, persons with intellectual disabilities, as "they have come to suspect there is real gold in those barren hills after."[32] In response to a staff billing related to the new community centers, the Committee on Relations with Local Clinical Groups Executive Committee organized a letter-writing campaign among professionals. Psychologists resented the medical establishment's expansion into community care.[33] Those in the APA Central Office felt this effort had "given psychology a

---

28. The group consisted of Theodore Blau, Nicholas Cummings, Raymond Fowler, Mervin Grevitz, Ernest Lawrence, Marvin Metsky, C. J. Rosecrans, S. Don Schultz, Eugene Shapiro, Max Seigel, Robert Weitz, Jack Wiggins, Rogers Wright, and Francis Young.

29. E. Lowell Kelley, Lewis Goldberg, Donald Fiske, and James Kilkowski, "Twenty-Five Years Later: A Follow-up of the Graduate Students in Clinical Psychology Assessed in the VA Selection Research Project," *American Psychologist* 33, no. 8 (1978): 746–755.

30. California State Psychology Association, "1962 Political Action Booklet for Local Psychological Associations and Individual Psychologists." American Psychological Association Records, Manuscript Division, Library of Congress, Washington, DC. [Here after cited as APA papers], Box 106.

31. APA papers, Box 96.

32. George Kelly to Joe Margolin, February 24, 1964. APA Papers, Box 95.

33. Committee on Relations with Local Clinical Groups Executive Committee, "Action for Community Mental Health," March 16, 1965. APA Papers, Box 96.

black eye on the Hill," for the letters, coming largely from private practitioners in Southern California, misunderstood the bill.[34] The hope of embedding the psychological profession within Great Society programs marked the beginning of a ten-year battle over control of the APA.

An exclusively male group within an increasingly feminized profession, the Dirty Dozen took their name from an overtly macho 1967 film set during World War II about a renegade band of criminals-turned-commandos who would do anything to get the job done. One member recalled: "The adoption of the name stemmed from the group's discovery that the academics in the APA were utilizing their faculty emoluments to control the organization, and 'The Dozen' committed to being just as 'Dirty.'"[35] Unlike contemporary movements in psychology, the Dirty Dozen developed no formal apparatus of their own: no bylaws, no procedures, no dues. A singular commitment to "politicizing" the APA to advance their professional interests united them. They sought to infiltrate existing committees with the goal of securing the organization's highest elected office. Annual conventions followed by telephone calls provided the network with its infrastructure as they mobilized to take over the organization and make it their own.

In 1969, the Black radicals and the white professionals formed something of a tentative coalition, born out of a common enemy. Both rejected an overly academic APA as irrelevant to the urgent needs of clinical care. As future ABPsi president Thomas Hilliard observed, too many APA sessions revolved around "running rats" or "the sex lives of a fly," topics a world apart from his clients' needs.[36] As part of their efforts to gain a foothold within the APA organizational structure, white professionals like Theodore Blau chaired the multiracial Commission on Accelerating Black Participation in Psychology, which was convened in response to the 1969 student protest.[37] Finally, both groups saw the scientist-practitioner ideal outlined at the Boulder conference as outdated and unable to meet the spiraling demands for mental health services. Members of both groups participated in creating, staffing, and later accrediting standalone training institutes independent of universities, starting with the California School of Professional Psychology in 1969. In 1973, Hilliard served on the steering committee for the Vail conference,

---

34. Arthur H. Brayfield to Jennie Ciccarello, April 27, 1965. APA Box 96.

35. Rogers H. Wright, "The Rise of Professionalism within American Psychology and How It Came to Be: A Brief History of the Dirty Dozen," in Rogers H. Wright and Nicholas A. Cummings, *The Practice of Psychology: The Battle for Professionalism*. Phoenix: Zeig, Tucker & Thisen, Inc., 2001, 1–58, 2.

36. "The Human Condition" interview circa 1973. https://itunes.apple.com/us/itunes-u/the-human-condition/id919554926?mt=10, 16:30

37. Theodore Blau, "APA Commission on Accelerating Black Participation in Psychology." *American Psychologist* 25, no. 12 (1970): 1103–1104.

which was established to reconsider "the patterns and levels of professional training," in which twenty-five Black delegates participated.[38]

The presidency of Kenneth Clark, who succeeded Albee, exemplified how these interests held together. Clark became a national celebrity with his testimony in the *Brown v. Board of Education* case (1954) where he demonstrated the psychic toll of segregation on Black children using differently colored dolls. In 1954, the APA did not endorse Clark's testimony (the organization did not even formally recognize this tremendous public victory for its science). The discipline did not reclaim the Black psychologist as its own until the late 1960s as the civil rights movement gained prominence and respectability among white liberals.[39] As APA president, Clark (who never joined ABPsi) oversaw a number of initiatives dedicated to social justice and the diversification of the profession, especially for women. The most substantive and long-standing of these initiatives was the APA's Board of Social and Ethical Responsibility for Psychology, created in 1973. The Board was established in response to demands to address institutionalized racism within the organization, but its mission advanced professional interest by enhancing the discipline's social relevance.[40]

The uneasy alliance soon fractured with the two groups taking divergent paths after the Vail conference concluded. One of the conference's stated goals had been to make professional training more "socially responsive." However, it failed to deliver on both this promise and the recommendations made by the Black psychologists in attendance to embed future training in community-based programs.[41] Instead, the main outcome was the legitimation of the Doctorate of Psychology (PsyD) credential as an alternative practitioner-scholar model of training. The fallout from Vail exemplified what ABPsi president Ruth King described as "a lack of responsiveness by APA to the concerns of Black professional psychologists and the mental health needs of the Black community."[42] She saw the two organizations as irreparably parting ways due to the "failure of APA to recognize the new Black movement as a viable problem-solving modality."[43]

38. Thomas O. Hilliard, "Professional Training and Minority Groups," in Maurice Korman (ed.), *National Conference on Levels and Patterns of Professional Training in Psychology*. Washington, DC: American Psychological Association, 1976, 41–49.

39. Ludy Benjamin and Ellen Crouse, "The American Psychological Association's Response to *Brown v. Board of Education*: The Case of Kenneth B. Clark," *American Psychologist* 57, no. 1 (2002): 38–50.

40. Wade Pickren and Henry Tomes, "The Legacy of Kenneth B. Clark to the APA: The Board of Social and Ethical Responsibility for Psychology," *American Psychologist* 57, no. 1 (2002): 51–59.

41. William D. Peirce, Thomas Hilliard, Floyd Wylie, James Dobbins, and Mildred Buck, "Community Mental Health and the Black Community: A Position Statement," *Interamerican Journal of Psychology* 6, no. 1–2 (1972): 135–136.

42. Ruth King to Dalmus Taylor, May 19, 1977. APA Papers.

43. Ruth E. King, "Highlights in the Development of ABPsi," *Journal of Black Psychology* 4, no. 1–2 (1978): 9–24, 11.

After 1973, the Dirty Dozen's attention narrowed to controlling the APA's political infrastructure to advance their interests as autonomous, accredited, and, most importantly, remunerated professionals. In contrast, the ABPsi leadership consistently undercut psychology's pretensions to a disinterested and aloof profession. Its members sought to embed the discipline in society and to subjugate psychological authority to forms of deliberative community control.

WESTSIDE STORY

The Community Mental Health Act also facilitated this more radical experiment with democratizing psychological care by providing funding for treatment outside of psychiatric institutions. The community psychology movement, officially launched at the all-white Swampscott Conference in 1965, proposed a dramatic shift in perspective "from the amelioration of illness to preventive intervention at the community level." Attendees articulated an optimistic psychology dedicated "to optimal realization of human potential through planned social action." They rejected the "medical model" inherited from psychiatry and opposed indiscriminate hospitalizations. They even deemed outpatient psychotherapy as too costly and insufficient as the psychologist's only possible intervention. Community psychology also entailed a renunciation of "exclusive prerogatives and professional rights." When it came to mental health, doctoral education was not a necessary credential, and treatment often depended on a more distributed network of care by laypersons.[44] At a time when clinicians lobbied at the state level for licensing legislation restricting the term *psychologist* to accredited members of their guild, community psychologists eschewed narrow professionalism. In other words, community psychologists took seriously the 1960s sociological critique of psychiatric authority and sought to develop alternative treatment programs for mental illness which saw it as rooted in economic inequality and social discrimination.[45] Others viewed deinstitutionalization more skeptically, noting that many psychiatric patients lacked the very family supportive care in the community that was required. By leaving their care to an ill-defined community, deinstitutionalization risked abandoning society's most vulnerable.[46]

44. Chester Bennett, "Community Psychology: Impressions of the Boston Conference on the Education of Psychologists for Community Mental Health," *American Psychologist* 20, no. 10 (1965): 832–835.

45. Michael E. Staub, *Madness Is Civilization: When the Diagnosis Was Social, 1948–1980*. Chicago: University of Chicago Press, 2011.

46. Gerald N. Grob, *From Asylum to Community: Mental Health Policy in Modern America*. Princeton, NJ: Princeton University Press, 1991, 239–272; Martin Summers, *Madness in the City of Magnificent Intentions: A History of Race and Mental Illness in the Nation's Capital*. Oxford: Oxford University Press, 2019, 277–309; Nic John Ramos, "Pathologizing the

The Ronald Reagan governorship brought mental health to the forefront of California politics. Upon his inauguration in January 1967, he announced dramatic cuts to the state budget, with the largest cut affecting the Department of Mental Hygiene. Because of decreases in confinement since the peak year of 1959, the staffing of the state hospitals, which Reagan colorfully denounced as tax-funded "hotels," seemed ripe for culling in the name of economy.[47] Reagan's cutbacks met with pushback across the aisle, but the bipartisan Lanterman–Petris–Short Act, passed later that year, accelerated the trend of relocating psychiatric services outside the hospital. The act enshrined new civil liberties for those deemed mentally ill by curtailing involuntary commitments for indefinite periods without recourse to review. A model for legislation in other jurisdictions granting patients a "right to treatment," by reserving hospitalization to persons in acute crisis, the Act also bolstered Reagan's efforts to minimize state functions. California's push against long-term, "custodial" warehousing came from the confluence of two lines of libertarian thought, the civil liberties of the antipsychiatry movement and the free market austerity of opponents to the welfare state.

The Westside Community Mental Health Center in San Francisco was one of the largest and boldest experiments in community psychology. William Goldman, a psychiatrist at Mount Zion Hospital and a self-described Jewish radical, found inspiration in the 1963 Act. It allowed him to secure NIMH funding in 1967 to coordinate the extensive mental health services in the Westside area, ranging from inpatient psychiatric hospitals to private psychotherapeutic practices to drug rehabilitation centers. The catchment zone was heterogeneous, including the hippie enclave around Haight-Ashbury to Japantown to the predominantly African American Fillmore District. Goldman wanted the new Westside consortium to represent all the communities it served rather than advance narrow medical interests. As a junior faculty member at San Francisco State University, his wife Ruth supported the 1968 strike led by the Third World Liberation Front, a student movement seeking to add Ethnic Studies to diversify the cultural representation on campus.[48] Westside would follow a similar path.[49]

Alongside holding extensive consultation sessions and establishing a Community Advisory Board, Goldman insisted that the newly created Central

---

Crisis: Psychiatry, Policing, and Racial Liberalism in the Long Community Mental Health Movement." *Journal of the History of Medicine and Allied Sciences* 74, no. 1 (2019): 57–84.

47. Philip M. Boffey, "California: Reagan and the Mental Health Controversy," *Science* 161, no. 3848 (1968): 1329–1331.

48. Ruth Goldman and William Goldman, *Passing the Torch: Supporting Tomorrow's Leaders*. Lanham, MD: Hamilton Books, 2018.

49. In this regard, it represented a bolder and better funded successor to the LaFargue Clinic in Harlem. See Dennis Doyle, "'Where the Need Is Greatest': Social Psychiatry and Race-Blind Universalism in Harlem's Lafargue Clinic, 1946–1958," *Bulletin of the History of Medicine* (2009): 746–774; Gabriel M. Mendes, *Under the Strain of Color: Harlem's Lafargue Clinic and the Promise of an Antiracist Psychiatry*. Ithaca, NY: Cornell University Press, 2015.

Office coordinating services across institutions would be staffed primarily by Black professionals. Accordingly, he recruited five Black psychologists to manage this storefront office, providing a visible and accessible presence in the neighborhood. The Central Office's design differed from that of the psychiatric hospital as "floor space is wide open and staff workers are readily available to anyone who calls at the office." This staff included a paid "community organizer" to further foster contact and involvement in operations.[50] The first person to fulfill this role, Thomatra Scott, held no advanced degrees but had spent a lifetime in unions and in youth organizing as part of a pledge "to break the back of the status quo to bring about community change."[51] Once these hires were in place, Goldman resigned as director, ceding control of operations to the new leadership. Westside's Central Office became what the *San Francisco Examiner* called the "headquarters for one of America's most successful black braintrusts."[52] As Hilliard's brother recalled, he joined Westside because in his previous job "he did not find the consciousness or the critical mass of African leadership that he needed. With an estimated 50 Black psychologists employed directly or indirectly at the Westside Community Mental Health Center in the 1970s, San Francisco was the ideal place for him."[53] The whole Bay Area became the "fountainhead" for ABPsi activism, with members living in Oakland, working at Westside in San Francisco, and teaching and recruiting from local universities like Stanford and Berkeley.

In San Francisco, the most militant voice for community control came from the Black Panther Party (BPP), whose leadership the Center contacted as part of its early consultation efforts but received no response. Founded across the bay in Oakland by Huey P. Newton and Bobby Seale in 1966 as an armed, self-defense group against police brutality and its excessive surveillance of the Black community, the BPP offered a fulsome critique of the "white power structure" grounded in a Marxist-inspired, Pan-Africanist, Third World internationalism. Newton and Seale began as workers for a youth program, an extension of Lyndon Johnson's "War on Poverty." The BPP represented a grassroots alternative to this state intervention, one intended to liberate America's Black population rather than subdue it.[54] At the heart of the Panther ideology was the ideal of self-determination for people of African descent as articulated in their 1967 Ten-Point Program. By 1968, the party had expanded its remit to "serve the people" by provisioning

---

50. William Goldman, "San Francisco Westside: A Community Mental Health Center Serves the People," *Mental Health Program Reports* 5 (1971): 174–187, 181.

51. "Activist for Youth," *San Francisco Examiner*, March 16, 1975, 3.

52. Jim Wood, "The IQ Bias Battle," *San Francisco Examiner*, September 24, 1972.

53. Asa Hilliard III, "Thomas O. Hilliard, PhD," in Robert L. Williams (ed.), *History of the Association of Black Psychologists: Profiles of Outstanding Black Psychologists*. Bloomington, IN: AuthorHouse, 2008, 187–196, 192.

54. Robert O. Self, *American Babylon: Race and the Struggle for Postwar Oakland*. Princeton, NJ: Princeton University Press, 2003, 217–255.

impoverished communities in need, starting with a free breakfast program for children and expanding to include the establishment of People's Free Medical Clinics. The weekly *Black Panther* newspaper also exposed and criticized the exploitation of Black bodies by the white medical establishment such as the Tuskegee Syphilis Experiment.[55] Through these concrete programs and their militant rhetoric of anticolonialism, revolutionary struggle, and control, the Panthers both inspired and clashed with those associated with Westside.

The Panthers viewed psychology with ambivalence. As a Black organization dedicated to revolutionary action, they borrowed from the Martinique-born psychiatrist Franz Fanon's psychoanalytic theory for the colonialized psyche. Yet they viewed white psychiatry and neurology as pernicious tools of oppression operating under the cloak of science.[56] Despite the Panthers' distrust of the state, they did not embrace the deinstitutionalization of psychiatric facilities as the liberation of the mad. The release of patients was another instance of the "fascist" state's divestment from the needy, one disproportionately affecting Black neighborhoods. "Pig Governor" Reagan's cutbacks of health services represented a "slow genocide trick" by "funneling thousands of mentally retarded and mental ill (criminally deranged) patients into Black and other poor oppressed communities." Tensions came to a head in August 1970 when a white resident at a Black-run halfway house physically assaulted a Black child. The girl's mother took her to the Kaiser Hospital, the family's designated health care provider through the father's employee insurance. Thinking the girl had been sexually molested, Kaiser staff refused to treat her and referred the family to the public hospital. When the mother contacted the police, they dismissed out-of-hand the assault as a minor spat between two children. The incident came to be seen as a dual insult emanating from a racist medical system: the intrusion of inadequately provisioned mentally ill "foreigners" into the Black neighborhood threatened the children's safety, followed by white hospital staff ignoring the concerns of Black benefits-holders.[57]

As the newly opened Westside had been holding outreach sessions declaring its desire to meet community needs, "one afternoon a delegation of young Black men wearing tams and daishikis came into our storefront administrative office and forcefully let it be known that our mental health center had an opportunity to contribute to the community's mental health."[58] The Westside Central Office agreed to mediate. Newly appointed as director of clinical services, William D. Pierce arranged a meeting with Kaiser Permanente's board of directors to express community concerns over the family's treatment. As soon as members of the Westside

---

55. Alondra Nelson, *Body and Soul: The Black Panther Party and the Fight against Medical Discrimination*. Minneapolis: University of Minnesota Press, 2011.

56. Huey P. Newton, "The Black Panthers," *The Black Panther*, August 23, 1969, 9–10.

57. "Five Year Old Black Child Attacked by Mental Deranged Maniac," *The Black Panther*, September 12, 1970, 2.

58. William M. Bolman, "Community Control of the Community Mental Health Center: II. Case Examples," *American Journal of Psychiatry* 129, no. 2 (1972): 181–186, 182.

team sat down with the Kaiser representatives, "the doors to this sumptuously appointed conference room opened and in marched a troop of Black Panthers in full uniform. They encircled the huge conference table and stood motionless with arms folded until the brief meeting ended. The Kaiser officials quickly agreed to change the policy about providing services to families of paying members regardless of the causal circumstances."[59] This encounter at Kaiser Permanente offices revealed Westside's unique position in terms of the politics of mental health. Community psychology formed a recognized conduit between the marginalized and the establishment. The Center created opportunities for advocacy that had been unavailable only a few years earlier. They sought to dismantle oppressive systems, often willfully negligent of Black concerns. Westside advanced a program of empowerment autonomous from the street-level militancy of the Black Panthers. Yet, the Party's adjacency mattered, with the visible presence of armed militants giving calls for community control considerable heft.

Black psychologists adopted much of the Panthers' rhetoric and tactics. In 1970, ABPsi issued its own "ten-point program," asking for a series of commitments from white-dominant psychology departments to increase Black representation among students and faculty. The organization moved "to break the 'quasi-dependency symbiotic with APA." In 1972, ABPsi broke with its tradition of holding its meetings in conjunction with the APA. Self-determination rather than acceptance from the white establishment became the priority.[60]

Despite the mediation with Kaiser Permanente, residents questioned whose interests the Westside Center served. Along with a Black-managed Central Office, the consortium established the city's first 24-hour crisis center to address community members in acute distress.[61] Yet, the white psychiatrists at Mount Zion remained sensitive of the continued gap between their approach and community demand. In 1971, Edward M. Weinshel, the director of residency training, noted how Mount Zion's "exclusively psychoanalytic" reputation "might deter prospective Black trainees from applying."[62] Such comments echoed a prevailing "common sense" among clinicians that the poor could insufficiently express themselves verbally and lacked the capacity of inner reflection demanded by insight-oriented therapies. It also spoke to the reality that building community care required looking beyond the boundaries of the psychiatric establishment. Addiction to narcotics created the greatest divide. The psychoanalytic psychiatrists felt it beneath them, but community representatives consistently rated it as the most pressing mental health issue they faced.

59. Harold Dent, "A Tribute to Bill Pierce," *Psych Discourse* 2016.

60. Williams, "A History of the Association of Black Psychologists," 18–20.

61. Goldman, "San Francisco Westside," 179–180.

62. Edward M. Weinshel to University of California School of Medicine Dean, July 14, 1971, UCSF Black Caucus Records. Permalink: https://calisphere.org/item/ff6e9c3c-655a-4722-a871-526cc7c03e4c

Among the first requests made by the Community Advisory Board was the inclusion of "indigenous self-help drug treatment programs as full members of the consortium."[63] Reality House differed in many ways from other drug treatment facilities available in the Bay Area. It was run by LeRoy Looper, an ex-convict and former addict without advanced degrees. Inspiration came from Rogers's *Client Center Therapy* (1951), which Looper had read in the prison library. Upon his release, he began a prisoner's outreach program and an addiction treatment center in New York City before relocating to San Francisco in 1968. Group therapy sessions focused on "reconstructing an individual's lifestyle into one that is meaningful and productive both for the individual and for society."[64] Looper took Rogerian empathy and radicalized it. At Reality House, equality and acceptance came from the shared, lived experiences of addiction and imprisonment between the lay therapist and the client.[65] Looper welcomed "anybody who wants to kick a habit, who feels tired, oppressed, lonely" and offered the impoverished a rational therapy focused on "what's going on his life now" rather than probing the psychic depths going back to childhood.[66]

His political commitments had two major consequences for those who received treatment. First, unlike the controversial Synanon, Reality House did not sequester those it treated. Looper expected them to remain connected to their former social lives as therapy focused on confronting the challenges faced in one's daily environment. Reality House formed a supportive community, but not one enclosed onto itself. The second striking feature was Looper's opposition to methadone. In 1965, a team of New York physicians suggested methadone could facilitate the safe withdrawal from heroine. Addiction was neither a moral failing nor caused by a sociopathic personality but was merely a biological condition treatable with pharmaceuticals. Methadone quickly captured scholarly and political attention as it made the outpatient treatment of opiate addicts feasible without requiring the time and labor of existing therapeutic community models.[67] The city of San Francisco expanded its methadone maintenance program in 1971.[68] Looper rejected this medical optimism, ever resistant to the state control that

---

63. "A Community Mental Health Consortium," *Hospital and Community Psychiatry* 21, no. 10 (1970): 329–332, 331.

64. *Directory of Drug Treatment Facilities in San Francisco*. San Francisco: Committee on Crime, 1970, 18.

65. "The Autobiography of LeRoy Looper" (1977). https://beyondchron.org/the-amazing-life-story-of-leroy-looper-1924-2011

66. "Refuge to Kick Drug Habit," *San Francisco Examiner*, September 22, 1969, 13.

67. On these alternatives, see Claire D. Clark, *The Recovery Revolution: The Battle over Addiction Treatment in the United States*. New York: Columbia University Press, 2017.

68. *San Francisco Public Health Annual Report 1971–1972*, 72–73.

lay behind it.[69] Methadone simply substituted one drug for another, one Looper deemed harder to quit. Methadone also came with dire consequences as a substance "controlled and doled out by the state, so that you become controlled by the state if you go into it . . . your private life is monitored and checked by the state."[70]

Such tensions between the state and the community pervaded the Westside project. The largest Black-led community health center in the country depended on support from the federal government in the form of continued NIMH funds for staffing. Peirce emerged as an acute observer (and critic) of the political economy of community psychology.[71] He rejected weaker concepts such as "participation" and "consultation" in favor of fulsome "community control," which entailed the capacity "to make decisions, set policy, and enforce and monitor priorities." Peirce's reasoned that "public funds equal community funds."[72] The Westside psychologists served as disloyal servants of the state. They translated community demands into language amenable for securing resources from federal agencies and yet sought to subvert their goals. At its height in the early 1970s, Westside became a psychic undercommons dedicated to not only community care but pride and self-determination.[73]

The psychologists at Westside soon expanded beyond providing clinical services to individuals in their catchment. Proper evaluations and psychotherapy benefited community members but merely targeted the symptoms rather than the underlying disease. In a lengthy radio interview conducted as ABPsi's president, Hilliard articulated his dual vision as a psychologist. His first role as a therapist was "to put clients that I see in touch with reality; guide them through the system." Yet, these individuals kept returning to his care as damaged as before. As a Black professional, he found it insufficient to remain in his office and manage the "casualties of an oppressive system." Society kept producing them at a faster rate, so true treatment necessarily involved restructuring the social, political, and economic order.[74] The Westside psychologists considered this daunting scale of intervention to be within their remit. Under the banner of the Bay Area ABPsi, they undertook three legal interventions starting in 1971. Clark's testimony in *Brown* established

---

69. On race and methadone, see Helena Hansen and Samuel K. Roberts, "Two Tiers of Biomedicalization: Methadone, Buprenorphine, and the Racial Politics of Addiction Treatments," *Critical Perspectives on Addiction* 14 (2012): 79–102.

70. "Facing Reality," *Good Times*, August 7, 1970, 14.

71. William D. Pierce, "Funding and Deinstitutionalization: The Impact on Minority Community Mental Health Centers," *Journal of Black Psychology* 4, no. 1–2 (1978): 82–90.

72. William D. Pierce, "The Concept of Community Control in Community Mental Health Delivery Systems," *Journal of Black Psychology* 2, no. 1 (1975): 35–43, 36–37.

73. Their actions resembled the actions of the fugitive intellectuals theorized in Fred Moten and Stefano Harney, "The University and the Undercommons: Seven Theses," *Social Text* 22, no. 2 (2004): 101–115.

74. "The Human Condition" interview circa 1973. https://itunes.apple.com/us/itunes-u/the-human-condition/id919554926?mt=10

an obvious precedent, but their involvement came from their immersion in the radical politics of northern California. They challenged the presumed "racial innocence" of post-Civil Rights liberal "law-and-order" ideology narrowly focused on racist intention rather than producing racialized disparities as its effect.[75]

Inspired by the diagnoses advanced by the BPP, these psychologists sought to dismantle the interlinked apparatus of the "disciplinary society" that disproportionately surveyed, tracked, and confined young Black men. They mounted a legal challenge to the use of standardized intelligence testing of Black children in California schools. They consulted on the voir dire process in the highly politicized Angela Davis trial to minimize the presence of racially prejudiced jurors. They offered expert testimony on the psychological effects of solitary confinement on behalf of the San Quentin Six prison activists. California, more so than any other state in the country, was seduced by the dream of human improvement through therapeutic interventions intended to correct the wayward deviant in schools and prisons. Westside psychologists revealed the lie behind this dream, showing it to be a eugenic nightmare with a price unequally extracted from Black lives.[76]

Several themes recurred across the Westside psychologists' legal actions. The most obvious one was the ubiquity of "bias," a term that conveyed at least a dual meaning in this context. First, bias connoted anti-Black prejudice. It was not simply an attitude contained in the individual psyche, but a pervasive phenomenon structuring society. Biases sedimented in the mundane classificatory practices of an interlocking set of institutions (schools, hospitals, courts, and prisons) which functioned as a singular system of racial oppression by unequally tracking, disciplining, and confining. Promoting Black mental health required dismantling this system. Bias also had strong methodological connotations. The Westside psychologists avoided both controlled experiments and standardized tests as interventions (both carried racialized baggage in the early 1970s) in favor of relying on their own trained and skilled clinical observations. Such a move was not innocent. It displayed a keen awareness of what Paul Meehl called "the cognitive activity of the clinician."[77] As was the case with Meehl, their cognitive psychology foregrounded the ubiquity of "human error," reflexively applied to the person of the clinician in their scientific activity and not simply reserved for the laypersons psychologists studied. Meehl touched off an ongoing debate about the

---

75. Naomi Murakawa, *The First Civil Right: How Liberals Built Prison America*. Oxford: Oxford University Press, 2014.

76. Pettit, Michael. "'Angela's Psych Squad': Black Psychology against the American Carceral State in the 1970s," *Journal of the History of the Behavioral Sciences* 58, no. 4 (2022): 365–382.

77. Paul Meehl, "The Cognitive Activity of the Clinician," *American Psychologist* 15, no. 1 (1960): 19–27.

comparative merit of subjective clinical judgments versus mechanical rules when making diagnostic predictions.[78]

Acutely aware that their judgments faced hostile publics who would not assume either their talent or their honesty, Black psychologists offered a disciplined, intersubjective judgment distributed across teams rather than housed in a singular, authoritative body. They performed "interrater agreement," even as they eschewed reporting measures of reliability.[79] They further emphasized process over outcome at the level of the cognizing individual and the social system. They championed processes that were consultative and democratic, open to the user (Davis and her legal team). Theirs was a community psychology informed by a cognitive science of intelligence as a polyvalent, emergent property scaffolded through social relations.

Another feature of their legal activism was their canny use of mass media. As journalists noted, the Westside psychologists held press conferences to publicize every action that had been undertaken. After Hilliard revealed their role in the Davis trial at the 1972 ABPsi meeting, his account circuited in a widely reprinted Associated Press story, leading to an extended photoessay in the glossy magazine *Ebony*. Black Power with its iconic Afro hairstyle, military uniforms, and salutes provided considerable fodder for white journalists looking for sensational stories on the political beat. Black militants carefully managed this attention to make visible the neglected plight of ordinary African Americans.[80] The ABPsi psychologists assumed much of the Panthers' program at a time when the Party faced an intense campaign of state suppression and internal political struggle. However, their self-fashioning as Black professionals departed greatly from the iconography of the gun-toting, bereted Panther. The Black press took a decided interest in their organizing. *Muhammad Speaks*, the weekly newspaper of the Nation of Islam, described the 1973 ABPsi conference as "possibly the most extensively educated Black people in the Western Hemisphere assembled." The four hundred delegates included fifty PhDs and another two hundred graduate students, but "the most conspicuous features of the group of Black educators was the unmistakable youthfulness of the 'doctors' and 'professors.'" Almost no one attending approached the age of fifty.[81] By this time, a number of ABPsi leaders had converted to Islam and relinquished their slave names. The following year,

---

78. Meehl himself opposed civil commitment on libertarian grounds. See Joseph M. Livermore, Carl P. Malmquist, and Paul E. Meehl, "On the Justifications for Civil Commitment," *University of Pennsylvania Law Review* 117, no. 1 (1968): 75–96.

79. Howard Tinsley and David Weiss, "Interrater Reliability and Agreement of Subjective Judgments," *Journal of Counseling Psychology* 22, no. 4 (1975): 358–376.

80. Jane Rhodes, *Framing the Black Panthers: The Spectacular Rise of a Black Power Icon*. Champaign: University of Illinois Press, 2017.

81. Nathaniel 10X, "Detroit Hosts Psychologists," *Muhammed Speaks*, September 21, 1973, 15.

ABPsi honored Elijah Muhammad as a "master psychologist" and invited Louis Farrakhan to address their annual convention.[82]

The Westside psychologists artfully performed their own Black intelligence, staging their bodies and minds before the media. Stories foregrounded their own respectability and achievement. These young Black men possessed doctorates and devised innovative legal strategies to bring justice to their community. Despite these achievements, newspaper narratives explained how these psychologists shared in the common experience of Black oppression. In a 1971 interview, Hilliard opened with his own experience of depression as a graduate student in Chicago when "he couldn't get a job, he couldn't pay the rent, and he couldn't concentrate on his dissertation."[83] Finally, newspaper stories dwelt on the sacrifices these psychologists made. A long story in the *San Francisco Examiner* explaining the group's opposition to intelligence testing noted that Arthur Dent, an educational psychologist and ABPsi member, refused to allow his own children to take the test even though his teachers had assumed they were destined for the gifted program. Fairness for the community allowed no exceptions.

In the 1970s, when forensic psychology remained protean with little canon or institutional form, the Westside psychologists implemented one radical possibility. Theirs was a forensic psychology informed by the Black freedom struggle, aligned with the prisoner rights movement, and dedicated to the abolition of the prison-industrial complex.[84] The utopia was short-lived. Community psychologists suffered from a lack of sustained support. Considerable federal money was available to establish community health centers, but funds quickly dwindled when it came to staffing them. Westside's Central Office found itself in this situation by 1976 as the original NIHM staffing grants expired.[85] The consortium continued to coordinate services and the leadership continued to collaborate by creating freestanding think tanks and consulting firms, but Westside no longer provided a fountainhead for their radical experiments with democracy.

THE TRIUMPH OF PROFESSIONALISM

The ruling in *Tarasoff v. Regents of the University of California* (1976) did much to undercut the radical future Hilliard envisioned, not only for forensic psychology but for the profession more broadly. In 1968, Prosenjit Poddar, an international student at Berkeley, met and started casually dating fellow student Tatiana Tarasoff.

---

82. Harold 4X, "Black Psychologists Honor Muhammad's Work," *Muhammad Speaks*, September 20, 1974, 5, 11.

83. Janet Chusmir, "The Whole Society Is the Patient," *Miami Herald*, May 14, 1971, 1B, 3B.

84. Thomas O. Hilliard, "Psychology, Law, and the Black Community," *Law and Human Behavior* 2, no. 2 (1978): 107–131.

85. Pierce, "Funding and Deinstitutionalization," 103; *Annual Report Department of Public Health City and County of San Francisco Fiscal Year* 1975–1976, 67.

She did not share his feelings and soon broke off their relationship. After Tarasoff left for summer vacation, a despondent Poddar eventually sought counseling from a psychologist at the university hospital. He confided his intent to kill Tarasoff to a psychologist, who had campus police detain Podder, but he was soon released, having been deemed rational. Upon Tarasoff's return from her vacation, Poddar stabbed her to death. Neither she nor her family had received advance warning of Podder's disclosure to the psychologist. Tarasoff's parents sued the therapist and his employer for negligence leading to Tatiana's death, citing the therapist's repeated failures to warn her of the imminent peril she faced. The therapist's defense was that any such warning would have required violating Podder's right to confidentiality as a client. The court found the argument wanting. Physicians' responsibilities, the court ruled, included "the duty to exercise reasonable care to protect others against dangers emanating from the patient's illness."[86]

Tarasoff sent ripples through the expanding psychology profession as members grappled with what the decision entailed for their culpability. The ruling represented an incursion by the state into the therapist–client relationship. It undercut the client-centered focus, which was so important to clinical psychology's postwar profession-building as a practice distinct from institutionalized care. The most pressing issue was what *Tarasoff* meant for the confidentiality deemed necessary to maintain a successful therapeutic relationship. A foreigner, a person of color, and an admitted murderer, Podder diverged from the affluent, mildly neurotic clients willingly immersing themselves in talk therapy. He much more closely resembled the formerly institutionalized psychiatric patient managed through drugs and behavior modification techniques now freed but without any family or community to provide the promised care. Clinical psychologists suddenly realized they were part of the criminal justice system without intending it.

Prior to the court's decision, APA's Board of Social and Ethical Responsibility for Psychology had convened a task force in response to "the national dialogue" on the criminal justice system and the role of mental health professionals in it.[87] ABPsi president George D. Jackson had suggested such a committee to his APA counterpart, although no ABPsi members would ultimately be invited to join.[88] APA selected John Monahan, a white community psychologist to chair the task force. Monahan's research on the dangerous tendency of mental health professionals to overpredict their patient's potential for violence was soon to be cited in the *Tarasoff* decision.[89] Drawing on survey results and their own deliberations, the committee raised a series of ethical challenges that emerged from psychologists'

---

86. *Tarasoff v. Regents of the University of California.* 17 Cal.3d 425 (1976) 551 P.2d 334, 131 Cal. Reporter 14.

87. June Tapp to Dick Boone, June 4, 1975, APA Papers Box 337.

88. Donald Campbell to George D. Jackson, June 16, 1975, APA Papers Box 337.

89. John Monahan and Lesley Cummings, "Social Policy Implications of the Inability to Predict Violence," *Journal of Social Issues* 31, no. 2 (1975): 153–164.

entanglement with the criminal justice system. Responding to the *Tarasoff* ruling delivered during its deliberations, the task force narrowed its focus to the question of who counted as "the client." Rogerian humanism insisted that it was the individual sitting across from the therapist. Therapy advanced through careful and individual face-work. *Tarasoff* revealed how all psychologists were embedded in complex systems. When Black APA staffer Carolyn Suber spoke to the committee about her own experience as an expert before the courts, she raised three areas of ethical conflict: the inappropriate use of tests on racialized clients; the need to inform defendants that a court subpoena might override the promised confidentiality of communication; and tensions surrounding "treatment" and advising defendants to accept the outcome of an injustice system in the hopes of a shorter sentence. Throughout her comments, Suber stressed that her "allegiance is to the client and not the defense attorney" and certainly not the system.[90] In contrast, the Task Force's final report reached very different conclusions about the question of the "client." It documented how psychologists necessarily fulfilled multiple roles in the justice system with varying priorities and loyalties. Rather than a singular focus, the ethical psychologist weighed the multiple obligations they must meet.[91]

The reaction to the *Tarasoff* decision was emblematic of how professional psychology extended its reach and yet narrowed its interests toward the end of the 1970s as the Dirty Dozen's political strategy began to pay dividends. In 1977, Missouri became the final state to pass legislation recognizing psychology as a licensed profession. The year 1977 was also a time of ecumenical reconciliation for clinicians. Decades of outcomes research had honed psychotherapy into a scientifically validated tool. New assessment techniques like meta-analysis communicated the effectiveness of psychotherapy to hostile outsiders. For a majority of clients, their mental health improved regardless of their therapist's theoretical orientation.[92] That same year, Theodore Blau became the first psychologist in independent practice elected as APA president. Nicholas Cummings, another of the Dirty Dozen, joined him two years later. In 1982, APA added a division dedicated wholly to "psychologists in private practice," joining those who were already focused on clinical psychology, psychotherapy, and health psychology. Within two years, the new division became the organization's third largest, closely trailing "general psychology" and "clinical psychology."

Building on these victories, the Dirty Dozen sought to transform the APA into a thoroughly "political" organization dedicated to professional interests. Politics meant something narrower to these professionals than it did to community psychologists like those affiliated with Westside. They focused mainly on

90. "Task Force on the Role of Psychology in the Criminal Justice System—Workshop on Psychology and the Courts, May 19, 1977—May 21, 1977," pages 5–6. APA Papers, Box 338.

91. "Report of the Task Force on the Role of Psychology in the Criminal Justice System," *American Psychologist* (1978): 1099–1113, quote 1100.

92. Mary Smith and Gene Glass, "Meta-analysis of Psychotherapy Outcome Studies," *American Psychologist* 32, no. 9 (1977): 752–760.

mobilizing dues-paying members to lobby their representatives in Washington to recognize psychology as a full-scale health profession. As Chief of Mental Health for the Kaiser Permanente Health Maintenance Organization in Oakland, Cummings's star rose as he became the expert on reconciling psychology with the demands of insurance. Along with the Dirty Dozen, a new cohort of largely Washington-based APA insiders insisted the time had come for the organization to take on a greater political role on the national stage. A failure to become systematically involved in the political process had hindered psychology's professional interests. The United States spent more on health care than any country in the world, and psychologists deserved their share of the pie. Accessing those resources required "psychologists to communicate effectively with policymakers of our nation health care and scientific research systems."[93]

Jimmy Carter's promise to contain health care costs while extending coverage offered much hope. Progress required silencing the still vexing question of whether psychotherapy counted as a "health service." Academics may disagree whether mental illness had an organic or a social origin, but remuneration for practitioners demanded setting aside such debates in favor of a united front aligned with medicine. Otherwise, psychology as a profession risked disappearing entirely in the new economic order.[94] Community psychologists like Albee continued to fiercely oppose such integration. The perennial organization man as enfant terrible went so far as to denounce the inclusion of psychotherapeutic services within national health insurance. The young, articulate "nouveau riche" obsessed with self-expression through self-examination loved individual psychotherapy. Government expenditures on such services diverted always limited funds away from preventative programs and investment in structural changes. Covering psychotherapy was not social medicine, but rather another instance of redistributing wealth from America's poorest to the most affluent.[95]

Carter's Presidential Commission on Mental Health captured these competing political visions. The Commission represented an attempt to reimagine the therapeutic state. Recent legal victories for institutionalized persons such as *Wyatt v. Stickney* (1971) and *O'Connor v. Donaldson* (1975) promised them a right to treatment. By speaking at once of "protecting human rights and guaranteeing freedom of choice" when designing and offering mental health services, the Commission captured the tensions over what psychology might become in the wake of psychiatry's lost professional monopoly.[96] Psychologists did much to shape

---

93. Patrick DeLeon, Gary VandenBos, and Alan Kraut, "Federal Legislation Recognizing Psychology," *American Psychologist* 39, no. 9 (1984): 933–946.

94. Patrick DeLeon, "Psychology and the Carter Administration," *American Psychologist* 32, no. 9 (1977): 750–751.

95. George Albee, "Does Including Psychotherapy in Health Insurance Represent a Subsidy to the Rich from the Poor?" *American Psychologist* 32, no. 9 (1977): 719–721.

96. *The President's Commission on Mental Health*, vol. 1 (Washington, DC: U.S. Government Printing Office, 1978), 10.

the Commission's final report which depicted mental illness as a social disease, born as much out of stress and inequity as any biological factor. Westside affiliate Wade Nobles contributed to a subpanel that not only recognized racial disparities in services and outcomes but also underscored the racism of previous governmental inquiries into Black families and community. Albee chaired the subpanel dedicated to "prevention" and offered a rousing manifesto for early childhood interventions as the key to future mental health. Perhaps among the most radical contributions, the Commission nevertheless resonated with his subpanel's judgment that "a society must also be measured by the steps it takes to prevent every form of preventable misfortune."[97]

Yet, radical voices like Albee's were increasingly marginal within an APA dedicated to consumer choice. This was a market-oriented ideology but not true free market libertarianism. The professionals still advocated for the expansion of state regulation and welfare provisions as these aligned with their monetary interest. However, as federal support for the community mental health centers waned, they became increasingly fixated on reimbursement from third-party insurance providers as the singular issue affecting their future. The nation's leading insurance companies continued to insist that compensation for psychologists required a referral and direct supervision from a medical professional. In 1971, the Dirty Dozen founded the Council for the Advancement of the Psychological Professions and Sciences (CAPPS) as "a national political-action arm" meant to address "the total range of public-policy matters that confront the profession."[98] Two years later, various state-level associations coordinated by CAPPS banded together to file a lawsuit against Blue Cross, claiming Blue Cross's position represented a conspiracy to restrain trade by maintaining a monopoly for psychiatrists to receive reimbursement for psychotherapy services. The unwillingness of APA's Central Office to back the lawsuit due to worries about potential liability led to a full-scale revolt of the professionals, with the Dirty Dozen mounting its first campaign to get one of their own elected president. Their ascendency led to a substantial reorientation in how APA and psychologists more broadly conceptualize public engagement. Reflecting on these changes led one APA insider concerned with questions of social justice to bemoan that "the air is full of CAPPS propaganda and it would be easy for the discussions to bog down in a mess of charges and counter-charges relating to health insurance, with no real consideration of the major issues in public policy formation which we ought to be exploring."[99]

In the years after 1973, the Dirty Dozen honed APA's focus onto national legislative politics with the aim of advancing narrow professional interests. In 1977, Marvin Metsky spearheaded the clinical division's efforts to get psychologists directly recognized under Medicare. He requested that each division member

97. *The President's Commission on Mental Health*, vol. 1, 1827.
98. Rogers H. Wright to Kenneth Little, April 28, 1971. APA Papers, Box 116.
99. Ross Stagner to Leona Tyler, July 24, 1973. APA Papers, Box 116.

write their representatives in Washington (of which 10 percent of them did) to support a proposed Medicare reform bill. Ultimately, the legislation failed, but Metsky's campaign provided the model for further lobbying efforts.[100] Leaders of the new division for health psychology (established in 1978 after APA convened a task force to demonstrate psychology's broader relevance to maintaining healthy habits and preventing physical illnesses) outlined a new "blueprint for activism." The problem with prior efforts was that they simply responded to imminent crises and then dissipated. To remedy this situation, they took advantage of their Washington location, "where physical access to federal resources is almost limitless," to convene monthly meetings on health broadly construed targeted at policymakers.[101] Closely aligned in terms of leadership and goals with the division for clinical psychology, health psychology offered a broader mandate. The field sought to go beyond psychotherapy for mental maladjustments to demonstrate the relevance of behavioral interventions for improving personal health. Never a formal lobby (due to APA's nonprofit status) and officially agnostic on the question of national health insurance, these APA insiders sought to interject a psychological perspective into the days' most pressing issues. Patrick DeLeon, a clinical psychologist with a law degree, became an influential conduit to the halls of power as Hawaii Senator Daniel Inouye's chief-of-staff.[102]

Expanding into new health markets also led the Dirty Dozen to cultivate more dubious patrons. Like the ABPsi psychologists, Blau had a keen interest in applying psychology to the law and a theory of addiction. The two came together starting in 1979 when he began serving as an expert on retainers for the tobacco industry. Officially, the grant sponsored his conducting a literature review on "the tobacco habit," a study that never appeared in any peer-reviewed journal.[103] At his client's behest, Blau leveraged his decades of clinical practice, his leadership in the APA, and his own experience as an ex-smoker both in court cases and before congressional committees. Blau's testimony made a firm distinction between drugs like heroin and tobacco.[104] Heroin involved physical dependency, but tobacco smokers varied in the extent of their use as well as "the severity of cession responses." For many, "the continuance of smoking appears more related to a wide range of psychosocial motives." For these reasons, neither the scientific literature nor Blau's own professional experience could lend support "justifying labeling it

---

100. Marvin Metsky, "Getting Our Feet Wet in National Politics," *Clinical Psychologist* 31 (Spring/Summer 1978): 10.

101. Patrick DeLeon, Anne O'Keefe, Gary VandenBos, and Alan Kraut, "How to Influence Public Policy: A Blueprint for Activism," *American Psychologist* 37, no. 5 (1982): 476–485, 479.

102. Rebecca A. Clay, "A Trailblazers Moves On," *APA Monitor* 43(1) (2012): 68.

103. Patrick M. Sirridge, November 13, 1979, https://www.industrydocuments.ucsf.edu/docs/#id=fgcy0050

104. Nancy D. Campbell, *Discovering Addiction: The Science and Politics of Substance Abuse Research*. Ann Arbor: University of Michigan Press, 2007.

or treating it as an addiction."[105] By placing tobacco in the realm of the merely psychological and subject to individual choice, Blau advanced industry interests at a time of heightened regulatory scrutiny.

The decision in a later lawsuit, *Virginia Academy of Clinical Psychologists and Robert J. Resnick v. Blue Shield of Virginia* (1980), gave clinical psychologists unprecedented autonomy in offering psychotherapy without the supervision of a psychiatrist. Robert Resnick, another future APA president, brought to suit, this time with APA's fulsome support. Upon appeal, the higher court ruled that "Any assertion that a physician must actually *supervise* the psychologist to assure the quality of psychotherapy treatment administered is refuted by the policy itself. The Blue Shield policy provides for payment to psychologists for psychotherapy if billed through *any* physician—not just those who regularly treat mental and nervous disorders. It defies logic to assume that the average family practitioner can supervise a licensed psychologist in psychotherapy, and there is no basis in the record for such an assumption."[106] "Virginia Blues" cases established psychologists as equals among mental health providers; a reality insurance companies needed to recognize.[107] Clinical psychology no longer fashioned itself as an alternative to biomedicine but instead as an option available to consumers within it.

Theirs was a pyrrhic victory. The first sign of trouble came with Ronald Reagan's election as president. His 1981 Omnibus Budget Reconciliation Act sought to curtail federal expenditures. Among its many targets, it repealed the Mental Health Systems Act, which Carter had signed into law just prior to the election. After a decade of lobbying, psychologists had finally secured federal recognition for the importance of their field and the interventions they offered. For a brief moment, it seemed psychotherapists would receive unfettered reimbursement. In less than a year, these inroads vanished without any substantial action taken.

This left psychologists at the mercy of an insurance industry that continued to look at the profession as a luxurious excess. Health maintenance organizations (HMOs) modeled on Kaiser Permanente emerged as a popular option to contain costs. Often secured through employers, HMO plans offered access to a suit of health services for a fixed annual fee. HMOs restricted both the client's choice of provider and the kinds and amount of services deemed reimbursable. "The New Yorker syndrome" (a term referring to articulate clients spending years in undirected, unproductive psychotherapy) became the insurance company's bane, and they sought to eliminate such waste. The fight over managed care

---

105. "Statement of Theodore H. Blau, PhD Presented before Subcommittee on Health and the Environment, House of Representatives," 1980, 3–6. Brown & Williamson Records; Master Settlement Agreement. https://www.industrydocuments.ucsf.edu/docs/rjfc0136

106. *Virginia Academy of Clinical Psychologists, and Robert J. Resnick, Ph.D. v. Blue Shield of Virginia, Blue Shield of Southwestern Virginia, and Neuropsychiatric Society of Virginia, Inc.*, 624 F.2d 476 (4th Cir. 1980).

107. Charles Kiesler and Michael Pallak. "The Virginia Blues," *American Psychologist* 35, no. 11 (1980): 953–954.

pitted the psychotherapist against the claims adjuster in determining the client's needs, a battle the psychologist typically lost. Having "won" psychotherapy from psychiatrists, psychologists now found new competition from less expensive psychiatric nurses and social workers.[108]

As the Dirty Dozen consolidated its control over the APA governance structure, they undertook concerted efforts to control psychology's public image to advance their professional interests. The creation in 1979 of the Committee on Legal Issues (COLI) offered a new platform for simultaneously expanding psychologists' social relevance and market share. Reporting to APA's Board of Directors, COLI advised the organization on priorities for involvement in legal proceedings. COLI expanded APA's role as frequent filer of *amicus curiae*, friendly third parties offering supportive expertise in legal cases. APA's amicus brief initially addressed issues directly relating to their expanding domain of professional expertise (e.g., the validity of psychometric tests, the forced institutionalization of patients, insurer's reimbursement of psychological services).[109] The brief filed in support of the defense in *New York v. Uplinger* (1984) marked a distinct change in direction. Citing the psychologist's expertise in "the nature and prevalence of variant sexual conduct," APA's attorneys publicly staged the organization's about-face regarding homosexuality. In conjunction with the American Psychiatric Association and the American Public Health Association, the nation's leading health organizations urged lawmakers to decriminalize sexual conduct between consenting adults in private. They emphasized that not only was sexual orientation immutable, but sexual minorities were healthy individuals entitled to the full rights of citizenship: employment, marriage, parenthood. Sexuality became the most frequent topic on which the APA submitted expert briefs. This legal activism served as a major public platform for advancing the organization's progressive self-image amid narrowing professionalism.[110]

As APA president in 1983, Max Siegel authorized the purchase of the glossy magazine *Psychology Today* to transform it into an official organ for the organization. This decision proved an utter failure. Members resented the costly investment made without their consent and many felt comfortable aligning their organization with a magazine whose profits came largely from cigarettes and alcohol advertisements. APA sold the magazine just four years later, at a loss of $16 million. This miscalculation forced APA to liquidate much of its Washington, DC, real estate to avoid bankruptcy.[111] Such moves further aggravated the

---

108. Melinda Henneberger, "Managed Care Changing Practice of Psychotherapy," *New York Times*, October 9, 1994, 1.

109. Patrick H. DeLeon and Jack Donahue, "Overview: The Growing Impact of Organized Psychology in the Judicial System," *Psychotherapy in Private Practice* 1(1) (1982): 109–122.

110. Lisa M. Diamond and Clifford J. Rosky, "Scrutinizing Immutability: Research on Sexual Orientation and US Legal Advocacy for Sexual Minorities," *The Journal of Sex Research* 53, no. 4–5 (2016): 363–391.

111. Robert Epstein, "Giving Psychology Away: A Personal Journey," *Perspectives on Psychological Science* 1, no. 4 (2006): 389–400, 392.

academics within APA. In 1988, after the clinicians defeated a motion to reorganize the APA, a large swath of largely cognitive psychologists defected to establish an independent American Psychological Society (named the Association for Psychological Science).[112]

Clinical psychology's increased market orientation did much to make short-term, goal-directed cognitive-behavioral therapy (CBT) the preferred method of treatment. Various "rational" psychotherapies had coexisted with psychoanalysis from the start, and clinical psychologists had long embraced "eclecticism." A pragmatic peace existed among various theoretical modalities. All therapies led to improved outcomes.[113] CBT appealed not only by focusing on immediate circumstances rather than the depths of the past, but by offering clinicians standardized inventories and manuals to guide their practice. This measurable and accountable checklist approach uniquely suited insurers' demands.[114] Periodic surveys of members of APA's Division 12 revealed distinct trends in their preferred theoretical orientations. The first survey in 1960 did not list "cognitive" as an option. It appeared as a notable alternative in surveys conducted in the early 1980s as clinicians looked to "therapy systems that emphasize the integration of affect, cognition, and behavior and stress intervention strategies more than heavily theoretical approaches."[115] CBT eclipsed psychodynamic approaches and soon thereafter, in 1995, became undisputed as the most popular orientation (Figure 3.4).[116]

Psychopharmacology posed an even greater challenge to clinical psychologists' market share.[117] A 1981 survey of registered doctoral-level psychologists found that 58 percent of respondents were uninterested in the right to prescribe medication.[118] At the 1984 APA meeting in Hawaii, Senator Inouye delivered a keynote address encouraging psychologists (and registered nurses) to pursue

---

112. Robin L. Cautin, "The Founding of the Association for Psychological Science: Part 1. Dialectical Tensions within Organized Psychology," *Perspectives on Psychological Science* 4, no. 3 (2009): 211–223.

113. Martin Seligman, "The Effectiveness of Psychotherapy: The *Consumer Reports* Study," *American Psychologist* 50, no. 12 (1995): 965–974.

114. Rachael I. Rosner, "Manualizing Psychotherapy: Aaron T. Beck and the Origins of Cognitive Therapy of Depression," *European Journal of Psychotherapy & Counselling* 20, no. 1 (2018): 25–47.

115. Darrell Smith, "Trends in Counseling and Psychotherapy," *American Psychologist* 37, no. 7 (1982): 802–809, 808.

116. John C. Norcross and Christie P. Karpiak, "Clinical Psychologists in the 2010s: 50 Years of the APA Division of Clinical Psychology," *Clinical Psychology: Science and Practice* 19, no. 1 (2012): 1–12.

117. Gardiner Harris, "Talk Doesn't Pay, So Psychiatry Turns Instead to Drugs," *New York Times*, March 6, 2011, 1, 25.

118. Loy O. Bascue and Martin Zlotowski, "Psychologists' Attitudes about Prescribing Medications," *Psychological Reports* 48, no. 2 (1981): 645–646.

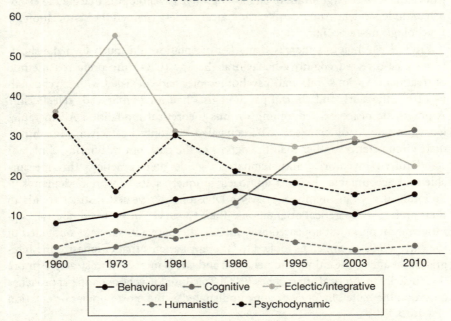

Figure 3.4 Preferred Theoretical Orientations among APA Division 12 Members. Data from Norcross & Karpiak (2010).

prescriptions privileges to improve health care access in underserved, rural areas.[119] Two years later, Eli Lily released Prozac, a generation of antidepressants. At the 1995 APA convention, its Council endorsed the policy that the practice of psychology included physical interventions. Prescribing medication fell within the clinician's training and competence, and this right would enhance consumer choice. Psychology was a complete mental health provider. Just as the American Psychiatric Association resisted psychologists' right to administer psychotherapy in the 1950s, the organization now lobbied against the psychologist's prescription privileges bills at the state level.[120] The pursuit of prescription privileges divided the rank and file like no other issue had done. For many clinicians, it represented a betrayal of psychology's unique vision, a capitulation of its therapeutic alternative to the biomedical establishment.[121] As Cummings ruefully observed, "It has not been easy for psychology, which struggled for many years to attain autonomy

---

119. Jan B. E. Leard-Hansson, "Psychologist-Prescribing Efforts: A Brief History," *Psychiatric News* 2001.

120. Ken Hausman, "More States Just Say No to Psychologist Prescribing," *Psychiatric News* (2003). https://psychnews.psychiatryonline.org/doi/full/10.1176/pn.38.8.0001a

121. John Brentar and John McNamara, "The Right to Prescribe Medication: Considerations for Professional Psychology," *Professional Psychology: Research and Practice* 22, no. 3

only to see the rules of the game change just as it became the preeminent psychotherapy profession."[122]

Support came, once again, from the American military. The demands of rehabilitating returning veterans had created the psychological profession from whole cloth after World War II and now this patron again promised access to the latest frontier of mental health. In 1988, Inouye proposed "a demonstration project" whereby already licensed military psychologists would receive additional training (and rights) to prescribe psychotropic medication independent of any physician. Inouye not only proposed the program, but members of his staff voluntarily enlisted in the military to participate in it.[123] Commenced in 1991, the program remained miniscule, involving a mere handful of psychologists. Its greatest importance lay in aligning the APA bureaucracy with psychologists embedded in the military at a time when many progressives questioned the value of the old alliance. As psychology entered the new millennium, its future as a profession once again seemed tied to appeasing military patrons.

CONCLUSION

The dominant narrative about postwar psychology which focuses on consolidation of the cognitive revolution obscures the centrality of clinical psychology's expansion to the subsequent history of the field. This demographic revolution and attendant diversification of the rank and file forever changed psychology. With growth came division. The postwar architects of professional psychology (like Carl Rogers and Albert Ellis) envisioned it as decidedly nonmedical. The growth of NIH funding and especially the problem of remuneration for those in private practice decisively realigned professional psychology to the biomedical establishment. The 1970s saw two major competitors for the politics of mental health, one dedicated to community control and the other to professional autonomy. Both pushed organized psychology into the realms of health and policy as it had never been imagined (or desired) by their academic counterparts since their mobilization during World War II. The dominance of the clinical seeded the ground for the affective, the hedonic, and the habitual to return to the psychological mainstream despite cognitive scientists' pronounced disinterest in these topics. The

---

(1991): 179–187; Steve C. Hayes and Elaine Heiby, "Psychology's Drug Problem: Do We Need a Fix or Should We Just Say No?" *American Psychologist* 51(3) (1996): 198–206; Elizabeth Cullen and Russ Newman, "In Pursuit of Prescription Privileges," *Professional Psychology: Research and Practice* 28, no. 2 (1997): 101–106.

122. Nicholas Cummings, "Impact of Managed Care on Employment and Training: A Primer for Survival," *Professional Psychology: Research and Practice* 26, no. 1 (1995): 10–15, 12.

123. Russ Newman, Randy Phelps, Morgan Sammons, Debra Dunivin, and Elizabeth Cullen, "Evaluation of the Psychopharmacology Demonstration Project: A Retrospective Analysis," *Professional Psychology: Research and Practice* 31, no. 6 (2000): 598–603.

triumph of narrow professionalism over community control ensured that this affective psychology would venerate the expertise of the psychologist's advantage at the expense of a public that was presumed to be faulty and deficient, betraying the field's postwar democratic promise. The resulting psychology certainly privatized social problems, attributing mental health to personal defects remedied through individualized care. But psychologists remade (or reasserted) themselves during this period.

Faced with a feminizing workforce and an eroding capacity to exercise autonomous clinical judgment, the APA leadership enshrined the image of the professional psychologist as an unquestioned white, male authority figure. Indeed, despite the dominant rhetoric of a feminized profession, the elected leadership remained resolutely male for decades. When it came to reflecting membership demographics, the situation worsened considerably over time. In 1972 and 1973, at the height of second wave feminism, the APA elected two women presidents in a row. Only three women were elected in the 1980s and only a single female president by the 1990s. It was only in the 2010s, as the APA experienced considerable internal crises, that women rather abruptly started to dominate its presidency. The candidate whose election started this reversal was Melba J. T. Vasquez, the organization's first Latina president in 2011. Indeed, racial representation at the highest level followed a nearly identical pattern. In 1971, APA members elected Kenneth Clark as their first Black president. Jessica Henderson Daniel followed as the second Black president in 2018. The timing of these elections suggests that the APA suffered not so much from a "glass ceiling" problem, but from what some social psychologists called the "glass cliff" wherein marginalized persons are granted leadership roles after an organization is in considerable jeopardy.[124]

Professionalism, then, was more than a numeric shift toward the number of applied psychologists. It was a political philosophy and a disposition toward the market related to and yet distinct from the neo-liberal policies taking hold around it. This philosophy consistently foregrounded the primacy of consumer choice. Born out of the VA system, psychologists never opposed government largesse; the warfare state allowed their rank to flourish, and questions around the staffing of federally funded community mental health centers led to their first political mobilization. But the client had the fundamental freedom to select a provider of their choice for mental health services. Recognized professions should compete equally in the market. This was a self-interested position as psychologists consistently opposed psychiatry's medical monopoly and autocratic methods. This freedom came with regulation in the form of licensure and accreditation. Government oversight maintained psychology as a well-regulated profession and provided a useful tool for combatting fledgling professions challenging psychologists from below. As part of advocating for consumer choice, psychologists championed a

---

124. Michelle K. Ryan and S. Alexander Haslam, "The Glass Cliff: Evidence that Women Are Over-Represented in Precarious Leadership Positions," *British Journal of Management* 16, no. 2 (2005): 81–90.

patient's "right to treatment" and opposed mere custodialism for institutionalized populations. These populations deserved care either as inpatients or better yet as clients living in the community. In the 1970s, professionals rallied around the possibility of universal health care, unlike medical organizations had in the 1930s. After its political failure with the election of Reagan, psychologists accommodated themselves to managed care and private insurance. They retained their ideological commitment to consumer choice but sundered it from older connections to patient rights. Professionalism now wholly operated by the logic of market.

Demands for racial justice did not disappear entirely. Entering the twenty-first century, psychology grappled with the paradoxes of racialized professionalism. As a legacy of early 1970s activism, the APA remained concerned with the representativeness of its membership and how it reflected the demographics of the clients it served. The organization continued to convene countless committees, task forces, and initiatives pondering the persistence of psychology's whiteness. Like most liberal American organizations, the APA needed to publicly reckon with its exclusionary history to stage its institutional morality.[125] Outcomes research provided "ethnic minority" psychologists with a valuable tool. Breaking psychotherapy into a series of testable variables allowed psychologist Stanley Sue to demonstrate how the ethnic identity of both the therapist and patient affected the treatment's outcome to the detriment of Black, Latino, Indigenous, and Asian American clients.[126] The Hilliard-led Black presence at the Vail conference had put the notion of the therapist's cultural competence on the training agenda. In the 1980s, Black feminist psychologists like Beverly Greene articulated sophisticated intersectional analyses of how race, gender, and sexuality structured the therapeutic relationship.[127] These approaches persisted as recognized, yet underdeveloped, aspects of training due to perennially limited time and resources. As psychology's democratic ambitions narrowed, its rank expanded to include those who demanded accountability to an even more diverse polity. However, this inclusivity had to accommodate itself to the narrow professionalism institutionalized by the Dirty Dozen.

---

125. Alondra Nelson, "The Social Life of DNA: Racial Reconciliation and Institutional Morality after the Genome," *The British Journal of Sociology* 69, no. 3 (2018): 522–537.

126. Stanley Sue, "Community Mental Health Services to Minority Groups: Some Optimism, Some Pessimism," *American Psychologist* 32, no. 8 (1977): 616–624.

127. Beverly A. Greene, "When the Therapist Is White and the Patient Is Black: Considerations for Psychotherapy in the Feminist Heterosexual and Lesbian Communities," *Women and Therapy* 5, no. 2–3 (1986): 41–65.

4

Vigilant Minds, Thoughtless Brains

Warfare, Welfare, and the Remaking of Cognition

When interviewed for an oral history project, Alan Baddeley, a long-time associate of the Applied Psychology Unit (APU) at Cambridge and its director from 1974 to 1996, recalled "a change in focus around the 1970s at the unit, from being essentially concerned with normal people under abnormal environments, to being concerned with people who had neuropsychological problems as a result of brain damage."[1] When psychologists generally speak of a revolutionary break separating behaviorism from cognitive science, they usually depict the subsequent transition to neuroscience as a more seamless transition, if not an inevitable outcome. On this reading, neurology provided the obvious physical platform on which cognitive programs ran. The turn to the brain did not represent a fundamental shift in theory; neuroimaging merely served as an innovative method for answering existing questions.[2] In contrast, Baddeley's recollection suggests a sharper break in thinking about thinking in the late twentieth century, one tied to a shift in the kind of bodies that mattered to psychologists.

The Medical Research Council (MRC) began funding the APU in 1944 as part of the war effort. The Unit's wartime studies of information flows in human–machine interactions became foundational to the cybernetic-inspired cognitive revolution of the 1950s. Committed to solving practical problems for paying clients, the APU quickly became an internationally recognized center for information-processing psychology. Its scientists returned concepts such as attention and memory to the psychological mainstream, granting them respectability by redefining them

---

1. Lois A. Reynolds and E. M. Tansey (eds.), *The MRC Applied Psychology Unit*. London: Wellcome Trust Centre for the History of Medicine at UCL, 2003, 23. Hereafter cited as APU Oral History.

2. The continuity between psychology and neuroscience is found in internal accounts like Margaret A. Boden, *Mind as Machine: A History of Cognitive Science*. Oxford: Oxford University Press, 2006 and critical, Foucauldian ones such as Nikolas Rose and Joelle M. Abi-Rached, *Neuro: The New Brain Sciences and the Management of the Mind*. Princeton, NJ: Princeton University Press, 2013.

in terms of the then novel communication theory. Although their models of the mind became a staple of introductory psychology textbooks, the existing historiography of the cognitive revolution largely neglects the Unit.[3] Sociologist Andrew Pickering's definition of cybernetics as "a postwar science of the adaptive brain" partly explains this neglect.[4] Computational methods feature prominently in twenty-first-century neuroscience in the form of imaging technologies, but as metaphors brains and computers had opposite historical trajectories for psychology.[5] At the height of the cognitive revolution, the APU psychologists deliberately skirted the reduction of mind to neurology but then abruptly reversed course in the 1980s. By emphasizing certain tensions and transitions, the historiography tends to ignore, the Unit provides a unique vantage point for considering the cognitive revolution and how it ended.

Encounters with three sets of bodies drove changes to cognitive theory at the APU.[6] As Baddeley observed, their theoretical models were extracted and then abstracted from a shifting pool of favored participants. These theory-laden bodies became available at different historical junctures as technological systems transformed the lives of ordinary Britons in ways both mundane and potentially catastrophic. Cognitive theory's three bodies were the vigilant military recruit, the "unskilled," female technology worker, and the amnesiac neuropsychological patient. The APU's mandate to advance basic science by addressing applied problems meant these shifts mirrored changes in postwar political economy. The bodies of interests and the tasks they performed reflected the transition from an imperial warfare state to the nationalization of industries to their subsequent privatization under neo-liberalism and the prioritization of health as an economic problem.[7] The changes at the APU did not represent the fate of cognitive science

---

3. The exception within the historiography of the cognitive revolution is Alan Collins, "From H=log sn to Conceptual Framework: A Short History of Information," *History of Psychology* 10, no. 1 (2007): 44–72.

4. Andrew Pickering, *The Cybernetic Brain: Sketches of Another Future*. Chicago: University of Chicago Press, 2010, 6.

5. On the role of imagining technologies in remaking personhood, see Anne Beaulieu, "Voxels in the Brain: Neuroscience, Informatics and Changing Notions of Objectivity," *Social Studies of Science* 31, no. 5 (2001): 635–680; Joseph Dumit, *Picturing Personhood: Brain Scans and Biomedical Identity*. Princeton, NJ: Princeton University Press, 2004; Simon Cohn, "Making Objective Facts from Intimate Relations: The Case of Neuroscience and Its Entanglements with Volunteers," *History of the Human Sciences* 21, no. 4 (2008): 86–103; Melissa M. Littlefield, *Instrumental Intimacy: EEG Wearables and Neuroscientific Control*. Baltimore: Johns Hopkins University Press, 2018.

6. On the embodiment of scientific knower, see Hélène Mialet, *Hawking Incorporated: Stephen Hawking and the Anthropology of the Knowing Subject*. Chicago: University of Chicago Press, 2012; Natasha Myers, *Rendering Life Molecular: Models, Modelers, and Excitable Matter*. Durham, NC: Duke University Press, 2015.

7. The APU is also strangely absent from Mathew Thomson, *Psychological Subjects: Identity, Culture, and Health in Twentieth-Century Britain*. Oxford: Oxford University Press, 2006.

as a whole, but the view from the Unit's home on Chaucer Road clarifies two key shifts in postwar psychology: the transfer of cybernetics from military to civilian life in 1950s and the seemingly strange death of the computer metaphor for cognition amid the personal computer revolution of the 1980s.

THE VIGILANT MIND

From the outset, the psychology pursued at the APU differed from that of its American contemporaries. Kenneth Craik, the young perceptual psychologist who served as the first director, held a dual fascination with human vision and mechanical engineering.[8] Indeed, he understood these two interests as a single one. In 1945, he argued that "electronic technology has recently added to man's own sense-organs artificial 'sensory devices.'" Radar and kindred technologies of war were not ungainly prosthetics for Craik. He felt that knowledge about humans and complex machines would advance if both were understood as "self-regulating systems." He described the human perceptual apparatus using the terminology for mechanical control systems. He embraced the cybernetic claim "to apply the same theory to the human operator in, for instance, flying an aircraft, and although the human being's behaviour is more flexible, more variable, and as a result less predictable, the analogy has been an extremely illuminating one."[9]

In addition to Craik's cybernetic visions, the experimental psychology of Frederic Bartlett served as a touchstone for the Unit. The unrivaled leader of British psychology at mid-century, the Cambridge professor served as the Unit's honorary director and its actual one following Craik's death in a bike accident in 1945. Bartlett pursued a psychology that was equally informed by his exposure to social anthropology and clinical neurology. He first gained fame for his book *Remembering* (1932), a response to the German psychologist Herrmann Ebbinghaus's influential *Memory* (1890). Ebbinghaus had established his famous "curve of forgetting" by memorizing a list of nonsense syllables and then testing himself at regular intervals to record his increasing inability to retrieve the list from his mind.[10] As Bartlett's substitution of the verb for the noun in his title suggested, he viewed remembering not as "the re-excitation of innumerable fixed, lifeless and fragmentary traces" but rather as "an imaginative reconstruction or construction."[11] Bartlett rejected long-standing "spatial" metaphors for memory

---

8. Alan Collins, "The Reputation of Kenneth James William Craik," *History of Psychology* 16, no. 2 (2013): 93–111.

9. K. J. W. Craik, "The Present Position of Psychological Research in Britain," *British Medical Bulletin*, 3(1–3) (1945): 24–26, 25.

10. Douwe Draaisma, *Metaphors of Memory: A History of Ideas about the Mind*. Cambridge: Cambridge University Press, 2000.

11. Frederic Charles Bartlett, *Remembering: A Study in Experimental and Social Psychology*, 1932; Cambridge: Cambridge University Press, 1995, 213.

as analogous to a repository of physical objects as well as Ebbinghaus's nonsense syllables method. Instead, Bartlett tasked participants with learning a simple story and then reproducing it. His participants "conventionalized" the narrative in the retelling, eliminating details and adapting the tale to their own experience using certain mental "schema" (a term borrowed from the neurologist Henry Head). Unlike his postwar successors, Bartlett refused to interpret such simplifications as mistakes; they illustrated the functional nature of memory as a social process of relating to one's group.[12]

Under Bartlett's leadership, the Department and the Unit essentially became one, but this unifying vision did not last. In the wake of his retirement in 1951, his institutional empire split, driven by interpersonal acrimony and methodological differences. The neuropsychologist Oliver Zangwill moved from Oxford to succeed Bartlett as the chair of the Cambridge Department. He arrived to find its facilities commingled with those of the Unit. Devoting so much space and resources to applied projects seemed unbefitting to an Oxbridge man at midcentury. In contrast to Zangwill's outside appointment, the medical doctor Norman Mackworth was promoted within the ranks of the APU to take over the director's role. Soon after assuming this position, he forced the MRC into purchasing a house on Chaucer Road to serve as the APU's new headquarters.[13] The move to a location that was a twenty-minute walk from campus spatialized the growing intellectual divide between Department and Unit, with each adopting distinct visions of how psychology, industry, and medicine fit together.

Zangwill conceptualized mental function in terms of its deficits and pathologies. He spent his formative years during the war at the Brain Injuries Unit of the Royal Infirmary Edinburgh, working alongside neurosurgeons and psychiatrists. He purposed psychology to fulfill the Infirmary's mission: the care and rehabilitation of injured soldiers to resettle them as working members of society.[14] A founding member of the Society for Experimental Psychology, Zangwill championed the close observation and assessment of individuals with brain damage reported in detailed case histories.[15] After the war, he looked to neurologists on the continent

---

12. On Bartlett's psychology and its renunciation during the cognitive revolution, see Elizabeth B. Johnston, "The Repeated Reproduction of Bartlett's Remembering," *History of Psychology* 4, no. 4 (2001): 341–366; James Ost and Alan Costall. "Misremembering Bartlett: A Study in Serial Reproduction," *British Journal of Psychology* 93, no. 2 (2002): 243–255; Alan Collins, "The Embodiment of Reconciliation: Order and Change in the Work of Frederic Bartlett," *History of psychology* 9, no. 4 (2006): 290–312; Brady Wagoner, *The Constructive Mind: Bartlett's Psychology in Reconstruction*. Cambridge, MA: Cambridge University Press, 2017.

13. Mackworth placed a £800 deposit on the house with MRC authorization. See APU Oral History, 52.

14. O. L. Zangwill, "Psychological Aspects of Rehabilitation in Cases of Brain Injury," *British Journal of Psychology* 37, no. 2 (1947): 60–69.

15. John Forrester, "If p, Then What? Thinking in Cases," *History of the Human Sciences* 9, no. 3 (1996): 1–25.

as his peers and built the field of neuropsychology through collaborations with hospital-based physicians in the new National Health Service (NHS).[16] These extensive connections to the world of clinical medicine did not guarantee Zangwill's enthusiasm for the kind of applied psychology pursued by the APU. As a reflection of the requirements of the military contracts that sustained it, the APU's staff expanded to include engineers, servicemen, and other nonpsychologists without advanced degrees, individuals Zangwill felt inappropriate for cross-appointment to his Department.[17]

In contrast to Zangwill's emphasis on relating deficits to lesions, the APU remained focused on what Bartlett called "highly skilled work" or the planned coordination of mental and physical activity by healthy individuals. Skilled performance resisted routinization through repetition, remaining flexible, anticipatory, and responsive to circumstances.[18] It required active *thinking*. Research in this vein began when Bartlett and Craik joined the Flying Personnel Research Committee in 1941. They focused on how fatigue affected the pilot's long-term ability to operate the controls of a plane. Bartlett rejected the notion that the methods used to measure "simple muscular fatigue" could capture the depletion of "mental effort."[19] Rather than disaggregate this complex job into a series of simpler tasks, Craik designed an early flight simulator, the Cambridge Cockpit, to replicate the full range of the pilot's mental performance under controlled but naturalistic conditions.[20]

Bartlett started from the demarcation of intellectual from manual work, valorizing the capacity of the mind over the limits of the body.[21] In 1951, he admonished the field of "industrial medicine" for its exclusive focus on "detailed studies of specific hazards which must be encountered in particular industries." In privileging the physical ailments and toxicological risks faced by manual laborers, industrial medicine neglected a host of maladjustments (such as fatigue, strain, and accident-causing errors) at the root of both workplace inefficiency and

16. Alan F. Collins, "An Intimate Connection: Oliver Zangwill and the Emergence of Neuropsychology in Britain," *History of Psychology* 9, no. 2 (2006): 89–112, 95–99.

17. On Zangwill's hostility to the APU, see Mackworth to Harold Himsworth, January 5, 1958, FD 1/8618: Unit Re-organization, 1957–1983, National Archives.

18. For a helpful distillation of Bartlett's unwritten theory of skill, see R. C. Oldfield, "Frederic Charles Bartlett: 1886–1969," *The American Journal of Psychology* 85, no. 1 (1972): 133–140, 137.

19. F. C. Bartlett, "Fatigue Following Highly Skilled Work," *Proceedings of the Royal Society of London. Series B-Biological Sciences* 131, no. 864 (1943): 247–257, 247.

20. D. Russell Davis, "The Disorganization of Behaviour in Fatigue," *Journal of Neurology, Neurosurgery, and Psychiatry* 9, no. 1 (1946): 23–29.

21. On the tensions among mental labor, skill, and mechanization, see Simon Schaffer, "Babbage's Intelligence: Calculating Engines and the Factory System," *Critical Inquiry* 21, no. 1 (1994): 203–227.

mental disease.[22] Those who followed Bartlett at the APU understood psychology as a natural science, a branch of biology, but likewise resisted reducing cognition to the physiology of the brain and nervous system. The psychological constituted a distinct level of analysis, one of increasing relevance in an automating society.

No skill captured the APU's interest like vigilance. "Attention," once a central concept of functionalist psychology, had become a controversial topic among American behaviorists due to its links to consciousness, intention, and the will.[23] Rebranded as "vigilance," attention returned to the center of psychological theory after World War II. Like "schema," the Cambridge psychologists borrowed vigilance from the neurologist Henry Head.[24] However, the term gained greater prominence and a new meaning as a result of their wartime work. Vigilance was both specialized military operation and an activity familiar to every patriotic Briton. Maintaining alertness carried moral connotations. Responding to Nazi denials of an imminent land invasion, Prime Minister Winston Churchill urged that "our sense of growing strength and preparedness must not lend to the slightest relaxation of vigilance or moral alertness."[25] Vigilance constituted a form of national service in this era of total war and the militarization of the home front.[26] It was a demanding and strenuous task, the kind of superior brainwork that allowed Britain to win the war against great odds.[27]

Mackworth made no secret of the military origins of his vigilance research. Like much scientific innovation at midcentury, its stated purpose was to address "problems relating to men fighting in a war."[28] He began his experiments on vigilance and its breakdown in 1943, before the formal creation of the APU, when the Royal Air Force (RAF) asked whether he could design an experiment "to determine the optimum length of watch for radar operators on anti-submarine

---

22. Bartlett, "The Bearing of Experimental Psychology upon Human Skilled Performance," *British Journal of Industrial Medicine* 8 (1951): 209–217, 216.

23. This disappearance is a striking example of how behaviorism undercut certain tenets of modernist personhood. See Jonathan Crary, *Suspensions of Perception: Attention, Spectacle, and Modern Culture*. Cambridge, MA: MIT Press, 1999.

24. Henry Head, "The Concept of Nervous and Mental Energy II: 'Vigilance,'; A Physiological State of the Nervous System," *British Journal of Psychology* 14 (1923): 126–147.

25. "Churchill Urges British Vigilance," *New York Times*, August 4, 1940, p. 1.

26. On the intertwined maintenance of reliable humans and machines in warfare, see Edward Jones-Imhotep, "Maintaining Humans" in Mark Solovey and Hamilton Cravens (eds.), *Cold War Social Science: Knowledge Production, Liberal Democracy, and Human Nature*. New York: Palgrave Macmillan, 2012, 175–95.

27. Jon Agar, *The Government Machine: A Revolutionary History of the Computer*. Cambridge, MA: MIT Press, 2003, 201–261. A history of the shifting place of Alan Turing, the women of Bletchley Park, and the Colossus computer in the popular memory of "the people's war" remains unwritten.

28. Mackworth, *Researches on the Measurement of Human Performance*. London: His Majesty's Stationary Office, 7.

patrol."[29] This essential security task placed certain demands on the human operator. A typical watch entailed "waiting for nothing to happen" as German U-boats surfaced at random and infrequent intervals. Because the rudimentary radar equipment had poor resolution, the operator needed to remain attentive to pinpoint the brief, unexpected blip on the screen. The military leadership worried that excessively long watches would lead radar operators to miss the telling signal. In this militarized setting, errors in judgment came with grave consequences and so became the psychologist's focus.

Mackworth engineered his Clock Test to simulate the demands of this task in the risk-free space of the Cambridge laboratory. As the name suggested, the apparatus consisted of a clockface with a pointer moving at regular intervals, except when it would irregularly skip and move two increments. Junior servicemen, both air force cadets and naval ratings, worked as the experimental subjects. Mackworth instructed these participants to press a response key whenever they witnessed any anomalous movements. Given this basic setup, Mackworth could test how watch length and other environmental conditions such as temperature affected this skilled performance. Despite the patronage of the Medical Research Council, Mackworth's experiments deliberately sidestepped the physiology or neurology underlying sustained vigilance, except for a single trial examining the effects of the amphetamine Benzedrine on the recruit's performance.[30]

The Services, especially the Navy, remained an everyday feature of life at the APU throughout the tenure of Mackworth's successor, Donald E. Broadbent, from 1958 to 1974. He, along with his two associate directors, E. C. Poulton and the mononymous (Reuben) Conrad, had all served in the armed forces during the Second World War and came to psychology through this common experience of mobilization. The APU was not an exclusively homosocial world. Women formed part of the paid staff from the start, very occasionally receiving credit as co-authors, but none obtained a leadership role until the 1990s. Much of the Unit's nonhierarchical management derived from a shared and homogeneous sociality. The Unit's leadership did not include any commissioned officers, but these psychologists felt comfortable among military men, a feature of APU life noticed by a younger generation. Reflecting on his time as a doctoral student with the group in the early 1970s, Graham Hitch recalled: "I was amazed to find that there was some sort of naval unit in Cambridge. Its sole purpose, as far as I could work out, was to provide, I think, 6 naval ratings per fortnight, to be tested at the unit." Although his own PhD was without military application, Hitch "was told that subjects were available and was asked whether I would like to use them. I think quite a large proportion of their time was used on non-military research while I was there."[31] Their omnipresence shaped the theoretical questions posed at the APU.

---

29. Mackworth, *Researches on the Measurement of Human Performance*, 12.

30. Mackworth, *Researches on the Measurement of Human Performance*, 30–36.

31. Graham Hitch APU Oral History, 29–30.

Most notably, Broadbent's famous "filter theory" of attention derived from military telecommunications. Broadbent took as his starting point humanity's encounter with complex technological systems. In such arrangements, the individual found themselves at the juncture of multiple, competing systems, each requiring their attention. His version of the vigilance test involved having naval ratings monitor poorly designed dials as loudspeakers blasted the sound of noisy machinery on a continual loop.[32] Much of Broadbent's own experimental program involved simulating the experience of receiving and responding to commands. He instructed participants to observe a series of divided sheets of paper, with different sections marked by a meaningless symbol. Mimicking military radio communication, a tape recording posed a sequence of yes–no questions about the sheet to the recruit coming from either one of two command positions. The participant had to both answer the question correctly and identify the source of the question.[33] The basic setup granted Broadbent considerable flexibility in how he could manipulate delivery of the messages. Originally, Broadbent used a loudspeaker to deliver the tape-recorded instructions. Using this setup, he tackled a series of problems arising from the demands of military radio communications: speaking and listening at the same time; prioritizing a new message when listening to one already in progress; managing the arrival of two simultaneous messages.[34] Each of these conflicts compromised the participant's ability to accurately respond.

In 1953, Broadbent introduced headphones into his experimental setup. This simple innovation concretized his cybernetic understanding of attention. Headphones not only further insulated the participant from their surroundings but allowed for simultaneous delivery of two distinct auditory messages, one to each ear. A favorite technique was to have the participant listen to long lists of digits and write them down as best they could. In the "dichotic listening" version of this task, "different material was recorded on the two tracks, so that one digit arrived at one of S's ears and another digit simultaneously at the other ear."[35] Stereophonic equipment enabled Broadbent to cast the human nervous system itself as a communication channel. Unlike the typical animal behavior setup, his experiments closely mimicked the lifeworld to meet his clients' requirements. However, these experiments reproduced a particular form of life and a historically specific experience of

---

32. Donald E. Broadbent, "Some Effects of Noise on Visual Performance," *Quarterly Journal of Experimental Psychology* 6, no. 1 (1954): 1–5.

33. Donald E. Broadbent, "Speaking and Listening Simultaneously," *Journal of Experimental Psychology* 43, no. 4 (1952): 267–273, 267.

34. Broadbent, "Speaking and Listening Simultaneously"; Broadbent, "Listening to One of Two Synchronous Messages," *Journal of Experimental Psychology* 44, no. 1 (1952): 51–55; Broadbent, "Failures of Attention in Selective Listening," *Journal of Experimental Psychology* 44, no. 6 (1952): 428–433.

35. Donald E. Broadbent, "The Role of Auditory Localization in Attention and Memory Span," *Journal of Experimental Psychology* 47, no. 3 (1954): 191–196, 194.

listening.[36] Soon to become an innocuous device for consuming music, stereo headphones were an exclusively military technology until 1958, the year when John C. Koss released the first commercial set.[37] Their use in the Cambridge laboratory helped constitute an individualized listener, isolated in a room and responsive to the orders they received. In striking contrast to his mentor Bartlett's account of remembering as a social activity, Broadbent made communication—of all things—a lonely, asocial affair.[38] Adhering to a modern acoustics move toward the abstraction of sound, Broadbent treated listening as the anonymous nervous system's encounter with militarized telecommunications technology.[39]

In articulating his filter theory, Broadbent never ventured far from these material arrangements. He eschewed "abstract symbols such as words or mathematical expressions" in favor of a simple mechanical analogy.[40] He visualized attention as a vertical, y-shaped tube with a swinging flap separating where the two arms met. The arms represented competing channels through which sensory information could enter as each was sufficiently wide to accommodate a single ball (representing information from various stimuli) at a time. This simple setup allowed Broadbent to represent different perceptual experiences. For example, two simultaneously dropped balls striking the flap at the same time created a jam where neither traveled into the main tube (e.g., noisy distraction). With two nonsimultaneously launched balls, the first took priority, knocking the flap and shutting out the competing ball/signal. A ball flung down one channel at a great velocity had an advantage over its competitor on the other channel.

Although Broadbent conceded that his mechanical model was "admittedly ludicrous as a description of what really happens in the brain," he refused to see this as a fault. The mechanical model appealed to him precisely because of this distance from nervous physiology. His fellow psychologists would never mistake it for "speculative neurology." Instead, his model directed readers to a functional explanation at the level of psychological description rather than an attempt to imagine its biological

---

36. Jonathan Sterne, *The Audible Past: Cultural Origins of Sound Reproduction*. Durham, NC: Duke University Press, 2003; Emily Thompson, *The Soundscape of Modernity: Architectural Acoustics and the Culture of Listening in America, 1900–1933*. Cambridge, MA: MIT Press, 2004; Edward Jones-Imhotep, "Malleability and Machines: Glenn Gould and the Technological Self," *Technology and Culture* 57, no. 2 (2016): 287–321.

37. Charles Stankievech, "From Stethoscopes to Headphones: An Acoustic Spatialization of Subjectivity," *Leonardo Music Journal* (2007): 55–59, 57.

38. On the historical irony of the cognitivists reconstructing this aspect of Bartlett, see Johnston, "Repeated Reproduction," 348–351.

39. This subject's experience of listening in the laboratory diverged markedly from that of the sophisticated concertgoers nineteenth-century psychophysicists used to discriminate tones. Alexandra Hui, *The Psychophysical Ear: Musical Experiments, Experimental Sounds, 1840–1910*. Cambridge, MA: MIT Press, 2013.

40. Broadbent, "A Mechanical Model for Human Attention and Immediate Memory," *Psychological Review* 64, no. 3 (1957): 205–215, 205.

basis.[41] Broadbent embraced the cybernetic concept of information processing for similar reasons. Cybernetics allowed him to consider the organism's internal states while remaining agnostic as to their material qualities.[42] In 1957, he explained: "The framing of psychological theories in terms of information flow does not commit us to any particular physiological mechanism, but it does leave the way open for a future filling it of detail when the neighbouring science becomes as advanced as we are."[43] Cybernetics provided psychologists with "an objective language for discussing events within the nervous system," a language "amenable to physiology without speculating in that science."[44] In terms of local institutional politics, information theory allowed the APU to preserve a domain separate from Zangwill's neurologically-oriented department.

A similar evasion of speculative neurology characterized Broadbent's *Perception and Communication*, published on both sides of the Atlantic the following year.[45] In this work he expanded on his "filter theory" of attention by redescribing human behavior using "terms originally developed for telephone engineering."[46] Tenuously employed and perhaps mindful of potential career prospects in psychology-rich America, he couched his analysis in the language of behaviorism, taking their key concepts (e.g., reinforcement, extinction) and challenging their validity in light of his experimental data and information theory. Rather than localize mental activity to specified brain regions, he schematized information processing in terms of "box and arrow" diagrams borrowed from mechanical engineering of complex communication systems.[47] Grounded in applied work on human performance, Broadbent conceded his was a "non-positivist approach" that "attempts to find out what happens inside the organism."[48] Such a perspective came easily to him "[o]wing perhaps to the accident that psychologists working on hearing

41. Broadbent, "Mechanical Model," 209–210.

42. When writing in more popular venues, Broadbent (or at least his editors) more readily made references to the brain. See Broadbent, "Attention and the Perception of Speech," *Scientific American*, 206, no. 4 (1962): 143–153.

43. Broadbent, "Information Theory and Older Approaches in Psychology," *Proceedings of the 15th International Congress of Psychology, Belgium* (1957):111–115, 114.

44. Broadbent, "Information Theory and Older Approaches in Psychology," 115.

45. On the importance of this publication strategy, see Broadbent, "Donald E. Broadbent," in Gardner Lindzey, *A History of Psychology in Autobiography* vol. 7. New York: Freeman, 1980, 39–73, 60.

46. Broadbent, *Perception and Communication*. Oxford: Pergamon Press, 1958, 36.

47. On the flowchart as model in cognitive science, see Joseph Dumit, "Plastic Diagrams: Circuits in the Brain and How They Got There" in David Bates and Nima Bassiri (eds.), *Plasticity and Pathology: On the Formation of the Neural Subject*. New York: Fordham University Press, 2016, 219–268.

48. Broadbent, *Perception and Communication*, 302

are naturally those in closest contact with telephone engineers."[49] Broadbent's version of cybernetics owed more to his immersion in the practical and material couplings of humans and machines rather than mathematical models.[50] He stated his principles qualitatively rather than as quantitative laws.

Among the new ideas suggested by information theory, a single one stood out for Broadbent: *capacity*, "a term representing the limiting quantity of information which can be transmitted through a given channel in a given time."[51] Where Bartlett had emphasized the mind's reconstructive powers, Broadbent focused on its failures. He envisioned the nervous system "as a single communication channel, so that it is meaningful to regard it as having a limited capacity."[52] The filtering mechanism served the needs of the nervous system as "an economical way of keeping down the amount of information passed through the main part of the mechanism."[53] It selected a single signal worthy of processing, discarding its competitors. Tasked by the Navy with understanding their noisy environments, Broadbent understood certain physical features (namely, a sound's intensity, pitch, and spatial localization) as the primary criteria for selecting a potential input for further consideration.[54]

Broadbent ignored how the potential semantic *meaning* carried by a signal affected its processing. In 1953, the telecommunications engineer Colin Cherry highlighted this neglect. Like Broadbent, Cherry had close ties to the military and an interest in cybernetics, having spent the war on radar research, but he illustrated this problem with an experience drawn from civilian life.[55] Cherry asked the reader to imagine themselves at that icon of midcentury sophistication, the cocktail party. Born out of American Prohibition, such happenings eschewed the stiff formality of the sit-down dinner in favor of an early evening, mixed-sex gathering centered around drink, wit, and gossip.[56] The din created by such conversations presented partygoers with a cognitive challenge; namely, "how do we recognize what one person is saying when others are speaking at the same

---

49. Broadbent, *Perception and Communication*, 5.

50. On the retention of "information" as a metaphor in cognitive psychology while jettisoning its mathematical underpinnings, see Alan Collins, "From $H=log\,sn$ to Conceptual Framework," 60.

51. Broadbent, *Perception and Communication*, 5.

52. Broadbent, *Perception and Communication*, 297.

53. Broadbent, *Perception and Communication*, 41.

54. Broadbent, *Perception and Communication*, 297.

55. Cherry became interested in the human factors in designing communication systems following a six-month visit to MIT in 1952 where he encountered the psychologist George Miller and the linguistic Roman Jakobson. See Carol Wilder, "A Conversation with Colin Cherry," *Human Communication Research* 3, no. 4 (1977): 354–362, 355.

56. See "The Cocktail Party: Hurrah?" *Life*, December 2, 1957, 134–142; Helen Markel, "How to Mix a Cocktail Party," *New York Times Magazine*, November 2, 1958, 15.

time?"[57] With this evocative example, Cherry shifted the problem of attention from the dutiful watchkeeper to the half-bored socialite seeking out the life of the party. A simple substitution, it underscored the very different ends for which human sought information.

Research into Cherry's "cocktail party problem" using meaningful messages on the dichotic listening task soon became a fixture of British experimental psychology. This research, also supported by MRC but through graduate fellowships, came from a younger generation that did not share the APU leadership's experience of military deployment. Their experiments tested civilians and demonstrated that when participants closely shadowed a message, "affective cues" broadcast on the secondary radio channel, like the person's own name, easily crossed the recognition threshold.[58] This contradicted the filter theory which posited that such a signal would quickly decay unanalyzed. In the 1960s, Oxford psychologist Anne Treisman proposed a significant revision to Broadbent's theory in light of the surprising fate of the "unattended message," arguing that "the channel filter attenuates irrelevant messages rather than blocks them completely."[59] British psychologists' fascination with the cocktail party effect spoke to the expansiveness of their cybernetic ambitions, their willingness to reconceptualize any mundane situation into the flow of information. As automation became a pressing political concern in the 1960s, the APU expanded beyond the militarized arrangements that originally sustained it.

GENTLEMEN OR PLAYERS?

Born out of wartime necessity, a unit dedicated to applied research fit uneasily within the academic culture of Cambridge. Its colleges, long the preserve of the clergy and gentry, played a central role in reproducing an antimaterialist nationalism that defined the English character as conservative, rustic, slow-moving and opposed to industry. In the postwar years, Oxbridge continued to embrace an ethos that married aristocratic values to those of professional service. The don served as a "moral gentleman" who formed the student's character through a liberal education that disparaged commercial careers and profit-making as philistine

---

57. E. Colin Cherry, "Some Experiments on the Recognition of Speech, with One and with Two Ears," *The Journal of the Acoustical Society of America* 25, no. 5 (1953): 975–979, 975–976.

58. Neville Moray, "Attention in Dichotic Listening: Affective Cues and the Influence of Instructions," *Quarterly Journal of Experimental Psychology* 11, no. 1 (1959): 56–60; Anne M. Treisman, "Contextual Cues in Selective Listening," *Quarterly Journal of Experimental Psychology* 12, no. 4 (1960): 242–248; C. I. Howarth and K. Ellis, "The Relative Intelligibility Threshold for One's own Name Compared with Other Names," *Quarterly Journal of Experimental Psychology* 13, no. 4 (1961): 236–239.

59. Anne M. Treisman, "Selective Attention in Man," *British Medical Bulletin* 20, no. 1 (1964): 12–16, 14.

pursuits. The Oxbridge man's role was to tame and civilize the forces set loose by industrialization.[60]

Rather than heralding a posthuman future, the APU's gentlemanly cybernetics reflected this English ambivalence about rapid technological change.[61] Although both Broadbent and Conrad served as founding members of the Ergonomics Research Society, a group dedicated to harmonizing men and machines, the anti-industrial ethos of Oxbridge continued manifesting itself within the Unit. It took shape in the recurring debate over how to balance the priorities of practical versus theoretical research. Drawing on his own vocabulary as a vision researcher, Mackworth described the successful balancing of the practical and the abstract as the Unit's "stereoscopic outlook."[62] Such an approach was not without its tensions. Members of the Unit made the distinction between "gentlemen" looking for recognition from the medieval university and "players" looking to have a practical impact on government policy and the management of industry. Given the MRC's mandate, Unit members could and should pursue both roles. However, Mackworth worried about where the Unit's "players" might come from, as academic men preferred "the scientific prestige that comes from the publication of basic scientific papers."[63]

As director, Broadbent continued this trend of conceptualizing the Unit's mission of domesticating work with advanced machines. His first report to the MRC described the APU's remit as dealing "with measurable aspects of human intellectual and manual performances under normal conditions, and also under a range of unusual environmental conditions." Despite reporting to the medical council, the Unit took the healthy, able-bodied, capable individual, "a man doing a job," as its primary object of analysis. Broadbent then divided this activity into four aspects, each illuminated by a different set of experiments: (1) "the background conditions of work"; (2) "the stimulus striking the senses"; (3) "the internal operations performed on this information"; and (4) "the execution of actions once they have been chosen."[64] In Broadbent's hands, psychology could both illuminate and augment skilled work with machines.

---

60. On the Victorian origins of this ethos, see Martin J. Wiener, *English Culture and the Decline of the Industrial Spirit, 1850–1980*. Cambridge: Cambridge University Press, 1981/200Fi4, 22–24.

61. Gentlemanly signifies the gendered and classed position of these psychologists. Rather than heralding transhumanism, their cybernetics, like Norbert Wiener's, concerned itself with "the human use of human beings." Liberal and humane, it was also distinct from the socialist planning described in Eden Medina, *Cybernetic Revolutionaries: Technology and Politics in Allende's Chile*. Cambridge, MA: MIT Press, 2011.

62. Mackworth to Harold Himsworth, January 5, 1958, FD 1/8618: Unit Re-organization, 1957–1983, National Archives.

63. Mackworth to Harold Himsworth, January 5, 1958, FD 1/8618: Unit Re-organization, 1957–1983, National Archives. The dichotomy between gentlemen and players had a long life within the Unit. See Broadbent, "Psychologists: Gentlemen or Players," *Bulletin of the British Psychological Society* 26, no. 91 (1973): 134–135.

64. APU Progress Report, 1954–1960, p. 4. Digitized versions of the APU's periodic progress reports to the MRC have been posted to the Unit's history page. http://www.mrc-cbu.cam.ac.uk/history/digital-archive/progress-reports

It was not simply the applied nature of the work that generated concerns, but the particular clients. Broadbent's acoustics research dovetailed with military needs, but others were less sanguine about these arrangements. In 1957, Conrad complained to the MRC that theoretically, interesting problems "have on occasion effectively been blocked because they could not be made to fit in current military requirements." Moreover, he worried about how military patronage shaped the Unit's reputation. "An impression is created that we are a para-military group, and our dependence on the Services makes us vulnerable to the effects of events which have nothing to do with science."[65] Such a reliance came at a cost. At the start of Broadbent's tenure as director, the APU staff included "engineers, Navy men and others whose scientific calibre in this field has not been particularly high." Their presence further distanced the Unit from the academic department. The Navy's provisions of experimental participants came with the demand that the Unit prioritize its projects. "Should the Navy or the Services for any reason cut off the supply, the unit would virtually cease to exist."[66] As Broadbent would later ruefully observe, relying on this sole client was a risky bet in an era of decolonization as "British defense budgets were, in the long run, likely to get tighter, since the country was already embarked on the incredible operation of liquidating the largest empire in history in the shortest time on record."[67] The largesse of the British "warfare state" allowed the APU to flourish, but its generosity always risked wavering.[68]

Overreliance on defense contracts became a more immediate concern after Harold Wilson's Labour government assumed office in 1964. His "white heat of the technological revolution" speech (1963) had promised to modernize Britain by creating a meritocratic society through automation and a greater investment in science. Overall, Wilson's government did increase spending on science and education, but it also altered priorities when it came to research and development in technology. Labour policy redirected funding away from the military and aviation projects supported by the Conservatives during the early phases of the Cold War.[69] This realignment of priorities toward the civilian branches of government targeted the very sector where the APU had its strongest connections.

Fortunately, Conrad had already been leading the APU's efforts to cultivate more civilian clients. This research addressed the problems of an automating society as telecommunication technologies extended beyond military personnel and became a mundane aspect of work and daily life. Instead of a militarized

65. Conrad to Himsworth, November 6, 1957, FD 1/8618: Unit Re-organization, 1957–1983, National Archives.

66. "Memorandum on Visit to the Applied Psychology Research Unit, Cambridge, 20th December 1960," FD 12/397, National Archives.

67. Broadbent, "Autobiography," 62.

68. On the expansion of governmental services through the pursuit of war, see David Edgerton, *Warfare State: Britain, 1920–1970*. Cambridge: Cambridge University Press, 2005.

69. David Edgerton, "The 'White Heat' Revisited: The British Government and Technology in the 1960s," *Twentieth Century British History* 7, no. 1 (1996): 53–82.

psychology, Conrad envisioned a psychology dedicated to the "interaction between the public and, generally, State-run complex technological systems."[70] As he noted, "[d]istant communication between people by letter or voice touches everyone." The universality of these communications systems necessitated the accessibility of their design so "that everyone understands how to use it, and is able to do so."[71] In practice, studying the United Kingdom's emerging computerized sector entailed collaborating with the civil service and nationalized industries, testing the abilities of a largely femininized yet unionized workforce.[72]

In the mid-1950s, Conrad began a long-standing collaboration with the General Post Office (GPO) focused on how workers and publics managed information loads.[73] Because the Department of State served as both the nation's mail service and telecommunications provider, working with the Post Office furnished Conrad with unique opportunities for studying everyday cognition. The GPO management had taken a keen interest in automation. In 1948, they hired a consultant physiologist and started an inhouse journal "to promote and extend knowledge of the operation and management of telecommunications." After a 1955 Royal Commission recommended civil servants' pay should be comparable to those in private industry, the GPO turned to "an intensive programme of mechanisation" to recoup the new labor costs.[74] Automation required mediating among the capacities and needs of workers, machines, and customers. Harmonizing these relations would ensure the smooth flow of the nation's information.

Sensitive to the needs of the user, Conrad's cybernetic ergonomics nevertheless adopted the managerial standpoint. A 1958 study, negotiated in advance with Union of Post Office Workers, assessed the level of traffic the telephonists operating the switchboard exchange could best handle. Too little traffic resulted in idle workers, but too much created logjams with prolonged wait times and abandoned calls.[75] The existing management and vocational literatures depicted the

---

70. R. Conrad, "Beyond Industrial Psychology," *Bulletin of the British Psychological Society* 20 (1967): 1–12, 12.

71. Conrad, "Experimental Psychology in the Field of Telecommunications," *Ergonomics* 3, no. 4 (1960): 289–295, 294.

72. Marie Hicks, *Programmed Inequality: How Britain Discarded Women Technologists and Lost Its Edge in Computing*. Cambridge, MA: MIT Press, 2017.

73. R. Conrad, "Performance of Telephone Operators Relative to Traffic Level." *Nature* 178, no. 4548 (1956): 1480–1481; R. Conrad and Barbara A. Hille, "Memory for Long Telephone Numbers," *Post Office Telecommunications Journal* 10 (1957): 37–39; R. Conrad, "Accuracy of Recall Using Keyset and Telephone Dial, and the Effect of a Prefix Digit." *Journal of Applied Psychology* 42, no. 4 (1958): 285–288.

74. *Post Office: Report and Commercial Accounts, 1957–1958*. London: Her Majesty's Stationary Office, 1958, 4.

75. R. Conrad and Barbara A. Hille. "Telephone Operators' Adaptation to Traffic Variations," *The Journal of the Institution of Electrical Engineers* 4 (1958): 10–14.

telephonist's work as tedious and repetitive, unskilled much like clerical work.[76] Except for a brief interlude after World War I when it employed veterans, the GPO exclusively hired young women, preferably still in their teens, as a cost-saving measure. Office matrons sought well-mannered, well-spoken "girls," preferably without previous employment, seeing them as being more malleable. These were poorly paid, short-term positions with little to no room for promotion. Young and necessarily single due to the Marriage Bar for Civil Service Workers, telephonists soon developed a reputation for frivolity and irresponsibility.[77] Unionized, these workers made modest gains as a result of their wartime service, but management continued to depict them as female obstacles in the smooth running of the nation's communication system.[78]

Conrad, finding that increased traffic had led to decreased operating time per call, concluded that "a substantial decrease in staff could be tolerated, without infringing [on] G.P.O. standard of service."[79] His GPO commission also led to research on "acoustic confusion" where Conrad examined the misrecollection of letters presented visually. Rather than being random errors due to the noise predicted by information theory, the mistakes largely stemmed from phonetic similarities.[80] Unlike the dominant image of these workers, Conrad presented operation of the exchange as a cognitively demanding task. His experiments quantified and measured the skill involved in this mental work. When it came to what cognitive labor was required, the feminine telephonist proved to be not so different from the masculine watchkeeper.[81]

Automation also transformed the GPO's other great responsibility, the seemingly more traditional mail service. With Britons posting approximately 9.7

---

76. Brenda Maddox, "Women and the Switchboard," in Ithiel de Sola Pool (ed.), *The Social Impact of the Telephone*. Cambridge, MA: MIT Press, 1977, 262–280; Kenneth Lipartito," When Women Were Switches: Technology, Work, and Gender in the Telephone Industry, 1890–1920," *American Historical Review* 99, no. 4 (1994): 1075–1111; Jennifer S. Light, "When Computers Were Women," *Technology and Culture* 40, no. 3 (1999): 455–483; Venus Green, *Race on the Line: Gender, Labor, and Technology in the Bell System, 1880–1980*. Durham, NC: Duke University Press, 2001.

77. Venus Green, "Race, Gender, and National Identity in the American and British Telephone Industries," *International Review of Social History* 46, no. 2 (2001): 185–205, 191–197.

78. Reforms included the repeal of the Marriage Ban in 1946. See Mark James Crowley, "Women Post Office Workers in Britain: The Long Struggle for Gender Equality and the Positive Impact of World War II," *Essays in Economic and Business History* 30 (2012): 77–92.

79. R. Conrad, "Experimental Psychology in the Field of Telecommunications," *Ergonomics* 3, no. 4 (1960): 289–295, 293.

80. R. Conrad and Audrey J. Hull, "Information, Acoustic Confusion and Memory Span," *British Journal of Psychology* 55, no. 4 (1964): 429–432.

81. Conrad assumed both female telephonists and male naval ratings would remember long spans of digits better than the national average; see Conrad, "Experimental Psychology in the Field of Telecommunications," 290.

billion letters per year in the late 1950s, the Post Office sought to introduce new technologies to rationalize their sorting and handling.[82] In 1959, Conrad began consulting on a pilot study using alphanumeric postcodes to demarcate delivery locations.[83] Any code needed to balance the demands of their efficient input into a computerized sorting system with the public's ability to recall these unfamiliar codes. In collaboration with his PhD student Alan Baddeley, Conrad translated research on information processing and the span of human memory to evaluate the design.[84] The pair recommended a code broken into two distinct chunks with components conveying meaningful information about the intended destination.[85]

Conrad's efforts to expand the APU's clientele proved successful. In 1960, the Royal Navy ranked first among the Unit's clients, accounting for approximately 50 percent of the work commissioned along with provisioning the necessary research subjects and equipment. A decade later, the Navy's proportion of contracted work had fallen to under 15 percent. This represented a relative decline rather than an absolute one. Broadbent insisted that it resulted from queries from an increasing variety of civilian clients rather than from a "falling demand from the Services, who have in some ways more pressing human problems than those met in days of simple equipment and more readily available manpower."[86] A wide swath of ordinary Britons now found themselves in cybernetic couplings of complex systems once unique to the war machine.[87] Conrad suggested the term "engineering psychology" to encompass this expansive line of research, extending well beyond the industrial factory and its workforce. Such a field would focus on "the behavior and abilities of people in an operating relationship to machines, equipment and larger technologically purposive systems."[88]

A 1971 documentary *With Man in Mind* staged the APU's gentlemanly cybernetics for the public. Long-time APU associate Muriel Woodhead directed the film (an inhouse production), and psychologist John Morton provided the

---

82. *Post Office: Report and Commercial Accounts, 1958–1959*. London: Her Majesty's Stationary Office, 1959, 3.

83. K. S. Holmes, "Ergonomics in the Post Office," *Conference on Ergonomics in Industry*. London: Her Majesty's Stationary Office, 1961, 90–91.

84. A. D. Baddeley, R. Conrad, and W. E. Thomson. "Letter Structure of the English Language," *Nature* 186, no. 4722 (1960): 414–416.

85. R. Conrad, "Designing Postal Codes for Public Use," *Ergonomics* 10, no. 2 (1967): 233–238.

86. APU Progress Report, 1964–1970, p. 4. Digitized versions of the APU's periodic progress reports to the MRC have been posted to the Unit's history page. http://www.mrc-cbu.cam.ac.uk/history/digital-archive/progress-reports

87. This fit the American pattern of social scientists moving from military to civilian patrons. See Mark Solovey, *Shaky Foundations: The Politics-Patronage-Social Science Nexus in Cold War America*. New Brunswick, NJ: Rutgers University Press, 2013; Heyck, *Age of System*, 51–80.

88. R. Conrad, "Beyond Industrial Psychology," *Bulletin of the British Psychological Society* 20 (1967): 1–12, 4.

score. The subject matter dealt exclusively with civilian life, emphasizing the everydayness of cognition in tasks such as dodging motor traffic, reading fine print, and working knobs and levers. Consisting of a rather dull series of lectures intercut with images of the domestic lives of white, middle-class Britons, the film repeatedly returned to the APU's central theme of the duality of human cognition. As Broadbent explained in the film's opening, omnipresent "human error" came at an increasingly high cost in a technological society. At the same time, he reminded viewers that "the human mind is thoughtful, imaginative, efficient, and remarkably versatile and flexible."[89] Speaking again to the camera at the film's conclusion, Broadbent declared his discipline necessary for taming the computer in the automating society. Psychology alone could "ensure the new technology is suited to human limitations, takes man into account, and enriches life instead of spoiling it."[90] An automating society was not an automated one. The APU's gentlemanly cybernetics flourished at the gaps between the everyday life and novel communications technologies, in the errors resulting from the persistent mismatch between people and machines. Midcentury neo-behaviorists had made the *automatic* telephone switchboard a central metaphor for the bodily wiring underlying their stimulus–response psychology.[91] Such automation was in progress in postwar Britain but was far from complete. The living telephonists Conrad studied were not mindless automata, but active, imperfect (and unionized) processors of information. As opposed the neo-behaviorist imagining of the automated switchboard, the cognitive psychology of the APU grew out of the mental work needed to make these human–machine couplings function in practice.

THE DREGS OF MEMORY

Despite these successes in embedding the APU into the computerization of British society, the Unit underwent a rather dramatic change in orientation after Alan Baddeley assumed the directorship in 1974. Although at the time of his application he was a professor at Stirling University, Baddeley came to the APU very much as an insider. He had received his PhD under Conrad and had worked as a researcher with the group between 1957 and 1966. Reflecting this experience, his application for the directorship noted "the trend from military to civilian applications" when it came to the kind of projects the APU undertook. Acknowledging this trend, Baddeley proposed that education should serve as the new focus for the Unit's activities. Pursuing applied research in this area would maintain the APU's historical strengths "in the fields of human information processing and of human

---

89. *With Man in Mind*, 0:45-1:30 http://www.mrc-cbu.cam.ac.uk/history/video

90. *With Man in Mind*, 14:30 http://www.mrc-cbu.cam.ac.uk/history/video

91. A wired, "automatic switchboard" showed how the organism "routes and distributes the impulses to individual muscles and glands in rather precisely graded amounts and sequences." Clark Hull, *Principles of Behavior*. New York: Appleton-Century-Crofts, 1943, 18.

performance under stress." Education fit especially well with his own expertise in memory and learning. He suggested that "our theoretical tools are probably now sufficiently developed to be usefully applied to the analysis of skills such as those involved [in] reading and arithmetic." For example, he felt the time was now ripe to bridge "our laboratory-bound concepts of long-term memory and the practical problem of teaching."[92] Education would allow the Unit to maintain its existing theoretical orientation and methods while opening the group to a host of potential new customers.

However, the Medical Research Council rejected his proposed focus on the grounds that it conflicted with the mandate of other funding bodies, namely, the Social Science Research Council (founded in 1965).[93] The necessity of different research councils to keep to their mandate was very much a live concern by 1974. After the Conservatives regained control of Parliament in 1970, they undertook a major review of the government's research and development policy. The resulting Rothschild Report (1971) proposed reorganizing support on a "customer-contractor" model. Transferring money for applied research from the scientific councils to the relevant government departments would "free" scientists to enter competitive bids to meet current governmental needs.[94] The Royal Society objected to the Report as an attack on the academic community's ability to decide its own research priorities, but newly appointed Secretary of State for Education Margaret Thatcher ultimately backed the recommendations for marketizing state functions.[95] In the wake of these developments, the MRC spoke defensively about the perceived gap between the projects it supported and the immediate needs of the Department of Health.[96] The heightened scrutiny following the Rothschild Report undoubtedly contributed to the MRC's reluctance to accept education as the APU's main focus.

Faced with this unexpected opposition to his original plan, Baddeley opted instead to organize research around neuropsychology. This alternative easily fit within the scope of the MRC, but it posed significant challenges. Namely, none of the APU affiliates expressed much interest in the topic. The practical problems suggested by human–machine interactions did not require this level of analysis and local institutional politics discouraged Unit members from adopting such a perspective. Indeed, psychologists at the APU lacked access to persons with cognitive deficits, a prerequisite for conducting neuropsychological studies in the

---

92. Alan Baddeley, "A Proposed Scientific Program for the Applied Psychology Unit, Cambridge" FD 7/972, National Archives.

93. Alan Baddeley, *Working Memories: Postmen, Divers and the Cognitive Revolution*. London: Routledge, 2018, 183–184.

94. *A Framework for Government Research and Development*. London: Her Majesty's Stationary Office, 1971.

95. Jon Agar, "Thatcher, Scientist," *Notes and Records of the Royal Society* 65, no. 3 (2011): 215–232.

96. M. F. Perutz, "Health and the Medical Research Council," *Nature* 235 (1972): 191–192.

1970s. The local teaching hospital, Addenbrooke's, was particularly weak in this area.[97] In other words, the turn to neuroscience did not represent an immediate extension evolution of the APU's theoretical interests, nor did it derive from the practical problems presented to them by any of their clients. Nor was it born out of strict necessity. Broadbent's 1970 report at the MRC noted the trend toward civilian clients, but he emphasized that military contracts still provided an adequate source of both financial support and problems worthy of investigation. Instead, the changes Baddeley instituted represented a pragmatic appeal to make the Unit's mission more legible to its patron the MRC at a time of political upheaval surrounding science funding.

Baddeley credited the clinical psychologist and a friend from their student days, Elizabeth Warrington, for inspiring this change in direction. Warrington had introduced him "to the theoretical power of the neuropsychological study of patients."[98] In the late 1960s, she had approached Baddeley about a possible collaboration. He responded with skepticism, confident that neurological cases were "likely too complex to provide useful theoretical models." Deeming the gap between experimental psychology and the clinic too wide for a productive collaboration, Baddeley "replied that it seemed unlikely that they [the patients] would be obliging enough to have their lesions in theoretically interesting locations and declined."[99] Nevertheless, he eventually relented and traveled to London to observe Warrington's work on the floor of the National Hospital, Queen Square. Unfamiliar with the world of clinical medicine, he was impressed when on his first visit "an elderly lady who was densely amnesiac" easily performed the cognitive task he presented to her.[100] Rather than the stereotype of total memory loss, Warrington's amnesiac patients gradually forgot in a manner not dissimilar to that outlined by Ebbinghaus. This suggested to Warrington and Baddeley a viable and unique platform to investigate the relationship between short-term and long-term memory.[101]

At the time, Queen Square served as the "centre of calculation" in the UK for persons struggling with neurological problems.[102] Queen Square was the place for the rare case, the undiagnosed struggling with spatial, reading, or language

---

97. APU Oral History, 51.

98. APU Oral History, 23.

99. Baddeley, *Working Memories*, 117.

100. Baddeley, *Working Memories*, 117.

101. Alan D. Baddeley and Elizabeth K. Warrington, "Amnesia and the Distinction between Long-and Short-Term Memory," *Journal of Verbal Learning and Verbal Behavior* 9, no. 2 (1970): 176–189; Baddeley and Warrington, "Memory Coding and Amnesia," *Neuropsychologia* 11, no. 2 (1973): 159–165; Elizabeth K. Warrington and Alan D. Baddeley, "Amnesia and Memory for Visual Location," *Neuropsychologia* 12, no. 2 (1974): 257–263.

102. Bruno Latour, *Science in Action: How to Follow Scientists and Engineers through Society*. Cambridge, MA: Harvard University Press, 1987, 215–257.

difficulties. These patients often experienced severe memory loss combined with the preservation of other major intellectual functions. Their amnesia came in multiple forms. Many of the individuals Warrington assessed were alcoholics suffering from the memory loss associated with Korsakoff syndrome. Others included those saved by modern medicine from devastating road accidents. Finally, some were survivors of modern medicine itself, with amnesia of iatrogenic origin following the vogue for psychosurgery to treat mental illness during the 1950s.[103] These varied neurological patients became the experimental platform for building a new psychology of thinking.[104]

Warrington had spent her entire career at the hospital, starting as a mere research assistant in 1954.[105] After completing her doctorate under Zangwill at the Institute for Neurology in 1960, she accepted the position of clinical psychologist at Queen Square. Hers was a low-status position compared to traditional academic appointments. Tasked with assessment rather than treatment, as the clinical psychologist on the ward floor she flew beneath the radar of her neurologist colleagues.[106] Neglect by the medical men gave Warrington the latitude to pursue her own research interests. She initially worked in the pattern set by Zangwill, publishing in medical journals with neurologists as co-authors. Her articles consisted of detailed, individual, clinical case studies. She most frequently published with the Oxford neurologist Marcel Kinsbourne.[107] Following his emigration to the United States in 1967, her network of collaborators expanded considerably. Her unique access to neurological cases and her expertise in clever assessment soon made her a valued collaborator for a number of male psychologists who quickly became the discipline's leaders in Britain: namely, Lawrence Weiskrantz, Tim Shallice, and Baddeley.

At this time, Warrington broke with Zangwill's pattern of research and increasingly aligned clinical neuropsychology with the new cognitive psychology.[108] Her

---

103. L. Stephen Jacyna and Stephen T. Casper (eds.), *The Neurological Patient in History*. Rochester: University Rochester Press, 2012.

104. On the realignment of the clinical and the experimental in the late modern hospital creating new objects and epistemic arrangements, see Peter Keating and Alberto Cambrosio, *Biomedical Platforms: Realigning the Normal and the Pathological in Late-Twentieth-Century Medicine*. Cambridge, MA: MIT Press, 2003.

105. "Interview with Professor Elizabeth Warrington," *Queen Square Alumnus Association Newsletter* 12 (2018). https://www.ucl.ac.uk/ion/alumni/queen-square-alumnus-association-newsletter-issue-12/interview-prof-elizabeth-warrington. Accessed February 23, 2020.

106. Elizabeth Warrington interviewed by Richard Thomas, Today Neuroscience, Tomorrow's History: A Video Archive Project, 2008. http://www.histmodbiomed.org/sites/default/files/55969.pdf

107. Between 1961 and 1966, Warrington and Kinsbourne coauthored nineteen research papers.

108. The commissioned history of Queen Square speaks obliquely of their "strained" relationship by the 1960s. See Simon Shorvon and Alastair Compston, *Queen Square: A History of the National Hospital and Its Institute of Neurology*. Cambridge: Cambridge University Press, 2018, 361.

role at Queen Square was to devise and apply forms of assessment of the individual who was difficult to classify. Lacking reliable tools, she borrowed the tasks generated by the emerging field of cognitive psychology and adopted them for the purpose of clinical diagnosis. More significantly, she deliberately introduced elements of experimental design into her studies of amnesia.[109] Rather than collect individual cases, she compared the performance of *groups* of amnesiacs with those of controls. Furthermore, she systematically varied the number of learning trials and the interval between exposure and recall, both of which were classic manipulations in the experimental study of verbal learning.[110]

Experimental design rather than clinical observation allowed Warrington "to pick up the dregs of memory."[111] In a pair of articles appearing in *Nature*, she and Weiskrantz publicized a "new method" for studying the long-term retention of certain kinds of memories among patients with amnesia. They repurposed a series of cards originally designed by Eugene S. Gollin to assess the cognitive development of children.[112] A sequence of five cards consisted of a common word or image presented by gradations of completeness, with detail increasing as the series progressed. After familiarizing the participant with the nature of the cards, the psychologist tasked them with identifying a word or an image as early as possible in the sequence.[113] Using the Gollin cards, Warrington and Weiskrantz argued that "amnesic subjects are not so forgetful as was once thought." When assessing with typical protocols of free recall, the patients with amnesia forgot the previously presented list of words within minutes. In contrast, when assessed with the Gollin cards, the patients recognized at an earlier stage of incompleteness words from the memorized list compared to novel control stimuli. They retained memories they could not freely or consciously recall. In these patients, amnesiac syndrome became a matter of retrieval rather than a memory's presence or absence in the storehouse of the mind.[114]

Warrington and Weiskrantz proposed a fundamental reconceptualization of the relationship between mind and brain. The brain retained memories that the conscious mind could not recall. However, subtle hints could retrieve said

---

109. Collins, "Zangwill," 98.

110. Elizabeth K. Warrington and L. Weiskrantz, "A Study of Learning and Retention in Amnesic Patients," *Neuropsychologia* 6, no. 3 (1968): 283–291.

111. Elizabeth Warrington interviewed by Richard Thomas, Today Neuroscience, Tomorrow's History: A Video Archive Project, 2008, p. 7. http://www.histmodbiomed.org/sites/default/files/55969.pdf

112. Eugene S. Gollin, "Developmental Studies of Visual Recognition of Incomplete Objects," *Perceptual and Motor Skills* 11, no. 3 (1960): 289–298.

113. Elizabeth K. Warrington and Lawrence Weiskrantz, "New Method of Testing Long-Term Retention with Special Reference to Amnesic Patients," *Nature* 217, no. 5132 (1968): 972–974.

114. Elizabeth K. Warrington and Lawrence Weiskrantz. "Amnesic Syndrome: Consolidation or Retrieval?" *Nature* 228, no. 5272 (1970): 628–630, quotation 628.

memories without the mind's knowledge. This cuing phenomenon became known as semantic priming and soon became a fixture of in verbal learning studies. "Unconsciousness" was an unpalatable term due to its psychoanalytic overtone, so cognitive psychologists adopted the language of the "implicit" to talk about knowledge without awareness, and they credited Ebbinghaus rather than Freud with the discovery of this realm.[115]

Having remade clinical neuropsychology in the image of cognitive science, Warrington now offered Baddeley a path to remake cognition in the image of the clinical. Her patients modeled how much so-called cognitive activity occurred in the absence of conscious thought. By 1981, Baddeley outlined the progress made in realigning the normal and the pathological at the APU. Underlying the Unit's various empirical projects was a core set of theoretical concepts, namely, the assumption that "cognitive behaviour reflects the operation of a number of sub-systems, and to use experimentation to analyse such systems into component parts." Such a statement signaled a new readiness to integrate the study of neuro-anatomical structures into the group's broadly functionalist outlook. Inspiration for localizing cognitive function into specified fleshy parts came from clinical neuropsychology. Despite this new theoretical orientation, Baddeley insisted that the Unit had not become dedicated to clinical research under his direction. Instead, he insisted that "[o]ur approach however has been to use data from the breakdown of cognitive function in the brain damaged patient in order to understand normal cognition."[116]

THE THOUGHTLESS BRAIN

In contrast to these successes, the Unit's strengths in computational theory and methods waned throughout the 1980s, despite the growing ubiquity of computers in everyday life.[117] A 1984 report noted that "the Unit continues to have an active interest in the application of artificial intelligence to cognitive psychology," as exemplified by staff member Philip Johnson-Laird's work on mental models. However, the APU's historical leadership in this area was "unlikely to continue to

115. Henry L. Roediger, "Implicit Memory: Retention without Remembering," *American Psychologist* 45, no. 9 (1990): 1043–1056.

116. "MRC Applied Psychology Unit Progress Report 1978–1981 and Report of Visiting Subcommittee," October 1981, FD 7/2465, National Archives.

117. This mirrored Britain's contemporaneous lost leadership in the computing. See Hicks, *Programmed Inequality*, 189–224. On the importance of working with computers to models of cognitive rationality, see Nathan Ensmenger, "Is Chess the Drosophila of Artificial Intelligence? A Social History of an Algorithm." *Social Studies of Science* 42, no. 1 (2012): 5–30; Janet Martin-Nielsen, "'It Was All Connected': Computers and Linguistics in Early Cold War America" in Mark Solovey and Hamilton Cravens (eds)., *Cold War Social Science*. New York: Palgrave, 2012, pp. 63–78; Joy Rohde. "Pax Technologica: Computers, International Affairs, and Human Reason in the Cold War." *Isis* 108, no. 4 (2017): 792–813.

flourish unless up-to-date computing facilities can be made available."[118] By 1989, contact with advanced computers had almost entirely dissipated. Research in this area was deemed increasingly futile as "the technology changes so rapidly that particular systems become obsolete before they have been adequately studied."[119] In contrast, the 1994 progress report affirmed that "health-related problems present an ideal opportunity for applying and enriching cognitive psychology."[120] This report also outlined efforts to establish a neuropsychological rehabilitation group and what became the Cambridge Cognitive Neuroscience Research Panel to recruit patients as volunteers for the Unit's experimental program. Both expected to benefit from plans to expand the neuroimaging facilities at Addenbrooke's.[121]

Baddeley's revisions of his influential model of "working memory" illuminate how cognition got recast in light of clinical and neuropsychological problems. Immediately prior to assuming the directorship, he had authored the first version of his model with his colleague Graham Hitch. There they understood short-term memory in functionalist terms, seeing it as "a limited capacity work space which can be divided between storage and control processing demands."[122] Certainly finite in its capacity, the mind was also a highly plastic system capable of reallocating those limited resources to prioritize certain tasks. The 1974 model of this "cognitive workspace" posited the existence of three components to achieve these goals: a "central executive" which functioned as "an attentional control system" and two subsidiary systems under its supervision dedicated to the temporary storage of visuospatial and phonological information, respectively, dubbed as "slave systems."[123]

Baddeley and Hitch's 1974 model represented something of a culmination of APU cybernetics. The linguistic shift from "short-term" to "working" memory prioritized function over biological structure.[124] "Working memory" also reflected the daily organization of work that Baddeley and his mentor Conrad encountered in their frequent collaborations with the GPO which provided the basis for the most empirical detailed component, the phonological loop. Their cognitive workspace was likewise a hierarchically organized system of processes and control

118. APU Progress Report, 1981–1984, p. 1.

119. APU Progress Report, 1985–1989, p. 5.

120. APU Progress Report, 1990–1994, p. 3.

121. APU Progress Report, 1990–1994, p. 4, 8, 90.

122. Alan D. Baddeley and Graham Hitch, "Working Memory," in Gordon Bower (ed.), *Psychology of Learning and* Motivation, volume 8 (New York: Academic Press, 1974), 47–89, 76.

123. Baddeley, *Working Memories*, 157–158.

124. A similar move occurred in one of the classic contributions to the cognitive revolution, George A. Miller, Eugene Galanter, and Karl H. Pribram, *Plans and the Structure of Behavior*. New York: Henry Holt, 1960. Surprisingly, this work is not cited. Baddeley later claimed to have "briefly dipped into it but did not read it, preferring a less speculative and more closely evidenced-based approach." See Baddeley, *Working Memories*, 157.

technologies exemplifying high modernist social science with its bureaucratic worldview.[125] Their model also relied on how engineers visualized the world. Schematizing the cognitive workspace using a box-and-arrow diagram allowed the pair to abstain from "speculative neurology" as Broadbent repeatedly urged.

Immersion in engineering also led Baddeley and Hitch to misconstrue the human mind in telling ways. It pushed them toward more conventional spatial metaphors of memory as storage, undercutting the radicalism of Bartlett's understanding of remembering as active reconstruction. More troubling, they borrowed the term "slave systems" under the control of a central executive from computing, despite the language's insensitivity and ultimate inaccuracy. The metaphor came late to engineering, after the abolition of human slavery. In 1904, the Scottish astronomer David Gill first used this language to describe a time-keeping device he introduced to the observatory at Cape Town. His instrument consisted of pendulum checking the movements of a subservient gear-based clock without diminishing its own exact measure. The metaphor only became ubiquitous, however, following World War II when it traveled into cybernetically infused communication theory. The analogy appealed in this arena because it captured the autonomy and "intelligence" of certain kinds of machines and their ability to keep their extensions in check.[126] Baddeley would quietly abandon the master–slave language, "partly under pressure from advocates of political correctness." At the same time, he acknowledged that the metaphor conveyed the wrong message as "these subsystems can be used to control the executive, a helpful alliance rather than a slave's revolt."[127] Baddeley's sustained ignorance surrounding the political violence permeating his preferred metaphor represented a kind of privilege. His linguistic choice revealed the unspoken and unquestioned whiteness of cybernetics as a high modernist undertaking, as well as the fundamental homogeneity of the social world from which it derived. Adopting the engineer's standpoint promised distance from the messiness of human affairs. Instead, it enabled psychological theory to be ignorant but not innocent of human history. In a Britain grappling with the legacies of empire, American hegemony, and what immigration from its former colonies meant for national identity, it was perhaps no accident that this insulation manifested itself in an unintended but deeply racialized slip.[128]

125. Heyck, *Age of System*, 18–50.

126. Ron Eglash, "Broken Metaphor: The Master-Slave Analogy in Technical Literature," *Technology and Culture* 48, no. 2 (2007): 360–369.

127. Baddeley, *Working Memories*, 157–158.

128. Paul Gilroy, *'There Ain't No Black in the Union Jack': The Cultural Politics of Race and Nation*. Chicago: University of Chicago Press, 1991; Chris Waters, "'Dark Strangers' in Our Midst: Discourses of Race and Nation in Britain, 1947–1963," *Journal of British Studies* 36, no. 2 (1997): 207–238; Roberta E. Bivins, *Contagious Communities: Medicine, Migration, and the NHS in Post-war Britain*. New York: Oxford University Press, 2015.

In 1974, considerable experimental data supported the existence of their two separate visual and semantic systems, but the nature of the central executive remained nebulous. In this regard, Baddeley and Hitch were far from alone. When psychologists revived the notion of "selective vigilance" in the 1950s, their behaviorist colleagues questioned who or what agent was selecting the information before it was processed. Especially in reaction to the New Look movement, they suggested that such theories posited the existence of a homunculus—a miniature but willful person operating in the head by selecting and storing information before it reached consciousness. Psychologists tried to avoid such metaphysical assumptions. In his field-shaping book *Cognitive Psychology* (1967), the American psychologist Ulric Neisser tried to put the homunculus critique to rest. He argued that "the stored-program computer has provided us with an alternative possibility, in the form of the *executive routine*." Unlike the much-parodied homunculus, such a program "does not carry out the tests or the searches or the constructions which are the task of the subroutines, and it does not include the stored information which the subroutines use. Indeed, the executive may take only a small fraction of the computing time and space allotted to the program as a whole, and it need not contain any very sophisticated processes. Although there is a real sense in which it 'uses' the rest of the program and the stored information, this creates no philosophical difficulties; it is not using itself."[129]

Baddeley, though familiar with Neisser's convenient solution, backtracked from it during his time as APU director. Understood as an acting agent and the seat of consciousness, his executive more closely resembled a watchful corporate manager than an inanimate computer program. More a metaphorical promise than an empirical reality, the nature of the "central executive" became Baddeley's overriding concern. Midcentury theories of attention dealt with "how information from the world is selected, filtered, and made available to awareness." In contrast, Baddeley's central executive dealt with "action and the capacity to *manipulate* and *control* such information."[130] His 1989 progress report posited "the attentional control of action" as the organizing principle for both the mind and his Unit's own research activity. The central executive lay at the heart of human intentionality and explained the errors involved in such a practical activity as driving a car. Reconceptualizing the central executive as "executive functions," Baddeley followed neurologists in localizing the organization of the self in the brain's frontal lobes.[131] This realignment allowed him to study the homunculus's function through the disorganization of behavior resulting from specific neurological deficits.

In this matter, Baddeley was greatly assisted by his colleague Tim Shallice, another of Warrington's frequent collaborators. Not among Baddeley's original

---

129. Ulric Neisser, *Cognitive Psychology*. New York: Appleton, 1967, 281.

130. Baddeley, *Working Memories*, 252.

131. APU Progress Report, 1985–1989.

appointments, Shallice came from London's Institute of Neurology to join the APU staff as a senior grade scientist in 1978.[132] Along with American cognitive psychologist Donald Norman, Shallice developed a model of the central executive which they called the Supervisory Attention System (SAS). Their model posited a dual form of action-taking, one of them routinized, automatic, unconscious; and the other attentional, deliberate, the very stuff of consciousness. Shallice and Norman, like most cognitivists, started with the mind's limited capacity to process information. However, this limit did not signify that all human action proceeded serially. Everyday life showed how the vast majority of bodily activities ran smoothly, automatically even, in parallel. In contrast, deliberative attentional interventions occurred infrequently, "only in cases where the action sequences are ill-specified, or in situations that are judged to be critical or dangerous that deliberate attentional control is required."[133] They unapologetically returned consciousness (and its absence), what they boldly and unambiguously called "the will" to psychology.[134] Originally circulated as a working paper linked to Norman's Center for Human Information Processing at UC San Diego, the primary evidence for this dual process system derived from the neurological patients Shallice studied in London. Individuals with frontal lobe lesions found it difficult to correct "known" errors when tested on an assortment of cognitive tasks. Otherwise functional, they persisted in making poor decisions because of their inability to plan and learn from their mistakes despite their "awareness" of these errors.[135]

Baddeley likewise advanced his theory of the central executive through further collaborations with clinicians dealing with chronic rehabilitative care. With clinical neuropsychologist Barbara Wilson, he published a clinical case of dysexecutive syndrome based on a patient (RJ) housed at the Rivermead Rehabilitation Centre. RJ was a former engineer who suffered from hemorrhages in both of his frontal lobes following a car accident. Behaviorally, he experienced great difficulty in breaking away from an activity, even when he was aware that he was repeating certain errors.[136] Baddeley understood the RJ study as an intervention against reductionism. Neurologists spoke of such cases as suffering from "frontal lobe syndrome." Yet, executive functions were wholly modular, nor were they precisely localized in that region. Despite a new interest in neuroanatomical structures, Baddeley suggested that the functional description "dysexecutive syndrome" was

132. Starting in 1969, Warrington and Shallice co-authored over 30 papers together.

133. Donald A. Norman and Tim Shallice, "Attention to Action: Willed and Automatic Control of Behavior," *Center for Human Information Processing Technical Report* no. 99 (1980), 26.

134. Norman and Shallice, "Attention to Action," 24–25.

135. Timothy Shallice, "Specific Impairments of Planning," *Philosophical Transactions of the Royal Society of London. B, Biological Sciences* 298, no. 1089 (1982): 199–209.

136. Alan Baddeley and Barbara Wilson, "Frontal Amnesia and the Dysexecutive Syndrome," *Brain and Cognition* 7, no. 2 (1988): 212–230.

more apt.[137] The APU's focus had decidedly shifted from the competent worker completing tasks to the failures of organizational control found in patients.

This realignment with medicine and neuroscience was not unique to a generation of new arrivals at the APU. If anything, the career of Baddeley's former mentor underwent an even more pronounced transformation along these lines. The death of his wife in 1968 led Conrad to abandon both Cambridge and industrial ergonomics as he searched for more meaningful work. After a period of contemplative solitude, he requested a secondment (i.e., temporary assignment) to the Royal National Throat, Nose, and Ear Hospital where he could retrain.[138] Conrad intended to apply his expertise on acoustics and memory to the question of language acquisition among children born with profound hearing loss. He adapted his experimental techniques for assessing verbal learning to ascertain the medium of memory among the deaf. "Oralism"—the ideology that deaf persons ought to emulate the language of the hearing population through lip reading and hearing aids—dominated the education of these children, much to their detriment as Conrad found. His encounter with these schoolchildren pushed him to conceive of a verbal memory store filled not with the traces of auditory sounds, but with written words, fingerspellings, and hand gestures.[139] By 1979, he emerged as a leading proponent of sign language and more importantly of "let[ting] the children choose." In his role of advocate, Conrad insisted that "we have to start with the brain," a stance notably at odds with earlier APU pronouncements. Drawing upon neurolinguistics, he argued that the developing child experienced a "critical period" (until the age of seven) in which neuroplasticity allowed for the inborn disposition toward language acquisition to develop. Enforcing oralist norms that condemned sign as "crude" and "repulsive" gestures, inferior to the richness of the spoken word, ignored the complex medium of these children's minds. Moreover, the delays it introduced unnecessarily narrowed the developmental window. The hearing's prejudicial equation of language with sound disadvantaged these children when they were at their most vulnerable.[140]

Conrad's career change sprang from a painful, personal experience, but his new interest also reflected a changing understanding of health and disability among psychologists and policymakers. As Warrington had done with the patients at Queen Square, Conrad demonstrated that individuals previously deemed defective possessed sophisticated cognitive systems. Their minds could accomplish much if accommodated on their own terms. This recognition, with its fundamentally

137. Alan Baddeley, "Exploring the Central Executive," *Quarterly Journal of Experimental Psychology Section A* 49, no. 1 (1996): 5–28.

138. He published a brief collaboration in this area in 1965, but it became his primary focus after 1970. Dorothy Bishop, "Quality and Longevity," *The Psychologist* 29, no. 7 (2016): 578–579.

139. R. Conrad, "Short-Term Memory Processes in the Deaf," *British Journal of Psychology* 61, no. 2 (1970): 179–195.

140. R. Conrad, "Let the Children Choose," *International Journal of Pediatric Otorhinolaryngology* 1, no. 4 (1980): 317–329, 327.

anti-eugenic stance, coincided with a time when persons with disabilities were asserting their political rights in new ways. In 1970, Parliament passed the Chronically Sick and Disabled Persons Act, which placed new obligations on local authorities to make accessibility provisions. Like the community care movement in the United States, the Act marked a move away from segregating people with disabilities in exclusionary institutions toward designing public space and services to maximize access. An incomplete project in the 1970s, the Act created a political vocabulary to assist persons with disabilities in asserting their rights and live their lives on their own terms. The scientists at the APU stood mainly as witnesses to this self-advocacy, but it shaped the research they conducted in profound ways.[141]

The APU's increased dependence on hospitals also reflected the political economy of research under Margaret Thatcher. By the 1980s, the beleaguered NHS remained one of the few nationalized industries, the kind of contractors APU had always found most amenable, whether military or civilian. The NHS also represented the last bastion of the postwar welfare state, one that continued to shape Britons' daily lives.[142] Indeed, pride in the NHS became a respectable form of "banal nationalism" across the political aisle.[143] The singular health service's unique centrality meant it provided the last refuge for ordinary Britons to make demands on the state. The rise of neuropsychology and its attendant medicalization of cognitive psychology represented a tacit acknowledgment of this new political reality.

These encounters fundamentally recast the kind of questions the APU psychologists posed. When first proposed in 1974, the central executive was a deliberately amorphous catchall, an unspecified diagram box, a blank space in the mind. Baddeley posited it to help make sense of the action undertaken by the so-called peripheral slave systems, which constituted the bulk of his empirical investigations.[144] The executive itself was central but experimentally intractable and so uninteresting. It signified the presence of obvious but vaguely defined mind-stuff. Once posited, however, the central executive acquired a life of its own. It proved a seductive metaphor. By the 1990s, Shallice, Baddeley, and others returned to the seemingly discredited Victorian notion of the will and made it a core principle of the new cognitive neuroscience.[145] This attentive, controlling, conscious will was not only spatialized but localized in certain neurological substrates, certain caveats

141. Alex Mold, *Making the Patient-Consumer: Patient Organisations and Health Consumerism in Britain*. Manchester: Manchester University Press, 2016.

142. Jennifer Crane, "'Save Our NHS': Activism, Information-Based Expertise and the 'New Times' of the 1980s," *Contemporary British History* 33, no. 1 (2019): 52–74.

143. Michael Billig, *Banal Nationalism*. Thousand Oaks: Sage, 1995.

144. Robert H. Logie, "Retiring the Central Executive," *Quarterly Journal of Experimental Psychology* 69, no. 10 (2016): 2093–2109.

145. Robert Kugelmann, "Willpower," *Theory and Psychology* 23, no. 4 (2013): 479–498.

notwithstanding.[146] If not a betrayal of postwar APU cybernetics, it did represent a significant departure in terms of theory, practice, and priorities.

In large part because of the spreading computerization studied by the APU at midcentury, attention had become an acute matter of concern in postindustrial societies.[147] Baddeley's neuralization of executive (dys)function became a hallmark of the cognitive "epidemics" of late modernity: attention deficit disorder, autism spectrum disorder, and even depression.[148] In the new millennium, business theorists began talking about an "attention economy" and the challenge of capturing people's eyeballs amid the proliferation of entertaining technologies.[149] Baddeley came to understand his cognitive workspace as less hierarchically organized than he previously assumed, mirroring the shift from the bureaucratized midcentury nationalized industry to the more flexible workplaces of late modernity. In light of these studies, he added a new component, the episodic buffer, to his working memory model to account for this new awareness of awareness's importance.[150] He ceased referring to the phonological loop and visuospatial sketchpad as "slave systems" as "these subsystems can be used to control the executive, a helpful alliance rather than a slave's revolt."[151] Being more flexible, the central executive became synonymous with psychologists' conception of the self. Executive functions encompassed the individual's ability to focus, divide, and switch their attention when completing complex tasks.[152] Attentional action was scarce, but this very scarcity made it invaluable. Attention became the very locus of human agency in a distracted world, a moralized homunculus to manage the self's most challenging tasks.[153]

146. Alan Baddeley, "Working Memory and Conscious Awareness," in Alan F. Collins, Susan E. Gathercole, Martin A. Conway, and Peter E. Morris (eds.), *Theories of Memory*. New York: Psychology Press, 1993, 11–28.

147. Herbert Simon, "Designing Organizations for an Information-Rich World," in Martin Greenberger (ed.), *Computers, Communications, and the Public Interest*. Baltimore: Johns Hopkins University Press, 1971, 37–52.

148. Andrew Lakoff, "Adaptive Will: The Evolution of Attention Deficit Disorder." *Journal of the History of the Behavioral Sciences* 36, no. 2 (2000): 149–169; Gregory Hollin, "Constructing a Social Subject: Autism and Human Sociality in the 1980s," *History of the Human Sciences* 27, no. 4 (2014): 98–115.

149. Thomas H. Davenport and John C. Beck, *The Attention Economy: Understanding the New Currency of Business*. Cambridge, MA: Harvard Business Press, 2001.

150. Alan Baddeley, "The Episodic Buffer: A New Component of Working Memory?" *Trends in Cognitive Sciences* 4, no. 11 (2000): 417–423.

151. Baddeley, *Working Memories*, 157.

152. Baddeley, *Working Memories*, 255–260.

153. Alan Baddeley, "Exploring the Central Executive," *The Quarterly Journal of Experimental Psychology: Section A* 49, no. 1 (1996): 5–28, 8–9.

This realignment with neurology fundamentally changed psychology at the APU, but probably saved the Unit from closure. In 1996, the MRC decided that experimental psychology no longer quite fit within its remit. For example, human–computer interaction seemed more like a topic of industrial than medical research. As a result, it withdrew support from two other psychology units in the UK and instructed the Cambridge group to fully redirect its research to neuroscience.[154] Two years later, the APU formally changed its name to the Cognition and Brain Sciences Unit soon after Baddeley's retirement as director.[155]

COMPUTATIONAL PARADOX REVISITED

This realignment of the experimental and the clinical, the cognitive and the neurological, soon spread beyond the APU. It began through networks that connected Britain to its former empire. In 1977, Endel Tulving received a Commonwealth Fellowship to travel from provincial Canada to spend a sabbatical year visiting colleagues in the United Kingdom. At the time, Tulving ranked among the world's leading taxonomists of memory. At the University of Toronto, he presided over the Ebbinghaus Empire, a fierce group of experimental psychologists who idolized their German namesake and emulated his methodological precedent. They spoke of different memory systems and levels of processing, but rarely addressed their underlying neurological substrate. In the comparatively cash-strapped Canadian university system of the 1960s, Tulving turned to the cheap technology of photocopied lists of words to identify various memory systems. In England, Tulving, soon joined by his star graduate student Daniel Schacter, not only learned of the excitement generated by Warrington's experiments but familiarized themselves with her techniques.[156]

Upon returning to Toronto, Tulving and Schacter did two things that transformed how North American psychologists approached memory. First, they replicated Warrington's priming effect experiment with healthy undergraduates.[157] It was especially through Schacter that "semantic priming" and what he soon called "implicit memory" came to be understood as common features of healthy cognitive functioning.[158] Implicit cognition found a welcome reception among

---

154. Michael Day, "British Psychology Faces Oblivion," *New Scientist*, October 5, 1996.

155. Baddeley had already announced his intention to retire as director in the 1994 report.

156. On the Toronto psychologists' encounter with Warrington, see Daniel L. Schacter, *Searching for Memory: The Brain, the Mind, and the Past*. New York: Basic Books, 1996, 163–165.

157. Endel Tulving, Daniel L. Schacter, and Heather A. Stark. "Priming Effects in Word-Fragment Completion Are Independent of Recognition Memory," *Journal of Experimental Psychology: Learning, Memory, and Cognition* 8, no. 4 (1982): 336–342.

158. Daniel L. Schacter, "Implicit Memory: History and Current Status," *Journal of Experimental Psychology: Learning, Memory, and Cognition* 13, no. 3 (1987): 501–518.

both clinical personnel and psychologists as it captured the kind of "automatic" *not thinking*, which both fields saw as the root of much human behavior. Second, Tulving and Schacter established a "Unit for Memory Disorders" for conducting cognitive experiments on individuals suffering with amnesia.[159] In 1983, the Baycrest Hospital north of the university opened its Behavioural Neurology Unit, a first in Canada, followed by the creation of the Rotman Research Institute in 1989. The Toronto psychologists cultivated extensive relationships with the hospital, turning the Ebbinghaus Empire into a hub for cognitive neuroscience. Upon his retirement from the University of Toronto in 1992, Tulving became a full-time member of the Rotman Institute's staff. In other words, the neuralization of cognition at Toronto closely mirrored the experience at the APU. This dual move would do much to braid the neurological to the automatic, placing both at the center of the psychological agenda.

These changes illuminate the local practicalities that drove this abrupt shift in thinking about thinking as the Cold War ended. Baddeley's plan to make education the Unit's new focus fit squarely within the APU's culture of gentlemanly cybernetics while extending their reach to a heretofore untouched branch of the public sector.[160] Its rejection by the MRC understandably came as a surprise. The APU switched to neuropsychology at the behest of its patron rather than as a gradual outcome of internal developments. This begs question of why their brand of computational cognitive psychology ceased being deemed "medical" when it had been beforehand. The diversification of science funding with different councils covering separate domains offers a partial explanation. However, broad changes in the political economy of Britain made the APU and other psychologists increasingly dependent on health money. In important respects, the two major classes of clients who previously provided financial support were no longer available after 1980. Détente, the end of empire, and shifting Labour government priorities meant the military had fewer resources to dedicate to human factor research deemed marginal to its core mission. Thatcher's privatization of formerly nationalization industries broke up the sector Conrad made his focus. In 1981, her government split the GPO into the Royal Mail and British Telecom, privatizing the latter in 1984. Throughout its history, the APU sought out clients from the private sector, but it always achieved its greatest successes with government ones, whether military or civilian. These contracts dissipated under Thatcher's marketization of science and state functions.[161] In contrast, health care in the form of the NHS remained in the public sector as well as occupying an increasingly prominent economic role.

159. On the founding of the Unit for Memory Disorders, see Schacter, *Searching for Memory*, 134.

160. As historian Mathew Thomson argues, the mental landscape of the British child was an expanding matter of concern in the 1970s. See Matthew Thomson, *Lost Freedom: The Landscape of the Child and the British Post-War Settlement*. Oxford: Oxford University Press, 2013.

161. On the withering of collaborative opportunities after privatization, see Baddeley, *Working Memories*, 250–251.

Turning to neuroscience was neither obvious nor inevitable. In 1974, the APU lacked access to the needed subjects and technologies. Neuropsychology's empirical techniques and theories were largely unfamiliar, if not unappealing. However, pressure from their primary patron led a new generation at the Unit to cultivate these relationships. Starting in the late 1970s, they realigned experimental psychology and clinical neuropsychology, generating new models of memory and attention in the process. Such a realignment would have deep repercussions for what counted as good, cutting-edge psychology in the twenty-first century. The reorientation of methods and research questions meant that when functional magnetic resonance imaging (fMRI) became readily available at the turn of the millennium, the easy transfer of medical equipment from research hospitals to academic psychology laboratories seemed obvious if not self-evident. It could happen automatically, without much thought.

5

Why Linda Was Not a Feminist

Expertise, Activism, and the Crisis of Confidence

The distinction British neuropsychology made between "implicit" and "explicit" memory proved foundational to what became known as dual process theories. These models posited the existence of two reasoning systems: one fast, associative, automatic, unconscious; the other slow, rule-based, deliberative, conscious. Dual process theories were old and, in many ways, synonymous with psychology itself, with both William James and Sigmund Freud endorsing such views of the mind. But this understanding soon became marginalized and then forgotten in scientific psychology, only to return with a vengeance in the late 1990s, often cloaked in the language of promissory neuroscience.[1] During this revival, the Nobel laureate Daniel Kahneman became the most prominent dual process theorist.[2] At the Hebrew University of Jerusalem during the 1970s, together with Amos Tversky he developed a research program focused on heuristics and biases in thinking, culminating with prospect theory. His program challenged the expected utility theory in economics and more broadly the algorithmic, mechanical rationality of Cold War action intellectuals.[3]

The famous Linda Problem, first introduced in 1983, exemplified Kahneman and Taversky's approach to understanding the fallacies of human judgments

---

1. Natasha Dow Schüll and Caitlin Zaloom, "The Shortsighted Brain: Neuroeconomics and the Governance of Choice in Time," *Social Studies of Science* 41, no. 4 (2011): 515–538; David E. Melnikoff and John A. Bargh, "The Mythical Number Two," *Trends in Cognitive Sciences* 22, no. 4 (2018): 280–293; C. J. Valasek, "Divided Attention, Divided Self: Race and Dual-mind Theories in the History of Experimental Psychology," *Science, Technology, and Human Values* (2021): 01622439211054455.

2. Kahneman, *Thinking Fast and Slow*. New York: Farrar, Straus, and Giroux, 2011.

3. Paul Erickson, Judy L. Klein, Lorraine Daston, Rebecca Lemov, Thomas Sturm, and Michael D. Gordin, *How Reason Almost Lost Its Mind: The Strange Career of Cold War Rationality*. Chicago: University of Chicago Press, 2013; Floris Heukelom, *Behavioral Economics: A History*. Cambridge: Cambridge University Press, 2014; Michael Lewis, *The Undoing Project: A Friendship that Changed the World*. New York: Penguin, 2016.

Governed by Affect. Michael Pettit, Oxford University Press. © Oxford University Press 2024.
DOI: 10.1093/oso/9780197621851.003.0006

when the mind largely runs on automatic. They presented participants with the following description of a fictional person: "Linda is 31 years old, single, outspoken and very bright. She majored in philosophy. As a student, she was deeply concerned with issues of discrimination and social justice, and also participated in antinuclear demonstrations." They then asked participants to rank a variety of statements about Linda in the order of their likelihood. Respondents tended to rank the conjunction of attributes "Linda is a bank teller and is active in the feminist movement" as more likely than either attribute appearing in isolation. The conjoined statement appeared to be more representative of her person as a whole, even though statistically speaking, she more likely possessed only one of the attributes.[4] People failed at reasoning by succumbing to quick, appeasing, intuitive shortcuts instead of slowing their thinking sufficiently to contemplate the problem to solve it correctly.

Such simple demonstrations of people's incapacity to reason properly galvinized a wide of range of psychologists by offering them an exciting means of intervening in the most pressing issues of the day. Gone was the layperson functioning as a deliberative chess expert carefully testing hypotheses about the world.[5] Instead of striving for "balance," the default decision makers became an easily swayed, unthinking beast ruled by pleasing dispositions. People reacted first based on their wants and later rationalized their choices.[6] Dual process theories themselves came to serve as a convenient mental shortcut for talking about the irrationality of the public, the fallibility of experts, and the appeal of behavioral experiments backed by Big Data to sort out various planetary crises. Statistician Andrew Gelman evocatively described the ascendancy of this point of view as a behaviorist "counterrevolution," decrying the antidemocratic sensibilities it imported into a host of social sciences.[7]

The history of the "affect heuristic" helps clarify how the reign of Cold War rationality ended. Kahneman made this heuristic the centerpiece of the dual process model he presented in his 2002 Nobel laureate address, but it did not number among the cognitive shortcuts he and Tversky first proposed in the

---

4. Amos Tversky and Daniel Kahneman, "Extensional versus Intuitive Reasoning: The Conjunction Fallacy in Probability Judgment," *Psychological Review* 90, no. 4 (1983): 293–315, 297.

5. Gerd Gigerenzer, "From Tools to Theories: A Heuristic of Discovery in Cognitive Psychology," *Psychological Review* 98, no. 2 (1991): 254–267; Jamie Cohen-Cole, *The Open Mind: Cold War Politics and the Sciences of Human Nature*. Chicago: University of Chicago Press, 2014.

6. Jonathan Haidt, "The Emotional Dog and Its Rational Tail: A Social Intuitionist Approach to Moral Judgment," *Psychological Review* 108, no. 4 (2001): 814–834.

7. https://statmodeling.stat.columbia.edu/2015/01/30/cognitive-vs-behavioral-psychology-economics-political-science. On the supposed demise of the behavioral sciences, see Jefferson D. Pooley, "A 'Not Particularly Felicitous' Phrase: A History of the 'Behavioral Sciences' Label," *Serendipities* 1, no. 1 (2016): 38–81.

1970s.[8] Reflecting the norms of Cold War cognitivism, their program was decidedly cool, focusing on how the computational limits of the human mind led to its failed grasp of probability. The availability and representativeness of information caused biased decisions, not its emotional color.[9] Coined by Kahneman's friend and sometime collaborator Paul Slovic, the affect heuristic was only added to the taxonomy of mental heuristics after 2000.[10] Yet, its reach quickly expanded. Kahneman understood that much of System 1 (automatic, quick thinking) fell under the power of affective dispositions. It opened up a new hedonic psychology of decision making, organized around primitive, precognitive judgments of like/dislike, good/bad, pleasure/pain. This represents a remarkable, historical shift *within* the field of judgment and decision making (JDM), an instance in a wider emotional or affective revolution that was felt across the human sciences.

Named and canonized at the turn of the millennium, the affect heuristic reflected how experts responded to the contentious domestic politics of the détente phase of the Cold War. Originally synonymous with nuclear dread, the affect heuristic grew out of public opposition to the expansion of power plants on American soil, a distrust of experts as neutral arbitrators of evidence, and the opposition from states to federal authority. The mounting nuclear controversy surrounding the construction of domestic nuclear power plants soon attracted a team of cognitive psychologists attached to the Oregon Research Institute (ORI): Slovic, Sarah Lichtenstein, and Baruch Fischhoff, all of whom were interested in the proliferation of technological risks characteristic of the post-scarcity, consumer-oriented societies of the détente period. These researchers captured the polyvalence, if not the contradictions, of the post-1960s social sciences. The ORI and its successor, Decision Research, owed their existence to the largesse of the Cold War state. On the other hand, members of the Oregon group brought to their experimental designs their experiences as active members in the feminist, civil rights, and peace movements. Grappling with the messy contradictions between venerating Cold War expertise and the post-1960s demands for grassroots democracy generated

---

8. Daniel Kahneman, "A Perspective on Judgment and Choice: Mapping Bounded Rationality." *American Psychologist* 58, no. 9 (2003): 697–720.

9. Summarizing their field in the 1970s, Slovic, Fischhoff, and Lichtenstein wrote: "Because of limited information-processing capacity and ignorance of the rules for optical information-processing and decision making, people's judgments are subject to systematic biases." See Paul Slovic, Baruch Fischhoff, and Sarah Lichtenstein, "Behavioral Decision Theory," *Annual Review of Psychology* 28, no. 1 (1977): 1–39, 14. Kahneman likewise became interested in emotion in the 1980s, after his break with Tversky, through his "undoing project" or how sentiments of regret shaped the mental simulation of altering events. See Lewis, *The Undoing Project*, 289–310.

10. Melissa L. Finucane, Ali Alhakami, Paul Slovic, and Stephen M. Johnson, "The Affect Heuristic in Judgments of Risks and Benefits," *Journal of Behavioral Decision Making* 13, no. 1 (2000): 1–17; Daniel Kahneman and Shane Frederick, "Representativeness Revisited: Attribute Substitution in Intuitive Judgment" in T. Gilovich, D. Griffin, and D. Kahneman (eds.), *Heuristics of Intuitive Judgment: Extensions and Applications*. New York: Cambridge University Press, 2002, 49–81.

not only the affective heuristic itself but much of the duality found in psychology's dual process theories. Finally, their story explains why antinuclear activism, the feminist movement, and the mathematical abilities of women were so readily available to Kahneman and Tversky in 1983.

COGNITION HEATS UP

Tversky and Kahneman's "heuristics and biases approach" ranks among the most influential research programs in the postwar social sciences.[11] In the 1950s and 1960s, optimistic cognitive scientists excitedly reported on how the mind worked. Human reasoning was imperfect, or "bounded," but early cognitive science tended to catalogue the mind's successes. That chess experts occasionally lost did not demonstrate their irrationality but the limits of their computational capacity.[12] In contrast, Tversky and Kahneman gave unprecedented attention to the mundane, yet persistent, failures of these very same processes, documenting where they broke down and betrayed the thinking organism's overconfident judgments. As psychologists Gerd Gigerenzer and Henry Brighton note, "In the 1970s, the term *heuristic* acquired a different connotation, undergoing a shift from being regarded as a method that makes computers smart to one that explains why people are not smart."[13] Indeed, Kahneman and Tversky's first collaborative paper reveled in the irony that fellow mathematical psychologists frequently failed to grasp the statistical reasoning they preached.[14] At the time, both men were unknowns in psychology employed at the Hebrew University and found themselves on the periphery of the discipline's ever expanding empire. Yet, each of their subsequent collaborative articles became a citation classic by revealing a different cognitive bias. For example, people predicted the frequency of an event based on the availability of information and its readiness in coming to mind rather than its actual frequency.[15] Their research program soon attracted a wide, interdisciplinary audience. Reflecting on their 1974 *Science* paper, they noted how it got reprinted

---

11. This section is based on a citation analysis of Tversky and Kahneman's articles from the 1970s, as well as a co-citation analysis of different subfield journals using the Web of Science database.

12. On *homo adaptivus* as a "limited, error-controlled organic machine," see Hunter Heyck, *Age of System: Understanding the Development of Modern Social Science*. Baltimore: Johns Hopkins University Press, 2015, quote 85.

13. Gerd Gigerenzer and Henry Brighton, "Homo heuristicus: Why Biased Minds Make Better Inferences," *Topics in Cognitive Science* 1, no. 1 (2009): 107–143, 109.

14. Amos Tversky and Daniel Kahneman, "Belief in the Law of Small Numbers," *Psychological Bulletin* 76, no. 2 (1971): 105–110.

15. Amos Tversky and Daniel Kahneman. "Judgment under Uncertainty: Heuristics and Biases," *Science* 185, no. 4157 (1974): 1124–1131.

in volumes dedicated to "economics, public policy, statistics, and cognitive science."[16] Notably absent from their list was their own field of psychology.

Tversky and Kahneman's work had a telling trajectory through their home discipline. In the 1970s, Kahneman and Tversky published exclusively in either cognitive science or generalist journals (e.g., *Science, Cognitive Science, Psychological Review*), but the preponderance of their early citations did not appear in these venues. Instead, citation metrics reveal two distinct and enthusiastic audiences for their work in the 1970s. The first was their occasional collaborators at the ORI, who shared their interest in mathematical psychology and judgment and decision making (JDM). Such an early reception was unsurprising given that Kahneman and Tversky wrote many of their papers during a 1972 sabbatical in Oregon and one of their graduate students soon after joined the group. Social psychology, a field that long trafficked in the failings of human reasoning, provided the second and even wider audience. At the time, social psychologists were keenly reorganizing their field after the supposed "crisis" it underwent in the late 1960s. They sought to distance themselves from the previous decade's unethical dramaturgy and the contaminations between the experimenter's expectations and the participant's response while still demonstrating the broader relevance of their work.[17] A new generation sought to remodel their field on the successes of cognitive psychology, with Tversky and Kahneman providing the field with its cognitive theory. Surveying the citations in the prestigious *Journal of Personality and Social Psychology* during this period reveals scant reference to the work of George Miller, Jerome Bruner, Noam Chomsky, Jean Piaget, or Herbert Simon (fewer than a half dozen citations each scattered across the decade).

Here the concept of bias loomed large. For statisticians and mathematical psychologists, the term "bias" has a technical meaning, distinct from lay connotations of "prejudice." Bias simply refers to the difference between an estimate and the true (and often unknowable) parameter.[18] However, the conceptual slippage between bias and prejudice did not simply result from the public's misunderstanding of psychological science. The cognitive revolution posited the human subject as a lay scientist testing their hypotheses. If scientists dealt with imperfect empirical data, then so too did laypeople. The task of the social psychologist became that of identifying and naming these errors in people perception, the most

---

16. Amos Tversky and Daniel Kahneman, "This Week's Citation Classic: Judgment under Uncertainty," *Current Contents* 14, April 4, 1983, 22.

17. Cathy Faye, "American Social Psychology: Examining the Contours of the 1970s Crisis." *Studies in History and Philosophy of Science Part C: Studies in History and Philosophy of Biological and Biomedical Sciences* 43, no. 2 (2012): 514–521; Jill Morawski, "Epistemological Dizziness in the Psychology Laboratory: Lively Subjects, Anxious Experimenters, and Experimental Relations, 1950–1970," *Isis* 106, no. 3 (2015): 567–597.

18. A similar conception of statistic bias underwrote Cold War weapons systems; see Donald MacKenzie, *Inventing Accuracy: A Historical Sociology of Nuclear Missile Guidance*. Cambridge, MA: MIT Press, 1990, 355–361.

famous example being Lee Ross's "fundamental attribution error" of confusing the demands of the situation with a person's inner character.[19] In *Human Inference* (1980), Ross and Michigan psychologist Richard Nisbett argued that processing errors underwrote the kind of destructive behaviors that interested social psychologists: intergroup conflict, social apathy, the dissonance between action and belief, prejudice.[20] Ross and Nisbett addressed a wide range of problems, but at its core their social cognition resided two fundamental convictions: (1) people, even experts, were overconfident in evaluating their own sound judgment and abilities; and (2) experimental psychologists possessed a unique ability to expose said errors using carefully designed laboratory procedures. Reviewing Ross and Nisbett's book, George A. Miller and Nancy Cantor noted that one could caricature their position as "We educated citizens of this advanced industrial society are not nearly as rational as we think we are"—a cynical view anticipated by Sigmund Freud but quite alien to the optimism of early cognitive scientists like Miller.[21] Theirs was hardly a novel one for psychologists. The notion of cognitive bias was already available to psychologists familiar with the clinical realm. Aaron Beck and Albert Ellis had already begun remaking mood disorders into disordered cognition riddled with the intrusion of automatic thoughts. What Kahneman and Tversky accomplished was, first, showing that the kinds of errors identified by clinicians had a level of generality and second, applying this clinical perspective to new classes of people and problems where they had previously not held sway. Distorted thinking was found not only in pathological but also in healthy, even expert, decision making.

The new social cognition represented a psychology of diminished expectations, a lost faith in democratic self-rule. Its pessimism resonated with the diagnosis of cultural malaise offered by Jimmy Carter in his prime time "crisis of confidence" speech of 1979. In that speech, the U.S. president addressed a nation that was still reeling from the revelations of the Watergate scandal, the superpower's unanticipated defeat in Vietnam, and the surprising inflation following the Organization of the Petroleum Exporting Countries (OPEC) oil embargo. Carter spoke of ordinary Americans' losing faith "not only in government itself but in the ability as citizens to serve as the ultimate rulers and shapers of our democracy."[22] The cultural

---

19. Lee Ross, "The Intuitive Psychologist and His Shortcomings: Distortions in the Attribution Process," in Leonard Berkowitz (ed.), *Advances in Experimental Social Psychology*, vol. 10. New York: Academic Press, 1977, 173–220.

20. Richard Nisbett and Lee Ross, *Human Inference: Strategies and Shortcomings of Social Judgment*. Englewood Cliffs, NJ: Prentice-Hall, 1980.

21. George A. Miller and Nancy Cantor. "A Book Review of R. Nisbett and L. Ross, Human Inference: Strategies and Shortcomings of Social Judgment," *Social Cognition* 1 (1982): 83–93, 87.

22. "Transcript of the President's Address to Country on Energy Problems," *New York Times*, July 16, 1979, A10.

pessimism of Carter's speech certainly resonated with the changes in how social psychologists viewed the individual.

In 1978, social psychologist Ellen Langer captured this mood when she dismissed the prevalent image in her field of "man or woman as a creature who, for the most part, attends to the world about him or her and behaves on the basis of reasonable inference drawn from such attention." Instead, she stated, "behavior is actually accomplished much of the time without paying attention to the substantive details of the 'informative' environment."[23] Langer deemed the notion of a contemplative subject carefully balancing competing cognitions as a flattering illusion. Her evidence suggested that most people acted without knowing. By the 1980s, her fellow social psychologists spoke of how "cognitive misers" hoarded scarce mental resources much like the Wall Street financier hoarded wealth. The social psychologists' turn to the mind's hidden recesses also reflected the practicalities of conducting research in the era. As concerns about state surveillance heightened privacy concerns after Watergate, ordinary people proved more reticent to volunteer their attitudes and opinions.[24] This mindset led social scientists to invest more in techniques that went beyond awareness, candor, and self-revelation. They sought to circumvent the knowing subject reliably relating their own thoughts.

Social psychologists grappling with these problems provided Kahneman and Tversky with their first enthusiastic audience and, in turn, how their work got read within this field framed its subsequent reception. This audience allowed them to move from the comparative academic periphery at Hebrew University to some of the most influential departments in America. Tversky's star particularly rose through his connection with social psychology. In 1978, he joined Ross at Stanford as a professor, a move that strained his relationship with Kahneman. Stanford social cognition erased the humility that was apparent in the heuristics and biases approach wherein scientists were reflexively subject to these errors, much like everyone else was. It reinscribed the "psychologist's advantage": the scientist's unique position in diagnosing human fallibilities while somehow remaining aloof from those same dynamics.[25] Put more crudely, hot cognition perpetuated the erotics

---

23. Ellen Langer, Arthur Blank, and Benzion Chanowitz, "The Mindlessness of Ostensibly Thoughtful Action: The Role of "Placebic" Information in Interpersonal Interaction," *Journal of Personality and Social Psychology* 36, no. 6 (1978): 635–642, 635. See also Shayna Fox Lee, "Psychology's Own Mindfulness: Ellen Langer and the Social Politics of Scientific Interest in 'Active Noticing,'" *Journal of the History of the Behavioral Sciences* 55, no. 3 (2019): 216–229.

24. On the dramatic increase on the nonresponse rate to both political and commercial polling over the 1970s, see Charlotte G. Steeh, "Trends in Nonresponse Rates, 1952–1979," *Public Opinion Quarterly* 45, no. 1 (1981): 40–57.

25. Karl E. Scheibe, "Metamorphoses in the Psychologist's Advantage," in J. G. Morawski (ed.), *The Rise of Experimentation in American Psychology*. New Haven, CT: Yale University Press, 1988, 53–71.

of the social psychologist's desire to be the smartest dude in the room.[26] However, this pessimistic interpretation of the incommensurability of cognitive biases with deliberative democracy was not the only one available. Attending to the reading Tversky and Kahneman received in Eugene, Oregon, reveals a different set of political possibilities for the heuristics and biases approach.

FEAR AND FRIENDSHIP IN THE ATOMIC AGE

For many, dropping the bomb on Hiroshima marked the start of a new era, and throughout the Cold War social scientists debated the prevalence of the atomic age's "nuclear anxiety" and its psychological consequences for the American population.[27] The U.S. government's policy of secrecy, particularly the management and restriction of information about nuclear power in the name of national security, heightened existing worries.[28] Having failed to maintain a nuclear monopoly, the Eisenhower administration piloted Operation Candor and Atoms for Peace in 1953. Rather than maintaining nuclear secrecy, the administration opted to distribute information about energy to select civilian groups and to obtain assent from the public through education.[29] Yet, the Eisenhower administration's own "New Look" policy of mass retaliation using nuclear weapons undercut its espousal of peace. Even the signing of the Strategic Arms Limitation Talks 1 (SALT 1) in 1969 curtailing the imminent threat of nuclear proliferation failed to eliminate the worries of ordinary citizens. Nuclear energy tapped into deeper cultural anxieties regarding the instability raised by the transmutation of matter.

26. Henderikus J. Stam, H. Lorraine Radtke, and Ian Lubek, "Strains in Experimental Social Psychology: A Textual Analysis of the Development of Experimentation in Social Psychology." *Journal of the History of the Behavioral Sciences* 36, no. 4 (2000): 365–382; Ian Nicholson, "'Shocking' Masculinity: Stanley Milgram, 'Obedience to Authority,' and the 'Crisis of Manhood' in Cold War America." *Isis* 102, no. 2 (2011): 238–268; Peter Hegarty, *Gentlemen's Disagreement: Alfred Kinsey, Lewis Terman, and the Sexual Politics of Smart Men*. Chicago: University of Chicago Press, 2013, 107–111.

27. Paul Boyer, *By the Bomb's Early Light: American Thought and Culture at the Dawn of the Atomic Age*. New York: Pantheon, 1985.

28. Itty Abraham, *The Making of the Indian Atomic Bomb: Science, Secrecy and the Postcolonial State*. Cambridge, MA: Zed Books, 1998; Peter Galison, "Secrecy in Three Acts," *Social Research* 77, no. 3 (2010): 970–974; Alex Wellerstein, *Restricted Data: The History of Nuclear Secrecy in the United States*. Chicago: University of Chicago Press, 2021.

29. Ira Chernus, "Operation Candor: Fear, Faith, and Flexibility," *Diplomatic History* 29, no. 5 (2005): 779–809; John Krige, "Atoms for Peace, Scientific Internationalism, and Scientific Intelligence," *Osiris* 21, no. 1 (2006): 161–181; Jacob Darwin Hamblin, "Exorcising Ghosts in the Age of Automation: United Nations Experts and Atoms for Peace," *Technology and Culture* 47, no. 4 (2006): 734–756.

For many, the term "nuclear" became synonymous with the extermination of all life on earth.[30]

Nuclear power gained new salience following the 1973 oil shock as the United States sought to secure its energy independence.[31] Domestic power plants seemed to be a key strategic resource as the oil-producing nations mobilized their access to this scarce resource as a means of exerting political power.[32] However, neither this need nor détente quelled concerns about the long-term, potentially catastrophic consequences of splitting the atom. The mounting opposition reflected lingering Cold War anxieties about weapons, new environmentalist sensibilities, and a growing suspicion of government authority.[33] To assuage public fears, the newly renamed Nuclear Regulatory Commission (NRC) charged MIT physicist Norman Rasmussen with investigating the risks posed by commercial plants. Released in 1975, the so-called Rasmussen Report, WASH-1400, "Reactor Safety Study," documented the superior health and environmental benefits of nuclear power vis-a-vis its fossil fuel counterparts and the high improbability (actuarially speaking) of a disaster given the current safety standards.[34] The report was thorough, well documented, cool in tone—and utterly unpersuasive.[35] Despite technical assessments demonstrating the safety of nuclear systems and the unlikelihood of accidents, a vocal minority of Americans organized to curtail the expansion of domestic power plants. The public's obstinate skepticism led federal regulators to abandon the model of an "informed and careful public" deliberating the value of a nuclear future. After the engineers and actuaries failed, they turned to psychologists to explain this irrationality and formulate a persuasion strategy.[36]

Concerns about the safety of nuclear power were particularly acute in Eugene, Oregon, a university town that had become a welcoming home for various environmental, cooperative, counterculture movements. In 1968, Eugene voters approved a measure allowing their local utility company to sell bonds to fund

---

30. Historian Spencer Weart argues nuclear energy tapped into deeper cultural anxieties the instability raised by the transmutation of matter Spencer R. Weart, *Nuclear Fear: A History of Images*. Cambridge, MA: Harvard University Pres, 1988.

31. Meg Jacobs, *Panic at the Pump: The Energy Crisis and the Transformation of American Politics in the 1970s*. New York: Wang and Hill, 2016.

32. Christopher R. W. Dietrich, *Oil Revolution: Anticolonial Elites, Sovereign Rights, and the Economic Culture of Decolonization*. New York: Cambridge University Press, 2017.

33. Jeremi Suri, *Power and Protest: Global Revolution and the Rise of Détente*. Cambridge, MA: Harvard University Press, 2009.

34. "Reactor Safety Study: An Assessment of Accident Risks in U.S. Commercial Nuclear Power Plants," WASH-1400 (NUREG 75/014), U.S. Nuclear Regulatory Commission, 1975.

35. Brian Balogh, *Chain Reaction: Expert Debate and Public Participation in American Commercial Nuclear Power 1945–1975*. Cambridge: Cambridge University Press, 1991, chapter 8.

36. On the wider tensions among public trust, expert judgment, and actuarial reasoning, see Theodore M. Porter, *Trust in Numbers: The Pursuit of Objectivity in Science and Public Life*. Princeton, NJ: Princeton University Press, 1995.

the construction of a nuclear power plant. Life in the affluent society demanded increased energy consumption, and nuclear power promised a safe and reliable source to meet these wants. In a remarkable reversal, two years later the same constituency voted in favor of a four-year moratorium on building any nuclear plants. The new measure came from a petition submitted by the Eugene Future Power Committee, a civic group organized in 1969 around the nuclear issue.[37] "The Oregon System," with its robust tradition for direct democracy using ballot initiatives dating back to the Progressive Era, made the tension between voters (publics) and bureaucrats (experts) particularly acute.[38]

The nuclear controversy soon came to the attention of a group of cognitive psychologists affiliated with the Oregon Research Institute (ORI).[39] The ORI was a uniquely Cold War creature: "a nonprofit organization devoted primarily to basic research in the behavioral sciences."[40] Dependent on federal government research grants and military contracts, it differed from universities and hospitals with its focus on fundamental rather than applied research.[41] Psychologist Paul Hoffman founded the ORI in 1960 to free himself from teaching responsibilities. An aviator during World War II and still sporting a crewcut decades later, Hoffman proved adept at securing federal support for his institute through military contracts that sustained social science research during the first phase of the Cold War.[42] He soon built a team of likeminded researchers interested in the emerging field of human JDM. Much of their work is built on Minnesota psychologist Paul Meehl's critique of clinical judgment and its fuzzy criteria for reading the mind. They sought to undermine the clinician's preference for making decisions based on the experience of the vivid case rather than the patterned behavior revealed by actuarial

---

37. Daniel Pope, "'We Can Wait. We Should Wait.' Eugene's Nuclear Power Controversy, 1968–1970." *Pacific Historical Review* 59, no. 3 (1990): 349–373.

38. On the long history of direct democracy in Oregon, see Robert D. Johnston, *The Radical Middle Class: Populist Democracy and the Question of Capitalism in Progressive Era Portland, Oregon*. Princeton, NJ: Princeton University Press, 2003.

39. At the time, organized psychology's engagement with the problems of the atomic age had waned. See J. G. Morawski and Sharon E. Goldstein. "Psychology and Nuclear War: A Chapter in Our Legacy of Social Responsibility," *American Psychologist* 40, no. 3 (1985): 276–284.

40. Dan Sellard, "Joe Doakes and the Oregon Research Institute," *Eugene Register-Guardian*, August 29, 1965, 3EE.

41. On the ORI's unique status as a recipient for government grants, see Wayne Morse, "Labor-Hew Appropriation Bill: Oregon Research Institute Problem," *Congressional Record* 112, 1966, 23836.

42. Mark Solovey, *Shaky Foundations: The Politics-Patronage-Social Science Nexus in Cold War America*. New Brunswick, NJ: Rutgers University Press, 2013. In this regard, their research program successfully bridged what Hunter Heyck identifies as the two systems of social science patronage in the Cold War. See Hunter Heyck, *Age of System: Understanding the Development of Modern Social Science*. Baltimore: Johns Hopkins University Press, 2015, chapter 2.

tables.[43] The team soon included Paul Slovic, recruited in 1964 as a graduate of the University of Michigan's mathematical psychology program. There Slovic had studied under Ward Edwards, and his labmates included Sarah Lichtenstein (PhD, 1962) and Amos Tversky (PhD, 1965). When Lichtenstein's then husband received an academic appointment at the University of Oregon in 1966, Slovic eagerly recruited her to join him at the ORI.

Together Lichtenstein and Slovic developed a series of experiments on preference reversals. They presented participants with different gambling scenarios and found that respondents "frequently chose one bet from a pair of bets and subsequently bid more for the bet they did not choose."[44] How the psychologist framed the bets and bids altered the participants' decision rather than the participants consistently selecting the one that would yield the greatest expected utility. This violated the tenets of Cold War game theory. In 1973, Lichtenstein and Slovic published a rather unique replication study. Exemplifying their increased interest in studying risk in more realistic scenarios, they reproduced the experiment on the floor of the Four Queens Casino in Las Vegas with real gamblers and genuine bets.[45] Their behavioral evidence soon attracted the interest—and ire—of economists.[46]

Throughout this period, Lichtenstein and Slovic remained in contact with Tversky. In 1970, on his way to a sabbatical year at Stanford's Center for Advanced Study, Tversky stopped by Eugene to reminisce with his graduate school friends, play some basketball, and share with them his excitement over a new line of research he had started in Jerusalem. The following year, he returned with Kahneman where they spent another leave year as visiting scientists at the ORI. The initial suggestion that Slovic might serve as their co-author quickly faded due to the intensity of the Tversky–Kahneman collaboration. In 1973, Slovic secured a Fulbright fellowship to make a reciprocal trip, but the surprise Egyptian invasion on the eve of Yom Kippur curtailed his time at the Hebrew University.

For Kahneman and Tversky, this failure of military intelligence exemplified the fallibility of human decision making as nothing else had done. Despite Israel's ultimate victory in the Yom Kippur War, the federal government's inability to

---

43. See Paul J. Hoffman, "The Paramorphic Representation of Clinical Judgment," *Psychological Bulletin* 57, no. 2 (1960): 116–131; Lewis R. Goldberg, "Man versus Model of Man: A Rationale, plus Some Evidence, for a Method of Improving on Clinical Inferences," *Psychological Bulletin* 73, no. 6 (1970): 422–432; Robyn M. Dawes, and Bernard Corrigan, "Linear Models in Decision Making," *Psychological Bulletin* 81, no. 2 (1974): 95–106.

44. Sarah Lichtenstein and Paul Slovic, "Reversals of Preference between Bids and Choices in Gambling Decisions," *Journal of Experimental Psychology* 89, no. 1 (1971): 46–55, 54.

45. Sarah Lichtenstein and Paul Slovic, "Response-induced Reversals of Preference in Gambling: An Extended Replication in Las Vegas," *Journal of Experimental Psychology* 101, no. 1 (1973): 16–20.

46. Paul Slovic, "Psychological Study of Human Judgment: Implications for Investment Decision Making," *The Journal of Finance* 27, no. 4 (1972): 779–799; David M. Grether and Charles R.

predict the incursion and prevent the war through a preemptive strike shattered the nation's image of invincibility. Many Israelis, Kahneman and Tversky included, remembered the Yom Kippur War in terms of *mehdal*: an overconfident shortcoming, an error of omission, or "as something which went wrong, yet did not have to go wrong."[47] The war made real the costs of making errors of judgment under uncertainty and solidified their shared pessimism regarding human rationality.[48] Attempts to remedy the situation only worsened their opinion of expertise. In 1975, Zvi Lanir recruited Kahneman to serve as a consultant to Israel's Ministry of Foreign Affairs. Together they designed a report for Israeli government decision makers on how to effectively convey information about the risks posed by various external threats. They visualized risk levels as a dial on a cockpit dashboard designed to ease information processing. Kahneman abandoned the consultancy after delivering the first report, primarily because the intelligence community's unwillingness to heed numerical, weighted evaluations of potential risks had further diminished his faith in the soundness of expert judgment.[49]

If the war disrupted the possibility of further collaboration, Slovic did not consider the visit futile: in that visit he met their promising graduate student, Baruch Fischhoff, whom he persuaded to join the ORI staff. Born in Detroit, Fischhoff had been accepted into the mathematical psychology program at Michigan upon finishing his degree at Wayne State University in 1967. Instead, he opted to leave the United States with the intention of spending the rest of his life on a kibbutz in Israel. This decision was the product of his engagement with the civil rights and youth movements and his keen desire to participate in a social organization dedicated to an "egalitarian lifestyle."[50] This mindset drew him to the Hashomer Hatzair youth movement with its values of "commitment, cooperation, spirituality, feminism, environmentalism, and the independence of young people." He became further radicalized following the murder of Detroit civil rights activist Viola Liuzzo in Selma, Alabama, in 1965.[51] Fischhoff first joined the Gal On kibbutz and then moved to Lahav, but he abandoned the movement after three years, frustrated by "the exaggerated claims of understanding political processes that

---

Plott. "Economic Theory of Choice and the Preference Reversal Phenomenon," *The American Economic Review* 69, no. 4 (1979): 623–638.

47. Charles S. Liebman, "The Myth of Defeat: The Memory of the Yom Kippur War in Israeli Society," *Middle Eastern Studies* 29, no. 3 (1993): 399–418, 413.

48. Lewis, *The Undoing Project*, 236–265.

49. Zvi Lanir and Daniel Kahneman, "An Experiment in Decision Analysis in Israel in 1975," *Studies in Intelligence* 50, no. 4 (2006): 11–19.

50. Olivier Klein, Peter Hegarty, and Baruch Fischhoff, "Hindsight 40 Years on: An Interview with Baruch Fischhoff," *Memory Studies* 10, no. 3 (2017): 249–260, 252.

51. "Distinguished Scientific Awards for an Early Career Contribution to Psychology: 1980," *American Psychologist* 36 (1981): 74–87, 75.

permeated the political discussions to which I had long subjected myself."[52] He then enrolled in the graduate program in psychology at Hebrew University where "the challenge for participating graduate students was to find a heuristic to call one's own."[53] Inspired by his interests in politics and history, Fischhoff developed what he coined "hindsight bias": the tendency to see past events as inevitable when future events seem unknowable and are filled with contingency.[54]

Fischhoff was not alone in the effort to reconcile cognitive science and egalitarian politics. By the mid-1970s, Sarah Lichtenstein formally separated from her husband and became active in the woman's movement. In 1976, she was named president of the Eugene Human Rights Commission for Women. Eschewing the then popular feminist image of the "bra burner," Lichtenstein subscribed to what would become known as "choice feminism," a stance that resonated with her scientific research on decision making. When interviewed about the Commission, she stated, "I believe sex discrimination will be eliminated when women have genuine options and choices and the freedom to make those choices. I believe in diversity. I don't think all women ought to be housewives. I don't think all women should work."[55] In 1982, she became a public representative on the advisory committee to a task force investigating gender pay equity among Oregon state employees (professors excluded).[56]

Intensive, egalitarian collaboration characterized the scientific friendship of the Oregon trio. Lichtenstein related an anecdote from graduate school in which her and Slovic's mutual advisor insisted that he be listed as first author of an article they co-authored "because he, being a man, would have to earn a living."[57] In contrast, their work on preference reversal listed Lichtenstein first (making a subtle feminist gesture in 1971), and authorship order rotated among the group. Slovic described their work process as follows. He took primary responsibility for identifying problems in need of solving, and Lichtenstein specialized in the more analytic side, carefully designing experiments and selecting the proper statistical analysis to reveal the underlying phenomena. Fischhoff also contributed to experimental design, but he excelled as a fluent, evocative writer. But unwilling

---

52. Baruch Fischhoff, "An Early History of Hindsight Research," *Social Cognition* 25 (2007): 10–13, 10.

53. Fischhoff, "An Early History of Hindsight Research," 10.

54. Baruch Fischhoff, "Hindsight Is not Equal to Foresight: The Effect of Outcome Knowledge on Judgment under Uncertainty," *Journal of Experimental Psychology: Human Perception and Performance* 1, no. 3 (1975): 288–299.

55. Don Floyd, "Women's Rights Leader Marvels at Discrimination," *Eugene Register-Guardian*, March 16, 1976, 1C.

56. Sarah Lichtenstein, "Comparable Worth as Multiattribute Utility," talk given at the Judgment and Decision Society Meeting, November 11, 1984. Decision Research Report 85-1.

57. Interview with Lichtenstein cited in William Poundstone, *Priceless: The Myth of Fair Value (and How to Take Advantage of It)*. New York: Hill and Wang, 2010, chapter 10.

to maintain clean lines among these roles, together they wrote, critiqued, and retyped up to ten drafts of each paper in an iterative process.

Their egalitarianism brought their working lives to a crisis point in 1976, when the ORI split over governance issues. Many of the ORI's staff opposed what they saw as Hoffman's autocratic, intrusive, and callous managerial style. For example, he objected to the countercultural habits of certain staff members, seeking to remove them from the ORI who opted to live in a commune. Hoffman complained to the press about "our share of troublemakers . . . a group that was Marxist in its orientation. They did not understand where research ends and management begins."[58] Publicly, he named no names. However, Slovic, Lichtenstein, and Fischhoff became the first team to break with Hoffman. Although grants were formally made to the ORI and not individual researchers, each project required specific expertise to complete it. This allowed them to take their existing financial support and seed their own independent organization, Decision Research.

The perception of technological risks became the centerpiece of the new institute. Their visit to the casino floor proved no fluke as the team increasingly focused on elucidating the cognitive processes underlying "societal risk taking." A self-described optimist, Slovic advocated a diffusionist model of public outreach. "Perhaps an awareness of our limitations," he mused in 1972, "coupled with sophisticated methods of decision analysis, will enable us to minimize many of the judgmental biases."[59] Their outlook grew more pessimistic throughout the decade. A proper reading of the 1950s cognitive science revealed a very different picture of human nature, one in which limited storage capacity and cognitive strain compromised the processing of information. Particularly relevant were the cognitive shortcuts (e.g., availability, anchoring, and representativeness) Tversky and Kahneman had recently identified. Echoing how their preference reversal research undercut existing economic models of rationality, they targeted the Chicago economist Frank Knight's vision of the knowledgeable risk-taker as an overly "optimistic assessment of human capacities."[60]

Among all the societal risks that existed, none loomed larger than nuclear power. In 1972, during the drafting the Rasmussen Report, Slovic had joined the "risk and public response task force" sponsored by the Atomic Energy Commission.[61] In the wake of the Report's failure to quell public opposition, the Oregon team

---

58. Mike Stahlberg, "Oregon Research Institute Reported Ailing," *Eugene Register-Guardian*, April 20, 1977, 1B–2B.

59. Paul Slovic, "From Shakespeare to Simon: Speculations—and Some Evidence—about Man's Ability to Process Information," *Oregon Research Institute Bulletin*, 12, no. 2 (1972): 1–19, 14.

60. Sarah Lichtenstein, Paul Slovic, Baruch Fischhoff, Mark Layman, and Barbara Combs, "Judged Frequency of Lethal Events," *Journal of Experimental Psychology Human Learning & Memory* 4, no. 6 (1978): 551–578, 577.

61. "High-Level Radioactive Waste Management and Its Alternatives," WASH-1297. Atomic Energy Commission, 1974, 80.

"began to get calls from various government agencies, the gist of which was 'We've had the best technical analysts study Problem X. However, the public doesn't believe their analyses. The public must be crazy. You're psychologists, tell us what to do.'"[62] The team was uniquely positioned to address the controversy as experts legible to the government and capable of securing major grants from both military and civilian patrons. Indeed, Decision Research continued to receive Defense Advanced Research Projects Agency (DARPA) money through its Cybernetics Technology Office years after passage of the 1973 Mansfield Amendment limited funds to projects of direct military relevance. The team became adept at making their research legible to the demands of their patrons in the federal government during the period of the Cold War largesse. At the same time, Eugene was both geographically and culturally far from the major centers of power along the eastern seaboard, and the group's sustained involvement in local, left-wing, countercultural movements sensitized them to the public's resistance to nuclear power. This engagement with grassroots, deliberative, egalitarian movements ran through their lives and into the very design of their experiments.

In 1978, the trio published their "psychometric paradigm" whereby they asked participants to rate the perceived risk and perceived benefit of host technologies. The nuclear engineer Chauncey Starr had suggested that consumer choices offered a "revealed preference" for risk and people opposed technologies over which they exerted little to no personal control.[63] The Oregon psychologists put Starr's theory to the test, asking their participants to take the time to contemplate a host of technologies and then evaluate each of them on nine scales measuring the risk's voluntariness, immediacy, novelty, severity, and so forth. The scales would give each novel technology its own personality profile. They recruited local members of the League of Women Voters and their spouses, a group to which Slovic's wife belonged. Founded in 1920, the League continued to support women's political engagement. Its remit extended beyond formal voting rights and encouraged its members to engage in civic life.[64] Central to the League's agenda were its antinuclear opposition in Eugene and its vision of the nuclear industry's threat to future life as a feminist issue.[65] For example, Jane Novick, the secretary for the Future Power Committee, was a League member and the organization had endorsed the plant construction moratorium measure as far back as 1970.[66] The

---

62. "Distinguished Scientific Awards for an Early Career Contribution to Psychology: 1980," 76.

63. Chauncey Starr, "Social Benefit versus Technological Risk," *Science* (1969): 1232–1238.

64. Marisa Chappell, "Rethinking Women's Politics in the 1970s: The League of Women Voters and the National Organization for Women Confront Poverty," *Journal of Women's History* 13, no. 4 (2002): 155–179.

65. More broadly, see Dorothy Nelkin, "Nuclear Power as a Feminist Issue," *Environment: Science and Policy for Sustainable Development* 23, no. 1 (1981): 14–39.

66. Pope, "Eugene's Nuclear Power Controversy," 361.

Oregon psychologists selected these participants not for their representativeness of the general population, but rather because they constituted "an extremely thoughtful, articulate, and influential group of private citizens." These were "the private citizen[s] most heavily engaged in the public policy-making process."[67] They represented "the best-informed citizens in the community"[68] In other words, the psychologists drew upon their local connections to assess the attitudes of an engaged and informed electorate.[69]

Although the citizen panel's risk perception differed from the actuarial assessment of experts, it was patterned and predictable. Laypeople opposed technologies that they perceived as falling outside their personal control and that came with potentially catastrophic effects. In the grid space of their factor analysis, nuclear power uniquely stood out.[70] People had difficulty properly processing information about the frequency of rare and unlikely events, causing lay evaluations to diverge from those of experts. The mind's reliance on the availability heuristic as a cognitive shortcut made attempts to overcome this "perception gap" nearly impossible. This normal mode of thinking meant that the very act of demonstrating the safeguards protecting community members from highly improbable disasters made the very possibility of such catastrophes available in people's minds. Because of the cognitive arms race introduced by the availability heuristic, the Oregon group advised policymakers that they needed to accept their own cognitive limitations when estimating the occurrence of rare events and allow for the expression of legitimate societal concerns. Persuasive words would not convert the public. Trust was a long-term prospect built through an unblemished safety record, a responsible government agency, and a heighted public appreciation of the technology's benefit.[71] Indeed, no sooner than this advice appeared in print than the 1979 accident at the Three Mile Island reactor occurred, seemingly to validate the public's inarticulate fear of the highly improbable.

In the 1970s, Slovic, Lichtenstein, and Fischhoff made no mention of affect; the word did not appear in their vocabulary. Nuclear opposition resulted not

---

67. Baruch Fischhoff, Paul Slovic, Sarah Lichtenstein, Stephen Read, and Barbara Combs. "How Safe Is Safe Enough? A Psychometric Study of Attitudes Towards Technological Risks and Benefits," *Policy Sciences* 9, no. 2 (1978): 127–152, 133.

68. Sarah Lichtenstein, Paul Slovic, Baruch Fischhoff, Mark Layman, and Barbara Combs, "Judged Frequency of Lethal Events," *Journal of Experimental Psychology: Human Learning and Memory* 4, no. 6 (1978): 551–578, 554.

69. Surveying an engaged citizenry resonated with early polling theory; see Sarah E. Igo, *The Averaged American: Surveys, Citizens, and the Making of a Mass Public*. Cambridge, MA: Harvard University Press, 2007.

70. Paul Slovic, Baruch Fischhoff, and Sarah Lichtenstein. "Rating the Risks," *Environment* 21, no. 3 (1979): 14–39.

71. Paul Slovic, Sarah Lichtenstein, and Baruch Fischhoff, "Images of Disaster: Perception and Acceptance of Risks from Nuclear Power," in Gordon T. Goodman and William D. Rowe (eds.), *Energy Risk Management*. London: Academic Press, 1979, 223–245.

from defective, secretive, or disingenuous motivations, but was the inevitable product of the manner in which healthy organisms processed information.[72] Their explanations favored cognitivism's decidedly cool and rationalistic explanations, namely, "the imaginability and memorability of the hazard."[73] However, something closely resembling affect was hiding in plain sight. Among their nine scales for measuring risk perception was one dedicated to "Common-dread: Is this a risk that people have learned to live with and can think about reasonably calmly, or is it one that people have a great dread for—on the level of a gut reaction?"[74] This dread, an existential, inarticulate, gut reaction, came to saturate their later analysis of risk. The concept came from the nuclear industry's dismissal of the public's supposed hysteria, but it took on new meaning for these psychologists. Such attitudes were not irrational, given the fundamental unknowability of the future and experts' overconfidence in their own predictive abilities.[75] The public possessed a richer conceptualization of risk than the experts. Risky feelings sensed and effectively communicated dangers, which eluded technical assessments, actuarial tables, and computational analysis.

GENDERING JUDGMENT

The team's turn to the League of Women Voters as an emotive yet reasonable public resonated with a very different study of human judgment that was then taking place at the same time across the country: Carol Gilligan's feminist challenge to her mentor Lawrence Kohlberg's cognitive model of moral development. Starting in the late 1950s, Kohlberg oversaw a cognitive revolution in the field of moral psychology. Building on the work of Jean Piaget, he posited a six-stage, sidewise sequence of moral development by presenting a sample of teenage boys from the Chicago suburbs with a series of hypothetical dilemmas and then scoring the youth's reasoning process as revealed by an interview. A classic hypothetical written by Kohlberg and reanalyzed by Gilligan involved a man named Heinz who stole a lifesaving drug for his dying wife from an unscrupulous pharmacist, who overcharged for the treatment. The problem asked children to ponder whether Heinz was justified in his actions and to provide their reasoning. Moral development, as measured by the quality of the boys' reasoning in such cases culminated

---

72. Nisbett and Ross contemporaneously made a similar move in staking out the ground for social cognition. See Nisbett and Ross, *Human Inference*.

73. Slovic, Fischhoff, and Lichtenstein, "Rating the Risks," 38.

74. Fischhoff et al., "How Safe Is Safe Enough?" 133.

75. Baruch Fischhoff, Paul Slovic, and Sarah Lichtenstein, "Knowing with Certainty: The Appropriateness of Extreme Confidence," *Journal of Experimental Psychology: Human Perception and Performance* 3, no. 4 (1977): 552–564.

in something akin to Immanuel Kant's categorical imperative.[76] An ethics of justice as fairness universally applied dovetailed neatly with the consensus liberalism espoused by Kohlberg's contemporaries at Harvard such as the political philosopher John Rawls.[77]

However, the presumed universality of Kohlberg's cognitivism was unraveling as a younger generation of women entering the field of psychology tried to replicate his findings. They noted that women seemed to be largely stuck at stage three, unable to subsume their immediate, interpersonal duties to more general, societal obligations. Rather than seeing women trapped at an inferior level of moral development, perhaps the flaw lay in the measure and its presumed hierarchy of reasoning.[78] Kohlberg's cognitive developmental psychology proved a ready target for feminist interventions.[79] It trafficked in long-standing tropes of women as moral educators, but ones whose domain remained confined to the domestic sphere due to their embeddedness in familial concerns rather than seeking to achieve civic-minded disinterestedness.[80]

Carol Gilligan began her career as Kohlberg's research assistant but soon emerged as his most influential critic.[81] Upon completing her PhD in 1966, she first chose to abandon academia in favor of a life combining professional dance, motherhood, and social activism. She returned as a part-time instructor after becoming "very engaged in all of the liberation movements of the sixties": the civil rights and voter registration, the Vietnam War protests, and the antinuclear movement. By the 1970s, her consciousness had expanded along with that of other women in these movements as they "started talking to each other in a completely

---

76. Lawrence Kohlberg, "The Development of Children's Orientations Toward a Moral Order I. Sequence in the Development of Moral Thought," *Vita Humana* 6, no. 1-2 (1963): 11–33.

77. Katrina Forrester, *In the Shadow of Justice: Postwar Liberalism and the Remaking of Political Philosophy*. Princeton, NJ: Princeton University Press, 2019. On the political assumptions implicit in Kohlberg's model, see Edmund V. Sullivan, "A Study of Kohlberg's Structural Theory of Moral Development: A Critique of Liberal Social Science Ideology," *Human Development* 20, no. 6 (1977): 352–376.

78. The charge that a sex bias impaired Kohlberg's schema predated Gilligan's famous book. See Constance Boucher Holstein, "Irreversible, Stepwise Sequence in the Development of Moral Judgment: A Longitudinal Study of Males and Females," *Child Development* 47, no. 1 (1976): 51–61.

79. Kohlberg's own moral behavior excluded women from the field when he sexually assaulted at least one female graduate student. Nicholas Kristof, "It's Taken 5 Decades to Get the Ph.D. Her Abusive Professor Denied Her," *New York Times*, May 25, 2019.

80. Linda K. Kerber, "Separate Spheres, Female Worlds, Woman's Place: The Rhetoric of Women's History," *Journal of American History* 75, no. 1 (1988): 9–39.

81. Lawrence Kohlberg and Carol Gilligan, "The Adolescent as a Philosopher: The Discovery of the Self in a Postconventional World," *Daedalus* 100, no. 4 (1971): 1051–1086.

different way about our experience."[82] At Harvard University, she brought this activist consciousness to bear on the field of developmental psychology.[83] Building on Kohlberg's concerns but seeking to be relevant to more immediate issues, Gilligan first planned to interview male Harvard students regarding their decisions when confronted by the draft upon graduation. With the repeal of the draft lottery in 1973, military service in Vietnam presented a less pressing moral quandary. Conveniently however, the Supreme Court's decision in *Roe v. Wade* that same year created a new dilemma for Harvard's female students, one that Gilligan's male mentor deemed uninteresting.[84] Gilligan interviewed twenty-nine local women contemplating an abortion, in the first trimester of their pregnancy and again a year later.[85]

Like Kohlberg, much of Gilligan's argument relied on a careful evaluation of the reasoning offered by her participants when considering real-life dilemmas or hypotheticals. However, she rejected her mentor's coding scheme as sexist. For example, she offered a very different reading of the Heinz dilemma among the developing adolescents she interviewed. Citing the example of "Amy," Gilligan argued that this young woman did not see the story as "a math problem with humans but a narrative of relationship that extends over time"[86] Instead, her participants responded in gendered but equally "reasonable" ways: "these two children see two very different moral problems—Jake a conflict between life and property that can be resolved by logical deduction, Amy a fracture of human relationship that must be mended with its own thread. Asking different questions that arise from different conceptions of the moral domain, the children arrive at answers that fundamentally diverge, and the arrangement of these answers as successive stages on a scale of increased moral maturity calibrated by the logic of the boys' response misses the different truth revealed in the judgment of the girl."[87] Gilligan staged the tension between the abstract and the concrete, the general and the personal, in women's reasoning, their potential objectivity. "Thus in all of the women's descriptions, identity is defined in a context of relationship and

82. Carol Gilligan, Interview by Leeat Granek [Video Recording], Psychology's Feminist Voices Oral History and Online Archive Project. New York, September 15, 2009. http://www.feministvoices.com/assets/Feminist-Presence/Gilligan/Carol-Gilligan-Oral-History.pdf

83. On Gilligan's role in the feminist origins of life course developmental psychology, see Susanne Schmidt, *Midlife Crisis: The Feminist Origins of a Chauvinist Cliché*. Chicago: University of Chicago Press, 2020, 139–151.

84. "Carol Gilligan," Psychology's Feminist Voices interview, p. 7.

85. Carol Gilligan and Mary Field Belenky, "A Naturalistic Study of Abortion Decisions," *New Directions for Child and Adolescent Development*, no. 7 (1980): 69–90.

86. Carol Gilligan, *In a Different Voice: Psychological Theory and Women's Development*. Cambridge, MA: Harvard University Press, 1982, 28.

87. Gilligan, *In a Different Voice*, 31.

judged by a standard of responsibility and care. Similarly, morality is seen by these women as arising from the experience of connection and conceived as a problem of inclusion rather than one of balancing claims."[88] Reflecting the wider concerns of the woman's movement, Gilligan sought to undercut such dichotomies between public and private, reason and emotion.

Gilligan's *In a Different Voice* (1982) became a widely reviewed, national bestseller and a controversial work among her fellow feminists. At issue was her extrapolation from her small, fairly homogeneous Boston-area samples to a more general psychology of women. Her feminist readers worried that the ethics of care implied an "essential" and essentializing female way of grappling with the world, one that inverted Kohlberg's sexist hierarchy but left women fundamentally governed by their emotions.[89] Gilligan demurred. "The different voice I describe is characterized not by gender but theme. Its association with women is an empirical observation, and it is primarily through women's voices that I trace its development. But this association is not absolute, and the contrasts between male and female voices are presented here to highlight a distinction between two modes of thought and to focus a problem of interpretation rather than to represent a generalization about either sex."[90] Rather than posit an essential femininity, she listened to how a particular set of women reasoned due to their socialization at the distinct historical juncture she observed. Her interviews revealed *a* different voice rather than *the different* one.

The Oregon group's approach shared Gilligan's common feminist starting point of listening to women's voices, voices that were often marginalized in civic deliberation. By attending to such "different voices," both Gilligan's research and that of the Oregon group called into question previously universal models of sound reasoning and good judgment. This resulted in heeding shared, communal concerns beyond individual choices and addressing relational, distributive questions of harm. Their common approach also entailed a shift in focus from ingeniously devised "hypothetical" scenarios to asking participants to evaluate the "real-life" risk-filled choice they actually faced in their daily lives.[91] The Oregon group further insisted that their psychometric approach offered a democratic alternative to more "politically conservative" forms of risk assessment, such as Starr's revealed preferences method. Rather than privileging the existing social and economic status quo, directly soliciting the expressed preferences of citizens allowed psychologists to track and represent changing values and articulate new norms. Moreover, their consultative approach allowed them to address distributional

---

88. Gilligan, *In a Different Voice*, 160.

89. See "*In a Different Voice*: An Interdisciplinary Forum, Reply" *Signs* 11(2) (1986): 324–333.

90. Gilligan, *In a Different Voice*, 2.

91. See also Norma Haan, "Hypothetical and Actual Moral Reasoning in a Situation of Civil Disobedience," *Journal of Personality and Social Psychology* 32, no. 2 (1975): 255–270.

questions of who in society has to bear the risks and who receives the benefits.[92] These feminist commitments allowed these psychologists to reveal the consensus undergirding early cognitive science's model of rationality and the mind as a false consensus, if not a forced one.[93] The gender of the rational "intuitive scientist" of Cold War cognition went unmarked but in practice defaulted to males. By the late 1970s, the disembodiness of his reason was an increasingly untenable fiction. Seeing this individual not only as cognitively limited and bounded like Simon's chessplayer but biased in a fundamental way reflected feminist concerns about the discriminatory effects of male bias in science (the paragon of human rationality), employment, and everyday life.[94]

The reception of Gilligan's book sheds some light on the Oregon group's resistance to equating antinuclear opposition with (mere) feelings. Even Gilligan's feminist readers tended to "equate care with feelings, which they oppose to thought, and imagine caring as passive or confined to some separate sphere."[95] Similarly, in the first published critique of the sex bias in Kohlberg's stepwise sequence, Constance Holstein spoke of "the problem of where to categorize irrational but morally relevant emotions such as compassion, sympathy, and love."[96] In contrast, Gilligan sought to overcome this long-standing dichotomy between feminized affect and masculine cognition. She intended to "describe care and justice as two moral perspectives that organize both thinking and feelings and empower the self to take different kinds of action in public as well as private life."[97] Any such realignment had just begun by the late 1970s. At times, decision making informed by emotions still connoted an inferior, partial, reactive, and feminine form of irrationality; the very imaginary in which the nuclear power industry trafficked. The psychometric paradigm also suggested that wisdom resided in affective decisions, but the Oregon group proved more hesitant to follow such implications. If they did not follow Gilligan in legitimizing and elevating this alternative mode of reasoning, they at least sought to create a space for understanding and depathologizing the psychology behind public resistance.

---

92. Baruch Fischhoff, Paul Slovic, and Sarah Lichtenstein, "Weighing the Risks: Risks: Benefits Which Risks Are Acceptable?" *Environment: Science and Policy for Sustainable Development* 21, no. 4 (1979): 17–38.

93. On the 1970s feminist challengers to the consensus liberalism of early cognitivism, see Cohen-Cole, *The Open Mind*, 217–252.

94. Rae Carlson, "Where Is the Person in Personality Research?" *Psychological Bulletin* 75, no. 3 (1971): 203–219; Sandra L. Bem and Daryl J. Bem. "Does Sex-Biased Job Advertising 'Aid and Abet' Sex Discrimination?" *Journal of Applied Social Psychology* 3, no. 1 (1973): 6–18.

95. Gilligan, "Reply," *Signs* 11, no. 2 (1986): 324–333, 326.

96. Holstein, "Irreversible, Stepwise Sequence in the Development of Moral Judgment," 61.

97. Gilligan, "Reply," *Signs* 11, no. 2 (1986): 324–333, 326.

IN THE SHADOW OF YUCCA MOUNTAIN

In the 1980s, Slovic further simplified the factor space of the psychometric paradigm to one axis relating to the information available about the hazard (its unknowability) and one relating to dread. This dread scale latter predicted where the public's choices diverged from the engineer–experts.[98] This wordless, nearly inexpressible, feeling succinctly communicated the public's fears and trepidations about making decisions involving technologies with long-term, involuntary, and potentially catastrophic consequences. This amplification of affect's role in decision making occurred as the Cold War reheated in the late 1970s and nuclear winter once again loomed as a possibility. In December 1979, the Soviet Union invaded Afghanistan, bringing an end to détente. Opinion polls recorded a renewed support for defense spending, a change in attitude that Ronald Reagan successfully channeled in his successful presidential bid in 1980.[99] A 1981 Gallup Poll found that 70 percent of those surveyed believed nuclear war was possible, with 30 percent rating the risk as good or certain. The Reagan administration's more hawkish stance soon created its own backlash in the form of the international nuclear freeze movement. In June 1982, a million people gathered in Central Park in the largest demonstration in U.S. history.[100] Understanding the motivation of this suddenly revived social movement provided a platform for Fischhoff's collaboration with social psychologists. Their analysis of the divergent "images of nuclear war" held by activists, experts, and world leaders further blurred the distinction between the affective and the cognitive.[101]

The immediate impetus for the psychometric paradigm's redesign, however, was Slovic's return to the Las Vegas area in 1986 to assess a very different risky bet that he and Lichtenstein had done a decade beforehand. The long-term storage of the waste produced by nuclear reactors was a technically difficult problem and a contentious political issue. The political valence of antinuclear activism mutated over the course of the 1970s from the near exclusive purview of the pacifist Left to include forms of antistatist populism distrustful of government oversight.[102] The Nuclear Waste Policy Act (1982) sought to address this resistance by outlining the process for selecting a centralized facility for the permanent, underground storage of 75,000 tons of the nation's radioactive waste. To avoid contaminating the soil and water table, the site required specific geological qualities, seismic stability

---

98. Paul Slovic, "Perception of Risk," *Science* 236, no. 4799 (1987): 280–285, 282.

99. For a summary of contemporary polling data, see Daniel Yankelovich and Larry Kaagan, "Assertive America," *Foreign Affairs* 59, no. 3 (1980): 696–713, 701.

100. David Cortright, *Peace: A History of Movements and Ideas*. New York: Cambridge University Press, 2008, 126–154.

101. Susan T. Fiske, Baruch Fischhoff, and Michael A. Milburn, "Images of Nuclear War," *Journal of Social Issues* 39, no. 1 (1983): 1–197.

102. See Natasha Zaretsky, *Radiation Nation: Three Mile Island and the Political Transformation of the 1970s*. New York: Columbia University Press, 2018.

above all. Perhaps the most daunting aspect of this engineering project was its time scale: there was a need to secure surrounding environment for ten thousand years as the waste decayed. In 1984, the Energy Department identified three potential sites for the repository: Deaf Smith County in the Texas Panhandle; the Hanford nuclear reservation in Washington State; and Yucca Mountain near the Nevada test site. All three states fiercely opposed their selection. Regional tensions arose as Western states were being asked to house waste that was largely produced by eastern states to meet the needs of their citizens. To assuage the concerns of the selected states, the Energy Department promised $500 million to support research on the feasibility of each site, with a final, evidence-based decision made in 1990.[103]

In the Nevada case, Yucca Mountain was not only proximate to the test site but lay only a hundred miles from Las Vegas, the state's main tourist attraction. The gamblers' haven exemplified a new U.S. economy where tourism supplanted industrial manufacturing as the source of local wealth. This economy of leisurely consumption required protecting and projecting certain images beyond its physical boundaries of place.[104] As a spokesperson for Nevada's governor put it: "we don't want to replace the neon glow of Las Vegas with a radioactive glow."[105] The relationship with the Department of Energy quickly deteriorated, with the state governments challenging the federal authority's evaluation methods and willingness to share information.[106] In December 1987, as part of a deficit-reducing bill, Congress selected Yucca Mountain as the sole candidate, agreeing to examine the other sites only if the Yucca site did not prove feasible.[107] After the Nevada legislature passed two bills opposing the site's selection, the state's attorney general filed suit in federal court to prevent construction of the repository.[108] The state also used the promised funds from the Energy Department to hire experts to demonstrate the project's inappropriateness.

Slovic alone joined this project. Reagan-era cuts to the National Science Foundation (NSF) made securing salary support from grants increasingly difficult. By the mid-1980s, Fischhoff had joined the faculty at Carnegie Mellon University, and Lichenstein had turned from science to support the electoral campaigns of

---

103. "U.S. Names 3 Sites for Atomic Study," *New York Times*, December 20, 1984, A24.

104. Hal Rothman, *Neon Metropolis: How Las Vegas Started the Twenty-first Century*. London: Routledge, 2002.

105. Karen Galatz, cited in Iver Peterson, "Issue of National Nuclear Waste Dump Polarizes Three States," *New York Times*, January 25, 1985, A10.

106. John H. Gervers, "The NIMBY Syndrome: Is It Inevitable?" *Environment: Science and Policy for Sustainable Development* 29, no. 8 (1987): 18–43.

107. Susan F. Rasky "Accord Is Reached on Nuclear Dump," *New York Times*, December 18, 1987, A32; Rasky, "Nevada May End Up Holding the Nuclear Bag," *New York Times*, December 20, 1987, E4.

108. "Nevada Sues to Block Nuclear Waste Dump," *New York Times*, December 28, 1989, A19.

female candidates for office. Slovic remained at Decision Research but also accepted a professorship at the University of Oregon. By this time, he ranked among the nation's leading authorities on risk. His name frequently appeared in newspaper stories across the United States deliberating various risks and their management, whether the issue involved seatbelts in cars, chemical exposure, or nuclear power. At a time when Kahneman and Tversky remained focused on intellectual battles within academia, Slovic embraced his role in risk analysis. Indeed, prior to Kahneman's 2003 Nobel Prize award, Slovic was the most prominent voice in the mass media in explaining cognitive heuristics and biases. Many of these newspaper stories framed the singular public's response to risk in its irrationality, even if Slovic demurred from this view, insisting that "It's not fair to call public perception of risk irrational, just because it differs from that of experts."[109]

Because of Slovic's capacity as a risk analyst, James Chalmers and James Flynn approached him to join an interdisciplinary team of social scientists (including economists, sociologists, psychologists, anthropologists, and geographers) dedicated to studying the potential social and economic impact of the Yucca site selection. Although the funding came from the Energy Department, the team worked in opposition to its experts. The contentious nature of the project led to considerable scrutiny from hostile observers and resulted in one of the largest consultative social science projects of its era, with numerous waves of telephone surveys and hundreds of reports.[110]

In the reports to the Nevada Nuclear Waste Project Office (NWPO), the team largely abandoned the cognitivist language Slovic had employed during the 1970s. He no longer framed opposition to nuclear power in terms of the "availability" of information or the individual's inability to comprehend the reasoning of probability theory. Emotions and images served as the primary drivers of the public's decision making. In part, Slovic's turn to emotions involved recognition of the failure of the 1970s informational campaigns to sway public opinion. His strategy also met the needs of his new patron. He was fundamentally embedded in an advertising campaign. Las Vegas's continued growth as a favored tourist destination depended on its national reputation. In the postindustrial economy, the management of image and impressions counted for everything.

The team began with a conventional telephone survey of random samples of Nevadans and people residing in the rest of the country. The questions asked respondents to form an attitude toward the national repository: its necessity, safety, and economic consequences. The survey called upon them to reason out the benefits and the costs.[111] The results proved unsatisfactory. Slovic's own

109. Malcolm W. Browne, "In the Human Equation, Risk Is Risk Endured," *New York Times*, March 30, 1980, E22.

110. Paul Slovic, "Remembering Jim Flynn," *Risk Analysis* 33 (2013): 183–185.

111. Howard Kunreuther, William H. Desvousges, and Paul Slovic. "Nevada's Predicament: Public Perceptions of Risk from the Proposed Nuclear Waste Repository." *Environment* 30, no. 8 (1988): 16–33.

research made the respondents question whether self-reported attitudes accurately predicted people's behavioral choices. The project demanded immediate and unsavory reactions to associating Las Vegas with nuclear waste.

Obtaining these kind of reactions required a change in method. His own research with Lichtenstein on the construction of preferences demonstrated how attitudes were often formed, rather than being simply revealed, through the contingencies of the elicitation process. The very framing of the questions could produce a different response. Slovic switched from his standardized psychometric rating scales to a time-sensitive word association technique. In telephone interviews, his team asked respondents to quickly free associate using Las Vegas and "nuclear waste repository" as images. Rapid word association tests has a venerable history in psychology, going back to Francis Galton in the nineteenth century. However, these tests became more closely associated with Carl Jung, psychoanalysis, and related projective techniques to plumb hidden, psychic depths.[112] Slovic and his team conceded as much, noting that "we reveal ourselves through associations in ways we might find difficult to do if we were required to spell out the full propositions behind these associations through answers to questions."[113] Peering beneath people's polite veneer revealed "pervasive qualities of dread, revulsion, and anger; the raw materials of stigmatization and political opposition."[114] The 1978 psychometric study called upon an informed public to carefully consider and deliberate on the risk posed by different technologies. In the shadow of Yucca Mountain, Slovic demanded the public's immediate, barely conscious, emotional reactions under constrained time pressure.

Slovic's perspective on risk remained resolutely psychological, but after Yucca Mountain he increasingly talked about politics. He refused to equate an affective public with an irrational one. No senator or congressperson wanted the national repository site in their backyard despite its purported economic benefits. Sensational media coverage certainly amplified subjective risk perception about rare, ill-understood events, but in 1986 Chernobyl had demonstrated how the statistically unlikely still came with real consequences.[115] Given recent history, the

---

112. Peter Hegarty, "Homosexual Signs and Heterosexual Silences: Rorschach Research on Male Homosexuality from 1921 to 1969," *Journal of the History of Sexuality* 12, no. 3 (2003): 400–423; Peter Galison, "Image of Self," in Lorraine Daston (ed.), *Things that Talk: Object Lessons from Art and Science*. Cambridge, MA: MIT Press, 2004, 257–296; Naamah Akavia, *Subjectivity in Motion: Life, Art, and Movement in the Work of Hermann Rorschach*. London: Routledge, 2012; Katherine A. Hubbard, *Queer Ink: A Blotted History towards Liberation*. London: Routledge, 2019.

113. Paul Slovic, Mark Layman, and James H. Flynn, "What Comes to Mind When You Hear the Words 'Nuclear Waste Repository'? A Study of 10,000 Images," Report Prepared for Nevada Agency for Nuclear Projects Yucca Mountain Socioeconomics Project, November 1990, 4.

114. Slovic, Layman, and Flynn, "What Comes to Mind," 23.

115. Roger E. Kasperson, Ortwin Renn, Paul Slovic, Halina S. Brown, Jacque Emel, Robert Goble, Jeanne X. Kasperson, and Samuel Ratick. "The Social Amplification of Risk: A Conceptual Framework," *Risk Analysis* 8, no. 2 (1988): 177–187.

American people had good reason to doubt the efficacy of federal regulators to protect them. Beyond the lost confidence in government following the Watergate scandal, the American public had lived through a history of bureaucratic mismanagement of nuclear waste that had rightly damaged trust. Affective judgments intuitively grasped information from a situation that experts tended to downplay and ignore. In the Yucca Mountain case, the federal government had stoked such emotional reactions by subverting its own deliberate process in selecting a site.[116]

If the recognition of affect in decision making derived from the messy politics of nuclear siting, its formal naming as a heuristic owed much to the return to the laboratory and an elegance for experimental design harkening back to the work on preference reversals. Slovic credits the dissertation of his student Ali Siddiq Alhakami for the breakthrough. In practice, beneficial technologies often carry high risks, and with great risk comes great reward, but the human mind prefers more dichotomous thinking, seeing costs and benefits as inversely correlated. Back in the lab, Al Alhakami and Slovic artificially manipulated the undergraduate participants' impression of different technologies by providing them with new information about either their cost or their benefit. Informing the participants about the costs made them instantly reevaluate the benefits and vice versa; an effect magnified under time pressure. Put simply, people made snap decisions regardless of whether they liked or disliked an object and assigned other informational attribute retrospectively to justify their existing feelings.[117]

COLD WAR, HOT HAND

Tracing the science of decision making through the Oregon group clarifies a number of interpretive issues central to the recent history of psychology. Three issues seem worth underscoring. First, these psychologists exemplify the polyvalence of what counted as "Cold War Social Science" and its legacy. Moreover, they offer a unique vantage point for understanding the wider shift from cognition to affect starting in the détente phase of the Cold War. Finally, they presented an alternative to the contemporary politics of cognitive biases, behavioral economics, and dual process theories more generally.

Historians Joel Isaac, David Engerman, and Mark Solovey have each dissuaded scholars from talking about a monolithic Cold War social science whose mission was driven solely by the interests of the military-industrial complex. Instead, they advocate a more pluralistic vision of a variety of social sciences in the Cold

---

116. Paul Slovic, James H. Flynn, and Mark Layman, "Perceived Risk, Trust, and the Politics of Nuclear Waste," *Science* 254, no. 5038 (1991): 1603–1607.

117. Ali Siddiq Alhakami and Paul Slovic, "A Psychological Study of the Inverse Relationship between Perceived Risk and Perceived Benefit," *Risk Analysis* 14, no. 6 (1994): 1085–1096.

War.[118] Despite their admonitions, the old image persists. A certain set of sites continue to loom large in the historical imagination: Harvard Yard, the RAND Corporation, Carnegie Tech's Graduate School of Industrial Administration, the beltway.[119] However, a psychologist on the witness stand demonstrating the utility of differently colored dolls as a projective test, the Esalen Institute overlooking Big Sur, the feminist rap group converting private hurts into public action were all Cold War assemblages. How does one reconcile the view from Harvard Yard and the view from Esalen to understand their dialectic and the frequent flows among them? Thinking through the cultural politics of détente helps us develop this perspective. Inspired by nuclear dread and the fear of annihilation, the affect heuristic hardly counts as a "groovy" endeavor.[120] Nevertheless, its genealogy drives home the necessity of holding together the military-industrial complex, the counterculture, and the exchanges between them in the making of the social sciences in Cold War America.[121]

The shift at Decision Research from cognitive processing to affective dispositions was far from unique. If the mid-1950s saw a cognitive revolution, the new attention to how cognitive biases necessarily compromised good reasoning signaled the start of an affective counterrevolution that returned unthinking, automatic behavior to the center of psychology. Notably, the turn to affect did not begin with "biology's gift" of anticipatory neuroscience, which remained a largely British endeavor in the 1970s.[122] Instead, it first derived from psychologists' immersion in a host of applied and clinical problems. Here the local environmental and feminist opposition to nuclear power exemplifies the historical shift in conceptualizing human decision making from information deficits to affect-governed choices. Having been repackaged in the twenty-first century as the more general affect heuristic, the fear, dread, and revulsion inspired by atomic power were transmitted into a host of post-Cold War scenarios.

Indeed, part of the underwrittenness of the affective revolution is a clear understanding of its political consequences. The cognitive revolution occurred at

---

118. Joel Isaac, "The Human Sciences in Cold War America," *The Historical Journal* 50, no. 3 (2007): 725–746; David C. Engerman, "Social Science in the Cold War," *Isis* 101, no. 2 (2010): 393–400; Mark Solovey, "Cold War Social Science: Specter, Reality, or Useful Concept?" in Solovey and Hamilton Craven (eds.), *Cold War Social Science*. New York: Palgrave Macmillan, 2012, pp. 1–22.

119. For a more capacious view than is typical of the recent literature, see Ellen Herman, *The Romance of American Psychology: Political Culture in the Age of Experts*. Berkeley: University of California Press, 1995.

120. David Kaiser and W. Patrick McCray, eds., *Groovy Science: Knowledge, Innovation, and American Counterculture*. Chicago: University of Chicago Press, 2016.

121. On these waves of Cold War science, see Jon Agar, "What Happened in the Sixties?" *British Journal for the History of Science* 41, no. 4 (2008): 567–600.

122. Constantina Papoulias and Felicity Callard, "Biology's Gift: Interrogating the Turn to Affect," *Body and Society* 16, no. 1 (2010): 29–56.

consensus liberalism's high point and reflected its principles of universality, openness, and sound individual reason.[123] The affective revolution happened after the collapse of utopian schemes on both sides of the Cold War and against the background of post-Watergate skepticism of federal authority, the energy crisis, neoliberal deregulation, the War on Terror, and the polarizing, tribalizing culture wars of red versus blue state politics. Research leading to the affect heuristic initially took inspiration from the democratic inclusiveness of feminist activism, but the concept was canonized amid the conservative antistatism of the 1980s. This substitution of countercultural challenge for a policy science fit for deregulation was not unique but reflected psychology's changing role in public affairs.

Today, "libertarian paternalism" represents the most visible political substantiation of the new psychology, centered at the University of Chicago, with the economist Richard Thaler and the legal scholar Cass Sunstein (former colleagues of and later advisors to Barack Obama).[124] In this context, affective science (represented by the behavioral nudge as fashionable public policy intervention) carries antidemocratic consequences wherein experts decry the very possibility of self-rule due to the masses' psychological failings. Because the people cannot be trusted to make informed, rational decisions, governments must create a choice architecture to nudge them onto the proper track.[125] Paternalistic institutions must engineer ways for them to *unconsciously, automatically* realize the proper goals (to sustain the system). Obama famously campaigned on hope, but hope quickly floundered thanks to congressional intransigence. His own electoral victory signaled the power of data analysts and behavioral science as new tools of governance.[126] In 2015, Obama established the Social and Behavioral Science Office. Nudges flourished as a political intervention amid the utter hopelessness of the jobless recovery, climate change, and governmental gridlock.

Despite the rhetoric of *dual* processes, the interventions behavior scientists recommended inevitably focused on manipulating System 1 (the fast, automatic, affective) into making better decisions. This is especially true of programs targeting the global poor.[127] Little remains of cognitivism and its rational, educable human nature. Analyzing the rhetorical strategies used by Kahneman and Tversky, fellow decision scientist Lola Lopes noted: "The idea

---

123. Cohen-Cole, *The Open Mind*.

124. Cass R. Sunstein and Richard H. Thaler, "Libertarian Paternalism Is not an Oxymoron," *The University of Chicago Law Review* (2003): 1159–1202.

125. On the ethics of nudges, see Evan Selinger and Kyle Whyte. "Is There a Right Way to Nudge? The Practice and Ethics of Choice Architecture," *Sociology Compass* 5, no. 10 (2011): 923–935.

126. Zeynep Tufekci, "Engineering the Public: Big Data, Surveillance and Computational Politics," *First Monday* 19, no. 7 (2014). https://firstmonday.org/ojs/index.php/fm/article/view/4901

127. World Bank, *World Development Report 2015: Mind, Society, and Behavior*. Washington, DC: The World Bank, 2015.

that people-are-irrational-and-science-has-proved-it is useful propaganda for anyone who has rationality to sell."[128] For his part, Kahneman remained ambivalent about his policy role, often taking a bemused and deflationary stance when asked about specific interventions.[129] In public speech, he expounded a rather fatalistic, tragicomic worldview. Pity poor humans unable to exceed their cognitive failings where even the simple pursuit of happiness often proved illusionary![130] Inevitability and ironic distance pervade his writing. This hopelessness is a central ingredient in how the research was communicated as it gained popularity with the punditry.

In countercultural Eugene, Slovic, Lichtenstein, and Fischhoff shared Kahneman's psychological views but rejected his quietism. They carefully balanced a recognition of the epistemic failings of both the public and the presuppositions of "expert systems" while retaining faith in deliberative democracy. The Oregon group insisted on holding together what other substantiations of JDM pulled apart. Nature rendered people cognitively limited and affectively predisposed, but a democracy has responsibility for creating the spaces for consultation and deliberation despite these limits. The Oregon group actively resisted against the antidemocratic implications of cognitive biases. Instead, they consistently mobilized their research in this area into conscious-raising efforts (later countering psychic numbing rather than behavioral nudges as policymakers embraced their psychology).[131] If one of the political outcomes (or appeals) of Kahneman and Tversky's heuristics and biases approach was an elevation of computerized, statistical decision making above overconfident localized expertise, then Slovic, Lichtenstein, and Fischhoff represent the counterexample. Cost-benefit analysis and risk assessment of nuclear power plants were actuarially sound (e.g., the Rasmussen Report), but it nevertheless failed to solve the political problem of public opposition.

The Oregon group's initial presentation of the laypeople's ranking of risks was not dissimilar from Tversky's famous analysis of "hot hand" in basketball.[132] There the smart, cool-headed, all-knowing cognitive psychologist assumed epistemic

---

128. Lola L. Lopes, "The Rhetoric of Irrationality," *Theory & Psychology* 1, no. 1 (1991): 65–82, 78.

129. On Kahneman's agnosticism in the political dispute between Sunstein and Slovic, see Kahneman, *Thinking Fast and Slow*, chapter 13.

130. Daniel Kahneman, Alan B. Krueger, David Schkade, Norbert Schwarz, and Arthur A. Stone. "Would You Be Happier If You Were Richer? A Focusing Illusion," *Science* 312, no. 5782 (2006): 1908–1910.

131. Paul Slovic, "'If I Look at the Mass I Will Never Act'": Psychic Numbing and Genocide," *Judgment and Decision Making* 2, no. 2 (2007): 79–95.

132. Reflecting on his 1970s research, Slovic was "struck by how harshly we came down on the public." See Slovic, "Understanding Perceived Risk: 1978–2015," *Environment: Science and Policy for Sustainable Development* 58, no. 1 (2016): 25–29, 25.

superiority over the rabid fan. He debunked the superstitious "belief" in winning streaks with the statistical "cold facts" that players do not have a better chance of making multiple shots in a row.[133] The fan's feverish resistance to this truth represents another instance of the layperson's irrationality and the psychologist's superiority. Part of Kahneman and Tversky's legacy was to transform every scenario, every possible problem, into a similar game. The same year as Tversky's hot hand article appeared, his grad student co-author Robert Vallone, along with Stanford colleagues Lee Ross and Mark Lepper, published their influential formulation of the "hostile media phenomenon." After an initial pilot study that used coverage of the Carter–Reagan election failed to generate sufficient heat in their participants, they turned to the Middle East. They selected Stanford undergraduates for their pro-Israeli and Palestinian attitudes and showed them clips of news coverage of the 1982 massacre of Palestinian refugees in Beirut perpetrated by a Christian militia. At issue was the invading Israeli army's culpability in the massacre. In a powerful illustration of motivated, affective cognition, both groups perceived the coverage as biased against their preferred side.[134]

Both the hot hand and hostile media studies undercut the reflexivity of the cognitive bias approach. Instead of being subject to the same processes, these studies repositioned the psychologist as the cool, neutral evaluator of the hot, motivated, and deficient public. The psychologist's toolbox provided them alone with capacity to sort through the biases wrought by humanity's limited cognitive machinery. And yet, was a democratic citizenry's right to decide their long-term fate equivalent to the feverish delusions of fandom? The Oregon group seemingly answered No. Expertise, when it came to knowing the future of complex systems, was always limited. Handling nuclear waste did not entail a one-off decision like the one in the Linda problem, but a society calculating risk on an awesome, inconceivable time scale.[135] Nuclear temporality raised questions of intergenerational justice, with those now living constraining the choices of those not yet conceived.

At the same time, the social cognition approach the Oregon group championed facilitated social psychology's retreat from the everyday and the reconstitution of the laboratory as a curated, pastoral garden for cultivating psychic truth.[136] In contrast to contemporary alternatives such as community psychology, theirs was a policy-relevant science, but one increasingly distant from social activism and movements.

---

133. Thomas Gilovich, Robert Vallone, and Amos Tversky, "The Hot Hand in Basketball: On the Misperception of Random Sequences," *Cognitive Psychology* 17, no. 3 (1985): 295–314.

134. Robert Vallone, Lee Ross, and Mark Lepper, "The Hostile Media Phenomenon: Biased Perception and Perceptions of Media Bias in Coverage of the Beirut Massacre," *Journal of Personality and Social Psychology* 49, no. 3 (1985): 577–585.

135. Gerd Gigerenzer, "How to Make Cognitive Illusions Disappear: Beyond 'Heuristics and Biases,'" *European Review of Social Psychology* 2, no. 1 (1991): 83–115.

136. Steven Conn, "Back to the Garden: Communes, the Environment, and Antiurban Pastoralism at the End of the Sixties," *Journal of Urban History* 36, no. 6 (2010): 831–848.

Most importantly, social cognition relocated the locus from the social psychologist's gaze from overt conduct in lived situations to how the lone individual perceived others in the inner recesses of their mind. The rise of social cognition tracked the psychologist's waning interest in material, lived social problems in favor of abstract and highly generalized scenarios.

The particular history of nuclear regulation and its psychologization remind us that declarations of "human irrationality" have a history and politics.[137] They famously flourished in fin-de-siècle Vienna amid the crisis of liberalism, leading a generation of modernist intellectuals to retreat into the recesses of private life.[138] They reemerged from the contentious politics of the 1960s as a wider range of citizens asserted their rights, breaking down the "vital center" consensus established by white males after World War II. Public irrationality was the rhetoric of the establishment (here the nuclear industry). *The very reason it turned to psychological expertise* in the 1970s was the inability of such a stance to handle its own public relations fiascos. It represented the breakdown and failure of the deliberative decision making promised if never fully delivered by Project Candor in 1953. By the 1980s, even psychologists schooled in the new social movements adopted public irrationality as their own. Like psychoanalysis before it, social cognition represented a tool for diagnosing social ills while withdrawing from the messiness of social life and political action. It reinscribed the expert's ability to stand aloof and judge (while boldly proclaiming the fallibility of all human judgment). Today, we live in the shadow of behavioral technologies born out of the hopelessness provoked by potential nuclear disaster. Ironically, revisiting the history of the Oregon group might offer a glimmer of hope. Among their contemporaries, they uniquely held together the ubiquity of cognitive biases and the necessity of deliberative, democratic institutions.

---

137. On the ubiquity of self-deception as a foundational assumption for psychology, see Michael Pettit, *The Science of Deception: Psychology and Commerce in America*. Chicago: University of Chicago Press, 2013.

138. Carl E. Schorske, *Fin-de-Siècle Vienna: Politics and Culture*. New York: Vintage, 1981.

6

Rethinking the Politics of Self-Esteem

In 1976, social psychologist William McGuire took his colleagues to task for a conceptual confusion at the heart of their field. He argued that for much of the twentieth century American psychologists too readily conflated self-concept (personal identity as a whole) with evaluative self-esteem, "as if our thoughts about ourselves are concerned almost entirely with how good we are."[1] Self-esteem, more so than any other word or concept, captured the growth of the psychological society, the psy-disciplines' expansion beyond treatment of psychopathology in institutionalized settings toward ordinary adjustment while they simultaneously universalized mental distress seeing individuals inhabiting "sick societies." The *APA Dictionary of Psychology* defines self-esteem as "the degree to which the qualities and characteristics contained in one's self-concept are perceived to be positive. It reflects a person's physical self-image, view of his or her accomplishments and capabilities, and values and perceived success in living up to them, *as well as the ways in which others view and respond to that person*."[2] Self-esteem revolves around humanity's dual existence as egotistical yet social beings, self-interested while requiring approval from others. Much of the appeal of self-esteem lies in this very capaciousness. For this reason, it has ranked among the most frequently studied psychological constructs. A 2002 survey found over 20,000 articles examining self-esteem.[3] These two aims of description and critique are often in tension, which explains why self-esteem has been such a central yet loaded concept for psychologists.

---

1. William J. McGuire and A. Padawer-Singer, "Trait Salience in the Spontaneous Self-concept," *Journal of Personality and Social Psychology* 33, no. 6 (1976): 743–754, 743.

2. Gary VandenBos, *APA Dictionary of Psychology*. Washington, DC: APA, 2015. Italics added.

3. Timothy A. Judge, Amir Erez, Joyce E. Bono, and Carl J. Thoresen, "Are Measures of Self-Esteem, Neuroticism, Locus of Control, and Generalized Self-Efficacy Indicators of a Common Core Construct?," *Journal of Personality and Social Psychology* 83, no. 3 (2002): 693–710.

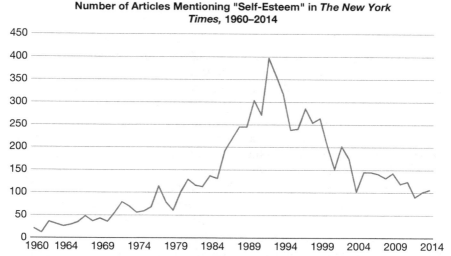

Figure 6.1 Articles per year mentioning "self-esteem" in *The New York Times*, 1960–2014.

Self-esteem's cultural salience in the United States seems to have tapered off since the early 1990s. Around this same time, the language of expert-driven self-help seemingly shifted with the rise of a new set of interrelated terms centered on self-regulation and self-control.[4] These latter terms dropped self-esteem's dialogical, relational aspect. This historical shift reflected psychologists' own adaptation to their political environment. Self-esteem in a modern sense coalesced out of the deprivations of the Great Depression and the political crises this crisis provoked. The concept's fate became tied to the capacities of the liberal welfare state to repair the psychic damage done to its citizens, rendering them both more equal under the law and more productive in their daily existence. Western democracies, especially the United States, hit peak self-esteem in the early 1990s. Since then, psychologists have lost faith in their capacity to give away self-worth to improve society. Instead, they have preached a neo-Victorian gospel of self-reliance. At a time when social mobility became more difficult, when inherited social inequality became more entrenched, psychologists likewise abandoned their Keynesian model of human capital and embraced its neo-liberal counterpart.

---

4. Jeremy T. Burman, Christopher D. Green, and Stuart Shanker, "On the Meanings of Self-Regulation: Digital Humanities in Service of Conceptual Clarity," *Child Development* 86, no. 5 (2015): 1507–1521.

ORIGINS

Contemporary psychologists usually trace the popularity of self-esteem as an intervention to combat the excesses of the 1960s counterculture and the permissiveness of the human potential movement. The term actually dates to the seventeenth century, and a notion of self-love long served as a fixture of Western literature on moral philosophy, self-improvement, and pedagogy. For example, most phrenologists counted self-esteem among the faculties found on the contours of the skull.[5] A materialist worldview in which various mental faculties were constituted by physical organs or components of the brain, phrenology was not wholly deterministic. For a modest fee, consultant phrenologists offered their customers a reading of their mental abilities based on the shape of their skull. Using this guidance, the customer could cultivate certain traits/organs while orienting their lives around their inborn strengths. The phrenological systems of the Austrian Johan Spurzheim, Scottish George Combe, and the American Fowler brothers all recognized self-esteem as one of humanity's basic faculties. Each distinguished between self-esteem as a form of self-respect, reliance, and nobility from the neighboring faculty of approbativeness, the desire for praise from others.

The phrenologists were hardly alone in keeping self-worth apart from the approval of others. Self-reliance defined Victorian advice literature. Samuel Smiles's bestselling *Self-Help* (1859) crystallized this genre, which was aimed at working men with upward aspirations. An advocate of classic (laissez-faire) liberalism, Smiles preached a gospel of personal uplift through thrift, good character, and perseverance. He insisted that working men already possessed these qualities; they simply needed to apply their inner energies properly. He argued, "Help from without is often enfeebling in its effects, but help from within invariably invigorates."[6] The book reflected Smiles's retreat from the radical reforms of the Chartist movement to instead focus on the cultivation of one's inner life rather than strive for social change.[7]

At the turn of the twentieth century, a generation of newly professionalized social scientists questioned this neat cleavage between the self and society. Writing in response to the dissolution of older "island communities" of small-town life through urbanization and the integration of the national market, American social scientists like George Herbert Mead and Charles Horton Cooley championed a dialogical, "looking glass" theory of human nature. Individualism was illusionary;

---

5. John Van Wyhe, *Phrenology and the Origins of Victorian Scientific Naturalism*. Burlington, VT: Ashgate, 2004.

6. Samuel Smiles, *Self-Help*. London: John Murray, 1859/1914, 1.

7. Robert J. Morris, "Samuel Smiles and the Genesis of *Self-Help*: The Retreat to a Petit Bourgeois Utopia," *The Historical Journal* 24, no. 1 (1981): 89–109.

the self was constituted by an interdependent web of relations.[8] In his *Principles of Psychology* (1890), William James dissolved the phrenological distinction between self-esteem and approbativeness. Rather than a fixed and distinct faculty, James argued self-esteem arose from the conflict between our outer "social self" as judged by others and our inner "spiritual self." He even provided a formula: "Self-esteem = Success/Pretensions." James's definition was domain-specific. In his example, he experienced mortification when someone else demonstrated superior knowledge of human psychology because he had "staked my all on being a psychologist." He felt nothing similar when proven deficient in his knowledge of the Greek language because he had no pretensions of being a skilled linguist.[9] Nevertheless, James placed social comparison at the heart of self-esteem. It was something a person received from others, a gift to be given or withdrawn.

GAINING SELF-ESTEEM

Although these turn-of-the-century concepts were later reclaimed by certain psychologists, these ideas did little to increase the popularity of self-esteem outside of the discipline. Historian Christopher Lasch argues that the widespread investment in the concept of self-esteem "took shape in the '30s, when the designers of an emerging welfare state were trying to convince the public that poverty and unemployment should not be attributed to lack of individual enterprise, that the system (not the individual) was at fault, that dependence on public relief was no disgrace, and that self-help was an illusion."[10] This interest in self-esteem shared a common cultural nexus as the New Look approach to perception. Both derived from how left-leaning émigré intellectuals tried to comprehend the psychological roots of the catastrophes that posed an existential threat to their lives. Building on the insights of the "looking glass" tradition of their adopted country, they understood one's self-evaluation as deriving from the perceptions of others. These psychologists gave primacy to social relationships in identity-formation (starting with but extending beyond the developmental niche of the nuclear family with its Oedipal dynamics). Two fundamentally different interpretations of self-esteem emerged: one grounded in the neo-Freudian critique of classic psychoanalysis, and the other in how social action researchers came to understand the nature of prejudice. For those within the neo-Freudian tradition, twentieth-century America represented a society wherein humanity's basic biological needs were met but the uneven distribution of abundance under capitalism led to anxiety-driven competition over status. Those inspired by social action research extended this line of

---

8. Jeffrey Sklansky, *The Soul's Economy: Market Society and Selfhood in American Thought, 1820–1920*. Chapel Hill: University of North Carolina Press, 2002.

9. William James, *The Principles of Psychology*. New York: Holt, 1890, 311.

10. Christopher Lasch, "For Shame," *The New Republic*, August 10, 1992, 29–34, 32.

thinking, understanding inequality as distributed along artificial lines separating racialized groups. Prejudice extracted a psychic toll from everyone but placed an especially high burden on the marginalized. At stake in these interpretations was the question of whether self-esteem posed a universal challenge for all or whether it was a problem particular to the minoritized group.

Neo-Freudianism

The popularization of self-esteem owed much to the vogue for neo-Freudian social theory in the United States in the late 1930s and 1940s. Leading contributors to this movement included Alfred Adler, Erich Fromm, Harry Stack Sullivan, Franz Alexander, and especially Karen Horney. These renegade analysts broke with Freud by questioning whether the biological libido was the origin of neuroses. In its place, they put feelings of anxiety, exacerbated by the competitive culture of industrial society. Neuroticism did not result from pathological psychosexual development; rather, it proliferated as mental disturbance symptomatic of capitalism. They rejected Freud's tragic view of human nature, championing a liberated self pursuing its own wants. Their theories circulated through a new genre of mass market books combining self-help with political analysis that made Fromm and Horney intellectual celebrities. Neo-Freudianism as a distinct intellectual movement existed for only a brief spell. By the late 1950s, its chief advocates found themselves under attack from the Freudian orthodoxy. In part due to their success in the book trade, the neo-Freudians eschewed the demands of professionalism and organized in an increasingly sect-like manner that limited their ability to influence medical practice.[11] The neo-Freudians failed to secure a stable niche within the American institutions of medicine or academia. When it came to the training of psychiatrists as medical doctors, the "orthodox" ego psychology held sway.[12]

Even after the movement's supposed demise, however, neo-Freudianism continued to exert a tremendous influence on postwar social science.[13] Clinical psychologists such as Carl Rogers and Albert Ellis eschewed Freud's emphasis on unconscious depths and childhood traumas in favor of the neo-Freudian emphasis on personal adjustment to immediate circumstances. They viewed the pursuit of self-esteem (defined in terms of approval by others) as the great source of neuroticism. Rogers made the gift of what he called "unconditional positive regard" from the therapist the prerequisite of a successful treatment. Personal growth required

---

11. Neil G. McLaughlin, "Why Do Schools of Thought Fail? Neo-Freudianism As a Case Study in the Sociology of Knowledge," *Journal of the History of the Behavioral Sciences* 34, no. 2 (1998): 113–134.

12. Dagmar Herzog, *Cold War Freud*. Cambridge: Cambridge University Press, 2017.

13. Edward J. Gitre, "The Great Escape: World War II, Neo-Freudianism, and the Origins of US Psychocultural Analysis," *Journal of the History of the Behavioral Sciences* 47, no. 1 (2011): 18–43.

acceptance of one's own flawed state. This new clinical psychology flourished outside of the medical establishment, notably, in the counseling services offered by universities, schools, and social service agencies.[14]

Abraham Maslow represented the clearest example of the sustained neo-Freudian influence on psychological theory. Throughout his career, he returned to the themes of dominance, recognition, and esteem as he moved from comparative to humanistic psychology. While studying dominance hierarchies in monkeys as a graduate student, a colleague jokingly referred to him as the "Apostle of Adler to the Apes."[15] By the late 1930s, Maslow switched focus from animal aggression to human sexuality, developing a questionnaire for measuring what he tentatively called "self-esteem" in college women.[16] Echoing Adler and Horney, Maslow argued for a "remarkably close relationship between dominance and sexuality, so close indeed that we are now inclined to consider sexuality as a sub-pattern in the total dominance syndrome."[17] He translated this early empirical work into his famous theory of motivation, listing self-esteem among the fundamental needs in contemporary society. According to Maslow, esteem had two facets. The first involved how the individuals related to themselves, including "the desire for strength, for achievement, for adequacy, for confidence in the face of the world, and for independence and freedom." The second facet revolved around the perception of others: "the desire for reputation or prestige (defining it as respect or esteem from other people), recognition, attention, importance or appreciation."[18] Maslow's hierarchy of needs, especially the pyramid graphic created by consultant Charles McDermid in 1960, became a staple of management theory, school curricula, and self-help guidance.[19] It placed the gaining of esteem from others near the pinnacle of humanity's fundamental motivations.

14. Tom McCarthy, "Great Aspirations: The Postwar American College Counseling Center," *History of Psychology* 17, no.1 (2014): 1–18.

15. William Morton Wheeler to Maslow, November 5, 1935, Abraham Maslow Papers, Akron, Box M4406, folder 3.

16. Abraham H. Maslow, "A Test for Dominance-Feeling (Self-Esteem) in College Women," *The Journal of Social Psychology* 12, no. 2 (1940): 255–270.

17. Maslow, "Self-esteem (Dominance-Feeling) and Sexuality in Women," *The Journal of Social Psychology* 16, no. 2 (1942): 259–294, 259.

18. Maslow, "A Theory of Human Motivation," *Psychological Review* 50, no. 4 (1943): 370–396, 381–382.

19. Dallas Cullen, "Maslow, Monkeys and Motivation Theory," *Organization* 4, no. 3 (1997): 355–373; Kira Lussier, "Of Maslow, Motives, and Managers: The Hierarchy of Needs in American Business, 1960–1985," *Journal of the History of the Behavioral Sciences* 55, no. 4 (2019): 319–341; Todd Bridgman, Stephen Cummings, and John Ballard. "Who Built Maslow's Pyramid? A History of the Creation of Management Studies' Most Famous Symbol and Its Implications for Management Education," *Academy of Management Learning and Education* 18, no. 1 (2019): 81–98.

Social Action Research

Self-esteem proved equally salient to the tradition of social action research initiated by Kurt Lewin. Rather than a universal attribute, Lewin and his followers argued that low self-esteem derived from a particular social history of exclusion and marginalization. It was symptomatic of how minority groups internalized the negative stereotypes about them circulating through the dominant culture. In 1941, Lewin published an influential article on Jewish self-hatred. The topic was a perennial one for diasporic Jews, one that was given new urgency in the wake of the Holocaust.[20] Lewin's theory derived from his own lived experience of exile in the United States: he had fled his native Germany following the Nazi seizure of power in 1933. He addressed the psychological plight of assimilated Jews living as minorities in alien societies without a state of their own. Individuals who embraced the norms and lifestyle of the dominant society suffered from lower self-esteem compared to those who were still immersed in their traditional religious and cultural matrix. Self-hatred represented the adoption by the culturally assimilated of the dominant culture's antisemitic stereotypes.[21]

Lewin soon extended his interpretation of Jewish self-hatred to encompass the plight of all minority groups. This expanded view lay at the foundation of intergroup relations as a distinct area of social psychology; its central tenet was "that so-called minority problems are majority problems."[22] This tenet went against the orthodoxy of the interwar period when psychologists, embracing eugenics, justified white supremacy by pointing to innate racial differences in intelligence and personality among peoples. By the 1940s, psychologists argued against their older beliefs, holding that group differences in aptitude and achievement derived from the effects of prejudicial treatment. Indeed, they came to see a belief in innate group differences as symptomatic of prejudice, a social pathology. Because of dominant group prejudice, minorities suffered from a lack of confidence, which in turn inhibited the minoritized individual's capacity to improve. Prejudice not only resulted in laws barring minorities from accessing spaces and resources, but also seeped beneath the skin to deform the self-image of the marginalized. As a practical solution to structural inequality, Lewin suggested "raising the self-esteem of the minority groups is one of the most strategic means for the improvement of intergroup relations."[23] A change in outlook must serve as the prerequisite for any social amelioration.

---

20. Susan A. Glenn, "The Vogue of Jewish Self-Hatred in Post-World War II America," *Jewish Social Studies* (2006): 95–136.

21. Kurt Lewin, "Self-hatred among the Jews," *Contemporary Jewish Record* 4 (1941): 219–232.

22. Lewin, "Action Research and Minority Problems," *Journal of Social Issues* 2, no. 4 (1946): 34–46, 45.

23. Lewin, "Action Research and Minority Problems," 45.

Lewin mentioned African Americans in passing, but his psychosocial account soon permeated liberals' understanding of the effects of segregation.[24] In the late 1930s, Columbia graduate student Ruth Horowitz conducted the first study of racial identity as an aspect of the self-consciousness developed in young children.[25] Kenneth and Mamie Clark soon extended Horowitz's techniques while questioning her "wish fulfillment" interpretation of Black children's preference for white images. They used then fashionable projective techniques, perhaps most famously differently colored dolls, and asked which body images the children identified with and which they aspired to be.[26] The Clarks initially studied Black children in a segregated Washington, DC, nursery, examining how age and skin tone affected racial preference.[27] They soon extended their analysis to a regional comparison by recruiting children from semi- and nonsegregated preschools in New York City.[28] In their initial reports, the Clarks found the children in the northern sample most readily identified with white images but held this identification was psychologically healthier than passively accepting the darker images.

In 1951, Robert L. Carter, a lawyer for the National Association for the Advancement of Colored People (NAACP), approached Kenneth Clark for assistance with the legal challenge to the Southern segregation of schools. The NAACP wanted to undercut the doctrine of separate but equal by demonstrating that even if the facilities were structurally equal, separate education itself caused genuine harm. As historian Daryl Michael Scott argues, Carter's strategy placed a large burden on psychological research. It required proving (1) Southern Black children possessed damaged psyches, (2) the damage derived from school itself rather than from broader social forces, and (3) this damage compromised the Black students' ability to learn.[29] The result was the social science statement on the effects of

---

24. John P. Jackson Jr, *Social Scientists for Social Justice: Making the Case against Segregation.* New York: New York University Press, 2001.

25. Ruth E. Horowitz, "Racial Aspects of Self-Identification in Nursery School Children," *The Journal of Psychology* 7, no. 1 (1939): 91–99.

26. Kenneth B. Clark. and Mamie Clark, "Racial Identification and Preference in Negro Children," In E. L. Hartley (Ed.), *Readings in Social Psychology*. New York: Holt, Rinehart, and Winston, 1947, 169–178.

27. Kenneth B. Clark. and Mamie Clark, "The Development of Consciousness of Self and the Emergence of Racial Identification in Negro Preschool Children," *The Journal of Social Psychology* 10, no. 4 (1939): 591–599; Kenneth B. Clark and Mamie Clark, "Skin Color as a Factor in Racial Identification of Negro Preschool Children," *The Journal of Social Psychology* 11, no. 1 (1940): 159–169.

28. Kenneth B. Clark and Mamie Clark, "Segregation as a Factor in the Racial Identification of Negro Pre-School Children: A Preliminary Report. *The Journal of Experimental Education* 8, no. 2 (1939): 161–163.

29. Daryl Michael Scott, *Contempt and Pity: Social Policy and the Image of the Damaged Black Psyche, 1880–1996*. Chapel Hill: University of North Carolina Press, 1997, 122.

segregation. This document drew together the evidence from the Clarks's Northern and Southern samples to document how segregation, prejudice, and discrimination damaged the personality developmental of all children, those in both the majority and minority groups. Through state-sanctioned segregation, he argued, "minority children learn the inferior status to which they are assigned." As a result, "the minority group child is thrown into a conflict with regard to his feelings about himself and his group.... This conflict and confusion leads to self-hatred and rejection of his own group."[30] In 1954, the American Psychological Association was remarkably indifferent to Clark's involvement in the *Brown* case, not even acknowledging it in various communications with him.[31] However, the framework his testimony provided soon created one of the discipline's most researched domains.

SELF-ESTEEM AS EXPERIMENT WITH DEMOCRACY

The *Brown* decision inspired an avalanche of research at the intersection of psychology, sociology, and psychiatry. Child development took on new relevance as the Soviet Union's launch of the Sputnik satellite in 1957 made the perceived backwardness of American education a pressing concern. Supported by the National Institute for Mental Health (NIMH), sociologist Milton Rosenberg and psychologist Stanley Coopersmith began massive surveys of the role played by self-esteem in schools.[32] Their books soon became some of the most cited works of the postwar social sciences, with Coopersmith's *Antecedents to Self-Esteem* (1967) cited over 10,000 times and Rosenberg's even more influential *Society and the Adolescent Self-Image* collecting over 46,000 citations since 1965.[33] A major reason for Rosenberg's enduring impact was his inclusion of a convenient and frequently administered 10-item scale. It asked participants the extent to which they agreed with statements such as "All in all, I am inclined to feel that I am a failure," "I feel that I'm a person of worth, at least on an equal plane with others," "I am able to do things as well as most other people." These items assessed what Rosenberg later called "global self-esteem," an individual's overall self-evaluation across domains.[34]

30. "Appendix to Appellants' Briefs: The Effects of Segregation and the Consequences of Desegregation: A Social Science Statement," 1952, 4.

31. Ludy T. Benjamin Jr. and Ellen M. Crouse. "The American Psychological Association's Response to *Brown v. Board of Education*: The Case of Kenneth B. Clark," *American Psychologist* 57, no. 1 (2002): 38–50.

32. Milton Rosenberg, *Society and the Adolescent Self-image*. Princeton, NJ: Princeton University Press, 1965; Sheldo Coppersmith, *The Antecedents of Self-esteem*. San Francisco: W. H. Freeman, 1967.

33. Google scholar results, May 2021.

34. Morris Rosenberg, Carmi Schooler, Carrie Schoenbach, and Florence Rosenberg, "Global Self-Esteem and Specific Self-Esteem: Different Concepts, Different Outcomes," *American Sociological Review* 60, no. 1 (1995): 141–156.

In 1965, the Lyndon Johnson administration introduced Head Start, a federal project designed to mitigate the damaging effects of poverty through early childhood interventions into health, nutrition, and especially education. At the time, social scientists offered a variety of explanations for America's persistent inequality. A 1965 report authored by Johnson's Assistant Secretary of Labor Daniel Patrick Moynihan blamed the intransigency of Black poverty on the community's pathological family structure with its absence of strong father figures.[35] In *Equality of Educational Opportunity* (1966), a report mandated by the 1964 Civil Rights Act, sociologist James Coleman controversially documented dramatic disparities in educational outcomes across racial lines, opening an unending debate about how best to assess the role of teachers, students, and schools.[36] In general, social scientists came to the pessimistic conclusion that the desegregation of schools alone was insufficient to advance social mobility.[37]

Self-concept appealed to progressive educators by offering an alternative to mere intelligence, represented by scores on a standardized test. Interest in self-esteem and a host of related interventions like Robert Rosenthal's "Pygmalion effect" of teacher expectancy flourished in the wake of Berkeley psychologist Arthur Jensen's revival of claims about the relationship between IQ and race.[38] Rather than genetic smartness predetermining an individual's destiny, psychologists and progressives could point to a host of societal factors mediating success while suggesting compensatory interventions.

Project Self-Esteem (1968–1970) in Pittsburgh exemplified this moment of coupling racialized self-image with academic performance. The project started in 1966 when the residents of the effectively segregated Hill District expressed dissatisfaction with the quality of instruction their children received from local elementary schools. These parents advocated teaching Black history to give their children a sense of pride and identity which the white-focused curriculum denied them. Black history was originally intended as an afterschool program housed in community churches, but the local and national protests following the assassination of Martin Luther King Jr. in 1968 led the Pittsburgh School Board to introduce Black history as part of the regular curriculum in three elementary schools.[39] These efforts came to the attention of two researchers at the neighboring University of Pittsburgh: Eugene Davis, a Black doctoral candidate in education, and Sanford

---

35. Ruth Feldstein, *Motherhood in Black and White: Race and Sex in American Liberalism, 1930–1965*. Ithaca, NY: Cornell University Press, 2000.

36. Leah N. Gordon, "If Opportunity Is Not Enough: Coleman And His Critics in the Era of Equality of Results," *History of Education Quarterly* 57, no. 4 (2017): 601–615.

37. Walter G. Stephan, "School Desegregation: An Evaluation of Predictions Made in *Brown v. Board of Education*," *Psychological Bulletin* 85, no. 2 (1978): 217–38.

38. Robert Rosenthal and Donald B. Rubin, "Interpersonal Expectancy Effects: The First 345 Studies." *Behavioral and Brain Sciences* 1, no. 3 (1978): 377–386.

39. On the creation of independent schools for teaching Black history to decolonize the mind, see Russell Rickford, *We Are an African People: Independent Education, Black Power, and the*

Golin, the Psychology Department's white director of clinical training. In the pilot study, the fifth-grade participants proved more responsive to exposure through Black art, music, and dance than the formal history lectures, so the project adopted this mode of instruction.[40] Golin secured NIMH funding to design an enhanced curriculum, recruit Black instructors and role models, and evaluate the program's efficacy by training members of the university's Black Action Society to perform the required psychological tests. Each element of the program's design aimed to empower Black individuals and to build community resources. For example, funding secured from philanthropic foundations allowed for the hiring of instructors from the Black Arts Movement, such as Harlem-based choreographer Bob Johnson. He remained in the city after the project's completion, founding the Pittsburgh Black Theatre Dance Ensemble and teaching in the university's new Black Studies program.

Reflecting the values of community psychology, "decision making power with regard to the content and conduct of the programs would reside in members of the Black community." For example, as a white psychologist schooled in the Moynihan Report, Golin wanted to include "father-absence" as a variable affecting self-esteem. However, community consultation led him to recognize his failure to appreciate the structure of the extended Black family. He modified this variable to the "frequency of changes of principle caretaker."[41] Project Self-Esteem, which included the production of a documentary entitled "I am Someone" and training of the children to perform African dance at the Pittsburgh Folk Festival, proved exceedingly popular with teachers, students, and parents alike. Golin came to the project from a culture of poverty, seeing largely deprivation in the degrading housing stock adjacent to his university. His initial grant described these children as "indigent," a term he dropped in subsequent reports.[42] Project Self-Esteem promised to transform the mental well-being not only of the Hill District community but also that of the white psychologist who came to realize the richness of Black culture.

Modeled on the plight of racialized groups, the circle of those prone to low self-esteem expanded in the ensuing decades as the consciousness-raising efforts

---

Radical Imagination. New York: Oxford University Press, 2016. On mobilizing children in Pittsburgh's civil rights movement, see James Collins, "Taking the Lead: Dorothy Williams, NAACP Youth Councils, and Civil Rights Protests in Pittsburgh, 1961–1964," *Journal of African American History* 88, no. 2 (2003): 126–137.

40. On the Black Arts movement as a mode of raising historical and national consciousness, see James Edward Smethurst, *The Black Arts Movement: Literary Nationalism in the 1960s and 1970s*. Chapel Hill: University of North Carolina Press, 2005.

41. Sanford Golin, Eugene Davis, Edward Zuckerman, and Nelson Harrison, "Psychology in the Community: Project Self-esteem," *Psychological Reports* 26, no. 3 (1970): 735–740, 737.

42. Sanford Golin, "The Self-Esteem and Goals of Indigent Children. Progress Report" (1969). https://files.eric.ed.gov/fulltext/ED036586.pdf

of the 1960s led to the self-identification of more and more groups as suffering from prejudice, marginalization, and trauma. Responding to a 1969 cover story on "The Homosexual in America," a letter writer to *Time* Magazine made the connection apparent. Walking the line between solidarity and appropriation, John Ungaretti argued: "The 'problem of homosexuality' is misnamed. More accurate is the 'problem of a society that refuses to accept (embrace?) minority behavior.' The Indian experienced that problem; it killed him. The black man experienced that problem; it enslaved and ghettoized him."[43] In the early 1970s, radical social psychologists understood antihomosexual prejudice in universalizing terms, linking it to other forms of discrimination. Antihomosexual attitudes were symptomatic of a more general "hereditarian bias in our culture," an authoritarian tendency to maintain the status quo through racial discrimination, a double standard between the sexes, and a resistance to sexual liberation.[44]

The white New York therapist George Weinberg drew upon his own clinical background when he popularized the term "homophobia" to capture this social hostility born out of fear.[45] As mental health professionals retreated in the 1970s from the notion that homosexuality represented a psychopathology, clinicians like Weinberg argued that psychology still had a positive role to play.[46] The stigma surrounding AIDS crystallized this new relationship between gay pride and clinical psychology. Statistically speaking, gay and lesbians suffered from a higher prevalence of mental disorders compared to their heterosexual counterparts. This was not due to some innate defect or pathological development. Rather, gays and lesbians still required extensive psychological care because they suffered from the stresses stemming from their encounters with the heterosexual majority's prejudicial attitudes.[47] The therapist's new role was to help the healthy homosexual cope with the psychic damage caused by trenchant societal bias.

By the late 1980s, self-esteem came to be seen as a uniquely "girl problem," an often racially coded phrase used to debate the limits of second-wave feminism.[48] In the 1970s, the women's movement centered on empowering women to find fulfillment

---

43. John Ungaretti, "Letter to the Editor," *Time*, 94, November 7, 1969, 11. On the harms of transforming indigenous demands for sovereignty into psychosocial trauma, see Dian Million, *Therapeutic Nations: Healing in an Age of Indigenous Human Rights*. Tucson: University of Arizona Press, 2013.

44. A. P. MacDonald, "A Time for Introspection," *Professional Psychology* 4 (1973): 35–42.

45. George H. Weinberg. *Society and the Healthy Homosexual*. New York: Macmillan, 1972.

46. Peter Hegarty, *A Recent History of Lesbian and Gay Psychology: From Homophobia to LGBT*. London: Routledge, 2017; Deborah Weinstein, "Sexuality, Therapeutic Culture, and Family Ties in the United States after 1973," *History of Psychology* 21, no. 3 (2018): 273–289.

47. Ilan H. Meyer, "Minority stress and Mental Health in Gay Men," *Journal of Health and Social Behavior* 36 (1995): 38–56.

48. Alexandra Rutherford, "Feminism, Psychology, and the Gendering of Neoliberal Subjectivity: From Critique to Disruption," *Theory and Psychology* 28 (2018): 619–644.

beyond their traditional roles confined in the home by pursuing education and employment. Its members organized consciousness-raising groups where women pooled their individual experiences of hurt to reveal structural, gender-based discrimination. By the mid-1980s, the feminist metaphor of "the glass ceiling" received a widespread airing in business and management circles, conveying the unspoken barriers preventing women from ascending the hierarchies of sectors dominated by white men.[49] Much of this literature located the blame in these women's psychology: their attitudes, their leadership style, their divided commitments to work and the home.[50]

Low self-esteem, acquired in adolescence, lay at the root of each of these problems. In 1991, the American Association of University Women released a large-scale report documenting the precipitous drop in white girls' assertiveness, confidence, and self-worth during adolescence. Surprisingly, their Black counterparts retained much of their perceived self-worth. Reversing 1960s criticisms of the "pathological" Black family, one advisor to the study suggested that these matrifocal units headed by strong, working mothers gave young women role models to emulate. Another consultant, developmental psychologist Carol Gilligan, focused on the unique educational challenges facing women in a world tailored to meet men's needs.[51] Gilligan's "difference feminism" represented a deliberate break with 1970s woman's liberation, which rejected the strict dichotomy between masculinity and femininity.[52] Gilligan argued that women could truly find success only after society listened to and accepted the "different voice" in which they thought and spoke. Amid this contestation over feminism's future, a seemingly novel "strange disease" captured the damaging effects of society's harmful attitudes toward women. Known among specialist physicians since the 1870s, anorexia nervosa started receiving unprecedented coverage in newspapers, glossy magazines, and popular books over a century later. Another "girl problem," the wasting disease captured how young women somatized low self-esteem, putting their lives in danger. Its prevalence inspired a massive research literature on "body image" as a psychological construct and the harmful effects of the mass media's distorting representations of women.[53]

---

49. C. Hymowitz and T. D. Schelhardt, "The Glass-Ceiling: Why Women Can't Seem to Break the Invisible Barrier that Blocks Them from Top Jobs," *The Wall Street Journal*, March 24, 1986, D1, D4–D5.

50. Jessica Ringrose, "Successful Girls? Complicating Post-Feminist, Neoliberal Discourses of Educational Achievement and Gender Equality," *Gender and Education* 19 (2007): 471–489.

51. Suzanne Daley, "Little Girls Lose Their Self-Esteem on the Way to Adolescence," *New York Times*, January 9, 1991, B6.

52. Anne Constantinople, "Masculinity-Femininity: An Exception to a Famous Dictum?," *Psychological Bulletin* 80, no. 5 (1973): 389–407; Sandra L. Bem and Daryl J. Bem, "Does Sex-biased Job Advertising "Aid and Abet" Sex Discrimination?" *Journal of Applied Social Psychology* 3, no. 1 (1973): 6–18; Jill G. Morawski, "The Measurement of Masculinity and Femininity: Engendering Categorical Realities," *Journal of Personality* 53, no. 2 (1985): 196–223.

53. Joan Jacobs Brumberg, *Fasting Girls: The Emergence of Anorexia Nervosa As a Modern Disease*. Cambridge, MA: Harvard University Press, 1988.

By 1980, social psychologists understood the pursuit of self-esteem as the defining feature of the human psyche. The modern individual was "constantly on the alert, dodging, protecting, feinting, distorting, denying, forestalling, and coping with potential threats to his self-esteem."[54] A psyche organized around its own defense and prone to self-enhancement came with grave cognitive consequences. Evoking a salient set of metaphors from the late Cold War, Anthony Greenwald suggested this organization resembled that of a totalitarian state. Cognitive biases allowed for a contented life by censoring the information available from the outside world into a form that most appeased the system.[55] Where much clinical psychology insisted on putting the client in touch with reality to improve their mental health, these social psychologists highlighted the self-protective nature of the human mind which insulated the individual from a harmful world through self-affirming illusions.[56] High self-esteem felt good but came at the cost of a largely fabricated self-image.

PEAK ESTEEM

Self-esteem peaked in the popular consciousness in the first half of the 1990s (see Figure 6.1). During this period, psychologists and journalists spoke of a shadowy "self-esteem movement" bent on wrecking American society. The timing was no accident, coming in the wake of Ronald Reagan's presidency, the collapse of the New Deal coalition, and the dismantling of America's modest welfare state. This period is known for its hyperindividualism and championing of the marketplace following the collapse of the Soviet Union. Many self-esteem advocates shared these views. The psychotherapist Nathaniel Branden promoted a version of self-esteem that combined humanistic psychology and the Objectivist philosophy of his former lover, author and philosopher Ayn Rand.[57] However, self-esteem's effervescence is better understood as a response to this political climate than as a direct reflection of it.

In 1986, state assemblyman John Vasconcellos secured a budget line for the California Task Force to Promote Self-Esteem. The press initially mocked Vasconcellos's task force as a typical example of Californian excess. One newspaper profile described Vasconcellos as "a longtime psychotherapy patient and psychological workshop participant."[58] Nevertheless, he insisted on the financial

---

54. Milton Rosenberg, *Conceiving the Self.* New York: Basic Books, 1979, 260.

55. Anthony G. Greenwald, "The Totalitarian Ego: Fabrication and Revision of Personal History," *American Psychologist* 35, no. 7 (1980): 603–618.

56. Shelley E. Taylor and Jonathon D. Brown, "Illusion and Well-being: A Social Psychological Perspective on Mental Health," *Psychological Bulletin* 103, no. 2 (1988): 193–210.

57. Nathaniel Branden, *The psychology of Self-Esteem: A New Concept of Man's Psychological Nature.* New York: Bantam Books, 1969.

58. Jacques Leslie, "The Unsettled Self-Esteem of John Vasconcellos," *Los Angeles Times,* August 23, 1987.

prudence of his idea. Improving self-esteem was a preventative measure that would lessen people's welfare dependency in the future. He even added researching the importance of "personal and social responsibility" to the task force's mandate to appease conservative legislators. Soon even skeptical journalists expressed surprise at the enthusiasm Vasconcellos's task force elicited from the heterogeneous mass demanding to participate. It quickly became the most popular task force in the state's history, with hundreds of volunteers of various genders, races, sexual orientations, religious beliefs, and political affiliations eager to participate in its proceedings. These public hearings identified "additional areas of concern" where social inequality intersected with self-esteem. Racism was the most prominent of these. Others included the effects of aging in a society where personal worth was inevitably tied to one's productivity and achievement, how the stigma surrounding AIDS affected survivability, and how to assist the disabled to "assume a fully human role within our society."[59]

Its final report, *Towards a State of Esteem* (1990), rejected the popular equation of self-esteem with "highly individualistic narcissism." Reflecting a political compromise among its members, the Task Force defined self-esteem as "appreciating my own worth and importance and having the character to be accountable for myself and to act responsibly towards others."[60] In nurturing self-worth, families came first, followed by schools. The report enumerated a host of social pathologies caused by low self-esteem: drug and alcohol abuse; crime and violence; poverty and welfare dependency; academic failure; and teenage pregnancy. It equated building self-esteem with a "social vaccine" that "empowers us to live responsibly" by inoculating individuals from the psychic pain caused by the everyday experience of sexism, racism, agism, poverty, and homophobia.[61] The Task Force concluded by emphasizing the individual's embeddedness "in the wider communities of which are all a part—neighborhoods, schools, workplaces, professional societies, and social, service, political, and religious groups." The goal of improve self-esteem was the creation of "a new environment of health and growth and community."[62] It recommended incorporating self-esteem training into the curriculum of public schools, expanding substance abuse programs and community-based juvenile delinquency prevention programs. To support nurturing families, public and private industry was urged to offer "jobsite child care, flextime work schedules, job sharing, and parental leave."[63] In terms of

---

59. California Task Force to Promote Self-Esteem and Personal and Social Responsibility, *Toward a State of Self-esteem*. Sacramento: California State Department of Education, 1990, 42.

60. *Towards a State of Self-Esteem*, 1.

61. *Towards a State of Self-Esteem*, 4

62. *Towards a State of Self-Esteem*, 13

63. *Towards a State of Self-Esteem*, 8.

practical recommendations, the report repeatedly returned to the state's therapeutic capacities to improve the lives of its most vulnerable citizens.

The feminist activist Gloria Steinem numbered among the Task Force's more prominent admirers. Two years after the final report appeared, she published *The Revolution Within: A Book of Self-Esteem* (1992), a combination of memoir and self-help tract.[64] In the 1970s, Steinem became a national icon for her contributions to the women's movement, helping found *Ms.* magazine and the National Women's Political Caucus. Two decades later, her focus shifted to self-improvement. She felt her early career attended to the "external barriers" facing women to the neglect of the inner, emotional ones that inhibited their success. Before the feminist revolution could achieve structural transformations in society, ordinary women must liberate their minds.

A new genre of television show fueled this fascination with self-esteem. In 1986, Oprah Winfrey made her national debut. Produced outside the network system and sold in syndication, her talk show soon overturned the soap opera's fifty-year reign over the daytime airwaves. By 1993, the Oprah Winfrey Show attracted fifteen million daily viewers. Her show delved into a range of struggles at the intersection of social issues and intimate matters. The format entailed active participation from a live studio audience consisting largely of middle-aged, affluent, yet ethnically diverse women.[65] Audience members asked questions of the guests on stage, but more importantly they shared their own stories. The successful format exemplified the psychologization of politics and the reduction of structural issues to personal problems.[66] Her weekday confessional drew upon the therapeutic ethos of humanistic psychology while further democratizing its power relations. Her show featured (and turned into celebrities) a range of paramedical experts, but the daytime talk show became a platform for the marginalized and the silenced to speak about what they deemed significant.[67] As a woman of color, Winfrey publicly and repeatedly staged her history of childhood sexual abuse, discrimination, and struggles with weight control. Personal trauma became ubiquitous, if not trendy. The testifying, damaged survivor struggling to reclaim herself became its own kind of expert. This granted Winfrey unprecedented popularity and influence, if not respect. A scathing *New York Times Magazine* profile in 1989 mocked her tendency to reduce all of the world's problems to a "lack of self-esteem."[68] Winfrey seemed nonplussed by this chastisement from the heart of the white establishment. The following June, at the height of her national celebrity,

---

64. Gloria Steinem, *Revolution from Within: A Book of Self-esteem*. New York: Knopf, 1992.

65. On the innovations of Winfrey's format, see Jane Shattuc, *The Talking Cure: TV Talk shows and Women*. London: Routledge, 1997, 2–3.

66. Janice Peck, *Age of Oprah: Cultural Icon for the Neoliberal Era*. London: Routledge, 2008.

67. Shattuc, *The Talking Cure*, 113.

68. Barbara Grizzuti Harrison, "The Importance of Being Oprah," *New York Times*, June 11, 1989,

the ABC network aired a special that she hosted and produced, *In the Name of Self-Esteem*.[69]

In the early 1990s, the left-wing of the Democratic Party (represented by Vasconcellos as statesman, Steinem as public intellectual, and Winfrey as celebrity-patron) embraced self-esteem. They did so in the age of Clintonian Third Way centrism as the Personal Responsibility and Work Opportunity Reconciliation Act (1996) rolled back welfare by putting a lifetime limit on the number of years one could receive benefits, discouraging support for single mothers, and tying benefits to workfare programs.[70] Writing amid these changes, the political theorist Barbara Cruikshank saw the self-esteem movement as emblematic of a new politics of hyperindividuality. Nevertheless, these progressives embraced self-esteem as a theory about the affective costs of inequity. A diverse set of constituents flocked to the California Task Force in hopes of securing resources for their communities. They volunteered their time because self-esteem functioned as a legible (to the white, expert establishment) vehicle for expressing the hurt caused by unthinking, structural privilege. That much of the action centered in California was no accident. The state witnessed not only the radicalism of the counterculture, but also Reagan's governorship where he first tested his antistatist policies. Self-esteem programs served as the means of shoring up the gains of the welfare state at the moment of its collapse.

Convened amid the Reagan Revolution, the California Task Force recalled some of the more progressive recommendations of the Carter administration's never implemented Commission on Mental Health (1978), transmitting its progressive vision of a preventative investment in people into a more austere era. Both documents identified continued inequity along racial and gender lines as major causes of mental distress and called for redistributing resources to social programs as early interventions at the social rather than individual level. Indeed, both reports highlighted the community as the locus of mental health instead of casting it as a personal attribute. The California Task Force sought to carry over the therapeutic impulses of the welfare state, a concerted move against the mounting neoliberalism of Reagan's America.

THREE CRITIQUES OF LIBERAL SELF-ESTEEM

Self-esteem was not without costs. These progressives proposed an uneasy amalgam of Keynesian investment by the state and neoliberal human capital theory. Citizens were valuable human resources whose potential structural inequality compromised. Like all gifts, self-esteem came with certain reciprocal obligations.[71] The state gave away positive self-regard through public education

---

69. Eva Illouz, *Oprah Winfrey and the Glamour of Misery: An Essay on Popular Culture*. New York: Columbia University Press, 2003, 171.

70. Gwendolyn Mink, *Welfare's End*. Ithaca, NY: Cornell University Press, 1998.

71. Marcel Mauss, *The Gift: Forms and Functions of Exchanges in Archaic Societies*. London: Cohen & West, 1966.

and social programs on the promise of future returns in terms of human productivity. These self-esteem programs flourished in disciplinary contexts targeting the poor and the marginalized. Rather than a vanguard for a neoliberal self, the vogue for self-esteem is better understood as an effect of how the post-1960s social justice movements entered the political mainstream and accommodated themselves to the moderating demands of the party system and an emerging consensus about the primacy of markets in determining worth. Aspirational toward social change, self-esteem nevertheless represented a dampening of the promised structural transformation in favor individual adaptation. By the 1990s, concerns about the limits of self-esteem coalesced into three lines of political critique. Each critique carried methodological implications, latching onto different areas of empirical research for support.

The first critique might be called the problem of unearned self-worth. The historian turned cultural critic Christopher Lasch offered the most sophisticated expression of this viewpoint. His surprising bestseller *The Culture of Narcissism* (1979) made him a leading critic of America's psychotherapeutic culture and its effects on civic life.[72] However, notions about unearned worth permeated neoconservative and libertarian commentary by the late 1980s. Lasch famously raised the psychoanalytic diagnosis of narcissistic personality disorder in the individual to the level of society. He built on a line of cultural critique that viewed the 1970s as "the me decade" when Americans of the baby boom generation renounced the morals traditionally anchoring society in favor of hedonistic forms of self-exploration. The cultivation of a deep, authentic "self" became a good onto itself.[73] In this line of thinking, self-esteem research was both the cause and effect of America's cultural decline. As early as 1965, a letter to the *New York Times* complained about an "increasingly common fallacy," warning "self-esteem cannot result from government subsidy." Instead, "it is the result of achieving self-betterment (economic or cultural) through one's own efforts and abilities."[74] According to this view, one cannot give away positive self-regard as a gift to others. Individuals must strive and struggle to earn it. Freely given self-worth corrupts morality and breeds dependency, infantilism, entitlement, and ultimately narcissism. The crudest form of this critique is found in popular catchphrases such as "Everyone gets a trophy" and "You are not a beautiful and unique snowflake," the latter from Chuck Palahnuik's popular satire of self-help culture *Fight Club*.[75]

The methodological counterpart to this first critique was the distinction between correlation and causation in psychology. According to psychology's central dogma, only experiments establish causal relations by eliminating any

---

72. Christopher Lasch, *The Culture of Narcissism*. New York: Norton, 1979.

73. Susanne Schmidt, *Midlife Crisis: The Feminist Origins of a Chauvinist Cliché*. Chicago: University of Chicago Press, 2020.

74. Charles E. Brunn, "Basis of Self-esteem," *New York Times*, July 9, 1965, 28.

75. Chuck Palahniuk, *Fight Club*. New York: Owl Books, 1996, 134.

confounding factors and determining the direction of the relationship. In contrast, almost all the empirical research on self-esteem relied on questionnaires administered to existing populations. These designs established a correlation between high self-esteem and positive outcomes, but they cannot determine the direction of the relationship.[76] Moreover, some experimental designs suggested the dangers of unearned self-esteem as "grandiose self-views" might lead to more aggressive behavior.[77]

The second line of critique came from the political left and questioned "the myth of empowerment."[78] Steinem's turn to self-esteem did much to crystallize this view. Her critics contended that her embrace of yoga, art, and psychotherapy confused consciousness-raising as an end rather than as a means. Reviewing Steinem's memoir, Deidre English suggested "[t]he strategic vision of social revolution here has been all but been replaced with a model of personal recovery." English feared this change in tactics. Tackling structural issues like sexual discrimination, pay gaps, and harassment would make American women feel better, not the quietude of focusing on personal improvement. Indeed, Steinem's newfound attention to inner life "may perpetrate a double bind in which some women are convinced they can't achieve anything because now their self-esteem—like their weight, their hair, their clothes, and their nails —is constantly in need of fixing."[79] Rather than an awakening change, the cult of self-improvement was a trap that made individuals responsible for augmenting their abilities and adjusting to the system.[80]

These political concerns about an exclusive and universalizing focus on personal growth resonated with the research conducted by cultural psychologists. In the early 1990s, Hazel Markus and Shinobu Kitayama popularized the contrast between Western self-concept which stressed independence from obligations and Eastern ones which saw the individual embedded in a web of interdependent relations. Self-esteem was emblematic of this dichotomy, a reflection of American hyperindividualism rather than constituting a human universal. Markus and Kitayama recommended that the term "should perhaps be replaced by self-satisfaction, or by a term that reflects the realization that one is fulfilling the

---

76. Jerald Bachman and Patrick O'Malley, "Self-esteem in Young Men: A Longitudinal Analysis of the Impact of Educational and Occupational Attainment," *Journal of Personality and Social Psychology* 35, no. 6 (1977): 365–380.

77. Brad J. Bushman and Roy F. Baumeister, "Threatened Egotism, Narcissism, Self-Esteem, and Direct and Displaced Aggression: Does Self-Love or Self-Hate Lead to Violence?" *Journal of Personality and Social Psychology* 75, no. 1 (1998): 219–229.

78. Dana Becker, *The Myth of Empowerment: Women and the Therapeutic Culture in America*. New York: New York University Press, 2005.

79. Deidre English, "She's Her Weakness Now," *New York Times*, February 2, 1992, BR3.

80. Barbara Cruikshank, *The Will to Empower: Democratic Citizens and Other Subjects*. Ithaca, NY: Cornell University Press, 1999.

culturally mandated task."[81] Rather than personal fulfillment, this self-satisfaction "among those with interdependent selves may be based in some large measure on their capacity to exert control over their own desires and needs so that they can indeed belong and fit in."[82]

The third critique questioned the ethics and effectiveness of self-esteem's reliance on "damage narratives." This critique emerged from the marginalized communities studied by social action researchers who disagreed with how liberal social scientists represented them as fundamentally broken and defined their communities by this damage. The Unangax̂ education scholar Eve Tuck is the clearest advocate of this position, though it has roots tracing back to the Black Power movement's break with liberal civil rights activism. In an influential open letter, Tuck argued that much social science research on marginalized communities has an implicit theory of social change, one she traced back to the Clarks and the *Brown* case. In the litigation framework, compensation requires proof of harm. The scientist surveys the marginalized community to document its members' pain and loss "in order to obtain particular political or material gains."[83] Communities participate in this extractive process in the hopes of building the case for change, but most often this never occurs. Instead, this research traffics in narrow, stereotypical images of these communities as only pathological and broken rather than showing their cultural richness, strength, and resilience. Although often well-intentioned, Tuck called for a moratorium on such research, for these narratives risked distorting how those in power understand these communities.

The problematic nature of the damage narrative drew empirical support from what could be called the paradox of Black self-esteem. Following the NAACP strategy in *Brown*, it became a truism that American Blacks suffered from low self-esteem, but the empirical literature revealed a more complicated picture.[84] Rosenberg noted this possibility as early as 1965. An unpublished validation study for his scale conducted by Melvin Ember among the nursing staff of a Washington-area mental hospital found that Black respondents scored higher than their white counterparts.[85] A 1970 replication of the Clarks' doll study found Black children now preferred the darker doll. The authors posited a historical change in Black self-esteem itself linked to the civil rights movement having successfully elevated

---

81. Hazel R. Markus and Shinobu Kitayama, "Culture and the Self: Implications for Cognition, Emotion, and Motivation," *Psychological Review* 98, no. 2 (1991): 224–253, 230.

82. Markus and Kitayama, "Culture and the Self," 242.

83. Eve Tuck, "Suspending Damage: A Letter to Communities," *Harvard Educational Review* 79, no. 3 (2009): 409–428, 413.

84. Jennifer Crocker and Brenda Major, "Social Stigma and Self-esteem: The Self-Protective Properties of Stigma," *Psychological Review* 96 (1989): 608–630.

85. Rosenberg, *Society and the Adolescent Self-image*, 63.

individual pride.[86] Others questioned whether global self-esteem (as measured by instruments like the Rosenberg Scale) was the correct measure for the effects of racial prejudice. The pre-1970 literature conflated personal self-esteem (how the individual values themselves) and racial self-esteem (how they value the group to which they belong).[87] Since the 1970s, studies have consistently found American Blacks to possess elevated global self-esteem if low Group Identity.[88] However, in the 1990s, the social psychologist Claude Steele's "stereotype threat" experiments helped maintain self-esteem as a crucial site of prejudice. Mere exposure to certain negative images pertaining to their group inhibited individuals' subsequent performance on a cognitive task.[89]

PSYCHOLOGISTS TAKE CONTROL

By the late 1990s, psychologists joined the anti-self-esteem bandwagon. Dethroning this false god proved instrumental to how a network of psychological scientists moved beyond the university to directly address a wide range of publics through a new genre of "evidence-based" self-help amplified by both old and new media. Martin Seligman led the way. As APA president in 1998, he outlined a new future for psychology, one that broke with biomedicine's mental illness model and instead emphasized health, character, and inner strength.[90] Seligman performed considerable boundary work to demarcate his "positive psychology" from the vast literature devoted to self-esteem. For example, one of his earliest ventures into the mass market book trade had devoted an entire chapter to "shattering the simplistic formulas of the self-esteem movement." Going forward, Seligman would retain Vasconcellos's immunization metaphor, but notably rebrand it a "psychological vaccine" rather than a "social" one.[91]

Self-control or "emotion regulation" lay at the heart of this emerging field. Under this rubric, psychologists offered the public a cluster of overlapping constructs relevant to improving their lives: emotional intelligence, self-efficacy, grit, delay

---

86. Joseph Hraba and Geoffrey Grant, "Black Is Beautiful: A Reexamination of Racial Preference and Identification," *Journal of Personality and Social Psychology*, 16, no. 3 (1970): 398–402.

87. William E. Cross Jr. *Shades of Black: Diversity in African-American identity*. Philadelphia: Temple University Press, 1991.

88. Judith R. Porter and Robert E. Washington, "Black Identity and Self-Esteem: A Review of Studies of Black Self-concept, 1968–1978," *Annual Review of Sociology* 5 (1979): 53–74.

89. Claude M. Steele, "A Threat in the Air: How Stereotypes Shape Intellectual Identity and Performance," *American Psychologist* 52, no. 6 (1997): 613–629.

90. Martin E. Seligman and Mihaly Csikszentmihalyi, "Positive Psychology: An Introduction," *American Psychologist* 55, no. 1 (2000): 5–14.

91. Martin E. Seligman, *The Optimistic Child: A Proven Program to Safeguard Children Against Depression and Build Lifelong Resilience*. New York: HarperPerennial, 1995.

of gratification, and resilience. In part, this terminological pluralism reflected a greater refinement of the more generic self-esteem into more precise measures. It also represented the attempt by different labs to brand their own unique intervention for increased citations and public accolades. Despite this variation, each construct placed a common emphasis on securing an "internal locus of control" for lifelong mental health. Largely promoted by university-based social and developmental psychologists, this literature built upon dual process theories of cognition. Control, now localized and materialized in the form of healthy executive function (following the research of Alan Baddeley), was a rare and besieged resource in the facing of the overwhelming automaticity. Success required making wise choices, which in turn depended on reining in emotional excess.[92]

This supposedly new and evidence-based gospel of self-control represented the culmination of how psychologists negotiated the politics (and bad press) surrounding behavior modification. Both behavior analysts (following B. F. Skinner) and behavior therapists (following Joseph Wolpe) had cast a wide range of social and psychological problems in terms of the human organism's maladjustment to its environment. They also offered a host of practical interventions, agnostic to psychopathology's hidden etiology, for managing these problems. Their technologies of control altered the reinforcers in the troubled person's surrounding environment to encourage more desirable outcomes. Presented as psychology's greatest gift to mass society, by the mid-1970s, behavior modification experienced a series of rejections from the wider public. Critics underscored what they saw as the approach's authoritarian underpinnings, especially in connection with programs targeting the often-overlapping categories of marginalized groups and captive populations such as prisoners and institutionalized patients. Behavior modification involved imposing the powerful on those under their control, asserting the dominant's group's vision of normality rather than curing any "disease." The gay liberation campaign against aversion therapy for homosexuality represented perhaps the most successful of these efforts, but the equation of behavior modification with totalitarian torture became commonplace in both the American counterculture and the halls of government. In the wake of these vehement criticisms, psychologists did not abandon the behavior modification project so much as rebrand it.

Social learning theory offered the key to negotiating this settlement. Behavior modification put a premium on control as a means of achieving desired ends. However, it offered a self-help remarkably devoid of any "self." Radical behaviorism dismissed the existence of such an agentful creature capable of selecting their fate as a humanistic fiction.[93] A core self on which behavior modification operated (and which volunteered to undertake this alteration of their conduct)

---

92. Wilhelm Hofmann, Brandon J. Schmeichel, and Alan D. Baddeley, "Executive Functions and Self-Regulation," *Trends in Cognitive Sciences* 16, no. 3 (2012): 174–180.

93. Alexandra Rutherford, *Beyond the Box: BF Skinner's Technology of Behaviour from Laboratory to Life, 1950s–1970s*. Toronto: University of Toronto Press, 2009, 102–117.

was precisely what social learning theory came to provide. This eclectic theory first gained widespread prominence through Stanford psychologist Albert Bandura's experiments on aggression in children. His research captured the imagination of policymakers as civil liberties concerns about personal expression collided with preoccupations with maintaining "law and order." In this charged political context, Bandura offered a tidy explanation of crime and violence in a language that appealed in turn to both liberals and conservatives. In a culture increasingly obsessed with the damaging effects of bad media (first comic books and television, later popular music and videogames), Bandura provided the mechanism whereby consumption became conduct. The results of his iconic Bobo doll studies, where children learned to imitate the violence an adult teacher perpetuated on the titular doll, made it into the columns of the *New York Times*, the *Congressional Record*, and presidential commissions as evidence of the effects of bad influences.[94]

Bandura retained behaviorism's emphasis on malleability, adaptation, and control, and he initially aligned himself with the behavior modifiers.[95] His was a largely situationist account with one essential caveat that acquired greater and greater emphasis in the coming decades and that allowed him to jettison much of behaviorism's problematic antihumanism. In 1974, while serving as APA president, Bandura brokered something of a compromise among behaviorists and cognitivists, clinicians and academics on the eve of their splintering.[96] Unlike radical behaviorists, social learning theorists came to emphasize cognitions as moderating variables in the organism's interactions with the environment. Amid the political contestation over "behavior modification" in prisons and elsewhere, social learning theory preserved choice, free will, and, most of all, personal responsibility. This final aspect became more pronounced throughout the 1970s. According to Bandura's Stanford colleague Walter Mischel, these learned cognitive coping skills counted among the most psychologically interesting things, neither inborn traits nor sociological situations. Cognitive skills (acquired thinking and coping strategies) explained how individual persons uniquely mediated between their inherited constitution and their dynamic circumstances.[97] People were not wholly the product of their environments (under "stimulus control" in the language of behaviorism), but they possessed the inner capacity to moderate and mitigate external influences.

This modified behavior modification found a receptive audience among the eclectic therapeutic underground of clinical practitioners who were beginning to

---

94. *Mass Media and Violence: A Report to the National Commission on the Causes and Prevention of Violence*. Washington, DC: US Government Printing Office, 1969.

95. Albert Bandura, *Principles of Behavior Modification*. New York: Holt, Rinehart, & Winston, 1969.

96. Albert Bandura, "Behavior Theory and the Models of Man," *American Psychologist* 29, no. 12 (1974): 859–869.

97. Walter Mischel, "Toward a Cognitive Social Learning Reconceptualization of Personality," *Psychological Review* 80, no. 4 (1973): 252–283.

dominate the APA. The product of elite research universities, from the start, social learning theory was developed as a clinically relevant theory of personality amenable to those trained as scientist-practitioners and exemplified the realignment of clinical and experimental priorities. In the clinical realm, as behavior therapists started to add the label "cognitive" to their approach, their practice shifted. Instead of merely desensitizing the patient toward a specific phobic object, cognitive-behavioral therapy (CBT) offered a kind of generalized training of the client, so that they learned more general coping skills applicable to a variety of situations in their lives.[98] Along with this attention to pliable cognitive skills came a new embrace of "the self," a concept that adherent behaviorists insisted was at best a fiction. In 1977, Bandura coined the term "self-efficacy" to describe those skills central to both social learning theory and cognitive-behavior therapy which allowed the person to succeed.[99] His term tellingly conjoined the language of personhood with the terminology derived from pharmaceutical testing. In a fundamentally corrupt society awash in the lures of Mammon, the self would serve as a *sanctuary* of goodness and resistance. Success hinged on possessing those cognitive skills to flexibly adapt to the environment without succumbing to its immediate temptations.

Two decades later, positive psychology represented the latest twist in this negotiated settlement between psychologists and liberal society. By the time Seligman launched his new force in psychology, CBT had become the favored theoretical framework for practicing clinicians. His approach definitively detached self-help from mental illness and universalized it as a set of cognitive skills needed by all. This move also created a marketplace or a platform for psychological wares aligned with but autonomous from the institutions of biomedicine. Psychology was fundamentally about healthy life, but it did not depend on medical doctors. Clinical psychologists offered cognitive skills as their own nostrums to compete with pharmaceuticals.

Seligman promised the APA practitioners a distinctly psychological approach to mental health, making good on the clinicians' desire for alignment with the institutions of biomedicine while preserving their autonomy from its medical "illness" model. He offered a vision of a psychological practice that was oriented toward the healthy life but did not depend on medical doctors. Often couched in the language of anticipatory neuroscience, the interventions he proposed eschewed the pharmaceuticals that had become increasingly popular with patients. They did so without abandoning the psychotherapeutic practitioner's preference for interventions with the individual clients, unlike the more sociological inclination of 1970s community psychology. Positive psychology bolstered the clinical practitioners' hard-won status as a health professional while offering them

---

98. Marvin R. Goldfried, "Systematic Desensitization as Training in Self-Control." *Journal of Consulting and Clinical Psychology* 37, no. 2 (1971): 228–234.

99. Bandura, "Self-efficacy: Toward a Unifying Theory of Behavioral Change," *Psychological Review* 84, no. 2 (1977): 191–215.

services distinct from those of their medical competition. Positive psychology promised a way of expanding psychology's market beyond the problems of mental illness by selling a universal set of cognitive skills needed by all. They instructed their clients in obtainable cognitive skills as their own nostrums to compete with pharmaceuticals. In a fundamentally corrupt, consumerist society, the self would serve as a *sanctuary* of goodness and resistance. Success hinged on possessing those cognitive skills to flexibly adapt to the environment without succumbing to its immediate temptations.

Pitched as a universal, "colorblind" approach grounded in careful laboratory experiments rather than shared, communal common sense, these interventions had a contested (if often hidden) history. For example, the foundational concept of "resilience" had roots in the Black psychology movement, a precedent Seligman failed to acknowledge.[100] When Thomas Hilliard explained how prisoners endured the deprivations of solitary confinement in the mid-1970s, he noted how they drew from the strength and "resiliency" of a shared culture and interpersonal bonds that in times past had allowed Black people to survive slavery.[101] Few psychologists took note of this interpretation at the time. Resilience reentered psychology through child development where it was understood as an individual attribute distributed unevenly through "at-risk" populations.[102] The first support came from Emmy Werner's longitudinal study of how children born into poverty in Hawaii flourished later in life. She noted how, when faced with "adverse" circumstances, "resilient children and youth appear to be skillful in selecting and identifying with resilient models and sources of support" compared to their less successful peers.[103] Even more influential was a longitudinal program conducted at the University of Minnesota on the children of persons with schizophrenia who did not contract the disease. Adversity did not doom these children. They successfully adapted and avoided succumbing to their parent's debility.[104] In other words, resilience came after "the empire of trauma" wherein long-standing psychic damage became an expected outcome of adverse circumstances.[105] Along with

---

100. Wade E. Pickren, "Light through a Cultural Lens: Decolonizing the History of Psychology and Resilience." In *The Challenges of Cultural Psychology*, London: Routledge, 2018, pp. 220–236.

101. Thomas O. Hilliard, "A Psychological Evaluation of the Adjustment Center Environment at San Quentin Prison," *Journal of Black Psychology* 2, no. 2 (1976):75–82.

102. Suniya S. Luthar, Dante Cicchetti, and Bronwyn Becker, "The Construct of Resilience: A Critical Evaluation and Guidelines for Future Work," *Child Development* 71, no. 3 (2000): 543–562.

103. Emmy E. Werner and Ruth S. Smith. *Vulnerable, but Invincible: A Longitudinal Study of Resilient Children and Youth*. New York: McGraw-Hill, 1982, 104.

104. Ann S. Masten, Karin M. Best, and Norman Garmezy, "Resilience and Development: Contributions from the Study of Children Who Overcome Adversity," *Development and Psychopathology* 2, no. 4 (1990): 425–444.

105. Didier Fassin and Richard Rechtman. *The Empire of Trauma: An Inquiry into the Condition of Victimhood*. Princeton, NJ: Princeton University Press, 2009.

positive psychology, resilience gained real traction following the September 11 terrorist attacks, as the American nation itself proved resilient to outside threats and quickly resumed normality through consumerism while exporting its shared "trauma" in the form of wars on foreign soil.[106]

Resilience was a highly amorphous commodity; which even its lead theorist described as a kind of "ordinary magic."[107] Developmental psychologists differed over what attributes best preserved those at risk. When Werner first outlined the policy implications of resilience in 1995, her recommendation echoed those of the California Task Force. To bolster resilience in young children, as a society, she said, "we need to decrease their exposure to potent risk factors and increase their competencies and self-esteem, as well as the sources of support they can draw upon."[108] In this formulation, competencies and self-esteem traveled together and largely came as gifts given by others. Just three years later, in 1998, the Minnesota developmentalists urged much greater caution about equating resilience, competence, and self-esteem. They cautioned: "Efforts to boost self-esteem to improve competence will not work if self-esteem is the result of competence rather than a cause of it. One could end up with a group of misbehaving children who think very highly of themselves."[109] Their skepticism toward self-esteem and a new demand for self-regulation quickly spread.

Tellingly, when the newly formed Association for Psychological Science (APS) announced its first ventures into the realm of guiding public policy (having just abandoned the APA to avoid such extrascientific entanglements), it included a Task Force on Self-Esteem. The inclusion of self-esteem as a nostrum among perennial bugbears such as herbal remedies, projective tests, and classroom size hinted at psychologists' growing incredulity toward their once favored construct.[110] Led by the social psychologist Roy Baumeister, the APS tasked the team with reviewing the existing literature on the effectiveness of self-esteem to improve the human condition. In their 2003 report, they found self-esteem wanting

---

106. On American resilience, see George A. Bonanno, Sandro Galea, Angela Bucciarelli, and David Vlahov. "Psychological Resilience after Disaster: New York City in the Aftermath of the September 11th Terrorist Attack," *Psychological Science* 17, no. 3 (2006): 181–186. On the exportation of resilience to the war zone, see Lamia Mounir Moghnieh, "Infrastructures of Suffering: Trauma, Sumud and the Politics of Violence and Aid in Lebanon," *Medicine Anthropology Theory* 8, no. 1 (2021): 1–26.

107. Ann S. Masten, "Ordinary Magic: Resilience Processes in Development," *American Psychologist* 56, no. 3 (2001): 227–238.

108. Emmy E. Werner, "Resilience in Development," *Current Directions in Psychological Science* 4, no. 3 (1995): 81–84.

109. Ann Masten and J. Douglas Coatsworth. "The Development of Competence in Favorable and Unfavorable Environments: Lessons from Research on Successful Children," *American Psychologist* 53, no. 2 (1998): 205–220, 213.

110. Robert A. Bjork and Stephen J. Ceci. "The Birth of *Psychological Science in the Public Interest*," *APS Observer*, 13 (2000), 5-14.

on almost every measure. They found certain *correlations*, but self-esteem failed to predict improved attainment in a *causal* manner.[111]

Fortunately, Baumeister had what he later called "the real deal."[112] In 1998, his lab announced the results of their first ego depletion experiment. The experimental condition first tasked the participants with exerting self-control (e.g., eating radishes while resisting the temptation of ever-present and delicious smelling cookies). The effort to withstand the cookies' appeal drained the will. When given a subsequent cognitive task (a challenging puzzle), these participants more readily abandoned it than those who were previously allowed to eat the cookies.[113] The failure of cookie-resistance to activate a "self-control module" available on the second task led Baumeister to reject the cognitive science's information-processing model as a framework. Instead of a trainable program that improved with subsequent performances, willpower functioned like a muscle, one that was susceptible to fatigue. This suggested an energy model of self-regulation reminiscent of Freud, with the brain looking to conserve resources following a taxing exercise.[114]

Sugary treats would serve as an omnipresent feature of experiments trying to capture this energistic, embodied mind. America's multibillion-dollar weight-loss industry provided an obvious inspiration and market for willpower research.[115] Baumeister rarely strayed from this context of discovery. For example, a later experiment appearing in the field-leading *Psychological Science* seemingly conflated glucose (the most common simple sugar) with how the experimenters happened to administer it (by offering naturally sweetened lemonade). The published study bizarrely heralded the unique benefits of lemonade as a replenishing "brain fuel" for overly taxed executive functions.[116] In other words, Baumeister designed experiments ready-made for the self-help market and subsequent media hype.

111. Roy F. Baumeister, Jennifer D. Campbell, Joachim I. Krueger, and Kathleen D. Vohs, "Does High Self-Esteem Cause Better Performance, Interpersonal Success, Happiness, Or Healthier Lifestyles?" *Psychological Science in the Public Interest* 4, no. 1 (2003): 1–44.

112. Roy F. Baumeister, "Conquer Yourself, Conquer the World," *Scientific American* 312(4) (2015): 60–65, 60.

113. Mark Muraven, Dianne M. Tice, and Roy F. Baumeister. "Self-control as a Limited Resource: Regulatory Depletion Patterns." *Journal of Personality and Social Psychology* 74, no. 3 (1998): 774–789.

114. Roy F. Baumeister, "Ego Depletion and Self-Control Failure: An Energy Model of the Self's Executive Function," *Self and Identity*, 1, no. 2 (2002): 129–136.

115. Starting in the 1970s, industry leaders like Weight Watchers incorporated elements of cognitive-behavioral therapy into their program. See Jessica Parr, '"Act Thin, Stay Thin': Commercialization, Behavior Modification, and Group Weight Control," *Journal of the History of the Behavioral Sciences* 55, no. 4 (2019): 342–357.

116. Emer J. Masicampo and Roy F. Baumeister. "Toward a Physiology of Dual-Process Reasoning and Judgment: Lemonade, Willpower, and Expensive Rule-Based Analysis," *Psychological Science* 19, no. 3 (2008): 255–260.

Baumeister was not alone in turning away from computational models of the mind toward older, "biological" ones of limited energies. He drew strength from the soon to be famous marshmallow test. At Stanford during the 1960s, Mischel had tested the ability of preschoolers to control their immediate impulses. The researcher presented each child with two possible rewards (either one marshmallow or two) and a bell. He then explained that if the child waited for the researcher's return, they could have both marshmallows, but if they rang the bell they would only enjoy one. In the late 1980s, Mischel released the longitudinal results of his "marshmallow test," first conducted on children at the Stanford daycare. As he predicted decades earlier, those capable of self-imposed delay of gratification achieved better academic performances and personal successes later in life.[117]

As was the case with Baumeister, Mischel's inspiration came from Freud. Mischel initially sought to recast the psychoanalytic in terms of social learning principles. By the 1990s, without altering his model, he excised the original psychoanalytic references and couched his research in anticipatory neuroscience. Working with posttraumatic stress disorder (PTSD) researcher Jennifer Metcalfe, he speculated about the physiological basis for dual process theories: the distinction between the brain's hot, fast, affect-driven system under stimulus control and a more rarely used, cool, completive, cognitive system of self-control. Success in life hinged on mastering and cultivating the latter system to allow for better decision making. Metcalfe and Mischel "deliberately eschewed most references to the abundant findings from brain research that tempt speculations about differences in the brain structures within which the hot and cool systems may have their primary locations." Despite a lack of empirical evidence, they found the neural network model an appealing heuristic as "metaphors could evolve into more tangible forms."[118]

Psychologists equivocated over whether this capacity for emotional regulation represented a set of teachable cognitive skills or an inborn trait that naturally varied among individuals. Mischel's earliest studies emphasized the former along with the particular demands of the experimental situation. As the longitudinal data from his preschoolers became available, he and his collaborators instead posited the existence of "a stable and seemingly basic cognitive and social competence that may have extensive implications for the individual's cognitive and social coping and adaptation."[119] A few years later, these skills became even more punctuated and internalized as "processing structures characterized by stable cognitive-affective organizations in the processing system that become

---

117. Walter Mischel, Yuichi Shoda, and Philip K. Peake, "The Nature of Adolescent Competencies Predicted by Preschool Delay of Gratification," *Journal of Personality and Social Psychology* 54, no. 4 (1988): 687–696.

118. Janet Metcalfe and Walter Mischel, "A Hot/Cool-System Analysis of Delay of Gratification: Dynamics of Willpower," *Psychological Review* 106, no. 1 (1999): 3–19.

119. Mischel, Shoda, and Peake, "The Nature of Adolescent Competencies Predicted by Preschool Delay of Gratification," 695.

activated when the individual encounters relevant situational features."[120] Mischel exemplified a general shift from conceptualizing strength as something borrowed from community-held resources to seeing it as the possession of an individual, their personal style of interacting their environment.

Children remained the crucial focus for the new affective science. Recommended interventions got pushed earlier and earlier into the life course so as not the waste any human capital.[121] Psychologists soon analogized self-control as emotional regulation to a kind of social intelligence, especially as they uncovered correlations between variations of this personal contribution and performance on standardized tests. In 2005, McKinsey consultant turned developmental psychologist Angela Duckworth predicted that steady determination outdid raw IQ when it came to future success.[122] Two years later, she identified this noncognitive trait as "grit," the combination of long-term passion with perseverance.[123] Her 2013 TED talk on grit went viral, accumulating over fourteen million views over a five-year period.

The new science of self-control marked a deliberate break with psychologists' earlier advocacy of self-esteem. The evolutionary psychologist Steven Pinker suggested such a narrative, writing "the very idea of self-control has acquired a musty Victorian odor. The Google Books Ngram Viewer shows that the phrase actually rose in popularity in the nineteenth century but began to free fall around 1920, cratering in the 1960s, the era of "doing your own thing," "letting it all hang out," and "taking a walk on the wild side."[124] Here Pinker parroted a familiar line of the conservative critique where the expansion of personal freedoms since the 1960s inevitably led to a cultural decline requiring new disciplinary, punitive controls to save society form itself.[125]

---

120. Walter Mischel and Yuichi Shoda, "A Cognitive-Affective System Theory of Personality: Reconceptualizing Situations, Dispositions, Dynamics, and Invariance in Personality Structure," *Psychological Review* 102, no. 2 (1995): 246–268, 263.

121. Executive function entered pediatrics around 2000 with Donald R. Royall, Edward C. Lauterbach, Jeffrey L. Cummings, Allison Reeve, Teresa A. Rummans, Daniel I. Kaufer, W. Curt LaFrance, Jr, and C. Edward Coffey. "Executive Control Function: A Review of Its Promise and Challenges for Clinical Research. A Report from the Committee on Research of the American Neuropsychiatric Association," *The Journal of Neuropsychiatry and Clinical Neurosciences* 14, no. 4 (2002): 377–405.

122. Angela L. Duckworth and Martin E. Seligman, "Self-discipline Outdoes IQ in Predicting Academic Performance of Adolescents," *Psychological Science*, 16, no. 12 (2005): 939–944.

123. Angela L. Duckworth, Christopher Peterson, Michael D. Matthews, and Dennis R. Kelly, "Grit: Perseverance and Passion for Long-Term Goals," *Journal of Personality and Social Psychology* 92, no. 6 (2007): 1087–1101.

124. Steven Pinker, "No, Thanks," *New York Times*, September 4, 2011, A18.

125. David Garland, *The Culture of Control: Crime and Social Order in Contemporary Society*. Chicago: University of Chicago Press, 2002.

If mid-twentieth-century psychologists worried about the emotional toll of modernity's competitive ethos, their twenty-first-century counterparts saw humans overflowing in excessive, positive affect. This abundance of good feelings overwhelmed the dual process system found in the brain. Natural selection had carved humans into frugal decision-makers adhering to their gut instincts. The economy of our mental machinery came at a cost. It made us hedonic automata largely beholden to their primordial dispositions. More precisely, human decision making suffered from too many pleasing, satiating affects that strengthened the ego by confirming its prior convictions. Cognition (e.g., cold, careful deliberation) was a precious resource in need of conservation. Those who managed their cognitions in a distracted world would succeed.

Self-control theorists smuggled over many crucial assumptions from self-esteem. First, the APS Task Force concurred with the California Task Force regarding the nature of the damage, offering a nearly identical symptomology of the broken state of American society (e.g., failing schools, addiction, teen pregnancy). Like self-esteem, self-regulation transferred certain tasks like academic performance and decisions about risk from the cognitive to the affective domain. This appealed to policymakers and parents by explaining personal success beyond inborn intelligence. The impetus for this line of thought came from *New York Times* science journalist Daniel Goleman's bestseller *Emotional Intelligence* (1995). Goleman offered a liberal counterweight to Richard Herrnstein and Charles Murray's *The Bell Curve* (1994), which equated crime and poverty with racialized differences in (cognitive) intelligence.[126] His book brought the work of Mischel and other psychologists to new audiences, including educators and policymakers, for the first time. Goleman's central theme was the necessity of emotional monitoring and management in sound decision making. This move beyond innate intelligence gained traction among liberals in response to the resurgent emphasis on standardized testing following George W. Bush's No Child Left Behind Act (2002).[127]

Through self-regulation interventions such as ego depletion, grit, and delay of gratification, psychologists maintained the myth of empowerment. If one could master these skills, one could achieve future success. Even conservatives like David Brooks, who as an editor at the *Wall Street Journal* had overseen its public defense of *The Bell Curve*, converted to emotional intelligence as life's great predictor.[128] As a

---

126. Daniel Goleman, *Emotional Intelligence: Why It Can Matter More than IQ*. New York: Bantam, 1995. On emotional intelligence as the new racial science, see Michael E. Staub, *The Mismeasure of Minds: Debating Race and Intelligence Between Brown and the Bell Curve*. Chapel Hill, NC: UNC Press Books, 2018, 109–138.

127. On the persistent mismatch between social science policy recommendations across the political spectrum and the lived experience of schools, see Charles M. Payne, *So Much Reform, So Little Change: The Persistence of Failure in Urban Schools*. Cambridge, MA: Harvard Education Press, 2008.

128. On Brooks's editorial work supporting *The Bell Curve*, see Linda S. Gottfredson, "Mainstream Science on Intelligence: An Editorial with 52 Signatories, History, and Bibliography," *Intelligence* 24, no. 1 (1997): 13–23, 17.

biweekly columnist for the *New York Times*, Brooks assembled an influential narrative linking the psychology of self-control to America's economic future. In a 2006 editorial, the self-professed "scientific imbecile" explained his recent immersion in "books on psychology and brain function."[129] They held the key to human capital formation which enabled a departure from the politics of old.[130] Globalization meant Americans needed certain traits to compete in the new postindustrial "cognitive age."[131] Instead of pursuing economic justice by funding schools or redistributing wealth through taxation, equality could be achieved by teaching the habits, skills, and mental traits persons needed to succeed. Only one test mattered for predicting future success: the marshmallow test. Brooks encouraged moving beyond the IQ as a measure of merit and returned to character (variously operationalized as delay of gratification, grit, and willpower) as the great underwriter of human achievement. This recommendation would strengthen family and marriage as the nucleus of human capital formation and promote a socially conservative but economically progressive politics.[132] The interventions Brooks recommended soon gained a prominent place in the curriculum of the charter school movement, such as the influential Knowledge is Power Program (KIPP) network.[133] There Mischel found willing collaborators for conducting research instead of the bureaucratic "tough defense system in place that closed New York's public schools to invasion and scrutiny," limiting research opportunities on their students.[134] KIPP programs even retained the older immunization metaphor, but Vasconcellos's "social vaccine" became privatized: the self-efficacy contained within each child's "growth mindset" rather than a shared feeling distributed throughout the community.

If self-control refurbished the myth of empowerment, these psychologists concurred with conservative social critics when it came to the havoc wrought by unearned esteem. Baumeister went further, highlighting the untold dark side of elevated self-esteem. It encouraged people to experiment, leading them to attempt risky, antisocial behaviors.[135] Echoing Lasch's famous cultural jeremiad, two of Baumeister's collaborators published a popular book arguing that America faced a narcissism epidemic driven by the millennial generation's addiction to immediate

---

129. David Brooks, "Of Love and Money," *New York Times*, May 25, 2006, 27.

130. David Brooks, "Psst! 'Human Capital,'" *New York Times*, November 13, 2005, C12.

131. David Brooks, "The Cognitive Age," *New York Times*, May 2, 2008, A21.

132. David Brooks, "Marshmallows and Public Policy," *New York Times*, May 7, 2006, D3.

133. Bethany Moreton, "S'More Inequality: The Neoliberal Marshmallow and the Corporate Reform of Education," *Social Text* 32, no. 3 (2014): 29–48.

134. Walter Mischel, *The Marshmallow Test: Mastering Self-Control*. New York: Little, Brown, 2014, 163.

135. Roy F. Baumeister, Todd F. Heatherton, and Dianne M. Tice. "When Ego Threats Lead to Self-Regulation Failure: Negative Consequences of High Self-Esteem," *Journal of Personality and Social Psychology* 64, no. 1 (1993): 141–156.

self-aggrandizement, a hunger stoked by social media and digital technologies.[136] Taken together, self-regulation advocates retained the hyperindividualism condemned by radical critics of self-esteem and the diagnosis of the fundamental "brokenness" from damage narratives, but married them to the conservative conviction that self-worth either came as an inborn trait or else must be earned through achievement rather than received as a gift given.

The new science of self-control certainly found ready patrons and audiences within America's growing evangelical communities. The John Templeton Foundation (JTF) had a particularly cozy relationship with Seligman and his associates starting in 1996. Supported by the money and vision of the namesake conservative investment banker, the JTF declared its mission to be the reconciliation of science with spirituality. The Foundation provided Seligman's Positive Psychology Center with several multimillion-dollar grants.[137] This largess allowed the positive psychology movement to (somewhat) wean itself off federal government support in the form of NIHM grants and to promote a vision of the person independent of the medical model of mental illness. Positive psychologists revived moral character as a fixed attribute predictive of personal success, a concept that psychologists had declared dead at the end of the 1920s.[138] Despite their loosely Freudian origins, the concepts of "ego depletion" and "delay of gratification" were easily assimilated into a conservative Christian understanding of temptation. Google search trends indicate that Mischel's marshmallow test only became a cultural shorthand following the release of a widely imitated viral video in September 2009.[139] Often mistaken for footage of the original Stanford experiment, the film was independently produced by Texas-based Igniter Media, a content provider for evangelical churches and ministers.[140] Character as self-control appealed to both facets of modern conservativism: the free market championing of individual choice on the one hand and the reempowerment of the patriarchal family as the true source of authority and social stability on the other.[141]

---

136. Jean M. Twenge and W. Keith Campbell, *The Narcissism Epidemic: Living in the Age of Entitlement*. New York: Simon and Schuster, 2009.

137. Daniel Horowitz, *Happier? The History of a Cultural Movement That Aspired to Transform America*. New York: Oxford University Press, 262–265.

138. Christopher Peterson and Martin E. P. Seligman. *Character Strengths and Virtues: A Handbook and Classification*. New York: Oxford University Press, 2004. On the failure of "character education" in the 1920s. see Michael Pettit, *Science of Deception: Psychology and Commerce in America*. Chicago: University of Chicago Press, chapter 6.

139. https://trends.google.com/trends/explore?date=all&geo=US&q=%22marshmallow%20test%22

140. https://www.youtube.com/watch?v=QX_oy9614HQ

141. On the duality in terms of public policy, see Melinda Cooper, *Family Values: Between Neoliberalism and the New Social Conservatism*. Cambridge, MA: MIT Press, 2017.

Positive psychology's theories of character-anchored willpower represented a species of "cruel optimism" for much of the intended audience.[142] Future-oriented and cloaked in promissory neuroscience, these theories traffic in nostalgia. They recalled, if not quite revivifies, long exhausted cultural scripts about individual free will and self-determination as the one true pathway to success. These self-help nostrums dangled the promise of social mobility at a time when ascending society's strata became increasingly impossible. After all, psychology's new-found enthusiasm for self-possession coincided with the revival of what economist Thomas Piketty called "patrimonial capitalism."[143] Starting in the 1970s, neo-liberal economic policies returned Western democracies to the nineteenth-century pattern of a widening gap between inherited wealth versus wages. Piketty's term underscores a particular feature of the current predicament: declining social mobility. Once again, wealth was increasingly being transmitted through families from one generation to the next.

At the tail end of the postwar period when tax policies and the Great Society programs led to a brief narrowing of inequality, economists and psychologists first uncovered the "paradoxical" disconnect between capital and happiness once basic needs were met.[144] Studying the aftermath of lottery wins and disabling accidents, social psychologist Philip Brickman argued that because people adapted themselves to a "hedonic treadmill," windfalls or losses did not alter the individual's long-term affective outlook.[145] Positive psychology crystallized around the distinction (if not the outright dichotomy) between material circumstance and "subjective well-being." In 2006, fresh from his Nobel Prize award, Daniel Kahneman dismissed the widespread conviction that greater income improved mood as the "focusing illusion," and yet another cognitive bias prevalent among the masses. The rich undoubtedly found satisfaction but did not experience greater moment-to-moment joy than the less fortunate. People paid too much attention to money as the singular gateway to true happiness when pleasure necessarily remained transitory.[146] The exact political message of such studies remained ambiguous. Urging people to focus less on the accumulation of material goods could certainly be read as a potential critique of America's obsession with status and money.

---

142. Lauren Berlant, *Cruel Optimism*. Durham, NC: Duke University Press, 2011.

143. Thomas Piketty, *Capital in the Twenty-First Century*. Cambridge, MA: Harvard University Press, 2014.

144. Richard A. Easterlin, "Does Economic Growth Improve the Human Lot? Some Empirical Evidence," in P. A. David and M. W. Reder (eds.), *Nations and Households in Economic Growth*. New York: Academic Press, 1974, 89–125.

145. Philip Brickman, Dan Coates, and Ronnie Janoff-Bulman, "Lottery Winners and Accident Victims: Is Happiness Relative?" *Journal of Personality and Social Psychology* 36, no. 8 (1978): 917–927.

146. Daniel Kahneman, Alan B. Krueger, David Schkade, Norbert Schwarz, and Arthur A. Stone. "Would You Be Happier If You Were Richer? A Focusing Illusion," *Science* 312, no. 5782 (2006): 1908–1910.

Studies like Kahneman's encouraged the cultivation of one's inner character rather than fruitlessly pursuing comparisons with others. But his position could also support quietude about growing social disparities, suggesting that the poor ought to be content with their lot.

Some happiness researchers did reassess matters after the 2008 financial crisis. These psychologists suddenly discovered historical data (from the widely utilized General Social Survey) indicating a strong correlation among America's less affluent between increasing unhappiness and the expanding income gap since the 1970s as their perceptions of fairness deteriorated.[147] It seemed that money mattered to those who were increasingly doing without.

Nevertheless, at the very historical juncture when it became increasingly difficult for individuals to climb the social ladder based on their own merits, psychologists switched from advocating the wide distribution of self-esteem as a "social vaccine" to individualized self-control. The new psychology of self-regulation, supposedly underwritten by the latest discoveries in neuroscience, was oddly reminiscent of the Victorians' moral psychology, replete with willpower, character, and self-reliance.[148] Education as a developmental growth continued serving as the great vector for promoting mobility by bestowing upon the disadvantaged the skills needed for future employment. However, public policy shifted from seeing education as a widely distributed social good to a wholly individualized form of human capital formation. Schools were expected to do all the work of solving society's inequities when every other part of society was organized to maintain said inequality. They were set up to fail.

LOSING CONTROL

Backed by the obligatory *New York Times* bestseller authored by an academic psychologist or better yet the viral TED talk, self-control interventions exemplified this twenty-first century trend toward hackable science. This built upon but pushed beyond an earlier generation of the behavior modifier's propensity for practical applications targeting specific symptoms rather than underlying syndromes. Rather than deriving predictions from a coherent, cumulative theory, a host of social psychologists dedicated their labs to identifying odd, surprising, and counterintuitive findings that just happened to have direct implications for enhancing individual performance in an ever-competitive society. This knowledge then circulated in a highly modularized and carefully packaged form as a set of discrete techniques or rather branded tricks for self-improvement, or what became known colloquially as "life hacks." These self-control interventions soon proved hackable in a second

---

147. Oishi Shigehiro, Selin Kesebir, and Ed Diener, "Income Inequality and Happiness," *Psychological Science* 22, no. 9 (2011): 1095–1100.

148. Robert Kugelmann, Willpower. *Theory and Psychology* 23, no. 4 (2013): 479–498.

sense: the product of "p-hacking," questionable research practices and data manipulation that allowed a desired, yet phantasmagorical, phenomenon to first materialize.

Granted unprecedented attention as a cure-all following the 2008 financial collapse, self-control fell into crisis much like self-esteem had before it. Undoubtedly, ego depletion fared the worst.[149] The well-publicized phenomenon became one of the first targets of the replication efforts spreading throughout social psychology. A multi-lab, preregistered replication involving over two thousand participants across twenty-three independent laboratories concluded that "if there is any effect, it is close to zero."[150] In other words, ego depletion failed to reach the methodological threshold for convincing psychological science. After participating in the multi-lab replication, one prominent depletion researcher reflected, "As someone who has been doing research for nearly twenty years, I now can't help but wonder if the topics I chose to study are in fact real and robust. Have I been chasing puffs of smoke for all these years?"[151]

Problems quickly spread. As the marshmallow test became a cultural icon, the interpretation of its results became more ambiguous. Did it reveal an inborn personality trait or a set of learned cognitive skills that allowed the individual to triumph over their circumstances? Alternatively, did performance on the test reveal simply reflect the participant's social circumstances with children raised in rich environments happy to wait as life had a habit of rewarding them? In other words, was self-control the cause or the effect? An experiment that administered the test to kindergarten-aged children assigned to either a reliable or unreliable condition suggested the latter.[152] Using a larger and more diverse sample, the researchers argued that controlling for socioeconomic demographics accounted for much of the variation predicted by the original study instead of any identifiable cognitive skill.[153] As had Mischel at one point. The marshmallow test was not Mischel's first foray into youthful decision making. Before his arrival at Stanford, he spent a year

---

149. Evan C. Carter and Michael E. McCullough, "Publication Bias and the Limited Strength Model of Self-Control: Has the Evidence for Ego Depletion Been Overestimated?" *Frontiers in Psychology* 5 (2014): 823.

150. Martin S. Hagger, Nikos L. D. Chatzisarantis, Hugo Alberts, Calvin O. Anggono, Cedric Batailler, Angela R. Birt, Ralf Brand, et al. "A Multilab Preregistered Replication of the Ego-Depletion Effect," *Perspectives on Psychological Science* 11, no. 4 (2016): 546–573, 558.

151. Michael Inzlicht, "Reckoning with the Past," (2016) http://michaelinzlicht.com/getting-better/2016/2/29/reckoning-with-the-past

152. Celeste Kidd, Holly Palmeri, and Richard N. Aslin. "Rational Snacking: Young Children's Decision-Making on the Marshmallow Task Is Moderated by Beliefs about Environmental Reliability," *Cognition* 126, no. 1 (2013): 109–114.

153. Tyler W. Watts, Greg J. Duncan, and Haonan Quan. "Revisiting the Marshmallow Test: A Conceptual Replication Investigating Links Between Early Delay of Gratification and Later Outcomes," *Psychological Science* 29, no. 7 (2018): 1159–1177. For an earlier, largely neglected

in Trinidad, then a British colony, where he became interested in the behavioral differences between children of African and East Indian descent. Those raised in unstable households rationally opted for immediate rewards as the world rarely made good on its promise of a future windfall.[154] In other words, the ability to delay gratification represented the learned behavior of the affluent rather than an independent trait that which predicted future success.

A notable feature of much of the self-control literature was the evasion of its own social history. Theories of resilience started with experiences of racialized, impoverished, colonial subjects, whether in Trinidad or in the then American territory of Hawaii. This starting point is striking given the overwhelming WEIRDness of psychology's subjects. American psychologists extracted, then abstracted, "strength" from these contexts. As early as 2000, Werner complained about the growing capaciousness of "resilience" among her peers, with the widespread "assumption that you can use wholesale intervention to make everyone resilient, which, of course, is the opposite of what we originally found in the first place."[155] Instead of an embedded set of reciprocal community relations, the new affective science rendered coping into an entirely individual cognitive skill—a learnable mindset but also a commodity, not only for the child whose human capital it built, but for the psychologists who marketed this remarkable gift.

In 2003, Baumeister's APS Task Force chastised psychologists' complicity with the vogue for self-esteem. They suggested that "perhaps psychologists should reduce their own self-esteem a bit and humbly resolve that next time they will wait for a more thorough and solid empirical basis before making policy recommendations to the American public."[156] Perhaps they should have exerted more self-control and delayed the gratification of quickly announcing its successor as, a mere fifteen years later, they found themselves in the same situation. Their theories and interventions had become fixtures of self-help books, viral online lectures, newspaper editorials, and classroom pedagogy. However, the "real deal" of self-control appeared to be almost spectral, even to scientists who had dedicated their careers to the phenomenon.

---

critique along these lines, see Curtis W. Banks, Gregory V. McQuater, Jenise A. Ross, and Wanda E. Ward, "Delayed Gratification in Blacks: A Critical Review," *Journal of Black Psychology* 9, no. 2 (1983): 43–56.

154. Walter Mischel, "Preference for Delayed Reinforcement: An Experimental Study of a Cultural Observation," *Journal of Abnormal and Social Psychology*, 56, no. 1 (1958): 57–61; Mischel, "Father-Absence and Delay of Gratification," *Journal of Abnormal and Social Psychology*, 63, no. 1 (1961): 116–124.

155. "Emmy E. Werner," Society for Research on Child Development Oral History Interview, May 31, 2000, 25. https://www.srcd.org/sites/default/files/file-attachments/werner_emmy_interview.pdf

156. Baumeister et al., "Does High Self-Esteem Cause Better Performance, Interpersonal Success, Happiness, Or Healthier Lifestyles?" 3.

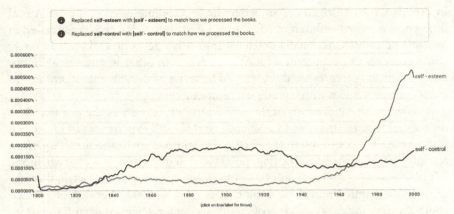

Figure 6.2 Word frequency of "self-esteem" and "self-control" in the Google Books Ngram Viewer corpus (1800–2000).

Despite the enthusiasm for self-control among experimental psychologists, pundits, and education reformers, self-esteem never entirely vanished. The feminist credo of empowerment would exert a particularly strong pull on the international philanthropy. The "girl effect," promoted by the Nike Foundation starting in the mid-2000s, promised the key to eliminating global poverty lay in empowering young women in the developing world as educators and entrepreneurs. Cold War modernization theorists had posited controlling birthrates would unlock economic growth.[157] The "girl effect" built on this logic, modifying it for leaner times. Rather than attempt to engineer society as a whole, micro-finance allowed developmental economists to target particular individuals and invest in their small-scale enterprise. Impoverished women were seen as more responsible to their families, communities, and businesses compared to men who were understood as wasting their money on needless vices. This philanthropic model centered on building up both the financial and human capital of the marginal and voiceless. It also represented the exportation of an entrepreneurial, postfeminist self on a global scale.[158]

Sociologist Jennifer Silva also found traces of its legacy in the domestic "mood economy" of working-class twenty-somethings in Richmond, Virginia, and Lowell, Massachusetts, far from the *New York Times* op-ed writer's gaze. Deindustrialization, exacerbated by the Great Recession, deprived these individuals of traditional *economic* markers of adulthood such as steady employment or homeownership. Instead, they drew upon what remained of the self-esteem apparatus (from school councilors to *The Dr. Phil Show*) to craft recovery

---

157. Michelle Murphy, *The Economization of Life*. Durham, NC: Duke University Press, 2017.

158. Alexandra Rutherford, "Feminism, Psychology, and the Gendering of Neoliberal Subjectivity: From Critique to Disruption," *Theory and Psychology* 28, no. 5 (2018): 619–644.

narratives for themselves where the overcoming of personal trauma, addiction, or abuse served as the key marker of maturity and independence.[159]

But self-esteem's power never resided entirely in the "merely" symbolic. Looking back to Pittsburgh, one clinical psychologist's brief foray into the reparative effects of Black consciousness certainly did not prevent the expropriation of housing to construct the new Civic Arena, nor did it stave off the mass unemployment resulting from a steel industry decimated by the offshoring of production. In the face of such destructive changes, talk of self-esteem continued because it proved an effective appeal for allocating material resources to underserved communities at the very moment when neoliberal policies encouraged the withdrawal of support from public institutions.

---

159. Jennifer M. Silva, *Coming up Short: Working-Class Adulthood in an Age of Uncertainty*. New York: Oxford University Press, 2013.

7

How Faces Became Special

Perceiving Others in a Digital Age

In their contribution to *The Handbook of Social Psychology* (1954) dedicated to "the perception of people," Harvard psychologists Jerome Bruner and Renato Tagiuri deemed looking at photographed faces largely irrelevant to their project. In a chapter setting out the field of social cognition, they carefully attended to the mental processes shaping social judgments, but a near century of research left them "wonder[ing] about the significance of studies of 'facial expression of emotion' in isolation. From the point of view of the adaptiveness of social behavior, it is rare to the vanishing point that judgment ever takes place on the basis of a face caught in a state similar to that provided by a photograph snapped at 20 milliseconds."[1] Fifty years later, another Cambridge-based psychologist came to the exact opposite conclusion. In 2006, Nancy Kanwisher remarked: "Faces are among the most important visual stimuli we perceive, informing us not only about a person's identity, but also about their mood, sex, age and direction of gaze. The ability to extract this information within a fraction of a second of viewing a face is important for normal social interactions and has probably played a critical role in the survival of our primate ancestors."[2] Theirs was more than a difference of opinion. Their disagreement represented a generational shift, a remarkable reevaluation of the salience, ecological validity, and evolutionary history of reading faces. Where the midcentury cognitive revolutionary dismissed face reading as a sideline for understanding social perception, his twenty-first century counterparts insisted that it constituted the most fundamental activity conducted by the human's primate brain. Along with the photographed face's new relevance came a considerable acceleration of the time in which social judgments

---

1. Jerome S. Bruner and Renato Tagiuri, "The Perception of People," *Handbook of Social Psychology*, vol. 2 (1954): 634–654.

2. Nancy Kanwisher and Galit Yovel, "The Fusiform Face Area: A Cortical Region Specialized for the Perception of Faces," *Philosophical Transactions of the Royal Society B: Biological Sciences*, 361, no. 1476 (2006): 2109–2128, 2109.

Governed by Affect. Michael Pettit, Oxford University Press. © Oxford University Press 2024.
DOI: 10.1093/oso/9780197621851.003.0008

got made. This demand for temporal resolution transformed mentation from a serial sequence of steps unfolding in the mind to a set of near instantaneous neural functions localized in space.

By the 1990s, it became commonplace for both computer and neuroscientists to assert that facial recognition represented a "special" kind of perception; such pronouncements were strikingly absent at the start of the cognitive revolution. This specialness emerged out of the crisis of the Cold War alliance between psychology and artificial intelligence (AI). This was a skill lying within the grasp of mere infants; humans recognized other people's faces easily, quickly, and without awareness. Yet, this ability proved elusive for even the most advanced digital minds. Ironically, the computer as an organizing metaphor petered out as psychologists' research practice became more digital. Between 1997 and 2002, two computerized technologies of visual display and the rapid recording of responses (functional Magnetic Resonance Imaging (fMRI) in neuroscience and the Implicit Association Test (IAT) in social psychology) capitalized on this human talent for face reading to measure thinking beyond awareness. Their widespread uptake occurred alongside the increased ubiquity of everyday biometrics emanating from the surveillance capitalism of the social web and the "War on Terror" security state. Embedded in an infrastructure of networked, digital communication, these technologies helped render face perception into the very ontology of the social while advancing the notion that much decision making and human action required minimal mental deliberation. Psychologists' newfound fascination with human faces operated simultaneously as an index, a vector, and an agent in this cultural shift to snap decisions based on fleeting glimpses.

GALTON SLEEPS IN R'LYEH

When Bruner and Tagiuri dismissed face reading as psychologically uninteresting, they were responding to a sporadic, century-old pursuit dating back to Charles Darwin. Darwin famously challenged the presumed human exceptionalism ubiquitous to Western culture by arguing for a continuity between humans and other animals much like his contemporary Charles Lyell argued for a continuity in the geological record. Not only humanity's physical form, but its conduct and even moral sense existed on a continuum with other species. Visual evidence concerning the emotions provided crucial support for Darwin's revolutionary claim. Through anecdotes, questionnaires, and especially then novel photographs, Darwin documented how other creatures (whether his beloved dog or the noble monkeys found in exotic lands) expressed themselves in a manner remarkably similar to the most civilized Briton. A series of photographs taken by the French neurologist Guillaume-Benjamin Duchenne lay at the heart of Darwin's *Expression of Emotions in Man and Animals* (1872). Duchenne attached electrodes to the faces of asylum patients in his care to produce a portrait gallery of basic, universal, and embodied affective expressions.[3]

Francis Galton shared his cousin's obsession with rendering universal truths from the human face. In 1878, he rehabilitated the discredited art of physiognomy with his first composite portrait. Galton rejected the physiognomist's discernment as unreliable. Instead, he sought to capture the essence of social types by exposing the pictures taken of multiple subjects on a single sheet of photosensitive paper. The overlap produced a singular, truer face than any idiosyncratic instance, and it did so without the liability of subjective human intervention. Galton's science trafficked in a specific genre of portraiture: the frontal, subordinated capture of a person's face associated with the institutional observation and recordkeeping of the criminal and the insane. His interest was indeed criminological, closely tied to his fascination with individuation through fingerprinting. The composite photograph revealed the "criminal type" underlying the variation of the particular. It also represented an alternative to the French police officer Alphonse Bertillon's identification system combining photographs with anthropomorphic measures on a single card and an extensive cataloguing system. Both Galton and Bertillon dreamed of an everyday biometrics in which photography, statistics, and readily available systems of data retrieval would survey and control the undesirable.[4] Galton never implemented his vision. It lay dormant, but like the undead his slumber was fitful. His dreams periodically percolated to the surface, inspiring a new generation of entrepreneurial physiognomists whose projects grabbed headlines before inevitably collapsing.

This boom–bust cycle made the eugenics-born pursuits of biometric control and affective universals seem like a failure by the 1950s. In reviewing the assorted Darwin-inspired studies of emotional expression, Bruner and Tagiuri found an unsystematic mess. They proposed an alternative. Instead of reading raw emotions captured in the blink of an eye, psychology should focus on sophisticated "impression formation." Huckster character analysts of the interwar period had used external signs (like hair color) to predict a person's personality, a move countered by psychometricians who showed how these popular measures failed to predict people's actual traits and behaviors. Bruner and Tagiuri proposed that psychologists go a step further. What were once dismissed as "errors" of judgment now became the very thing of interest. Everyone was their own psychologist. People went about the world constantly making intuitive assessments of others in hopes of piercing the veil of politesse. Their mind-reading abilities proved limited. Social convention camouflaged genuine expression and intentions, and so people

---

3. Phillip Prodger, *Darwin's Camera: Art and Photography in the Theory of Evolution.* Oxford: Oxford University Press, 2009.

4. Allan Sekula, "The Body and the Archive," *October* 39 (1986): 3–64; John Tagg, *The Burden of Representation: Essays on Photographies and Histories.* Minneapolis: University of Minnesota Press, 1988; Simon A. Cole, *Suspect Identities: A History of Fingerprinting and Criminal Identification.* Cambridge, MA: Harvard University Press, 2001.

developed techniques for reading the surfaces others presented. The postwar science of interpersonal relations would consider these very inferences made by gathering ambiguous information from the other people's bodies and behaviors. These social judgments required observing the whole, dynamic person (certainly their face, but also their body, demeanor, dress, and actions). Both "emotional expression" and "interpersonal relations" required categorizing information about persons, but, in the mid-1950s, the psychologist's look slowed from a darting glance to a thoughtful (if biased) stare.[5]

Face perception was also surprisingly marginal to the emerging field of pattern recognition. This branch of cognitive science, operating at the intersection of psychology and artificial intelligence, sought to build thinking machines by having them actively learn to perceive. By the mid-1950s, artificial intelligence researchers had achieved considerable success in programming computers to play complex, social games like chess and solving logical propositions. Machines could think. A greater challenge lay in whether computers could "select from their environment the things, or the relations, they are going to think about."[6] In 1958, Frank Rosenblatt, a psychologist at the Cornell Aeronautical Laboratory, proposed such a solution. His Perceptron algorithm looked to the brain as part of a living, biological system, with connections acquired over time by associating various perceived sensory inputs.[7] The *New York Times* covered the publication of Rosenblatt's article, a tribute rarely accorded to the *Psychological Review*. The story, rife with Cold War hype and anxieties about intelligent machines supplanting humanity, focused on a demonstration at the behest of Rosenblatt's patron, the U.S. Navy. It described "the embryo of an electronic computer" as "the first electronic device to think as the human brain." At first prone to mistakes, like every child, Perceptron would grow wiser with experience. Equipped with "a camera-eye lens to scan objects or survey situations," it would remember what it itself experienced rather than what humans fed it with punch cards. Rosenblatt promised future Perceptrons would even "recognize people and call out their names."[8]

Perceptron's celebrity inspired emulators and rivals, often backed by generous military contracts. A complementary approach was Pandemonium, programmed by Oliver Selfridge based out of the Lincoln Laboratory, a leading defense research facility housed at the Massachusetts Institute of Technology (MIT). Along with psychologist Ulric Neisser, Selfridge labored to make various human-generated patterns (from written letters to Morse code) machine readable. Once built, these machines would, in turn, explain how human perception worked. Faces were but

---

5. Bruner and Tagiuri, "The Perception of People."

6. Oliver G. Selfridge and Ulric Neisser, "Pattern Recognition," *Scientific American* 203 (August 1960): 60–69, 60.

7. Frank Rosenblatt, "The Perceptron: A Probabilistic Model for Information Storage and Organization in the Brain," *Psychological Review* 65 (1958): 386–408.

8. "Electronic 'Brain' Teaches Itself," *New York Times*, July 13, 1958, E9.

one relevant category of patterns. In a 1964 *Scientific American* article, Neisser introduced the process of visual search to a popular audience by asking his reader to scan an accompanying photograph of the 1961 Orange Bowl football game for what was probably the most recognizable face in America at the time: the recently assassinated president John F. Kennedy. Almost immediately detectable, Neisser confessed he remained "hard put to explain how that one face can be identified among so many."[9] But Neisser did not dwell on this enigma. His article immediately left this tricky (if not hard) problem behind by breaking it down into simpler, more tractable ones like scanning lists of letters or words in the laboratory. Neisser's presentation suggested the visual scanning of faces, and words formed a common problem met by a singular perceptual ability.

Although difficult to gauge as many records remain classified, it seems that even the expanding securing state deemed facial recognition a low priority.[10] In 1963, at the height of enthusiasm for perceptrons, the Central Intelligence Agency (CIA) started keeping tabs on related projects. As with the original Perceptron, funding came from the military, this time an Air Force contract to Scope Incorporated, a Virginia company. Conflex, "a conditioned reflex computer," combined a sensory matrix with a digital algorithm programmed to simulate brain mechanisms. The 1962 prototype demonstrated its learning by successfully identifying human photographs, but Conflex was sold as an all-purpose perceiver, sensitive to visuals, acoustics, pressure, and temperature.[11] A CIA memo outlined a range of possible uses for Conflex. Beyond "basic studies of biological response systems," it could be applied to "character recognition," "photographic image recognition," and "the prenormalization of photography reconnaissance data." In 1964, the latter application captured the interest of the CIA's National Photographic Interpretation Center (NPIC).[12] Established in 1961, NPIC provided the visual intelligence instrumental to the escalation of the Cuban Missile Crisis the following year. Recognizing human-made patterns in the landscape as snapped by distant, aerial cameras best met the needs of the Cold War security state. The primary threats came from territorially sovereign enemies with their burgeoning nuclear infrastructure rather than unfamiliar faces mingling in domestic crowds. In 1965, engineer Woody Bledsoe approached the CIA with plans for an automated facial recognition system. Funded for a few years through shadow corporations, his technology,

---

9. Ulric Neisser, "Visual Search," *Scientific American* 210 (June 1964): 94–103, 95.

10. Due to ongoing state secrecy, a full accounting is impossible. However, the sparse public record is telling.

11. Edward C. Driese, John S. Gerig, Malcolm R. Uffelman, and Richard E. Williams, "System for Classifying Minimally Constrained Stimuli," U.S. Patent 3,295,103, issued December 27, 1966.

12. Assistant for Plans and Development to Director, NPIC, "Report on Perceptron and Conflex Concerning Automated Image Recognition," April 2, 1963. https://www.cia.gov/library/readingroom/document/cia-rdp78b04770a002300030029-4

reminiscent of Bertillonage, likewise floundered.[13] In 1969, Marvin Minsky and Seymour Papert published a damning critique of the entire Perceptron enterprise which cooled interest in neural networks for over a decade.[14] Even before this, the most immediate problems facing Cold War cognitive scientists meant they found the Darwinian-Galtonian dream remarkably uninteresting.

SCRUTINIZING THE GAZE

The cognitive psychologists affiliated with MIT proved an exception to this early Cold War indifference to facial recognition. Psychology came late to the university, achieving departmental status only in 1964, two years after the MIT biophysicist Francis Schmitt coined the term "neuroscience" to refer to an emerging discipline focused on "mind, brain, and behavior."[15] Housed within an engineering school where practical problems inspired the cutting edge of research, the new department led by Hans-Lukas Teuber adopted this perspective, which was a very different orientation than the pure science ideal embraced by its North American counterparts at other elite universities. Receiving his PhD from Harvard's Department of Social Relations in 1946, Teuber spent the first half of his career at the Bellevue Medical Center in New York rehabilitating war veterans with brain injuries. He brought these connections to the department he built, cultivating close ties with clinical neurology at a time when such relationships were largely unknown among American psychologists.[16]

Teuber encouraged a number of his younger associates to pursue face perception. The first associate was PhD student Robert Yin. Inspiration came from the face's prominence in the ambiguous figures that captivated interwar Gestalt psychologists. This led Yin to consider the human visage both as a whole and as object whose perception was pliable to distortion through inversion. He tested this assumption by having participants memorize a dossier of studio photographs of rather nondescript men. Each photograph had a standardized pose, and the men lacked glasses, beards, or noticeable birthmarks. Yin had a second dossier of photographed objects; things typically seen from a singular orientation. When the participants flipped through yet another dossier, Yin compared their success

---

13. Shaun Raviv, "The Secret History of Facial Recognition," *Wired*, January 21, 2020. https://www.wired.com/story/secret-history-facial-recognition

14. Mikel Olazaran, "A Sociological Study of the Official History of the Perceptrons Controversy," *Social Studies of Science* 26, no. 3 (1996): 611–659.

15. Yvan Prkachin, "'The Sleeping Beauty of the Brain: Memory, MIT, Montreal, and the Origins of Neuroscience," *Isis* 112, no. 1 (2021): 22–44.

16. For example, Teuber became one of the first psychologists to study the famous amnesiac HM, along with colleagues at McGill University in Canada. Brenda Milner, Suzanne Corkin, and H-L. Teuber, "Further Analysis of the Hippocampal Amnesic Syndrome: 14-Year Follow-Up Study of HM," *Neuropsychologia* 6, no. 3 (1968): 215–234.

in recognizing familiar objects from the previous set (whether people or things) when presented upright or inverted. Both human and nonhuman stimuli were harder to recognize when inverted, but upside-down faces proved uniquely difficult to identify. The participants' verbal reports suggested what search strategies they pursued. Some looked for a distinguishing feature, but most relied on "some personal impression made by the face." Inversion disrupted this orientating anchor.[17] Along with this experiment with healthy participants, Yin conducted a complementary one with American veterans of the Korean War suffering from neurological injuries. Those with damage to the brain's right posterior performed more poorly when it came to recognizing faces compared to the controls. These same individuals performed better than the controls when the faces were inverted. Not only did the mind possess a face-specific pattern analyzer, but one seemingly localized in a specific region of the brain.[18] The inverted face paradigm and the clinical neuropsychology cases provided two of the major pillars of revived face perception research. Despite these promising findings, Yin represented yet another dead end for face perception. Upon receiving his PhD, he chose not to pursue a career in neuroscience. He abandoned perception research for the qualitative analysis of public policy, another telling indicator of face perception's marginal status at this time.

Teuber encouraged others at MIT to extend Yin's research. Susan Carey and Rhea Diamond turned from neurological patients to young children to understand how humans came to distinguish between so many faces at a glance. Yin's paradigm highlighted two possible strategies the mind used to represent faces: piecemeal (as an assemblage of distinct features) and configural (as a Gestalt whole). Carey and Diamond's cross-sectional design had children of different ages recognize variously inverted, obscured, and posed faces. Those under the age of ten relied on isolated features to identify people; those older switched to seeing faces as wholes. The human brain developed configural processing as it matured.[19]

Humans might only mature into holistic perception well into childhood, but a fascination with faces came much earlier. According to ethologically informed approaches to human development like John Bowlby's attachment theory, the child entered the world with an innate inclination toward the mother. Much of Bowlby's evidence came from research conducted by others on birds and monkeys, but his theory of a profound affective bond between mother and child honed by evolution inspired a wide range of experiments on young children.[20] In 1961, developmental

---

17. Robert Yin, "Looking at Upside-down Faces," *Journal of Experimental Psychology* 81, no. 1 (1969): 141–145, 145.

18. Yin, "Face Recognition by Brain-Injured Patients: A Dissociable Ability?" *Neuropsychologia* 8, no. 4 (1970): 395–402.

19. Susan Carey and Rhea Diamond, "From Piecemeal to Configurational Representation of Faces," *Science* 195, no. 4275 (1977): 312–314.

20. Marga Vicedo, *The Nature and Nurture of Love: From Imprinting to Attachment in Cold War America*. Chicago: University of Chicago Press, 2013.

psychologist Robert Fantz introduced what became known as the "preferential looking task" to unlock mental landscape of nonverbal participants, whether neonate chicks or human infants. These subjects could not verbally express their thoughts, but the direction of their gaze indicated what objects captured their attention and intentions. Frantz's method entailed presenting the infant with two stimuli with differing patterns of complexity and following the neonate's gaze to determine its preferred choice.[21] Infants actively and purposefully explored their world. They attended to the novel and scrutinized it. Rather than blank slates or passive machines, Fantz started a line of research suggesting wordless infants were born philosophers eager to acquire knowledge.

Others kept Frantz's equation of visual fixation with discerning attention but opted to present stimuli sequentially and measure the comparative duration of the neonate's gaze. One category of objects infants invariably encountered was other people's faces.[22] Babies also possessed faces of their own. How did their encounters with others shape their self-understanding? By using videotape recordings and by making the kinds of funny faces so many parents performed for their own babies, Andrew Meltzoff and M. Keith Moore found that an imitative ability came to children much sooner than existing cognitive theory suggested. Within a few weeks, infants could imitate a number of facial gestures modeled by an experimenter. This imitation required that the infant recognize these features in the experimenter and connect them to their equivalents on their own faces. Meltzoff and Moore rejected the ethological/attachment hypothesis of an innate releasing mechanism. Instead, human neonates were cognitively sophisticated beasts, receiving visual information from the world and proprioceptive data from their own bodies. More remarkably, the infant mind actively processed, compared, and organized these experiences into an imitative response, the foundation for future learning. Only days in this world, infants acquired the distinction between self and other while also grasping that some kind of relationship existed between them.[23]

Infancy research appealed to psychologists hoping to finally resolve the nature–nurture controversy and to parents seeking to unlock the mystery of their own child's unspoken thoughts. Following the infant's gaze allowed them to finally communicate (in a manner). Such designs became exceedingly popular among developmental psychologists but were rife with methodological problems. Convincing parents to hand over their newborns to a psychologist for a scientific experiment was always a challenge. This obstacle to recruitment meant sample sizes tended to be very small, making statistical inferences dubious at best. Many infants proved uncooperative, leading to the discarding of their data (as if a repeated

---

21. Robert L. Fantz, "Visual Experience in Infants: Decreased Attention to Familiar Patterns Relative to Novel Ones," *Science* 146, no. 3644 (1964): 668–670.

22. Jerome Kagan, Barbara A. Henker, Amy Hen-Tov, Janet Levine, and Michael Lewis, "Infants' Differential Reactions to Familiar and Distorted Faces," *Child Development* (1966): 519–532.

23. Andrew N. Meltzoff and M. Keith Moore, "Imitation of Facial and Manual Gestures by Human Neonates," *Science* 198, no. 4312 (1977): 75–78.

unwillingness to fix the gaze on the experiment's chosen object advanced no evidentiary claim). Finally, despite the presence of considerable instrumentation like video cameras and one-way mirrors to introduce forms of standardization and control, these experiments inevitably hinged upon adult researchers coding the rather ambiguous direction of the infant's gaze or the gestures they expressed.[24]

These caveats aside, three lines of research converged by the mid-1970s, suggesting face recognition constituted a "special ability" operating beyond conscious awareness: its seeming early ontogeny in human infants; Yin's inverted face paradigm; and neurological cases of patients with prosopagnosia or face blindness.[25] With the exception of the inverted face paradigm, none of this evidence derived from the kind of experimental designs characteristic of American cognitive science. Rather than military contracts, funding at MIT and elsewhere came from foundation grants dedicated to understanding health and the aging process at both ends of the lifespan. A new style of cognitive science coalesced in the 1970s with data taken not from the default healthy, adult male (or his mechanical analog), but from the embodied responses from a host of "special" populations aligned with applied clinical and developmental problems.

COMPUTATIONAL PARADOX

That humans (even infants) seemingly recognized faces was striking, as the task bested the most advanced artificial minds. The perceived gap between human and artificial minds became an increasingly pressing concern for cognitive scientists in the 1980s. The computer metaphor animated much postwar cognitive science. According to early advocates like Herbert Simon, the best way to figure out how the human mind worked was to build an artificial counterpart. Programming early computers to solve logical problems (like playing chess) revealed the limits of a universal, algorithmic rationality. The complexity of the decision environment meant neither human nor machine could calculate all possibilities in an efficient manner. Both relied on usually dependable rules of thumbs, heuristics, to cut off cumbersome and unlikely pathways to arrive at a quicker decision.[26] What interested Simon about cognition regardless of medium were those aspects that ran slowly and serially. In a 1980 address before the Sigma Xi honor society, Simon declared that "the systems we are examining operate rather slowly, and for many purposes we can ignore the detail beyond a resolution of tens to hundreds

---

24. Ruth Leys, *Newborn Imitation: The Stakes of a Controversy*. Cambridge: Cambridge University Press, 2020.

25. For a review canonizing these three lines while skeptically pointing to their inconclusiveness, see Hadyn D. Ellis, "Recognizing faces." *British Journal of Psychology* 66, no. 4 (1975): 409–426.

26. Hunter Crowther-Heyck, *Herbert A. Simon: The Bounds of Reason in Modern America*. Baltimore: Johns Hopkins University Press, 2005.

of milliseconds."[27] These thought processes were accessible through careful introspection and were verbalizable through self-reports. Analyzing the protocols written down as people solved advanced, logical puzzles allowed Simon to read the language of thought itself.[28] At the heart of his cognitive science was a strong analogy among the computer, the scientist, the chess player, and the layperson as knowers pursuing the same bounded but fundamentally rational decisions.

By 1980, Simon's younger contemporaries took the opposite point of view when it came to what mattered most about cognition. In one of the most cited articles ever published in the *Psychological Review*, social psychologists Richard Nisbett and Timothy Wilson presented a series of experiments demonstrating that participants were almost never aware of how their perceptual or memory processes functioned. Only the results of thinking appeared in subjective consciousness. Participants repeatedly failed to accurately report the effect of stimuli on their responses and tended to base their reports on pleasing, prior, unarticulated assumptions.[29] Social psychologist Robert Zajonc mounted an even more pointed challenge to cool cognition's ecological validity. Computational systems collected information, remembered it, and used it to achieve goals, but they had no emotional reaction to these objectives. In contrast, Zajonc conceived of "very few perceptions and cognitions in everyday life that do not have a significant affective component, that aren't hot, or in the very least tepid." In Zajonc's example, participants who he asked to scrutinize a series of photographed portraits later recognized more faces when instructed to judge the person's likeability than when they were asked to attend to factual features like estimating the length of the nose or the distance between the eyes. Rather than pointing to a deeper level of processing, this suggested to Zajonc the activation of a separate affective system.[30] Unlike many of his contemporaries, Zajonc did not look to computers for inspiration. He found supposedly complex social behaviors in cockroaches and other "simple" organisms.[31] Based on his research on mere (subliminal) exposure to phenomena, he insisted that "preferences need no inferences." Humans tended to make quick decisions based on their barely

---

27. Herbert A. Simon, "Studying Human Intelligence by Creating Artificial Intelligence," *American Scientist* 69, no. 3 (1981): 300–309, 302.

28. Kai Ericsson and Herbert Simon, "Verbal Reports as Data," *Psychological Review* 87, no. 3 (1980): 215–251.

29. Richard E. Nisbett, and Timothy DeCamp Wilson, "Telling More Than We Can Know: Verbal Reports on Mental Processes," *Psychological Review* 84, no. 3 (1977): 231–259.

30. Robert Zajonc, "Feeling and Thinking: Preferences Need No Inferences," *American Psychologist* 35, no. 2 (1980): 151–175, quote 153.

31. D. W. Rajecki, "Zajonc, Cockroaches, and Chickens, c. 1965–1975: A Characterization and Contextualization," *Emotion Review* 2, no. 4 (2010): 320–328.

articulated affective inclinations and subsequently used words to justify their choice.[32]

Such criticisms extended beyond territorial social psychologists defending their turf. In his *Scientific American* column in the 1980s, the cognitive scientist Douglas Hofstadter bemoaned the sorry state of artificial intelligence. After the funding crunch of the first AI winter of the mid-1970s, the field had seemingly lost its moorings in basic science. It now floundered by focusing on highly specialized, domain-specific "expert systems" designed to meet the immediate and overly specified demands of the industries that paid for them. Missing was the kind of general intelligence that allowed a living organism to survive. Where certain computer programs approached the level of chess champion, simple acts that came automatically to humans (like riding a bicycle) remained elusive. Progress for Hofstadter required augmenting the temporal resolution for observing thought. What happened inside the brain as a person almost immediately recognized their own mother was the psychologically interesting problem. Rather than complex problem solving, Hofstadter declared the "subcognitions" of the fleshy brain like "perception[,] is where it's at."[33]

The modeling of man on machine had long provoked concerns from humanists, but Hofstadter represented a critical voice from inside the AI community.[34] The late 1970s influx of funding for interdisciplinary cognitive science venues (conferences, journals, departments) ultimately created platforms where academics from disciplines with very different sensibilities became aware of their differences. Philosophers proved especially hostile to another (and comparatively well-financed) intrusion of psychology into their supposed domain of rational thinking. Psychologists, always the dominant party in this multidisciplinary matrix, turned inward, invoking vague computer metaphors without engaging much in concrete computational methods.[35] By the mid-1980s, these skirmishes led cognitive scientists to talk about a "computational paradox." Ironically, after thirty years of effort, "the rigorous application of methods and models drawn from

---

32. For more on Zajonc's advocacy of affect and automaticity against intentional, appraisalist theories of emotion, see Ruth Leys, *The Ascent of Affect: Genealogy and Critique.* Chicago: University of Chicago Press, 2017, 172–219.

33. Douglas R. Hofstadter, "Waking Up from the Boolean Dream, Or, Subcognition as Computation," *Metamagical Themas: Questing for the Essence of Mind and Pattern.* New York: Basic Books, 1985, 631–665.

34. Edward Jones-Imhotep, "The Ghost Factories: Histories of Automata and Artificial Life," *History and Technology* 36, no. 1 (2020): 3–29; Danielle Judith Zola Carr, "'Ghastly Marionettes' and the Political Metaphysics of Cognitive Liberalism: Anti-Behaviourism, Language, and the Origins of Totalitarianism," *History of the Human Sciences* 33, no. 1 (2020): 147–174.

35. Rafael Núñez, Michael Allen, Richard Gao, Carson Miller Rigoli, Josephine Relaford-Doyle, and Arturs Semenuks, "What Happened to Cognitive Science?" *Nature Human Behaviour* 3, no. 8 (2019): 782–791.

the computational realm has helped scientists to understand the ways in which human beings are not very much like these prototypical computers."[36]

Connectionism mounted a serious challenger to Simon's brand of slow, serial, explicit, logical computationalism. The 1986 publication of a massive collection *Parallel Distributed Processing* edited by David Rumelhart and James McClelland heralded the new approach.[37] Rather than start with the medium-agnostic program, connectionists, like Perceptron researchers before them, built their theory from the physical structure of the brain. Sustaining a living organism required countless tasks run in parallel distributed throughout its body. Much of this work (the beating heart, the breathing lungs, the seeing eyes) happened automatically, or at least beyond the threshold of awareness and without a conscious decision ever being made. Simon acknowledged that "the human sensory organs are obviously parallel devices in which many processes are going on simultaneously," but he dismissed this fact as irrelevant to the kind of cognitive theory he sought to build. Only those processes where deliberate attention was directed mattered to him.[38] Connectionism analogized cognitive processing to the associations formed by the neural networking of the brain, but the exact relationship between the two remained ambiguous. Connectionism gave psychology a stronger biological flavor, but the relationship was often as metaphorical as the computer before it. The movement's widest impact was to downplay concerns about reducing psychology to its neurological substrate.

Cool computationalism's hold on psychology further weakened in July 1990 when U.S. president George H. W. Bush announced "the decade of the brain." Backed by congressional mandate, the initiative aimed to raise general awareness about neuroscience while channeling considerable National Institutes of Health (NIH) funding into brain-based research. This new patronage accelerated a trend started by the release of Prozac in 1987, the first in a new generation of selective serotonin reuptake inhibitor antidepressant drugs. Within five years, over four and a half million Americans had been prescribed Prozac, setting off a psychopharmacological revolution that helped secure mental illnesses as brain disorders.[39] In the clinical context of depression, things like mood and affect were not sidelines or noise, but the very substance of the mind's function. This newly available generosity encouraged psychologists in areas of supposed basic research to align themselves with the imperatives of health care. Few alternatives

---

36. Howard Gardner, *The Mind's New Science: A History of the Cognitive Revolution*. New York: Basic Books, 1985, 44.

37. Michelle Gibbons, "Attaining Landmark Status: Rumelhart and McClelland's PDP Volumes and the Connectionist Paradigm," *Journal of the History of the Behavioral Sciences* 55, no. 1 (2019): 54–70.

38. Simon, "Studying Human Intelligence by Creating Artificial Intelligence," 302.

39. On the pharmaceutical industry's sponsorship of 1990s anti-stigma campaigns, see Loren Gaudet, "'Even Heroes Get Depressed': Sponsorship and Self-Stigma in Canada's Mental Illness Awareness Week," *Journal of Medical Humanities* 40, no. 2 (2019): 155–170.

for financial support were available to them after Ronald Reagan had decimated National Science Foundation (NSF) funding to psychology as a social science in 1981.[40] This funding environment also helped put to rest psychologists' ongoing worries about the dangers of speculative neurology outstripping available evidence.[41] Instead, progress lay in cultivating a forward-looking anticipatory neuroscience whose bold predictions may or not become true within the promised five- to ten-year window.

The computational paradox gave face perception a new relevance. The dwindling of psychology's Cold War alignment with artificial intelligence drew attention to the persistent distance between the minds of humans and machines. The future of computers did not lie in anthropomorphic emulation.[42] For example, in an article simultaneously published in the new *Journal of Cognitive Neuroscience* and the *Institute of Electronical and Electronic Engineers* in 1991, computer scientists Matthew Turk and Alex Pentland proposed a solution to the long-standing facial recognition problem. Their program decomposed photographed faces into a series of comparable eigenvectors that telling did not necessarily correspond to anthropomorphic categories like eyes, ears, and noses. Their connectionist model allowed for autonomous machine learning by abandoning the project of directly modeling human thought processes in favor of dramatically increasing computational power to levels beyond the limits of organic brains.[43] Conversely, the critical question for psychologists became what made the moody, affective, social thinking of the human unique. Rather than a strange curiosity, the infant's early and perhaps innate ability exemplified what humans accomplished easily and automatically. Facial recognition distinguished humans (or at least primates) from machines. It made us and our brains special.

"Their Own Private Patch of Real Estate in the Brain"

Deemed "special" by the early 1990s, Nancy Kanwisher made face perception central to the functional magnetic resonance imaging (fMRI) boom that remade psychology at century's end. Another graduate of MIT's (renamed) Department of Brain and Cognitive Sciences, Kanwisher began her career in 1986 as a vision researcher uninterested in face perception. The topic struck her as a minor sideline tangential to the real problem of general object perception. What did capture

---

40. Mark Solovey, *Social Science for What?: Battles over Public Funding for the "Other Sciences" at the National Science Foundation*. Cambridge, MA: MIT Press, 2020, 207–235.

41. Gregory A. Miller, "Mistreating Psychology in the Decades of the Brain," *Perspectives on Psychological Science* 5, no. 6 (2010): 716–743.

42. Rodney A. Brooks, "Intelligence without Representation," *Artificial Intelligence* 47, no. 1-3 (1991): 139–159.

43. Matthew Turk and Alex Pentland, "Eigenfaces for Recognition," *Journal of Cognitive Neuroscience* 3, no. 1 (1991): 71–86.

her imagination was the publication of the earliest fMRI graphs of neural activity in the human visual cortex on the cover of *Science* magazine in 1991. Seeing these images, so closely resembling photographs of brain activity itself, galvanized her. She returned to the Boston area from the west coast hoping to gain access to the novel technology housed at Massachusetts General Hospital, where it was used as a diagnostic tool for viewing the body's soft tissues.[44] Visualizing neural activity had been possible since 1924, when German psychiatrist Hans Berger made the first electroencephalograph (EEG) recording, but fMRI's voxel graphs promised greater verisimilitude than Berger's simple, continuous line.[45] fMRI also allowed far greater spatial precision than EEG's recording of electrical impulses by placing electrodes on the skull. The technology possessed a much finer temporal resolution than its immediate competitor, positronic emission tomography (PET), allowing for the capture of fleeting events in the cerebrum.[46]

Grantless and untenured with limited access to the machine, Kanwisher knew she needed to "score a big result fast."[47] This suddenly made face perception an attractive problem. It was tractable, even given her constraints. The existing clinical literature and preliminary imaging studies indicated the back right of the visual cortex was a promising place to conduct an expedient expedition. Kanwisher set out to resolve whether this region was involved specifically in the face perception or whether it simply became active during a more general perception of objects.

Kanwisher initially recruited twenty participants (including herself as the very first). Lying in the scanner, they looked at a mirror onto which various images were projected. For stimuli, Kanwisher pulled ninety photographs from Harvard's freshman "face book" and intermingled them with the presentation of ninety photographs of various objects.[48] A preliminary scan of her own visual cortex "found a promising blob on the bottom of my right hemisphere" when she looked

---

44. Nancy Kanwisher, "The Quest for the FFA and Where It Led," *Journal of Neuroscience* 37, no. 5 (2017): 1056–1061, 1058.

45. Rhodri Hayward, "The Tortoise and the Love-Machine: Grey Walter and the Politics of Electroencephalography," *Science in Context* 14, no. 4 (2001): 615–641; Kenton Kroker, *The Sleep of Others and the Transformations of Sleep Research*. Toronto: University of Toronto Press, 2007; Cornelius Borck, "Recording the Brain at Work: The Visible, the Readable, and the Invisible in Electroencephalography," *Journal of the History of the Neurosciences* 17, no. 3 (2008): 367–379; Melissa M. Littlefield, *Instrumental Intimacy: EEG Wearables and Neuroscientific Control*. Baltimore: Johns Hopkins University Press, 2018; Anthony Enns, "Visualizing Thoughts: Photography, Neurology and Neuroimaging." In *Mind Reading as a Cultural Practice*. New York: Palgrave Macmillan, 2020, 63–91.

46. Joseph Dumit, *Picturing Personhood: Brain Scans and Biomedical Identity*. Princeton, NJ: Princeton University Press, 2004.

47. Nancy Kanwisher, "The Quest for the FFA and Where It Led," 1058.

48. Nancy Kanwisher, Josh McDermott, and Marvin M. Chun, "The Fusiform Face Area: A Module in Human Extrastriate Cortex Specialized for Face Perception," *Journal of Neuroscience* 17, no. 11 (1997): 4302–4311, 4303.

at the faces but not the other objects.[49] As she continued running participants through the MRI, each produced their own idiosyncratic patterns of illumination when looking at faces. Data for five individuals needed to be thrown out because their excessive head movements created artifacts in the recordings. Kanwisher printed the remaining participants' activation maps and posted them along the wall outside her office.[50] A remarkable symmetry existed between the participant's task in the machine and her own as a scientist working outside of it. Both gazed at visual patterns to discriminate objects, whether faces or illuminated brain regions. As she paced the hallway scanning the gallery of voxelated brains, Kanwisher perceived a common set of blobs in a similar vicinity, what she dubbed the fusiform face area (FFA). After this visual inspection, she analyzed her results statistically. She split the data for each participant in half, using the average of the even-numbered runs for each subject to establish a baseline "localizer" for the region of interest (ROI), comparing them to and then using the face and object from odd runs. Kanwisher hoped to publicize the FFA results in either *Science* or *Nature*, but both journals rejected her article. Face perception still lacked general interest as late as 1997.[51]

Instead, it found a home in the *Journal of Neuroscience*. What made the paper a citation classic was not necessarily the topic of face perception, but the group's ROI technique for convincingly localizing mental function. Kanwisher claimed to have discovered a "module" in the brain that was uniquely specialized for face perception. This region selectively activated for one class of objects but not other stimuli. This "special-purpose cortical machinery" provided the strongest empirical evidence for the radical modularity of the mind.[52] Each mental process dwelled in its unique territory. Advances in cognitive science would come from identifying other regions of interest in the brain rather than conceptualizing the mind as a medium-agnostic, general-purpose problem-solver. Kanwisher's ROI technique was not wholly responsible for the trend, however, psychologists' use of fMRI skyrocketed after 1997 (see Figure 7.1). Generalist journals such as *Science*, *Nature*, and the *Proceedings of the National Academic of Sciences* soon welcomed this line of research. Articles on cognitive processes appearing in their pages had to contain the obligatory neuroimages, to the exclusion of behavioral

---

49. Kanwisher, "The Quest for the FFA and Where It Led," 1058.

50. On the embodiment of MRI reading, see Morana Alac, *Handling Digital Brains: A Laboratory Study of Multimodal Semiotic Interaction in the Age of Computers*. Cambridge, MA: MIT Press, 2011.

51. Kanwisher, "The Quest for the FFA and Where It Led," 1057.

52. Nancy Kanwisher, Josh McDermott, and Marvin M. Chun, "The Fusiform Face Area: A Module in Human Extrastriate Cortex Specialized for Face Perception," *Journal of Neuroscience* 17, no. 11 (1997): 4302–4311, 4310.

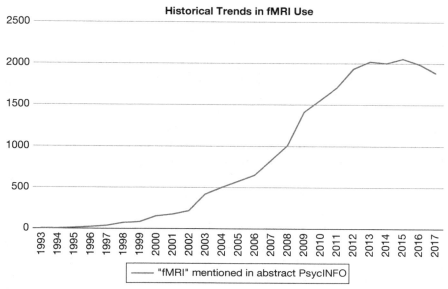

Figure 7.1 Historical Trends in fMRI Use.

observations. Some complained that the MRI machine had given birth to a "new phrenology."[53]

Along with talking about the brain's modular machines, a mixture of visual and spatial metaphors saturated Kanwisher's writing. Her goal was not so much to present a cognitive theory as to create a neural "map" or "portrait" to establish the "architecture of the mind." In one repeated turn of phrases, she argued that fMRI allowed scientists to determine which mental functions "get their own private patch of real estate in the brain."[54] Possessive individualism, the liberal theory guaranteeing freedom through self-ownership and seeing the securing of private property rights as the foundation for politics, long shaped how American psychologists conceived of personhood.[55] In equating mental modules with private property owners (hereditary aristocrats if these functions were innate at birth, capitalists if acquired through development), Kanwisher pushed the metaphor further than ever before. Now, these components of the brain, not the whole person, asserted exclusive privilege over their domain. As new discoveries revealed that these individual landowners possessed an increasing amount of the

---

53. William R. Uttal, *The New Phrenology: The Limits of Localizing Cognitive Processes in the Brain.* Cambridge, MA: MIT Press, 2001.

54. Kanwisher, "Functional Specificity in the Human Brain: A Window into the Functional Architecture of the Mind," *Proceedings of the National Academy of Sciences* 107, no. 25 (2010): 11163–11170, 11167.

55. Jeff Sugarman, "Psychologism as a Style of Reasoning and the Study of Persons," *New Ideas in Psychology* 44 (2017): 21–27.

brain's territory, little room was left for general purpose functions like rationality. Not only "society," but the "person" was an illusion, the effect of an array of self-possessed neural components. So ran the "massive modularity hypothesis" in evolutionary psychology.[56]

But not everyone agreed that Kanwisher had discovered a unique parcel of the brain wholly dedicated to recognizing other human faces. Criticisms came in two directions from her fellow fMRI users. The first critique focused on the specificity of the FFA, and the second on the localization of function to this one region.

Some rejected the notion that facial recognition represented an innate ability honed through evolution. Children learned to distinguish faces developmentally, so this mental function was better understood as an acquired form of expertise. Back in 1986, Diamond and Carey had found trained dog breeders to be susceptible to the inversion illusion when presented with pictures of different types of dogs as ordinary people when it came to faces.[57] The strongest support for this position came from Isabel Gauthier. As a graduate student at Yale, she trained participants to become experts in distinguishing among vaguely anthropomorphic, but nonsense, stimuli affectionately called "Greebles." These computerized drawings came with individual identities, possessed one of two genders, and belonged to one of five families. Inverting a Greeble compromised the trained expert's ability to recognize it, but the novices fared no worse. What appeared automatic was actually the product of "extensive practice."[58] Sure enough, when Greeble experts entered the MRI machine, the FFA lit up as they distinguished the various figures from one another.[59] Gauthier rejected the notion that this area constituted a uniquely specialized module with an independent function. It was the region responsible for a more general expert judgment of visual inputs. Rather than viewing facial recognition as a hot, affect-driven, primitive ability that evolved in the deep past, it was better understood as a cool, skilled performance, not so different than learning to play chess.

A second, even more damning, challenge came from NIH researcher James V. Haxby who rejected Kanwisher's fundamental assertion about the localization

---

56. John Tooby and Leda Cosmides, "The Psychological Foundations of Culture," in John Barkow, Leda Cosmides, and John Tooby (eds.), *The Adapted Mind*. New York: Oxford University Press, 1992, 19–136.

57. Rhea Diamond and Susan Carey, "Why Faces Are and Are Not Special: An Effect of Expertise," *Journal of Experimental Psychology: General* 115, no. 2 (1986): 107–117.

58. Isabel Gauthier and Michael J. Tarr, "Becoming a "Greeble" Expert: Exploring Mechanisms for Face Recognition," *Vision Research* 37, no. 12 (1997): 1673–1682.

59. Isabel Gauthier, Pawel Skudlarski, John C. Gore, and Adam W. Anderson, "Expertise for Cars and Birds Recruits Brain Areas Involved in Face Recognition," *Nature Neuroscience* 3, no. 2 (2000): 191–197. A recent meta-analysis supports the expertise hypothesis, despite Kanwisher's contention that such studies suffer from small effect sizes. See Edwin J. Burns, Taylor Arnold, and Cindy M. Bukach, "P-curving the Fusiform Face Area: Meta-analyses Support the Expertise Hypothesis," *Neuroscience and Biobehavioral Reviews* 104 (2019): 209–221.

of mental functions. When Haxby's team asked respondents to view pictures of human faces, cats, houses, chairs, scissors, shoes, and bottles, each category produced its own distinct pattern of maximum neural activation.[60] Psychologically speaking, the act of recognizing someone was not a singular function. It involved both hot affective responses and cool cognitive processes, including identifying the person, evaluating their emotional state, and tracking the gaze of their eyes. One would not expect this multiplicity of processes to occupy a single lot of neural real estate. Haxby's own imaging studies supported this multisystem model. Looking at human faces activated a pattern of brain regions that extended well beyond the FFA. Rather than seeing each function as owning a unique patch of exclusive property, Haxby saw mental processes distributed throughout the "commons" of the brain. This distributed network of responses worked collaboratively to encode the information the brain received from the world.[61]

Despite these often-heated debates, Kanwisher and her critics shared a host of assumptions. All concurred on the legitimacy of neuroimaging techniques, especially the then novel fMRI, for visualizing mental processes. Pursuing this line of research required that experimental psychologists build collaborative (if often subservient) relationships with radiologists in hospitals or other health care settings. In 1999, Dartmouth College became the first American university to house an MRI machine in an academic department for research purposes rather than for clinical diagnosis. However, scanner access remained expensive, and their ownership was largely monopolized by medical centers for the next decade, except at the wealthiest universities. Despite these obstacles, neuroimaging proved seductive to psychologists. This technology allowed them to circumvent unreliable verbal reports and messy behavioral measures in favor of the automatic and unobtrusive recording of physiological traces. Gone was Simon's preoccupation with the verbalizable language of thought as older questions about how the mind organized and accessed conceptual knowledge took a backseat. Bypassing the responding subject allowed these scientists to grapple with the speed and location of thought itself, even if the temporal resolution of these setups was no more precise than century-old attempts at mental chronometry in psychophysics.[62]

Beyond moving cognitive science into clinical settings like the Massachusetts General Hospital, establishing the validity of these techniques hinged upon making face perception a fundamental area of psychological research. The FFA was the first great success story of cerebral localization, and subsequent mappings pursued by Kanwisher and others followed its example. Inside the claustrophobic and noisy MRI machine, which was ever sensitive to the slightest movement on

---

60. James V. Haxby, M. Ida Gobbini, Maura L. Furey, Alumit Ishai, Jennifer L. Schouten, and Pietro Pietrini, "Distributed and Overlapping Representations of Faces and Objects in Ventral Temporal Cortex," *Science* 293, no. 5539 (2001): 2425–2430.

61. James V. Haxby, Elizabeth A. Hoffman, and M. Ida Gobbini, "The Distributed Human Neural System for Face Perception," *Trends in Cognitive Sciences* 4, no. 6 (2000): 223–233.

62. Jimena Canales, *A Tenth of a Second: A History*. Chicago: University of Chicago Press, 2010.

the participant's part, few other tasks beyond visual recognition seemed feasible. The machinery limited the execution of meaningful behaviors or the communication of complex, dynamic instructions. Mental tasks needed to be machine appropriate. Silently gazing at images projected on a screen provided the most reliable data. Measuring quick, affective responses played to fMRI's strengths as a method, but this setup allowed for remodeling so-called higher cognitive functions in light of this success. Written passages soon joined pictures, but the methodology of brief exposure followed by rapid recording remained. A widely cited 2001 *Science* article that came out of Princeton's new MRI research center had participants read dilemmas drawn from moral philosophy and then examine their neurological responses as they attempted to solve the problems. Rather than slowly reasoning toward consistent conclusions, the scanner showed that immediate, unarticulated affective responses guided people's moral decision making, which they later rationalized.[63] Kanwisher's graduate student, Rebecca Saxe, identified the cerebral location for people's "theory of mind" by having participants read short passages where they did and did not have to intuit other's intentions.[64]

Born out of the constraints placed on early fMRI research, Kanwisher's success with the FFA recast what counted as "the social" and "the cognitive." The particularity of this region suggested that all human cognition was fundamentally social at some primitive level. Modularity did not require innateness, but the two ideas frequently traveled together.[65] This association started not with the empiricism of new neuroimaging data, but with a cultural shift where psychologists reevaluated their field's relationship to biology, especially evolutionary theory. The commemorating of the centennial of Darwin's major books on humanity revived general interest in his approach to mental life.[66] The psychologist Paul Ekman developed a facial action coding system intended to extract affective universals beneath the vagaries of cultural decorum. Ekman's theory went against the stream of midcentury understanding of feelings as an effect of cognitive appraisal. According to this view, humans did not experience emotions until they had access to a label for them. This reduced emotions to cognitive states. In contrast to this intentional, deliberative model, psychologists started to see humans as first and foremost affective

---

63. Joshua D. Greene, R. Brian Sommerville, Leigh E. Nystrom, John M. Darley, and Jonathan D. Cohen, "An fMRI Investigation of Emotional Engagement in Moral Judgment," *Science* 293, no. 5537 (2001): 2105–2108.

64. Rebecca Saxe and Nancy Kanwisher, "People Thinking about Thinking People: The Role of the Temporo-Parietal Junction in 'Theory of Mind,'" *Neuroimage* 19, no. 4 (2003): 1835–1842.

65. Kanwisher, "The Quest for the FFA and Where It Led," 1059.

66. Erika Lorraine Milam, *Creatures of Cain: The Hunt for Human Nature in Cold War America*. Princeton, NJ: Princeton University Press, 2019.

beasts.[67] In the late 1980s, primatologists suggested the largeness of the human brain evolved not to cope with factual data from the environment, but to handle the ambiguous and affective-laden information produced by their complex social systems. Survival in early primate societies required forming coalitions and "the tactical deception" of competitors to secure food and mates. Human sociality began with the primitive ape's ability to recognize, read, and manipulate their conspecifics.[68]

This social brain hypothesis explained the presence of a region dedicated to facial recognition distinct from other objects, and imaging studies advanced the hypothesis's naturalized definition of the social.[69] As mediated by the fMRI machine, this definition further narrowed what counted as the social. Now it occurred entirely inside the lone individual's head as the mere thinking (or feeling) what the thoughts of others might be. In a remarkable reversal from the assumptions of Cold War AI, the material affordances of neuroimaging technology rendered a social, affect-laden activity the core exemplar of how to conduct basic cognitive science.

LOOKING WITH PREJUDICE

The field of social psychology independently underwent a near identical transformation in the second half of the 1990s. The Implicit Association Test (IAT) likewise "harvested" healthy participants' nonverbal thoughts as they rapidly judged the human faces flashed on a computer screen. Anthony Greenwald officially launched this research program with a 1992 *American Psychologist* article entitled "New Look 3." After two failed efforts in the late 1940s and mid-1970s, Greenwald declared the time had come for psychologists to fully embrace "unconscious cognition" as a legitimate topic. Harkening back to the immediate postwar years, Greenwald's revived New Look theory with a different source of support. Instead of drawing upon passé psychoanalytic theory, he turned to recent experiments on the unconscious retrieval of memory. The experiments Elizabeth Warrington initiated on implicit memory in amnesiacs provided the social psychologist with "a simple (cognitively less sophisticated) view of unconscious cognition."[70] Based

---

67. Paul Ekman and Wallace V. Friesen, *Facial Action Coding System*. Washington, DC: Consulting Psychologists Press, 1978. On the methodological limits of Ekman's program, see Leys, *The Ascent of Affect*, 76–128.

68. On the social brain hypothesis, see Nikolas Rose and Joelle Abi-Rached, *Neuro: The New Brain Sciences and the Management of the Mind*. Princeton, NJ: Princeton University Press, 2013, 141–162.

69. John D. Greenwood, *The Disappearance of the Social in American Social Psychology*. New York: Cambridge University Press, 2004.

70. Anthony G. Greenwald, "New Look 3: Unconscious Cognition Reclaimed," *American Psychologist* 47, no. 6 (1992): 766–779, 766. Jerome Bruner, one of the few surviving psychologists from the original movement, gave a rather dismissive review of Greenwald's attempt to build

out of the University of Washington, soon home to North America's leading implicit memory researchers Larry Jacoby and Henry L. Roediger III, Greenwald proposed a new direction for social cognition. The "implicit" was first and foremost about implicit *measures* of human reactions: the use of new digital technologies to record subjects without their awareness. This methodological preference soon blurred into how psychologists understood the persons they studied. Humans largely acted without awareness. The implicit ran together the unconscious, the automatic, and the uncontrolled. It benefited from the psychoanalytic residue surrounding the older New Look with its dual promise of psychic depth and social relevance while distancing itself from this troubled past by couching the latest findings in a vague, promissory neuroscience.

The revived New Look would reprioritize which topics mattered to social psychologists. The main lines of social cognition research focused on a small set of attributional errors, universal biases divorced from the subject's embeddedness in history and culture. Among the topics neglected, none loomed as large as intergroup prejudice did. In the previous issue of *American Psychologist*, Sandra Graham had documented how Black people had largely disappeared from social psychology journals in the 1980s, not only as authors but as participants. With the turn to "the effect of priming, reaction time, or other indicators of process, the traditionally social psychological issues pertinent to the study of African Americans have receded from view."[71] Greenwald, then, built upon an older tradition in social psychology where facial recognition was far from a universal human ability, but one that operated within the constraints of racial prejudice, and remade it for a digital age.[72] He attempted to retain the precision of cognitive measures and tasks while reconnecting the field to pressing social problems. In 1995, Greenwald and his frequent co-author Mahzarin R. Banaji published an extensive review of "implicit social cognition," demonstrating how these unarticulated processes affected people's attitudes, beliefs, and self-concept.[73]

Greenwald fashioned himself less as a theorist than as an innovative methodologist.[74] The real proof lay in the test. The IAT had the appearance of a game. However, gameplay differed from the slow, strategical maneuvering of chess. The IAT asked players to sort words and pictures into categories as quickly as possible

---

this genealogy, denying it had much to do with the unconscious. See Jerome Bruner, "Another Look at New Look 1," *American Psychologist* 47, no. 6 (1992): 780–783.

71. Sandra Graham, "'Most of the Subjects Were White and Middle Class': Trends in Published Research on African Americans in Selected APA Journals, 1970–1989," *American Psychologist* 47, no. 5 (1992): 629–639, 637.

72. Roy Malpass and Jerome Kravitz, "Recognition for Faces of Own and Other Race," *Journal of Personality and Social Psychology* 13, no. 4 (1969): 330–334.

73. Anthony Greenwald, and Mahzarin Banaji, "Implicit Social Cognition: Attitudes, Self-Esteem, and Stereotypes," *Psychological Review* 102, no. 1 (1995): 4–27.

74. Anthony G. Greenwald, "There Is Nothing So Theoretical As a Good Method," *Perspectives on Psychological Science* 7, no. 2 (2012): 99–108.

by pressing the appropriate button. In the test's most iconic form, it presented the user with anonymized faces that the user was instructed to sort into their proper racialized category. The crucial phase of the test intermingled racial categorization with an attribution carrying a strong affective valence (pleasant/unpleasant, good/bad). For example, in one round the user should hit the same key for black/pleasant and another key for white/unpleasant. The next round reversed these pairings. The measure of an implicit attitude came from the differences in reaction time on these different tasks. A greater delay in categorizing Black stimuli (whether faces, words, or names) as pleasant indicated a higher level of unconscious prejudice.[75] The IAT promised to deliver the psychic depth of older projective tests without the interpretative ambiguity of these methods. Thin, seemingly transparent, reaction time numbers replaced long, verbal self-reports. The IAT was a flexible, mobilizable technology rapidly deployable on a mass scale.

Much of the test's success depended on this distribution among the internet users of the first dot.com bubble. Wanting simultaneously to *test* and to *educate* the public, Greenwald, Banaji, and Nosek launched the Project Implicit website in October 1998.[76] Designed to mimic an interactive museum exhibit, the site offered visitors the opportunity to take a simplified version of the IAT. Participation exceeded expectations, with 600,000 respondents in the site's first 18 months of operation. By May 2002, the number of individual tests had risen to 1.2 million, reaching 13 million ten years later. One of the very first psychological tests implemented on a worldwide web is still largely accessed through dial-up connections; coverage in "old" media news segments like the NBC program *Dateline* and the Discovery Channel drove much of the early interest. Although not randomly selected from the general population, the masses of respondents proved more diverse than the typical samples of university undergraduates. Unlike laboratory participants, the website provided online users with "summary interpretation of their test performance by characterizing it as showing "strong," "medium," "slight," or "little or no" association of the type measured by each test."[77] The decision not to confine their analysis to the typical undergraduate population allowed the test's designers to make bold claims about the distribution of implicit biases throughout society. They noted the distinct lack of need for moderating variables to analyze online surveys. People expressed implicit biases based on age, gender, race, and political orientation.

---

75. Anthony G. Greenwald; Debbie E. McGhee, and Jordan L. K. Schwartz, "Measuring Individual Differences in Implicit Cognition: The Implicit Association Test," *Journal of Personality and Social Psychology* 74, no. 6 (1998): 1464–1480.

76. Brian A. Nosek, Mahzarin R. Banaji, and Anthony G. Greenwald, "E-research: Ethics, Security, Design, and Control in Psychological Research on the Internet," *Journal of Social Issues* 58, no. 1 (2002): 161–176.

77. Anthony G. Greenwald, Brian A. Nosek, and Mahzarin R. Banaji, "Understanding and Using the Implicit Association Test: I. An Improved Scoring Algorithm," *Journal of Personality and Social Psychology* 85, no. 2 (2003): 197–216, 198.

Thirty years after the civil rights movement and the Voting Rights Act (1965), the IAT captured and made visible the persistence of unspoken prejudice, despite public disavowal of racist beliefs among dominant groups.[78] Prejudice continued to brew inside people's minds and shape their actions, maintaining an injustice *system of power* through hegemonic consent.[79] The IAT buttressed the revival of political psychology following the contested presidential election of George W. Bush, or what one advocate called "the end of the end of ideology."[80] The test offered a powerful means of capturing and re-presenting to the participant *how* injustice clung to American society, omnipresent yet secreted away in the recess of the mind.

The IAT, one of dozens of proposed tasks designed to access "automatic" social judgments without a person's awareness, succeeded by establishing how psychologists might use the internet as a distributed network for conducting their research. The test's online circulation heralded a new era of extractive technologies known as "Big Data analytics," built off an internet culture of candid self-revelation. Twentieth-century social scientists struggled with recruiting participants willing to volunteer for their studies. Even prior to the introduction of caller identification technology, the response rates for telephone opinion polls dropped precipitously starting in the 1970s as ordinary Americans resented these unwanted intrusions into their private lives.[81] The computerization of long-available personal data (whether school, health, or financial records) allowed for their mobilization and monetization, often against the interests of the very users who first donated them.[82] These files, once presumed to belong to the administrative bodies that collected them, came under increased regulatory supervision as citizens sought to "own their own data" to shelter their lives from the gaze of an intrusive state and unscrupulous corporations.[83] Given this new ethos of protecting a right to privacy coming out of the 1970s, twenty-first century social scientists marveled at the semi-anonymous internet user's propensity for self-disclosure. Through new social media platforms and online retailers, people were willing to surrender the most intimate aspects of their inner selves in a format extractable by

---

78. John B. McConahay, Betty B. Hardee, and Valerie Batts, "Has Racism Declined in America? It Depends on Who Is Asking and What Is Asked," *Journal of Conflict Resolution* 25, no. 4 (1981): 563–579.

79. John T. Jost, Mahzarin R. Banaji, and Brian A. Nosek, "A Decade of System Justification Theory: Accumulated Evidence of Conscious and Unconscious Bolstering of the Status Quo," *Political Psychology* 25, no. 6 (2004): 881–919.

80. John T. Jost, "The End of the End of Ideology," *American Psychologist* 61(7) (2006): 651–670.

81. Charlotte G. Steeh, "Trends in Nonresponse Rates, 1952–1979," *Public Opinion Quarterly* 45, no. 1 (1981): 40–57.

82. Dan Bouk, "The History and Political Economy of Personal Data over the Last Two Centuries in Three Acts," *Osiris* 32, no. 1 (2017): 85–106.

83. Sarah E. Igo, *The Known Citizen: A History of Privacy in Modern America*, Cambridge, MA: Harvard University Press, 2018.

a "knowing capitalism" whose product increasingly became the very possession, analysis, and circulation of data.[84]

Distributed through this social web, the IAT served as a powerful new technology for drawing prejudice to the surface. The test also abstracted prejudice by defining it as an unconscious attitude found hidden, inaccessible, and somewhere inside the head.[85] By locating itself at the blurry boundary separating the unconscious and the merely unspoken, the IAT risked performing a kind of disappearing act. The test divorced prejudice from its moorings in the unequal access to material resources and the excessive scrutiny given to racialized populations. By making prejudice at once an individual attribute and a universal quality of humanity's tribal nature, the IAT erased the very conscious "possessive investment in whiteness."[86] Rather than a primitive relic, racism was deliberately reproduced because inequality was productive for some.[87] America's prejudices were not so much implicit but built into the infrastructure on which the country ran.

The IAT's psychologizing of discrimination rendered it under the skin but did not necessarily individualize it. A 1998 newspaper story published soon after Project Implicit's launch noted how Greenwald and Banaji "blame[d] the culture for saddling individuals with prejudices. No one has a choice about being exposed to the culture's values."[88] A *New York Times* story from the same year reported: "the researchers note that no evidence links a person's performance on the test with attitudes or behavior in the outside world. 'We like to think of it as an unconsciousness-raising tool,' Dr. Banaji said, a tool 'for increasing awareness or self-analysis. It should not be used to select individuals for jobs or to select a jury.'"[89] The very spectre of the IAT's use in these settings alarmed a small network of social psychologists. Fearful of recommendations implicit to the test (namely, "statist interventionist" supporting affirmative action hiring policies), these "market purist" libertarians mounted a significant (and frequently acrimonious) challenge to the IAT's predictive validity.[90] As the test's ability to reliably

---

84. Mike Savage and Roger Burrows, "The Coming Crisis of Empirical Sociology," *Sociology* 41, no. 5 (2007): 885–899.

85. Robert S. Steele and Jill G. Morawski, "Implicit Cognition and the Social Unconscious," *Theory and Psychology* 12, no. 1 (2002): 37–54.

86. George Lipsitz, *The Possessive Investment in Whiteness: How White People Profit from Identity Politics*. Philadelphia: Temple University Press, 2006.

87. Ruha Benjamin, *Race after Technology: Abolitionist Tools for the New Jim Code*. Cambridge: Polity, 2019.

88. Jerry Large, "You Can't Hide Your Prejudices," *Toronto Star*, October 22, 1998, D1.

89. Erice Goode, "A Computer Diagnosis of Prejudice," *New York Times*, October 13, 1998, F7.

90. Gregory Mitchell and Philip E. Tetlock, "Antidiscrimination Law and the Perils of Mindreading," *Ohio State Law Journal* 67 (2006): 1023–1121; Philip E. Tetlock and Gregory Mitchell. "Calibrating Prejudice in Milliseconds," *Social Psychology Quarterly* 71, no. 1 (2008): 12–16; Hart Blanton, James Jaccard, Jonathan Klick, Barbara Mellers, Gregory Mitchell,

predict an individual's subsequent prejudicial behavior became a contentious issue, a compromise was reached. The IAT's architects argued for its broad relevance to jurisprudence and employment but insisted that the test could not serve as a diagnosis of an individual's prejudicial intentions or actions.[91] Rather than an individual attribute, IAT became a technology for manifesting *collective guilt* and complicity when it came to racism.

Already a widely used social psychology tool, press coverage of the IAT (in op-ed pages and in science columns) increased dramatically in 2008 with Barack Obama's presidential campaign and the ongoing debate about whether America constituted a postracial society.[92] Amid the polarization of American politics around a blue/red state dichotomy, the cool reasonableness of Cold War consensus liberalism and its cognitivist counterpart seemed increasingly untenable propositions. The IAT provided a language and an imaginary for this resurgent tribalism. In 2014, *Washington Post* science reporter Chris Mooney, author of *The Republican War on Science*, published a map based on the data collected by the Project Implicit. Tellingly coding high IAT scores in red and low ones in blue, the map offered a spatialized picture of racism in America. It also produced a near identical visualization to the iconic map depicting the partisan state-by-state breakdown of the 2000 election; a repeated touchstone for recent political punditry.[93]

Mooney produced his map in the wake of the Ferguson uprising, a sustained protest set off by the fatal shooting of Michael Brown by a Ferguson, Missouri, police officer in August 2014. The incident crystallized decades-long complaints from African Americans about the over-policing of their communities, the devaluing of their lives by the state, and the steady growth of the carceral-industrial complex. Adherent consumers of the social psychology of automaticity when designing their campaign materials and economic policies, "implicit bias" came to frame the Obama administration's response to this crisis. As Stanford psychologist Jennifer Eberhardt had shown, it was not just that ordinary Americans held vague prejudicial attitudes toward African Americans, but "seeing Black" carried connotations of

---

and Philip E. Tetlock, "Strong Claims and Weak Evidence: Reassessing the Predictive Validity of the IAT," *Journal of Applied Psychology* 94, no. 3 (2009): 567–582; Frederick Oswald, Gregory Mitchell, Hart Blanton, James Jaccard, and Philip Tetlock, "Predicting Ethnic and Racial Discrimination: A Meta-Analysis of IAT Criterion Studies." *Journal of Personality and Social Psychology* 105, no. 2 (2013): 171–192.

91. Beth Azar, "IAT: Fad or Fabulous?" *APA Monitor* 39, no. 7 (2008): 44.

92. Jeffery Yen, Kevin Durrheim, and Romin W. Tafarodi, "'I'm Happy to Own My Implicit Biases': Public Encounters with the Implicit Association Test," *British Journal of Social Psychology* 57, no. 3 (2018): 505–523.

93. Chris Mooney, "Across America, Whites Are Biased and They Don't Even Know It," *Washington Post*, December 8, 2014.

criminality.[94] This unthinking, automatic association led to the disproportionate killing of Black suspects by trained police officers.[95] Juries deemed darker-skinned, Black defendants in capital cases more "deathworthy."[96] As part of its response to Ferguson, the U.S. Department of Justice under Attorney General Eric Holder provided $4.75 million in funding for a National Initiative for Building Community Trust and Justice, which included extensive "implicit bias training" for police departments.[97]

This unconscious decision making also featured prominently in one of the 2016 presidential debates, when the moderator Lester Holt raised the issue of "implicit bias" as the locus of prejudice among police officers. Democratic candidate Hillary Clinton responded, "I think implicit bias is a problem for everyone," a position congruent with the founders of the IAT.[98] The test initially elicited the ire of libertarians who worried that it sanctioned state interventions. Now, its embrace by the Democratic Party came under attack from radicals who feared its acquiescence. The test elided certain institutions' culpability for violence under the veil of a generalized prejudice. Indeed, participants in a qualitative analysis of IAT takers pointed to the test's evasion of similar structural materializations of prejudice.[99] Quantitative assessments showed the effectiveness of the training quickly dwindled over time.[100] Confessions by former officers suggested why. Few took the debiasing training seriously, and "the proctors let us cheat on whatever "tests" there are, and we all made fun of it later over coffee."[101] Framed as a mode of critique of a prejudicial society, in practice, the bureaucratization of the IAT functioned to increase spending on the police in the form of providing implicit bias training for officers instead of divestment and the reallocation of budget line to other services. Despite the many failures of these debiasing programs, the ubiquity of "implicit bias" in American liberal discourse and its contestation by

94. Jennifer L. Eberhardt, Phillip Atiba Goff, Valerie J. Purdie, and Paul G. Davies, "Seeing Black: Race, Crime, and Visual Processing," *Journal of Personality and Social Psychology* 87, no. 6 (2004): 876–893.

95. Eric Hehman, Jessica K. Flake, and Jimmy Calanchini, "Disproportionate Use of Lethal Force in Policing Is Associated with Regional Racial Biases of Residents," *Social Psychological and Personality Science* 9, no. 4 (2018): 393–401.

96. Jennifer L. Eberhardt, Paul G. Davies, Valerie J. Purdie-Vaughns, and Sheri Lynn Johnson, "Looking Deathworthy: Perceived Stereotypicality of Black Defendants Predicts Capital-Sentencing Outcomes," *Psychological Science* 17, no. 5 (2006): 383–386.

97. https://trustandjustice.org/

98. https://www.washingtonpost.com/video/politics/clinton-on-implicit-bias-in-policing/2016/09/26/46e1e88c-8441-11e6-b57d-dd49277af02f_video.html

99. Yen, Durrheim, and Tafarodi, '"I'm Happy to Own My Implicit Biases,'" 512–514.

100. Calvin Lai, Allison Skinner, Erin Cooley, Sohad Murrar, Markus Brauer, Thierry Devos, Jimmy Calanchini et al. "Reducing Implicit Racial Preferences: II. Intervention Effectiveness Across Time." *Journal of Experimental Psychology: General* 145, no. 8 (2016): 1001–1016.

101. https://medium.com/@OfcrACab/confessions-of-a-former-bastard-cop-bb14d17bc759

radicals and conservatives spoke to the remarkable inroads made by psychologists as they transformed their own field.

Between 1997 and 2002, recognizing human faces went from a marginal curiosity pursued within a specialized branch of perception research to residing at the very heart of psychology's two most utilized technoscientific instruments. The IAT for measuring social attitudes and the fMRI for localizing brain function derived from distinct theoretical problems but ended in an eerily similar *methodological* place. Beyond a certain kind of dustbowl instrumentalism, both entailed recording the nonverbal responses of the psychological participant as they very quickly evaluated somewhat anonymized faces. Their supposed atheoretical nature, the massiveness of the data they wrangled, and the claim to circumvent the participant's conscious intentions sold these instruments as psychology's new cutting edge.[102]

This parallel transformation of both cognitive and social psychology not only had consequences for psychological theory but also shaped more mundane conceptions of the person. Psychologists long debated what to call those individuals who entered their laboratories and surrendered their inner subjectivity to scientific analysis. In the behaviorist era, "subject" was the preferred terms for both humans and nonhuman animals. Starting in the 1970s, style manuals and ethical guidelines gradually encouraged the introduction of the term "participant," replacing the outdated "subject" to describe those who volunteered their data in a study. The new term better suited cognitivist and humanistic sensibilities as it connoted greater autonomy, consent, involvement, and awareness.[103] Active participation did not really characterize these latest research designs. The individuals contributing their data to the kinds of studies exemplified by IAT and fMRI were *respondents* who consented, but whose awareness was more an obstacle than a benefit to science.

Some psychologists bemoaned the loss of actual behavioral measures in favor of conveniently available "finger movements."[104] Such criticisms failed to appreciate how technologies like the fMRI and the IAT helped bring about a world where much of social life revolved around the push of a button as physical copresence became increasingly unnecessary for conducting everyday social and economic activity.[105] All kinds of interpersonal interactions were taking place on

---

102. On the disavowal of theory for method, see Anthony G. Greenwald, "There Is Nothing So Theoretical as a Good Method," *Perspectives on Psychological Science* 7, no. 2 (2012): 99–108.

103. Roger Bibace, Joshua W. Clegg, and Jaan Valsiner, "What Is in a Name? Understanding the Implications of Participant Terminology," *Integrative Psychological and Behavioral Science* 43, no. 1 (2009): 67–77.

104. Roy F. Baumeister, Kathleen D. Vohs, and David C. Funder, "Psychology As The Science of Self-Reports and Finger Movements: Whatever Happened to Actual Behavior?" *Perspectives on Psychological Science* 2, no. 4 (2007): 396–403.

105. David Lyon, *Surveillance Society: Monitoring Everyday Life*. Lanham, MD: Open University Press, 2001.

screens with feelings shared or withheld at the push of a button. However, only certain bodies were allowed to disappear in the age of the internet. Transactions at a distance vanished certain bodies, but this occurred alongside the persistence of heightened scrutiny of the Black body by the state and others.[106] Indeed, the computational algorithms that governed this digital infrastructure continued to parse the world in the manner of their biased programmers.[107]

MTURK AS THE HIDDEN ABODE OF PSYCHOLOGY

It was not only fellow denizens of the net who were being trained to fixate on other people's faces, but America's growing security apparatus. The police's gaze remained resolutely physiognomic, uninformed by the latest insights of cognitive theory. Identi-Kit, introduced by the California police in 1959, and Photo-Fit, designed by British characterologist Jacques Penry, aimed to improve the sketches of criminals. These technologies worked piecemeal, offering the eyewitness a sequential gallery of different features to choose when assembling a composite picture—a failure of method highlighted by legal inquiries like the Devlin Committee in the UK and psychologists by the mid-1970s.[108] Formal inquiries into the nature of legal evidence provided the impetus for psychologists to first pose the question of facial perception's specialness. Applied cognitive psychologists led by Elizabeth Loftus questioned the reliability of eyewitnesses as their memory of events proved malleable to even the slightest reframing of the questioning.[109] Alongside these criticisms, psychologists also offered their services as experts in those soft technologies of control. For example, in 1985, psychologist Paul Ekman began training workshops for law enforcement groups, teaching them to use his micro-expression coding system as a lie detector cultivated within the individual officer's mind.[110] However, the more visible component of this security apparatus involved new mechanical devices for screening bodies as hijackings and bombings from modular terrorist cells eclipsed nuclear

---

106. On "coded exposure," see Benjamin, *Race after Technology*, chapter 3.

107. On how the algorithmic perpetuates surveillances and discrimination, see Safiya Umoja Noble, *Algorithms of Oppression: How Search Engines Reinforce Racism*. New York: New York University Press, 2018.

108. Courtney E. Thompson, "Physogs: A Game with Consequences," *Endeavour* 43, no. 3 (2019): 100689.

109. Elizabeth F. Loftus, "Leading Questions and the Eyewitness Report," *Cognitive Psychology* 7, no. 4 (1975): 560–572.

110. Daniel Goleman, "Researchers Identify True Clues for Lying," *New York Times*, February 12, 1985, C1, C8.

strikes from competitive superpowers as the primary threats to the post-Cold War order.[111]

This surveillance state was not a phenomenon new to the late twentieth century; its reach was simply unequally distributed. It began with the poor, the disenfranchised, the deviant, the stateless. Immigration required visual inspection upon entry for fitness and a screening for race, sexuality, and ability.[112] Movement across state borders increasingly required documentation. The passport, which began as a diplomatic letter of introduction focused on communicating the issuer's authority to other foreign agents, became a required identification paper allowing its holder to travel.[113] This requirement coincided with the invention of the stateless person.[114] The provision of welfare benefits was always contingent on determining whether the recipients were "deserving" or "worthy." Such assessments required scrutinizing their employment, households, sexual history, and even bodily fluids for signs of immorality. This "compulsory visibility of the welfare poor" led to strategies of evasion, with recipients forging underground networks of "elicit" work, housing, and other activities. Combatting this "welfare fraud" involved computerized technologies of surveillance, a bureaucratic gaze reminiscent of Bertillonage.[115]

By the late 1990s, the American biometrics industry took off to meet the demands of coordinating this surveillance. State-level Department of Motor Vehicles offices became crucial test sites as they developed "smart" driver's licenses with holographic and biometric features designed to combat fake IDs. As part of this effort, they also created massive databases integrated across state lines to prevent people from acquiring multiple ID cards. This industry experimented with a host of other biometric measures, including optical fingerprinting and voice recognition. As part of the U.S. government's post-2001 War on Terror, the newly created Department of Homeland Security invested large sums of money to make automated surveillance a reality. Everyday biometrics came in the form of iris scans at airports, fingerprints to unlock phones, and the omnipresence of closed-circuit televisions in public spaces.[116] These surveillance systems collected

111. Lisa Stampnitzky, *Disciplining Terror: How Experts Invented 'Terrorism.'* New York: Cambridge University Press, 2013.

112. Douglas C. Baynton, *Defectives in the Land: Disability and Immigration in the Age of Eugenics*. Chicago: University of Chicago Press, 2016.

113. John C. Torpey, *The Invention of the Passport: Surveillance, Citizenship and the State*. Cambridge: Cambridge University Press, 2000.

114. Linda K. Kerber, "The Stateless as the Citizen's Other: A View from the United States," *American Historical Review* 112, no. 1 (2007): 1–34.

115. John Gilliom, *Overseers of the Poor: Surveillance, Resistance, and the Limits of Privacy*. Chicago: University of Chicago Press, 2001.

116. Kelly A. Gates, *Our Biometric Future: Facial Recognition Technology and the Culture of Surveillance*. New York: New York University Press, 2011.

a tremendous amount of digital data, but with computer programs still struggling with advanced pattern recognition, its classification often depended on the kind of cognitive skill that came automatically to humans.

To address the continuing gap between computers and humans hampering their own profits, Amazon.com, the online retailer turned multinational technology company, launched its Mechanical Turk (MTurk) service in 2005. The name came from an eighteenth-century hoax, a supposedly chess-playing automata that secretly housed a human controlling its movements. Amazon's "artificial artificial intelligence" adhered to the same logic, with hidden human workers giving automated systems their apparent smartness. The infrastructure of the digital economy was replete with Human Intelligence Tasks (HITs), beyond the capacity of current computation by machine. These HITs consisted largely of minute classificatory tasks requiring a decisive judgment (e.g., tagging human faces in digital photographs). Amazon originally built the platform to meet the internal need of identifying duplicate product pages that their algorithms could not. MTurk created a virtual marketplace for connecting businesses with underemployed humans willing "to sell their idle brains."[117] Jobs came as piecework, with a globally distributed pool of laborers entering competitive bids on HITs at pennies a task. Perhaps no "employment" better exemplified the paucity and precarity of the postindustrial gig economy.[118]

By 2010, academic psychologists saw the potential of adopting MTurk as a source for cheap, reliable data.[119] At the time, North American psychologists were increasingly being criticized for the unrepresentativeness of their typical samples, which were conveniently drawn from undergraduate psychology classes. The responses provided by these Western, Educated, Industrialized, Rich, Democratic (WEIRD) participants often poorly reflected how the rest of the world thought.[120] MTurk promised access to a more geographically, demographically, economically diverse pool. At the very least, MTurk samples were no worse than those pulled from college campuses. Rather than offering course credit, psychologists could compensate these online workers for mere pennies an experiment.[121] The ethics of employing participants at less than minimum wage never featured in the resulting methodological discussions. However, psychologists expressed some unease with

---

117. Jason Pontin, "Artificial Intelligence, With Help from the Humans," *New York Times*, March 25, 2007, B5.

118. Kathryn Zyskowski and Kristy Milland, "A Crowded Future: Working Against Abstraction on Turker Nation," *Catalyst: Feminism, Theory, Technoscience* 4, no. 2 (2018): 1–30.

119. Gabriele Paolacci, Jesse Chandler, and Panagiotis G. Ipeirotis, "Running Experiments on Amazon Mechanical Turk," *Judgment and Decision Making* 5, no. 5 (2010): 411–419.

120. Joseph Henrich, Steven J. Heine, and Ara Norenzayan, "The Weirdest People in the World?" *Behavioral and Brain Sciences* 33, no. 2–3 (2010): 61–83.

121. Michael Buhrmester, Tracy Kwang, and Samuel D. Gosling, "Amazon's Mechanical Turk: A New Source of Inexpensive, Yet High-Quality, Data?" *Perspectives on Psychological Science* 6, no. 1 (2011): 3–5.

these arrangements. Desirous of a readily available, cheap pool of respondents, psychologists did not fully trust these anonymous crowds. With the turn to online labor pools came a new measure, the instructional manipulation check (IMC). These simple items broke up the respondent's workflow by offering instructions contradicting those on neighboring items. A failure to pass the IMC often led to discarding that person's entire set of responses.[122] Unnervingly, MTurkers performed better on the IMC items than the university-recruited counterparts.[123] Amazon's punitive ranking algorithm for dependable Turkers proved more disciplining than the incentives psychologists offered their students.

The debate over the validity of MTurk as a recruitment tool excavated the rarely spoken about conditions of production in contemporary psychology as its physical laboratories came to resemble online environments. Methodologists frequently spoke of "demand characteristics," a problem identified by midcentury psychologists who worried about how overly compliant subjects would conform to the researcher's expectations.[124] The respondent presented a related but distinct problem in the digital age. IMCs tracked distractedness, not compliance, as speedy respondents clicked through to the end to receive credit (whether financial or academic) while expending a minimum of time and effort. Always few in number, the inattentive participants revealed the hidden abode of psychology.[125] At least two "economic" readings seem plausible. It was no accident that much of the methodological literature came from the decision science field started by Herbert Simon. These scientists reflexively drew upon his theory of bounded rationality to make sense of their research (or working) conditions. According to this view, experiments and surveys require substantial cognitive effort from participants, who receive little reward and so they turn to satisficing strategies as a shortcut.[126] Alternatively, an anthropological reading of this literature opens it as a "hidden transcript" of resistance to these scientists' dominant narrative. Political anthropologists like James C. Scott document the prevalence of actions such as poaching, evasion, and desertion among the peasantry. Scott interprets these "shirking" activities as a form of "everyday resistance," still political but

---

122. Daniel M. Oppenheimer, Tom Meyvis, and Nicolas Davidenko, "Instructional Manipulation Checks: Detecting Satisficing to Increase Statistical Power," *Journal of Experimental Social Psychology* 45, no. 4 (2009): 867–872.

123. David J., Hauser and Norbert Schwarz, "Attentive Turkers: MTurk Participants Perform Better on Online Attention Checks Than Do Subject Pool Participants," *Behavior Research Methods* 48, no. 1 (2016): 400–407.

124. Jill Morawski, "Epistemological Dizziness in the Psychology Laboratory: Lively Subjects, Anxious Experimenters, and Experimental Relations, 1950–1970," *Isis* 106, no. 3 (2015): 567–597.

125. On the hidden abode of production, see Karl Marx, *Capital*.

126. Jon A. Krosnick, "Response Strategies for Coping with the Cognitive Demands of Attitude Measures in Surveys," *Applied Cognitive Psychology* 5.3 (1991): 213–236.

distinct from conscious revolutionary action.[127] Inattentiveness and dereliction are forms of resistance to undesirable conditions. Here the laboratory experiment (whether physical or virtual) serves as a contested workplace where scientists struggle with respondents as they each pursue attempts to extract as much value from the situation.

CONCLUSION

These fraught relations were not unique to the experiments run through the MTurk platform, but they originated in and saturated the era's two most iconic technologies, the fMRI and IAT. From Kanwisher's experimental use of Harvard's freshman face book a few years before Mark Zuckerberg used it to create Facebook to Project Implicit's launching of an online test to facilitate self-knowledge, these psychologists anticipated and helped bring into being the infrastructure of this digital world. Born out of the psychology laboratory with its measurement apparatus, the observer glancing at computerized faces (and whose responses were amenable to automated "harvesting") became a mundane occurrence in the age of networked sociality.[128] Neither psychological science nor knowing capitalism wanted complex, ambiguous behavioral measures, preferring instead quick responses digitally recorded and analyzed on a mass scale.

In these simultaneously distant yet heated online environments, the appeal of both the IAT and fMRI resided in their claim to tap the automatic, the primitive, and the innate. Some perception researchers, namely, Isabel Gauthier, made the case for how face reading was a learned skill. Likewise, many IAT advocates insisted that what their test measured was a cultural artifact of prejudiced society. Nevertheless, the temporal resolution of these instruments promised a means of getting beyond the veneer of decorum to observe humanity's animal brain in action. These technologies promised to capture our hidden, base, instinctual, and hence true selves. Both groups of researchers repeatedly asserted the relevance of rapid face perception for understanding human sociality as a kind of tribalism. Society for these psychologists had deep roots in the competitive and dangerous "state of nature" where quick choices about friend or foe came with existential consequences.

When computer scientists finally made major advances in facial recognition software in the 2010s, they did so by modeling human perception, but not always in ways they intended. The publication of the computer scientist Fei-Fei Li's ImageNet database in 2009 did much to improve machine learning algorithms.

---

127. James C. Scott, *Domination and the Arts of Resistance: Hidden Transcripts*. New Haven, CT: Yale University Press, 1990.

128. Brian A.Nosek, Mahzarin R. Banaji, and Anthony G. Greenwald, "Harvesting Implicit Group Attitudes and Beliefs from a Demonstration Web Site," *Group Dynamics: Theory, Research, and Practice* 6, no. 1 (2002): 101–115.

She explicitly modeled her database on George A. Miller's WordNet, a massive dictionary used in computational psycholinguistics which organized terms by their semantic associations rather than by the alphabet. Due to time and budgetary constraints, Li relied on MTurkers to collect, categorize, and properly label the database's 3.2 million images.[129] Despite massive funding for security purposes, individuating human faces proved more difficult than general object recognition for both government and corporate algorithms. Computers floundered on the variability of aging, pose, expression, and illumination across images of the same person. Faces escaped detection because they were not just static, invariant objects but dynamic, emotional, expressive social tools. In 2015, Facebook's DeepFace algorithm declared success where others had failed. Achieving a 97.5 percent accuracy rate, it neared human levels. DeepFace succeeded in part due to its access to the massive pictorial archive donated to its parent company by Facebook users when they agreed to the terms of service.[130] This harvesting of user data raised ethical concerns, as did the technologies deployment by authoritarian regimes like the Chinese state's targeting of the Uyghur minority. A 2019 review by the U.S. National Institute of Standards and Technology found most facial recognition algorithms on the market seriously wanting. Due to the biased datasets on which they were trained, these algorithms had a significantly higher false positive rate when it came to ethnic minorities than whites. Like many other areas of Big Data analytics, facial recognition programs replicated the unconscious racial prejudices of their coders.[131] Computer and human minds again converged.

129. https://qz.com/1034972/the-data-that-changed-the-direction-of-ai-research-and-possibly-the-world

130. https://www.sciencemag.org/news/2015/02/facebook-will-soon-be-able-id-you-any-photo

131. https://www.technologyreview.com/2019/12/20/79/ai-face-recognition-racist-us-government-nist-study

8
The Coming Crisis of Affective Science

The summer of 2015 saw the release of two widely anticipated reports. Each called into question psychology's status as both an ethical helping profession and a reliable science. Strikingly different in their targets and methodology, both reports raised profound questions about the openness and transparency of psychology as they catapulted once hushed corridor talk into the dominant news story about the field.[1] First, in July, the APA released the Hoffman report, a damning independent investigation into the organization's "collusion" with the American Department of Defense (DoD) to allow its members to conduct "enhanced interrogations" (commonly known as torture) on foreign detainees in the ongoing War on Terror.[2] In late August, *Science* published the results of a massive, multisited collaboration that estimated the reproducibility of psychology to be roughly 39 percent.[3] Put simply, when independent teams of researchers attempted to replicate the results of the field's most celebrated studies, they most often could not. The findings of these reports sparked very public and deeply acrimonious debates, as they seemingly undercut the progress made following a period of tremendous growth for psychology. The new affective science had gained unprecedented cultural salience since the financial crisis of 2008 as the field proffered an unending supply of fixes for mitigating the dangers posed by unthinking, human automaticity. The

---

1. On corridor talk, see Gary Lee Downey, Joseph Dumit, and Sharon Traweek, "Corridor Talk," in *Cyborgs & Citadels: Anthropological Interventions in Emerging Sciences and Technologies.* Joseph Dumit and Gary Lee Downey (eds.). Santa Fe: School of American Research Press, 1998, 245–264.

2. David H. Hoffman and associates, *Report to the Special Committee of the Board of Directors of the American Psychological Association: Independent Review Relating to APA Ethics Guidelines, National Security Interrogations, and Torture (Revised)*. Chicago: Sidley Austin LLP, 2015. Retrieved from www.apa.org/independent-review/revised-report.pdf

3. Open Science Collaboration, "Estimating the Reproducibility of Psychological Science," *Science* 349, no. 6251 (2015): aac4716.

Hoffman report seemingly offered a kind of housecleaning with the dismissal of many APA employees seen as enabling torture. In contrast to this sense of closure, the *Science* report sent reverberations throughout the discipline, giving voice to the notion that psychology was entering into its own "crisis," which jeopardized the very future of the science and the profession.

The remarkable traction of replication as *the* crisis facing psychology (soon to the apparent exclusion of torture) was striking given that none of the issues the controversy raised were new. For decades, methodologists had flagged the problems associated with how psychologists collected their data and conducted statistical analyses. Such cautions appeared at regular intervals and became ubiquitous fixtures of research methods textbooks and expert task forces, even if leading journals continued to flaunt these norms. Given this steady state of affairs, why the sudden panic? Why did reproducibility come to constitute a crisis at the precise historical conjuncture that it did considering that the fragility of psychology's way of obtaining truthfulness lay hidden in plain sight for *decades*? How did a seemingly cumulative science come to feel phantasmagorical overnight? Something more than the proper use of statistics was at stake. Declaring something a crisis eradicates notions of historical precedence or continuity, yet crises inevitably revolve around questions of existing legitimacy, power, and hegemony. The replication crisis illuminated experimental psychologists' self-perception as scientists and the particular way in which they felt their discipline was "coming apart at the seams."[4] The crisis created a space for psychologists to express their anxieties about how their science had gone astray. The project of giving psychology away proved wildly successful, perhaps too successful. The open science movement that arose as a response to failed replication efforts represented in many ways a laudatory marshalling of intellectual and material resources toward self-examination, a temporary slowing of psychology's expansion into new domains in favor of introspective criticism. Below the surface brewed tensions between psychology and the ascendant field of neuroscience, the role of business schools as institutional niches for basic psychology, the redesign of psychological experiments to abet the writing of self-help and social policy, and the media ecology of the internet, which simultaneously amplified scientific hype and created sites for its very public dissection.

At the same time, the open science reformers' focus on methods represented something of an evasion of certain problems by concentrating disciplinary attention on others. The movement quickly reestablished a reified hierarchy among cognitive, social, and clinical psychology. In practice, these specialties increasingly operated in mutual isolation from each other, rendering certain problems immediate to one and irrelevant to other.[5] By focusing exclusively on laboratory

---

4. This perspective on crises derives from Stuart Hall, Charles Critcher, Tony Jefferson, John Clarke, and Brian Roberts. *Policing the Crisis: Mugging, the State and Law and Order*. London: Red Globe Press, 2013.

5. Replication crisis has focused on experimental (especially social) psychology, with little crossover with the clinical side. See Jennifer L. Tackett, Scott O. Lilienfeld, Christopher J. Patrick,

procedures and statistics and offering a highly metricized system for rewarding good behavior, the reformers implicitly argued that psychology's overextension into new realms of questionable relevancy was legitimate if the underlying methodology remained sound. In other words, framing the crisis in terms of replication also served as a way of not talking directly about certain transformations affecting psychology's place in the university and society.

Both crises resulted from the threefold transformation of postwar psychology. First, coming out of World War II, psychology embraced a new identity, that of a health science. This change began with the rapid proliferation of clinical psychologists but soon extended to other psychologists who offered a host of behavioral interventions to augment people's health and happiness. Psychology's place in this new arena was highly contested, and its expertise was not readily accepted. Second, as a result of attempts to secure a stronger foothold in the medical marketplace, psychologists much more aggressively cultivated publicity and policymakers starting in the late 1970s. This dual concern with health and policy and the demand to demonstrate immediate, practical utility led to the third transformation: psychologists' embrace of theories of unconscious, affective decision making. This certainly resonated with an interpretation advanced by an influential group of clinicians that leading mental illnesses like depression were in fact a cluster of cognitive distortions, but it expanded beyond this realm. The reembrace of the unconsciousness also reflected a shift in who psychologists understood as their subjects. Instead of analyzing the achievements of the cognitive elite like themselves, they increasingly sought to explain the emotional delusions of the masses beneath them. In contrast to the comparative optimism of postwar experimental psychologists, the omnipresence of cognitive failure captivated much of the field by the late 1990s.

Tracking both the long and the short history of replication and torture in psychology reveals what crisis talk both revealed and occluded. The 2010s certainly witnessed new, unprecedented demands for openness, transparency, and inclusion within the field of psychology. Yet, these dual crises unrolled across a highly uneven terrain. The increased specialization and intradisciplinary division also meant that considerable attention was given to making certain practices "open" while maintaining others as secretive and obscure. What exactly needed "openness" and how this openness should be achieved remained hotly debated.

COMBATIVE REPLICATION OR GENTLEMANLY SCIENCE

Psychologists, like other scientists, long upheld the ideal of the repeatability of an experiment, but the language of replication derived from the reception,

---

Sheri L. Johnson, Robert F. Krueger, Joshua D. Miller, Thomas F. Oltmanns, and Patrick E. Shrout, "It's Time to Broaden the Replicability Conversation: Thoughts for and from Clinical Psychological Science," *Perspectives on Psychological Science* 12, no. 5 (2017): 742–756.

appropriation, and in some quarters rejection of the (eu)geneticist R. A. Fisher's philosophy of research design. First outlined in 1925 and further refined a decade later, Fisher's approach to data analysis made slow but steady progress through psychology. Prior to 1940, a mere seventeen studies in psychology used Fisher's Analysis of Variance (ANOVA) technique. The situation changed dramatically after World War II as psychology underwent a period of near exponential growth.[6] Given the flood of publications and greater anonymity within the field resulting from the sudden expansion of graduate programs, editors required a simple standard for determining whether an article merited publication. The Neyman–Pearson adaptation of Fisherian statistics fit the bill.

Although the use of ANOVA became nearly ubiquitous, Fisher's early readers in psychology recognized the incongruity between his agricultural experiments on seed, fertilizer, and soil and the psychologists' entanglement with conscious, reactive humans. The example of the Latin Square nicely illustrates this gap. Fisher championed the Latin Square as a technique for implementing true randomization in experimental design. Each square on the grid represented a unique level (or better, a unique combination of levels) of the treatment. At the Rothamsted Experimental Station in the United Kingdom, Fisher implemented his experimental treatment spatially. The Latin Square was not a conceptual abstraction, but rather a practical way of organizing actual fields to test different combinations on their own plots of land. In contrast, the psychologist's problem was temporal. As Brent Baxter noted in 1941, their testing ground (whether undergraduate students or inbred lab rats) changed over time. They lived, they matured, they learned, and these were the very processes that concerned the psychologist. Like a modern Heraclitus, Baxter realized the very same psychological participant was never the same person twice. They became someone different with every passing moment.[7] Psychologists could adapt the Latin Square by randomly assigning subjects to different sequences of treatments to counterbalance any carryover effects, but this was something different in kind than Fisher's field growing synchronically.

The other translation issue centered on how to interpret the meaning of a statistically significant result. In his 1935 book, *The Design of Experiments*, Fisher recommended a cutoff point of $p < 0.05$. This meant that the observed difference between treatments or groups had a less than 5 percent likelihood to be due to chance. Fisher recommended interpreting such results as meaning an intervention was worthy of further testing and corroboration. For American psychologists, $p < 0.05$ became an accepted criterion for publication and implied the established reality of the phenomenon under consideration. Almost immediately,

---

6. Anthony J. Rucci and Ryan D. Tweney, "Analysis of Variance and the "Second Discipline" of Scientific Psychology," *Psychological Bulletin* 87.1 (1980): 166–184.

7. Brent Baxter, "Problems in the Planning of Psychological Experiments," *American Journal of Psychology* 54, no. 2 (1941): 270–280.

methodologists condemned this dependence on the "null ritual." Their criticisms began appearing in the discipline's leading journals with some frequency starting in 1960.[8] However, the $p < 0.05$ remained a touchstone for truth.

A final consequence of adopting ANOVA was the downplaying of the naturalistic observation. Instead, psychologists favored testing hypotheses through the administration of novel treatments. In the 1950s, the distinction between observational versus experimental studies was expressed as the two disciplines of psychology.[9] However, even this distinction became muted over time as the reward system in psychology privileged testing counterintuitive hypotheses using surprising manipulations.[10]

Among postwar experimental psychologists, only one community resisted the lure of the null ritual: behavior analysts. B. F. Skinner questioned the value of pulling a small sample from the population, exposing them to a single manipulation, and making an inference about the population based on any observed change.[11] Instead, Skinner advocated a science of total control to build the science of behavior. He favored examining the lives of *captive* nonhuman animals (especially pigeons and rats) in carefully crafted artificial environments. Skinner justified his rejection of "mechanized statistics" in his 1956 presidential address before the Eastern Psychological Association. Citing the practical success of his former students Keller Breland and Marion Breland, Skinner embraced "the engineering problem of the animal trainer" as an alternative for conducting psychological science. "No one goes to the circus to see the average dog jump through a hoop significantly oftener than untrained dogs raised under the circumstances."[12] Developing useful technologies like animal training required dependably conditioning and

---

8. On the "null ritual," Gerd Gigerenzer, "Mindless Statistics," *Journal of Socio-Economics* 33, no. 5 (2004): 587–606. Early criticisms included Jum Nunnally, "The Place of Statistics in Psychology," *Educational and Psychological Measurement* 20, no. 4 (1960): 641–650; William W. Rozeboom, "The Fallacy of the Null-Hypothesis Significance Test," *Psychological Bulletin* 57, no. 5 (1960): 416–428; David Bakan, "The Test of Significance in Psychological Research," *Psychological Bulletin* 66, no. 6 (1966): 423–437; David T. Lykken, "Statistical Significance in Psychological Research," *Psychological Bulletin* 70, no. 3 (1968): 151–159.

9. Lee J. Cronbach, "The Two Disciplines of Scientific Psychology," *American Psychologist* 12, no. 11 (1957): 671–684.

10. Paul Rozin, "What Kind of Empirical Research Should We Publish, Fund, and Reward?: A Different Perspective," *Perspectives on Psychological Science* 4, no. 4 (2009): 435–439.

11. On the rejection of causality, see Andrew S. Winston, "Cause into Function: Ernst Mach and the Reconstruction of Explanation in Psychology," in Christopher D. Green, Marlene Shore, and T. Thomas Teo (eds.), *The Transformation of Psychology: Influences of 19th-Century Philosophy, Technology, and Natural Science* (Washington, DC: American Psychological Association, 2001), 107–131.

12. B. F. Skinner, "A Case History in Scientific Method," *American Psychologist* 11, no. 5 (1956): 221–233, 228.

extinguishing specific patterns of behavior in individual organisms. Skinner famously championed the value of useful applications over scientific theories.[13] However, Skinner devoted considerable time to articulating a distinct and articulate philosophy of science.[14]

In place of the statistical analysis provided by null hypothesis testing, behavior analysts championed "direct replication," a term coined by Murray Sidman in his textbook *The Tactics of Scientific Research* (1960). According to Sidman, direct replication came in two forms: "by performing the experiment again with new subjects or by making repeated observations on the same subjects under each of several experimental conditions."[15] Sidman suggested direct replication could take two forms: intersubject (seeing how different participants respond to the same manipulation of conditions) or intrasubject (seeing how the same participants react to changing manipulations). Intrasubjective or intragroup replication was unique to behavioral analysts and took pride of place in Sidman's account. Establishing the laws of behavior required long-term observation of participants to establish their baseline and then reaction to modified conditions. Skinner famously recommended that "instead of studying a thousand rats for one hour each or a hundred rats for ten hours each the investigator is more likely to study one rat for a thousand hours."[16]

This philosophy of science served the behavior analysis community as the discipline of psychology increasingly embraced cognitivism. Rather than disappearing in the wake of linguistic master Noam Chomsky's withering critique of Skinner's *Verbal Behavior* (1957), behavior analysts moved increasingly into the applied realm. They offered a host of social technologies for managing institutionalized populations (e.g., the reward system known as the token economy) and models for addiction.[17] Here the intrasubject reproducibility of schedules of reinforcement proved key to their success, just as Skinner predicted when he described the work of his animal training protégés. Given the influence of operant conditioning principles in the design of persuasive technologies, perhaps no psychological theory had a greater impact on the form of the computerized lifeworld.[18]

---

13. B. F. Skinner, "Are Theories of Learning Necessary?," *Psychological Review* 57, no. 4 (1950): 193–216.

14. See Laurence D. Smith, *Behaviorism and Logical Positivism: A Reassessment of the Alliance*. Stanford, CA: Stanford University Press, 1986.

15. Sidman, *Tactics of Scientific Research: Evaluating Experimental Data in Psychology*. New York: Basic Books, 73.

16. B. F. Skinner, "Operant Behavior," in W.K. Honig (ed.), *Operant Behavior: Areas Of Research And Application*. New York: Appleton-Century-Co., 1966, 12–32, 21.

17. Alexandra Rutherford, *Beyond the Box: BF Skinner's Technology of Behaviour from Laboratory to Life, 1950s–1970s*. Toronto: University of Toronto Press, 2009.

18. B. J. Fogg, *Persuasive Technology: Using Computers to Change What We Think and Do*. Burlington, MA: Morgan Kaufmann, 2003.

"Conceptual replication" came from a very different disciplinary space: postwar social psychologists looked to another neo-behaviorist for their philosophy of science. Like other behaviorists, E. C. Tolman stayed true to the Watsonian prohibition against using introspection as a method. His experiments focused on measuring the overt activity of animals in carefully managed environments. However, Tolman rejected the dictum against discussing inner states. He posited the existence of "intervening variables" (mind stuff) mediating between environmental stimuli and the organism's response. One could even study these hypothetical "cognitive maps" if you operationalized their presence into a surrogate that was tractable and measurable in the world. Moreover, one could reoperationalize this psychic stuff into different "constructs" to create new scenario for theory-testing.[19] Originating in the circle of psychological theorists Tolman gathered at Berkeley, it became the dominant approach to social psychology during its postwar golden age.[20]

Inspired by the politics of the Popular Front and their mobilization against fascism during World War II, social psychologists sought to transform an older perceptual psychology into a science explaining prejudice, compliance, obedience, and other dangerous irrationalities. Initially taking the perceptual psychology's apparatus and deploying it to address psychoanalytically inspired questions, the character of social psychology experiments grew more dramaturgical in the distrustful, "looking-glass" culture of Cold War America.[21] Social psychologists pursued the ideal of experimental realism, wherein the subject became enthralled by the heightened drama of the laboratory situation, allowing the psychologist to extract genuine responses. Suspended between the ideals of the sober social scientists and the "ludicro-experimenters" who took pleasure in cleverly designed situations that tormented their subjects, they abided in a jocular culture of masculine displays of dominance.[22] Participants shocked recalcitrant learners, overheard potentially fatal seizures, played the role of prison guard or prisoner.

Perhaps no research group better exemplified these trends than the group that gathered around Leon Festinger's theory of cognitive dissonance. Trained by the

---

19. Many psychologists wanted to credit the physicist Percy Bridgman with this philosophy of science. However, it emerged from the disciplinary peculiarities of psychology. See Christopher D. Green, "Of Immortal Mythological Beasts: Operationism in Psychology," *Theory and Psychology* 2, no. 3 (1992): 291–320.

20. On Tolman's endorsement of Fisher's experimental design, see Richard S. Crutchfield and E. C. Tolman, "Multiple-variable Design for Experiments Involving Interaction of Behavior," *Psychological Review* 47, no. 1 (1940): 38–42.

21. Jill Morawski, "Epistemological Dizziness in the Psychology Laboratory: Lively Subjects, Anxious Experimenters, and Experimental Relations, 1950–1970," *Isis* 106, no. 3 (2015): 567–597.

22. Henderikus J., Stam, H. Lorraine Radtke, and Ian Lubek, "Strains in Experimental Social Psychology: A Textual Analysis of the Development of Experimentation in Social Psychology," *Journal of the History of the Behavioral Sciences* 36, no. 4 (2000): 365–382; Ian Nicholson, "'Shocking' Masculinity: Stanley Milgram, 'Obedience to Authority,' and the 'Crisis of Manhood' in Cold War America," *Isis* 102, no. 2 (2011): 238–268.

eminent Gestalt psychologist Kurt Lewin, Festinger assumed the role of guiding research on group dynamics following his mentor's death in 1947. Festinger posited that individuals strive toward a calm, equilibrium when it comes to their thoughts, feelings, and belief. When holding two conflicting beliefs, the individual must take action to resolve the tension, often by creating mental schema to justify their seemingly irrational thoughts. Festinger repeatedly demonstrated his theory in a series of dramatic studies, the most extreme of which was a secretive ethnography of a doomsday cult both before and after the proposed date for the flying saucer's arrival had passed.[23] Most cognitive dissonance experiments were more prosaic, usually taking place on university campuses and using undergraduate students. In the paradigmatic "forced compliance" experiment, Festinger and his associate James Carlsmith had undergraduates perform a tedious task. They found that those compensated with a dollar had a higher opinion of the work than those offered $20, as the participants in the first group needed greater justification of their wasted time.[24]

One of the more controversial cognitive dissonance studies, and perhaps the clearest manifestation of the jocular culture of postwar social psychology, was the "severity of initiation" experiment by Elliot Aronson and Judson Mills in 1959. Their hypothesis was that individuals who experienced a painful or embarrassing induction into a group would come to embrace their membership as compensation for the earlier psychic torment. This pair of male scientists recruited sixty-odd female undergraduates on the pretext of joining an existing discussion group dedicated to the psychology of sex. Using headphones, the participant listened to the fictitious group's banal conversation. In the severe initiation condition, joining the group required participants to read aloud "12 obscene words, e.g., fuck, cock, and screw. Ss also read aloud two vivid descriptions of sexual activity from contemporary novels." In the mild condition, they had to read aloud five generic words; the control one required no such introduction. The psychologists found that the students in the severe condition rated the dull conversation much more interesting than those in the other groups, confirming the prediction made by cognitive dissonance theory.[25]

By 1964, the cognitive character of Festinger's theory and its reliance on hidden "intervening variables" faced sustained criticism. Psychologists Natalia and Alphonse Chapanis argued that Festinger and his students failed to demonstrate that participants held the hypothesized "discrepant cognitions." For example, they offered three alternative ways of interpreting the severity of initiation

---

23. Henry W. Riecken, Stanley Schachter, and Leon Festinger, *When Prophecy Fails: A Social and Psychological Study of a Modern Group That Predicted the Destruction of the World.* New York: Harper & Row, 1956.

24. Leon Festinger and James M. Carlsmith, "Cognitive Consequences of Forced Compliance," *Journal of Abnormal and Social Psychology* 58, no. 2 (1959): 203–210.

25. Elliot Aronson and Judson Mills, "The Effect of Severity of Initiation on Liking for a Group," *Journal of Abnormal and Social Psychology* 59, no. 2 (1959): 177–181, 178.

experiment. Perhaps the college women were not the innocent sorority girls the male experimenters had presumed them to be, and what they observed was the *relief* that a supposedly embarrassing task only required everyday chatter. Or maybe the girls prided themselves on accomplishing what the psychologists called a difficult task. Finally, drawing out the psychosexual dynamics and sexism was built into the experiment but ignored in the original study, or maybe the girls experienced "the displacement of vicarious sexual pleasure from a discomfiting, but sexually arousing, situation to a more socially acceptable one?"[26] A year later, Milton Rosenberg suggested that the design of cognitive dissonance experiments were vulnerable to "evaluation apprehension" or the participants felt anxieties to perform well before the expert.[27] The Belgian psychologist Jozef M. Nuttin Jr. published what he called a "critical replication" of the Festinger and Carlsmith force compliance experiment with mixed results.[28] The most sustained criticism came from Daryl J. Bem, then an ambitious young social psychologist. In 1967, he published a series of replications of classic cognitive dissonance experiments, suggesting that his own self-perception theory offered a more parsimonious explanation of the results.[29]

The Festinger circle went to work to resolve the dissonance generated by these conflicting interpretations of their results. When Harold Gerard and Grover Mathewson published what they called a "replication" of the severity of the initiation experiment in 1966, they acknowledged the messiness of using sex talk as a manipulation to administer psychic pain. They proposed a simpler solution, one perhaps inspired by Stanley Milgram or maybe countless experiments on rats or the growing vogue for aversion therapy to cure homosexuality. They gave their subjects a series of electric shocks to prove the "suffering-leads-liking" hypothesis.[30] Despite the tenuousness of calling such an experiment a "replication" of the original, this new approach became canonized in Aronson and Carlsmith's influential methodology chapter in *The Handbook of Social Psychology* (1968). The pair heralded the superiority of what they now dubbed "conceptual replication" as a tool for repeatedly testing a hypothesis across a variety of situations.[31] Severity of

26. Natalia P. Chapanis and Alphonse Chapanis, "Cognitive Dissonance," *Psychological Bulletin* 61, no. 1 (1964): 1–22, 5.

27. Milton J. Rosenberg, "When Dissonance Fails," *Journal of Personality and Social Psychology* 1, no. 1 (1965): 28–42.

28. Jozef M. Nuttin, "Attitude Change after Rewarded Dissonant and Consonant 'Forced Compliance,'" *International Journal of Psychology* 1, no. 1 (1966): 39–57.

29. Daryl J. Bem, "Self-Perception," *Psychological Review* 74, no. 3 (1967): 183–200.

30. Harold B. Gerard and Grover C. Mathewson, "The Effects of Severity of Initiation on Liking for a Group: A Replication," *Journal of Experimental Social Psychology* 2, no. 3 (1966): 278–287.

31. Elliot Aronson and J. Merrill Carlsmith, "Experimentation in Social Psychology," in Gardner Lindzey and Elliot Aronson (eds.), *The Handbook of Social Psychology*. Reading, MA: Addison-Wesley, 1968, 1–79, 17.

initiation came to serve as the example of the advantages of conceptual over direct replication among social psychologists. If the original study remained locked in time (the effectiveness of its treatment being contingent on the presumed sexual repression of the 1950s coed), then reoperationalizing the intervening variable provided a means of retesting hypotheses generated by the underlying theory in a changing cultural landscape.[32] Conceptual replication promised to deliver a means of establishing the universality of psychic phenomena, freeing social psychology from the bounds of the culture that bore it.

By 1970, a disciplinary consensus existed. This consensus owed a considerable debt to how psychologists read the philosopher Karl Popper's arguments about how science advanced not through verifying theories but by rejecting poor ones using a process of falsification. Early proponents of Popper's approach within the discipline, namely the clinician Paul Meehl, insisted that falsification was distinct from widely practiced null hypothesis testing. However, the two quickly became conflated among a later generation of pop Popperians.[33] The goal of experimentation was to place one's cherished theories in true existential danger. On this reading, conceptual replications provided the more robust "risky test" of a theory (as they posed a new challenge for the predicted outcome under novel conditions), while direct replications were left to experiments mired in controversy.

Throughout this period, lone authors lamented the absence of venues for publishing (direct) replications, but little action was taken. Direct replications did occur during this era. Some even made it into print. However, psychologists deployed these replication efforts toward phenomena they deemed dubious and in need of debunking. Menstrual synchrony and the Mozart Effect numbered among the very few phenomena receiving the scrutiny of multiple direct replications. In 1971, the biopsychologist Martha McClintock published an article in *Nature* suggesting that friends living in the proximity experienced a synchronization in the onset of their menstrual cycles. Cited as the first tangible evidence for the existence of human pheromones, McClintock's article received lavish praise from sociobiologists eager to disabuse the notion of human exceptionalism. Menstrual synchrony circulated in human sexuality textbooks and popular magazines. By the 1980s, certain strands of the women's movement embraced the notion, a physical manifestation of the bonds of sisterhood. The only problem was that the majority of researchers who tried could not replicate McClintock's startling findings. By the 2010s, menstrual synchrony moved from sociobiological fact to feminist myth.[34] In a 1993 *Nature* article, psychologist Frances Rauscher described how

---

32. See Wolfgang Stroebe and Fritz Strack, "The Alleged Crisis and the Illusion of Exact Replication," *Perspectives on Psychological Science* 9, no. 1 (2014): 59–71.

33. Maarten Derksen, "Putting Popper to Work," *Theory and Psychology* 29, no. 4 (2019): 449–465.

34. Michael Pettit and Jana Vigor, "Pheromones, Feminism and the Many Lives of Menstrual Synchrony," *BioSocieties* 10, no. 3 (2015): 271–294.

exposure to a piece of classical music improved participants' spatial reasoning on a series of subsequent tasks.[35] It was soon dubbed "the Mozart Effect," but fellow psychologists failed to reproduce her findings in independent tests.[36]

A few features unite menstrual synchrony and the Mozart Effect. Both phenomena circulated well beyond the scientific literature, gaining considerable public fascination, if notoriety, among experts. They suggested that surprisingly small interventions could radically alter one's self. Experts deemed them more than technical errors because they seemed to inspire mass credulity. The public circulation of these phenomena, understood as popular myths, risked misrepresentation of an otherwise sound psychological science. Their seductive popularity demanded an active response to protect both the public and the profession. They were the psychological equivalent to physicists responding to cold fusion or N-Rays.[37] (Direct) replication belonged to managing controversy in the realm of pseudoscience. When it came to normal science, it had no recognized role.

These combative replications bolstered the psychologist's self-image as a member of a sophisticated science. Psychologists prided themselves on their unique training among the social sciences. They alone possessed advanced methods for both experimental design and statistical analysis. This training demarcated their field from others (psychoanalysis, sociology, qualitative methods). Sophisticated methods promised to protect psychologists from falling prey to pleasing biases. It also schooled them constantly detect said distorting biases in the everyday thinking of others. However, as Daniel Kahneman and Amos Tversky demonstrated in the early 1970s, probabilistic thinking in psychology was not particularly strong, even among their fellow mathematical psychologists who ought to know better.[38] A sizable literature followed suit, demonstrating that psychologists were far from immune in overestimating their own abilities in comprehending probability theory and evaluating their own research design.[39] This persistent gap between the psychologist's self-image of statistical sophistication and their practical naiveté when it came to mathematical matters proved highly exploitable. A psychological fact must derive from experiments amenable to quantitative analysis to isolate the salient variable from the surrounding noise of the world. This bestowed upon the

---

35. Frances H. Rauscher, Gordon L. Shaw, and Catherine N. Ky, "Music and Spatial Task Performance," *Nature* 365, no. 6447 (1993): 611.

36. Kenneth M. Steele, Karen E. Bass, and Melissa D. Crook, "The Mystery of the Mozart Effect: Failure to Replicate," *Psychological Science* 10, no. 4 (1999): 366–369. Clémentine Beauvais, "The 'Mozart Effect': A Sociological Reappraisal," *Cultural Sociology* 9, no. 2 (2015): 185–202.

37. Thomas F. Gieryn, *Cultural Boundaries of Science: Credibility on the Line*. Chicago: University of Chicago Press, 1999.

38. Amos Tversky and Daniel Kahneman, "Belief in the Law of Small Numbers," *Psychological Bulletin* 76, no. 2 (1971): 105–110.

39. Justin Kruger and David Dunning, "Unskilled and Unaware of It: How Difficulties in Recognizing One's Own Incompetence Lead to Inflated Self-Assessments," *Journal of Personality and Social Psychology* 77, no. 6 (1999): 1121–1134.

ordinary psychologist his smartness. But interpreting said data remained a murky, ill-understood affair, even among professed experts.

ALL THAT'S SOLID MELTS INTO AIR

And then things changed after 2008. The simultaneity of the financial crisis and the crisis over psychology's methods was no coincidence. The financial crisis reordered psychology much as it did the rest of the world.[40] The resulting recession exasperated tensions already present in the academic job market into a world of haves and have-nots. The proliferation of journal impact factor and its individuation via google scholar and h-index meant that success became an empirical and predictable matter like any other social science phenomenon.[41] Policymakers began using scientometrics to retrospectively evaluate the worth of scientific research programs in the 1970s.[42] By the 2000s, they became a basis for prospecting a young academic's future worth.[43] The ready availability of citation metrics encouraged scientists to game the system to magnify their influence.

A notable feature of the post-2008 academic landscape was the new inroads made by social psychologists (and with them theories of preconscious affect governing decisions) into business schools.[44] With their lucrative salaries and connections to the policy world, a business school appointment often transformed the research agendas of the parent discipline.[45] Bolstered by Kahneman's 2003 Nobel Prize and how the crash seemingly demonstrated the irrationality of markets, social psychologists joined the ranks of business school professors like never before. Their presence was not limited to behavioral economics, but also included a more generic social psychology of influence, the manipulation of behavior

---

40. Philip Mirowski, *Never Let a Serious Crisis Go to Waste: How Neoliberalism Survived the Financial Meltdown*. London: Verso Books, 2013.

41. Jorge E. Hirsch, "An Index to Quantify an Individual's Scientific Research Output," *Proceedings of the National academy of Sciences of the United States of America* 102.46 (2005): 16569; David van Dijk, Ohad Manor, and Lucas B. Carey, "Publication Metrics and Success on the Academic Job Market," *Current Biology* 24.11 (2014): R516–R517.

42. Michael Pettit, "The Great Cat Mutilation: Sex, Social Movements and the Utilitarian Calculus in 1970s New York City," *BJHS Themes* 2 (2017): 57–78.

43. Diana Hicks, Paul Wouters, Ludo Waltman, Sarah De Rijcke, and Ismael Rafols, "The Leiden Manifesto for Research Metrics," *Nature* 520, no. 7548 (2015): 429.

44. The entry of social psychology into business schools is distinct that involved in the field of industrial/organizational psychology, stretching back to the psychotechnics movement of the 1890s.

45. On business schools as important institutional niches for the social sciences that reoriented their research agenda, see Marion Fourcade and Rakesh Khurana, "From Social Control to Financial Economics: The Linked Ecologies of Economics and Business in Twentieth Century America," *Theory and Society* 42, no. 2 (2013): 121–159.

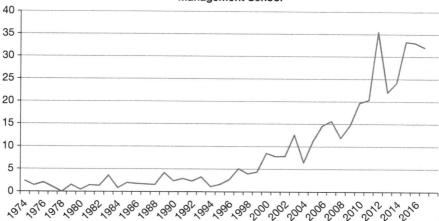

Figure 8.1 Percent of *Journal of Personality and Social Psychology* articles with at least one author affiliated with a business or management school.

through subtle cues beyond awareness. As social psychology increasingly aligned itself with business schools, the distinction between testing a psychological theory and testing psychological interventions fit for the self-help market became increasingly blurry. Psychologists aimed to publish in high-impact venues like *Science* and *Nature*, or at least *Psychological Science*, a journal founded in 1990 emulating their "short report" model. Business school psychologists had a disproportional presence in these "high-impact," yet supposedly "basic," psychology journals as well as the field-leading *Journal of Personality and Social Psychology* (see Figures 8.1 and 8.2). This further encouraged the circulation of psychological facts in a highly modularized, consumable form, detached from any general psychological theory to give meaning to the counterintuitive findings. The goal of crafting interventions ready-made for clickbait headlines or TED talks (if not public policy) exasperated certain pathologies in the discipline's reward structure.

In the era of TED-talk science, the affective science of embodied cognition, social priming, and other unconsciousness processes generated a palpable buzz. Yet, these studies did not travel as exemplars supporting a cumulative and coherent affective theory. Instead, psychologists presented these experiments as offering puzzling, counterintuitive insights into human conduct, which also happened to offer surprisingly simple and practical interventions for self-improvement. In other words, they transformed their social psychology labs into machines for generating easily implementable "life hacks." The presentation of this hackable science followed a similar pattern. In a once highly regarded experiment, John Bargh exposed undergraduates to words associated with the elderly and found they

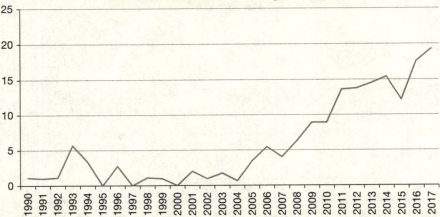

Figure 8.2 Percent of *Psychological Science* articles with at least one author affiliated with business or management school.

literally moved more slowly afterward.[46] In another embodied cognition experiment, Amy Cuddy and her associates took inspiration from the hypermasculine social world of the Harvard Business School, borrowing her experimental treatment from the Oliver Stone film *Wall Street* (1987). The study suggested striking a dominant pose for one minute, alerting an individual's self-confidence, encouraging them to engage in riskier behavior, and increasing their testosterone while lowering cortisol levels.[47] "Power posing" became an international sensation when Cuddy recorded a related TED talk in 2012 which soon accumulated 45 million views.[48] A final example of the new psychology was Roy Baumeister's ego depletion theory. Like Bargh, Baumeister argued evolution designed humans to largely run on automatic, with conscious decisions expending tremendous energy. Fortunately, Baumeister soon discovered a "brain fuel" to replenish the mind after such taxing activity: the glucose found in naturally sweetened lemonade.[49]

46. John A. Bargh, Chen, M., and Burrows, L. "Automaticity of Social Behavior: Direct Effects of Trait Construct and Stereotype Activation on Action," *Journal of Personality and Social Psychology* 71, no. 2 (1996): 230–244.

47. Dana R. Carney, Amy J. C. Cuddy, and Andy J. Yap, "Power Posing: Brief Nonverbal Displays Affect Neuroendocrine Levels and Risk Tolerance," *Psychological Science* 21, no. 10 (2010): 1363–1368.

48. https://www.ted.com/talks/amy_cuddy_your_body_language_shapes_who_you_are

49. Matthew T. Gailliot, Roy F. Baumeister, C. Nathan Dewall, Jon K. Maner, E. Ashby Plant, Dianne M. Tice, Lauren E. Brewer, and Brandon J. Schmeichel, "Self-Control Relies on Glucose as a Limited Energy Source: Willpower Is More than a Metaphor," *Journal of Personality and Social Psychology* 92, no. 2 (2007): 325–336.

Starting with a failed replication of Bargh's elderly priming effect in 2012, each of these studies soon became focal points of the replication movement.[50]

This modularized hackable science of discrete psychological facts circulated through a novel media ecology with certain affordances encouraging a dialectic between puffery and reform. Writing in the early years of online science communication, Bruce Lewenstein described an emerging set of channels for debating the merit of science which threatened the older, hierarchical distinctions between published and unpublished.[51] Semi-anonymous blogs and, later, Twitter created platforms for transmitting discussions of methodology to multiple, often heterogeneous, audiences. Media sociologists Alice E. Warwick and danah boyd offer a pertinent analysis of how communication on such platforms operate. Rather than viewing social media as limitless, open spaces, they describe how these spaces are bounded by certain conversational norms and "imagined audiences." Tweeting simultaneously involves *broadcasting* to an imagined general audience while also conversing with known followers who share common interests. Tweeting is simultaneous talking within a specific community and transmitting beyond it.[52] Science blogging similarly blurred the boundary between informal, gossipy conversations and formal, published criticism. Authors and commentators (sometimes signing their names, sometimes speaking anonymously) broadcast fairly technical analyses of recent studies to anyone with an internet connection.

What the *New York Times* first dubbed "neuroscience: under attack" in 2012 was actually the wider circulation of academic corridor talk to wider and more diffuse audiences.[53] For example, a poster at the Human Brain Mapping conference demonstrating the flaws in the statistical techniques used to analyze fMRI data by showing the brain activity of a dead salmon reached a wider audience than the original attendees, while simultaneously building Neuroskeptic as a platform for critical debate.[54] Popular science blogs also allowed researchers to boost methodological concerns appearing in more traditional outlets. On December 29, 2008, the British psychologist-blogger Vaughn Bell publicized what he called "a bombshell of a paper" forthcoming in *Perspective on Psychological Science* (*PPS*), describing "voodoo correlations" in much fMRI research.[55] In the comments

---

50. Stéphane Doyen, Olivier Klein, Cora-Lise Pichon, and Axel Cleeremans, "Behavioral Priming: It's All in the Mind, but Whose Mind?" *PloS One* 7, no. 1 (2012): e29081.

51. Bruce V. Lewenstein, "From Fax to Facts: Communication in the Cold Fusion Saga," *Social Studies of Science* 25, no. 3 (1995): 403–436.

52. Alice E. Marwick and danah boyd, "I Tweet Honestly, I Tweet Passionately: Twitter Users, Context Collapse, and the Imagined Audience," *New Media and Society* 13, no.1 (2011): 114–133.

53. Alissa Quart, "Neuroscience: Under Attack," *New York Times*, November 23, 2012. http://www.nytimes.com/2012/11/25/opinion/sunday/neuroscience-under-attack.html

54. http://blogs.discovermagazine.com/neuroskeptic/2009/09/16/fmri-gets-slap-in-the-face-with-a-dead-fish

55. https://mindhacks.com/2008/12/29/voodoo-correlations-in-social-brain-studies

section of another blog covering the *PPS* preprint, semi-anonymous readers repeatedly raised concerns about the reviewing standards for psychological science papers appearing in *Nature* and *Science*.[56]

Indeed, *PPS* quickly became the leading mainstream venue for publicizing concerns about psychology's reproducibility, often debunking articles published in its parent journal *Psychological Science*. Founded in 2006, *PPS*'s mission was to provide "an eclectic mix of provocative reports and articles, including broad integrative reviews, overviews of research programs, meta-analyses, theoretical statements, book reviews, and articles on topics such as the philosophy of science, opinion pieces about major issues in the field, autobiographical reflections of senior members of the field, and even occasional humorous essays and sketches."[57] Under the editorship of Barbara Spellman, the new journal *PPS* became a respectable and influential venue for such talk (while its parent journal *Psychological Science* became the focus of replication efforts). As these examples suggest, much of the debate initially focused on social neuroscience, an ascendant field threatening psychology's territory, and reflected psychologists' well-established worries about the hype of speculative neurology.

Then, in 2011, Daryl Bem reentered the fray. The long-time iconoclast, now a senior professor at Cornell, published decades worth of statistically significant experiments on pre-cognition or extrasensory perception (ESP) in the high-impact *Journal of Personality and Social Psychology*.[58] The reaction to Bem's paper was immediate and vitriolic. The intensity of the response reflected a betrayal of scientific norms by a senior disciplinary gatekeeper. Critics questioned the legitimacy of the peer review system which published what they viewed as a nonsense paper simply because it adhered to the rules of the game. Bem seemingly gamed the system to promote what social psychologists have long viewed as pseudoscience and had been trying to shake since the 1880s.

This led psychologists to look askance at more mainstream topics whose results seemed to be too good to be true. The overextended market of hackable science soon collapsed. Social priming became the first to fall, driven by the revelations in the autumn of 2011 that prolific Dutch psychologist Diederik Stapel had fabricated the data in over thirty of his papers.[59] Stapel exemplified the new affective science with a swell of readily applicable papers dealing with social priming, embodied cognition, and unconscious moral judgments. Discussions of his case galvanized

---

56. http://archives.sethroberts.net/blog/2008/12/28/voodoo-correlations-in-social-neuroscience

57. https://us.sagepub.com/en-us/nam/perspectives-on-psychological-science/journal201964#description

58. Daryl J. Bem, "Feeling the Future: Experimental Evidence for Anomalous Retroactive Influences on Cognition and Affect," *Journal of Personality and Social Psychology* 100, no. 3 (2011): 407–425.

59. http://retractionwatch.com/2011/10/31/stapel-report-finds-faked-data-in-at-least-30-papers-possibly-more

concerns about counterintuitive studies published in high-status venues. The attack focused on the psychology of the quick fix: "this one-minute pose will improve your feelings, behavior, biochemistry; drink naturally sweetened lemonade or "brain fuel" to strengthen your willpower to lose weight."

The Reproducibility Project tried a different tact. Rather than focusing studies that would provoke incredulity, they chose to retest a sample of high-profile but otherwise unremarkable experiments. In November 2011, Brian Nosek announced the project's launch on a new Google forum dedicated to the Open Science Framework in psychology.[60] He proposed a multisited team of international collaborators who would directly replicate the findings from studies published in 2008 issues of three prominent journals: (1) *Journal of Experimental Psychology: Learning, Memory, and Cognition*, (2) *Journal of Personality and Social Psychology*, and (3) *Psychological Science*. Replicators would attempt to follow the experiment's procedures exactly, contacting the original team for clarification as needed. The devastating results when published in *Science* attracted international headlines. When independent teams conducted direct replications of the field's highest profile studies, they were able to secure comparable results in only about a third of the cases.[61]

Nosek was no stranger to mobilizing the infrastructure of the internet to conduct massive, online research. He had made his reputation as a contributor to the Implicit Association Test (IAT), piloting its move from a laboratory setting onto a website during the first dot.com boom. The IAT became the first great success story of digitized social research. The viral popularity of the Project Implicit website led to the collection of data from hundreds of thousands of users while embedding its related construct "implicit bias" in political discourse. The internet served not only as a medium for communication, but also as a model for organization. It became an open platform for critique, collaboration, and data management. Reformers issued calls for greater data transparency by preregistering research designs in online archives, and they modeled their reform on the "open-source" movement in computer programming. They exemplified what anthropologist Christopher Kelty calls the recursive public sphere, "constituted by a shared imaginary of the technical and legal conditions of possibility for their own association."[62]

As the crisis widened and psychology's self-confidence seemed to be on the cusp of collapsing, Kahneman released on open letter warning about the consequences of failing to address mounting doubts about the validity of social priming. The Nobel laureate had given the phenomenon a prominent place in his 2011 bestseller *Thinking Fast and Slow*, having leaned heavily on publications in this area to

---

60. https://groups.google.com/forum/#!topic/openscienceframework/qWcal4bQynw

61. Open Science Collaboration, "Estimating the Reproducibility of Psychological Science," *Science* 349, no. 6251 (2015): aac4716.

62. Christopher Kelty, "Geeks, Social Imaginaries, and Recursive Publics," *Cultural Anthropology* 20, no. 2 (2005): 185–214.

explain how the fast and frugal "hot" system of affect-laden, unconscious decision making functioned. Kahneman now distanced himself from the field—his letter made clear that he did not identify as "a member of your community"—while warning of "a train wreck looming" if social psychologists did not get their house in order.[63]

In many ways, the competing sides in the replication crisis represented Kahneman's dual legacy in psychology. The research agenda of the combatants focused on different facets of his dual process theory as developed during distinct phases of his career. Kahneman and Tversky first made their reputation with research on how certain mental shortcuts (cognitive biases and heuristics) led to misinterpreting information. By the mid-1980s, the Kahneman–Tversky collaboration had frayed under pressure from personal jealousy and institutional distance. Relocated to the policy school at Princeton, Kahneman began formulating a very different science, a policy-oriented, "hedonic" science of happiness. The Kahneman–Tversky theories of the 1970s fell very much within the (limits to) information-process psychology of the cognitive revolution. By 2000, Kahneman came to suggest that the affective predisposition created a second (or hot, or fast) cognitive system, one largely running an automatic. In other words, the psychologists pushing for great transparency and reforms in data management practices saw themselves as heirs to Kahneman's work on faulty expert judgment, while those they criticized pursued the research on affect-laden automaticity which he had advocated since the 1990s.

Despite the efforts of Nosek and other reforms proposed to normalize open science practices, much of the psychological establishment continued to view replication efforts through a combative lens. Their response dwelled on the incivility among psychology's online methodologists. Given the highly modularized form psychological research had taken, they read replication efforts as individual attacks on particular persons or labs. Drawing upon their own field's imaginary of tribalized and unthinking digital mobs, the discipline's leaders stressed the damage done to careers by widely circulated claims of failed replication, especially to junior academics seeking tenure at the world's most elite institutions. Daniel T. Gilbert (a fixture of TED talks and PBS, but probably most famous for staging a series of "experiments" in a viral ad campaign encouraging people to save for the future with Prudential Financial) called the reformers the "replication police" and "shameless little bullies" on Twitter.[64] In an editorial, Princeton professor Susan Fiske, writing in her capacity as the president of the Association for Psychological

---

63. Daniel Kahneman, Open Email, September 26, 2012. Available at https://www.nature.com/polopoly_fs/7.6716.1349271308!/suppinfoFile/Kahneman%20Letter.pdf

64. https://twitter.com/dantgilbert/status/470199929626193921, May 24, 2014. Gilbert's twitter profile (once) read: "Professor of Psychology @Harvard, author of Stumbling on Happiness, host of PBS series This Emotional Life, and yes, that guy in the Prudential commercials." https://twitter.com/DanTGilbert (accessed September 19, 2017). He has since deleted the Prudential line (January 30, 2018).

Science (APS), called them "methodological terrorists."[65] Open science advocates denounced this rhetoric. However, even those who had once been sympathetic to the methodological reform suggested that unspoken and troubling gendered dynamics compromised the movement. Certainly, Cuddy (young, blonde, a former dancer) came under particularly harsh scrutiny.[66] Individual replication efforts often left the powerful male psychologists mentoring these students and pushing these research agendas unscathed. This led some to question the gender politics of the #bropenscience movement.

In contrast to the soon ridiculed power posing, the IAT's fate was telling. By 2015, it had become the most widely used (if controversial) measure in contemporary psychology. Like no other technique, it captured the rule of unconscious affect across all decision making. Nosek, who led most of psychology's Open Science initiatives, was one of its co-developers. When pushed in media interviews, Nosek has stated that he longer believes in the predictive validity of the test.[67] Given its prominence in psychology and Nosek's prominence within the open science circle, it is striking how little attention the IAT has received from the reproducibility efforts. The movement still concentrated on eliminating the latest versions of the Mozart Effect rather than directly grappling with the field's core phenomena.

Gilbert did not limit himself to tweeting his displeasure. With his long-term collaborator Timothy D. Wilson and Harvard statistician Gary King, Gilbert rebutted the dramatic claims of the 2015 multisited replication effort. After quibbling over a few instances where the replication efforts deviated from the original protocols, the team focused on the faulty logic of direct replication. First, they listed examples where the replication study deviated from the original. These were instances when European researchers relied on their undergraduates rather than on those attending the original American universities. Next, they raised the issue of statistical power. All experiments have a chance of missing the underlying phenomenon in a particular sample. If the researchers repeated the original studies a few dozen times, they would have had a higher likelihood of detecting the original (true) phenomenon. Finally, they raised the specter of bias. These lower status psychologists were motivated to prove their social betters wrong in the competitive game of twenty-first-century science.[68]

---

65. Susan T. Fiske, "Mob Rule or Wisdom of Crowds?" http://datacolada.org/wp-content/uploads/2016/09/Fiske-presidential-guest-column_APS-Observer_copy-edited.pdf

66. Susan Dominus, "When the Revolution Came for Amy Cuddy," *New York Times*, October 18, 2017. https://www.nytimes.com/2017/10/18/magazine/when-the-revolution-came-for-amy-cuddy.html

67. Jesse Singal, "Psychology's Racism Measuring Tool Isn't Up to the Job." https://www.thecut.com/2017/01/psychologys-racism-measuring-tool-isnt-up-to-the-job.html

68. Daniel T. Gilbert, Gary King, Stephen Pettigrew, and Timothy D. Wilson, "Comment on "Estimating the Reproducibility of Psychological Science,'" *Science* 351, no. 6277 (2016): 1037a.

These criticisms had some merit. Unlike the behavior analysts, no contemporary social psychologist engaged in intra-subject replications, examining how the same participants repeatedly responded to the same and slightly altered conditions. The logic of experimental psychology was quite different. With a sufficiently large sample (historically six to ten people per condition and increasingly fifty), any conveniently available human could substitute for another. Except few psychologists genuinely believed that.

In defending the tarnished reputation of psychology, this social science supergroup made some startling concessions. The justification of studying psychological phenomena in tightly controlled, unnaturalistic laboratories had always hinged on the claim to detect universal laws. The goal was *explaining* underlying mental processes, not *describing* the conduct of the persons at hand. Psychology never meant to generalize beyond the specific laboratory conditions and the particular participants tested. Although the authors would likely recoil at the notion, their response seemed to embrace the inevitability of "experimenter's regress," the inability to disentangle a phenomenon from the apparatus and conditions used to measure it.[69] In other words, the best defense mounted by some of the most prominent social scientists denied psychology ever pretended to generalize beyond its immediate circumstances. Who would dare claim otherwise? At best, the discipline had been engaged in a hundred-year ethnography—an extended thin description—of the American sophomore. They defended the validity of past psychological research by arguing for its fragility, if not its phantasmagorical nature.[70] Perhaps Bem was the most honest methodologist when he confessed: "If you looked at all my past experiments, they were always rhetorical devices. I gathered data to show how my point would be made. I used data as a point of persuasion, and I never really worried about, 'Will this replicate or will this not?'"[71]

The 2015 *Science* report had emphasized that failed replication formed a routine part of a healthy science, but a kindred study revealed more sinister signs of unspoken trouble. This latter study exemplified the dominant cultural logic of the day by turning psychologists' confidence in their peers into market. The study asked experts to act as "traders," investing more sums on those findings they forecasted would replicate. When money was on the line, psychologists predicted quite successfully which studies would or would not replicate. False positives were not randomly distributed throughout the literature but accumulated in a patterned

---

69. Harry M. Collins, *Changing Order: Replication and Induction in Scientific Practice*. Chicago: University of Chicago Press, 1985, chapter 4.

70. In this regard, they seemingly endorsed the views of the once heretical social constructionism of Kenneth J. Gergen, "Social Psychology as History, *Journal of Personality and Social Psychology* 26, no. 2 (1973): 309–320.

71. https://slate.com/health-and-science/2017/06/daryl-bem-proved-esp-is-real-showed-science-is-broken.html

manner, detectable to the expert.[72] In the aggregate, psychological experts were highly competent in determining in advance what counted as a sure bet, or, at least, they seemed remarkably competent in intuiting when something was amiss.

Few followed the Gilbert team's "defense" of experimental psychology by recognizing the profound historical contingency of the discipline's most cherished phenomenon. Indeed, open science advocates soon devised a system of badges to reward greater transparency in research conduct. This new set of metrics normalized open science practices but largely muted the potentially radical critique of disciplinary norms initially posed by the replication movement. Rather than disrupt psychology's business as usual, open science practices were quickly coopted into a research culture bent on overproduction, mechanized rule following, and metricized rewards. That this methodological quietude ultimately triumphed was perhaps unsurprising. Psychologists had good reason not to overly scrutinize their field's role in recent history.

"Safe, Legal, Ethical, and Effective"

The debate about overreplication ultimately obscured what was without doubt the most controversial mobilization of the new affective science: the purported role of psychologists in "enhanced interrogations" as part of the U.S. government's War on Terror following the September 11 attacks. In Afghanistan and Iraq, the Bush administration used the legal category of "enemy combatant" to justify the capture and detention of alleged members of terrorist organizations without granting these individuals prisoner-of-war rights under the Geneva Convention. In March 2004, images began to the circulate from the Abu Ghraib prison in Iraq depicting detainees suffering humiliating and degrading forms of physical abuse at the hands of their American military captors. From the outset, classic social psychology demonstrations showing how the demands of the situation led people to behave in monstrous ways provided journalists with a framework for talking about the abuses perpetrated at Abu Ghraib.[73] Blame lay in dehumanizing institutions and the pressure to conform rather than in any one individual's personal failings. Philip Zimbardo, the APA president in 2002, embraced this interpretation. He connected conditions at Abu Ghraib to those of his so-called Stanford Prison Experiment in lectures about the "the psychology of evil" and

---

72. Anna Dreber, Thomas Pfeiffer, Johan Almenberg, Siri Isaksson, Brad Wilson, Yiling Chen, Brian A. Nosek, and Magnus Johannesson, "Using Prediction Markets to Estimate the Reproducibility of Scientific Research," *Proceedings of the National Academy of Sciences* 112, no. 50 (2015): 15343–15347.

73. John Schwartz, "Simulated Prison in '71 Showed a Fine Line Between 'Normal' and 'Monster,'" *New York Times*, May 6, 2004, A20; Anahad O'Connor, "Pressure to Go Along with Abuse Is Strong, But Some Soldiers Find Strength to Refuse," *New York Times*, May 14, 2004, A9.

in expert witness testimony on behalf of the American soldiers put on trial.[74] As many Americans began to question the Bush administration's justification for war, psychological science seemed to offer a steady moral compass for a nation recovering from the disorienting excesses of patriotic fervor.

Instead of anchoring sound judgment, a very different link between these abuses and affective science crystallized a mere six months later. In November 2004, a front-page *New York Times* story detailed an International Committee of the Red Cross site visit report alleging that "the American military has intentionally used psychological and sometimes physical coercion 'tantamount to torture' on prisoners at Guantanamo Bay, Cuba." The report further identified the agents of this abuse as Behavioral Science Consultation Teams (BSCTs, or Biscuits), "composed of psychologists and psychological workers who advise the interrogators."[75] The release of the Red Cross report threatened to undo psychology's carefully cultivated public image as a helping health profession and provoked an immediate reaction within the APA leadership.

The American state's response to 9/11 did not represent a "state of exception," a moment of crisis when the sovereign oversteps the rule of law in the name of serving the public good.[76] Instead, political theorist Laleh Khalili documents how U.S. police action fit within a century-old pattern of liberal counterinsurgency, characterized by "the invocation of law and legality as structuring the conduct of war, an absolute dependence on a set of clearly defined procedures and administrative processes as means of ensuring regulatory and ethical compliance, and finally a discourse of humanitarian intent."[77] The Bush administration (largely through a set of infamous memos authored by Deputy Assistant Attorney General John Yoo in 2002) created an ad hoc regime that oscillated between international and domestic criminal law to grant the government maximum flexibility to pursue its strategy. Rather than a suspension of law or ethical codes, the bodies of the detainees held at Guantanamo Bay and other dark sites were precisely managed as "the requirements of discipline and the combined Taylorized and bureaucratization of the military has meant that the US military operates with reams of complex documents that break down the procedures of detention into infinitesimal elements concatenated together to make a process and, in doing so,

---

74. Melissa Dittmann, "Psychological Science Offers Clues to Iraqi Prisoner Abuse," *APA Monitor* 35, no. 7 (July/August 2004): 13; Melissa Dittmann, "What Makes Good People Do Bad Things," *APA Monitor* 35, no. 9 (October 2004): 68.

75. Neil A. Lewis, "Red Cross Finds Detainee Abuse in Guantanamo," *New York Times*, November 30, 2004, A1, A19.

76. Giorgio Agamben, *State of Exception*. Chicago: University of Chicago Press, 2005. Indeed, physical torture had become a surprisingly mundane feature of racialized policing in urban centers like Chicago. See Laurence Ralph, *The Torture Letters: Reckoning with Police Violence*. Chicago: University of Chicago Press, 2020.

77. Laleh Khalili, *Time in the Shadows: Confinement in Counterinsurgencies*. Stanford, CA: Stanford University Press, 2013, 4.

to eliminate the need for the soldiers to make on-the-spot decisions about vulnerable detainees."[78] Instead of the result of fast, affective, automatic unthinking of a national collective under attack, detainment was a calculated product of cool and sustained deliberation.

Khalili's analysis recasts the protracted debate within the APA over the ethics of psychologists' participation in interrogations. Ultimately, by involving only a small number of dues-paying members, convening a presidential task force, rewriting codes of conduct, and inventing novel psychological constructs, the APA made professional psychology indispensable to the process of rendering torture legal and ethical. Just as the Bush administration's policies had roots in earlier forms of counterinsurgency, APA's attempt to assert psychology's political utility after 9/11 also had a longer history. It represented the culmination of "the battle for professionalism" which dominated the organization since the 1970s. This version of the politics of mental health started from a coziness with an "inside the beltway," Washington perspective on affairs. It also derived from the same, almost pathological, need for policy relevance and the endless drive to market psychological expertise which drove the inflated claims at the heart of the replication crisis. Pushed by these multiple demands to show psychology in action, the APA leadership carefully recrafted its ethical code to position the profession as the liberal, even kind, face of counterinsurgency and torture.

The precise role psychologists played in interrogations and the nature of organized psychology's response remain contested and subject to ongoing lawsuits. The Hoffman report provided the most thorough narrative of this historical episode, and as a fact-gathering exercise it generated an extensive archive of semi-public utterances.[79] Following a resolution by its Board of Directors in November 2014, the APA secured the services of attorney David H. Hoffman to conduct an independent review of allegations that the organization deliberately crafted permissive ethical guidelines at the behest of the DoD, the Central Intelligence Agency (CIA), and other branches of the security state. Hoffman and his associates collated thousands of pages of internal communication and interviewed key players.

The least contested narrative ran as follows. Prior to the September 11 attacks, the U.S. military offered select personnel Survival, Evasion, Resistance, and Escape (SERE) training to evade capture and withstand torture if captured. In April 2002, the CIA granted a $81 million contract to Mitchell Jessen and Associates, a company led by two operational psychologists, James Mitchell and Bruce Jessen.[80] Former affiliates of the SERE program and current APA members, the

---

78. Khalili, *Time in the Shadows*, 141.

79. David H. Hoffman, *Report to the Special Committee of the Board of Directors of the American Psychological Association: Independent Review Relating to APA Ethics Guidelines, National Security Interrogations, and Torture*. Sidley Austin LLP, 2015. Retrieved from www.apa.org/independent-review/revised-report.pdf

80. "Operational" or "operative" psychology is the term adopted by applied psychologists working for the secret services; see Moritz Michels and Martin Wieser. "From Hohenschönhausen to

pair reverse-engineered the SERE training to instruct BSCTs in how to conduct interrogations. With much of the SERE training dating back to the 1950s, Mitchell and Jessen purportedly updated it by including elements of what psychologists called "learned helpless," a trendy revision to classical conditioning. Martin Seligman, the former APA president who coined the term "learned helplessness" in the late 1960s met twice with Mitchell and Jessen and delivered a lecture at the SERE school at their invitation.[81]

The APA's response to 9/11 was shaped by professional psychology's longstanding, and sometimes troubled, relationship with the U.S. military. The field of clinical psychology was born out of the shortage of psychiatrists to deal with the mental traumas experienced by returning soldiers after World War II. Over time, such a deep debt to the military was not without tension, especially as psychologists increasingly identified as "liberals" from the 1960s onward.[82] For example, in 1991, the APA Council of Representatives voted to prohibit the DoD from advertising in APA publications due to discriminatory policies preventing gay and lesbian persons from (openly) serving in the military.[83] Despite this setback, the military remained a crucial ally for the profession. The same year of the advertising prohibition, the DoD piloted the Psychopharmacology Demonstration Project (PDP), a program designed to train doctoral-level, licensed psychologists to prescribe psychotropic medications.[84] This small cadre of military psychologists could obtain prescription privileges, a professional right that was unavailable in the vast majority of U.S. jurisdictions. This project formally ended in 1997, and some of the PDP trainees would later head the BSCTs.[85]

These tensions shaped the APA's response to the 2001 terrorist attacks. In 2002, its Council of Representatives passed a resolution calling upon the entire psychology community to contribute to "an end to terrorism in all its manifestations." The resolution represented a mixture of interests. Some items focused on the affected population (e.g., the heightened "levels of stress, anxiety, fear, and insecurity" generated by the attacks and increased incidents of domestic hate crimes). Others called upon the APA to advocate "at the congressional and executive levels for increased use of behavioral experts and behavioral knowledge in dealing with

Guantanamo Bay: Psychology's Role in the Secret Services of the GDR and the United States," *Journal of the History of the Behavioral Sciences* 54, no. 1 (2018): 43–61.

81. Dan Aalbers, "Torture," in Thomas Teo (ed.), *Encyclopedia of Critical Psychology*. New York: Springer, 2014, 1973–1980.

82. On the liberalism of the American professoriate, see Neil Gross, *Why Are Professors Liberal and Why Do Conservatives Care?* Cambridge, MA: Harvard University Press, 2013.

83. Peter Hegarty, *A Recent History of Lesbian and Gay Psychology: From Homophobia to LGBT*. New York: Routledge, 2017, 46–48.

84. Russ Newman, Randy Phelps, Morgan Sammons, Debra Dunivin, and Elizabeth Cullen, "Evaluation of the Psychopharmacology Demonstration Project: A Retrospective Analysis," *Professional Psychology: Research and Practice* 31, no. 6 (2000): 598–603.

85. Dunivin was also married to the APA Director of Practice Russ Newman.

both the threat and impact of terrorism" and "increased support for behavioral research that will produce greater understanding of the roots of terrorism and the methods to defeat it."[86] However, the November 2004 Red Cross revelations raised serious concerns among the rank-and-file membership. In order to address these worries and to rehabilitate psychology's image, the organization's leadership convened a Presidential Task Force on Psychological Ethics and National Security (PENS) in April 2005. Its purported goal was to determine whether the existing code provided "adequate ethical guidance" to psychologists involved in national security investigations.[87] Rather than insulating the organization from the mounting criticism, the PENS Task Force further imbricated the psychological profession as a whole in the U.S. government's enhanced interrogation practices. Rather than restrict their involvement in national security policing, the final report controversially positioned psychologists as uniquely qualified to ensure that interrogations were "safe, legal, ethical, and effective."[88]

The PENS task force was deeply entangled with the project of making psychology a legitimate health profession. For example, the frequently used language of "safe and effective" came from the world of bureaucratic regulation, evidence-based medicine, and the evaluation of treatments. Namely, the 1962 Kefauver-Harris reforms of the Federal Drug Administration insisted that pharmaceutical manufacturers demonstrate their novel therapeutics were not only safe to the public but also effective treatments.[89] Likewise, the PDP psychologists repeatedly described themselves as "safe and effective" prescribers of medication.[90]

Along with this familiar rhetoric, the Task Force also advanced the novel claim that psychologists were somehow uniquely skilled at rendering interrogations legal and ethic.[91] This argument derived from a committee whose makeup was controversial from the outset. Rather than providing clear civilian oversight, the committee skewed (six to four) toward members with military affiliations or familial connections. For example, Russ Newman, director of the Practice Directorate,

---

86. https://www.apa.org/about/policy/chapter-4b

87. "Report of the American Psychological Association Presidential Task Force on Psychological Ethics and National Security," 1.

88. "Report of the American Psychological Association Presidential Task Force on Psychological Ethics and National Security," 8.

89. Jeremy Greene and Scott H. Podolsky, "Reform, Regulation, and Pharmaceuticals: The Kefauver-Harris Amendments at 50," *New England Journal of Medicine* 367, no. 16 (2012): 1481–1483.

90. Debra Lina Dunivin, "Experiences of a Department of Defense Proscribing Psychologist: A Personal Account," in Morgan T. Sammons, Ruth Ullmann Ed Paige, and Ronald F. Levant (eds.), *Prescriptive Authority for Psychologists: A History and Guide*. Washington, DC: APA, 2003, 103–115.

91. On torture expertise, see Alfred McCoy, *A Question of Torture: CIA Interrogation, from the Cold War to the War on Terror*. New York: Metropolitan Books, 2007; Lisa Stampnitzky, *Disciplining Terror: How Experts Invented "Terrorism."* New York: Cambridge University Press, 2013.

was named a nonvoting "observer," even though it was known that he was married to Lieutenant Colonel Debra Dunivin, a former PDP trainee and then the leader of a BSCT. In contrast, Olivia Moorehead-Slaughter, an African American child psychologist with experience on the Ethics Committee but having no involvement with national security issues, was named chair because "her diversity was important to the selection group."[92] Chosen to give the air of inclusivity, Moorehead-Slaughter was granted little agency by the APA leadership as Stephen Behnke, Director of the APA's Office of Ethics, ghostwrote her contributions. In interviews conducted as part of the Hoffman report, the pair conceded that "Behnke drafted or outlined nearly every correspondence Moorehead-Slaughter sent over the PENS listserv, offered an outline of comments and analysis ahead of the PENS meetings, and provided her talking points after the report received criticism from both inside and outside of the task force."[93] Indeed, Behnke had already articulated much of the organization's response in a June 9, 2005 email sent to the task force members two weeks before their formal meeting. There he borrowed the quadripartite formulation of "safe, legal, ethical, and effective" from a suggestion made by task force member Colonel L. Morgan Banks.[94] In turn, this language came directly from a memo released six months earlier by the DoD to describe the BSCTs' mission.[95]

Behnke was even bolder in public statements, asserting that psychologists were "in a unique position to assist in ensuring that processes are safe, legal, ethical, and effective for all participants."[96] In a 2007 statement submitted to the U.S. Senate Select Committee on Intelligence, Behnke, speaking on the organization's behalf, argued that "conducting an interrogation is inherently a *psychological* endeavor." Interrogations required "building rapport" where psychologists possessed credentialed expertise in "human behavior, motivations and relationships." This meant "psychology is central to this process because an understanding of an individual's belief systems, desires, motivations, culture and religion likely will be essential in assessing how best to form a connection and facilitate educing accurate, reliable and actionable intelligence."[97] His Senate testimony made evident how he understood that psychologists contributed to making interrogations effective. Elsewhere he addressed the issue of how psychological expertise contributed

92. Hoffman, *Report to the Special Committee*, 241.

93. Hoffman, *Report to the Special Committee*, 248.

94. Behnke to Moorehead-Slaughter, June 9, 2005, Hoffman Binder-1, 728-729. http://www.apa.org/independent-review/binder-1.pdf

95. Memorandum for JTF-GTMO-JIG-BSCT, December 10, 2004

96. Stephen Behnke, "Psychological Ethics and National Security: The Position of the American Psychological Association," *European Psychologist* 11, no. 2 (2006): 153–155, 154.

97. American Psychological Association, "Statement of the American Psychological Association on Psychology and Interrogations Submitted to the United States Senate Select Committee on Intelligence" September 21, 2007. https://www.apa.org/news/press/statements/senate-2007.pdf

to making them inherently more ethical. In articles published simultaneously in the *Monitor*, both APA president Gerry Koocher and Behnke suggested a deep familiarity with the process known as "behavioral drift" justified the presence of psychologists at these sites. Because psychologists possessed scientific expertise in this domain, they could monitor military and CIA interrogators (described in Koocher's editorial as typically young, female, and themselves the children of immigrants) and ensure the utmost ethical oversight.[98] Such an argument sounded appealing. Indeed, "behavioral drift" could have been a well-established psychological construct backed by considerable empirical evidence. The concept certainly did not seem out of place in a psychological science emphasizing the automaticity of much human conduct. However, the term was wholly of their invention, never appearing in the peer-reviewed, scientific literature prior to its coining in these two editorials. Nor did these publications inspire subsequent empirical research. In this regard, the new affective science gave the APA ethicists the cloak of legitimacy for their phantasmagorical creations.

In promising to make interrogations not only ethical but effective, the PENS task force repeatedly returned to the question of whose interests psychologists served or, in the language of the professions, "who was the client?" This was not the first time APA ethicists grappled with this question. A defining characteristic of "classic" professions like law and medicine is a shared emphasis on a service ideal to their paying client. Already by the 1960s, sociologists had noted how this traditional role was breaking down as professionals came to work for large organizations where such clear-cut two-party arrangements were increasingly scare.[99] For example, school psychologists, Koocher's own area of expertise, often experienced conflicting demands from the child, parent, and education system.[100] The client question was even more acute in policing contexts and became central to the Task Force on the Role of Psychology in the Criminal Justice System (1978). This task force began by surveying psychologists working in criminal justice settings, asking them about the ethics of (forced) rehabilitation and behavior modification. However, the responses revealed other tensions, namely, the conflict between the psychotherapist as "liberal humanist" and the "conservative" philosophy of institutions like parole boards. Correctional services paid their wages. However, these psychologists felt a professional obligation to protect

---

98. Gerald P. Koocher, "Varied and Valued Roles," APA Monitor 37, no. 7 (2006): 5; Stephen Behnke, "Ethics and Interrogations: Comparing and Contrasting the American Psychological, American Medical and American Psychiatric Association positions," *APA Monitor* 37, no. 7 (2006): 66.

99. Everett C. Hughes, "Professions," *Daedalus* 92, no. 4 (1963): 655–668.

100. Peter Kuriloff, "Law, Educational Reform, and the School Psychologist," *Journal of School Psychology* 13, no. 4 (1975): 335–348.

the vulnerable revelations made during psychotherapy, even if such confessions might inform their punishment.[101]

Convened in the wake of congressional censure of behavior modification programs in prisons and the *Tarasoff* decision in California, the 1978 task force asked tough questions about what psychology should become and whose needs the profession should serve. At the forefront were concerns about how certain legal obligations might necessitate breeching the privacy and confidentiality of the psychotherapeutic relationship.[102] The report entertained the possibility of domesticating the criminal justice setting to the established norms of the psychotherapeutic encounter in private practice. The committee deemed such maneuvers untenable given the expansion of psychology's professional domain. Psychologists' entry into the criminal justice system meant they had to fundamentally reconceive their social role and look beyond their default obligations, namely, "an individual, purchaser of psychological services."[103] The task force recommendations repeatedly erred on the side of placing constraints on how psychologists exercised their professional judgment. For example, it urged psychologists to keep to their proper knowledge domain. "Since it is not within the professional competence of psychologists to offer conclusions on matters of law, psychologists should resist pressure to offer such conclusions."[104] Furthermore, the report urged that "psychologists should be exceedingly cautious in offering predictions of criminal behavior for use in imprisoning or releasing offenders."[105] The 1978 task force consistently posited the psychologist as a limited agent, humbled by their new responsibilities and obligations.

In the intervening years, the APA code shifted from professional ethics designed to protect the public to guild ethics intended to protect its members from litigation.[106] Psychologists' adoption of multiple roles in various educational and legal contexts led to a 2002 amendment to the ethics code. Namely, the section on the potential conflicts between the professional code and the law added new language stating that in cases of unresolvable demands from these two bodies, "psychologists may adhere to the requirements of the law, regulations, or other

---

101. W. Glenn Clingempeel, Edward Mulvey, and N. Dickon Reppucci, "A National Study of Ethical Dilemmas of Psychologists in the Criminal Justice System" in John Monahan (ed.), *Who Is the Client? The Ethics of Psychological Intervention in the Criminal Justice System*. Washington, DC: APA, 1980, 126–153, 130.

102. Sarah E. Igo, *The Known Citizen: A History of Privacy in Modern America*. Cambridge, MA: Harvard University Press, 2018.

103. "Report of the Task Force on the Role of Psychology in the Criminal Justice System," *American Psychologist* 33 (1978): 1099–1113, 1101.

104. "Report of the Task Force on the Role of Psychology in the Criminal Justice System," 1105.

105. "Report of the Task Force on the Role of Psychology in the Criminal Justice System," 1108.

106. Kenneth S. Pope, "The Code Not Taken: The Path from Guild Ethics to Torture and Our Continuing Choices." *Canadian Psychology/Psychologie canadienne* 57, no. 1 (2016): 51–59.

governing legal authority."[107] Despite the timing, this amendment did not come at the bequest of the DoD. Rather, it derived from members' concerns that the expansive code exposed the liability of practitioners. Nevertheless, the new language ultimately subsumed the individual's moral responsibility as a professional to the demands of the state. The 2002 code "explicitly allowed psychologists to set aside any ethical responsibilities that were in irreconcilable conflict with various forms of governmental authority."[108] Although not written at the behest of the DoD, the revisions to the code opened a space for military psychologists to operate.

When the ethicists on the PENS task force returned to the client question in 2005, they did so with much greater confidence in the psychologists' knowledge and professional abilities. After Michael Gelles, a forensic psychologist with the Naval Criminal Investigative Service, first posed this question on the PENS listserv, task force members repeatedly returned to it. Drawing on his own professional experience, Gelles insisted that the "client" was not the individual detainee under observation but "the organization." He observed: "As psychologists broadened their role and became 'more visible' in the government, law enforcement and intelligence community there were new demands placed upon us, serving our client the 'organization' "[109] Behnke, writing as Moorehead-Slaughter, concurred, noting the variety of distinct services psychologists now provided; "the roles of operational consultants and health care providers are decidedly different and should be kept separate."[110] Koocher amplified this line of argument, evoking the psychologist's responsibility as a professional not only to the paying client but society as a whole. "In this case the client is the agency, government, and ultimately the people of the nation (at risk). The goal of such psychologists' work will ultimately be the protection of others (i.e., innocents) by contributing to the incarceration, debilitation, or even death of the potential perpetrator, who will often remain unaware of the psychologists' involvement."[111] Behnke/Moorehead-Slaughter followed by saying: "we might have ethical obligations even to individuals or entities who are not our clients." As ethicists, they needed to keep in view who counted as "the most vulnerable party" and serve their needs.[112] On the PENS listserv, the civilian leadership of the APA made clear that this was the nation at risk rather than any

---

107. "Ethical Principles of Psychologists and Code of Conduct," *American Psychologist* 57 (2002): 1060–1073, 1063.

108. Kenneth S. Pope and Thomas G. Gutheil. "Psychologists Abandon the Nuremberg Ethic: Concerns for Detainee Interrogations," *International Journal of Law and Psychiatry* 32, no. 3 (2009): 161–166.

109. Michael Gelles to PENS Task Force listserv, May 3, 2005. The entire contents of the PENS Task Force listserv has been publicly archived. http://www.ethicalpsychology.org/resources/PENS-listserv.php

110. Olivia Moorehead-Slaughter to PENS Task Force list, May 6, 2005.

111. Gerry Koocher to PENS Task Force listserv, May 6, 2005.

112. Olivia Moorehead-Slaughter to PENS Task Force listserv, May 10, 2005.

one prisoner undergoing interrogation. With each subsequent email, the living presence of the individual detainee faded from view.

The public reception of these ethical maneuvers was mixed at best. In 2006, Behnke wrote of "a 'left wing conspiracy' against the APA on this issue, something I've suspected for a long while but have become entirely convinced of now."[113] This conspiracy talk resonated with another moment when the "battle for professionalism" ideology manifested itself. Behnke professed admiration for the practical, worldly psychologists working for the security state in contrast to their moralistic, wordy counterparts in academia. He noted: "unlike some of our colleagues whose ability to generate prattle on this subject is apparently endless, you and Morgan have full-time work that is hugely demanding and important."[114]

However, the torture controversy was not limited simply to the professional branch of psychology, but rather cut to the core of the affective science being promoted by academics on the self-help circuit. Among the more contentious issues was the precise role of "learned helplessness" and the theory's developer, Martin Seligman, in America's extralegal torture program. Unlike the conveniently coined "behavioral drift," "learned helplessness" was a venerable theory with a respected pedigree binding together psychology as a science and practice. Seligman first proposed the term back in 1967 to describe the results of a behavioral experiment where harnessed dogs unable to escape an administered shock transferred this learned behavior to situations where they could avoid the shock.[115] Couched in the language of classic or Pavlovian conditioning, Seligman reformulated his theory in the 1970s to explain depression in humans.[116] This theory of depression became a key plank of CBT, the consensus modality that allowed psychologists to assert their domain over psychotherapy and wrestle it free from their professional rivals in psychiatry. Learned helplessness offered the expanding ranks of clinicians an account of depression operating wholly at the psychological rather than neurobiological level. Into the 1990s, after many cognitive psychologists abandoned the APA to form the rival Association for Psychological Science, Seligman remained the experimental psychologist ready to serve clinicians' needs.[117] This led to his election as APA president in 1998, long after this office had become a near monopoly of those working in private practice. As president, Seligman offered practicing psychologists a second gift to expand

---

113. Behnke to Koocher and Levant, July 9, 2006; Hoffman Report, Binder 2, p. 28. http://www.apa.org/independent-review/binder-2.pdf

114. Behnke to Debra L. Dunivan and Louie Morgan Banks, January 26, 2007, Hoffman Report, Binder 2, p. 135. http://www.apa.org/independent-review/binder-2.pdf

115. Martin E. Seligman and Steven F. Maier, "Failure to Escape Traumatic Shock," *Journal of Experimental Psychology* 74, no. 1 (1967): 1–9.

116. Lyn Abramson, Martin Seligman, and John Teasdale, "Learned Helplessness in Humans: Critique and Reformulation," *Journal of Abnormal Psychology* 87, no. 1 (1978): 49–74.

117. Martin Seligman, "The Effectiveness of Psychotherapy: The Consumer Reports Study," *American Psychologist* 50, no. 12 (1995): 965–974.

their market share: "positive psychology," a supposedly new way of viewing mental health by emphasizing the individual's character, strength, and resilience. In sum, the torture controversy implicated the person who in the recent past had done the most to secure psychology's prominence in the public sphere.

Reeling from the 9/11 attack, Seligman took action. The precise nature of the action taken remains a matter of dispute. In mid-December, he convened a meeting of twelve professors at his home to discuss what contributions they could make to the emergent War on Terror. Four members of the American intelligence community also happened to attend this private event, including James Mitchell and Kirk Hubbard. Seligman stated that he did not invite them and did not know who did.[118] In April 2002, he delivered a lecture on learned helplessness to the SERE School in San Diego. The Hoffman report suggested that Seligman possessed a naïveté which strained credulity, concluding that "it would have been difficult not to suspect that one reason for the CIA's interest in learned helplessness was to consider how it could be used in the interrogation of others."[119] After the report's release, Seligman remained defiant. In 2018, he claimed to have no memory whatsoever of the second meeting at his own home with Mitchell, Hubbard, and Bruce Jessen, writing "I have wracked my brain for many years trying to conjure up any memory at all of this meeting, but with no success."[120] Despite this convenient lapse in memory, Seligman denied any wrongdoing.

Instead, Seligman seemingly derived rather different moral lessons from the encounter between organized psychology and psychological torture. According to his writings, from his perspective, this episode represented the capture of the Association over which he once presided by the antiwar left. "The antiwar activists have scared the pants off many APA members. Psychologists—scientists, practitioners, and centrist social activists—have learned that co-operating with the government—particularly with the Department of Defense—is dangerous to one's career."[121] On Seligman's telling, he was a naïve patriot who dared support his country and its soldiers. The real victim of the torture controversy was the APA's mutually beneficial relationship with the American defense apparatus.

CONCLUSION

At first glance, the moral crisis over torture and the methodological crisis involving replication appear to have little in common. One centered on the APA, professional ethics, and psychology's standing as a helping profession. The other centered on

---

118. Martin Seligman, "The Hoffman Report, the Central Intelligence Agency, and the Defense of the Nation: A Personal View," *Health Psychology Open* 5, no. 2 (2018): 1–9, 2.

119. Hoffman, *Report to the Special Committee*, 49.

120. Seligman, "The Hoffman Report," 3.

121. Seligman, "The Hoffman Report," 8.

the APS, dwelled on methodology, and raised questions about psychology's status as an empirical science. However, certain shared features draw these two crises together. In their unique ways, both crises derived from psychology's unremitting expansiveness, the constant demand to demonstrate its necessary utility to new domains. Late modern psychology knew no boundaries. Its pliable expertise applied to every conceivable situation. A depth of knowledge and a sensitivity to contextual circumstances were unnecessary luxuries—except psychological expertise did not go unquestioned. New forms of communication that dissolved the boundaries once separating gentlemanly scientists from unruly publics provided the venues for promoting psychology and calling out the overselling of its claims. The disdain for epistemic modesty characteristic of the late modern academic entrepreneur overproducing their wares led to both crises.[122] In this regard, both crises revolved around the openness of psychology.

Both crises also cast large shadows of ignorance. Even after the dust had settled in both instances, much remained as uncertain as when the crises began. Replication efforts had led many to question some of psychology's cherished findings, but few studies seemed definitive by very design. Similarly, the question of culpability for torture remained highly contested despite the Hoffman report's pursuit of accountability and the considerable archive this investigation produced. Instead, the dual crises of the 2010s revealed how morally and epistemologically vacuous psychology had become. Affective science offered psychologists a fluid vocabulary for producing convenient facts for whatever audience desired them. Whether "power poses" for liberal feminists trying to climb the corporate leader or "behavioral drift" for ethicists justifying the presence of APA members at dark sites, psychologists' penchant for overproduction meant facts were available to all sides. Psychology flourished in a culture of pervasive bullshit, as the philosopher Harry Frankfurt defines the term. Frankfurt distinguished bullshit from outright falsehood in so far as the bullshitter is utterly indifferent to the truthfulness of their claims.[123] On this reading, psychology succeeded while stuck in a cycle of perpetual crisis because it functioned as science-looking technology for providing persuasive results without any regard for the truth. Most the bullshit produced by psychologists was benign. However, the benign bullshit provided cover for the harmful because not even psychologists could tell the difference anymore.

Indeed, the banality of the majority studies masked the troubling message underwriting much affective science. As both a science at the level of theory and a profession at the level of practice, psychologists adopted modes of relating to their fellow citizens with profoundly antidemocratic commitments. The moral and epistemological crises that engulfed psychology did not represent "states of exception" but rather represented the culmination of a consistent sequence of political

---

122. Thomas Teo, "Academic Subjectivity, Idols, and the Vicissitudes of Virtues in Science: Epistemic Modesty Versus Epistemic Grandiosity." In *Psychological Studies of Science and Technology*. New York: Palgrave Macmillan, 2019, 31–48.

123. Harry G. Frankfurt, *On Bullshit*. Princeton, NJ: Princeton University Press, 2009.

choices made by the field's leadership. The task of securing the profession's place in an expanding and highly competitive health market after the 1970s led the leaders of organized psychology to embrace a view of the public as cognitively lacking. This view derived from their own research on the ubiquity of cognitive bias in human thought but got inflected by broader lost faith in democratic self-governance in favor of technocratic rule. After some genuine experiments with democratic experimental designs, securing psychology's place led to a reification of the psychologist's advantage. Psychologists were uniquely positioned to reveal human ignorance and offer rational guidance. This move downplayed the reflexivity about the human knower emanated in much cognitive science. Instead, the public became a tribal, affective beast, unknowingly beholden to its own disposition. Yet, psychologists remained all too human. This picture of humans offered by psychologists was not so much incorrect but inadequately applied to psychologists themselves. The twenty-first-century crises resulted from concerted attempts to evade this recent history. Rather than a universal science of basic human motivation, the new affective psychology was a culturally peculiar formation and a rather unstable one at that.

APPENDIX

I generated Figures 8.3 and 8.4 by searching for the terms "business" or "management" in the address field in the Web of Science database entries for the respective journals. Caveat: Correlation does not imply causation, and the directionality problem is rife here.

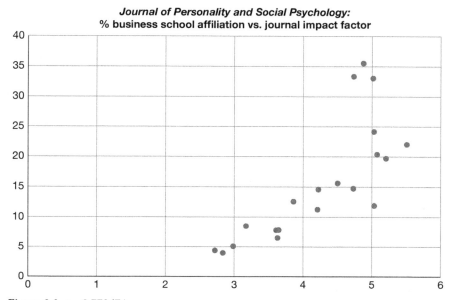

Figure 8.3 $r = 0.770674$

Journal of Personality and Social Psychology: percent business school affiliation vs. journal impact factor.

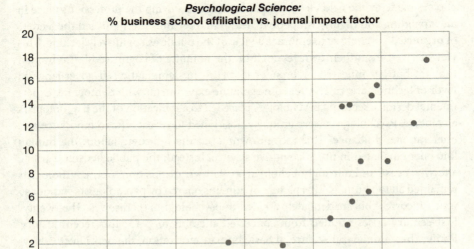

Figure 8.4 $r = 0.843346$
Psychological Science: percent business school affiliation vs. journal impact factor.

Conclusion

It remains undecided whether the crises of the 2010s will spell the end of affective science's quiet revolution both within psychology and across late modern society. That psychologists will continue investing in affect is almost certain. A pliable and capacious meta-theory, affective science fulfills multiple purposes, seemingly delivering on a long-standing dream of a total psychology unifying the experimental and the clinical, the social and the perceptual, the domains of the affective, the behavioral, the cognitive. Affective science promises to overcome the specter of fission haunting postwar psychology, even if it largely exists as a series of modularized interventions tailored to particular problems rather than to a formalized grand theory. Given its remarkable flexibility, psychologists seemingly have little impetus to jettison affective science in toto even if many of its cherished studies prove unreproducible and its leading proponents have found themselves mired in charges of torture. The affective likewise holds tremendous appeal for policymakers and social commentators across the political spectrum. For some, it provides a means of going beyond the austere, instrumental, imperial, masculine discourse of Western rationality to recognize the pull of embodied ways of knowing, as diffracted through the differences of race, gender, ability, and orientation. Ironically, for others, affect offers a tidy (if always modifiable) explanation for why smart people succeed and why the majority remain trapped in their irrational stupidity in need of expert guidance. Realized in an age of specialization and hyperproductivity, the tremendous cultural work performed by affective science often goes unnoticed because of its modularized diffusion across countless sites and publics who have given their own meaning.

Fragmentation also obscured a set of transformations that fundamentally recast relations between the discipline of psychology and the society its practitioners inhabited, altering both in the process. This book has attempted to tell this very history. While a comprehensive, global account remains impossible, this book has presented some of the major sources for affective science at length and has also followed the consequences of its adoption—a multisited history to help make sense of the recent past. Underlying the varied and local stories told, the book traces the arc of three key changes.

First, coming out of the 1970s, psychology definitively aligned itself with the problems of health even if it continued to have ambivalent relations with the institutions of biomedicine. Professions in private practice dominated the discipline's major organizational body both numerically and politically. The rise of clinical psychology is the most obvious index, along with the adoption of cognitive-behavioral therapy (CBT), as an ecumenical, theory-light, and evidence-based regime of treatment. However, this transformation was not confined to the clinical profession. Salaried, university-based, social and developmental psychologists turned over their laboratories to test those cognitive skills needed to obtain self-control as the key to emotional regulation. By the late 1990s, these same experimental psychologists adopted medical neuroimaging technology as their favored tool for probing mental function. Virtually no area of psychology was untouched by the new imperative toward health as the new mode of normality. This organization of psychology around the problems of health reflected a wider societal realignment concerning the priorities of application over theory, the triumph of technology over basic science.

This new identity as a health-minded profession led to a cultivated conspicuousness when it came to giving away psychological knowledge. To encourage healthy lifestyles, psychologists' wares needed to reach the public in a medical marketplace crowded with alternatives. Without doubt, the psyche and its failings had long been an object of fascination, but public enthusiasm left most psychologists uneasy if not consternated. The comparative largesse bestowed on the postwar university meant it could use its own reward structure to insulate academics from the market. But the imperatives of health meant that even those psychologists ensconced in their ivory tower found themselves engaging the lay audiences more directly than ever before. The discipline's long-standing public relations problem moved to the center of its organizational efforts as psychologists forged new relationships with all levels of government, commercial corporations, paying clients, and a heterogeneous range of persons capable of recasting their lived experience in psychological terms.

This cultivation of new publics raised a serious, if largely unanswerable, question: to whom was psychology responsible? As a discipline increasingly organized around solving practical problems rather than generating general theory, psychologists accrued debts to innumerable patrons and found themselves enmeshed in a web of often conflicting obligations. In postwar America, the psychology profession began with the durable fiction of mutuality between counselor and client who met each other as equals. A profound reciprocity defined the professional ethos and the psychologist's self-fashioning. Intimacy, frankness, and mutuality underwrote therapeutic success. However, such quaint interpersonal relations were soon dwarfed by the systems and structures in which psychologists found themselves embedded. In response, the 1970s witnessed a broad range of experiments with democracy as psychologists mobilized their science to make large-scale systems accountable to marginalized persons. The rank of psychologists diversified during these years as persons schooled in the new social movements (civil rights, feminism, gay liberation) entered graduate programs and brought with them their radical sensibilities and demands for societal change. These experiments with democracy were diverse but were united by research designs intended to empower a range of lay publics by giving them instruments to amplify their voice. These bold experiments with democracy which flourished in the 1970s serve as a timely reminder that the current configuration of knower and known found in psychology was not inevitable, but rather represented a disciplinary choice with a history.

In contrast, the affective science that consolidated in the late 1990s offered a very different solution, representing something of an antidemocratic counterrevolution. Affective science derived its view of the person from a cognitive arms race between scientists and their subjects, one defined by their mutual suspicion and distrust. Psychologists revived behavioristic (if not strictly behaviorist) interpretations of their data which denied the research subject's capacity for accurate self-knowledge and even rational self-rule. A profound suspicion surrounding experts and the state pushed psychologists to adopt new technologies of elicitation which circumvented knowing self-disclosure in favor of automatic, implicit, unconscious responses. In a telling slippage between favored research methods and generalized theory, psychologists upheld the results of these studies as evidence that ordinary people made poor judgments and largely acted without unawareness. They ran on automatic, beholden to their powerful affective dispositions.

THE NET EFFECT OF THESE THREE TRANSFORMATIONS

This history reveals then how psychologists came to serve as both architects and critics of the late modern attention economy. The computer as a metaphor for the mind may not convince as it once did, but the pairing of human psyches and digital technology has been indelibly productive for both. In building the social web, computer engineers openly drew upon psychology's theories of automaticity to make their designs intuitive (if not addictive) to the user. The affordance of its digitized mediascape provided psychologists with new opportunities for circulating their increasingly modularized science to a host of new publics. The lines separating participant, client, and audience blurred, as did those separating research and treatment. Psychology has been built into the very infrastructure of our digital culture. If cognitive science upheld the superiority of the algorithmic over human irrational judgment, the digital infrastructure that psychology helped design is troublingly biased in profoundly human ways. At the same time, the "openness" of these online platforms with their unique demands for public accountability has also subjected psychology to unprecedented scrutiny and critique. For this reason, affective science's immediate fate seems to be one of getting locked in a perpetual cycle of hype and incredulity.

BIBLIOGRAPHY

Archival Collections Consulted

Records of the American Psychological Association, Library of Congress.
Report to the Special Committee of the Board of Directors of the American Psychological Association, Independent Review Relating to APA Ethics Guidelines, National Security in Interrogations, and Torture, Supplementary Materials. https://www.apa.org/independent-review
Albert Ellis Papers, Rare Book and Manuscript Library, Columbia University Libraries.
David Krech Papers, Archives for the History of American Psychology, The Cummings Center for the History of Psychology, University of Akron.
Abraham Maslow Papers, Archives for the History of American Psychology, The Cummings Center for the History of Psychology, University of Akron.
Medical Research Council Archives, National Archives, Kew.
Herbert A. Simon Papers, Carnegie Mellon University, https://digitalcollections.library.cmu.edu/cmu-collection/herbert-simon

Published Works

Aalbers, Dan. "Torture." In Thomas Teo (ed.), *Encyclopedia of Critical Psychology*. New York: Springer, 2014, 1973–1980.
Abbott, Andrew. *The System of Professions: An Essay on the Division of Expert Labor*. Chicago: University of Chicago Press, 1988.
Abdi, Yusuf Omer. "The Problems and Prospects of Psychology in Africa." *International Journal of Psychology* 10, no. 3 (1975): 227–234.
Abelove, Henry. "Freud, Male Homosexuality, and the Americans." In Henry Abelove, Michèle Aina Barale, and David M. Halperin (eds.), *The Lesbian and Gay Studies Reader*. New York: Routledge, 1993, 381–393.
Abraham, Itty. *The Making of the Indian Atomic Bomb: Science, Secrecy and the Postcolonial State*. Cambridge, MA: Zed Books, 1998.
Abraham, Tara. *Rebel Genius: Warren S. McCulloch's Transdisciplinary Life in Science*. Cambridge, MA: MIT Press, 2016.
Abramson, Lyn, Martin Seligman, and John Teasdale. "Learned Helplessness in Humans: Critique and Reformulation." *Journal of Abnormal Psychology* 87, no. 1 (1978): 49–74.

Agamben, Giorgio. *State of Exception*. Chicago: University of Chicago Press, 2005.
Agar, Jon. *The Government Machine: A Revolutionary History of the Computer*. Cambridge, MA: MIT Press, 2003, 201–261.
Agar, Jon. "Thatcher, Scientist." *Notes and Records of the Royal Society* 65, no. 3 (2011): 215–232.
Agar, Jon. "What Happened in the Sixties?" *British Journal for the History of Science* 41, no. 4 (2008): 567–600.
Ahmed, Sara. *Complaint!* Durham, NC: Duke University Press, 2021.
Ahmed, Sara. *Cultural Politics of Emotion*. Edinburgh: Edinburgh University Press, 2004.
Ahmed, Sara. *The Promise of Happiness*. Durham, NC: Duke University Press, 2010.
Akavia, Naamah. *Subjectivity in Motion: Life, Art, and Movement in the Work of Hermann Rorschach*. London: Routledge, 2012.
Alac, Morana. *Handling Digital Brains: A Laboratory Study of Multimodal Semiotic Interaction in the Age of Computers*. Cambridge, MA: MIT Press, 2011.
Albee, George. "Does Including Psychotherapy in Health Insurance Represent a Subsidy to the Rich from the Poor?" *American Psychologist* 32, no. 9 (1977): 719–721.
Albee, George. "The Uncertain Future of Clinical Psychology." *American Psychologist* 25, no. 12 (1970): 1071–1080.
Alhakami, Ali Siddiq, and Paul Slovic. "A Psychological Study of the Inverse Relationship Between Perceived Risk and Perceived Benefit." *Risk Analysis* 14, no. 6 (1994): 1085–1096.
American Psychological Association (APA). "Ethical Principles of Psychologists and Code of Conduct." *American Psychologist* 57 (2002): 1060–1073.
American Psychological Association (APA). "Report of the Task Force on the Role of Psychology in the Criminal Justice System." *American Psychologist* 33 (1978): 1099–1113.
Amouroux, Rémy. "Beyond Indifference and Aversion: The Critical Reception and Belated Acceptance of Behavior Therapy in France." *History of Psychology* 20, no. 3 (2017): 313–329.
Arnett, Jeffrey Jensen. "The Neglected 95%, a Challenge to Psychology's Philosophy of Science." *American Psychologist* 64, no. 6 (2009): 571–574.
Aronson, Elliot, and J. Merrill Carlsmith. "Experimentation in Social Psychology." In Gardner Lindzey and Elliot Aronson (eds.), *The Handbook of Social Psychology*. Reading, MA: Addison-Wesley, 1968, 1–79.
Aronson, Elliot, and Judson Mills. "The Effect of Severity of Initiation on Liking for a Group." *Journal of Abnormal and Social Psychology* 59, no. 2 (1959): 177–181.
Ash, Mitchell G. "Psychology and Politics in Interwar Vienna: The Vienna Psychological Institute, 1922–1942," in Mitchell G. Ash and William R. Woodward (eds.), *Psychology in Twentieth-Century Thought and Society*. New York: Cambridge University Press, 1987, 143–164.
Azar, Beth. "IAT: Fad or Fabulous?" *APA Monitor* 39, no. 7 (2008): 44.
Bach, George R. "The Marathon Group: Intensive Practice of Intimate Interaction." *Psychological Reports* 18, no. 3 (1966): 995–1002.
Bachman, Jerald, and Patrick O'Malley. "Self-esteem in Young Men: A Longitudinal Analysis of the Impact of Educational and Occupational Attainment." *Journal of Personality and Social Psychology* 35, no. 6 (1977): 365–380.

Baddeley, Alan. "Exploring the Central Executive." *Quarterly Journal of Experimental Psychology Section A* 49, no. 1 (1996): 5–28.

Baddeley, Alan. "Working Memory and Conscious Awareness." In Alan F. Collins, Susan E. Gathercole, Martin A. Conway, and Peter E. Morris (eds.), *Theories of Memory*. New York: Psychology Press, 1993, 11–28.

Baddeley, Alan. "The Episodic Buffer: A New Component of Working Memory?" *Trends in Cognitive Sciences* 4, no. 11 (2000): 417–423.

Baddeley, Alan. *Working Memories: Postmen, Divers and the Cognitive Revolution*. London: Routledge, 2018.

Baddeley, A., D. R. Conrad, and W. E. Thomson. "Letter Structure of the English Language." *Nature* 186, no. 4722 (1960): 414–416.

Baddeley, Alan D., and Graham Hitch. "Working Memory." In Gordon Bower (ed.), *Psychology of Learning and Motivation*, volume 8. New York: Academic Press, 1974, 47–89.

Baddeley, Alan D., and Elizabeth K. Warrington. "Amnesia and the Distinction between Long-and Short-Term Memory." *Journal of Verbal Learning and Verbal Behavior* 9, no. 2 (1970): 176–189.

Baddeley, Alan D., and Elizabeth K. Warrington. "Memory Coding and Amnesia." *Neuropsychologia* 11, no. 2 (1973): 159–165.

Baddeley, Alan, and Barbara Wilson. "Frontal Amnesia and the Dysexecutive Syndrome." *Brain and Cognition* 7, no. 2 (1988): 212–230.

Bakan, David. "Behaviorism and American Urbanization." *Journal of the History of the Behavioral Sciences* 2, no. 1 (1966): 5–28.

Bakan, David. "The Test of Significance in Psychological Research." *Psychological Bulletin* 66, no. 6 (1966): 423–437.

Baker, David B., and Ludy T. Benjamin, Jr. "The Affirmation of the Scientist-Practitioner: A Look Back at Boulder." *American Psychologist* 55, no. 2 (2000): 241–247.

Balogh, Brian. *Chain Reaction: Expert Debate and Public Participation in American Commercial Nuclear Power 1945–1975*. Cambridge: Cambridge University Press, 1991.

Bandura, Albert. "Behavior Theory and the Models of Man." *American Psychologist* 29, no. 12 (1974): 859–869.

Bandura, Albert. *Principles of Behavior Modification*. New York: Holt, Rinehart, & Winston, 1969.

Bandura, Albert. "Self-efficacy: Toward a Unifying Theory of Behavioral Change." *Psychological Review* 84, no. 2 (1977): 191–215.

Banks, Curtis W., Gregory V. McQuater, Jenise A. Ross, and Wanda E. Ward. "Delayed Gratification in Blacks: A Critical Review." *Journal of Black Psychology* 9, no. 2 (1983): 43–56.

Bargh, John A., M. Chen, and L. Burrows. "Automaticity of Social Behavior: Direct Effects of Trait Construct and Stereotype Activation on Action." *Journal of Personality and Social Psychology*, 71, no. 2 (1996): 230–244.

Baritz, Loren. *The Servants of Power: A History of the Use of Social Science in American Industry*. Middletown, CT: Wesleyan University Press, 1960.

Bartlett, F. C. "The Bearing of Experimental Psychology upon Human Skilled Performance." *British Journal of Industrial Medicine* 8 (1951): 209–217.

Bartlett, F. C. "Fatigue Following Highly Skilled Work." *Proceedings of the Royal Society of London. Series B-Biological Sciences* 131, no. 864 (1943): 247–257.

Bascue, Loy O., and Martin Zlotowski. "Psychologists' Attitudes about Prescribing Medications." *Psychological Reports* 48, no. 2 (1981): 645–646.

Bauer, Heike. *The Hirschfeld Archives: Violence, Death, and Modern Queer Culture*. Philadelphia: Temple University Press, 2017.

Baumeister, Roy F. "Conquer Yourself, Conquer the World." *Scientific American* 312, no. 4 (2015): 60–65.

Baumeister, Roy F. "Ego Depletion and Self-Control Failure: An Energy Model of the Self's Executive Function." *Self and Identity* 1, no. 2 (2002): 129–136.

Baumeister, Roy F., Jennifer D. Campbell, Joachim I. Krueger, and Kathleen D. Vohs. "Does High Self-Esteem Cause Better Performance, Interpersonal Success, Happiness, or Healthier Lifestyles?" *Psychological Science in the Public Interest* 4, no. 1 (2003): 1–44.

Baumeister, Roy F., Todd F. Heatherton, and Dianne M. Tice. "When Ego Threats Lead to Self-Regulation Failure: Negative Consequences of High Self-Esteem." *Journal of Personality and Social Psychology* 64, no. 1 (1993): 141–156.

Baumeister, Roy F., Kathleen D. Vohs, and David C. Funder, "Psychology as the Science of Self-Reports and Finger Movements: Whatever Happened to Actual Behavior?" *Perspectives on Psychological Science* 2, no. 4 (2007): 396–403.

Baxter, Brent. "Problems in the Planning of Psychological Experiments." *The American Journal of Psychology* 54, no. 2 (1941): 270–280.

Bayer, Ronald. *Homosexuality and American Psychiatry: The Politics of Diagnosis*. Princeton, NJ: Princeton University Press, 1987.

Baynton, Douglas C. *Defectives in the Land: Disability and Immigration in the Age of Eugenics*. Chicago: University of Chicago Press, 2016.

Beaulieu, Anne. "Voxels in the Brain: Neuroscience, Informatics and Changing Notions of Objectivity." *Social Studies of Science* 31, no. 5 (2001): 635–680.

Beauvais, Clémentine. "The 'Mozart Effect': A Sociological Reappraisal." *Cultural Sociology* 9, no. 2 (2015): 185–202.

Beck, Aaron T. "Thinking and Depression: I. Idiosyncratic Content and Cognitive Distortions." *Archives of General Psychiatry* 9, no. 4 (1963): 324–333, 328.

Beck, Aaron T., Calvin H. Ward, Mock Mendelson, Jeremiah Mock, and John Erbaugh. "An Inventory for Measuring Depression." *Archives of General Psychiatry* 4, no. 6 (1961): 561–571.

Beck, Ulrich. *Risk Society: Towards a New Modernity*. Thousand Oaks, CA: SAGE, 1992.

Becker, Dana. *The Myth of Empowerment: Women and the Therapeutic Culture in America*. New York: New York University Press, 2005.

Behnke, Stephen. "Ethics and Interrogations: Comparing and Contrasting the American Psychological, American Medical and American Psychiatric Association positions." *APA Monitor* 37, no. 7 (2006): 66.

Behnke, Stephen. "Psychological Ethics and National Security: The Position of the American Psychological Association." *European Psychologist* 11, no. 2 (2006): 153–155.

Bem Daryl J. "Feeling the Future: Experimental Evidence for Anomalous Retroactive Influences on Cognition and Affect." *Journal of Personality and Social Psychology* 100, no. 3 (2011): 407–425.

Bem, Daryl J. "Self-Perception." *Psychological Review* 74, no. 3 (1967): 183–200.

Bem, Sandra L., and Daryl J. Bem. "Does Sex-Biased Job Advertising 'Aid and Abet' Sex Discrimination?" *Journal of Applied Social Psychology* 3, no. 1 (1973): 6–18.

Benjamin, Ludy T., Jr. "A History of Clinical Psychology as a Profession in America (and a Glimpse at Its Future)." *Annual Review of Clinical Psychology* 1 (2005): 1–30, 10–14.

Benjamin, Ludy T., Jr., and Ellen M. Crouse. "The American Psychological Association's Response to *Brown v. Board of Education*: The Case of Kenneth B. Clark." *American Psychologist* 57, no. 1 (2002): 38–50.

Benjamin, Ruha. *Race after Technology: Abolitionist Tools for the New Jim Code*. Cambridge: Polity, 2019.

Bennett, Chester. "Community Psychology: Impressions of the Boston Conference on the Education of Psychologists for Community Mental Health," *American Psychologist* 20, no. 10 (1965): 832–835.

Berlant, Lauren. *Cruel Optimism*. Durham, NC: Duke University Press, 2011.

Berlyne, David E. "American and European Psychology." *American Psychologist* 23, no. 6 (1968): 447–452.

Bibace, Roger, Joshua W. Clegg, and Jaan Valsiner. "What Is in a Name? Understanding the Implications of Participant Terminology." *Integrative Psychological and Behavioral Science* 43, no. 1 (2009): 67–77.

Bilalić, Merim, Kieran Smallbone, Peter McLeod, and Fernand Gobet. "Why Are (the Best) Women So Good at Chess? Participation Rates and Gender Differences in Intellectual Domains." *Proceedings of the Royal Society B: Biological Sciences* 276, no. 1659 (2009): 1161–1165.

Billig, Michael. *Banal Nationalism*. Thousand Oaks, CA: Sage, 1995.

Bishop, Dorothy. "Quality and Longevity." *The Psychologist* 29, no. 7 (2016): 578–579.

Bivins, Roberta E. *Contagious Communities: Medicine, Migration, and the NHS in Postwar Britain*. New York: Oxford University Press, 2015.

Bjork, Robert A., and Stephen J. Ceci. "The Birth of *Psychological Science in the Public Interest*," *APS Observer*, 13 (2000): 5-14.

Blanton, Hart, James Jaccard, Jonathan Klick, Barbara Mellers, Gregory Mitchell, and Philip E. Tetlock. "Strong Claims and Weak Evidence: Reassessing the Predictive Validity of the IAT." *Journal of Applied Psychology* 94, no. 3 (2009): 567–582.

Blau, Theodore. "APA Commission on Accelerating Black Participation in Psychology." *American Psychologist* 25, no. 12 (1970): 1103–1104.

Boden, Margaret A. *Mind as Machine: A History of Cognitive Science*. Oxford: Oxford University Press, 2006.

Boffey, Philip M. "California: Reagan and the Mental Health Controversy." *Science* 161, no. 3848 (1968): 1329–1331.

Bolman, William M. "Community Control of the Community Mental Health Center: II. Case Examples." *American Journal of Psychiatry* 129, no. 2 (1972): 181–186.

Bonanno, George A., Sandro Galea, Angela Bucciarelli, and David Vlahov. "Psychological Resilience after Disaster: New York City in the Aftermath of the September 11th Terrorist Attack." *Psychological Science* 17, no. 3 (2006): 181–186.

Borck, Cornelius. "Recording the Brain at Work: The Visible, the Readable, and the Invisible in Electroencephalography." *Journal of the History of the Neurosciences* 17, no. 3 (2008): 367–379.

Bouk, Dan. "The History and Political Economy of Personal Data over the Last Two Centuries in Three Acts." *Osiris* 32, no. 1 (2017): 85–106.

Boyer, Paul. *By the Bomb's Early Light: American Thought and Culture at the Dawn of the Atomic Age.* New York: Pantheon, 1985.

Brancale, Ralph, Albert Ellis, and Ruth R. Doorbar. "Psychiatric and Psychological Investigations of Convicted Sex Offenders: A Summary Report." *American Journal of Psychiatry* 109, no. 1 (1952): 17–21.

Branden, Nathaniel. "The Benefits and Hazards of the Philosophy of Ayn Rand: A Personal Statement." *Journal of Humanistic Psychology* 24, no. 4 (1984): 39–64.

Branden, Nathaniel. *The Psychology of Self-Esteem: A New Concept of Man's Psychological Nature.* New York: Bantam Books, 1969.

Brattain, Michelle. "Race, Racism, and Antiracism: UNESCO and the Politics of Presenting Science to the Postwar Public." *American Historical Review* 112, no. 5 (2007): 1386–1413.

Brentar, John, and John McNamara. "The Right to Prescribe Medication: Considerations for Professional Psychology." *Professional Psychology: Research and Practice* 22, no. 3 (1991): 179–187.

Brickman, Philip, Dan Coates, and Ronnie Janoff-Bulman. "Lottery Winners and Accident Victims: Is Happiness Relative?" *Journal of Personality and Social Psychology* 36, no. 8 (1978): 917–927.

Bridgman, Todd, Stephen Cummings, and John Ballard. "Who Built Maslow's Pyramid? A History of the Creation of Management Studies' Most Famous Symbol and Its Implications for Management Education." *Academy of Management Learning and Education* 18, no. 1 (2019): 81–98.

Brinkmann, Svend, and Steinar Kvale. "Confronting the Ethics of Qualitative Research," *Journal of Constructivist Psychology* 18, no. 2 (2005): 157–181.

Broadbent, Donald. E. "Attention and the Perception of Speech." *Scientific American* 206(4) (1962): 143–153.

Broadbent, Donald. E. "Donald E. Broadbent." In Gardner Lindzey, *A History of Psychology in Autobiography* vol. 7. New York: Freeman, 1980, 39–73.

Broadbent, Donald E. "Failures of Attention in Selective Listening." *Journal of Experimental Psychology* 44, no. 6 (1952): 428–433.

Broadbent, Donald. E. "Information Theory and Older Approaches in Psychology." *Proceedings of the 15th International Congress of Psychology, Brussels, Belgium* (1957):111–115.

Broadbent, Donald E. "Listening to One of Two Synchronous Messages." *Journal of Experimental Psychology* 44, no. 1 (1952): 51–55.

Broadbent, Donald. E. "A Mechanical Model for Human Attention and Immediate Memory." *Psychological Review* 64, no. 3 (1957): 205–215.

Broadbent, Donald E. "Psychologists: Gentlemen or Players," *Bulletin of the British Psychological Society* 26, no. 91 (1973): 134–135.

Broadbent, Donald E. "The Role of Auditory Localization in Attention and Memory Span." *Journal of Experimental Psychology* 47, no. 3 (1954): 191–196.

Broadbent, Donald E. "Some Effects of Noise on Visual Performance." *Quarterly Journal of Experimental Psychology* 6, no. 1 (1954): 1–5.

Broadbent, Donald E. "Speaking and Listening Simultaneously." *Journal of Experimental Psychology* 43, no. 4 (1952): 267–273.

Bronstein, Carolyn. *Battling Pornography: The American Feminist Anti-Pornography Movement, 1976–1986*. Cambridge: Cambridge University Press, 2011.

Brooks, Rodney A. "Intelligence without Representation." *Artificial Intelligence* 47, no. 1–3 (1991): 139–159.

Brown, Kate. "Gridded Lives: Why Kazakhstan and Montana Are Nearly the Same Place. *American Historical Review*, 106, no. 1 (2001): 17–48.

Brumberg, Joan Jacobs. *Fasting Girls: The Emergence of Anorexia Nervosa As a Modern Disease*. Cambridge, MA: Harvard University Press, 1988.

Bruner, Jerome S. "Another Look at New Look 1." *American Psychologist* 47, no. 6 (1992): 780–783.

Bruner, Jerome S. "The Course of Cognitive Growth." *American Psychologist* 19, no. 1 (1964): 1–15.

Bruner, Jerome S. "Jerome S. Bruner," in Gardner Lindzey (ed.), *A History of Psychology in Autobiography*, vol. 4. San Francisco: W. H. Freeman, 1980, 75–151.

Bruner, Jerome S. "IV. Perceptual Theory and the Rorschach Test," *Journal of Personality* 17, no. 2 (1948): 157–168.

Bruner, Jerome S. "On Perceptual Readiness." *Psychological Review* 64, no. 2 (1957): 123–152.

Bruner, Jerome S., and Cecile C. Goodman, "Value and Need as Organizing Factors in Perception." *Journal of Abnormal and Social Psychology* 42, no. 1 (1947): 33–44.

Bruner, Jerome S., Jacquelin J. Goodnow, and George A. Austin. *A Study of Thinking*. New York: Wiley, 1956.

Bruner Jerome S., and Leo Postman. "Emotional Selectivity in Perception and Reaction." *Journal of Personality* 16, no. 1 (1947): 69–77.

Bruner, Jerome S., and Renato Tagiuri. "The Perception of People." In Gardner Lindzey (ed.), *The Handbook of Social Psychology*, vol. 2. Cambridge, MA: Addison-Wesley, 1954, 634–654.

Buchanan, Roderick D. "Legislative Warriors: American Psychiatrists, Psychologists, and Competing Claims over Psychotherapy in the 1950s." *Journal of the History of the Behavioral Sciences* 39, no. 3 (2003): 225–249.

Buchanan, Roderick D., Jr. "On Not "Giving Psychology Away": The Minnesota Multiphasic Personality Inventory and Public Controversy over Testing in the 1960s." *History of Psychology* 5, no. 3 (2002): 284–309.

Buhle. Mari Jo. *Feminism and Its Discontents: A Century of Struggle with Psychoanalysis*. Cambridge, MA: Harvard University Press, 2009, 206–239.

Buhrmester, Michael. Tracy Kwang, and Samuel D. Gosling, "Amazon's Mechanical Turk: A New Source of Inexpensive, Yet High-Quality, Data?" *Perspectives on Psychological Science* 6, no. 1 (2011): 3–5.

Burgin, Angus. *The Great Persuasion: Reinventing Free Markets since the Depression*. Cambridge, MA: Harvard University Press, 2012.

Burman, Jeremy T., Christopher D. Green, and Stuart Shanker. "On the Meanings of Self-Regulation: Digital Humanities in Service of Conceptual Clarity." *Child Development* 86, no. 5 (2015): 1507–1521.

Burns, Edwin J., Taylor Arnold, and Cindy M. Bukach. "P-curving the Fusiform Face Area: Meta-Analyses Support the Expertise Hypothesis." *Neuroscience and Biobehavioral Reviews* 104 (2019): 209–221.

Burns, Jennifer. *Goddess of the Market: Ayn Rand and the American Right*. Oxford: Oxford University Press, 2009.

Bushman, Brad J., and Roy F. Baumeister. "Threatened Egotism, Narcissism, Self-Esteem, and Direct and Displaced Aggression: Does Self-Love or Self-Hate Lead to Violence?" *Journal of Personality and Social Psychology* 75, no. 1 (1998): 219–229.

California Task Force to Promote Self-Esteem and Personal and Social Responsibility. *Toward a State of Self-esteem*. Sacramento: California State Department of Education, 1990, 42.

Campbell, Nancy D. *Discovering Addiction: The Science and Politics of Substance Abuse Research*. Ann Arbor: University of Michigan Press, 2007.

Canaday, Margot. *The Straight State: Sexuality and Citizenship in Twentieth-Century America*. Princeton, NJ: Princeton University Press, 2009.

Canales, Jimena. *A Tenth of a Second: A History*. Chicago: University of Chicago Press, 2010.

Capshew. James H. *Psychologists on the March: Science, Practice, and Professional Identity in America, 1929–1969*. Cambridge: Cambridge University Press, 1999.

Capshew, James H., and Ernest R. Hilgard. "The Power of Service: World War II and Professional Reform in the American Psychological Association." In Evans, Rand B.; Sexton, Virginia Staudt; Cadwallader, Thomas C. (eds.), *The American Psychological Association: A Historical Perspective*. Washington, DC: American Psychological Association, 1992, pp. 149–175.

Carey, Susan, and Rhea Diamond, "From Piecemeal to Configurational Representation of Faces." *Science* 195, no. 4275 (1977): 312–314.

Carlson, Rae. "Where Is the Person in Personality Research?" *Psychological Bulletin* 75, no. 3 (1971): 203–219.

Carney, Dana R., Amy J. C. Cuddy, and Andy J. Yap. "Power Posing: Brief Nonverbal Displays Affect Neuroendocrine Levels and Risk Tolerance." *Psychological Science* 21, no. 10 (2010): 1363–1368.

Carr, Danielle Judith Zola. "'Ghastly Marionettes' and the Political Metaphysics of Cognitive Liberalism: Anti-Behaviourism, Language, and the Origins of Totalitarianism." *History of the Human Sciences* 33, no. 1 (2020): 147–174.

Carroll, David W. *Purpose and Cognition: Edward Tolman and the Transformation of American Psychology*. New York: Cambridge University Press, 2017.

Carter, Evan C., and Michael E. McCullough, "Publication Bias and the Limited Strength Model of Self-Control: Has the Evidence for Ego Depletion Been Overestimated?" *Frontiers in Psychology* 5 (2014): 823.

Cautin, Robin L. "The Founding of the Association for Psychological Science: Part 1. Dialectical Tensions Within Organized Psychology." *Perspectives on Psychological Science* 4, no. 3 (2009): 211–223.

Chabris, Christopher F., and Mark E. Glickman. "Sex Differences in Intellectual Performance: Analysis of a Large Cohort of Competitive Chess Players." *Psychological Science* 17, no. 12 (2006): 1040–1046.

Chapanis Natalia P., and Alphonse Chapanis. "Cognitive Dissonance." *Psychological Bulletin* 61, no. 1 (1964): 1–22.

Chappell, Marisa. "Rethinking Women's Politics in the 1970s: The League of Women Voters and the National Organization for Women Confront Poverty." *Journal of Women's History* 13, no. 4 (2002): 155–179.

Charness, Neil. "The Impact of Chess Research on Cognitive Science." *Psychological Research* 54, no. 1 (1992): 4–9.

Charness, Neil, and Yigal Gerchak, "Participation Rates and Maximal Performance: A Log-Linear Explanation for Group Differences, such as Russian and Male Dominance in Chess." *Psychological Science* 7, no. 1 (1996): 46–51.

Chernus, Ira. "Operation Candor: Fear, Faith, and Flexibility." *Diplomatic History* 29, no. 5 (2005): 779–809.

Cherry, E. Colin. "Some Experiments on the Recognition of Speech, with One and with Two Ears." *Journal of the Acoustical Society of America* 25, no. 5 (1953): 975–979.

Cherry, Frances. *Stubborn Particulars of Social Psychology: Essays on the Research Process*. London: Routledge, 1995.

Cirino, Sérgio, Rodrigo Miranda, and Robson Cruz. "The Beginnings of Behavior Analysis Laboratories in Brazil: A Pedagogical View." *History of Psychology* 15, no. 3 (2012): 263–272.

Clark, Claire D. *The Recovery Revolution: The Battle over Addiction Treatment in the United States*. New York: Columbia University Press, 2017.

Clark, Kenneth B., and Mamie Clark. "The Development of Consciousness of Self and the Emergence of Racial Identification in Negro Preschool Children." *Journal of Social Psychology* 10, no. 4 (1939): 591–599.

Clark, Kenneth B., and Mamie Clark. "Racial Identification and Preference in Negro Children." In E. L. Hartley (ed.), *Readings in Social Psychology*. New York: Holt, Rinehart, and Winston, 1947, 169–178.

Clark, Kenneth B., and Mamie Clark. "Segregation as a Factor in the Racial Identification of Negro Pre-school Children: A Preliminary Report." *Journal of Experimental Education* 8, no. 2 (1939): 161–163.

Clark, Kenneth B., and Mamie Clark. "Skin Color As a Factor in Racial Identification of Negro Preschool Children." *Journal of Social Psychology* 11, no. 1 (1940): 159–169.

Clark, Kenneth E. "The APA Study of Psychologists." *American Psychologist* 9, no. 3 (1954): 117–120.

Clingempeel, W. Glenn, Edward Mulvey, and N. Dickon Reppucci. "A National Study of Ethical Dilemmas of Psychologists in the Criminal Justice System." In John Monahan (ed.), *Who Is the Client? The Ethics of Psychological Intervention in the Criminal Justice System*. Washington, DC: APA, 1980, 126–153.

Cohen-Cole, Jamie *The Open Mind: Cold War Politics and the Sciences of Human Nature*. Chicago: University of Chicago Press, 2014.

Cohn, Simon. "Making Objective Facts from Intimate Relations: The Case of Neuroscience and Its Entanglements with Volunteers." *History of the Human Sciences* 21, no. 4 (2008): 86–103.

Cole, Simon A. "From the Sexual Psychopath Statute to 'Megan's Law': Psychiatric Knowledge in the Diagnosis, Treatment, and Adjudication of Sex Criminals in New Jersey, 1949–1999." *Journal of the History of Medicine and Allied Sciences* 55, no. 3 (2000): 292–314.

Cole, Simon A. *Suspect Identities: A History of Fingerprinting and Criminal Identification*. Cambridge, MA: Harvard University Press, 2001.

Collins, Alan F. "An Intimate Connection: Oliver Zangwill and the Emergence of Neuropsychology in Britain." *History of Psychology* 9, no. 2 (2006): 89–112, 95–99.

Collins, Alan. "The Embodiment of Reconciliation: Order and Change in the Work of Frederic Bartlett." *History of Psychology* 9, no. 4 (2006): 290–312.

Collins, Alan. "From H=log s (n) to Conceptual Framework: A Short History of Information." *History of Psychology* 10, no. 1 (2007): 44–72.

Collins, Alan. "The Reputation of Kenneth James William Craik." *History of Psychology* 16, no. 2 (2013): 93–111.

Collins, Harry M. *Changing Order: Replication and Induction in Scientific Practice*. Chicago: University of Chicago Press, 1985.

Collins, James. "Taking the Lead: Dorothy Williams, NAACP Youth Councils, and Civil Rights Protests in Pittsburgh, 1961–1964." *Journal of African American History* 88, no. 2 (2003): 126–137.

Conn, Steven. "Back to the Garden: Communes, the Environment, and Antiurban Pastoralism at the End of the Sixties." *Journal of Urban History* 36, no. 6 (2010): 831–848.

Conrad, R. "Accuracy of Recall Using Keyset and Telephone Dial, and the Effect of a Prefix Digit." *Journal of Applied Psychology* 42, no. 4 (1958): 285–288.

Conrad, R. "Beyond Industrial Psychology." *Bulletin of the British Psychological Society* 20 (1967): 1–12.

Conrad, R. "Designing Postal Codes for Public Use." *Ergonomics* 10, no. 2 (1967): 233–238.

Conrad, R. "Experimental Psychology in the Field of Telecommunications." *Ergonomics* 3, no. 4 (1960): 289–295.

Conrad, R. "Let the Children Choose." *International Journal of Pediatric Otorhinolaryngology* 1, no. 4 (1980): 317–329.

Conrad, R. "Performance of Telephone Operators relative to Traffic Level." *Nature* 178, no. 4548 (1956): 1480–1481.

Conrad, R. "Short-Term Memory Processes in the Deaf." *British Journal of Psychology* 61, no. 2 (1970): 179–195.

Conrad, R., and Barbara A. Hille. "Memory for Long Telephone Numbers." *Post Office Telecommunications Journal* 10 (1957): 37–39.

Conrad, R., and Barbara A. Hille. "Telephone Operators' Adaptation to Traffic Variations." *Journal of the Institution of Electrical Engineers* 4 (1958): 10–14.

Conrad, R., and Audrey J. Hull. "Information, Acoustic Confusion and Memory Span." *British Journal of Psychology* 55, no. 4 (1964): 429–432.

Constantinople, Anne. "Masculinity-Femininity: An Exception to a Famous Dictum?" *Psychological Bulletin* 80, no. 5 (1973): 389–407.

Cooper, Melinda. *Family Values: Between Neoliberalism and the New Social Conservatism*. Cambridge, MA: MIT Press, 2017.

Coppersmith, Sheldon. *The Antecedents of Self-esteem*. San Francisco: W. H. Freeman, 1967.

Cortright, David. *Peace: A History of Movements and Ideas*. New York: Cambridge University Press, 2008.

Craik, K. J. W. "The Present Position of Psychological Research in Britain." *British Medical Bulletin* 3, no. 1–3 (1945): 24–26.

Crane, Jennifer. "'Save our NHS': Activism, Information-Based Expertise and the 'New Times' of the 1980s." *Contemporary British History* 33, no. 1 (2019): 52–74.

Crary, Jonathan. *Suspensions of Perception: Attention, Spectacle, and Modern Culture*. Cambridge, MA: MIT Press, 1999.

Crocker, Jennifer, and Brenda Major. "Social Stigma and Self-Esteem: The Self-Protective Properties of Stigma." *Psychological Review* 96, no. 4 (1989): 608–630.

Cronbach, Lee J. "The Two Disciplines of Scientific Psychology." *American Psychologist* 12, no. 11 (1957): 671–684.

Cross, William E., Jr. *Shades of Black: Diversity in African-American Identity*. Philadelphia: Temple University Press, 1991.

Crowley, Mark James. "Women Post Office Workers in Britain: The Long Struggle for Gender Equality and the Positive Impact of World War II." *Essays in Economic and Business History* 30 (2012): 77–92.

Crowther-Heyck, Hunter. *Herbert A. Simon: The Bounds of Reason in Modern America*. Baltimore: Johns Hopkins University Press, 2005.

Cruikshank, Barbara. *The Will to Empower: Democratic Citizens and Other Subjects*. Ithaca, NY: Cornell University Press, 1999.

Crutchfield, Richard S., and E. C. Tolman, "Multiple-Variable Design for Experiments Involving Interaction of Behavior." *Psychological Review* 47, no. 1 (1940): 38–42.

Cullen, Dallas. "Maslow, Monkeys and Motivation Theory." *Organization* 4, no. 3 (1997): 355–373.

Cullen, Elizabeth, and Russ Newman. "In Pursuit of Prescription Privileges." *Professional Psychology: Research and Practice* 28, no. 2 (1997): 101–106.

Cummings, Nicholas. "Impact of Managed Care on Employment and Training: A Primer for Survival." *Professional Psychology: Research and Practice* 26, no. 1 (1995): 10–15, 12.

Cushman, Philip. *Constructing the Self, Constructing America: A Cultural History of Psychotherapy*. Reading, MA: Addison-Wesley, 1995;

Cvetkovich, Ann. *Archive of Feelings*. Durham, NC: Duke University Press, 2003.

Danziger, Kurt. *Constructing the Subject: Historical Origins of Psychological Research*. New York: Cambridge University Press, 1990.

Danziger, Kurt. "Universalism and Indigenization in the History of Modern Psychology" in Adrian Brock (ed.), *Internationalizing the History of Psychology*. New York: New York University Press, 2006, 208–225.

Davenport, Thomas H., and John C. Beck. *The Attention Economy: Understanding the New Currency of Business*. Cambridge, MA: Harvard Business Press, 2001.

Davies, William. *The Happiness Industry: How the Government and Big Business Sold Us Well-Being*. London: Verso Books, 2015.

Davis, D. Russell. "The Disorganization of Behaviour in Fatigue." *Journal of Neurology, Neurosurgery, and Psychiatry* 9, no. 1 (1946): 23–29.

Davison, Gerald. "Homosexuality: The Ethical Challenge." *Journal of Consulting and Clinical Psychology* 44, no. 2 (1976): 157–162.

Davison, Kate. "Cold War Pavlov: Homosexual Aversion Therapy in the 1960s." *History of the Human Sciences* 34, no. 1 (2021): 89–119.

Dawes Robyn M., and Bernard Corrigan. "Linear Models in Decision Making." *Psychological Bulletin* 81, no. 2 (1974): 95–106.

De Grazia, Victoria. *Irresistible Empire: America's Advance through Twentieth-Century Europe*. Cambridge, MA: Harvard University Press, 2005.

De Laet, Marianne, and Annemarie Mol. "The Zimbabwe Bush Pump: Mechanics of a Fluid Technology." *Social Studies of Science* 30, no. 2 (2000): 225–263.

DeLeon, Patrick. "Psychology and the Carter Administration." *American Psychologist* 32, no. 9 (1977): 750–751.

DeLeon, Patrick H., and Jack Donahue. "Overview: The Growing Impact of Organized Psychology in the Judicial System." *Psychotherapy in Private Practice* 1, no.1 (1982): 109–122.

DeLeon, Patrick, Anne O'Keefe, Gary VandenBos, and Alan Kraut. "How to Influence Public Policy: A Blueprint for Activism." *American Psychologist* 37, no. 5 (1982): 476–485.

DeLeon, Patrick, Gary VandenBos, and Alan Kraut. "Federal Legislation Recognizing Psychology." *American Psychologist* 39, no. 9 (1984): 933–946.

Denning, Michael. *The Cultural Front: The Laboring of American Culture in the Twentieth Century*. London: Verso, 1997.

Derksen, Maarten. "Putting Popper to Work." *Theory and Psychology* 29, no. 4 (2019): 449–465.

Desjarlais, Robert R. *Counterplay: An Anthropologist at the Chessboard*. Berkeley: University of California Press, 2011.

Diamond, Lisa M., and Clifford J. Rosky. "Scrutinizing Immutability: Research on Sexual Orientation and US Legal Advocacy for Sexual Minorities." *Journal of Sex Research* 53, no. 4–5 (2016): 363–391.

Diamond, Rhea, and Susan Carey. "Why Faces Are and Are Not Special: An Effect of Expertise." *Journal of Experimental Psychology: General* 115, no. 2 (1986): 107–117.

Dietrich, Christopher R. W. *Oil Revolution: Anticolonial Elites, Sovereign Rights, and the Economic Culture of Decolonization*. New York: Cambridge University Press, 2017.

DiGiuseppe, Raymond A., Norman J. Miller, and Larry D. Trexler, "A Review of Rational-Emotive Psychotherapy Outcome Studies." *The Counseling Psychologist* 7, no. 1 (1977): 64–72.

Dittmann, Melissa. "Psychological Science Offers Clues to Iraqi Prisoner Abuse." *APA Monitor* 35, no. 7 (July/August 2004): 13

Dittmann, Melissa. "What Makes Good People Do Bad Things." *APA Monitor* 35, no. 9 (October 2004): 68.

Dodge, Raymond. "An Improved Exposure Apparatus." *Psychological Bulletin* 4, no. 1 (1907): 10–13.

Downey, Gary Lee, Joseph Dumit, and Sharon Traweek. "Corridor Talk." In *Cyborgs & Citadels: Anthropological Interventions in Emerging Sciences and Technologies*, Joseph Dumit and Gary Lee Downey (eds.). Santa Fe: School of American Research Press, 1998, 245–264.

Downing, Lisa, Iain Morland, and Nikki Sullivan, *Fuckology: Critical Essays on John Money's Diagnostic Concepts*. Chicago: University of Chicago Press, 2015.

Doyen, Stéphane, Olivier Klein, Cora-Lise Pichon, and Axel Cleeremans, "Behavioral Priming: It's All in the Mind, but Whose Mind?" *PloS One* 7, no. 1 (2012): e29081.

Doyle, Dennis. "'Where the Need Is Greatest': Social Psychiatry and Race-Blind Universalism in Harlem's Lafargue Clinic, 1946–1958." *Bulletin of the History of Medicine* (2009): 746–774.

Draaisma, Douwe. *Metaphors of Memory: A History of Ideas about the Mind*. Cambridge: Cambridge University Press, 2000.

Dreber, Anna, Thomas Pfeiffer, Johan Almenberg, Siri Isaksson, Brad Wilson, Yiling Chen, Brian A. Nosek, and Magnus Johannesson. "Using Prediction Markets to

Estimate the Reproducibility of Scientific Research." *Proceedings of the National Academy of Sciences* 112, no. 50 (2015): 15343–15347.

Duckworth, Angela L., Christopher Peterson, Michael D. Matthews, and Dennis R. Kelly. "Grit: Perseverance and Passion for Long-Term Goals." *Journal of Personality and Social Psychology* 92, no. 6 (2007): 1087–1101.

Duckworth, Angela L., and Martin E. Seligman, "Self-discipline Outdoes IQ in Predicting Academic Performance of Adolescents." *Psychological Science* 16, no. 12 (2005): 939–944.

Dumit, Joseph. *Picturing Personhood: Brain Scans and Biomedical Identity*. Princeton, NJ: Princeton University Press, 2004.

Dumit, Joseph. "Plastic Diagrams: Circuits in the Brain and How They Got There." In David Bates and Nima Bassiri (eds.), *Plasticity and Pathology: On the Formation of the Neural Subject*. New York: Fordham University Press, 2016, 219–268.

Dunivin, Debra Lina. "Experiences of a Department of Defense Proscribing Psychologist: A Personal Account." In Morgan T. Sammons, Ruth Ullmann Ed Paige, and Ronald F. Levant (eds.), *Prescriptive Authority for Psychologists: A History and Guide*. Washington, DC: APA, 2003, 103–115.

D'Zurilla, Thomas, and Marvin Goldfried. "Problem Solving and Behavior Modification." *Journal of Abnormal Psychology* 78, no. 1 (1971): 107–126.

Easterlin, Richard A. "Does Economic Growth Improve the Human Lot? Some Empirical Evidence." In P. A. David and M. W. Reder (eds.), *Nations and Households in Economic Growth*. New York: Academic Press, 1974, 89–125.

Eberhardt, Jennifer L., Paul G. Davies, Valerie J. Purdie-Vaughns, and Sheri Lynn Johnson. "Looking Deathworthy: Perceived Stereotypicality of Black Defendants Predicts Capital-Sentencing Outcomes." *Psychological Science* 17, no. 5 (2006): 383–386.

Edgerton, David. "The 'White Heat' Revisited: The British Government and Technology in the 1960s." *Twentieth Century British History* 7, no. 1 (1996): 53–82.

Edgerton, David. *Warfare State: Britain, 1920–1970*. Cambridge: Cambridge University Press, 2005.

Edwards, Paul N. *Closed World: Computers and the Politics of Discourse in Cold War America*. Cambridge, MA: MIT Press, 1996.

Eghigian, Greg. "Deinstitutionalizing the History of Contemporary Psychiatry." *History of Psychiatry* 22, no. 2 (2011): 201–214.

Eglash, Ron. "Broken Metaphor: The Master–Slave Analogy in Technical Literature." *Technology and Culture* 48, no. 2 (2007): 360–369.

Ekman, Paul, and Wallace V. Friesen. *Facial Action Coding System*. Washington, DC: Consulting Psychologists Press, 1978.

Elias, Gabriel. "A Clinician Answers Guthrie." *American Psychologist* 5, no. 9 (1950): 495.

Ellis, Albert. "Are Homosexuals Necessarily Neurotic?" *One: The Homosexual Magazine* 3, no. 4 (1955): 8–12.

Ellis, Albert. "A Weekend of Rational Encounter." *Rational Living* 4, no. 2 (1969): 1–8.

Ellis, Albert. "Changing Rational-Emotive Therapy (RET) to Rational Emotive Behavior Therapy (REBT)." *Journal of Rational-Emotive and Cognitive-Behavior Therapy* 13, no. 2 (1995): 85–89.

Ellis, Albert. "Homosexuality: The Right to Be Wrong," *Journal of Sex Research* 4, no. 2 (1968): 96–107.

Ellis, Albert. *Is Objectivism a Religion?* New York: Lyle Stuart, 1968.

Ellis, Albert. "On the Cure of Homosexuality." *International Journal of Sexology* 55 (1952): 135–138.
Ellis, Albert. "Outcome of Employing Three Techniques of Psychotherapy." *Journal of Clinical Psychology* 13 (1957): 344–350.
Ellis, Albert. "Questionnaire versus Interview Methods in the Study of Human Love Relationships." *American Sociological Review* 12, no. 5 (1947): 541–553.
Ellis, Albert. "Rational-Emotive Therapy and Cognitive Behavior Therapy: Similarities and Differences." *Cognitive Therapy and Research* 4, no. 4 (1980): 325–340.
Ellis, Albert. "Rational Psychotherapy." *Journal of General Psychology* 59 (1958): 35–49, 35.
Ellis, Albert. "The Effectiveness of Psychotherapy with Individuals Who Have Severe Homosexual Problems." *Journal of Consulting Psychology* 20 (1956): 191–195.
Ellis, Albert. "The Private Practice of Psychotherapy: A Clinical Psychologist's Report." *Journal of General Psychology* 58 (1958): 207–216.
Ellis, Albert. *Reason and Emotion in Psychotherapy*. New York: Lyle Stuart, 1962.
Ellis, Hadyn D. "Recognizing Faces." *British Journal of Psychology* 66, no. 4 (1975): 409–426.
Engerman, David C. "Social Science in the Cold War." *Isis* 101, no. 2 (2010): 393–400.
Enns, Anthony. "Visualizing Thoughts: Photography, Neurology and Neuroimaging," in Schlicht, Laurens, Carla Seemann, and Christian Kassung (eds.) *Mind Reading as a Cultural Practice*. New York: Palgrave Macmillan, 2020, 63–91.
Ensmenger, Nathan. "Is Chess the Drosophila of Artificial Intelligence? A Social History of an Algorithm." *Social Studies of Science* 42, no. 1 (2012): 5–30.
Epstein, Robert. "Giving Psychology Away: A Personal Journey." *Perspectives on Psychological Science* 1, no. 4 (2006): 389–400.
Erickson, Paul. *The World the Game Theorists Made*. Chicago: University of Chicago Press, 2015.
Erickson, Paul, Judy L. Klein, Lorraine Daston, Rebecca Lemov, Thomas Sturm, and Michael D. Gordin. *How Reason Almost Lost Its Mind: The Strange Career of Cold War Rationality*. Chicago: University of Chicago Press, 2013.
Ericsson, Kai, and Herbert Simon, "Verbal Reports as Data." *Psychological Review* 87, no. 3 (1980): 215–251.
Ervin, Sam. "Why Senate Hearings on Psychological Tests in Government." *American Psychologist* 20, no. 11 (1965): 879–880.
Esterberg, Kristin Gay. "From Illness to Action: Conceptions of Homosexuality in *The Ladder*, 1956-1965." *Journal of Sex Research* 27, no. 1 (1990): 65–80, 74.
Eyal, Gil. *The Autism Matrix*. London: Polity, 2010.
Eysenck, Hans J. "The Effects of Psychotherapy: An Evaluation." *Journal of Consulting Psychology* 16, no. 5 (1952): 319–324.
Fantz, Robert L. "Visual Experience in Infants: Decreased Attention to Familiar Patterns Relative to Novel Ones." *Science* 146, no. 3644 (1964): 668–670.
Farmer, Ashley D. *Remaking Black Power: How Black Women Transformed an Era*. Chapel Hill: University of North Carolina Press Books, 2017.
Fassin, Didier, and Richard Rechtman. *The Empire of Trauma: An Inquiry into the Condition of Victimhood*. Princeton, NJ: Princeton University Press, 2009.
Faye, Cathy. "American Social Psychology: Examining the Contours of the 1970s Crisis." *Studies in History and Philosophy of Science Part C: Studies in History and Philosophy of Biological and Biomedical Sciences* 43, no. 2 (2012): 514–521.

Feldstein, Ruth. *Motherhood in Black and White: Race and Sex in American Liberalism, 1930–1965*. Ithaca, NY: Cornell University Press, 2000.
Festinger, Leon, and James M. Carlsmith. "Cognitive Consequences of Forced Compliance." *Journal of Abnormal and Social Psychology* 58, no. 2 (1959): 203–210.
Fichter, Manfred, and Hans-Ulrich Wittchen. "Clinical Psychology and Psychotherapy: A Survey of the Present State of Professionalization in 23 Countries." *American Psychologist* 35, no. 1 (1980): 16–25.
Finison, Lorenz J. "Psychologists and Spain." *American Psychologist* 32, no. 12 (1977): 1080–1084.
Finison, Lorenz J. "The Psychological Insurgency: 1936–1945." *Journal of Social Issues* 42, no. 1 (1986): 21–33.
Finucane, Melissa L. Ali Alhakami, Paul Slovic, and Stephen M. Johnson. "The Affect Heuristic in Judgments of Risks and Benefits." *Journal of Behavioral Decision Making* 13, no. 1 (2000): 1–17.
Fischhoff, Baruch. "An Early History of Hindsight Research." *Social Cognition* 25 (2007): 10–13.
Fischhoff, Baruch. "Hindsight Is Not Equal to Foresight: The Effect of Outcome Knowledge on Judgment under Uncertainty." *Journal of Experimental Psychology: Human Perception and Performance* 1, no. 3 (1975): 288–299.
Fischhoff, Baruch, Paul Slovic, and Sarah Lichtenstein. "Knowing with Certainty: The Appropriateness of Extreme Confidence." *Journal of Experimental Psychology: Human Perception and Performance* 3, no. 4 (1977): 552–564.
Fischhoff, Baruch, Paul Slovic, and Sarah Lichtenstein. "Weighing the Risks: Risks: Benefits which Risks Are Acceptable?" *Environment: Science and Policy for Sustainable Development* 21, no. 4 (1979): 17–38.
Fischhoff, Baruch, Paul Slovic, Sarah Lichtenstein, Stephen Read, and Barbara Combs. "How Safe Is Safe Enough? A Psychometric Study of Attitudes towards Technological Risks and Benefits." *Policy Sciences* 9, no. 2 (1978): 127–152.
Fiske, Susan T., Baruch Fischhoff, and Michael A. Milburn. "Images of Nuclear War." *Journal of Social Issues* 39, no. 1 (1983): 1–197.
Fleck, Christian. *A Transatlantic History of the Social Sciences: Robber Barons, the Third Reich and the Invention of Empirical Social Research*. London: Bloomsbury, 2011.
Fogg, B. J. *Persuasive Technology: Using Computers to Change What We Think and Do*. Burlington, MA: Morgan Kaufmann, 2003.
Forman, Paul. "The Primacy of Science in Modernity, of Technology in Postmodernity, and of Ideology in the History of Technology." *History and Technology* 23, no. 1–2 (2007): 1–152.
Forrester, John. "If p, Then What? Thinking in Cases." *History of the Human Sciences* 9, no. 3 (1996): 1–25.
Forrester, Katrina. *In the Shadow of Justice: Postwar Liberalism and the Remaking of Political Philosophy*. Princeton, NJ: Princeton University Press, 2019.
Fourcade, Marion, and Rakesh Khurana. "From Social Control to Financial Economics: The Linked Ecologies of Economics and Business in Twentieth Century America." *Theory and Society* 42, no. 2 (2013): 121–159.

Fox Lee, Shayna. "Psychology's Own Mindfulness: Ellen Langer and the Social Politics of Scientific Interest in 'Active Noticing.'" *Journal of the History of the Behavioral Sciences* 55, no. 3 (2019): 216–229.

Frankfurt, Harry G. *On Bullshit*. Princeton, NJ: Princeton University Press, 2009.

Fraterrigo, Elizabeth. *Playboy and the Making of the Good Life in Modern America*. Oxford: Oxford University Press, 2009.

Freedman, Estelle B. "'Uncontrolled Desires': The Response to the Sexual Psychopath, 1920–1960." *Journal of American History* 74, no. 1 (1987): 83–106.

Frenkel-Brunswik, Else. "Intolerance of Ambiguity as an Emotional and Perceptual Personality Variable." *Journal of Personality* 18, no. 1 (1949): 108–143.

Frenkel-Brunswik, Else. "Psychoanalysis and Personality Research." *Journal of Abnormal and Social Psychology* 35, no. 2 (1940): 176–197, 192.

Fuechtner, Veronika. "Indians, Jews, and Sex: Magnus Hirschfeld and Indian Sexology." Fuechtner, Veronika, and Mary Rhiel (eds.) in *Imagining Germany, Imagining Asia: Essays in Asian-German Studies*. Rochester, NY: Camden House, 2013, 111–30.

Gailliot, Matthew T., Roy F. Baumeister, C. Nathan Dewall, Jon K. Maner, E. Ashby Plant, Dianne M. Tice, Lauren E. Brewer, and Brandon J. Schmeichel. "Self-Control Relies on Glucose as a Limited Energy Source: Willpower Is More than a Metaphor." *Journal of Personality and Social Psychology* 92, no. 2 (2007): 325–336.

Galison, Peter. "Image of Self." On Lorraine Daston (ed.), *Things That Talk: Object Lessons from Art and Science*. Cambridge, MA: MIT Press, 2004, 257–296.

Galison, Peter. "The Ontology of the Enemy: Norbert Wiener and the Cybernetic Vision." *Critical Inquiry* 21, no. 1 (1994): 228–266;

Galison, Peter. "Secrecy in Three Acts." *Social Research* 77, no. 3 (2010): 970–974.

Gardner, Howard. *The Mind's New Science: A History of the Cognitive Revolution*. New York: Basic Books, 1985.

Garland, David. *The Culture of Control: Crime and Social Order in Contemporary Society*. Chicago: University of Chicago Press, 2002.

Gates, Kelly A. *Our Biometric Future: Facial Recognition Technology and the Culture of Surveillance*. New York: New York University Press, 2011.

Gaudet, Loren. "'Even Heroes Get Depressed': Sponsorship and Self-Stigma in Canada's Mental Illness Awareness Week." *Journal of Medical Humanities* 40, no. 2 (2019): 155–170.

Gauthier, Isabel, Pawel Skudlarski, John C. Gore, and Adam W. Anderson. "Expertise for Cars and Birds Recruits Brain Areas Involved in Face Recognition." *Nature Neuroscience* 3, no. 2 (2000): 191–197.

Gauthier, Isabel, and Michael J. Tarr, "Becoming a 'Greeble' Expert: Exploring Mechanisms for Face Recognition." *Vision Research* 37, no. 12 (1997): 1673–1682.

Gerard, Harold B., and Grover C. Mathewson. "The Effects of Severity of Initiation on Liking for a Group: A Replication." *Journal of Experimental Social Psychology* 2, no. 3 (1966): 278–287.

Gergen, Kenneth J. "Social Psychology as History." *Journal of Personality and Social Psychology* 26, no. 2 (1973): 309–320.

Gervers, John H. "The NIMBY Syndrome: Is It Inevitable?" *Environment: Science and Policy for Sustainable Development* 29, no. 8 (1987): 18–43.

Geuter, Ulfried. *The Professionalization of Psychology in Nazi Germany*. Translated by Richard J. Holmes. 1984. New York Cambridge University Press, 1992.

Gibbons, Michelle. "Attaining Landmark Status: Rumelhart and McClelland's PDP Volumes and the Connectionist Paradigm." *Journal of the History of the Behavioral Sciences* 55, no. 1 (2019): 54–70.

Gieryn, Thomas F. *Cultural Boundaries of Science: Credibility on the Line.* Chicago: University of Chicago Press, 1999.

Gigerenzer, Gerd. "From Tools to Theories: A Heuristic of Discovery in Cognitive Psychology." *Psychological Review* 98, no. 2 (1991): 254–267.

Gigerenzer, Gerd. "How to Make Cognitive Illusions Disappear: Beyond 'Heuristics and Biases.'" *European Review of Social Psychology* 2, no. 1 (1991): 83–115.

Gigerenzer, Gerd. "Mindless Statistics." *Journal of Socio-Economics* 33, no. 5 (2004): 587–606.

Gigerenzer, Gerd, and Henry Brighton. "Homo heuristicus: Why Biased Minds Make Better Inferences." *Topics in Cognitive Science* 1, no. 1 (2009): 107–143.

Gigerenzer, Gerd, and Julian N. Marewski. "Surrogate Science: The Idol of a Universal Method for Scientific Inference." *Journal of Management* 41, no. 2 (2015): 421–440.

Gigerenzer, Gerd, Zeno Swijtink, Theodore Porter, Lorraine Daston, and Lorenz Kruger. *The Empire of Chance: How Probability Changed Science and Everyday Life.* Cambridge: Cambridge University Press, 1989

Gilbert, Daniel T., Gary King, Stephen Pettigrew, and Timothy D. Wilson. "Comment on 'Estimating the Reproducibility of Psychological Science.'" *Science* 351, no. 6277 (2016): 1037a.

Gilligan, Carol. *In a Different Voice: Psychological Theory and Women's Development.* Cambridge, MA: Harvard University Press, 1982.

Gilligan, Carol. "Reply." *Signs* 11, no. 2 (1986): 324–333.

Gilligan, Carol, and Mary Field Belenky. "A Naturalistic Study of Abortion Decisions." *New Directions for Child and Adolescent Development*, no. 7 (1980): 69–90.

Gilliom, John. *Overseers of the Poor: Surveillance, Resistance, and the Limits of Privacy.* Chicago: University of Chicago Press, 2001.

Gilovich, Thomas, Robert Vallone, and Amos Tversky. "The Hot Hand in Basketball: On the Misperception of Random Sequences." *Cognitive Psychology* 17, no. 3 (1985): 295–314.

Gil-Riaño, Sebastián. "Relocating Anti-Racist Science: The 1950 UNESCO Statement on Race and Economic Development in the Global South." *British Journal for the History of Science* 51, no. 2 (2018): 281–303.

Gilroy, Paul. *'There Ain't No Black in the Union Jack': The Cultural Politics of Race and Nation.* Chicago: University of Chicago Press, 1991.

Gitre, Edward J. "The Great Escape: World War II, Neo-Freudianism, and the Origins of US Psychocultural Analysis." *Journal of the History of the Behavioral Sciences* 47, no. 1 (2011), 18–43.

Glenn, Susan A. "The Vogue of Jewish Self-Hatred in Post-World War II America." *Jewish Social Studies* (2006): 95–136.

Goldberg, Lewis R. "Man versus Model of Man: A Rationale, Plus Some Evidence, for a Method of Improving on Clinical Inferences." *Psychological Bulletin* 73, no. 6 (1970): 422–432.

Goldfried, Marvin R. "Systematic Desensitization as Training in Self-Control." *Journal of Consulting and Clinical Psychology* 37, no. 2 (1971): 228–234.

Goldiamond, Israel. "Indicators of Perception: I. Subliminal Perception, Subception, Unconscious Perception: An Analysis in Terms of Psychophysical Indicator Methodology." *Psychological Bulletin* 55, no. 6 (1958): 373–411.

Goldman, Ruth, and William Goldman. *Passing the Torch: Supporting Tomorrow's Leaders*. Lanham, MD: Hamilton Books, 2018.

Goldman, William. "San Francisco Westside: A Community Mental Health Center Serves the People." *Mental Health Program Reports* 5 (1971): 174–187.

Goleman, Daniel. *Emotional Intelligence: Why It Can Matter More Than IQ*. New York: Bantam, 1995.

Golin, Sanford, Eugene Davis, Edward Zuckerman, and Nelson Harrison. "Psychology in the Community: Project Self-esteem." *Psychological Reports* 26, no. 3 (1970): 735–740.

Gollin, Eugene S. "Developmental Studies of Visual Recognition of Incomplete Objects." *Perceptual and Motor Skills* 11, no. 3 (1960): 289–298.

Gordon, Leah N. "If Opportunity Is Not Enough: Coleman and His Critics in the Era of Equality of Results." *History of Education Quarterly* 57, no. 4 (2017): 601–615.

Gottfredson, Linda S. "Mainstream Science on Intelligence: An Editorial with 52 Signatories, History, and Bibliography." *Intelligence* 24, no. 1 (1997): 13–23, 17.

Graham, Sandra. '"Most of the Subjects Were White and Middle Class': Trends in Published Research on African Americans in Selected APA Journals, 1970–1989." *American Psychologist* 47, no. 5 (1992): 629–639.

Green, Christopher D. "Of Immortal Mythological Beasts: Operationism in Psychology." *Theory and Psychology* 2, no. 3 (1992): 291–320.

Green, Christopher D. "Where Did the Word 'Cognitive' Come from Anyway?" *Canadian Psychology* 37, no. 1 (1996): 31–39.

Green, Christopher D. "Why Psychology Isn't Unified, and Probably Never Will Be." *Review of General Psychology* 19, no. 3 (2015): 207–214.

Green, Venus. "Race, Gender, and National Identity in the American and British Telephone Industries." *International Review of Social History* 46, no. 2 (2001): 185–205.

Green, Venus. *Race on the Line: Gender, Labor, and Technology in the Bell System, 1880–1980*. Durham, NC: Duke University Press, 2001.

Greene, Beverly A. "When the Therapist Is White and the Patient Is Black: Considerations for Psychotherapy in the Feminist Heterosexual and Lesbian Communities." *Women and Therapy* 5, no. 2–3 (1986): 41–65.

Greene, Jeremy, and Scott H. Podolsky. "Reform, Regulation, and Pharmaceuticals: The Kefauver-Harris Amendments at 50." *New England Journal of Medicine* 367, no. 16 (2012): 1481–1483.

Greene, Joshua D., R. Brian Sommerville, Leigh E. Nystrom, John M. Darley, and Jonathan D. Cohen. "An fMRI Investigation of Emotional Engagement in Moral Judgment." *Science* 293, no. 5537 (2001): 2105–2108.

Greenwald, Anthony G. "New Look 3: Unconscious Cognition Reclaimed." *American Psychologist* 47, no. 6 (1992): 766–779.

Greenwald, Anthony G. "There Is Nothing So Theoretical As a Good Method." *Perspectives on Psychological Science* 7, no. 2 (2012): 99–108.

Greenwald, Anthony G. "The Totalitarian Ego: Fabrication and Revision of Personal History." *American Psychologist* 35, no. 7 (1980): 603–618.

Greenwald, Anthony, and Mahzarin Banaji. "Implicit Social Cognition: Attitudes, Self-Esteem, and Stereotypes." *Psychological Review* 102, no. 1 (1995): 4–27.
Greenwald, Anthony G., Brian A. Nosek, and Mahzarin R. Banaji. "Understanding and Using the Implicit Association Test: I. An Improved Scoring Algorithm." *Journal of Personality and Social Psychology* 85, no. 2 (2003): 197–216.
Greenwald, Anthony G., Debbie E. McGhee, and Jordan L. K. Schwartz. "Measuring Individual Differences in Implicit Cognition: The Implicit Association Test." *Journal of Personality and Social Psychology* 74, no. 6 (1998): 1464–1480.
Greenwood, John D. *The Disappearance of the Social in American Social Psychology*. New York: Cambridge University Press, 2003.
Greenwood, John D. "Understanding the 'Cognitive Revolution' in Psychology." *Journal of the History of the Behavioral Sciences* 35, no. 1 (1999): 1–22.
Grether, David M., and Charles R. Plott. "Economic Theory of Choice and the Preference Reversal Phenomenon." *The American Economic Review* 69, no. 4 (1979): 623–638.
Grob, Gerald N. "Public Policy and Mental Illnesses: Jimmy Carter's Presidential Commission on Mental Health." *The Milbank Quarterly* 83, no. 3 (2005): 425–456.
Grob, Gerald N. *From Asylum to Community: Mental Health Policy in Modern America*. Princeton, NJ: Princeton University Press, 1991.
Grogan, Jessica. *Encountering America: Humanistic Psychology, Sixties Culture and the Shaping of the Modern Self*. New York: Harper Perennial, 2013.
Gross, Neil. *Why Are Professors Liberal and Why Do Conservatives Care?* Cambridge, MA: Harvard University Press, 2013.
Grossberg, John. "Behavior Therapy: A Review." *Psychological Bulletin* 62, no. 2 (1964): 73–88.
Ha, Nathan. "Detecting and Teaching Desire: Phallometry, Freund, and Behaviorist Sexology." *Osiris* 30, no. 1 (2015): 205–227.
Haan, Norma. "Hypothetical and Actual Moral Reasoning in a Situation of Civil Disobedience." *Journal of Personality and Social Psychology* 32, no. 2 (1975): 255–270.
Hacking, Ian. *The Taming of Chance*. Cambridge: Cambridge University Press, 1990.
Hagger, Martin S., Nikos L. D. Chatzisarantis, Hugo Alberts, Calvin O. Anggono, Cedric Batailler, Angela R. Birt, Ralf Brand, et al. "A Multilab Preregistered Replication of the Ego-Depletion Effect." *Perspectives on Psychological Science* 11, no. 4 (2016): 546–573, 558.
Haidt, Jonathan. "The Emotional Dog and Its Rational Tail: A Social Intuitionist Approach to Moral Judgment." *Psychological Review* 108, no. 4 (2001): 814–834.
Haidt, Jonathan. "The New Synthesis in Moral Psychology." *Science* 316, no. 5827 (2007): 998–1002, 998.
Hall, Stuart. "Encoding/Decoding" in Stuart Hall, Dorothy Hobson, Andrew Lowe, and Paul Willis (eds.), *Culture, Media, Language*. London: Hutchinson, 1980, pp. 128–138.
Hall, Stuart, Charles Critcher, Tony Jefferson, John Clarke, and Brian Roberts. *Policing the Crisis: Mugging, the State and Law and Order*. Bloomsbury, UK: Red Globe Press, 1978/2013.
Hamblin, Jacob Darwin. "Exorcising Ghosts in the Age of Automation: United Nations Experts and Atoms for Peace." *Technology and Culture* 47, no. 4 (2006): 734–756.

Hansen, Helena, and Samuel K. Roberts. "Two Tiers of Biomedicalization: Methadone, Buprenorphine, and the Racial Politics of Addiction Treatments." *Critical Perspectives on Addiction* 14 (2012): 79–102.

Haraway, Donna. *Primate Visions: Gender, Race, and Nature in the World of Modern Science*. London: Routledge, 1989.

Haraway, Donna. *Simians, Cyborgs, and Women: The Reinvention of Nature*. New York: Routledge, 1991.

Harcourt, Bernard E. "From the Asylum to the Prison: Rethinking the Incarceration Revolution." *Texas Law Review* 84 (2005): 1751–1786.

Harrington, Anne, and John Dunne. "When Mindfulness Is Therapy: Ethical Qualms, Historical Perspectives." *American Psychologist* 70, no. 7 (2015): 621–631.

Harris, Ben. "Jewish Quotas in Clinical Psychology? The Journal of Clinical Psychology and the Scandal of 1945." *Review of General Psychology* 13, no. 3 (2009): 252–261.

Hauser, David J., and Norbert Schwarz. "Attentive Turkers: MTurk Participants Perform Better on Online Attention Checks Than Do Subject Pool Participants." *Behavior Research Methods* 48, no. 1 (2016): 400–407.

Haxby, James V., Elizabeth A. Hoffman, and M. Ida Gobbini. "The Distributed Human Neural System for Face Perception." *Trends in Cognitive Sciences* 4, no. 6 (2000): 223–233.

Haxby, James V., M. Ida Gobbini, Maura L. Furey, Alumit Ishai, Jennifer L. Schouten, and Pietro Pietrini. "Distributed and Overlapping Representations of Faces and Objects in Ventral Temporal Cortex." *Science* 293, no. 5539 (2001): 2425–2430.

Hayes, Steve C., and Elaine Heiby. "Psychology's Drug Problem: Do We Need a Fix or Should We Just Say No?" *American Psychologist* 51, no. 3 (1996): 198–206.

Hayles, N. Katherine. *How We Became Posthuman: Virtual Bodies in Cybernetics, Literature, and Informatics*. Chicago: University of Chicago Press, 1999.

Hayward, Rhodri. "The Tortoise and the Love-Machine: Grey Walter and the Politics of Electroencephalography." *Science in Context* 14, no. 4 (2001): 615–641.

Head, Henry. "The Concept of Nervous and Mental Energy II: 'Vigilance'; A Physiological State of the Nervous System." *British Journal of Psychology* 14 (1923): 126–147.

Hečlo, Hugh. "The Sixties' False Dawn: Awakenings, Movements, and Postmodern Policy-Making." *Journal of Policy History* 8, no. 1 (1996): 34–63.

Hegarty, Peter. *Gentlemen's Disagreement: Alfred Kinsey, Lewis Terman, and the Sexual Politics of Smart Men*. Chicago: University of Chicago Press, 2013.

Hegarty, Peter. "Homosexual Signs and Heterosexual Silences: Rorschach Research on Male Homosexuality from 1921 to 1969." *Journal of the History of Sexuality* 12, no. 3 (2003): 400–423.

Hegarty, Peter. *A Recent History of Lesbian and Gay Psychology: From Homophobia to LGBT*. London: Routledge, 2017;

Hehman, Eric, Jessica K. Flake, and Jimmy Calanchini. "Disproportionate Use of Lethal Force in Policing Is Associated with Regional Racial Biases of Residents." *Social Psychological and Personality Science* 9, no. 4 (2018): 393–401.

Heider, Karl G. "The Rashomon Effect: When Ethnographers Disagree." *American Anthropologist* 90, no. 1 (1988): 73–81.

Heims, Steven J. *Constructing a Social Science for America: The Cybernetics Group 1946–1953*. Cambridge, MA: MIT Press, 1991.

Henrich, Joseph, Steven J. Heine, and Ara Norenzayan. "The Weirdest People in the World?" *Behavioral and Brain Sciences* 33, no. 2–3 (2010): 61–83.
Herman, Ellen. *The Romance of American Psychology: Political Culture in the Age of Experts*. Oakland: University of California Press, 1995.
Herzog, Dagmar. *Cold War Freud*. Cambridge: Cambridge University Press, 2017.
Heukelom, Floris. *Behavioral Economics: A History*. Cambridge: Cambridge University Press, 2014.
Heyck, Hunter. *Age of System: Understanding the Development of Modern Social Science*. Baltimore: Johns Hopkins University Press, 2015.
Hicks, Diana, Paul Wouters, Ludo Waltman, Sarah De Rijcke, and Ismael Rafols. "The Leiden Manifesto for Research Metrics." *Nature* 520, no. 7548 (2015): 429.
Hicks, Marie. *Programmed Inequality: How Britain Discarded Women Technologists and Lost its Edge in Computing*. Cambridge, MA: MIT Press, 2017.
Hilliard, Asa, III. "Thomas O. Hilliard, PhD." In Robert L. Williams (ed.), *History of the Association of Black Psychologists: Profiles of Outstanding Black Psychologists*. Bloomington, IN: AuthorHouse, 2008, 187–196.
Hilliard, Thomas O. "Professional Training and Minority Groups." In Maurice Korman (ed.), *National Conference on Levels and Patterns of Professional Training in Psychology*. Washington, DC: American Psychological Association, 1976, 41–49.
Hilliard, Thomas O. "Psychology, Law, and the Black Community." *Law and Human Behavior* 2, no. 2 (1978): 107–131.
Hirsch, Jorge E. "An Index to Quantify an Individual's Scientific Research Output." *Proceedings of the National academy of Sciences of the United States of America* 102, no. 46 (2005): 16569.
Hochberg, Julian E., and Henry Gleitman. "Towards a Reformulation of the Perception-Motivation Dichotomy." *Journal of Personality* 18 (1949): 180–191.
Hoffman, David H., and Associates. *Report to the Special Committee of the Board of Directors of the American Psychological Association: Independent Review Relating to APA Ethics Guidelines, National Security Interrogations, and Torture (Revised)*. Chicago: Sidley Austin LLP, 2015. Retrieved from www.apa.org/independent-rev iew/revised-report.pdf
Hoffman, Paul J. "The Paramorphic Representation of Clinical Judgment." *Psychological Bulletin* 57, no. 2 (1960): 116–131.
Hofmann, Wilhelm, Brandon J. Schmeichel, and Alan D. Baddeley. "Executive Functions and Self-Regulation." *Trends in Cognitive Sciences* 16, no. 3 (2012): 174–180.
Hofstadter, Douglas R. "Waking up from the Boolean Dream, Or, Subcognition as Computation." *Metamagical Themas: Questing for the Essence of Mind and Pattern*. New York: Basic Books, 1985, 631–665.
Hogan, Michael J. *The Marshall Plan: America, Britain and the Reconstruction of Western Europe, 1947–1952*. Cambridge: Cambridge University Press, 1987.
Hollin, Gregory. "Constructing a Social Subject: Autism and Human Sociality in the 1980s." *History of the Human Sciences* 27, no. 4 (2014): 98–115.
Holmes, K. S. "Ergonomics in the Post Office." *Conference on Ergonomics in Industry*. London: Her Majesty's Stationary Office, 1961, 90–91.
Holstein, Constance Boucher. "Irreversible, Stepwise Sequence in the Development of Moral Judgment: A Longitudinal Study of Males and Females." *Child Development* 47, no. 1 (1976): 51–61.

Horney, Karen. *Self-Analysis*. New York: Norton, 1942.

Horowitz, Daniel. *Betty Friedan and the Making of* The Feminine Mystique: *The American Left, the Cold War, and Modern Feminism*. Amherst: University of Massachusetts Press, 1998.

Horowitz, Daniel. *Happier?: The History of a Cultural Movement that Aspired to Transform America*. Oxford: Oxford University Press, 2017.

Horowitz, Ruth E. "Racial Aspects of Self-Identification in Nursery School Children." *Journal of Psychology* 7, no. 1 (1939): 91–99.

Horwitz, Allan V., and Jerome C. Wakefield, *The Loss of Sadness: How Psychiatry Transformed Normal Sorrow into Depressive Disorder*. Oxford: Oxford University Press, 2007.

Howard, Ann, Georgine Pion, Gary Gottfredson, Pamela Flattau, Stuart Oskamp, Sheila Pfaffin, Douglas Bray, and Alvin Burstein. "The Changing Face of American Psychology: A Report from the Committee on Employment and Human Resources." *American Psychologist* 41, no. 12 (1986): 1311–1327.

Howarth, C. I., and K. Ellis. "The Relative Intelligibility Threshold for One's Own Name Compared with Other Names." *Quarterly Journal of Experimental Psychology* 13, no. 4 (1961): 236–239.

Hraba, Joseph, and Geoffrey Grant. "Black Is Beautiful: A Reexamination of Racial Preference and Identification." *Journal of Personality and Social Psychology* 16, no. 3 (1970): 398–402.

Hubbard, Katherine A. *Queer Ink: A Blotted History towards Liberation*. London: Routledge, 2019.

Hughes, Everett C. "Professions." *Daedalus* 92, no. 4 (1963): 655–668.

Hui, Alexandra. *The Psychophysical Ear: Musical Experiments, Experimental Sounds, 1840–1910*. Cambridge, MA: MIT Press, 2013.

Hull, Clark. *Principles of Behavior*. New York: Appleton-Century-Crofts, 1943.

Igo, Sarah E. *The Averaged American: Surveys, Citizens, and the Making of a Mass Public*. Cambridge, MA: Harvard University Press, 2007.

Igo, Sarah E. *The Known Citizen: A History of Privacy in Modern America*. Cambridge, MA: Harvard University Press, 2018.

Illouz, Eva. *Saving the Modern Soul: Therapy, Emotions, and the Culture of Self-Help*. Oakland: University of California Press, 2008.

Illouz, Eva. *Oprah Winfrey and the Glamour of Misery: An Essay on Popular Culture*. New York: Columbia University Press, 2003, 171.

Individual Rights and the Federal Role in Behavior Modification: A Study. Prepared by the Staff of the Subcommittee on Constitutional Rights of the Committee on the Judiciary, United States Senate, Ninety-Third Congress, Second Session. Washington, DC: U.S. Government Printing Office, 1974.

Innis, Nancy K. "Lessons from the Controversy over the Loyalty Oath at the University of California." *Minerva* 30, no. 3 (1992): 337–365.

Isaac, Joel. "The Human Sciences in Cold War America." *The Historical Journal* 50, no. 3 (2007): 725–746.

Isaac, Joel. *Working Knowledge: Making the Human Sciences from Parsons to Kuhn*. Cambridge, MA: Harvard University Press, 2012.

Jackson, John P., Jr. *Social Scientists for Social Justice: Making the Case Against Segregation*. New York: New York University Press, 2001.

Jacobs, Meg. *Panic at the Pump: The Energy Crisis and the Transformation of American Politics in the 1970s*. New York: Wang and Hill, 2016.
Jacyna, L. Stephen and Stephen T. Casper (eds.). *The Neurological Patient in History*. Rochester, NY: University Rochester Press, 2012.
James, William. *The Principles of Psychology*. New York: Holt, 1890.
Jay, Martin. *The Dialectical Imagination: A History of the Frankfurt School and the Institute of Social Research, 1923–1950*. Berkeley: University of California Press, 1973/1996.
Johnson, David K. *The Lavender Scare: The Cold War Persecution of Gays and Lesbians in the Federal Government*. Chicago: University of Chicago Press, 2009.
Johnson, Paul Christopher. *Automatic Religion: Nearhuman Agents of Brazil and France*. Chicago: University of Chicago Press, 2021.
Johnston, Elizabeth B. "The Repeated Reproduction of Bartlett's Remembering." *History of Psychology* 4, no. 4 (2001): 341–366.
Johnston, Elizabeth, and Ann Johnson. "Balancing Life and Work by Unbending Gender: Early American Women Psychologists' Struggles and Contributions." *Journal of the History of the Behavioral Sciences* 53, no. 3 (2017): 246–264.
Johnston, Robert D. *The Radical Middle Class: Populist Democracy and the Question of Capitalism in Progressive Era Portland, Oregon*. Princeton, NJ: Princeton University Press, 2003.
Jones-Imhotep, Edward. "The Ghost Factories: Histories of Automata and Artificial Life." *History and Technology* 36, no. 1 (2020): 3–29.
Jones-Imhotep, Edward. "Maintaining Humans." In Mark Solovey and Hamilton Cravens (eds.), *Cold War Social Science: Knowledge Production, Liberal Democracy, and Human Nature*. New York: Palgrave Macmillan, 2012, 175–195.
Jones-Imhotep, Edward. "Malleability and Machines: Glenn Gould and the Technological Self." *Technology and Culture* 57, no. 2 (2016): 287–321.
Jost, John T. "The End of the End of Ideology." *American Psychologist* 61, no. 7 (2006): 651–670.
Jost, John T., Mahzarin, R. Banaji, and Brian A. Nosek. "A Decade of System Justification Theory: Accumulated Evidence of Conscious and Unconscious Bolstering of the Status Quo." *Political Psychology* 25, no. 6 (2004): 881–919.
Judge, T. A., A. Erez, J. E. Bono, and C. J. Thoresen. "Are Measures of Self-Esteem, Neuroticism, Locus of Control, and Generalized Self-Efficacy Indicators of a Common Core Construct?" *Journal of Personality and Social Psychology* 83, no. 3 (2002): 693–710.
Kagan, Jerome, Barbara A. Henker, Amy Hen-Tov, Janet Levine, and Michael Lewis. "Infants' Differential Reactions to Familiar and Distorted Faces." *Child Development* (1966): 519–532.
Kahneman, Daniel. "Maps of Bounded Rationality: Psychology for Behavioral Economics." *American Economic Review* 93, no. 5 (2003): 1449–1475.
Kahneman, Daniel. "A Perspective on Judgment and Choice: Mapping Bounded Rationality." *American Psychologist* 58, no. 9 (2003): 697–720.
Kahneman, Daniel. *Thinking Fast and Slow*. New York: Farrar, Straus, and Giroux, 2011.
Kahneman, Daniel, and Shane Frederick. "Representativeness Revisited: Attribute Substitution in Intuitive Judgment." In T. Gilovich, D. Griffin, and D. Kahneman (eds.), *Heuristics of Intuitive Judgment: Extensions and Applications*. New York: Cambridge University Press (2002), 49–81.

Kahneman, Daniel, Alan B. Krueger, David Schkade, Norbert Schwarz, and Arthur A. Stone. "Would You Be Happier If You Were Richer? A Focusing Illusion." *Science* 312, no. 5782 (2006): 1908–1910.

Kaiser, David. "Booms, Busts, and the World of Ideas: Enrollment Pressures and the Challenge of Specialization." *Osiris* 27, no. 1 (2012): 276–302.

Kaiser, David and W. Patrick McCray (eds.). *Groovy Science: Knowledge, Innovation, and American Counterculture*. Chicago: University of Chicago Press, 2016.

Kanwisher, Nancy. "Functional Specificity in the Human Brain: A Window into the Functional Architecture of the Mind." *Proceedings of the National Academy of Sciences* 107, no. 25 (2010): 11163–11170.

Kanwisher, Nancy. "The Quest for the FFA and Where It Led." *Journal of Neuroscience* 37, no. 5 (2017): 1056–1061, 1058.

Kanwisher, Nancy, Josh McDermott, and Marvin M. Chun. "The Fusiform Face Area: A Module in Human Extrastriate Cortex Specialized for Face Perception." *Journal of Neuroscience* 17, no. 11 (1997): 4302–4311.

Kanwisher, Nancy, and Galit Yovel. "The Fusiform Face Area: A Cortical Region Specialized for the Perception of Faces." *Philosophical Transactions of the Royal Society B: Biological Sciences* 361, no. 1476 (2006): 2109–2128.

Kasperson, Roger E., Ortwin Renn, Paul Slovic, Halina S. Brown, Jacque Emel, Robert Goble, Jeanne X. Kasperson, and Samuel Ratick. "The Social Amplification of Risk: A Conceptual Framework." *Risk Analysis* 8, no. 2 (1988): 177–187.

Katz, Martin M., Steven K. Secunda, Robert M. A. Hirschfeld, and Stephen H. Koslow. "NIMH Clinical Research Branch Collaborative Program on the Psychobiology of Depression." *Archives of General Psychiatry* 36, no. 7 (1979): 765–771.

Keating, Peter, and Alberto Cambrosio. *Biomedical Platforms: Realigning the Normal and the Pathological in Late-Twentieth-Century Medicine*. Cambridge, MA: MIT Press, 2003.

Kelley, E. Lowell, Lewis Goldberg, Donald Fiske, and James Kilkowski. "Twenty-Five Years Later: A Follow-up of the Graduate Students in Clinical Psychology Assessed in the VA Selection Research Project." *American Psychologist* 33, no. 8 (1978): 746–755.

Kelty, Christopher. "Geeks, Social Imaginaries, and Recursive Publics." *Cultural Anthropology* 20, no. 2 (2005): 185–214.

Kerber, Linda K. "Separate Spheres, Female Worlds, Woman's Place: The Rhetoric of Women's History." *Journal of American History* 75, no. 1 (1988): 9–39.

Kerber, Linda K. "The Stateless As the Citizen's Other: A View from the United States." *American Historical Review* 112, no. 1 (2007): 1–34.

Khalili, Laleh. *Time in the Shadows: Confinement in Counterinsurgencies*. Stanford, CA: Stanford University Press, 2013.

Kidd, Celeste, Holly Palmeri, and Richard N. Aslin. "Rational Snacking: Young Children's Decision-Making on the Marshmallow Task Is Moderated by Beliefs about Environmental Reliability." *Cognition* 126, no. 1 (2013): 109–114.

Kiesler, Charles, and Michael Pallak. "The Virginia Blues." *American Psychologist* 35, no. 11 (1980): 953–954.

Kim, Susanna, and Alexandra Rutherford. "From Seduction to Sexism: Feminists Challenge the Ethics of Therapist–Client Sexual Relations in 1970s America." *History of Psychology* 18, no. 3 (2015): 283–296.

King, Ruth E. "Highlights in the Development of ABPsi." *Journal of Black Psychology* 4(1-2) (1978): 9–24, 11.
Kittrie, Nicholas N. *The Right to Be Different: Deviance and Enforced Therapy.* Baltimore: Johns Hopkins University Press, 1971.
Klein, Elise, and China Mills. "Psy-Expertise, Therapeutic Culture and the Politics of the Personal in Development." *Third World Quarterly* 38, no. 9 (2017): 1990–2008.
Klein, Olivier, Peter Hegarty, and Baruch Fischhoff. "Hindsight 40 Years on: An Interview with Baruch Fischhoff." *Memory Studies* 10, no. 3 (2017): 249–260.
Klerman, Gerald L., and Myrna M. Weissman. "Increasing Rates of Depression." *Journal of the American Medical Association* 261, no. 15 (1989): 2229–2235.
Kline, Ronald R. *The Cybernetics Moment: Or Why We Call Our Age the Information Age.* Baltimore: Johns Hopkins University Press, 2015.
Kohlberg, Lawrence. "The Development of Children's Orientations Toward a Moral Order I. Sequence in the Development of Moral Thought." *Vita Humana* 6, no. 1–2 (1963): 11–33.
Kohlberg, Lawrence, and Carol Gilligan. "The Adolescent as a Philosopher: The Discovery of the Self in a Postconventional World." *Daedalus* 100, no. 4 (1971): 1051–1086.
Koocher, Gerald P. "Varied and Valued Roles." *APA Monitor* 37, no. 7 (2006): 5.
Kosofsky Sedgwick, Eve. *Touching Feeling: Affect, Pedagogy, Performativity*. Durham, NC: Duke University Press, 2003.
Krech, David. "David Krech" in Gardner Lindzey (ed.), *A History of Psychology in Autobiography*, vol. 3. Englewood Cliffs, NJ.: Prentice-Hall, 1974, pp. 221–250.
Krech, David. "A Note on Fission." *American Psychologist* 1, no. 9 (1946): 402–404.
Krech, David. "Notes toward a Psychological Theory." *Journal of Personality* 18, no. 1 (1949): 66–87.
Krige, John. *American Hegemony and the Postwar Reconstruction of Science in Europe.* Cambridge, MA: MIT Press, 2008.
Krige, John. "Atoms for Peace, Scientific Internationalism, and Scientific Intelligence." *Osiris* 21, no. 1 (2006): 161–181.
Kripal, Jeffrey J. *Esalen: America and the Religion of No Religion*. Chicago: University of Chicago Press, 2011.
Kroker, Kenton. *The Sleep of Others and the Transformations of Sleep Research.* Toronto: University of Toronto Press, 2007.
Krosnick, Jon A. "Response Strategies for Coping with the Cognitive Demands of Attitude Measures in Surveys." *Applied Cognitive Psychology* 5, no. 3 (1991): 213–236.
Kruger, Justin, and David Dunning. "Unskilled and Unaware of It: How Difficulties in Recognizing One's Own Incompetence Lead to Inflated Self-Assessments." *Journal of Personality and Social Psychology* 77, no. 6 (1999): 121–1134.
Kugelmann, Robert. "Willpower." *Theory and Psychology* 23, no. 4 (2013): 479–498.
Kunreuther, Howard, William H. Desvousges, and Paul Slovic. "Nevada's Predicament: Public Perceptions of Risk from the Proposed Nuclear Waste Repository." *Environment* 30, no. 8 (1988): 16–33.
Kuriloff, Peter. "Law, Educational Reform, and the School Psychologist." *Journal of School Psychology* 13, no. 4 (1975): 335–348.
Lai, Calvin, Allison Skinner, Erin Cooley, Sohad Murrar, Markus Brauer, Thierry Devos, Jimmy Calanchini, et al. "Reducing Implicit Racial Preferences: II. Intervention

Effectiveness Across Time." *Journal of Experimental Psychology: General* 145, no. 8 (2016): 1001–1016.

Lakoff, Andrew. "Adaptive Will: The Evolution of Attention Deficit Disorder." *Journal of the History of the Behavioral Sciences* 36, no. 2 (2000): 149–169.

Langer, Ellen, Arthur Blank, and Benzion Chanowitz. "The Mindlessness of Ostensibly Thoughtful Action: The Role of 'Placebic' Information in Interpersonal Interaction." *Journal of Personality and Social Psychology* 36, no. 6 (1978): 635–642.

Lanir, Zvi, and Daniel Kahneman. "An Experiment in Decision Analysis in Israel in 1975." *Studies in Intelligence* 50, no. 4 (2006): 11–19.

Lasch, Christopher. *The Culture of Narcissism*. New York: Norton, 1979.

Lasch, Christopher. "For Shame." *The New Republic*, August 10, 1992, 29–34.

Latham, Michael E. *Modernization As Ideology: American Social Science and "Nation Building" in the Kennedy Era*. Chapel Hill: University of North Carolina Press, 2000.

Latour, Bruno. *Science in Action: How to Follow Scientists and Engineers through Society*. Cambridge, MA: Harvard University Press, 1987.

Leahey, Thomas H. "The Mythical Revolutions of American Psychology." *American Psychologist* 47, no. 2 (1992): 308–318.

Leonard, Robert. *Von Neumann, Morgenstern, and the Creation of Game Theory: From Chess to Social Science, 1900–1960*. Cambridge: Cambridge University Press, 2010.

Lester, Andrew. "'This Was My Utopia': Sexual Experimentation and Masculinity in the 1960s Bay Area Radical Left." *Journal of the History of Sexuality* 29, no. 3 (2020): 364–387.

Lewenstein, Bruce V. "From Fax to Facts: Communication in the Cold Fusion Saga." *Social Studies of Science* 25, no. 3 (1995): 403–436.

Lewin, Kurt. "Action Research and Minority Problems." *Journal of Social Issues* 2, no. 4 (1946): 34–46.

Lewin, Kurt. "Self-hatred among the Jews." *Contemporary Jewish Record* 4 (1941): 219–232.

Lewis, Abram J. "'We Are Certain of Our Own Insanity': Antipsychiatry and the Gay Liberation Movement, 1968–1980." *Journal of the History of Sexuality* 25, no. 1 (2016): 83–113.

Lewis, Michael. *The Undoing Project: A Friendship that Changed the World*. New York: Penguin, 2016.

Leys, Ruth. *The Ascent of Affect: Genealogy and Critique*. Chicago: University of Chicago Press, 2017.

Leys, Ruth. *Newborn Imitation: The Stakes of a Controversy*. Cambridge: Cambridge University Press, 2020.

Lezaun, Javier, Fabian Muniesa, and Signe Vikkelsø. "Provocative Containment and the Drift of Social-Scientific Realism." *Journal of Cultural Economy* 6, no. 3 (2013): 278–293.

Lichtenstein, Sarah, and Paul Slovic. "Response-induced Reversals of Preference in Gambling: An Extended Replication in Las Vegas." *Journal of Experimental Psychology* 101, no. 1 (1973): 16–20.

Lichtenstein, Sarah, and Paul Slovic. "Reversals of Preference between Bids and Choices in Gambling Decisions." *Journal of Experimental Psychology* 89, no. 1 (1971): 46–55.

Lichtenstein, Sarah, Paul Slovic, Baruch Fischhoff, Mark Layman, and Barbara Combs. "Judged Frequency of Lethal Events." *Journal of Experimental Psychology Human Learning and Memory* 4, no. 6 (1978): 551–578.

Liebman, Charles S. "The Myth of Defeat: The Memory of the Yom Kippur War in Israeli Society." *Middle Eastern Studies* 29, no. 3 (1993): 399–418.

Light, Jennifer S. "When Computers Were Women." *Technology and Culture* 40, no. 3 (1999): 455–483.

Lipartito, Kenneth. "When Women Were Switches: Technology, Work, and Gender in the Telephone Industry, 1890–1920." *American Historical Review* 99, no. 4 (1994): 1075–1111.

Lipsitz, George. *The Possessive Investment in Whiteness: How White People Profit from Identity politics.* Philadelphia: Temple University Press, 2006.

Littlefield, Melissa M. *Instrumental Intimacy: EEG Wearables and Neuroscientific Control.* Baltimore: Johns Hopkins University Press, 2018.

Livermore, Joseph M., Carl P. Malmquist, and Paul E. Meehl. "On the Justifications for Civil Commitment." *University of Pennsylvania Law Review* 117, no. 1 (1968): 75–96.

Loftus, Elizabeth F. "Leading Questions and the Eyewitness Report." *Cognitive Psychology* 7, no. 4 (1975): 560–572.

Logie, Robert H. "Retiring the Central Executive." *Quarterly Journal of Experimental Psychology* 69, no. 10 (2016): 2093–2109.

Looper, LeRoy. "The Autobiography of LeRoy Looper" (1977). https://beyondchron.org/the-amazing-life-story-of-leroy-looper-1924-2011

Lopes, Lola L. "The Rhetoric of Irrationality." *Theory and Psychology* 1, no. 1 (1991): 65–82.

Luborsky, Lester, Barton Singer, and Lise Luborsky. "Comparative Studies of Psychotherapies: Is it True that Everyone Has Won and All Must Have Prizes?" *Archives of General Psychiatry* 32, no. 8 (1975): 995–1008.

Lunbeck, Elizabeth. *The Americanization of Narcissism.* Cambridge, MA: Harvard University Press, 2014.

Lussier, Kira. "Of Maslow, Motives, and Managers: The Hierarchy of Needs in American Business, 1960–1985." *Journal of the History of the Behavioral Sciences* 55, no. 4 (2019): 319–341.

Luthar, Suniya S., Dante Cicchetti, and Bronwyn Becker. "The Construct of Resilience: A Critical Evaluation and Guidelines for Future Work." *Child Development* 71, no. 3 (2000): 543–562.

Lutz, Catherine. "Epistemology of the Bunker: The Brainwashed and Other New Subjects of Permanent War." In Joel Pfister and Nancy Schnog (eds.), *Inventing the Psychological: Toward a Cultural History of Emotional Life in America.* New Haven, CT: Yale University Press, 1997, 245–267.

Lykken, David T. "Statistical Significance in Psychological Research." *Psychological Bulletin* 70, no. 3 (1968): 151–159.

Lyon, David. *Surveillance Society: Monitoring Everyday Life.* Lanham, MD: Open University Press, 2001.

Lyotard, Jean-François. *The Postmodern Condition: A Report on Knowledge.* Minneapolis: University of Minnesota Press, 1984.

MacDonald, A. P. "A Time or Introspection." *Professional Psychology* 4 (1973): 35–42.

MacKenzie, Donald. *Inventing Accuracy: A Historical Sociology of Nuclear Missile Guidance.* Cambridge, MA: MIT Press, 1990.

Mackworth, N. A. *Researches on the Measurement of Human Performance.* London: His Majesty's Stationary Office, 1948.

Maddox, Brenda. "Women and the Switchboard." In Ithiel de Sola Pool (ed.), *The Social Impact of the Telephone*. Cambridge, MA: MIT Press, 1977, 262–280.

Madsen, Ole Jacob. *The Psychologization of Society: On the Unfolding of the Therapeutic in Norway*. London: Routledge, 2018.

Mahoney, Michael. "Reflections on the Cognitive-Learning Trend in Psychotherapy." *American Psychologist* 32, no. 1 (1977): 5–13.

Mahoney, Michael J., Aaron T. Beck, Marvin R. Goldfried, and Donald Meichenbaum. "Editorial." *Cognitive Therapy and Research* 1, no. 1 (1977): 1–3.

Makari, George. *Revolution in Mind: The Creation of Psychoanalysis*. New York: HarperCollins, 2008.

Malpass, Roy, and Jerome Kravitz. "Recognition for Faces of Own and Other Race." *Journal of Personality and Social Psychology* 13, no. 4 (1969): 330–334.

Mandler, George. "Origins of the Cognitive (R)evolution." *Journal of the History of the Behavioral Sciences* 38, no. 4 (2002): 339–353.

Marinelli, Lydia, and Andreas Mayer. *Dreaming by the Book: Freud's 'The Interpretation of Dreams' and the History of the Psychoanalytic Movement*. New York: Other Press, 2003.

Marks, Harry M. *The Progress of Experiment: Science and Therapeutic Reform in the United States, 1900–1990*. Cambridge: Cambridge University Press, 2000.

Marks, Sarah. "CBT in Britain: Historical Development and Contemporary Situation." In Windy Dryden (ed.), *Cognitive Behaviour Therapies*. London: Sage, 2012, 1–24.

Markus, Hazel R., and Shinobu Kitayama. "Culture and the Self: Implications for Cognition, Emotion, and Motivation." *Psychological Review* 98, no. 2 (1991): 224–253.

Martin, George R. R. "The Computer Was a Fish." *Analog Science Fiction/Science Fact*, July 1972, 61–74.

Martin-Nielsen, Janet. '"It Was All Connected': Computers and Linguistics in Early Cold War America" in Mark Solovey and Hamilton Cravens (eds.). *Cold War Social Science*. New York: Palgrave, 2012, 63–78.

Marwick Alice E., and danah boyd. "I Tweet Honestly, I Tweet Passionately: Twitter Users, Context Collapse, and the Imagined Audience." *New Media and Society* 13, no.1 (2011): 114–133.

Masicampo, Emer J., and Roy F. Baumeister. "Toward a Physiology of Dual-Process Reasoning and Judgment: Lemonade, Willpower, and Expensive Rule-Based Analysis." *Psychological Science* 19, no. 3 (2008): 255–260.

Maslow, Abraham H. "Self-esteem (Dominance-Feeling) and Sexuality in Women." *Journal of Social Psychology* 16, no. 2 (1942): 259–294.

Maslow, Abraham H. "A Test for Dominance-Feeling (Self-Esteem) in College Women." *Journal of Social Psychology* 12, no. 2 (1940): 255–270.

Maslow, Abraham H. "A Theory of Human Motivation." *Psychological Review* 50, no. 4 (1943): 370–396, 381–382.

Mass Media and Violence: A Report to the National Commission on the Causes and Prevention of Violence. Washington, DC: US Government Printing Office, 1969.

Masten, Ann S. "Ordinary Magic: Resilience Processes in Development." *American Psychologist* 56, no. 3 (2001): 227–238.

Masten, Ann S., Karin M. Best, and Norman Garmezy, "Resilience and Development: Contributions from the Study of Children Who Overcome Adversity." *Development and Psychopathology* 2, no. 4 (1990): 425–444.

Masten Ann S., and J. Douglas Coatsworth. "The Development of Competence in Favorable and Unfavorable Environments: Lessons from Research on Successful Children." *American Psychologist* 53, no. 2 (1998): 205–220.

Maton, Kenneth, Jessica Kohout, Marlene Wicherski, George Leary, and Andrey Vinokurov. "Minority Students of Color and the Psychology Graduate Pipeline: Disquieting and Encouraging Trends, 1989–2003." *American Psychologist* 61, no. 2 (2006): 117–131.

Mauss, Marcel. *The Gift: Forms And Functions of Exchanges in Archaic Societies.* London: Cohen & West, 1966.

May, Elaine Tyler. *Homeward Bound: American Families in the Cold War Era.* New York: Basic Books, 1988.

Mayer, Andreas. *Sites of the Unconscious: Hypnosis and the Emergence of the Psychoanalytic Setting.* Chicago: University of Chicago Press, 2013.

Mayes, Rick, and Allan V. Horwitz. "DSM-III and the Revolution in the Classification of Mental Illness." *Journal of the History of the Behavioral Sciences* 41, no. 3 (2005): 249–267.

McCabe, David P., and Alan D. Castel. "Seeing Is Believing: The Effect of Brain Images on Judgments of Scientific Reasoning." *Cognition* 107, no. 1 (2008): 343–352.

McCarthy, Tom. "Great Aspirations: The Postwar American College Counseling Center." *History of Psychology* 17, no. 1 (2014): 1–18.

McConahay, John B., Betty B. Hardee, and Valerie Batts. "Has Racism Declined in America? It Depends on Who Is Asking and What Is Asked." *Journal of Conflict Resolution* 25, no. 4 (1981): 563–579.

McConnell, James, Richard Cutler, and Elton McNeil. "Subliminal Stimulation: An Overview." *American Psychologist* 13, no. 5 (1958): 229–242.

McCoy, Alfred. *A Question of Torture: CIA Interrogation, from the Cold War to the War on Terror.* New York: Metropolitan Books, 2007.

McGuire, Danielle L. *At the Dark end of the Street: Black Women, Rape, and Resistance.* New York: Vintage, 2010.

McGuire, William J., and A. Padawer-Singer. "Trait Salience in the Spontaneous Self-Concept." *Journal of Personality and Social Psychology* 33, no. 6 (1976): 743–754.

McLaughlin, Neil G. "Why Do Schools of Thought Fail? Neo-Freudianism As a Case Study in the Sociology of Knowledge." *Journal of the History of the Behavioral Sciences* 34, no. 2 1998): 113–134.

Medina, Eden. *Cybernetic Revolutionaries: Technology and Politics in Allende's Chile.* Cambridge, MA: MIT Press, 2011.

Meehl, Paul. "The Cognitive Activity of the Clinician." *American Psychologist* 15, no. 1 (1960): 19–27.

Meeker, Martin. "Behind the Mask of Respectability: Reconsidering the Mattachine Society and Male Homophile Practice, 1950s and 1960s." *Journal of the History of Sexuality* 10, no. 1 (2001): 78–116.

Melnikoff, David E., and John A. Bargh. "The Mythical Number Two." *Trends in Cognitive Sciences* 22, no. 4 (2018): 280–293.

Meltzoff, Andrew N., and M. Keith Moore. "Imitation of Facial and Manual Gestures by Human Neonates." *Science* 198, no. 4312 (1977): 75–78.

Mendes, Gabriel M. *Under the Strain of Color: Harlem's Lafargue Clinic and the Promise of an Antiracist Psychiatry.* Ithaca, NY: Cornell University Press, 2015.

Metcalfe, Janet, and Walter Mischel. "A Hot/Cool-System Analysis of Delay of Gratification: Dynamics of Willpower." *Psychological Review* 106, no. 1 (1999): 3–19.

Metsky, Marvin. "Getting Our Feet Wet in National Politics." *Clinical Psychologist* 31 (Spring/Summer 1978): 10.

Metzl, Jonathan, and Anna Kirkland (eds.). *Against Health: How Health Became the New Morality*. New York: New York University Press, 2010.

Meyer, Ilan H. "Minority Stress and Mental Health in Gay Men." *Journal of Health and Social Behavior* 36 (1995): 38–56.

Meyerowitz, Joanne (ed.). *Not June Cleaver: Women and Gender in Postwar America, 1945–1960*. Philadelphia: Temple University Press, 1994.

Mialet, Hélène. *Hawking Incorporated: Stephen Hawking and the Anthropology of the Knowing Subject*. Chicago: University of Chicago Press, 2012.

Michels, Moritz, and Martin Wieser. "From Hohenschönhausen to Guantanamo Bay: Psychology's Role in the Secret Services of the GDR and the United States." *Journal of the History of the Behavioral Sciences* 54, no. 1 (2018): 43–61.

Milam, Erika Lorraine. *Creatures of Cain: The Hunt for Human Nature in Cold War America*. Princeton, NJ: Princeton University Press, 2020.

Miller, George A. "The Cognitive Revolution: A Historical Perspective." *Trends in Cognitive Sciences* 7, no. 3 (2003): 141–144.

Miller, George A. "The Magical Number Seven, Plus or Minus Two: Some Limits on our Capacity for Processing Information." *Psychological Review* 63, no. 2 (1956): 81–97.

Miller, George A., Jerome S. Bruner, and Leo Postman. "Familiarity of Letter Sequences and Tachistoscopic Identification." *Journal of General Psychology* 50, no. 1 (1954): 129–139.

Miller, George A., and Nancy Cantor. "A Book Review of R. Nisbett and L. Ross, Human Inference: Strategies and Shortcomings of Social Judgment." *Social Cognition* 1 (1982): 83–93, 87.

Miller, George A., Eugene Galanter, and Karl H. Pribram. *Plans and the Structure of Behavior*. New York: Henry Holt, 1960.

Miller, Gregory A. "Mistreating Psychology in the Decades of the Brain." *Perspectives on Psychological Science* 5, no. 6 (2010): 716–743.

Million, Dian. *Therapeutic Nations: Healing in an Age of Indigenous Human Rights*. Tucson: University of Arizona Press, 2013.

Milner, Brenda, Suzanne Corkin, and H-L. Teuber. "Further Analysis of the Hippocampal Amnesic Syndrome: 14-Year Follow-Up Study of HM." *Neuropsychologia* 6, no. 3 (1968): 215–234.

Mink, Gwendolyn. *Welfare's End*. Ithaca, NY: Cornell University Press, 1998.

Mirowski, Philip. *Never Let a Serious Crisis Go to Waste: How Neoliberalism Survived the Financial Meltdown*. London: Verso Books, 2013.

Mischel, Walter. "Father-Absence and Delay of Gratification." *Journal of Abnormal and Social Psychology* 63, no. 1 (1961): 116–124.

Mischel, Walter. *The Marshmallow Test: Mastering Self-Control*. New York: Little, Brown, 2014, 163.

Mischel, Walter. "Preference for Delayed Reinforcement: An Experimental Study of a Cultural Observation." *Journal of Abnormal and Social Psychology* 56, no. 1 (1958): 57–61.

Mischel, Walter. "Toward a Cognitive Social Learning Reconceptualization of Personality." *Psychological Review* 80, no. 4 (1973): 252–283.
Mischel, Walter, and Yuichi Shoda, "A Cognitive-Affective System Theory of Personality: Reconceptualizing Situations, Dispositions, Dynamics, and Invariance in Personality Structure." *Psychological Review* 102, no. 2 (1995): 246–268.
Mischel, Walter, Yuichi Shoda, and Philip K. Peake, "The Nature of Adolescent Competencies Predicted by Preschool Delay of Gratification." *Journal of Personality and Social Psychology* 54, no. 4 (1988): 687–696.
Mitchell, Gregory, and Philip E. Tetlock. "Antidiscrimination Law and the Perils of Mindreading." *Ohio State Law Journal* 67 (2006): 1023–1121.
Moghaddam, Fathali. "Psychology in the Three Worlds: As Reflected by the Crisis in Social Psychology and the Move Toward Indigenous Third-World Psychology." *American Psychologist* 42, no. 10 (1987): 912–920.
Moghnieh, Lamia Mounir. "Infrastructures of Suffering: Trauma, Sumud and the Politics of Violence and Aid in Lebanon." *Medicine Anthropology Theory* 8, no. 1 (2021): 1–26.
Mold, Alex. *Making the Patient-Consumer: Patient Organisations and Health Consumerism in Britain*. Manchester: Manchester University Press, 2016.
Monahan, John, and Lesley Cummings. "Social Policy Implications of the Inability to Predict Violence." *Journal of Social Issues* 31, no. 2 (1975): 153–164.
Morawski, Jill. "Epistemological Dizziness in the Psychology Laboratory: Lively Subjects, Anxious Experimenters, and Experimental Relations, 1950–1970." *Isis* 106, no. 3 (2015): 567–597.
Morawski, Jill G. "The Measurement of Masculinity and Femininity: Engendering Categorical Realities." *Journal of Personality* 53, no. 2 (1985): 196–223.
Morawski, J. G., and Sharon E. Goldstein. "Psychology and Nuclear War: A Chapter in Our Legacy of Social Responsibility." *American Psychologist* 40, no. 3 (1985): 276–284.
Moray, Neville. "Attention in Dichotic Listening: Affective Cues and the Influence of Instructions." *Quarterly Journal of Experimental Psychology* 11, no. 1 (1959): 56–60
Moreton, Bethany. "S'More Inequality: The Neoliberal Marshmallow and the Corporate Reform of Education." *Social Text* 32, no. 3 (2014): 29–48.
Morris, Robert J. "Samuel Smiles and the Genesis of Self-Help; the Retreat to a Petit Bourgeois Utopia." *The Historical Journal* 24, no. 1 (1981), 89–109.
Moscovici, Serge. "Quelles histoires?" *Canadian Psychology* 33, no. 3 (1992): 540–547.
Moscovici, Serge, and Ivana Marková. *The Making of Modern Social Psychology: The Hidden Story of How an International Social Science Was Created*. Cambridge: Polity Press, 2006.
Moten, Fred, and Stefano Harney. "The University and the Undercommons: Seven Theses." *Social Text* 22, no. 2 (2004): 101–115.
Moyn, Samuel. *The Last Utopia: Human Rights in History*. Cambridge, MA: Harvard University Press, 2012.
Murakawa, Naomi. *The First Civil Right: How Liberals Built Prison America*. Oxford: Oxford University Press, 2014.
Muraven, Mark, Dianne M. Tice, and Roy F. Baumeister. "Self-control as a Limited Resource: Regulatory Depletion Patterns." *Journal of Personality and Social Psychology* 74, no. 3 (1998): 774–789.
Murphy, Michelle. *The Economization of Life*. Durham, NC: Duke University Press, 2017.

Murray, Christopher J. L., Alan D. Lopez, and World Health Organization. *The Global Burden of Disease: A Comprehensive Assessment of Mortality and Disability from Diseases, Injuries, and Risk Factors in 1990 and Projected to 2020*. World Health Organization, 1996.

Murray, Heather. *Asylum Ways of Seeing: Psychiatric Patients, American Thought and Culture*. Philadelphia: University of Pennsylvania Press, 2022.

Myers, Natasha. *Rendering Life Molecular: Models, Modelers, and Excitable Matter*. Durham, NC: Duke University Press, 2015.

Neisser, Ulric. *Cognitive Psychology*. New York: Appleton-Century-Crofts, 1967.

Neisser, Ulric. "The Imitation of Man by Machine." *Science* 139, no. 3551 (1963): 193–197.

Neisser, Ulric. "Visual Search." *Scientific American* 210 (June 1964): 94–103.

Nelkin, Dorothy. "Nuclear Power as a Feminist Issue." *Environment: Science and Policy for Sustainable Development* 23, no. 1 (1981): 14–39.

Nelson, Alondra. *Body and Soul: The Black Panther Party and the Fight against Medical Discrimination*. Minneapolis: University of Minnesota Press, 2011.

Nelson, Alondra. "The Social Life of DNA: Racial Reconciliation and Institutional Morality after the Genome." *The British Journal of Sociology* 69, no. 3 (2018): 522–537.

Newell, Allen, J. C. Shaw, and H. A. Simon. "Chess-Playing Programs and the Problem of Complexity." *IBM Journal of Research and Development* 2, no. 4 (1958): 320–335.

Newman, Russ, Randy Phelps, Morgan Sammons, Debra Dunivin, and Elizabeth Cullen. "Evaluation of the Psychopharmacology Demonstration Project: A Retrospective Analysis." *Professional Psychology: Research and Practice* 31, no. 6 (2000): 598–603.

Nichols, Lawrence T. "Social Relations Undone: Disciplinary Divergence and Departmental Politics at Harvard, 1946–1970." *American Sociologist* 29, no. 2 (1998): 83–107.

Nicholson, Ian. "Baring the Soul: Paul Bindrim, Abraham Maslow and 'Nude Psychotherapy,'" *Journal of the History of the Behavioral Sciences* 43, no. 4 (2007): 337–359.

Nicholson, Ian. "'Shocking' Masculinity: Stanley Milgram, 'Obedience to Authority,' and the 'Crisis of Manhood' in Cold War America." *Isis* 102, no. 2 (2011): 238–268.

Nisbett, Richard, and Lee Ross. *Human Inference: Strategies and Shortcomings of Social Judgment*. Englewood Cliffs, NJ: Prentice-Hall, 1980.

Nisbett, Richard E., and Timothy DeCamp Wilson. "Telling More Than We Can Know: Verbal Reports on Mental Processes." *Psychological Review* 84, no. 3 (1977): 231–259.

Noble, Safiya Umoja. *Algorithms of Oppression: How Search Engines Reinforce Racism*. New York: New York University Press, 2018.

Noll, Richard. *The Jung Cult: The Origins of a Charismatic Movement*. New York: Simon and Schuster, 1997.

Norcross, John C., and Christie P. Karpiak. "Clinical Psychologists in the 2010s: 50 Years of the APA Division of Clinical Psychology." *Clinical Psychology: Science and Practice* 19, no. 1 (2012): 1–12.

Norman, Donald A., and Tim Shallice. "Attention to Action: Willed and Automatic Control of Behavior." *Center for Human Information Processing Technical Report* no. 99 (1980).

Nosek, Brian A., Mahzarin R. Banaji, and Anthony G. Greenwald. "E-research: Ethics, Security, Design, and Control in Psychological Research on the Internet." *Journal of Social Issues* 58, no. 1 (2002): 161–176.

Nosek, Brian A., Mahzarin R. Banaji, and Anthony G. Greenwald. "Harvesting Implicit Group Attitudes and Beliefs from a Demonstration Web Site." *Group Dynamics: Theory, Research, and Practice* 6, no. 1 (2002): 101–115.

Núñez, Rafael, Michael Allen, Richard Gao, Carson Miller Rigoli, Josephine Relaford-Doyle, and Arturs Semenuks. "What Happened to Cognitive Science?" *Nature Human Behaviour* 3, no. 8 (2019): 782–791.

Nunnally, Jum. "The Place of Statistics in Psychology." *Educational and Psychological Measurement* 20, no. 4 (1960): 641–650.

Nuttin, Jozef M. "Attitude Change after Rewarded Dissonant and Consonant 'Forced Compliance.'" *International Journal of Psychology* 1, no. 1 (1966): 39–57.

O'Connor, Cliodhna, and Helene Joffe. "How Has Neuroscience Affected Lay Understandings of Personhood? A Review of the Evidence." *Public Understanding of Science* 22, no. 3 (2013): 254–268.

Oishi, Shigehiro, Selin Kesebir, and Ed Diener. "Income Inequality and Happiness." *Psychological Science* 22, no. 9 (2011): 1095–1100.

Olazaran, Mikel. "A Sociological Study of the Official History of the Perceptrons Controversy." *Social Studies of Science* 26, no. 3 (1996): 611–659.

Oldfield, R. C. "Frederic Charles Bartlett: 1886–1969." *American Journal of Psychology* 85, no. 1 (1972): 133–140.

Open Science Collaboration. "Estimating the Reproducibility of Psychological Science." *Science* 349, no. 6251 (2015): aac4716.

Oppenheimer, Daniel M., Tom Meyvis, and Nicolas Davidenko. "Instructional Manipulation Checks: Detecting Satisficing to Increase Statistical Power." *Journal of Experimental Social Psychology* 45, no. 4 (2009): 867–872.

Ost, James, and Alan Costall. "Misremembering Bartlett: A Study in Serial Reproduction." *British Journal of Psychology* 93, no. 2 (2002): 243–255.

Oswald, Frederick, Gregory Mitchell, Hart Blanton, James Jaccard, and Philip Tetlock. "Predicting Ethnic and Racial Discrimination: A Meta-Analysis of IAT Criterion Studies." *Journal of Personality and Social Psychology* 105, no. 2 (2013): 171–192.

Padilla, Eligio, Russell Boxley, and Nathaniel Wagner. "The Desegregation of Clinical Psychology Training." *Professional Psychology* 4, no. 3 (1973): 259–264.

Pandora, Katherine. *Rebels within the Ranks: Psychologists' Critique of Scientific Authority and Democratic Realities in New Deal America*. Cambridge: Cambridge University Press, 2002.

Paolacci, Gabriele, Jesse Chandler, and Panagiotis G. Ipeirotis. "Running Experiments on Amazon Mechanical Turk." *Judgment and Decision Making* 5, no. 5 (2010): 411–419.

Papoulias, Constantina, and Felicity Callard. "Biology's Gift: Interrogating the Turn to Affect." *Body and Society* 16, no. 1 (2010): 29–56.

Parr, Jessica. "'Act Thin, Stay Thin': Commercialization, Behavior Modification, and Group Weight Control." *Journal of the History of the Behavioral Sciences* 55, no. 4 (2019): 342–357.

Payne, Charles M. *So Much Reform, So Little Change: The Persistence of Failure in Urban Schools*. Cambridge, MA: Harvard Education Press, 2008.

Peck, Janice. *Age of Oprah: Cultural Icon for the Neoliberal Era*. New York: Routledge, 2008.

Peirce, William D., Thomas Hilliard, Floyd Wylie, James Dobbins, and Mildred Buck. "Community Mental Health and the Black Community: A Position Statement." *Interamerican Journal of Psychology* 6, no. 1-2 (1972): 135–136.

Perutz, M. F. "Health and the Medical Research Council." *Nature* 235 (1972): 191–192.

Peterson, Christopher, and Martin E. P. Seligman. *Character Strengths and Virtues: A Handbook and Classification*. New York: Oxford University Press, 2004.

Pettit, Michael. "'Angela's Psych Squad': Black Psychology against the American Carceral State in the 1970s." *Journal of the History of the Behavioral Sciences* 58, no. 4 (2022): 365–382.

Pettit, Michael. "The Great Cat Mutilation: Sex, Social Movements and the Utilitarian Calculus in 1970s New York City." *BJHS Themes* 2 (2017): 57–78.

Pettit, Michael. *The Science of Deception: Psychology and Commerce in America*. Chicago: University of Chicago Press, 2013.

Pettit, Michael, and Jana Vigor. "Pheromones, Feminism and the Many Lives of Menstrual Synchrony." *BioSocieties* 10, no. 3 (2015): 271–294.

Pickering, Andrew. *The Cybernetic Brain: Sketches of Another Future*. Chicago: University of Chicago Press, 2010.

Pickren, Wade. "Liberating History: The Context of the Challenge of Psychologists of Color to American Psychology." *Cultural Diversity and Ethnic Minority Psychology* 15, no. 4 (2009): 425–433.

Pickren, Wade E. "Light through a Cultural Lens: Decolonizing the History of Psychology and Resilience." In Gordana Jovanović, Lars Allolio-Näcke, Carl Ratner, *The Challenges of Cultural Psychology*. New York: Routledge, 2018, pp. 220–236.

Pickren, Wade. *Psychology and Health: Culture, Place, History*. London: Routledge, 2019.

Pickren, Wade. "Tension and Opportunity in Post-World War II American Psychology." *History of Psychology* 10, no. 3 (2007): 279–299.

Pickren, Wade, and Henry Tomes. "The Legacy of Kenneth B. Clark to the APA: The Board of Social and Ethical Responsibility for Psychology." *American Psychologist* 57, no. 1 (2002): 51–59.

Pierce, William D. "The Concept of Community Control in Community Mental Health Delivery Systems." *Journal of Black Psychology* 2, no. 1 (1975): 35–43.

Pierce, William D. "Funding and Deinstitutionalization: The Impact on Minority Community Mental Health Centers." *Journal of Black Psychology* 4, no. 1–2 (1978): 82–90.

Piketty, Thomas. *Capital in the Twenty-First Century*. Cambridge, MA: Harvard University Press, 2014.

Pinker, Steven. "No, Thanks," *New York Times*, September 4, 2011, A18.

Plant, Rebecca Jo. "William Menninger and American Psychoanalysis, 1946–48." *History of Psychiatry* 16, no. 2 (2005): 181–202.

Poiger, Uta G. *Jazz, Rock, and Rebels: Cold War Politics and American Culture in a Divided Germany*. Oakland: University of California Press, 2000.

Pooley, Jefferson D. "A 'Not Particularly Felicitous' Phrase: A History of the 'Behavioral Sciences' Label." *Serendipities* 1, no. 1 (2016): 38–81.

Pope, Daniel. "'We Can Wait. We Should Wait.' Eugene's Nuclear Power Controversy, 1968–1970." *Pacific Historical Review* 59, no. 3 (1990): 349–373.

Pope, Kenneth S. "The Code Not Taken: The Path from Guild Ethics to Torture and Our Continuing Choices." *Canadian Psychology/Psychologie canadienne* 57, no. 1 (2016): 51–59.

Pope, Kenneth S., and Thomas G. Gutheil. "Psychologists Abandon the Nuremberg Ethic: Concerns for Detainee Interrogations." *International Journal of Law and Psychiatry* 32, no. 3 (2009): 161–166.

Porter, Judith R., and Robert E. Washington. "Black Identity and Self-Esteem: A Review of Studies of Black Self-Concept, 1968–1978." *Annual Review of Sociology* (1979): 53–74.

Porter, Theodore M. *The Rise of Statistical Thinking, 1820–1900*. Princeton, NJ: Princeton University Press, 1986.

Porter, Theodore M. *Trust in Numbers: The Pursuit of Objectivity in Science and Public Life*. Princeton, NJ: Princeton University Press, 1995.

Post Office: Report and Commercial Accounts, 1958–1959. London: Her Majesty's Stationary Office, 1959, 3.

Postman, Leo, and Jerome S. Bruner. "Multiplicity of Set as a Determinant of Perceptual Behavior." *Journal of Experimental Psychology* 39, no. 3 (1949): 369–377.

Poundstone, William. *Priceless: The Myth of Fair Value (and How to Take Advantage of It)*. New York: Hill and Wang, 2010.

Prkachin, Yvan. '"The Sleeping Beauty of the Brain': Memory, MIT, Montreal, and the Origins of Neuroscience." *Isis* 112, no. 1 (2021): 22–44.

Prodger, Phillip. *Darwin's Camera: Art and Photography in the Theory of Evolution*. Oxford: Oxford University Press, 2009.

Rajecki, D. W. "Zajonc, Cockroaches, and Chickens, c. 1965–1975: A Characterization and Contextualization." *Emotion Review* 2, no. 4 (2010): 320–328.

Ralph, Laurence. *The Torture Letters: Reckoning with Police Violence*. Chicago: University of Chicago Press, 2020.

Ramos, Nic John. "Pathologizing the Crisis: Psychiatry, Policing, and Racial Liberalism in the Long Community Mental Health Movement." *Journal of the History of Medicine and Allied Sciences* 74, no. 1 (2019): 57–84.

Rauscher, Frances H., Gordon L. Shaw, and Catherine N. Ky. "Music and Spatial Task Performance." *Nature* 365, no. 6447 (1993): 611.

Raviv, Shaun. "The Secret History of Facial Recognition." *Wired*, January 21, 2020. https://www.wired.com/story/secret-history-facial-recognition

Raz, Mical. *The Lobotomy Letters: The Making of American Psychosurgery*. Rochester, NY: University Rochester Press, 2013.

Rees, Amanda. *The Infanticide Controversy: Primatology and the Art of Field Science*. Chicago: University of Chicago Press, 2009.

Reisch, George A. *How the Cold War Transformed Philosophy of Science: to the Icy Slopes of Logic*. New York: Cambridge University Press, 2005.

Reynolds Lois A., and E. M. Tansey (eds.), *The MRC Applied Psychology Unit*. London: Wellcome Trust Centre for the History of Medicine at UCL, 2003, 23. Cited as APU Oral History.

Rhodes, Jane. *Framing the Black Panthers: The Spectacular Rise of a Black Power Icon*. Champaign: University of Illinois Press, 2017.

Rickford, Russell. *We Are an African People: Independent Education, Black Power, and the Radical Imagination*. New York: Oxford University Press, 2016.

Riecken, Henry W., Stanley Schachter, and Leon Festinger. *When Prophecy Fails: A Social and Psychological Study of a Modern Group That Predicted the Destruction of the World.* New York: Harper & Row, 1956.

Rieff, Philip. *The Triumph of the Therapeutic: Uses of Faith after Freud.* Chicago: University of Chicago Press, 1987.

Ringrose, Jessica. "Successful Girls? Complicating Post-Feminist, Neoliberal Discourses of Educational Achievement and Gender Equality." *Gender and Education* 19, no. 4 (2007): 471–489.

Rizzoli, Valentina, Paula Castro, Arjuna Tuzzi, and Alberta Contarello. "Probing the History of Social Psychology, Exploring Diversity and Views of the Social: Publication Trend in the *European Journal of Social Psychology* from 1971 to 2016." *European Journal of Social Psychology* 49, no. 4 (2019): 671–687.

Robb, Christina. *This Changes Everything: The Relational Revolution in Psychology.* New York: Farrar, Straus, Giroux, 2006.

Robins, Richard W., Samuel D. Gosling, and Kenneth H. Craik. "An Empirical Analysis of Trends in Psychology." *American Psychologist* 54, no. 2 (1999): 117–128.

Rodgers, Daniel T. *Atlantic Crossings: Social Politics in a Progressive Age.* Cambridge, MA: Harvard University Press, 1998.

Rodgers, Daniel T. *Age of Fracture.* Cambridge, MA: Harvard University Press, 2011.

Roediger, Henry L. "Implicit Memory: Retention without Remembering." *American Psychologist* 45, no. 9 (1990): 1043–1056.

Rogers, Carl R. "'Client-Centered' Psychotherapy." *Scientific American* 187, no. 5 (1952): 66–75.

Rogers, Carl R. "Interpersonal Relationships: U.S.A. 2000." *Journal of Applied Behavior Science* 4, no. 3 (1968): 265–280.

Rogers, Carl R. "The Use of Electrically Recorded Interviews in Improving Psychotherapeutic Techniques." *American Journal of Orthopsychiatry* 12, no. 3 (1942): 429–434.

Rohde, Joy. "Pax Technologica: Computers, International Affairs, and Human Reason in the Cold War." *Isis* 108, no. 4 (2017): 792–813.

Roiser, Martin, and Carla Willig. "The Strange Death of the Authoritarian Personality: 50 Years of Psychological and Political Debate." *History of the Human Sciences* 15, no. 4 (2002): 71–96.

Rose, Nikolas. *Inventing Our Selves: Psychology, Power, and Personhood.* Cambridge: Cambridge University Press, 1998.

Rose, Nikolas, and Joelle M. Abi-Rached. *Neuro: The New Brain Sciences and the Management of the Mind.* Princeton, NJ: Princeton University Press, 2013.

Rosenberg, Milton. *Conceiving the Self.* New York: Basic Books, 1979.

Rosenberg, Milton. *Society and the Adolescent Self-Image.* Princeton, NJ: Princeton University Press, 1965.

Rosenberg, Milton J. "When Dissonance Fails." *Journal of Personality and Social Psychology* 1, no. 1 (1965): 28–42.

Rosenberg, Morris, Carmi Schooler, Carrie Schoenbach, and Florence Rosenberg. "Global Self-Esteem and Specific Self-Esteem: Different Concepts, Different Outcomes." *American Sociological Review* 60, no. 1 (1995): 141–156.

Rosenblatt, Frank. "The Perceptron: A Probabilistic Model for Information Storage and Organization in the Brain." *Psychological Review* 65 (1958): 386–408.

Rosenthal, Robert, and Donald B. Rubin, "Interpersonal Expectancy Effects: The First 345 Studies." *Behavioral and Brain Sciences* 1, no. 3 (1978): 377–386.

Rosenzweig, Mark R. "Trends in Development and Status of Psychology: An International Perspective." *International Journal of Psychology* 17, no. 1–4 (1982): 117–140.

Rosner, Rachael I. "History and the Topsy-Turvy World of Psychotherapy." *History of Psychology* 21, no. 3 (2018): 177–186.

Rosner, Rachael I. "Manualizing Psychotherapy: Aaron T. Beck and the Origins of Cognitive Therapy of Depression." *European Journal of Psychotherapy and Counselling* 20, no. 1 (2018): 25–47.

Rosner, Rachael I. "The 'Splendid Isolation' of Aaron T. Beck." *Isis* 105, no. 4 (2014): 734–758.

Ross, Kristin. *Fast Cars, Clean Bodies: Decolonization and the Reordering of French culture*. Cambridge, MA: MIT Press, 1996.

Ross, Lee. "The Intuitive Psychologist and His Shortcomings: Distortions in the Attribution Process." In Leonard Berkowitz (ed.), *Advances in Experimental Social Psychology*, vol. 10. New York: Academic Press, 1977, 173–220.

Rothman, Hal. *Neon Metropolis: How Las Vegas Started the Twenty-first Century*. London: Routledge, 2002.

Royall, Donald R., Edward C. Lauterbach, Jeffrey L. Cummings, Allison Reeve, Teresa A. Rummans, Daniel I. Kaufer, W. Curt LaFrance Jr., and C. Edward Coffey. "Executive Control Function: A Review of Its Promise and Challenges for Clinical Research. A Report from the Committee on Research of the American Neuropsychiatric Association." *Journal of Neuropsychiatry and Clinical Neurosciences* 14, no. 4 (2002): 377–405.

Rozeboom, William W. "The Fallacy of the Null-Hypothesis Significance Test." *Psychological Bulletin* 57, no. 5 (1960): 416–428.

Rozin, Paul. "What Kind of Empirical Research Should We Publish, Fund, and Reward?: A Different Perspective." *Perspectives on Psychological Science* 4, no. 4 (2009): 435–439.

Rucci, Anthony J., and Ryan D. Tweney. "Analysis of Variance and the 'Second Discipline' of Scientific Psychology." *Psychological Bulletin* 87, no. 1 (1980): 166–184.

Rush, Augustus J., Aaron T. Beck, Maria Kovacs, and Steven Hollon. "Comparative Efficacy of Cognitive Therapy and Pharmacotherapy in the Treatment of Depressed Outpatients." *Cognitive Therapy and Research* 1, no. 1 (1977): 17–37.

Rutherford, Alexandra. *Beyond the Box: BF Skinner's Technology of Behaviour from Laboratory to Life, 1950s–1970s*. Toronto: University of Toronto Press, 2009.

Rutherford, Alexandra. "Feminism, Psychology, and the Gendering of Neoliberal Subjectivity: From Critique to Disruption." *Theory and Psychology* 28 (2018): 619–644.

Rutherford, Alexandra. '"Making Better Use of US Women': Psychology, Sex Roles, and Womanpower in post-WWII America." *Journal of the History of the Behavioral Sciences* 53, no. 3 (2017): 228–245.

Rutherford, Alexandra. *Psychology at the Intersections of Gender, Feminism, History, and Culture*. New York: Cambridge University Press, 2021.

Rutherford, Alexandra. "The Social Control of Behavior Control: Behavior Modification, Individual Rights, and Research Ethics in America, 1971–1979." *Journal of the History of the Behavioral Sciences* 42, no. 3 (2006): 203–220.

Ryan, Michelle K., and S. Alexander Haslam. "The Glass Cliff: Evidence that Women Are Over-Represented in Precarious Leadership Positions." *British Journal of Management* 16, no. 2 (2005): 81–90.

Samelson, Franz. "From 'Race Psychology' to 'Studies In Prejudice': Some Observations on the Thematic Reversal in Social Psychology." *Journal of the History of the Behavioral Sciences* 14, no. 3 (1978): 265–278.

Sanford, R. Nevitt. "The Effects of Abstinence from Food upon Imaginal Processes: A Preliminary Experiment." *Journal of Psychology* 2, no. 1 (1936): 129–136;

Sanford, R. Nevitt. "The Effects of Abstinence from Food upon Imaginal Processes: A Further Experiment." *Journal of Psychology* 3, no. 1 (1937): 145–159.

Savage, Mike, and Roger Burrows. "The Coming Crisis of Empirical Sociology." *Sociology* 41, no. 5 (2007): 885–899.

Saxe, Rebecca, and Nancy Kanwisher. "People Thinking about Thinking People: The Role of the Temporo-Parietal Junction in 'Theory of Mind.'" *Neuroimage* 19, no. 4 (2003): 1835–1842.

Schacter, Daniel L. "Implicit Memory: History and Current Status." *Journal of Experimental Psychology: Learning, Memory, and Cognition* 13, no. 3 (1987): 501–518.

Schacter, Daniel L. *Searching for Memory: The Brain, the Mind, and the Past.* New York: Basic Books, 1996.

Schachter, Stanley, Josef Nuttin, Cecily De Monchaux, Paul H. Maucorps, Diedrich Osmer, Hubertus Duijker, Ragnar Rommetveit, and Joachim Israel. "Cross-Cultural Experiments on Threat and Rejection: A Study of the Organization for Comparative Social Research." *Human Relations* 7, no. 4 (1954): 403–439.

Schaffer, Simon. "Babbage's Intelligence: Calculating Engines and the Factory System." *Critical Inquiry* 21, no. 1 (1994): 203–227.

Scheibe, Karl E. "Metamorphoses in the Psychologist's Advantage," in J. G. Morawski (ed.), *The Rise of Experimentation in American Psychology*. New Haven, CT: Yale University Press, 1988, 53–71.

Scheibe, Karl. "The Psychologist's Advantage and Its Nullification: Limits of Human Predictability." *American Psychologist* 33, no. 10 (1978): 869–881.

Schmidt, Susanne. *Midlife Crisis: The Feminist Origins of a Chauvinist Cliché*. Chicago: University of Chicago Press, 2020.

Schorske, Carl E. *Fin-de-Siècle Vienna: Politics and Culture*. New York: Vintage, 1981.

Schruijer, Sandra G. L. "Whatever Happened to the 'European' in European Social Psychology? A Study of the Ambitions in Founding the European Association of Experimental Social Psychology." *History of the Human Sciences* 25, no. 3 (2012): 88–107.

Schüll, Natasha Dow, and Caitlin Zaloom, "The Shortsighted Brain: Neuroeconomics and the Governance of Choice in Time." *Social Studies of Science* 41, no. 4 (2011): 515–538.

Scott, Daryl Michael. *Contempt and Pity: Social Policy and the Image of the Damaged Black Psyche, 1880–1996*. Chapel Hill: University of North Carolina Press, 1997.

Scott, James C. *Domination and the Arts of Resistance: Hidden Transcripts*. New Haven, CT: Yale University Press, 1990.

Sedgwick, Eve Kosofsky. "How to Bring Your Kids Up Gay." *Social Text* 29 (1991): 18–27.

Segall, Marshall H., Donald T. Campbell, and Melville J. Herskovits. *The Influence of Culture on Visual Perception*. Indianapolis: Bobbs-Merrill, 1966.

Sekula, Allan. "The Body and the Archive." *October* 39 (1986): 3–64.
Selcer, Perrin. "The View from Everywhere: Disciplining Diversity in Post–World War II International Social Science." *Journal of the History of the Behavioral Sciences* 45, no. 4 (2009): 309–329.
Self, Robert O. *American Babylon: Race and the Struggle for Postwar Oakland*. Princeton, NJ: Princeton University Press, 2003.
Selfridge, Oliver G., and Ulric Neisser. "Pattern Recognition." *Scientific American* 203 (August 1960): 60–69.
Seligman, Martin. "The Effectiveness of Psychotherapy: The *Consumer Reports* Study." *American Psychologist* 50, no. 12 (1995): 965–974.
Seligman, Martin. "The Hoffman Report, the Central Intelligence Agency, and the Defense of the Nation: A Personal View." *Health Psychology Open* 5, no. 2 (2018): 1–9.
Seligman, Martin E. *The Optimistic Child: A Proven Program to Safeguard Children Against Depression and Build Lifelong Resilience*. New York: HarperPerennial, 1995.
Seligman, Martin E., and Mihaly Csikszentmihalyi. "Positive Psychology: An Introduction." *American Psychologist* 55, no. 1 (2000): 5–14.
Seligman, Martin E., and Steven F. Maier. "Failure to Escape Traumatic Shock." *Journal of Experimental Psychology* 74, no. 1 (1967): 1–9.
Selinger, Evan, and Kyle Whyte. "Is There a Right Way to Nudge? The Practice and Ethics of Choice Architecture." *Sociology Compass* 5, no. 10 (2011): 923–935.
Shallice, Timothy. "Specific Impairments of Planning." *Philosophical Transactions of the Royal Society of London. B, Biological Sciences* 298, no. 1089 (1982): 199–209.
Shamdasani, Sonu. "'Psychotherapy': The Invention of a Word." *History of the Human Sciences* 18, no. 1 (2005): 1–22.
Shamdasani, Sonu. *Cult Fictions: C. G. Jung and the Founding of Analytical Psychology*. London: Routledge, 2003;
Shattuc, Jane. *The Talking Cure: TV Talk shows and Women*. London: Routledge, 1997.
Shaw, Brian. "Comparison of Cognitive Therapy and Behavior Therapy in the Treatment of Depression." *Journal of Consulting and Clinical Psychology* 45, no. 4 (1977): 543–551.
Sherif, Muzafer. "A Study of Some Social Factors in Perception." *Archives of Psychology* 187 (1935).
Shiffrin, Richard M., and Walter Schneider. "Controlled and Automatic Human Information Processing: II. Perceptual Learning, Automatic Attending and a General Theory." *Psychological Review* 84, no. 2 (1977): 127–190.
Shorvon, Simon, and Alastair Compston. *Queen Square: A History of the National Hospital and its Institute of Neurology*. Cambridge: Cambridge University Press, 2018.
Sidman, Murray. *Tactics of Scientific Research: Evaluating Experimental Data in Psychology*. New York: Basic Books, 1960.
Silva, Jennifer M. *Coming Up Short: Working-Class Adulthood in an Age of Uncertainty*. Oxford: Oxford University Press, 2013.
Silverman, Chloe. *Understanding Autism: Parents, Doctors, and the History of a Disorder*. Princeton, NJ: Princeton University Press, 2011.
Simon, Herbert "Designing Organizations for an Information-Rich World." In Martin Greenberger (ed.), *Computers, Communications, and the Public Interest*. Baltimore: Johns Hopkins University Press, 1971, 37–52.

Simon, Herbert A. "Motivational and Emotional Controls of Cognition." *Psychological Review* 74, no. 1 (1967): 29–39.

Simon, Herbert A. "Studying Human Intelligence by Creating Artificial Intelligence." *American Scientist* 69, no. 3 (1981): 300–309.

Simon, Herbert A., and Michael Barenfeld. "Information-Processing Analysis of Perceptual Processes in Problem Solving." *Psychological Review* 76, no. 5 (1969): 473–483.

Simon, Herbert A., and William G. Chase. "Skill in Chess." *American Scientist* 61, no. 4 (1973): 394–403.

Simpkins, Gary, and Phillip Raphael. "Black Students, APA, and the Challenge of Change." *American Psychologist* 25, no. 5 (1970): xxi.

Skinner, B. F. "Are Theories of Learning Necessary?" *Psychological Review* 57, no. 4 (1950): 193–216.

Skinner, B. F. *Beyond Freedom and Dignity*. Indianapolis, IN: Hackett Publishing, 1971/2002.

Skinner, B. F. "A Case History in Scientific Method." *American Psychologist* 11, no. 5 (1956): 221–233, 228.

Skinner, B. F. "Operant behavior." In W. K. Honig (ed.), *Operant behavior: Areas of research and application*. New York: Appleton-Century-Co., 1966, 12–32.

Sklansky, Jeffrey. *The Soul's Economy: Market Society and Selfhood In American Thought, 1820–1920*. Chapel Hill: University of North Carolina Press, 2002.

Sloman, Steven A. "The Empirical Case for Two Systems of Reasoning." *Psychological Bulletin* 119, no. 1 (1996): 3–22.

Slovic, Paul. "'If I Look at the Mass I will Never Act': Psychic Numbing and Genocide." *Judgment and Decision Making* 2, no. 2 (2007): 79–95.

Slovic, Paul. "Perception of Risk." *Science* 236, no. 4799 (1987): 280–285.

Slovic, Paul. "Psychological Study of Human Judgment: Implications for Investment Decision Making." *Journal of Finance* 27, no. 4 (1972): 779–799.

Slovic, Paul. "Remembering Jim Flynn." *Risk Analysis* 33 (2013): 183–185.

Slovic, Paul. "Understanding Perceived Risk: 1978–2015." *Environment: Science and Policy for Sustainable Development* 58, no. 1 (2016): 25–29.

Slovic, Paul, Baruch Fischhoff, and Sarah Lichtenstein. "Behavioral Decision Theory." *Annual Review of Psychology* 28, no. 1 (1977): 1–39.

Slovic, Paul, Baruch Fischhoff, and Sarah Lichtenstein. "Rating the Risks." *Environment* 21, no. 3 (1979): 14–39.

Slovic, Paul, James H. Flynn, and Mark Layman. "Perceived Risk, Trust, and the Politics of Nuclear Waste." *Science* 254, no. 5038 (1991): 1603–1607.

Slovic. Paul, Sarah Lichtenstein, and Baruch Fischhoff. "Images of Disaster: Perception and Acceptance of Risks from Nuclear Power." In Gordon T. Goodman and William D. Rowe (eds.), *Energy Risk Management*. London: Academic Press, 1979, 223–245.

Smethurst, James Edward. *The Black Arts Movement: Literary Nationalism in the 1960s and 1970s*. Chapel Hill: University of North Carolina Press, 2005.

Smiles, Samuel. *Self-Help*. London: John Murray, 1859/1914.

Smith, Darrell. "Trends in Counseling and Psychotherapy." *American Psychologist* 37, no. 7 (1982): 802–809.

Smith, Laurence D. *Behaviorism and Logical Positivism: A Reassessment of the Alliance*. Stanford, CA: Stanford University Press, 1986.

Smith, M. Brewster. "Else Frenkel-Brunswik" in Barbara Sicherman and Carol Hurd Green (eds.), *Notable American Women: The Modern Period*. Cambridge, MA: Harvard University Press, 1980, 250–252.

Smith, Mary, and Gene Glass, "Meta-Analysis of Psychotherapy Outcome Studies." *American Psychologist* 32, no. 9 (1977): 752–760.

Sokal, Michael M. "The Gestalt Psychologists in Behaviorist America." *American Historical Review* 89, no. 5 (1984): 1240–1263.

Solovey, Mark. "Cold War Social Science: Specter, Reality, or Useful Concept?" In Mark Solovey and Hamilton Craven (eds.), *Cold War Social Science*. New York: Palgrave Macmillan, 2012, 1–22.

Solovey, Mark. *Shaky Foundations: The Politics-Patronage-Social Science Nexus in Cold War America*. New Brunswick, NJ: Rutgers University Press, 2013, 120–127.

Solovey, Mark. *Social Science for What?: Battles over Public Funding for the "Other Sciences" at the National Science Foundation*. Cambridge, MA: MIT Press, 2020, 207–235.

Spear, Joseph H. "Prominent Schools or Other Active Specialties? A Fresh Look at Some Trends in Psychology." *Review of General Psychology* 11, no. 4 (2007): 363–380.

Spencer, Robyn C. *The Revolution Has Come: Black Power, Gender, and the Black Panther Party in Oakland*. Durham, NC: Duke University Press, 2016.

Stam, Henderikus J., H. Lorraine Radtke, and Ian Lubek, "Strains in Experimental Social Psychology: A Textual Analysis of the Development of Experimentation in Social Psychology." *Journal of the History of the Behavioral Sciences* 36, no. 4 (2000): 365–382.

Stampnitzky, Lisa. *Disciplining Terror: How Experts Invented 'Terrorism'*. New York: Cambridge University Press, 2013.

Stankievech, Charles. "From Stethoscopes to Headphones: An Acoustic Spatialization of Subjectivity." *Leonardo Music Journal* 17, no. 1 (2007): 55–59.

Stark, Luke. "Albert Ellis, Rational Therapy, and the Media of 'Modern' Emotional Management." *History of the Human Sciences* 30, no. 4 (2017): 54–74.

Starr, Clarence. "Social Benefit versus Technological Risk." *Science* (1969): 1232–1238.

Staub, Michael E. *Madness Is Civilization: When the Diagnosis Was Social, 1948–1980*. Chicago: University of Chicago Press, 2011.

Staub, Michael E. *The Mismeasure of Minds: Debating Race and Intelligence Between Brown and the Bell Curve*. Chapel Hill, NC: UNC Press Books, 2018.

Stearns, Peter N. *American Cool: Constructing a Twentieth-Century Emotional Style*. New York: New York University Press, 1994.

Steeh, Charlotte G. "Trends in Nonresponse Rates, 1952–1979." *Public Opinion Quarterly* 45, no. 1 (1981): 40–57.

Steele, Claude. M. "A Threat in the Air: How Stereotypes Shape Intellectual Identity and Performance." *American Psychologist* 52, no. 6 (1997): 613–629.

Steele, Kenneth M., Karen E. Bass, and Melissa D. Crook. "The Mystery of the Mozart Effect: Failure to Replicate." *Psychological Science* 10, no. 4 (1999): 366–369.

Steele, Robert S., and Jill G. Morawski. "Implicit Cognition and the Social Unconscious." *Theory and Psychology* 12, no. 1 (2002): 37–54.

Stein, Marc. *Sexual Injustice: Supreme Court Decisions from Griswold to Roe*. Chapel Hill: University of North Carolina Press, 2010.

Stephan, Walter G. "School Desegregation: An Evaluation of Predictions Made in *Brown v. Board of Education*." *Psychological Bulletin* 85, no. 2 (1978): 217–238.

Sterne, Jonathan. *The Audible Past: Cultural Origins of Sound Reproduction*. Durham, NC: Duke University Press, 2003.

Stroebe, Wolfgang, and Fritz Strack. "The Alleged Crisis and the Illusion of Exact Replication." *Perspectives on Psychological Science* 9, no. 1 (2014): 59–71.

Strub, Whitney. *Obscenity Rules: Roth v. United States and the Long Struggle over Sexual Expression*. Lawrence: University Press of Kansas, 2013.

Sue, Stanley. "Community Mental Health Services to Minority Groups: Some Optimism, Some Pessimism," *American Psychologist* 32, no. 8 (1977): 616–624.

Sugarman, Jeff. "Psychologism as a Style of Reasoning and the Study of Persons." *New Ideas in Psychology* 44 (2017): 21–27.

Sullivan, Edmund V. "A Study of Kohlberg's Structural Theory of Moral Development: A Critique of Liberal Social Science Ideology." *Human Development* 20, no. 6 (1977): 352–376.

Summers, Martin. *Madness in the City of Magnificent Intentions: A History of Race and Mental Illness in the Nation's Capital*. New York: Oxford University Press, 2019.

Sunil, Bhatia. *Decolonizing Psychology: Globalization, Social Justice, and Indian Youth Identities*. New York: Oxford University Press, 2017.

Sunstein, Cass R., and Richard H. Thaler. "Libertarian Paternalism Is not an Oxymoron." *The University of Chicago Law Review* (2003): 1159–1202.

Suri, Jeremi. *Power and Protest: Global Revolution and the Rise of Détente*. Cambridge, MA: Harvard University Press, 2009.

Szasz, Thomas S. *Law, Liberty, and Psychiatry: An Inquiry into the Social Uses of Mental Health practices*. New York: Macmillan, 1963.

Tackett, Jennifer L., Scott O. Lilienfeld, Christopher J. Patrick, Sheri L. Johnson, Robert F. Krueger, Joshua D. Miller, Thomas F. Oltmanns, and Patrick E. Shrout. "It's Time to Broaden the Replicability Conversation: Thoughts for and from Clinical Psychological Science." *Perspectives on Psychological Science* 12, no. 5 (2017): 742–756.

Tagg, John. *The Burden of Representation: Essays on Photographies and Histories*. Minneapolis: University of Minnesota Press, 1988.

Tarasoff v. Regents of the University of California. 17 Cal.3d 425 (1976) 551 P.2d 334, 131 Cal. Reporter 14.

Taylor, Charles. *Sources of the Self: The Making of the Modern Identity*. Cambridge, MA: Harvard University Press, 1989.

Taylor, Shelley E., and Jonathon. D. Brown, "Illusion and Well-Being: A Social Psychological Perspective on Mental Health." *Psychological Bulletin*, 103, no. 2 (1988): 193–210.

Teo, Thomas. "Academic Subjectivity, Idols, and the Vicissitudes of Virtues in Science: Epistemic Modesty Versus Epistemic Grandiosity." In Kieran C. O'Doherty, Lisa M. Osbeck, Ernst Schraube, and Jeffery Yen (eds.), *Psychological Studies of Science and Technology*. New York: Palgrave Macmillan, 2019, pp. 31–48.

Teo, Thomas. "Backlash against American Psychology: An Indigenous Reconstruction of the History of German Critical Psychology." *History of Psychology* 16, no. 1 (2013): 1–18.

Teo, Thomas. "Homo Neoliberalus: From Personality to Forms of Subjectivity." *Theory and Psychology* 28, no. 5 (2018): 581–599.

Tetlock, Philip E., and Gregory Mitchell. "Calibrating Prejudice in Milliseconds." *Social Psychology Quarterly* 71, no. 1 (2008): 12–16.

The President's Commission on Mental Health, vol. 1. Washington, DC: U.S. Government Printing Office, 1978.

Thompson, Courtney E. "Physogs: A Game with Consequences." *Endeavour* 43, no. 3 (2019): 100689.

Thompson, Emily. *The Soundscape of Modernity: Architectural Acoustics and the Culture of Listening in America, 1900–1933*. Cambridge, MA: MIT Press, 2004.

Thompson, Evan. *Why I Am not a Buddhist*. New Haven, CT: Yale University Press, 2020.

Thomson, Mathew. *Lost Freedom: The Landscape of the Child and the British Post-War Settlement*. Oxford: Oxford University Press, 2013.

Thomson, Mathew. *Psychological Subjects: Identity, Culture, and Health in Twentieth-Century Britain*. Oxford: Oxford University Press, 2006.

Tikhomirov, O. K., and E. D. Poznyanskaya. "An Investigation of Visual Search as a Means of Analyzing Heuristics." *Soviet Psychology* 5, no. 2 (1966): 3–15.

Tinsley, Howard, and David Weiss. "Interrater Reliability and Agreement of Subjective Judgments." *Journal of Counseling Psychology* 22, no. 4 (1975): 358–376.

Tolman, Edward Chace. "Psychological Man." *Journal of Social Psychology* 13, no. 1 (1941): 203–218.

Tomkins, Silvan. "The Quest for Primary Motives: Biography and Autobiography of an Idea." *Journal of Personality and Social Psychology* 41, no. 2 (1981): 306–329, 314.

Tontonoz, Matthew. "Sandor Rado, American Psychoanalysis, and the Question of Bisexuality." *History of Psychology* 20, no. 3 (2017): 263–289.

Tooby, John, and Leda Cosmides. "The Psychological Foundations of Culture." In John Barkow, Leda Cosmides, and John Tooby (eds.), *The Adapted Mind*. New York: Oxford University Press, 1992, 19–136.

Torpey, John C. *The Invention of the Passport: Surveillance, Citizenship and the State*. Cambridge: Cambridge University Press, 2000.

Treisman, Anne M. "Contextual Cues in Selective Listening." *Quarterly Journal of Experimental Psychology* 12, no. 4 (1960): 242–248.

Treisman, Anne M. "Selective Attention in Man." *British Medical Bulletin* 20, no. 1 (1964): 12–16.

Tuck, Eve. "Suspending Damage: A Letter to Communities." *Harvard Educational Review* 79, no. 3 (2009): 409–428.

Tufekci, Zeynep. "Engineering the Public: Big Data, Surveillance and Computational Politics." *First Monday* 19, no. 7 (2014).

Tulving, Endel, Daniel L. Schacter, and Heather A. Stark. "Priming Effects in Word-Fragment Completion Are Independent of Recognition Memory." *Journal of Experimental Psychology: Learning, Memory, and Cognition* 8, no. 4 (1982): 336–342.

Turk, Matthew, and Alex Pentland. "Eigenfaces for Recognition." *Journal of Cognitive Neuroscience* 3, no. 1 (1991): 71–86.

Tversky, Amos, and Daniel Kahneman. "Belief in the Law of Small Numbers." *Psychological Bulletin* 76, no. 2 (1971): 105–110.

Tversky, Amos, and Daniel Kahneman. "Extensional versus Intuitive Reasoning: The Conjunction Fallacy in Probability Judgment." *Psychological Review* 90, no. 4 (1983): 293–315.

Tversky, Amos, and Daniel Kahneman. "Judgment under Uncertainty: Heuristics and Biases." *Science* 185, no. 4157 (1974): 1124–1131.

Tversky, Amos, and Daniel Kahneman. "This Week's Citation Classic: Judgment under Uncertainty." *Current Contents* 14, April 4, 1983, 22.

Twenge, Jean M., and W. Keith Campbell. *The Narcissism Epidemic: Living in the Age of Entitlement*. New York: Simon and Schuster, 2009.

Uttal, William R. *The New Phrenology: The Limits of Localizing Cognitive Processes in the Brain*. Cambridge, MA: MIT Press, 2001.

Valasek, C. J. "Divided Attention, Divided Self: Race and Dual-mind Theories in the History of Experimental Psychology." *Science, Technology, and Human Values* (2021): 01622439211054455.

Valentine, David. *Imagining Transgender: An Ethnography of a Category*. Durham, NC: Duke University Press, 2007.

Vallone, Robert, Lee Ross, and Mark Lepper. "The Hostile Media Phenomenon: Biased Perception and Perceptions of Media Bias in Coverage of the Beirut Massacre." *Journal of Personality and Social Psychology* 49, no. 3 (1985): 577–585.

van Dijk, David, Ohad Manor, and Lucas B. Carey. "Publication Metrics and Success on the Academic Job Market." *Current Biology* 24, no. 11 (2014): R516–R517.

van Strien, Pieter J. "The American 'Colonization' of Northwest European Social Psychology after World War II." *Journal of the History of the Behavioral Sciences* 33, no. 4 (1997): 349–363.

Van Wyhe, John. *Phrenology and the Origins of Victorian Scientific Naturalism*. Burlington, VT: Ashgate, 2004.

Vicedo, Marga. *The Nature and Nurture of Love: From Imprinting to Attachment in Cold War America*. Chicago: University of Chicago Press, 2013.

Vidal, Fernando. "Brainhood, Anthropological Figure of Modernity." *History of the Human Sciences* 22, no. 1 (2009): 5–36.

Virginia Academy of Clinical Psychologists, and Robert J. Resnick, Ph.D. v. Blue Shield of Virginia, Blue Shield of Southwestern Virginia, and Neuropsychiatric Society of Virginia, Inc., 624 F.2d 476 (4th Cir. 1980).

Wagnleitner, Reinhold. *Coca-Colonization and the Cold War: The Cultural Mission of the United States in Austria after the Second World War*. Chapel Hill: University of North Carolina Press, 1994.

Wagoner, Brady. *The Constructive Mind: Bartlett's Psychology in Reconstruction*. Cambridge, MA: Cambridge University Press, 2017.

Waidzunas, Tom. *The Straight Line: How the Fringe Science of Ex-Gay Therapy Reoriented Sexuality*. Minneapolis: University of Minnesota Press, 2015.

Warrington, Elizabeth K., and Alan D. Baddeley, "Amnesia and Memory for Visual Location." *Neuropsychologia* 12, no. 2 (1974): 257–263.

Warrington, Elizabeth K., and L. Weiskrantz. "A Study of Learning and Retention in Amnesic Patients." *Neuropsychologia* 6, no. 3 (1968): 283–291.

Warrington, Elizabeth K., and Lawrence Weiskrantz. "Amnesic Syndrome: Consolidation or Retrieval?" *Nature* 228, no. 5272 (1970): 628–630.

Warrington, Elizabeth K., and Lawrence Weiskrantz. "New Method of Testing Long-term Retention with Special Reference to Amnesic Patients." *Nature* 217, no. 5132 (1968): 972–974.

Waters, Chris. '"Dark Strangers' in Our Midst: Discourses of Race and Nation in Britain, 1947–1963." *Journal of British Studies* 36, no. 2 (1997): 207–238.

Watts, Tyler W., Greg J. Duncan, and Haonan Quan. "Revisiting the Marshmallow Test: A Conceptual Replication Investigating Links between Early Delay of Gratification and Later Outcomes." *Psychological Science* 29, no. 7 (2018): 1159–1177.

Weart, Spencer R. *Nuclear Fear: A History of Images*. Cambridge, MA: Harvard University Press, 1988.

Weinberg. George H. *Society and the Healthy Homosexual*. New York: Macmillan, 1972.

Weinstein, Deborah. "Sexuality, Therapeutic Culture, and Family Ties in the United States after 1973." *History of Psychology* 21, no. 3 (2018): 273–289.

Wellerstein, Alex. *Restricted Data: The History of Nuclear Secrecy in the United States*. Chicago: University of Chicago Press, 2021.

Werner, Emmy E. "Resilience in Development." *Current Directions in Psychological Science* 4, no. 3 (1995): 81–84.

Werner, Emmy E., and Ruth S. Smith. *Vulnerable, but Invincible: A Longitudinal Study of Resilient Children and Youth*. New York: McGraw-Hill, 1982.

White, Joseph. "Toward a Black Psychology." *Ebony*, September 1970, 45–52.

Wiener, Martin J. *English Culture and the Decline of the Industrial Spirit, 1850–1980*. 1981; Cambridge: Cambridge University Press, 2004.

Wierzbicka, Anna. *Imprisoned in English: The Hazards of English as a Default Language*. New York: Oxford University Press, 2013.

Wilder, Carol. "A Conversation with Colin Cherry." *Human Communication Research* 3, no. 4 (1977): 354–362.

Williams, Robert. "A History of the Association of Black Psychologists: Early Formation and Development." *Journal of Black Psychology* 1, no. 1 (1974): 9–24.

Williams, William Appleman. *The Tragedy of American Diplomacy*. New York: Norton, 1959.

Wilson, Jeff. *Mindful America: Meditation and the Mutual Transformation of Buddhism and American Culture*. Oxford: Oxford University Press, 2014.

Winston, Andrew S. "Cause into Function: Ernst Mach and the Reconstruction of Explanation in Psychology," in Christopher D. Green, Marlene Shore, and Thomas Teo. (Eds.), *The Transformation of Psychology: Influences of 19th-Century Philosophy, Technology, and Natural Science*. Washington, DC: American Psychological Association, 2001, 107–131.

Winston, Andrew. "'The Defects of His Race': E. G. Boring and Antisemitism in American Psychology, 1923–1953." *History of Psychology* 1, no. 1 (1998): 27–51.

Winston, Andrew S. "Value Neutrality and SPSSI: The Quest for Policy, Purity, and Legitimacy." *Journal of Social Issues* 67, no. 1 (2011): 59–72.

World Bank. *World Development Report 2015: Mind, Society, and Behavior*. Washington, DC: The World Bank, 2015.

Wright, Rogers. "The Rise of Professionalism within American Psychology and How It Came to Be: A Brief History of the Dirty Rogers H. Dozen." In Rogers Wright and Nicholas A. Cummings, *The Practice of Psychology: The Battle for Professionalism*. Phoenix: Zeig, Tucker & Thisen, 2001, 1–58.

Yankelovich, Daniel, and Larry Kaagan. "Assertive America." *Foreign Affairs* 59, no. 3 (1980): 696–713.

Yen, Jeffery. "Authorizing Happiness: Rhetorical Demarcation of Science and Society in Historical Narratives of Positive Psychology." *Journal of Theoretical and Philosophical Psychology* 30, no. 2 (2010): 67–78.

Yen, Jeffery, Kevin Durrheim, and Romin W. Tafarodi. "'I'm Happy to Own My Implicit Biases': Public Encounters with the Implicit Association Test." *British Journal of Social Psychology* 57, no. 3 (2018): 505–523.

Yin, Robert. "Face Recognition by Brain-Injured Patients: A Dissociable Ability?" *Neuropsychologia* 8, no. 4 (1970): 395–402.

Yin, Robert. "Looking at Upside-Down Faces." *Journal of Experimental Psychology* 81, no. 1 (1969): 141–145.

Young Jacy L., and Peter Hegarty, "Reasonable Men: Sexual Harassment and Norms of Conduct in Social Psychology." *Feminism and Psychology* 29, no. 4 (2019): 453–474.

Zajonc, Robert. "Feeling and Thinking: Preferences Need no Inferences." *American Psychologist* 35, no. 2 (1980): 151–175.

Zangwill, O. L. "Psychological Aspects of Rehabilitation in Cases of Brain Injury." *British Journal of Psychology* 37, no. 2 (1947): 60–69.

Zaretsky, Natasha. *Radiation Nation: Three Mile Island and the Political Transformation of the 1970s*. New York: Columbia University Press, 2018.

Zyskowski, Kathryn, and Kristy Milland. "A Crowded Future: Working Against Abstraction on Turker Nation." *Catalyst: Feminism, Theory, Technoscience* 4, no. 2 (2018): 1–30.

INDEX

For the benefit of digital users, indexed terms that span two pages (e.g., 52–53) may, on occasion, appear on only one of those pages.
Figures are indicated by an italic f following the page number.

AABT. *See* Association for the Advancement of Behavior Therapy
ABPsi. *See* Association of Black Psychologists
Abu Ghirab, 283–84
academics and practitioners, tension between, 100–2
academics, social psychologists in
  addressing social priming validity, 279–80
  hackable science market, 278–79
  IAT fate, 281–82
  post-2008 academic landscape, 274–77
  psychology reproducibility, 277–78
  Reproducibility Project, 279
  tarnished psychology reputation, 282–83
  viewing replication efforts through combative lens, 280–81
Adler, Alfred, 196
administrative research, 21–22
Adorno, Theodor, 21–22
affect heuristic, history of, 162–63
affective revolution, 8–12
affective science, 1, 16–20, 294–95
  coming crisis of, 263–95
  in TED-talk science era, 275–77
  as uniquely American story, 18–26
African American Fillmore District, 107
AI. *See* artificial intelligence
Albee, George, 100–3, 105, 118–19

Alexander, Franz, 196
Alfred P. Sloan Foundation, 52–53
Allport, Gordon W., 35
Amazon.com, 259
American Association of University Women, 204
American Economic Review, 12
American Prohibition, 138–39
American Psychiatric Association (APA), 90–91, 122
American Psychological Association (APA), 5–6, 29–30, 60–61, 96
  Board of Social and Ethical Responsibility 116–17
  controlling public image of psychology, 122
  Council of Representatives, 286–87
  enshrining psychologist image, 126
  magazine purchase, 122–23
  membership repetitiveness, 127
  preferred theoretical orientations, 124f
  response to 9/11 attacks, 286–87
  triumph of professionalism and, 117–21
American Psychologist, 12, 27, 249–50
American Public Health Association, 122
American red and blue, 12–18
Analysis of Variance (ANOVA), 265–66
ANOVA. *See* Analysis of Variance
Antecedents to Self-Esteem (Coopersmith), 200

anti-self-esteem, field
   capital-happiness disconnect, 224–25
   children as crucial focus, 219–20
   cruel optimism, 224
   ego depletion experiments, 218–19
   emotion regulation at heart of, 212–13
   evangelical communities, 223
   maintaining myth of empowerment, 221–22
   modified behavior modification, 213–15
   new science of self-control, 220–21
   positive psychology, 215–16
   resilience, 216–17
   reviewing literature, 217–18
   untold dark side of self-esteem, 222–23
anticipatory neuroscience, 10
APA Dictionary of Psychology, 192
APA. *See* American Psychiatric Association; American Psychological Association
Applied Psychology Unit (APU)
   change in orientation at, 145–50
   expanding clientele of, 144
   human–machine couplings, 139–45
   medicine-neuroscience alliance, 150–58
   overview, 128–30
   primary object of analysis, 140
   psychology pursued at, 130–39
   realignments spreading beyond, 158–60
APS Task Force, 227
APS. *See* Association for Psychological Science
APU. *See* Applied Psychology Unit
Aronson, Elliot, 270
Art and Science of Love, The (Ellis), 74
artificial intelligence (AI), 231
Association for Psychological Science (APS), 217–18, 227, 280–81, 292–93
Association for the Advancement of Behavior Therapy (AABT), 88–89
Association of Black Psychologists (ABPsi), 95, 102, 110
Atlas Shrugged (Rand), 71–72
atomic age, fear/friendship in age of
   egalitarian collaboration, 172–74
   Eisenhower administration, 168–69
   Fischhoff-Lichtenstein-Slovic report, 175–77

   Lichtenstein-Slovic experiments, 171
   nuclear power concerns, 169–71
   risk perceptions, 174–76
   Yom Kippur War, 171–72
Atomic Energy Commission, 174–75
Atoms for Peace, 168–69
attentional control of action, 153
Aubert, Vilhelm, 55–56
Authoritarian Personality, The (TAP), 37–38
autonomous man, abolition of, 87
aversion therapy, 90–91

Bach, George, 76
Baddeley, Alan, 128, 129–30, 145–50
Bakan, David, 17–18
Banaji, Mahzarin R., 250
banal nationalism, 156
Barker, Elver, 80–81
Bartlett, Frederic, 130–31, 132–33
Baumeister, Roy, 217–18, 275–77
Beck Depression Inventory, 18
Beck, Aaron T., 83–84, 165–66
behavioral drift, 288–89, 292–93, 294
Behavioral Science Consultation Teams (BSCTs), 284, 285–86
behaviorists, 1–2, 27–28, 48–49, 88–89, 93–94, 133, 144–45, 214
behavior modification, 87–89, 96–97, 116, 213–15, 289–90
Behavioural Neurology Unit, Baycrest Hospital, 158–59
Behnke, Stephen, 287–89, 291–92
Bell Curve, The (Murray), 221–22
Bell, Vaughn, 277–78
Bem, Daryl J., 270–71, 278
Berkeley Barb, 60, 61–62
Berkeley Psychology Department, 41–42
Berlyne, David, 56–57
Bertillon, Alphonse, 232
Beyond Freedom and Dignity (Skinner), 87
bias, term, 113–14, 165–66
Big 5, 18
Big Data, 3, 12–13, 252–53
Big Money, experiment, 34–35
Big Sur, 187
Bindrim, Paul, 76–78

biologization, 9–10
Black Arts Movement, 201–2
Black Panther Party, 87–88
Black Panther Party (BPP), 108–10, 113
Blau, Theodore, 104–5, 117, 120–21
Blue Shield, 121
Boring, E. G., 35
Boulder, Colorado, APA conference in, 97–98
Bowlby, John, 236–37
BPP. See Black Panther Party
Brain and Behavioral Science, 52–53
Branden, Nathaniel, 205
Brighton, Henry, 164–65
Broadbent, Donald E., 144
  Ergonomics Research Society and, 140–41
  vigilant military recruiting and, 134–39
Brooks, David, 221–22
Brown, 112–13, 200
Brown v. Board of Education, 105
Brown, Kate, 20–21
Brown, Michael, 254–55
Browne, Harry, 71
Bruner, Jerome, 27–28, 31, 34–35, 165, 230–31
Brunswik, Egon, 37
BSCTs. *See* Behavioral Science Consultation Teams
bubble, psychology, 98–99
Bühler, Karl, 37
Bush, George H. W., 241–42
Bush, George W., 252
business schools, social psychologists, 274–75

California School of Professional Psychology, 104–5
California Task Force to Promote Self-Esteem, 205–7, 208
Cambridge Cognitive Neuroscience Research Panel, 150–51
Campbell, Donald T., 55
Cantor, Nancy, 165–66
capacity, term, 138
capital-happiness disconnect, 224–25
CAPPS. *See* Council for the Advancement of the Psychological Professions and Sciences
Carey, Susan, 236, 246
Carlsmith, James, 270
Carter, Jimmy, 95–96, 117–18, 166–67
Carter, Robert L., 199–200
Catholic Church, 77–78
CBT. *See* cognitive-behavioral therapy
Center for Cognitive Studies, Harvard, 52
Center for Human Information Processing, UC San Deigo, 153–54
Center for the Study and Reduction of Violence, 87–88
Central Intelligence Agency (CIA), 234–35
Chalmers, James, 184
Champanis, Natalia and Alphonse, 270–71
Cherry, Colin, 138–39
chess
  as analogy, 52–53
  appeal of, 49
  cognitive science departing from New Look, 47–48
  Cold War heating, 46
  establishing cognition, 50–51
  homo adaptivus, 47
  making evident limits of cognitive systems, 49–50
  MIT symposium, 46–47
  modeling rationality, 60–61
  in new cognitivist imaginary, 48
  passion of, 51–52
  as ready-at-hand platform, 48–49
  slow deliberateness of, 50
Chess Playing Automaton, 48
Chomsky, Noam, 165, 268
Chronically Sick and Disabled Persons Act, 155–56
Churchill, Winston, 133
CIO. *See* Congress of Industrial Organizations
Clark, Kenneth, 105, 126, 199
Clark, Mamie, 199
Client Center Therapy (Rogers), 111
clinical neuropsychology, 148–49, 150, 235–36
clinical psychology, 23, 27, 62–63, 71–72, 116, 117, 119–20, 205, 286, 298
  achieving autonomy, 68
  championing, 67–68

clinical psychology (*cont.*)
   cleavage between experimental psychology and, 4
   defining expertise, 98
   gay pride and, 203
   hierarchy, 264–65
   increased market orientation of, 97
   neo-Freudianism, 196–97
   obscuring centrality of, 125–26
   social world of, 74–75
   specializing in, 102
   triumph of, 96
Clinton, Hillary, 255–56
Clintonian Third Way, 208
Clock Test, 134
coca-colonization
   hypernationalism emergence, 53
   shaping, 55–58
   social psychology, 53–54
   UNESCO race statement, 54
cocktail party problem (Cherry), 138–39
Cognitive Psychology (Neisser), 52–53
cognition, cooling, 40–42
cognitive behavior modification, 88–89
cognitive bias, origins of
   atomic age prevalence, 168–77
   gendering judgment, 177–81
   heuristics and biases approach, 164–68
   Linda Problem, 161–62
   tracing science of decision-making, 186–91
   Yucca Mountain, 182–86
cognitive biases, 7
Cognitive Psychology (Neisser), 153
cognitive revolution, 4, 7, 27–28, 31, 42, 60–61
   and RET, 68–73
cognitive science, 4–5, 7, 10–11, 15–18
Cognitive Science, 52–53
cognitive theory, 7, 165, 237, 241, 245–46, 257–58
   three bodies of, 129–30
cognitive workspace, 151–52, 157
cognitive-behavioral therapy (CBT), 91–93, 123, 214–15, 298
Cold War Social Science, 186
Coleman, James, 201

COLI. *See* Committee on Legal Issues
combative replication, 273–74
Combe, George, 194
Commission on Accelerating Black Participation in Psychology, 104–6
Commission on Mental Health, 208
Committee for Research on Problems of Sex (CPRS), 65
Committee on Legal Issues (COLI), 122
Committee on Relations with Local Clinical Groups Executive Committee, 103–4
Committee on Science and Professional Ethics and Conduct, APA, 74–75
Committee on Transnational Socia Psychology, 56
Communist Party, 30, 32, 40–42
Community Advisory Board, 107–8, 111
Community Mental Health Act, 103–4, 106
companionate marriage, 66
complete psychological theory, 31–32
complete theory, 59
computational paradox, face reading and, 238–42
conceptual replication, 269, 271–72
Conference for the Experimental Analysis of Behavior, 86
Conflex, 234–35
Congress of Industrial Organizations (CIO), 32
connectionism, 241
Conrad, Reuben, 134
cool computationalism, 241–42
cool, American, 12–18
cool, red and blue, 12–18
Cooley, Charles Horton, 194
Cordelia, *King Lear*, 38
Cornell Aeronautical Laboratory, 233
Cosmopolitan, 81–82
Council for the Advancement of the Psychological Professions and Sciences (CAPPS), 119
Cox, E. E., 40–41
CPRS. *See* Committee for Research on Problems of Sex
Craik, Kenneth, 130

Creative Marriage (Ellis), 74
critiques, self-esteem
  damage narratives, 211–12
  myth of empowerment, 210–11
  unearned self-worth, 209–10
cruel optimism, 224
Cruikshank, Barbara, 208
Cuban Missile Crisis, 234–35
cuckoo bird, postwar clinical psychologist as, 100–2
Cuddy, Amy, 275–77
cultural front, Unamerican science of, 55–58
Culture of Narcissism, The (Lasch), 209
Cummings, Nicholas, 117, 123–25
curve of forgetting, 130–31
cybernetics, 2–3, 59, 137–39, 151–52, 156–57
  definition of, 128–29
  gentlemanly, 140, 144–45, 159
  nervous system and, 136–37
  transfer of, 129–30
  whiteness of, 152

damage narratives, self-esteem and, 211–12
Daniel, Jessica Henderson, 126
Darwin, Charles, 231–32
Dateline, 251
Davis, Angela, 113–14
Davis, Eugene, 201–2
Deaf Smith County, Texas, 182–83
Decision Research, 163–64, 174–75, 183–84, 187
DeepFace, 261–62
defense contracts, overreliance on, 141
delay of gratification, 212–13, 219, 221–22, 223
DeLeon, Patrick, 119–20
Dellums, Ron, 95
demand characteristics, 260–61
democracy, experimenting with, 200–5
Denning, Michael, 32
Department of Defense (DoD), 263–64
Department of Homeland Security, USA, 258–59
Department of Mental Hygiene, 107

Descartes, René, 16–17
Desjarlais, Robert, 50–51
Diagnostic and Statistical Manual (DSM), 90–91
Diamond, Rhea, 236, 246
Dior, Christian, 31
direct replication, 268, 272–73
Dirty Dozen, 103–4, 117–18
disciplinary society, 113
Doctorate of Psychology (PsyD), 105–6
doctorates, granting, 99*f*
DoD. *See* Department of Defense
dominance- feeling, 65
dot.com boom, 279
dregs of memory, 145–50
DSM. See *Diagnostic and Statistical Manual*
Duchenne, Guillaume-Benjamin, 231–32
Dunivin, Debra, 287–88

Eagleton, Thomas, 92
East Bay Sexual Freedom League, 60
East Coast Homophile Organization, 80–81
Eastern Psychological Association, 267–68
Ebbinghaus Empire, 158–59
Ebbinghaus, Herrmann, 44, 130–31
Eberhardt, Jennifer, 254–55
Ebony, periodical, 102, 113–14
Edwards, Paul, 48
Edwards, Ward, 170–71
EEG. *See* electroencephalograph
ego depletion, 218–19, 221–22, 223, 226, 275–77
Ekman, Paul, 8, 257–58
electroencephalograph (EEG), 242–43
Elias, Gabriel, 27
Ellis, Albert, 60, 165–66, 196–97
  Beck-Ellis alliance, 83–93
  challenging authority of, 78–81
  cognitive revolution of, 68–73
  RCTs appealing to, 90
  sexual revolution of, 73–83
  and women's liberation movement, 81–83
Emotional Intelligence (Goleman), 221
Engerman, David, 186–87

engineering psychology, 144
English, Deidre, 210
enhanced interrogation. *See* torture
Equal Rights Amendment, 87–88
Equality of Educational Opportunity (Coleman), 201
Ergonomics Research Society, 140
Ervin, Sam, Jr., 87–88
Esalen Institute, 75–76
Esalen retreat, controversy, 75–77
ESESP. *See* European Society for Experimental Social Psychology
Esquire, 74
Eugene Future Power Committee, 169–70
Eugene Human Rights Commission for Women, 173
Euguene, Oregon, 169–70
European Society for Experimental Social Psychology (ESESP), 56
executive (dys)function, 157
executive function, 12
exogamous sex, 78
experimenting from the left, 32, 40
　Big Money experiment, 34–36
　double political intervention, 35
　Frenkel-Brunswik ideology, 37–40
　intolerance to ambiguity, 36–37
　psychology composition shift, 33–34
Expression of Emotions in Man and Animals (Darwin), 231–32
Eysenck, Hans, 85

face reading, 261–62
　boom-bust cycle of, 231–35
　computational paradox, 238–42
　fMRI and, 242–49
　Mechanical Turk and, 257–61
　overview, 230–31
　prejudice and, 249–57
　scrutinization of, 235–38
Facebook, 261–62
Fanny Hill, 74
Fanon, Franz, 109
Fantz, Robert, 236–37
Fascism, identifying, 39
Federal Communications Commission, 45
Festinger, Leon, 53–54, 269–72

FFA. *See* fusiform face area
filter theory, 135, 136, 137–38
financial crisis (2008), 274–75
Fischhoff, Baruch, 163–64, 172–73
Fisher, R. A., 265–66
Fiske, Susan, 280–81
Flying Personnel Research Committee, 132
Flynn, James, 184
fMRI. *See* functional magnetic resonance imaging
Frankfurt, Harry, 294
Frenkel-Brunswik, Else, 28–29, 31, 34, 42
Freud, Sigmund, 11, 61–62, 161
Friedan, Betty, 63–64
Fromm, Erich, 196
frontal lobe syndrome, 154–55
functional magnetic resonance imaging (fMRI), 160
　criticisms of, 246–47
　establishing validity of, 247–48
　face reading and, 242–49
　higher cognitive functions, 247–48
　historic trends in use of, 245f
　purpose of, 245–46
　social brain hypothesis, 248–49
functional Magnetic Resonance Imaging (fMRI), 231
fundamental attribution error, 165–66
fusiform face area (FFA), 243–44

Galton, Francis, 185, 232–35
Garvey, Marcus, 102
Gauthier, Isabel, 246
Gelles, Michael, 291–92
Gelman, Andrew, 162
General Post Office (GPO), 142, 143
gentlemanly science, 265–74
geopolitics, 55–57
Gerard, Harold, 271–72
"Gift to My Daughter, A" (Browne), 71
Gigerenzer, Gerd, 164–65
Gilbert, Daniel T., 280–81
Gill, David, 152
Gilligan, Carol, 177–81, 204
girl effect, 228
glass cliff, 126
Gleitman, Henry, 31, 45

Goldfried, Marvin, 89
Goldman, William, 107–8
Goleman, Daniel, 221
Gollin, Eugene S., 149, 201–2
Goodman, Cecile, 34–35
Google Books Ngram Viewer, 220
GPO. *See* General Post Office
Graduate School of Industrial Administration, Carnegie Tech, 186–87
Graham, Sandra, 250
Great Depression, 28–29, 193
Greebles, 246
Greenwald, Anthony, 205, 249–51
grit, 212–13, 220, 221–22
Groot, Adriaan de, 48–49

hackable science, 225–26, 275–77, 278–79
Haidt, Jonathan, 11–12
Hakami, Al, 186
Hall, Stuart, 21–22
Handbook of Social Psychology, The, 230–31, 271–72
Hanford nuclear reservation, 182–83
Harvard Yard, 52–53, 186–87
Hazar, Hashomer, 172–73
Haxby, James V., 246–47
Head Start, 201
Head, Henry, 133
headphones, introduction of, 135–36
health maintenance organizations (HMOs), 121–22, 161, 164–65, 167–68, 171
Heinz, dilemma involving, 177–78, 179–80
Herskovits, Melville, 55
heuristics and biases approach, 164–68
Hidden Persuaders, The (Packard), 45
Hilliard, Thomas, 95–96, 104–5
hindsight bias, 172–73
Hirschfeld, Magnus, 66
historical approach, psychology, 12–18
Hitch, Graham, 134, 151
HITs. *See* Human Intelligence Tasks
HMOs. *See* health maintenance organizations
Hochberg, Julian, 31, 45
Hoffman, David H., 285

Hoffman, Paul, 170–71
Hofstadter, Douglas, 240
Holder, Eric, 254–55
Holocaust, 198
Holstein, Constance, 181
Holt, Lester, 255–56
homo adaptivus, 47
homophobia, term, 203
Homosexual Law Reform Society, 79–80
homosexuality, 122, 202–3
 curing, 213
 declassifying, 90–91
 defense of, 66–67, 78–80
 as disorder, 90–91
Hooker, Evelyn, 78–79, 90–91
Horney, Karen, 65, 67–68, 196
Horowitz, Ruth, 199
hostile media studies, 186–91
hot hand, 186–91
House Un-American Activities Committee (HUAC), 40–41
HUAC. *See* House Un-American Activities Committee
Hubbard, Kirk, 293
Hull, Clark Hull, 27–28
Human Inference (Ross/Michigan), 165–66
Human Intelligence Tasks (HITs), 259
human mind, misconstruing, 152
Huxley, T. H., 16–17
hypernationalism, emergence of, 53–54

IAT. *See* Implicit Association Test
ICW. *See* Institute of Child Welfare
Identi-Kit, 257–58
If This Be Sexual Heresy (Ellis), 74
Igniter Media, 223
IMC. *See* instructional manipulation check
Implicit Association Test (IAT), 18, 231, 249–53, 254, 255–56, 261, 279
In a Different Voice (Gilligan), 180
In the Name of Self-Esteem, 208
Independent, The, 74
indigenous psychologies, 57
infants, research on, 237–38
inference revolution, 2–3
influence-pressure, 76
Inouye, Daniel K., 123–25

Institute for Neurology, 148
Institute for Rational Living, 68–69
Institute for Social Relations, 55–56
Institute of Child Welfare (ICW), 37
Institute of Electronical and Electronic Engineers, 242
instructional manipulation check (IMC), 259–60
International Committee of the Red Cross, 284
interrater agreement, 114
intervening variables, 269, 270–71
intolerance to ambiguity, personality-centered science, 36–37
Isaac, Joel, 186–87
Izard, Carroll, 8

Jackson, George D., 116–17
Jacoby, Larry, 249–50
Jaensch, Erich, 39
James, William, 11–12, 17–18, 161, 194
JDM. *See* judgment and decision making
Jensen, Arthur, 201
Jessen, Bruce, 285–86, 293
Jewish self-hatred, 198
John Templeton Foundation (JTF), 223
Johnson-Laird, Philip, 150–51
Journal of Abnormal and Social Psychology, 42
Journal of Applied Behavior Analysis, 86
Journal of Cognitive Neuroscience, 242
Journal of Experimental Psychology: Learning, Memory, and Cognition, 279
Journal of Neuroscience, 244–45
Journal of Personality, 41–42
Journal of Personality and Social Psychology, 165, 274–75, 275f, 279, 295f
Journal of Personality, The, 31
JTF. *See* John Templeton Foundation
judgment and decision making (JDM), 162–63, 165
judgment, gendering, 177–81

Kahneman, Daniel, 12, 161–62, 164–68, 171, 273–74
Kaiser Permanente, 109–10, 117–18, 121–22

Kant, Immanuel, 177–78
Kanwisher, Nancy, 230–31, 242–44
Kelty, Christopher, 279–80
Kennedy, John F., 103–4, 233–34
Khalili, Laleh, 284–85
King, Gary, 281
King, Martin Luther, Jr., 102, 201–2
King, Ruth, 105–6
Kinsbourne, Marcel, 148
Kinsey, Alfred, 65
KIPP. *See* Knowledge Is Power Program
Kitayama, Shinobu, 210–11
Klein, George, 31
Knowledge Is Power Program (KIPP), 221–22
Kohlberg, Lawrence, 177–79
Koocher, Gerry, 288–89, 291–92
Korsakoff syndrome, 147–48
Koss, John C., 135–36
Krech, David, 30–33
Krechevsky, Isidore. *See* Krech, David
Ku Klux Klan, 95

Langer, Ellen, 167
Lanir, Zvi, 171–72
Lanterman–Petris–Short Act, 107
Lasch, Christopher, 195–96, 209
Latin Square, 266
Lavender Scare, 63–64
League of Women Voters, 177–78
learned helplessness, 285–86, 292–93
Lepper, Mark, 188–89
Lewenstein, Bruce, 277
Lewin, Kurt, 53–54, 198–99, 269–70
Leys, Ruth, 8, 10–11
Li, Fei-Fei, 261–62
libertarian paternalism, 188
Lichtenstein, Sarah, 163–64, 170–71, 173
life hacks, 225–26, 275–77
Life Magazine, 31, 75–76
Lily, Eli, 123–25
Linda Problem, 161–62
Liuzzo, Viola, 172–73
Loftus, Elizabeth, 257–58
looking glass, theory, 194, 269
Looper, LeRoy, 111–12
Lopes, Lola, 188–89

love doctrine, 66
Lyell, Charles, 231–32

machine, modeling of human on, 238–42
Mackworth, Norman, 131, 134
"Magical Number Seven, Plus or Minus Two" (Miller), 46–47
Mahoney, Michael, 83
Mansfield Amendment, 174–75
Markus, Hazel, 210–11
Marriage Bar for Civil Service Workers, 142–43
Marshall Plan, 40–41
marshmallow test, 219
Maslow, Abraham, 65, 197
Massachusetts Institute of Technology (MIT), 233–34
Mattachine Review, 78–79
Mattachine Society, 78–79
Matthewson, Grover, 271–72
McClelland, James, 31, 241
McClintock, Martha, 272–73
McDermid, Charles, 197
McGuire, William, 192
Mead, George Herbert, 194–95
Mechanical Turk (MTurk), 259–61
mechanized statistics, 267–68
medical model, alternatives to, 5, 9–10
Medical Research Council, 146
medication, prescribing, 123–25
Meehl, Paul, 113–14, 170–71, 272
mehdal, 171–72
Meichenbaum, Donald, 89
Meltzoff, Andrew, 237
Memoirs v. Massachusetts, 74
Memory (Ebbinghaus), 130–31
Menlo Park, 64–65
menstrual synchrony, 272–73
Mental Health Systems Act, 95–96, 121
mental health, contemporary embrace of, 14
messages, encoding of, 21–22
meta-theory, 4–5, 7, 8–9, 14, 297
Metcalfe, Jennifer, 219
methodological terrorists, 280–81
Metsky, Marvin, 119–20

Milgram, Stanley, 271–72
Miller, Arlynn, 81–82
Miller, George A., 42–43, 46, 102, 165–66, 261–62
Mills, Judson, 270
mind-brain relationship, reconceptualization of, 149–50
Minsky, Marvin, 234–35
Mischel, Walter, 214, 219–20
Mitchell, James, 285–86, 293
Moghaddam, Fathali, 57–58
Monahan, John, 116–17
mood economy, 228–29
Mooney, Chris, 254–55
Moore, M. Keith, 237
Moorehead-Slaughter, Olivia, 287–88, 291–92
Morton, John, 144–45
Moscovici, Serge, 56–57
motherliness, rejection of, 38–39
Mount Zion Hospital, 107, 110
Moynihan Report, 201, 202
Moynihan, Daniel, 201
Mozart Effect, 272–73, 281
MRC. *See* Medical Research Council
Ms. magazine, 207
MTurk. *See* Mechanical Turk
Muhammad Speaks, 114–15
Muhammad, Elijah, 114–15
Murphy, Gardner, 31
Murray, Charles, 221
Murray, Henry A., 35
myth of empowerment, self-esteem and, 210–11

NAACP. *See* National Association for the Advancement of Colored People
Nathaniel Branden Institute (NBI), 71–72
National Association for the Advancement of Colored People (NAACP), 199–200
National Health Service (NHS), 131–32, 156
National Initiative for Building Community Trust and Justice, 254–55
National Institute of Mental Health (NIMH), 10, 11, 200
National Institutes of Health (NIH), 93–94, 241–42

National Photographic Interpretation Center (NPIC), 234–35
National Science Foundation (NSF), 183–84, 241–42
Nature, 149, 244–45, 272–73, 274–75
Naval Criminal Investigative Service, 291–92
NBI. *See* Nathaniel Branden Institute
Neisser, Ulric, 52, 153, 233–34
neo-Freudianism, 196–97
net effect, three transformations, 299
neuroscience, 10–11, 235
Neurotic Personality of Our Time (Horney), 65
Nevada Nuclear Waste Project Office (NWPO), 184
New Deal, 32
New Left, 13–14
"New Look 3" (Greenwald), 249–50
New Look, movement
    acquiring narrower meaning, 27–29
    championing vision of, 29–33
    chess, 46–53
    coca-colonization of mind, 53–58
    cooling of cognition, 40–45
    erasure of, 40–42
    experimenting from the left, 33–40
    revival of, 249–50
    taking up Depression-era studies, 33–34
New York Psychoanalytic Society, 67–68
New York Society of Clinical Psychologists, 74–75
New York Times, 74, 209, 221, 225–26, 233, 253–54, 277–78, 284
New York Times Magazine, 207–8
New York v. Uplinger, 122
New Yorker syndrome, 121–22
Newell, Simon, 46–47, 48, 51–52
Newman, Russ, 287–88
NHS. *See* National Health Service
Nike Foundation, 228
NIMH. *See* National Institute of Mental Health
Nisbett, Richard, 165–66, 239–40
No Child Left Behind Act, 221
Nobles, Wade, 118–19
Norman, Donald, 153–54

Nosek, Brian, 279
NPIC. *See* National Photographic Interpretation Center
NRC. *See* Nuclear Regulatory Commission
NSF. *See* National Science Foundation
nuclear power, concerns regarding, 169–71
Nuclear Regulatory Commission (NRC), 169
Nuclear Waste Policy Act, 182–83
nude psychotherapy, 76–77
null ritual, 266–67
Nuttin, Jozef M., Jr., 271
NWPO. *See* Nevada Nuclear Waste Project Office

O'Connor v. Donaldson, 118–19
Obama, Barack, 188, 254
    administration, 254–55
Objectivism, dismissing, 71–72
Omnibus Budget Reconciliation Act, 121
"On Perceptual Readiness" (Bruner), 44–45
OPEC. *See* Organization of the Petroleum Exporting Countries
Open Science Framework, 279
Operation Candor, 168–69
oralism, 155
Oregon group, 163–64, 176, 180–81, 186, 189, 190–91
Oregon Research Institute (ORI), 163–64, 170–71
Oregon System, 169–70
Oregon trio. *See* Fischhoff, Baruch; Lichtenstein, Sarah; Slovic, Paul
Organization of the Petroleum Exporting Countries (OPEC), 166–67
ORI. *See* Oregon Research Institute
Origins and Development of the Incest Taboo, The (Ellis), 74

Packard, Vance, 45
Palahnuik, Chuck, 209
Pandemonium, 233–34
Papert, Seymour, 234–35
Parallel Distributed Processing, 241
Parsons, Talcott, 42–43
participant, term, 256
patrimonial capitalism, 224

pattern recognition, emerging field of, 233
PDP. *See* Psychopharmacology Demonstration Project
peak esteem, 205–8
Penry, Jacques, 257–58
PENS. *See* Psychological Ethics and National Security
Penthouse, 74
Pentland, Alex, 242
People's Free Medical Clinics, 109
Perception and Communication (Broadbent), 137–38
perception-centered New Look, 34, 36
Perceptron, 233–34
perceptual defense, controversy, 43–45
peripheral slave systems, 156–57
Perl, Fritz, 75–76
Personal Responsibility and Work Opportunity Reconciliation Act, 208
personality-centered New Look, 34, 36
Perspective on Psychological Science (PPS), 277–78
PhDs
  by specialty, 100*f*
  women obtaining, 99–100
Piaget, Jean, 165, 177–78
Pickering, Andrew, 128–29
Pierce, William D., 109–10
Piketty, Thomas, 224
Pillay, A. J., 66
Pittsburgh Black Theatre Dance Ensemble, 202
Playboy, 73, 81–82
players, 139–45
Poddar, Prosenjit, 115–16
Popper, Karl, 272
Popular Front, 5, 32, 59
Positive Affect and Negative Affect Schedule, 18
positive psychology, 215–16
Positive Psychology Center, 223
Postman, Leo, 31, 43–44
posttraumatic stress disorder (PTSD), 219
postwar psychology, 297–99
  Applied Psychology Unit, 128–59

cognitive bias, 161–91
coming crisis of affective science, 263–95
face reading, 230–62
meaning of reason and rationality in, 60–94
New Look origin story, 27
professionalism, 95–127
self-esteem, 192–229
threefold transformation of, 265
Poulton, E. C., 134
power poses, 294
power posing, 275–77
PPS. *See Perspective on Psychological Science*
practical psychology, 60–61
preferential looking task, 236–37
prejudice, looking for, 249–57
Presidential Commission on Mental Health, 118–19
Principles of Psychology, 194–95
Problem X, 174–75
Proceedings of the National Academic of Sciences, 244–45
professionalism
  overview, 95–97
  as political philosophy, 125–27
  psychology entry into, 98
  revolt of professionals, 97–106
  triumph of, 115–25
  in Westside (San Francisco), 106–15
Project Candor, 191
Project Implicit, 251, 253–54
Project Self-Esteem, 201–2
Prozac, 123–25, 241–42
psychoanalysis, 66
Psychological Clinic, Harvard, 35–36
psychological détente, 83–93
Psychological Ethics and National Security (PENS), 286–88
Psychological Laboratory, 35
Psychological Review, 46–47, 233, 239–40
psychological science, 19–20
Psychological Science, 218, 274–75, 278, 279, 296*f*
psychologist, term, 106
psychologist's advantage, 167–68

Psychologists' Committee of the
    Medical Bureau to Aid Spanish
    Democracy, 32–33
psychology
    affective revolution, 8–12
    American red and blue, 12–18
    biologization of, 9–10
    postwar transformations, 4–7
    in three worlds, 57
Psychology Today, 122–23
psychometric paradigm, 175–76, 182
psychopharmacology, 123–25
Psychopharmacology Demonstration
    Project (PDP), 286
PsyD. *See* Doctorate of Psychology
PTSD. *See* posttraumatic stress disorder
public relations, issue of, 87
public universities, behavior analysis in, 86
Pygmalion effect, 201

Queen Square, 147–48
questionnaire, clinical psychology, 84–85

RAF. *See* Royal Air Force
RAND Corporation, 46–47, 52–53, 186–87
Rand, Ayn, 71–72, 205
randomized controlled trials (RCTs), 89
Rasmussen Report, 169, 174–75
Rasmussen, Norman, 169
Rational Living, 83–84
rational psychotherapy, 60–61
rational-emotive therapy (RET), 60–62
Rauscher, Frances, 272–73
Rawls, John, 177–78
RCTs. *See* randomized controlled trials
Reagan, Ronald, 95–96, 107, 121, 205
Reality House, 111–12
Reason and Emotion in Psychotherapy
    (Ellis), 70–71, 74
red and blue, American, 12–18
Red Scare, 22–23, 29, 40–45
Red Vienna, 38–39
Reece Committee, 40–41
Reece, B. Carroll, 40–41
region of interest (ROI), 243–45
replication
    ANOVA use, 265–67

    avenues for publishing, 272–73
    combative, 265–74
    conceptual, 269, 271–72
    direct, 268, 272–73
    of initiation experiment, 271–72
    overview of, 263–65
Reproducibility Project, 279
Republican War on Science, The
    (Mooney), 254
resilience, 216–17
Resnick, Robert, 121
RET. *See* rational-emotive therapy
revolt, professionals
    background, 97–102
    Black revolt, 102
    clinical psychologist revolt, 103–4
    Commission on Accelerating Black
        Participation in Psychology, 104–5
*Revolution Within: A Book of Self-Esteem,
    The* (Steinem), 207
right to be sick, argument, 82–83
RJ, patient, 154–55
Roe v. Wade, 178–79
Roediger, Henry L., III, 249–50
Rogerian humanism, 116–17
Rogers, Carl, 67–68, 98, 196–97
Rogue, 74
ROI. *See* region of interest
Rokeach, Milton, 42
Roosevelt, Franklin Delano, 32
Rosenberg Scale, 211–12
Rosenberg Self-Esteem Scale, 18
Rosenberg, Milton, 200, 270–71
Rosenthal, Robert, 201
Ross, Lee, 165–66, 189–90
Rothschild Report, 146
Rotman Research Institute, 158–59
Royal Air Force (RAF), 133–34
Royal National Throat, Nose, and Ear
    Hospital, 155
Royal Society, 146
Rumelhart, David, 241

SALT 1. *See* Strategic Arms Limitation
    Talks 1
San Francisco Examiner, 107–8, 115
SAS. *See* Supervisory Attention System

Schacter, Daniel, 158–60
Schmitt, Francis, 235
Schneirla, T. C., 32–33
schools and systems approach, 1–4
schools, psychology approach, 1–4
Science, 164–65, 242–43, 244–45, 263–64, 274–75, 282–83
Scientific American, 233–34, 240
Scott, Daryl Michael, 199–200
Scott, James C., 260–61
Scott, Thomatra, 107–8
selective vigilance, 153
Self-Analysis (Ellis), 67–68
self-efficacy, term, 214–15
self-esteem
    articles mentioning, 193*f*
    critiques of, 208–12
    cultural salience of, 193
    definition, 192
    as experiment with democracy, 200–5
    gaining, 195–96
    human psyche and, 205
    losing control of, 225–29
    neo-Freudianism and, 196–97
    origins of, 194–95
    peaking of, 205–8
    perceiving as "girl problem," 203–4
    psychologists against, 212–25
    replication and, 226
    social action research and, 198–200
    word frequency of, 228*f*
Self-Help (Smiles), 194
self-help, promoting, 70–71
Selfridge, Oliver, 233–34
Seligman, Martin, 292–93
SERE. *See* Survival, Evasion, Resistance, and Escape
severity of initiation, experiment, 270
Sex and Single Man (Ellis), 74
Sex without Guilt (Stuart), 74
sex, postwar reconstruction of
    animating Ellis career, 63–64
    discrimination, 66–67
    Ellis-Maslow pair, 65–66
    panic over sex crimes, 64–65
    psychology in private practice, 67–68
sexual psychopaths, 64–65

sexual revolution, RET
    antagonizing clinical psychologists, 74–75
    building Manhattan practice, 73
    challenging Ellis authority, 78–81
    Esalen retreat controversy, 75–77
    exogamous sex, 78
    public image, 74–76
    women's liberation movement, 81–83
Shakow, David, 97–98
Shallice, Tim, 153–54
Shannon, Claude, 48
Shaw, J. C., 48
Sherif, Muzafer, 31, 33–34
Sidman, Murray, 268
Silva, Jennifer, 228–29
Simon, Herbert, 7, 46–47, 48, 165, 238–40
Skinner, B. F., 27–28, 86, 87, 213, 267–68
slave systems, term, 152
Slovic, Paul, 162–64, 170–71
Smiles, Samuel, 194
social action research, 198–200
Social and Behavioral Science Office, 188–89
Social and Ethical Responsibility for Psychology, 105
social psychology, 53–54
    Black people in, 250
    entry into business schools, 274–75
    European, 56–58
    IAT in, 249–50, 254–55
    Jewish self-hatred, 198
    on outskirts of cognitive empire, 53–54
    pursuing ideal of experimental realism, 269
    waning zest for, 41–42
Society and the Adolescent Self-Image (Rosenberg), 200
Society for the Psychological Study of Social Issues (SPSSI), 30, 32–33, 41–42
Society for the Scientific Study of Sex, 66
Society of Experimental Psychology, 131–32
sociobiology, competition from, 8–9
Solovey, Mark, 186–87
Special Interest Group in Information Theory, 46–47

speculative neurology, 10
  evasion of, 136–38
Sproul, Robert Gordon, 41–42, 90–91
SPSSI. *See* Society for the Psychological Study of Social Issues
Spurzheim, Johan, 194
Sputnik, 46
Stanford Prison Experiment, 283–84
Stapel, Diederik, 278–79
Strategic Arms Limitation Talks 1 (SALT 1), 168–69
Stearns, Peter, 14–15
Steinem, Gloria, 207
stereotype threat, 211–12
Stevens, S. S., 42–43
Stuart, Lyle, 74
Suber, Carolyn, 116–17
Sullivan, Harry Stack, 196
Sunstein, Cass, 188
Supervisory Attention System (SAS), 153–54
surveillance state, 257–59
Survival, Evasion, Resistance, and Escape (SERE), 285–86
Swampscott Conference, 106
systems-schools approach. *See* schools-systems approach
Szasz, Thomas, 72–73

tachistoscope, 43–44
Tactics of Scientific Research, The (Sidman), 268
Tagiuri, Renato, 230–31, 232–33
Tajfel, Henri, 56–57
talk therapy
  Beck-Ellis alliance, 83–85
  efficiency of, 85
  embracing RET, 83
Tarasoff v. Regents of the University of California, 115–17
Tarasoff, Tatiana, 115–16
Task Force on Sex Roles and Sex Bias Stereotyping on Psychotherapeutic Practice, 81–82
Teachers College, 64
Teuber, Hans-Lukas, 235–36
Thaler, Richard, 188

Thatcher, Margaret, 156
Theatre of Psychodrama, 74–75
therapeutic cultures, 93–94
  cognitive revolution, 68–73
  overview, 60–63
  postwar reconstruction of sex, 63–68
  psychological détente, 83–93
  sexual revolution, 73–83
Thinking Fast and Slow (Kahneman), 279–80
Third World Liberation Front, 107
Thorne, Richard, 60
tiger economies, 57–58
Time magazine, 202–3
Tolman, E. C., 27–28, 30, 269
Tomkins, Silvan, 8
torture
  ethical maneuvers and, 291–92
  and Khalili analysis, 284–85
  learned helplessness and, 292–93
  least contested narrative of, 285–86
  link between affective science and, 283–84
  overview of, 263–65
  and PENS Task Force, 286–92
  psychologist role in, 285, 288–92
  and US response to 9/11, 284–85
"Towards a Black Psychology" (White), 102
Towards a State of Esteem, 206–7
traffic, assessing, 142–43
transformations, postwar psychology, 4–7
  first transformation, 5–6
  second transformation, 6–7
  third transformation, 7
transvestism, 90–91
triumph of professionalism
  controlling public image of psychology, 122–23
  Dirty Dozen and, 117–21
  political visions, 117–21
  psychopharmacology and, 123–25
  Tarasoff ruling, 115–17
  "Virginia Blues" cases, 121–22
Tuck, Eve, 211
Tulving, Endel, 158–60
Turing, Alan, 48

Turk, Matthew, 242
Tversky, Amos, 164–68, 170–71, 273–74
Tyler, Elaine May, 63–64

unearned self-worth, self-esteem and, 209–10
Union of Post Office Workers, 142–43
United Nations, 53
United States Public Health Service (USPHS), 97
United States, as psychological society, 62–63
USPHS. *See* United States Public Health Service
utility of consciousness, 16–17

VA. *See* Veterans Administration
Vasconcellos, John, 205
Verbal Behavior (Skinner), 268
Veterans Administration (VA), 29–30, 97
Vietnam War, 85, 178–79
vigilance, branding of, 133–35
Village Voice, 74–75
Virginia Academy of Clinical Psychologists and Robert J. Resnick v. Blue Shield of Virginia, 121
Voting Rights Act, 252

Wall Street (film), 275–77
Warrington, Elizabeth, 147, 148–50, 155–56
Warwick, Alice E., 277
WASH-1400, 169
Washington Post, 254
Watergate, scandal, 85
Weinberg, George, 203
Weinshel, Edward M., 110
WEIRD. *See* Western, Educated, Industrialized, Rich, and Democratic

Weiskrantz, Lawrence, 148, 149–50
Werner, Emmy, 31, 227
Western, Educated, Industrialized, Rich, and Democratic (WEIRD), 20–21, 259–60
Westside Community Mental Health Center (San Francisco), 107–8
expansion, 112–13
legal activism, 113–15
professionalism in, 107–15
Swampscott Conference, 106
White, Joseph, 102
Wiener, Norbert, 48
Wilson, Barbara, 154–55
Wilson, Timothy D., 239–40, 281
Winfrey, Oprah, 207
With Man in Mind (documentary), 144–45
Witkin, Herman, 31
Wolpe, Joseph, 86
Woodhead, Muriel, 144–45
WordNet, 261–62
working memory, model, 151–52
World War II, 5, 18–19, 22, 29–30, 59, 61–62, 92–93, 104, 125–26, 133, 152, 265–66
writing from the Left, 32
Wyatt v. Stickney, 85, 118–19

Yerkes, Robert M., 65
Yin, Robert, 235
Yom Kippur War, 171–72
Yoo, John, 284–85
Yucca Mountain, 182–86

Zajonc, Robert, 8, 239–40
Zangwill, Oliver, 131–32, 148–49
Zimbardo, Philip, 283–84